ISRAEL

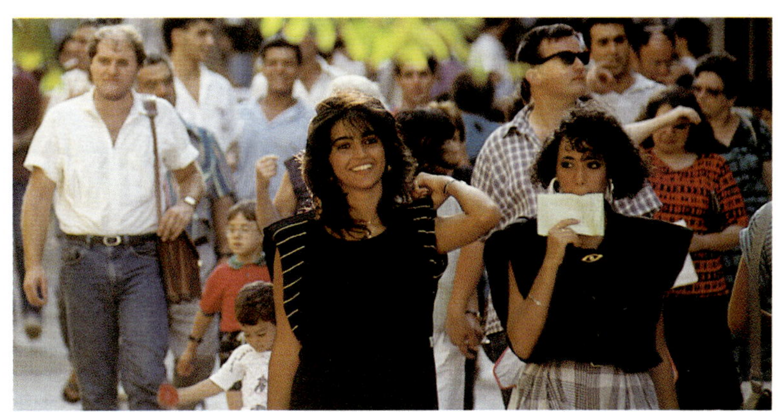

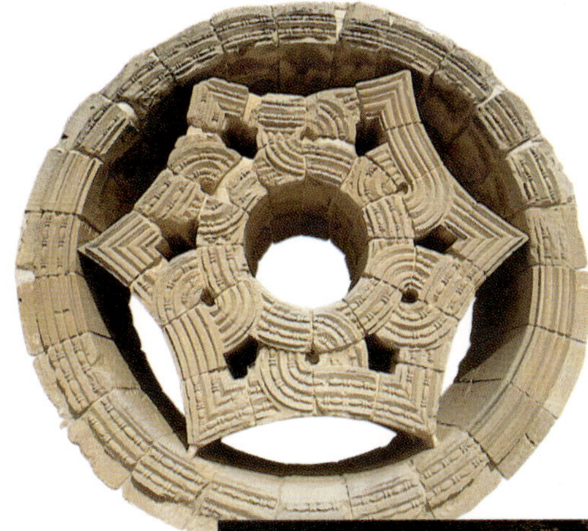

ISRAEL

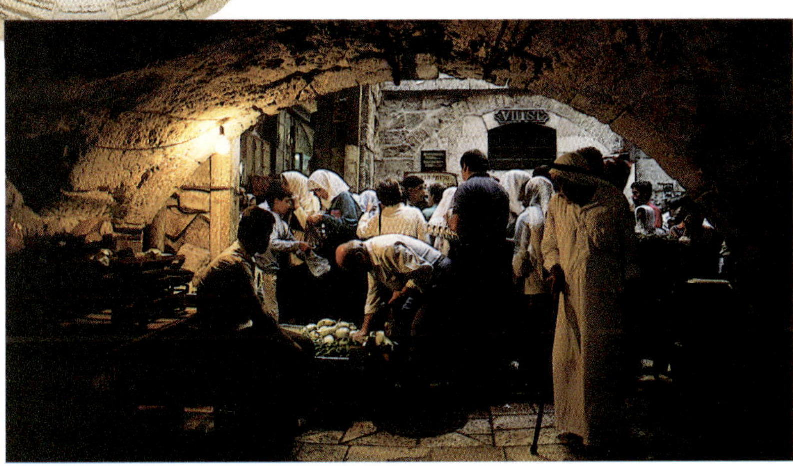

Text
Rachel Goldmann
Nicola Förg

Photography
Tom Krausz

Tauris Parke Books
London • New York

Contents

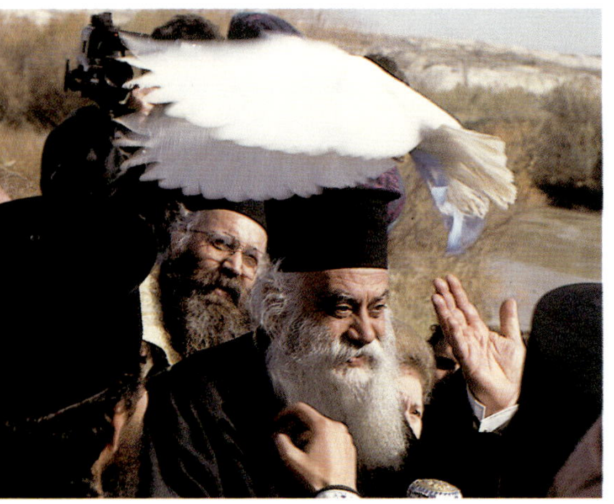

Greek Orthodox Monk on the River Jordan

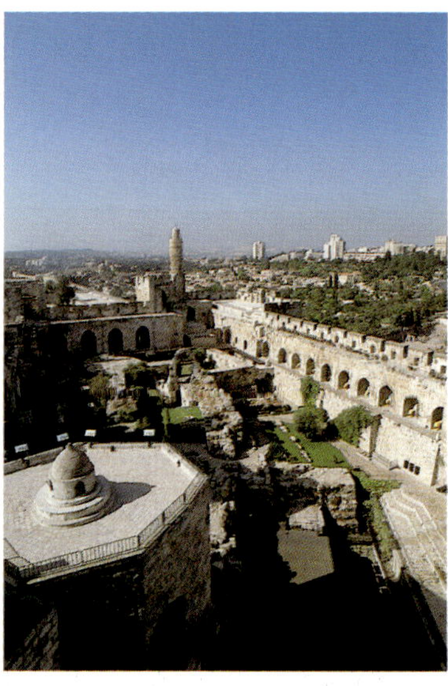

View from Jerusalem's Citadel

Chapel in Capernaum

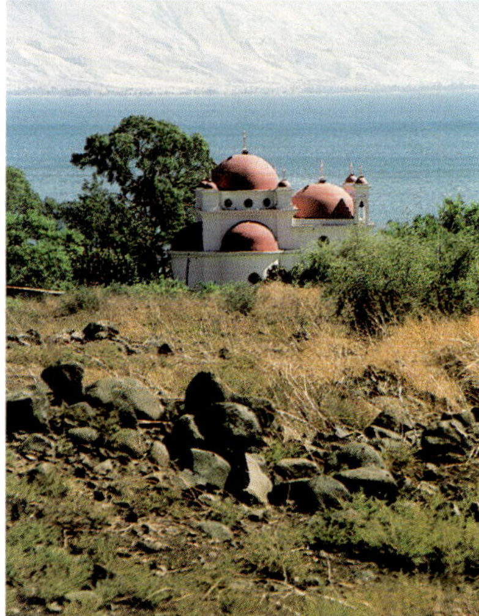

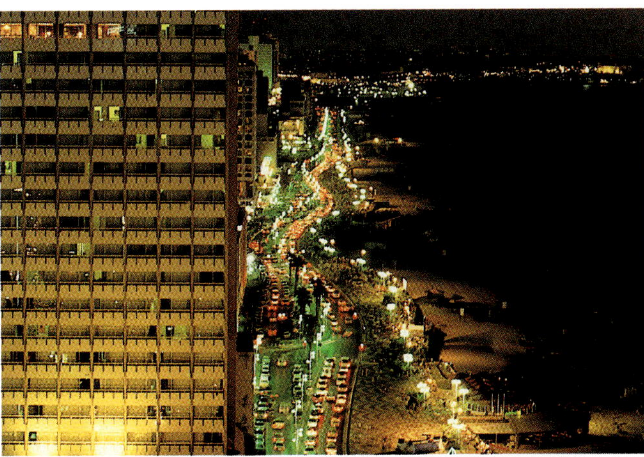

The rugged rock-face of the 'Temple of Hathor' in the Timna Valley

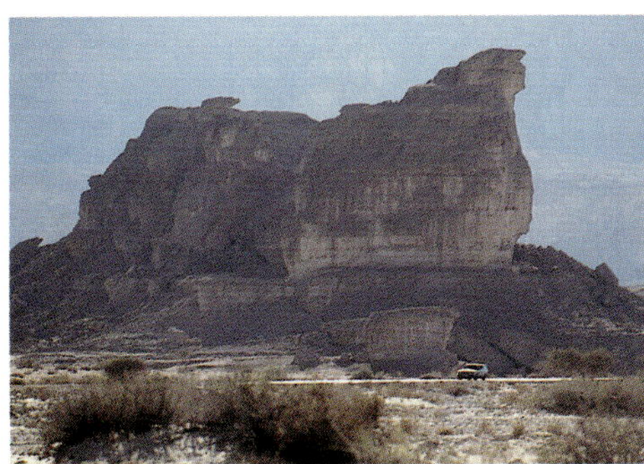

'The Sphinx' in Timna-Tal

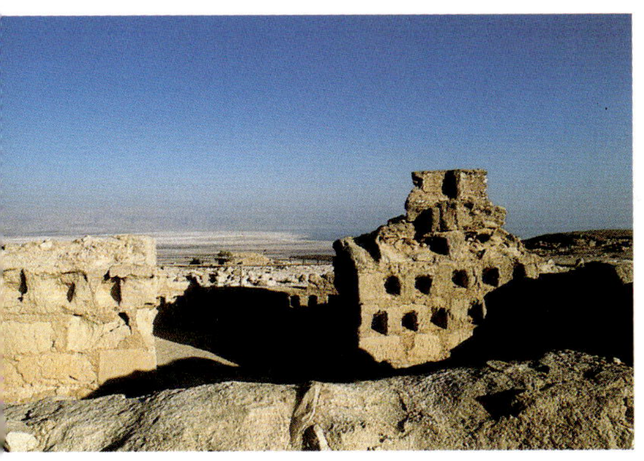

The round Columbarium in Masada

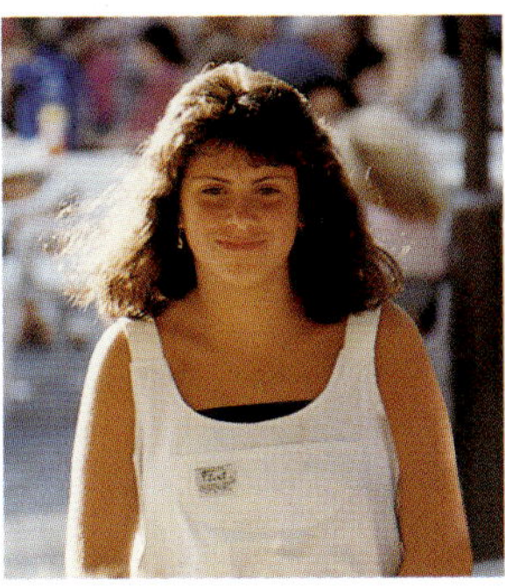

Israeli Woman in Jerusalem

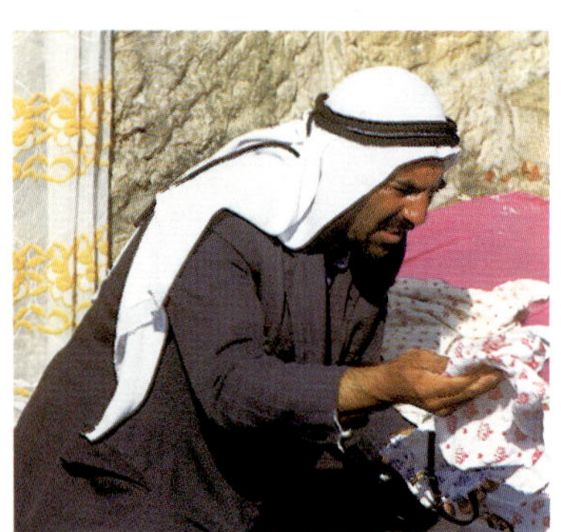

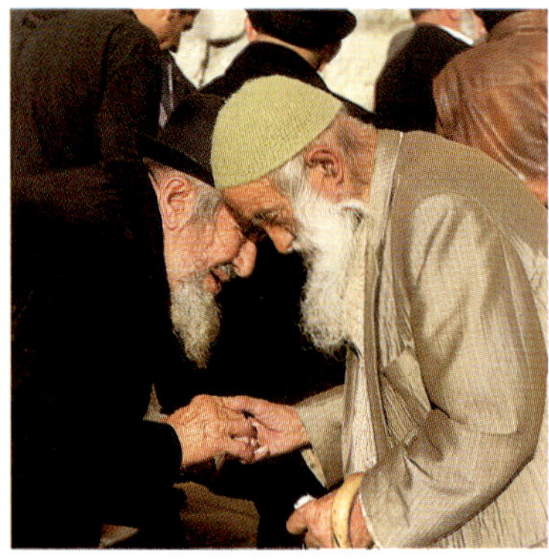

Oriental industriousness, fervent religious faith and a contrasting landscape from the gently undulating hills of Galilee (right) to the forbidding desert: Israel, a destination for pilgrims, scholars and holidaymakers, offers the greatest variety in the smallest of areas.

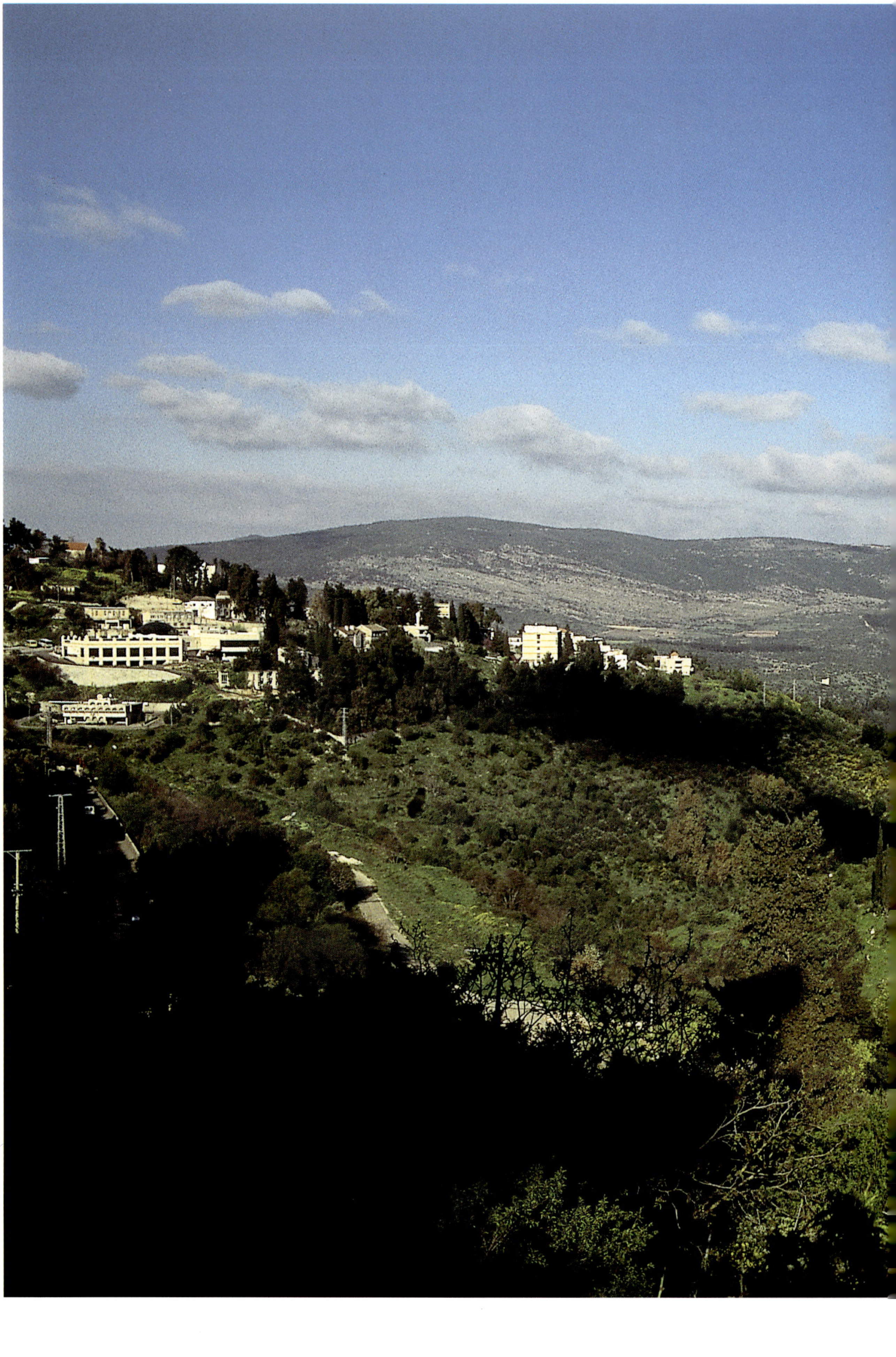

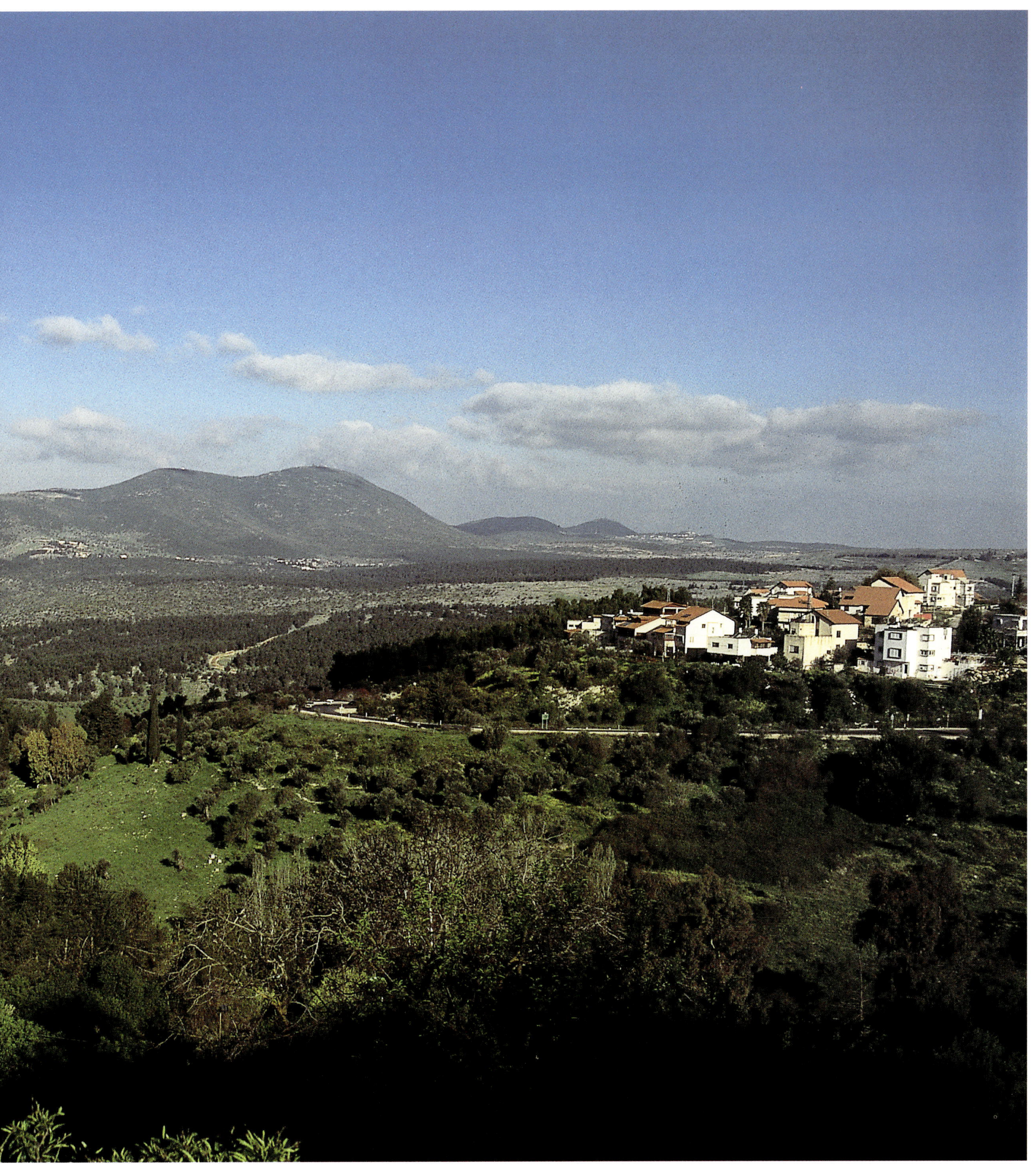

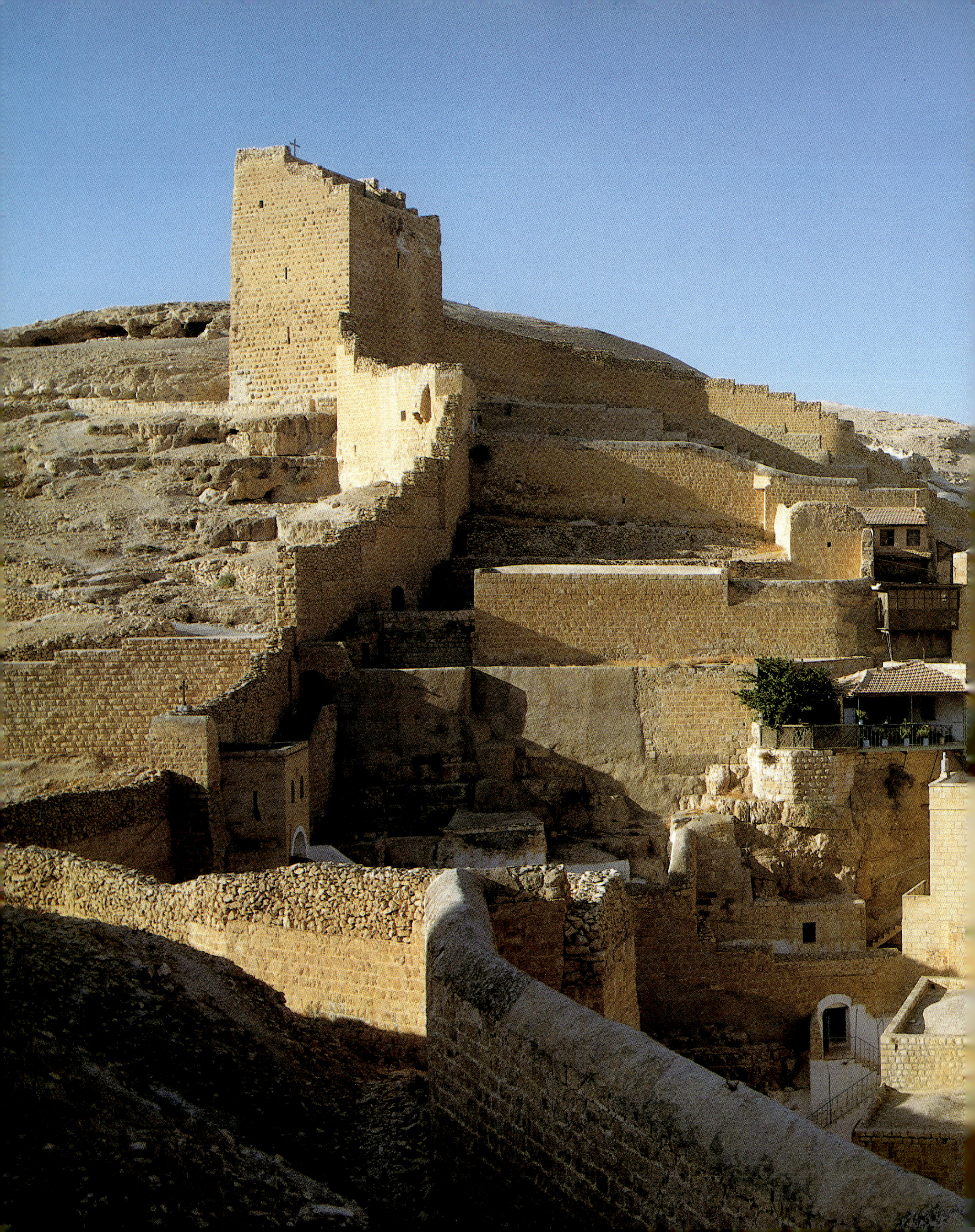

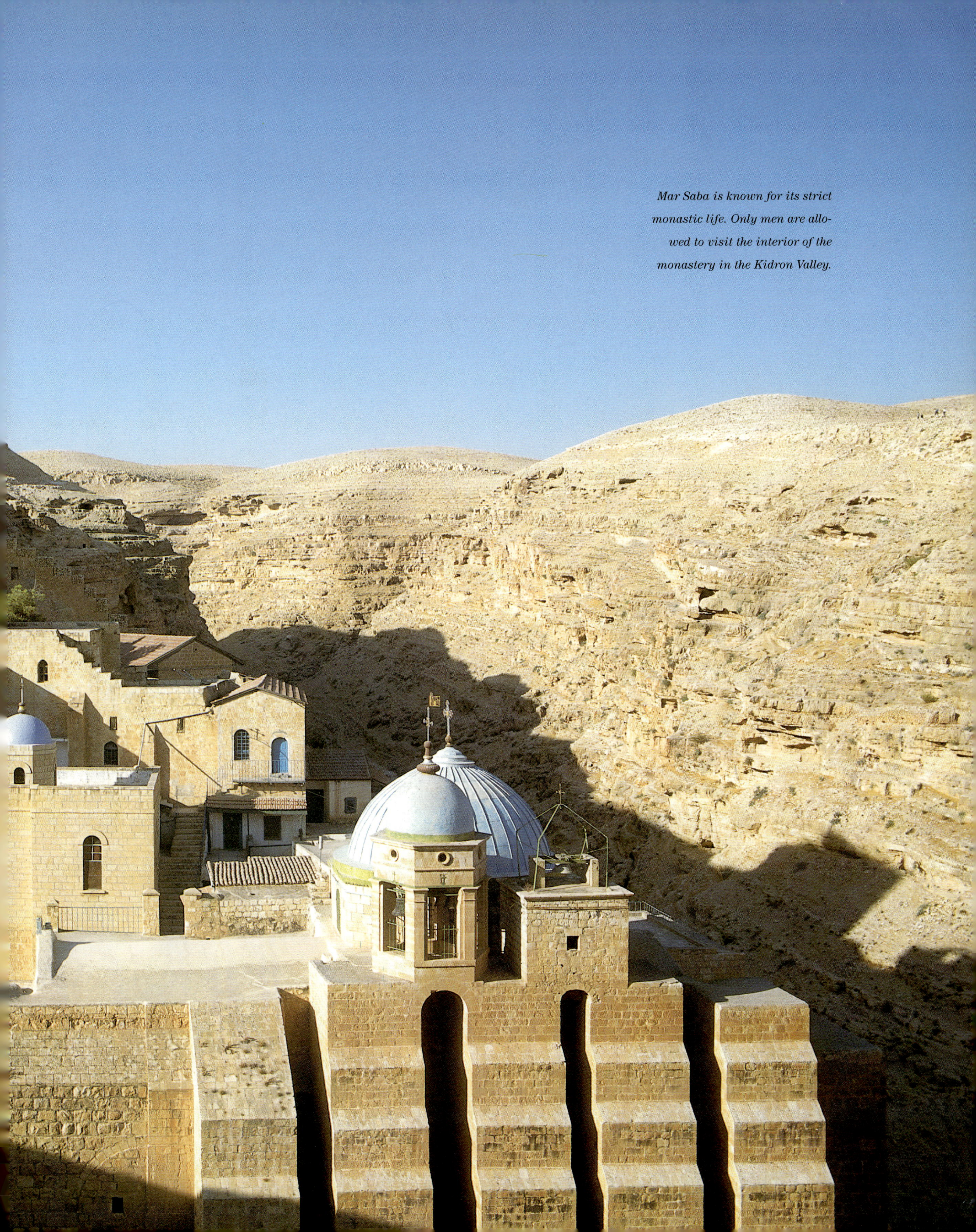

Mar Saba is known for its strict monastic life. Only men are allowed to visit the interior of the monastery in the Kidron Valley.

'We, the people of Israel – Jews, Muslims, Christians and Druze – dream of a peace that is bound to come one day.'

Chaim Herzog

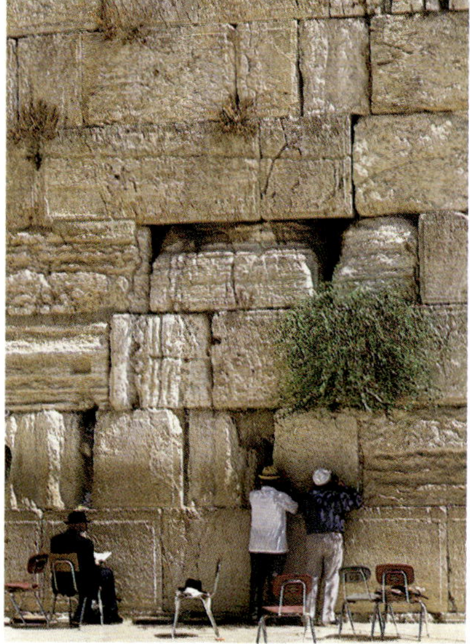

Unique, historic monuments reaching back over 40 centuries, modern city and at the same time Holy City for Jews, Christians and Muslims: **Jerusalem** is the name the Israelis give to their capital city – City of Peace.

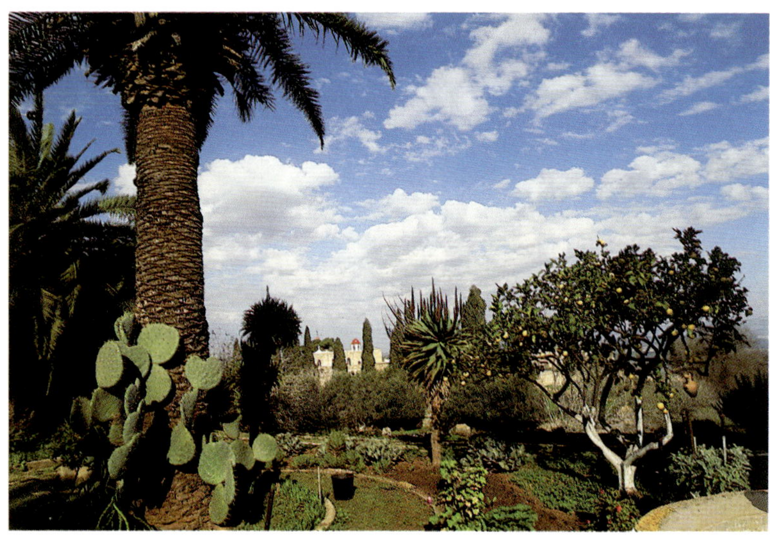

Israel's highest mountains and greenest valleys, the picturesque Sea of Galilee and the sites closely bound up with Jesus and the early Christians: travels through the **North and Galilee**.

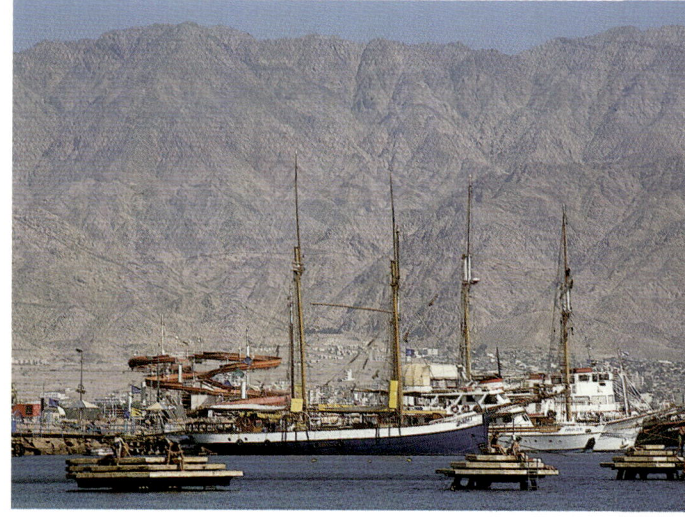

Long, sandy beaches, sparkling blue sea and a fascinating underwater world, adjoining barren mountains, deep gorges and the colours of the desert: **Southern Israel from the Negev to Eilat** awaits you with breathtaking natural phenomena.

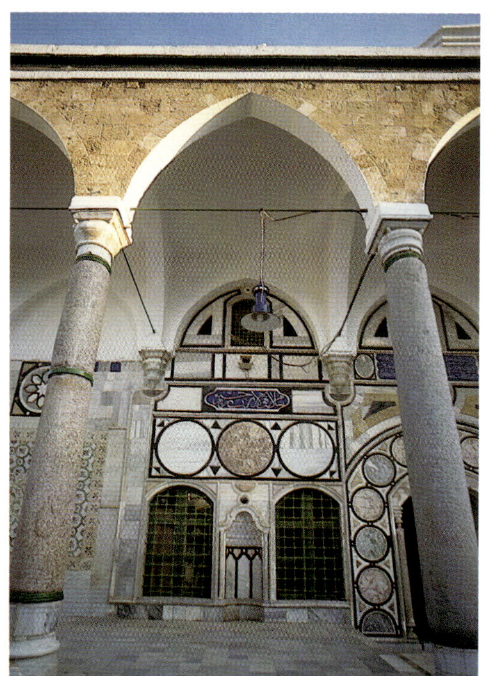

The crusader city of Acre, laden with historic references, and the lively city of Tel Aviv, modern beach resorts and spectacular excavation sites: attractions along the **Mediterranean coast**.

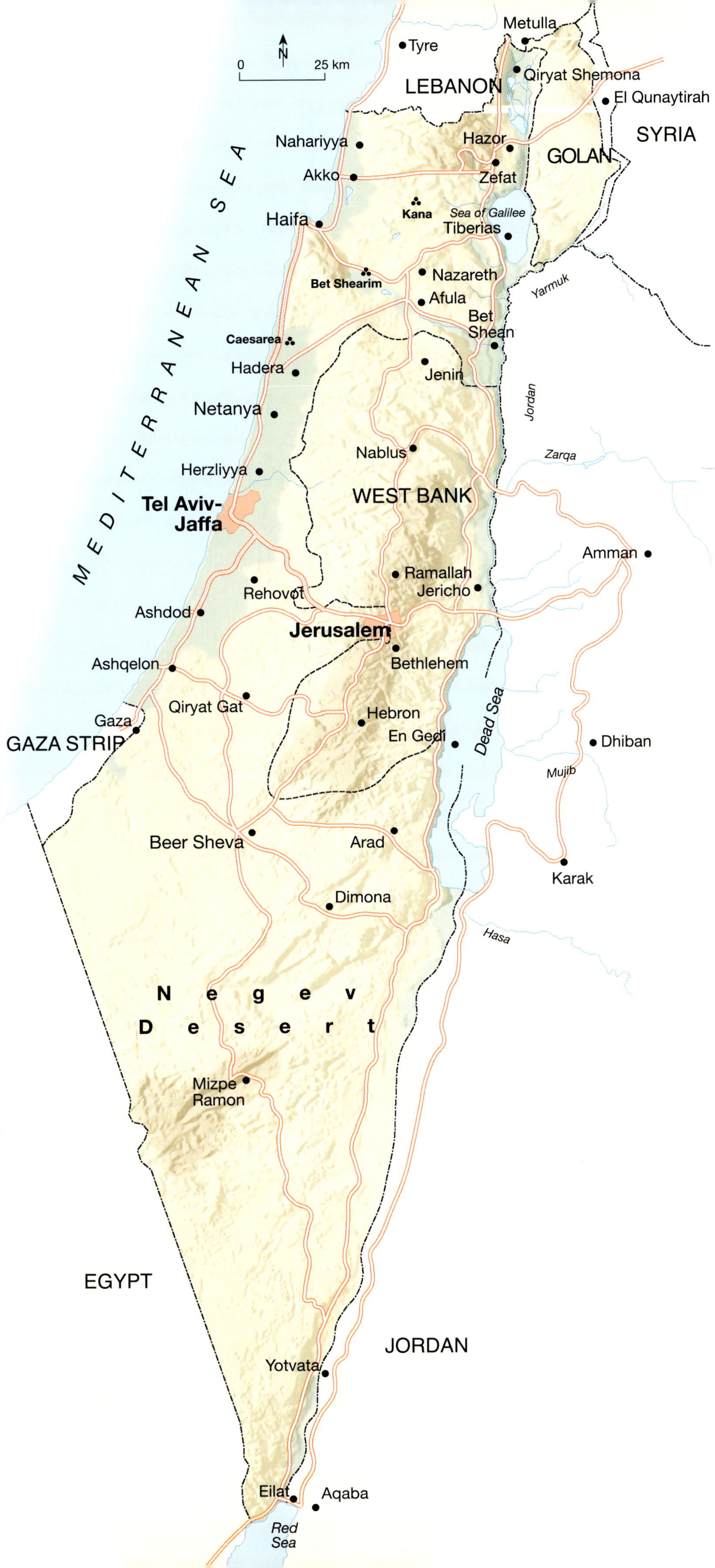

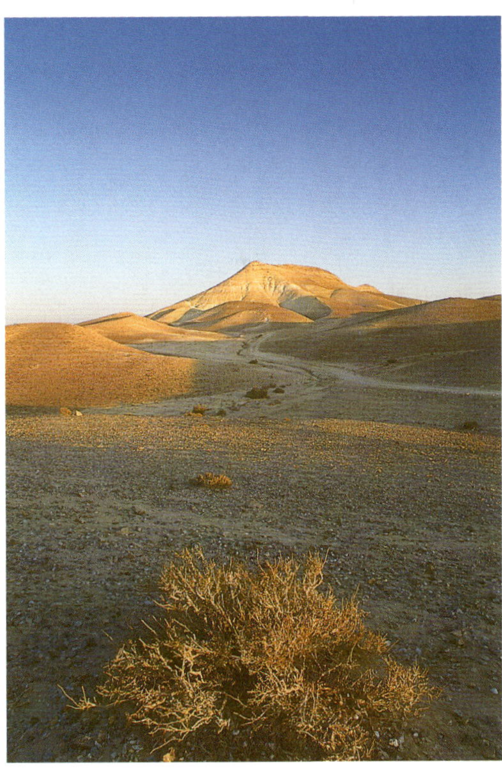

The lowest point on earth and the saltiest waters, Jericho - the oldest city on earth, the fortress of Masada – national pilgrimage site for Israelis: **The Dead Sea and the Judean Desert** are full of wonders.

Pioneers on Biblical Lands

There are many areas on our planet that still remain largely undiscovered. Israel is not one of them. Quite the contrary: no other country has been the subject of such intensive media reports, no other country is the subject of such violent debates and has people of such diverse origins expressing such firm views about it, some of whom have never been there.

To begin with, Israel is a young country – barely 50 years old – and a typical immigrant country. Between 1882 and 1948, the year of the declaration of the State, Jews emigrated to Palestine in six large waves. This continued after the founding of the State and resumed again in the 1990s after the surprising collapse of the Eastern Bloc countries.

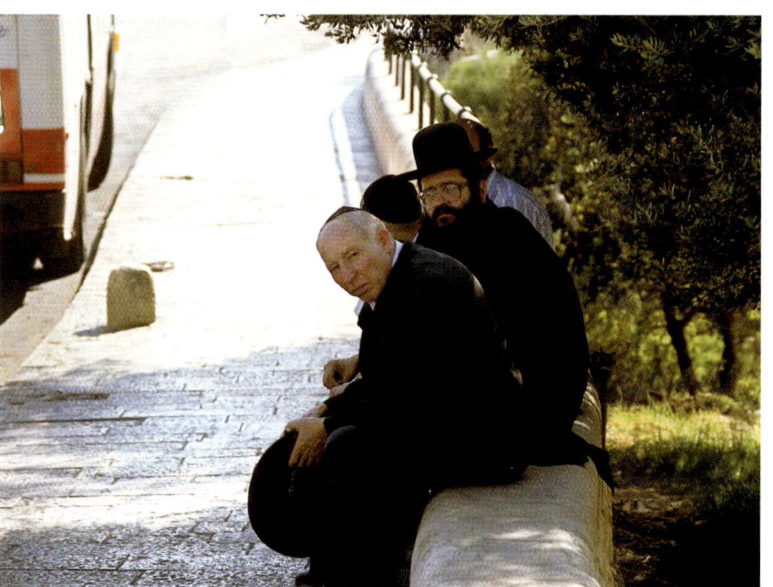

Jews make up the majority of Israel's inhabitants. They immigrated to this place from all over the world both before and after the founding of the State of Israel. Their religious identity as well as age and status in the family is recognised by the little cap or hat that they wear known as the 'kippah'.

The familiar slogan of 'A Land without a People for a People without a Land' which inspired the early immigrants of the nineteenth century, was part of the philosophy of Theodor Herzl and his Zionist followers and turned out to have serious consequences. For the country which was being populated by the Jews was by no means uninhabited and its Arab residents were none too pleased with their new neighbours, who almost overnight and with revolutionary zeal tried to catapult the strip of Palestinian land into the modern era. The resulting conflict has been raging for nearly 100 years, the conflict of a people's basic right to exist. It has still not been resolved and continues to dominate the news media since the murder of Yitzhak Rabin in 1995 and the faltering peace process. The election of Ehud Barak as Prime Minister in 1999 has raised new hopes.

Israel is a country with such a heterogeneous population of six million individuals that it is difficult for a visitor to gain a proper feel for it, let alone an understanding of its context and background. He is therefore likely to leave the country feeling even more ignorant than when he arrived. One way of gaining an insight into Israel is through its jokes and humour, which

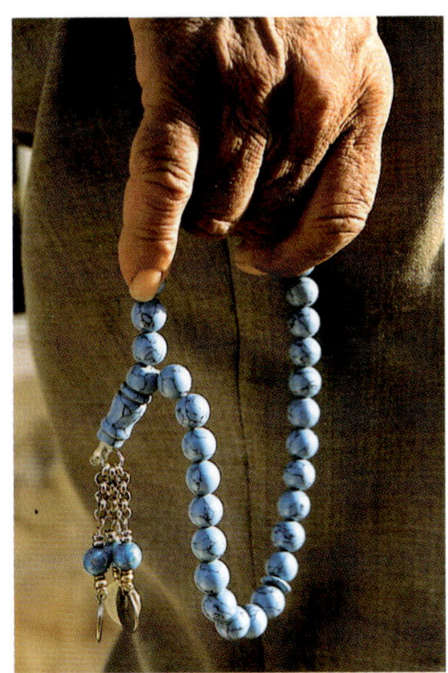

manage to prove, in their own charming way, that the nation doesn't take itself quite as seriously as one might be led to believe. Israel, at the cross-roads of three world religions, Christianity, Judaism and Islam as well as countless religious minorities, doesn't just make jokes about religion. Its targets include politics, the Holocaust and even the wars it has fought for its bare survival. Literary scholars and students of folklore have described the Jewish joke as being the very key to Jewish history and claim that Jews have been forced to flee from Judaism either into despair or humour.

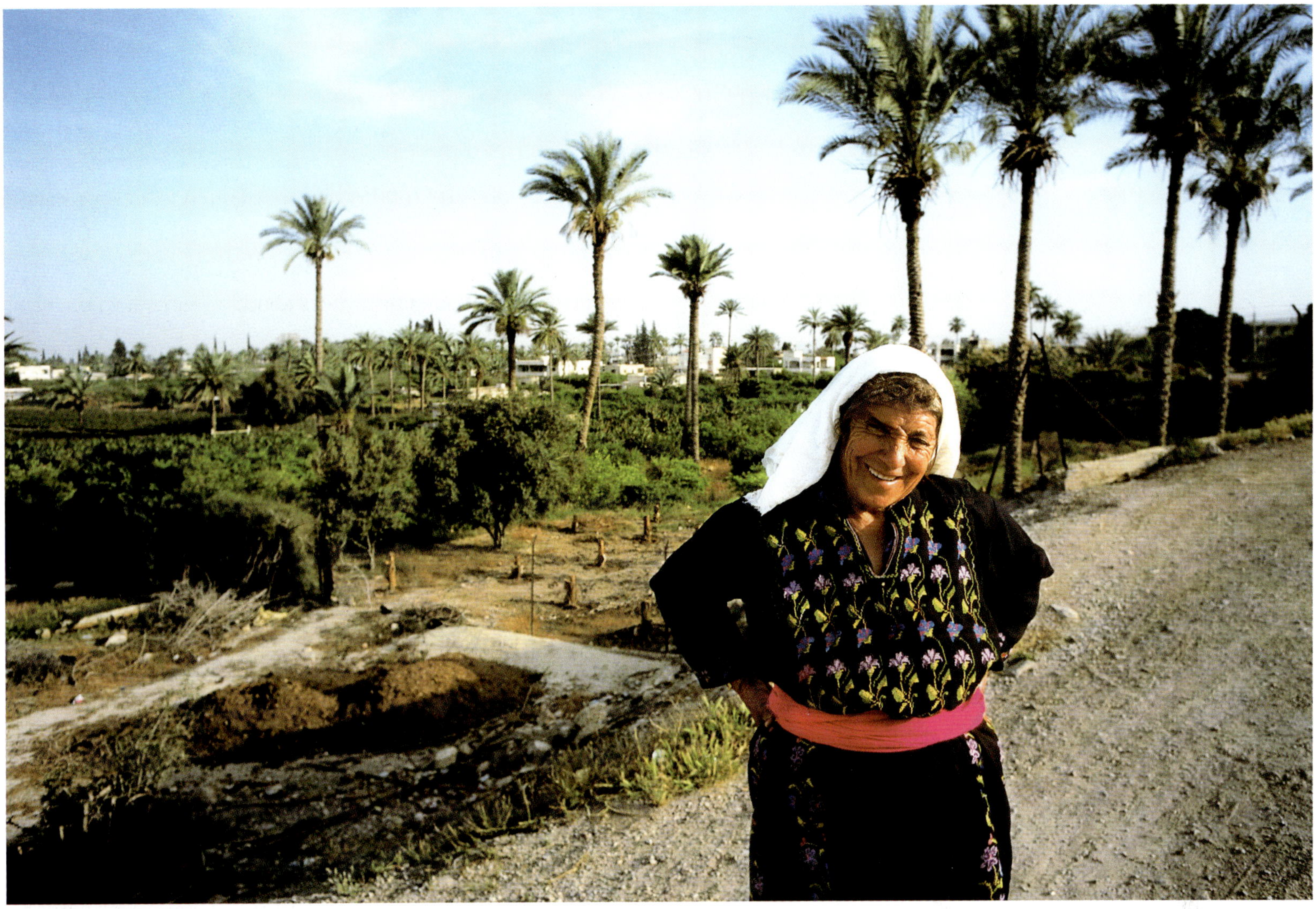

The writer Ephraim Kishon is probably one of Israel's most successful 'exports'. In the fictitious letter he wrote to President Anwar al Sadat after Egypt and Syria invaded Israel in 1973, resulting in the Yom Kippur War he said: 'If only you had invaded us on an ordinary weekday you would have found a nation of bad-tempered people, tired from their working day, stuffed full of steak and chicken. Yom Kippur, on the other hand, is a day of fasting, no one is working, people are calm and relaxed

Many Bedouin women hand embroider their dresses, both for special occasions and for every day, with floral or geometric patterns using age-old traditional styles (top). For a Muslim, allowing the prayer beads to slide through the hand is the same as saying a prayer. Each of the beads represents a surah[chapter] of the Koran (below).

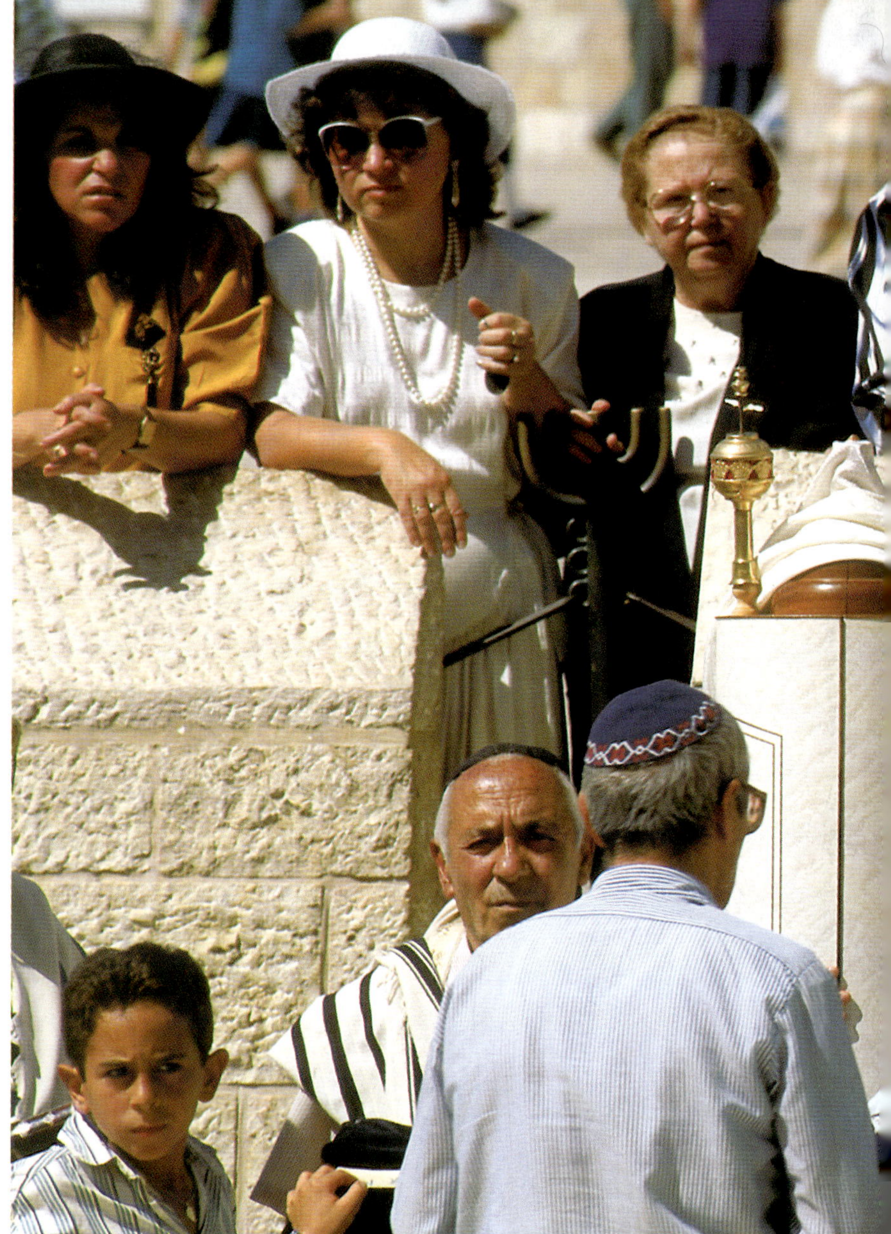

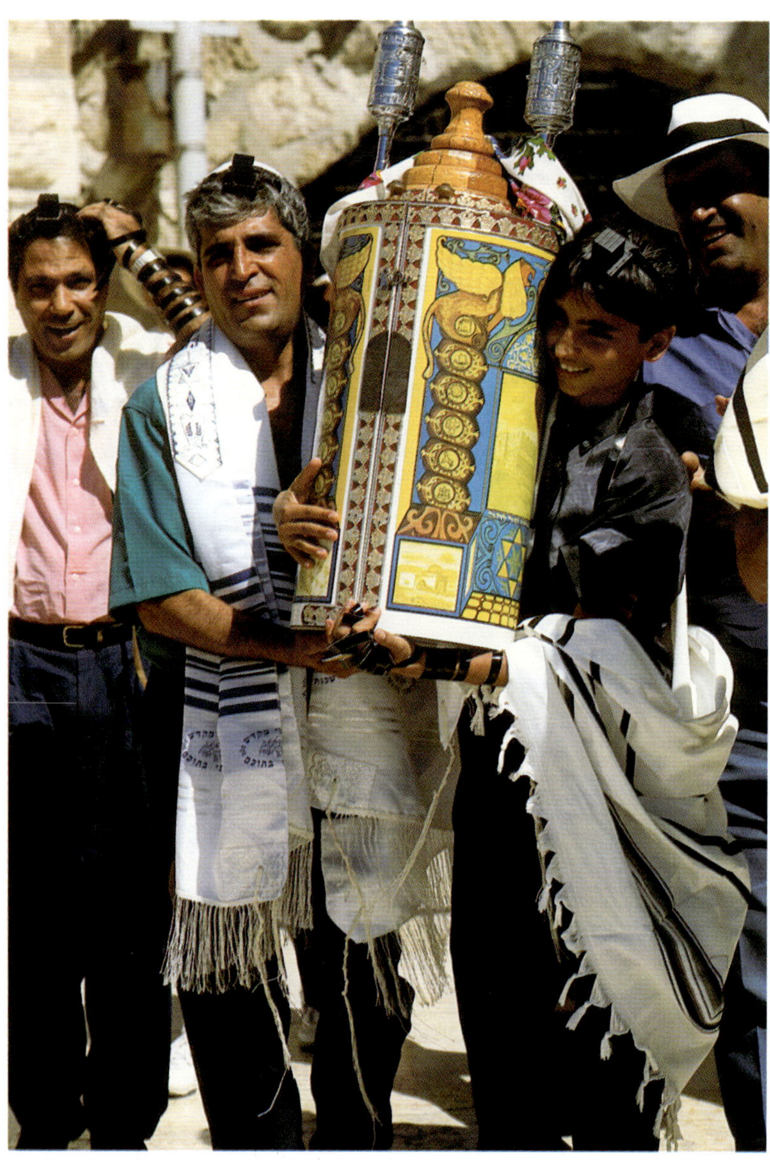

and are just raring to go into action again. You actually saved our lives, Anwar, by picking Yom Kippur. Anyway, at least we both learned something. From now on we'll pay more attention to your words and to our borders.' A touch of bitter irony which makes one thing clear: anyone who wants to meet that Israeli challenge head on should first throw out any prejudices. What is fatal about this country are its paradoxes: the more you know about it, the less you seem to understand it. However, it becomes a lot easier to understand when we take a look at the history of Zionism and the foundation of the State of Israel.

Theodor Herzl's Dream

Jews are probably the only people on earth who, over the centuries, preferred to suffer pogroms, suppression and expulsion rather than give up their religion and identity. And they are also probably the only people on earth who looked upon their own national liberation movement with scepticism, derision and rejection when it first started to emerge. Yet political Zionism is based on an understanding both simple and profound: living side-by-side in peace with non-Jews is not possible, and if the situation of the Jews should change then they would have to take their fate into their own hands rather than rely on tolerance from the world around them or on deliverance by the Messiah. Like so many before him, the Viennese journalist, Theodor Herzl (1860–1904) believed deeply that assimilation would be the solution and had even considered persuading the Jews of Vienna to go through a mass baptism in the city's St. Stephen's Cathedral. Constant anti-Semitic attacks, however, whether during the Dreyfuss trial which Herzl covered as a

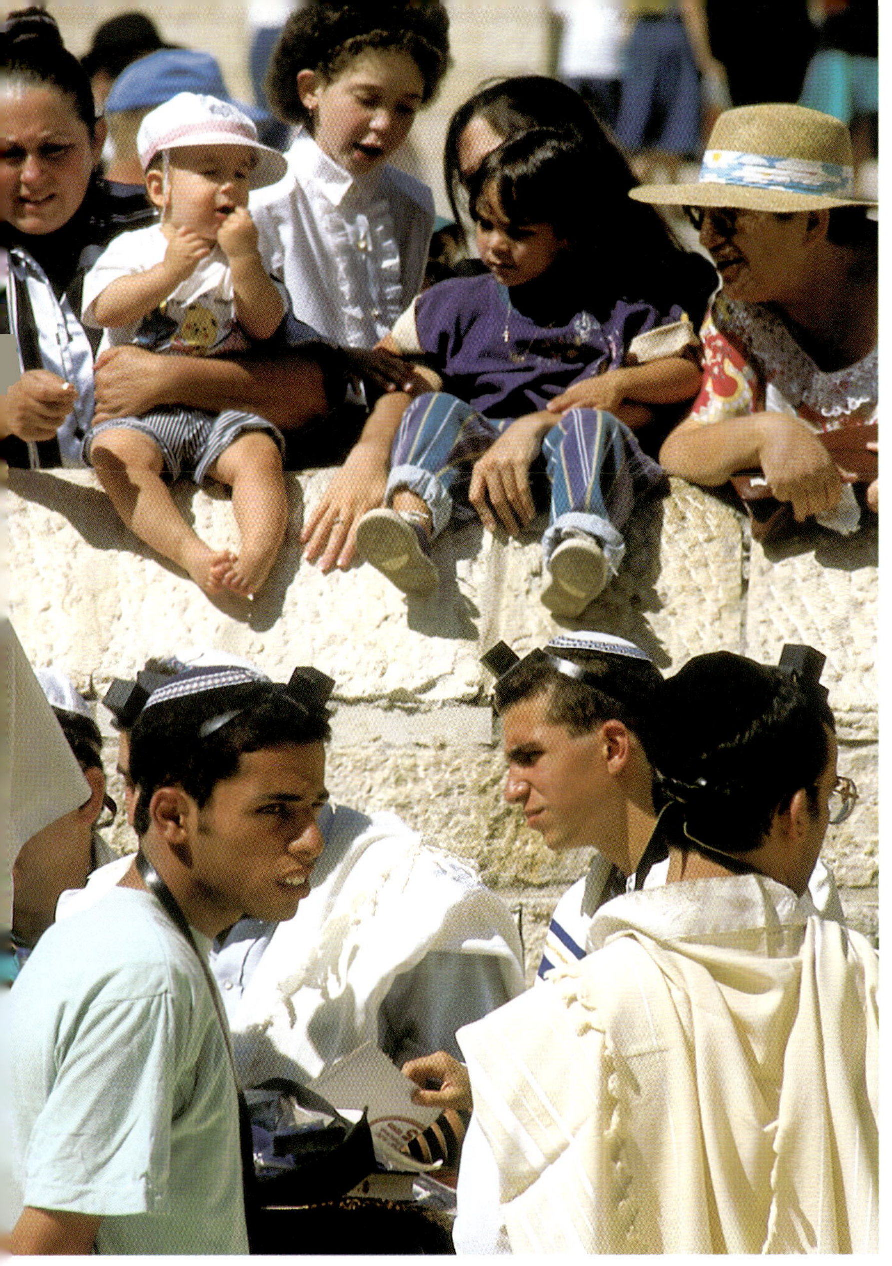

During the Bar Mitzvah festivities thirteen-year-old boys celebrate reaching the age of religious maturity. They may now for the first time as full members of the community read from the Torah which is contained in the highly decorated Ark.

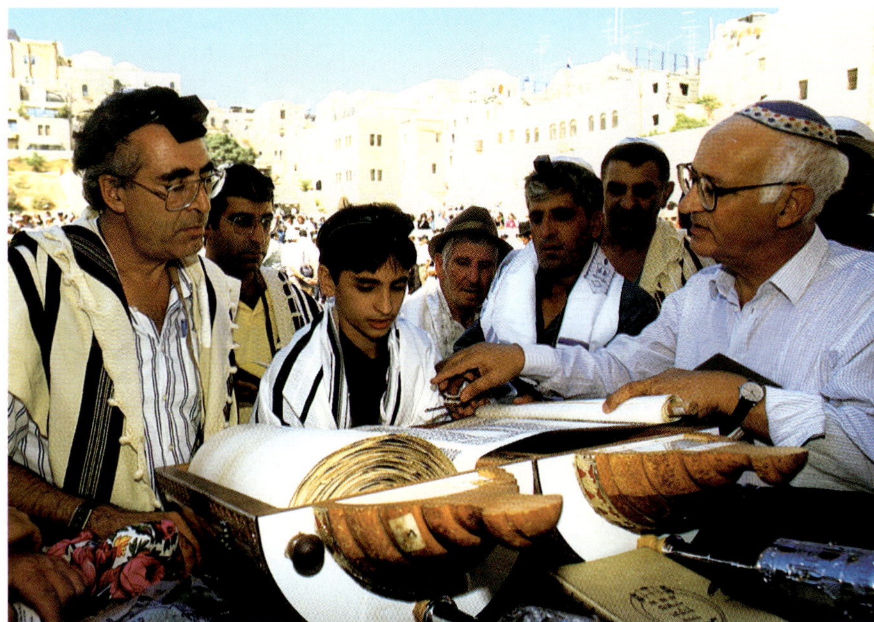

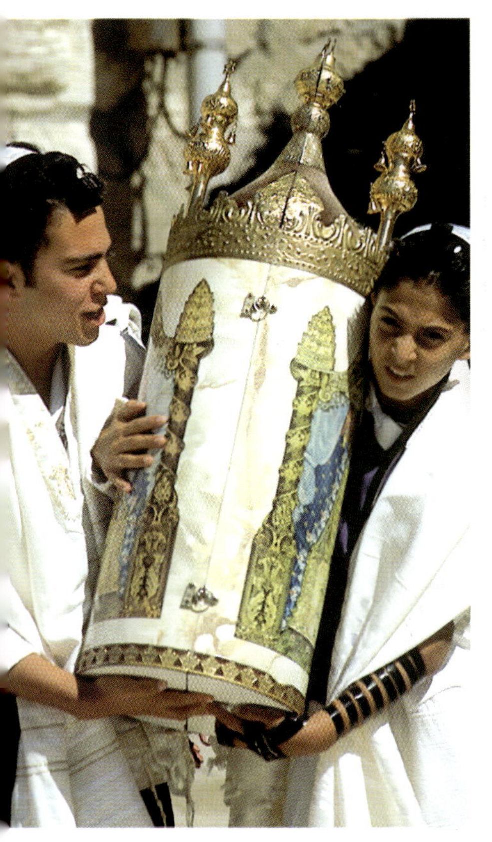

reporter in Paris, or in the form of insults and abuse on the street, made him realise that there was nothing for it but to flee. When his pamphlet *The Jewish State* was published in Vienna in 1896, the Jews who used to frequent the coffee houses were heard to say, 'Let Dr Herzl create a Jewish State, just so long as he appoints me ambassador to Vienna'. The majority of the Jewish population was critical of Herzl's ideas, while Orthodox Jewry rejected him as being dangerous and damaging.

After violent pogroms broke out again in Russia in 1880, the Russian doctor Leon Pinsker (1821–1891) also spoke out in favour of a return of the Jews to Palestine in his pamphlet entitled *Autoemancipation – An Exhortation to Members of his Race from a Russian Jew*. The little pamphlet did not attract much notice, but, by this time many Jews had themselves reached the conclusion that their intolerable situation could only be improved by emigrating. The majority of eastern European emigrants made their way to the United States, but around 1881 the first wave of immigrants arrived in the Holy Land. 'Creating

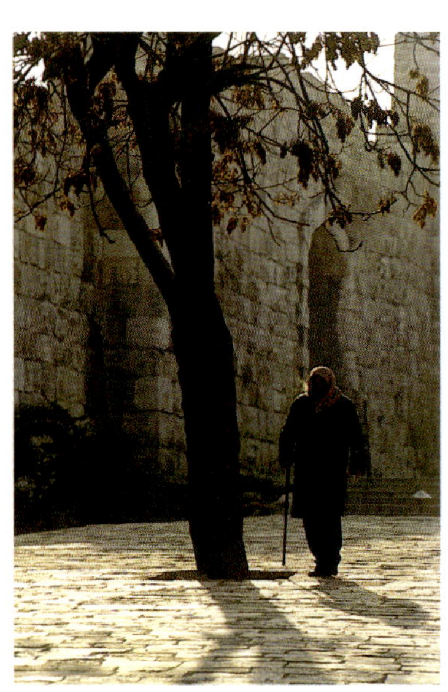

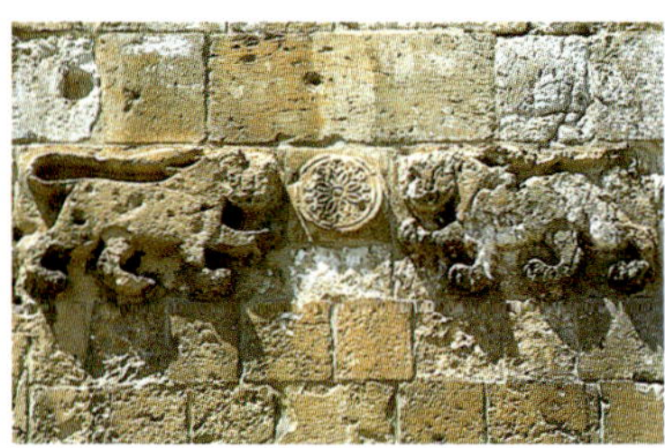

The impressive 16th century town walls surrounding the Old City of Jerusalem with its battlements, towers and embrasures. Eight gates including the New Gate (above) and the Lions' Gate (detail, below) lead into the Old City.

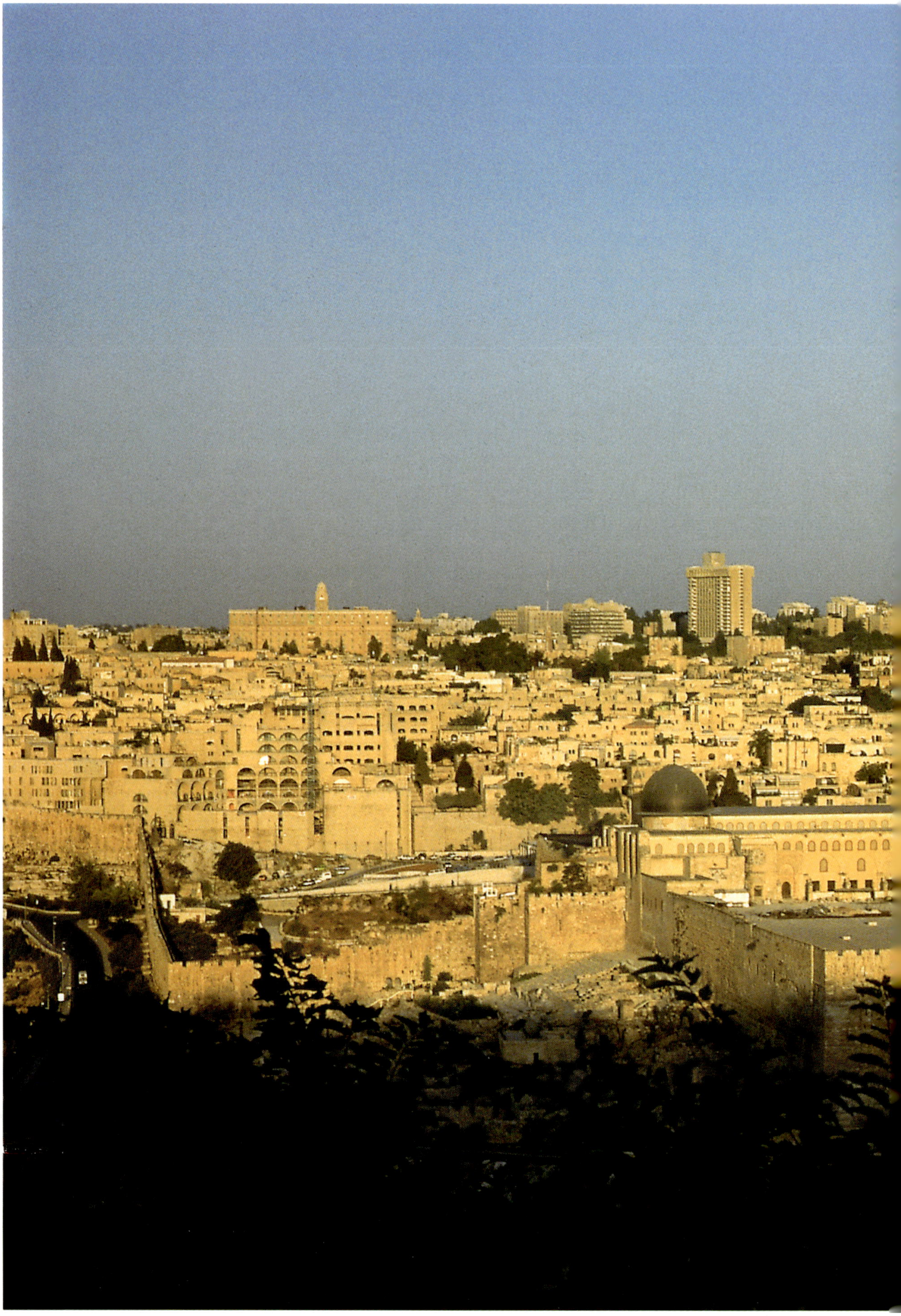

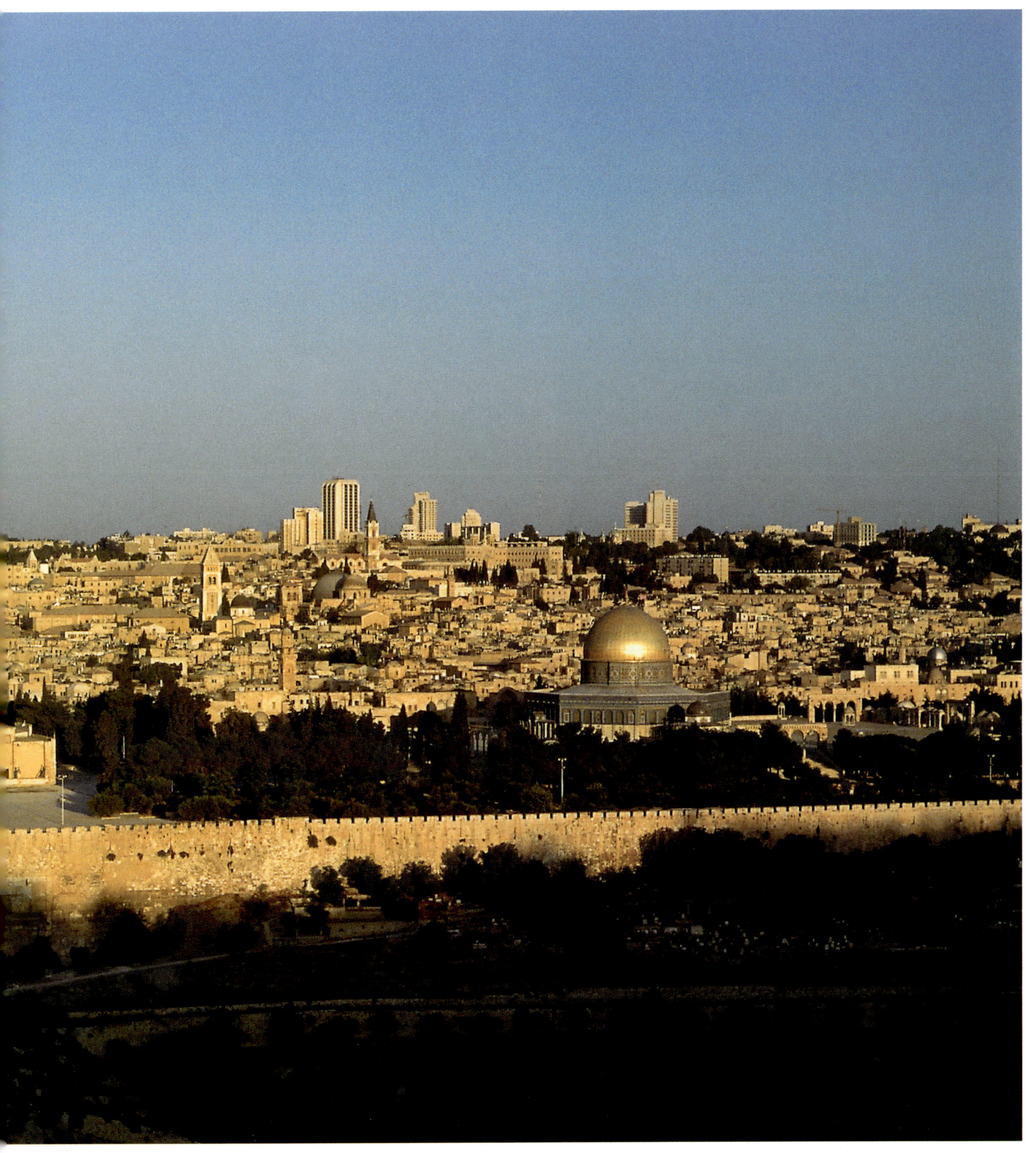

Martin Buber, Professor for Social Philosophy at the University of Jerusalem between 1938 and 1951 lived in the Talbiye District (left). The Church of All Nations was built at the foot of the Mount of Olives in 1924 (centre).

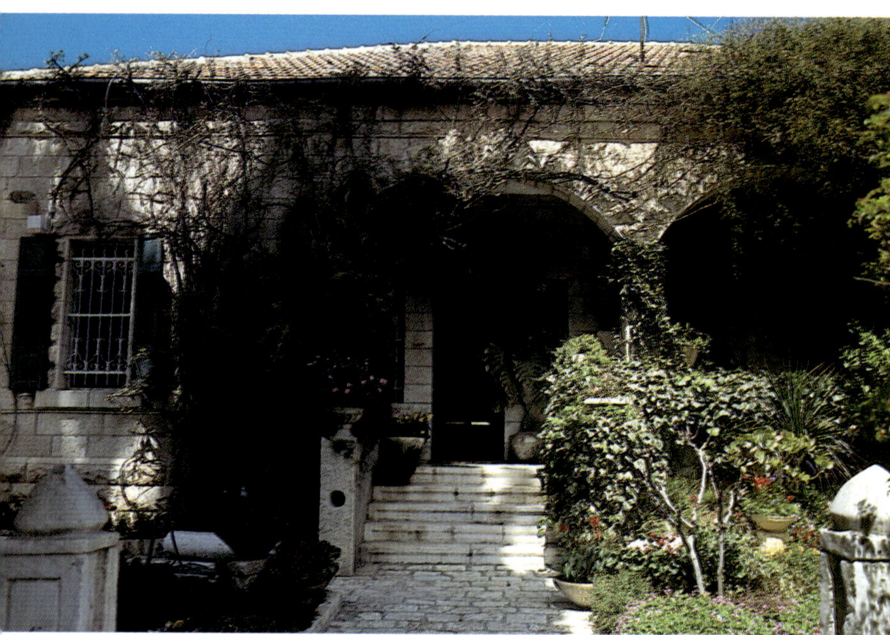

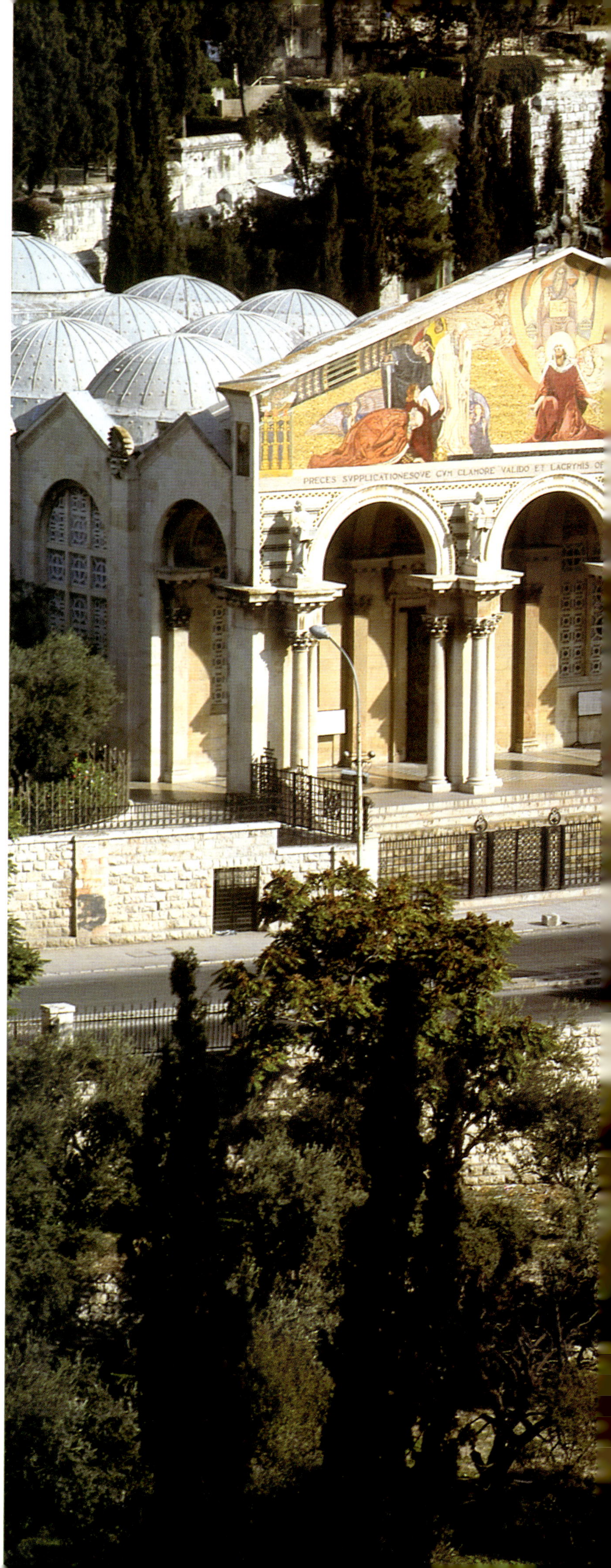

something with our own hands' was the motto of the early Zionists. Finally they would prove to the anti-Semites that Jews didn't only pore over books but were capable of becoming good farmers and soldiers. The catchword 'Jewish work', however, made many Arab rural workers very bitter, because it was their land which was often being sold behind their backs by Arab landowners to the Zionists. The *fellahins* who had tended their land for centuries were now seeing strangers tilling this same land. The early foundations for a Jewish State, but also for the Arab-Israeli conflict, had been laid.

Herzl was a dreamer as well as a strong believer in progress. His people should become 'normal' and should be freed of the burden of being the eternal outsider. The Land of Zion was to become a melting pot of nations, races and religions. In his novel *Old-New Land* he describes a vision of a new State, in which Zionists create a modern Garden of Eden in the desert, threaded with irrigation systems. And of course, in the novel, even the Arab inhabitants are grateful to the colonizers for their work.

One might speculate today on what the Holy Land would look like if the high-flown dreams of Herzl, the utopian, had come true. Or whether the State of Israel would have even existed

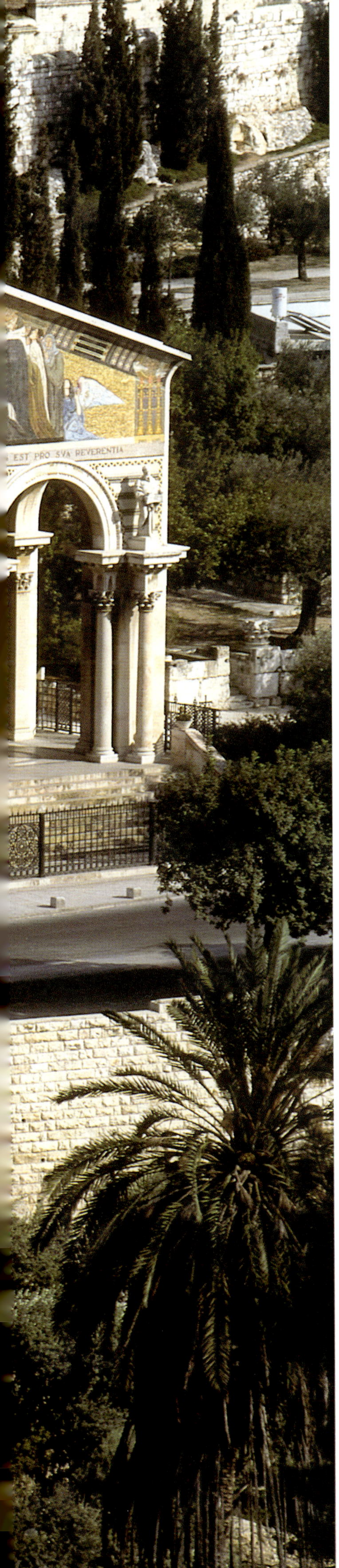

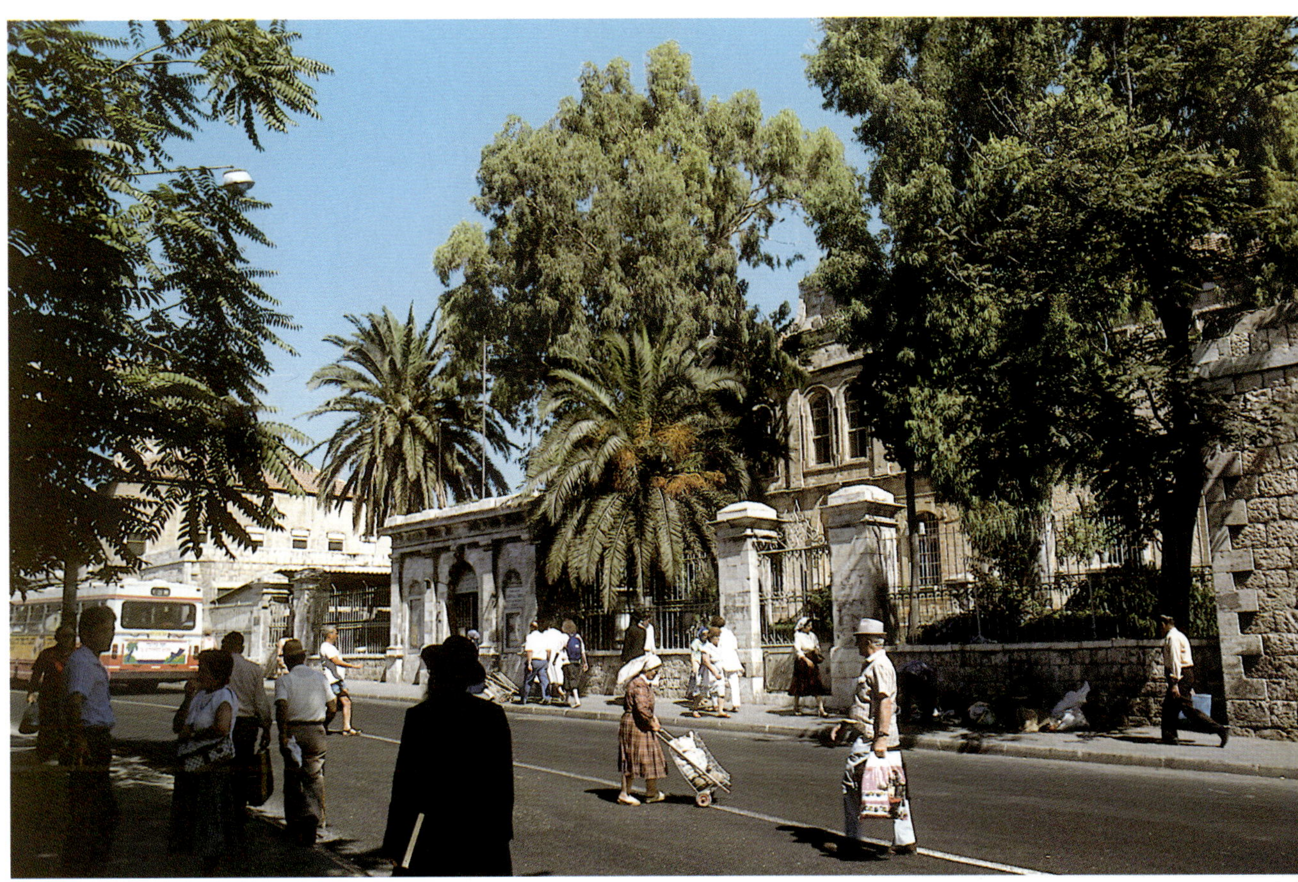

today if the immigrants of yesteryear had concentrated more on aesthetic ideas than on practical projects. The Jewish immigrants who arrived from Russia, Poland and finally from Nazi Germany were not particularly interested in converting the country into a social precedent for multi-cultural harmony. They wanted to create a new homeland in which it was quite normal to be Jewish, a safe refuge for the suppressed and persecuted, a country in which Jews were not at the mercy of foreign powers. If they were going to succeed, they would need more than a lot of dreams of nationalism; they needed a proper infrastructure for which they would have to work very hard.

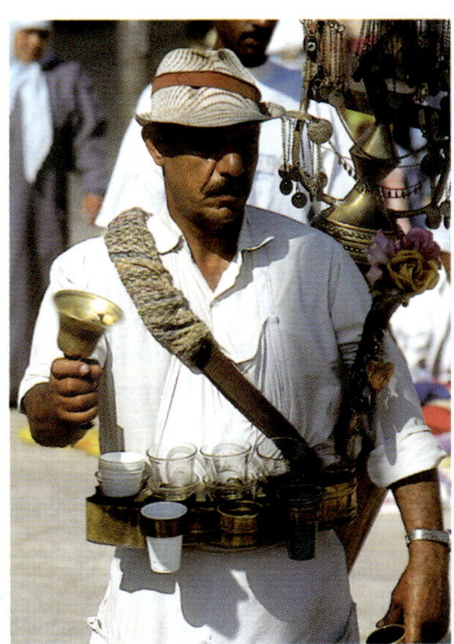

Outside the old city walls, Jerusalem is a picture of modernity, of 'unholiness'. But the tea and water vendors continue to remind us that this is the Orient.

The Founding of a Modern State

In 1917 Great Britain took over the administration of Palestine and in the so-called Balfour Declaration, the Zionist leader and later the first president of Israel, Chaim Weizmann (1874–1952) was promised that a 'Jewish Homeland' would be created in the British Mandate. The fact that we now had a western-looking country which had thrown off the shackles of ailing Turkish rule had an immediate effect on the Yishuv, the Jewish community in Palestine. The hitherto slumbering Near East awoke, both politically and economically. While industrial and agri-

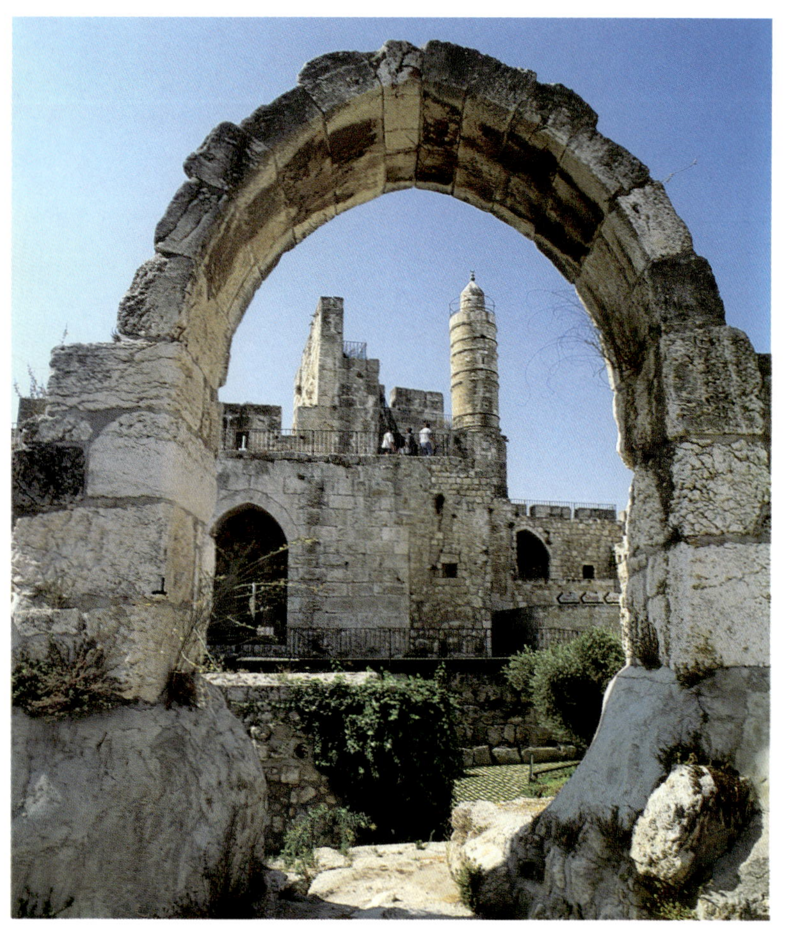

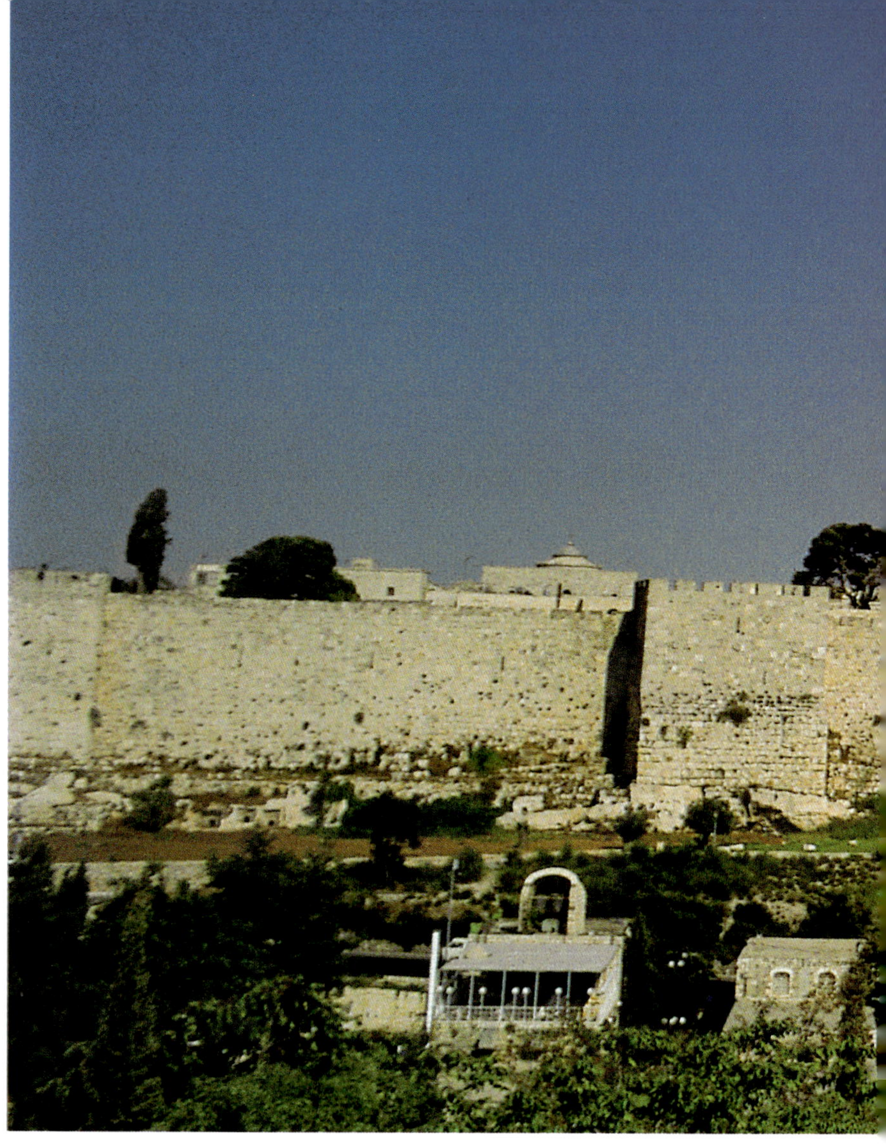

The Museum of the History of Jerusalem occupies a conveniently strategic position on a hill inside Jerusalem's imposing Citadel (above right); the Tower of David (above and centre) is part of the Citadel complex and in its present form dates back to the 14th century – it offers unparalleled views over the Old City. The focus for religious Jews in Jerusalem: Jews gather to pray at the Wailing Wall (below); in the Church of the Holy Sepulchre even Syrian Jacobites have their own chapel (page right, below).

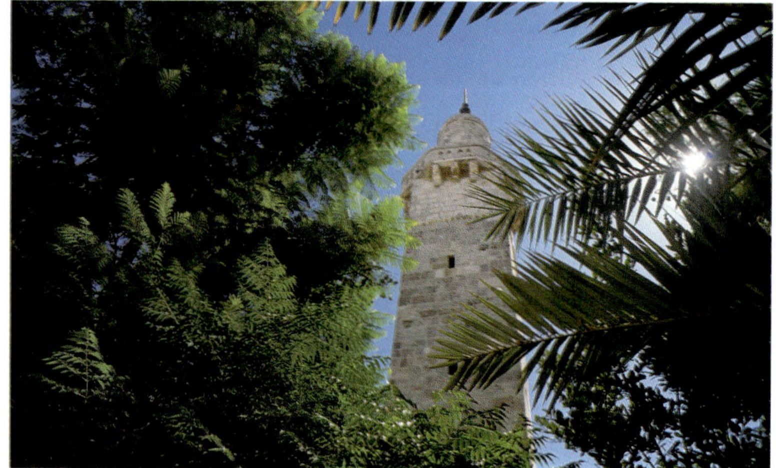

cultural collectives, the kibbutzim, were being established, newspapers and radio stations, writers' associations and theatres were also developing. And everyone who worked in these new establishments and whose mother-tongue was Yiddish, Russian, German or Polish was now using a new common language which had been reintroduced after 1880 by the philologist Eliezer Ben Yehuda (1858–1922): Ivrit, or modern Hebrew.

An industrial and agricultural infrastructure, its own language and under the circumstances, a surprisingly diverse and blossoming cultural life, these were only three of the pillars of the future Jewish State. The fourth and probably the most powerful to date, the army, was also created during this period and probably owes its existence to the British. Shortly after British Foreign Secretary Balfour (1848–1930) indicated his support to the Zionists for a future Jewish homeland, the British started giving the Arabs hope for their own state. As a result of this rather two-faced policy, tensions between Arabs and Jews intensified, leading to riots and revolts causing the deaths of hundreds of people on both sides. Following this, the British more or less nullified the Balfour Declaration and put a lid on immigration for Jews – a measure which was to prove disastrous given the fact that the Nazis were to seize power in Germany in 1933. This was not the end of the violent clashes. But it was now that the Yishuv settlers decided there was only one thing they could do. During the Arab uprising against Jewish immigration between 1936 and 1939, military underground organisations were formed which later became the basis for the Israeli army.

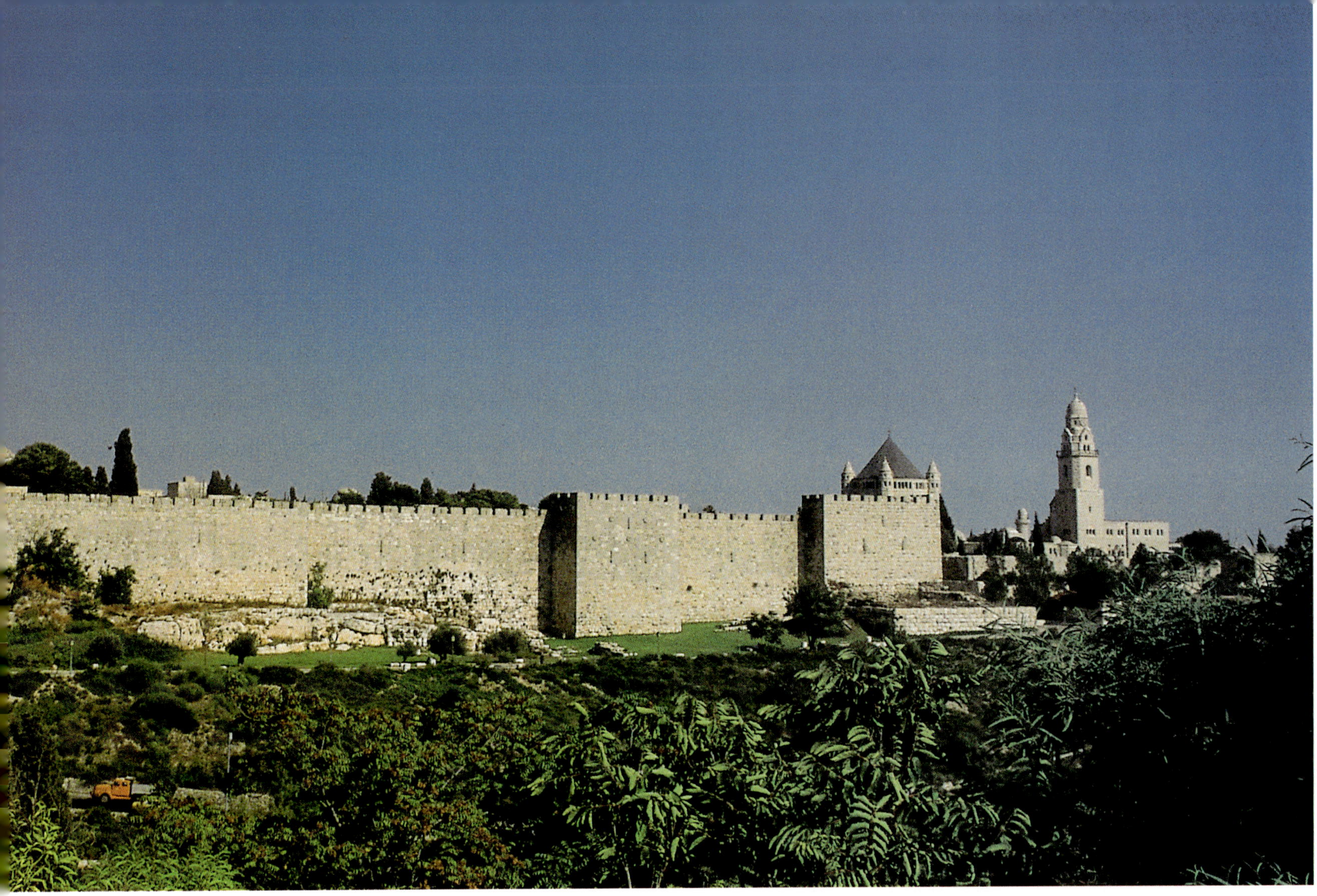

In 1947 the British handed over their mandate to the United Nations Special Committee on Palestine, which designed a plan for Palestine under which both Arabs and Jews should set up their own state. Israel's first Prime Minister David Ben-Gurion (1886–1973), ever the pragmatist, accepted the partition proposal. Understandably the League of the neighbouring Arab nations which was also acting for the splintered Palestinian national movement was against it, as it represented the interests of the relevant country rather than the cause of the Arabs living in Palestine.

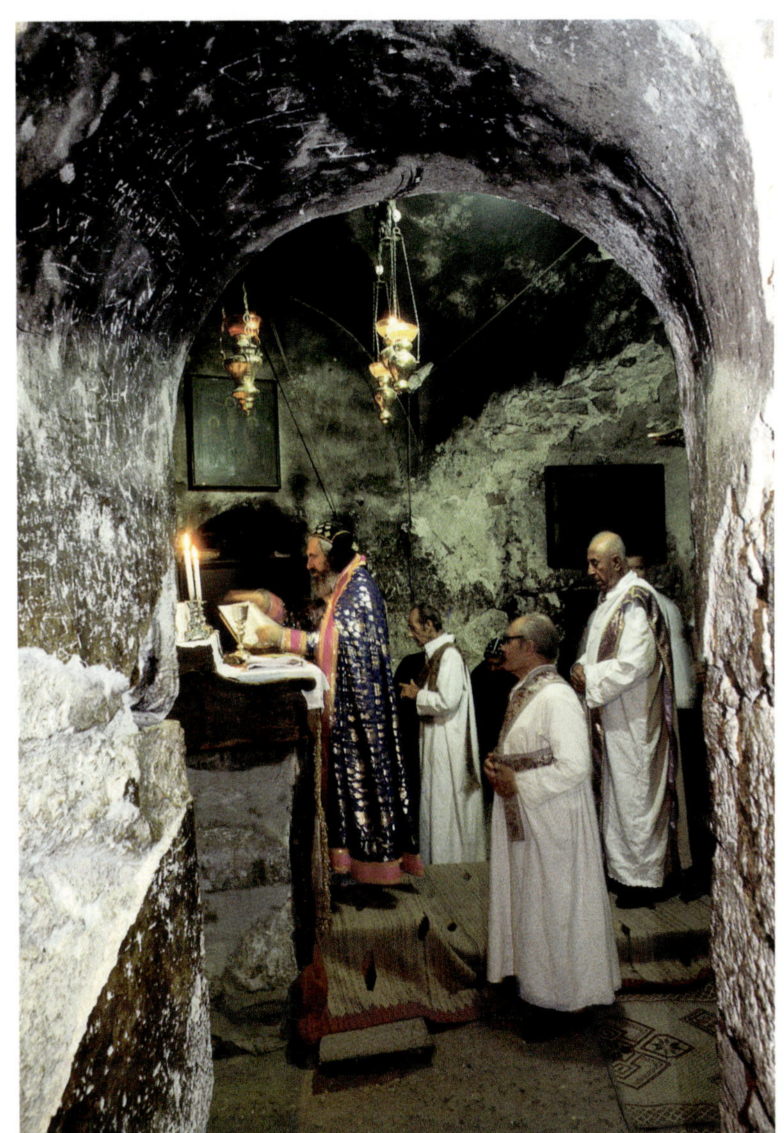

The Yad Vashem complex is a reminder of the Holocaust. The memorial wall was designed to simulate a ghetto wall (left). One of the most moving sculptures on the site is Nandor Glid's Dry Bones (right). The stone floor of the Hall of Remembrance is engraved with the names of 22 concentration camps (below).

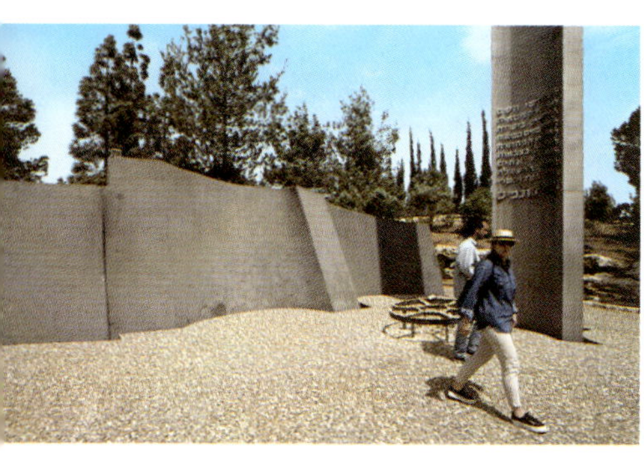

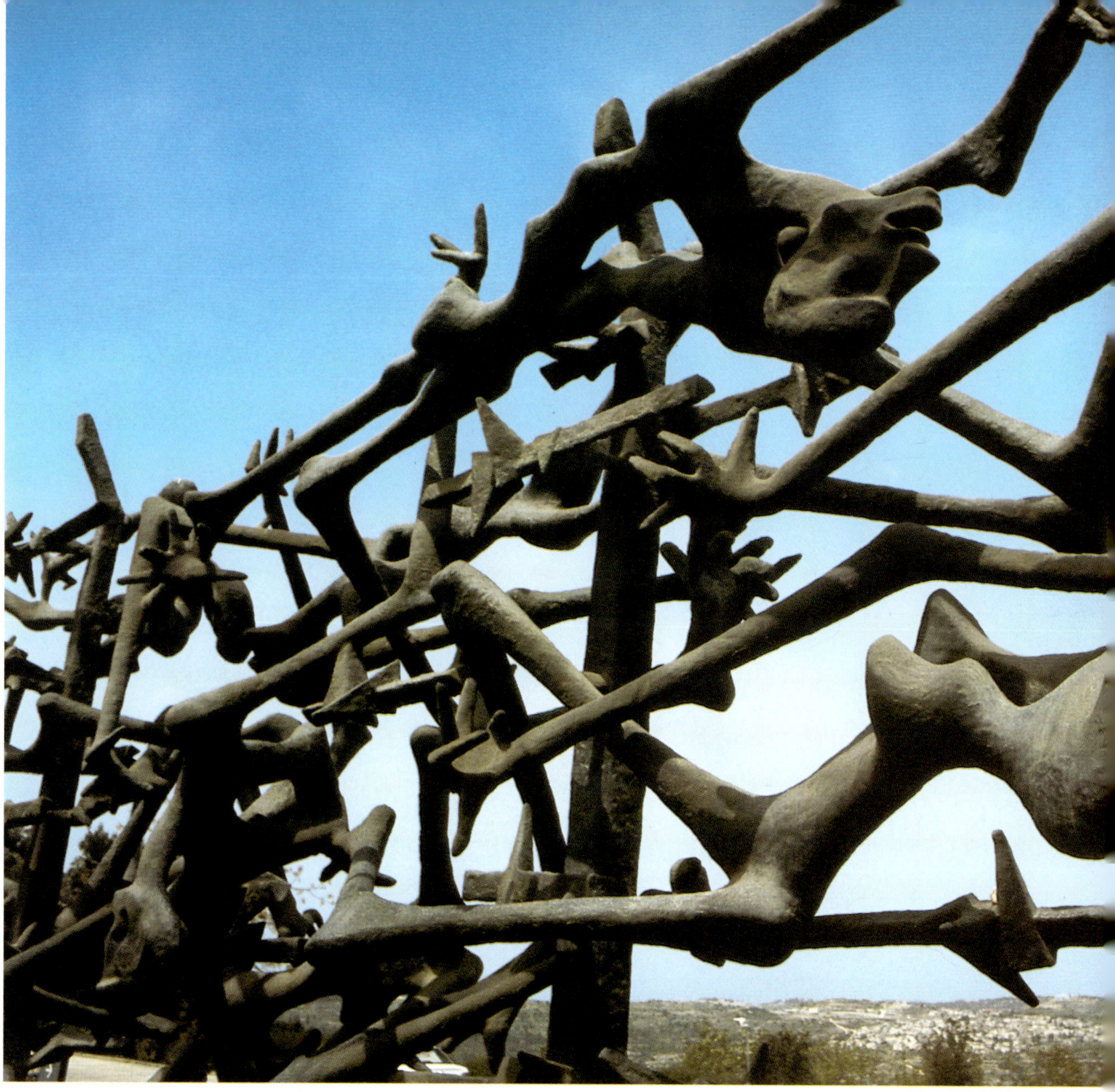

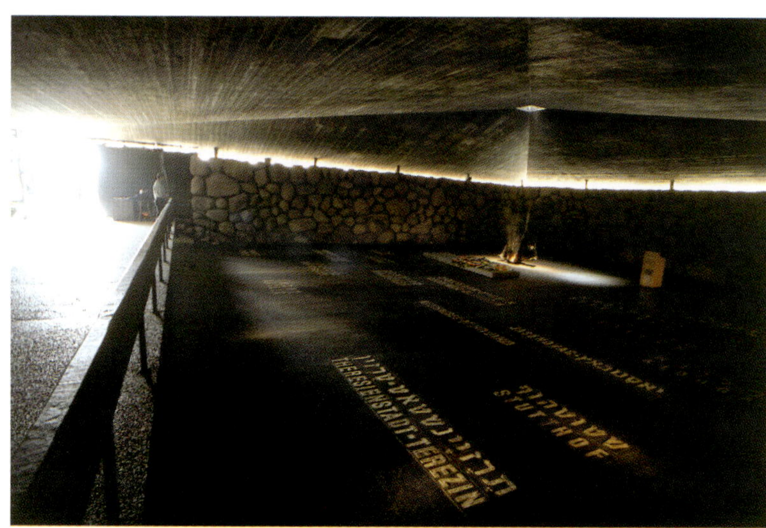

On 14 May 1948 the sovereign State of Israel was declared. One day later five Arab armies invaded Israel. The military organisations which had originally been formed to fight the British Mandate now proved to be Israel's salvation. Israel was able to keep the upper hand in the so-called War of Independence, while the Palestinians were temporarily obliged to bury hopes of their own state. Many fled, many were driven away by force, and many live in refugee camps to this day. In their history, the War of Independence has a different name: al-Nakhba or the Catastrophe.

At the time of the Declaration of Independence the infrastructure was already in place: hospitals, universities, factories, unions and an army. The Jewish State however received its most tremendous boost by what was probably the most horrific event in Jewish history, the Holocaust. Thousands of Jews who never in their wildest dreams would have thought of emigrating to Palestine before 1933 now had to flee from the Nazis. These Jews from German-speaking countries known as 'yekkes', made a major contribution to the Jewish State. They

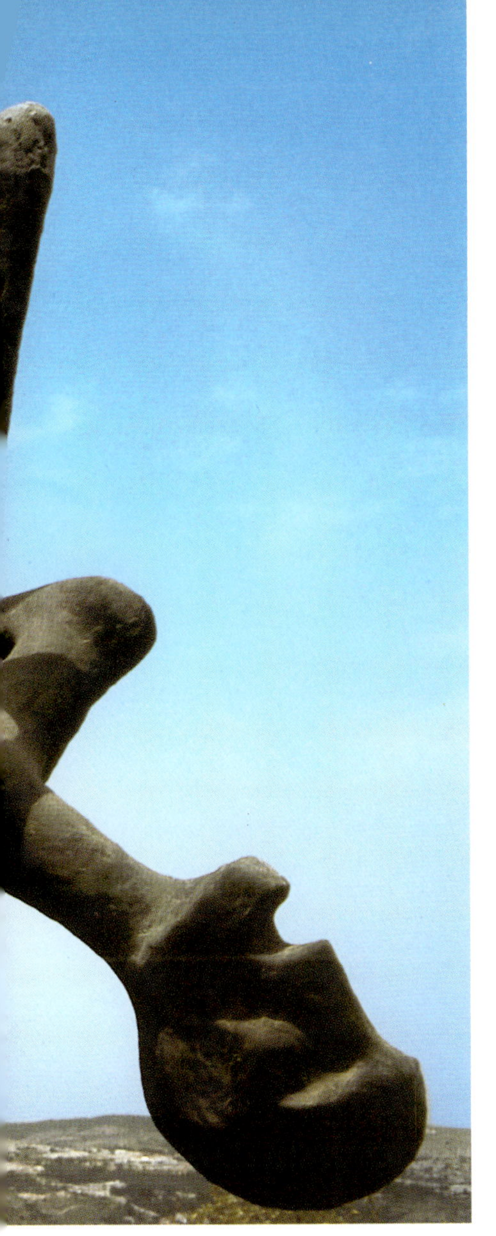

The Shrine of the Book houses the oldest known manuscript of the Old Testament in Hebrew (top). The Knesset, Israel's Parliament (below).

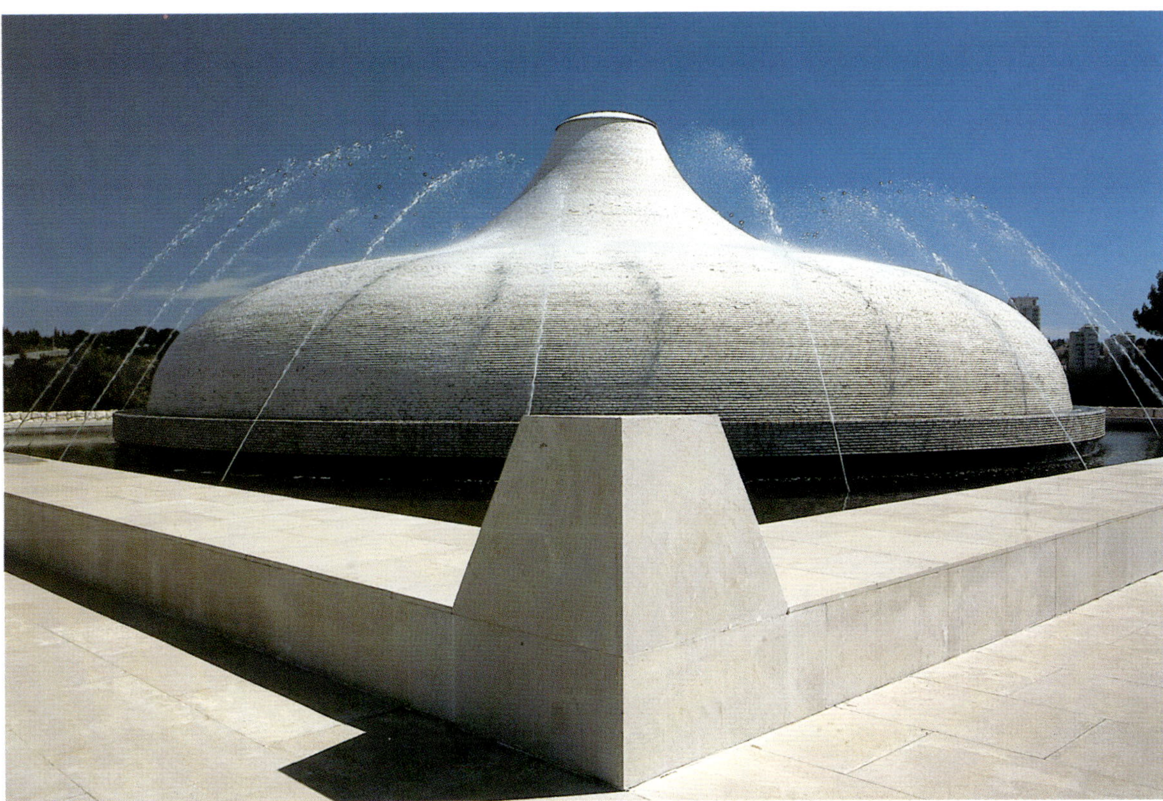

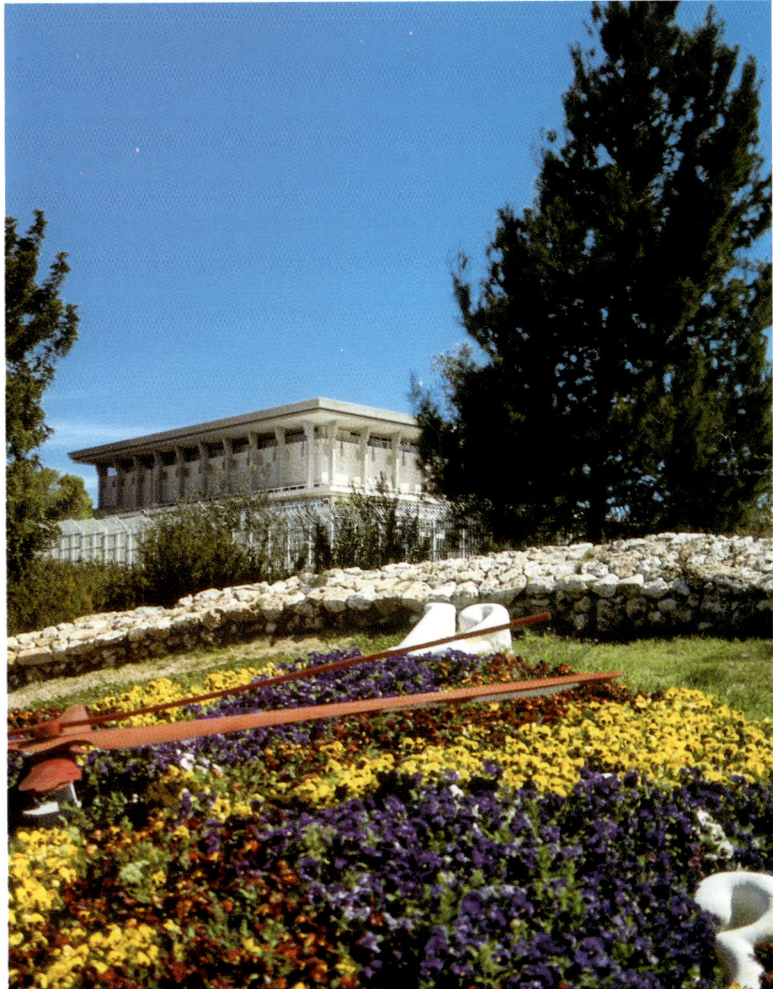

were particularly involved in setting up the judiciary and played a major role in establishing the Hebrew University in Jerusalem, which was initially run by professors from central Europe. And they brought something else – something the rough-and-ready pioneers had had little time for – politeness and good manners.

The Stony Path towards Normality

All Zionist thinkers, regardless of which political camp they belonged to and regardless of how they imagined the Jewish State had one idea in common: they skilfully used Jewish history to support the return of the people to Zion while breaking with at least a part of this history so that they could start a whole new chapter. Israel should be fully aware of its traditions, while at the same time leaving behind the traditions of the Diaspora. It is therefore not possible to say today whether Zionism has been a success. It is true that the Jewish State has been established, but there are still more people living in the Diaspora than in Israel. Israel was meant to break with

Continues on Page 26

History in Dates and Images:

4000 years of Israel

1800–1700 BC: Presumed to be the period when Abraham lived and when he went on the journey to the Promised Land.

1279–1212 BC: Ramses II rules Egypt. It was probably during his reign that Moses led the Israelites out of Egypt.

1200–1000 BC: The era of the Judges who acted as tribal leaders. The Israelites abandon their nomadic lifestyle, take up agriculture and settle in fortified cities.

c. 1000 BC: David is elected King of Israel.

965 BC: David dies. His son Solomon succeeds him.

From 963 BC: Solomon builds the Temple in Jerusalem. After his death in about 926, his kingdom is divided into Judah (south) and Israel (north).

772/721 BC: Israel is conquered by the Assyrians and becomes part of their empire. Ten of the 12 Tribes of Israel disappear during this period.

597 BC: The Babylonian King Nebuchadnezzar invades Judah and takes the upper echelons of Judean society into exile in Babylon.

587 BC: Jerusalem is besieged and then plundered by the Babylonians. The Temple is destroyed.

538 BC: The Israelites return from exile in Babylon and build the Second Temple which is consecrated around 516. Judah remains a Persian province.

332 BC: Alexander the Great conquers the area.

167 BC: Beginning of a three-year rebellion by the Maccabees against Hellenization.

63 BC: Conquered by the Roman general Pompey.

c. 40–4 BC: Reign of King Herod. Roman governors rule after his death. Jesus of Nazareth later crucified under Pontius Pilate.

66–73 AD: Revolt against Rome: The Second Temple is destroyed and the majority of the Jews are driven into exile.

132–135 AD: Simon Bar Kochba leads second revolt. The Emperor Hadrian defeats the rebels, renames Judah 'Palestine' and forbids Jews entry to the city of Jerusalem.

324 AD: The Roman Emperor Constantine occupies Palestine.

638 AD: Arabs conquer Jerusalem under the leadership of Caliph

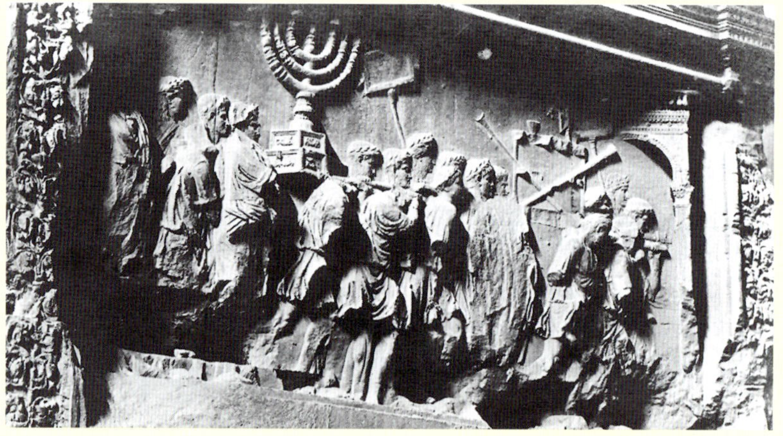

Theodor Herzl (1860–1940, above). The triumphal procession of Titus following the destruction of the Temple in 70 AD (relief on Titus's arch, Rome, below). Jewish immigrants in the port of Haifa, 1947 (right).

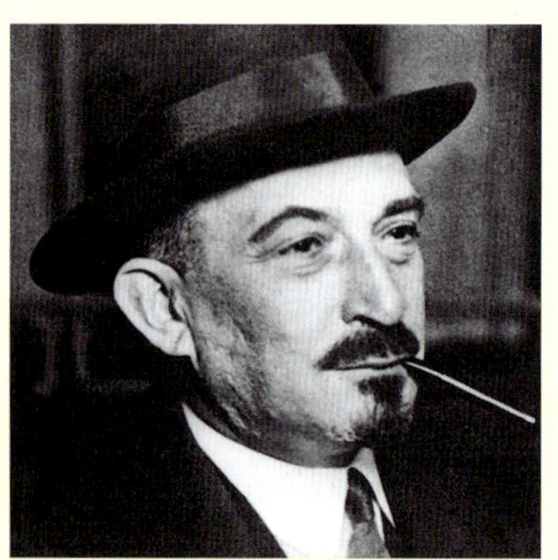

Chaim Weizmann (1874–1952).

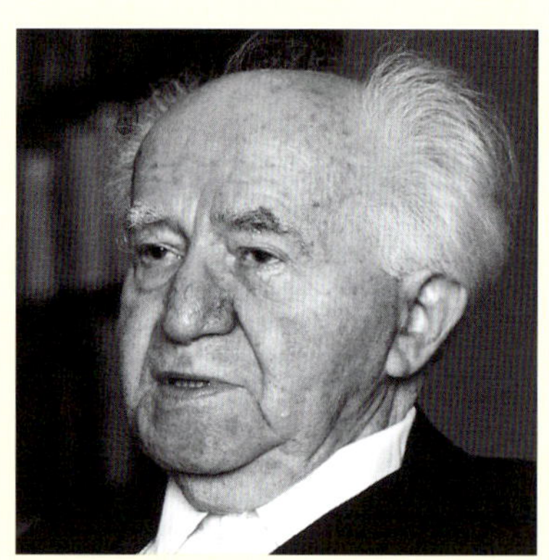

David Ben-Gurion (1886–1973).

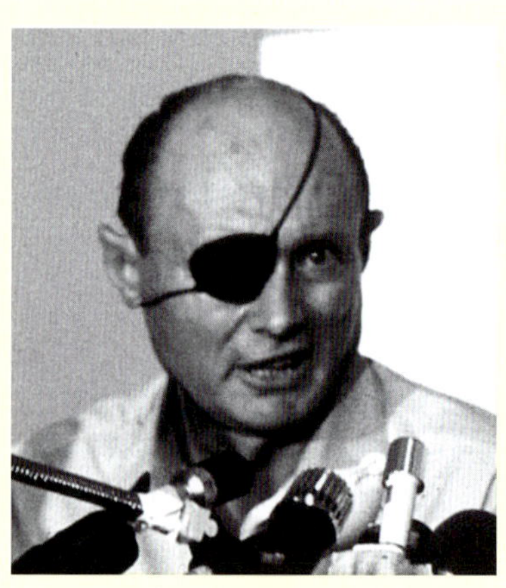

Moshe Dayan (1915–1981).

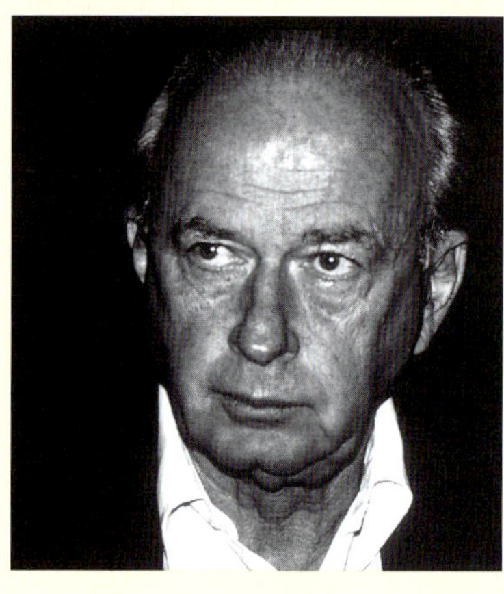

Yitzhak Rabin (1922–1995).

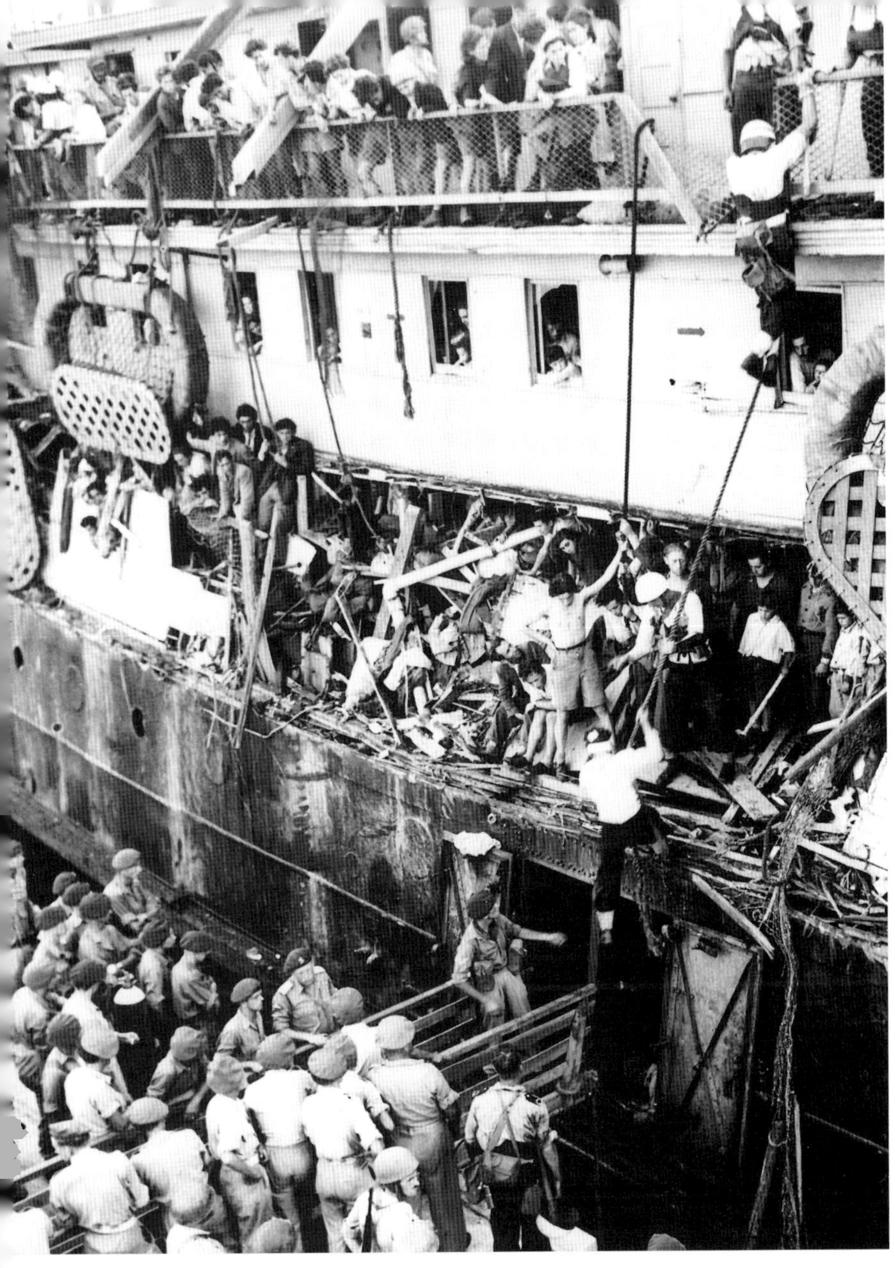

Omar. Jews are once again permitted to settle in the city.

1096–1099, 1147–1149, 1189–1192: Period of the first three Crusades and numerous massacres of Jews and Muslims by Crusaders. Establishment of the Crusader Kingdom of Jerusalem.

1291: Acre falls and the Mamelukes drive out the crusaders for good.

1516: Turks capture Palestine. A period of prosperity under Sultan Suleiman the Magnificent (1494–1566) is followed by centuries of neglect as a province of the Ottoman Empire.

1882–1903: First wave of Zionist immigration, followed by further periods of immigration in the years 1904 and 1914, 1919–1923, 1924–1928 and 1932–1939.

1897: First Zionist Conference in Basle, during which the demand for a 'Jewish State', proposed by the Viennese journalist Theodor Herzl, is formulated.

1917: The Balfour Declaration. The British are granted a Mandate for Palestine and Britain's Foreign Secretary, Arthur James Balfour, promises the Jews 'the establishment in Palestine of a national home for the Jewish people'.

1936/1937: Arab revolt against Zionist settlers.

1947: The UN proposes partition, under which both a Jewish and a Palestinian state would be established. The Arab League rejects this plan.

1948: Prime Minister Ben-Gurion declares the State of Israel on 14 May 1948. Invasion by five Arab armies. An armistice ends the War of Independence in January 1949.

1956: Following President Nasser of Egypt's nationalisation of the Suez Canal, French and British troops march into the canal zone. Israel conquers Sinai but returns the territory following pressure from the USA.

1967: The Six Day War begins on 6 June 1967. Israel captures East Jerusalem, the Sinai, the West Bank (West Jordan) and the Gaza Strip.

1973: The Yom Kippur War. Egypt and Syria attempt to recapture lost territories.

1977: The Labour Party loses its majority for the first time and cedes power to Menachem Begin, the candidate of the Israeli right wing.

1979: Begin and President Sadat of Egypt sign a peace treaty brokered their two countries, brokered by US President Carter.

1982: Israeli invasion of Lebanon. Establishment of a 'security zone' in south Lebanon.

1987: Beginning of the 'Intifada', the revolt by Palestinians in the occupied territories.

1993: On 13th September, Prime Minister Yitzhak Rabin and PLO chief Yassir Arafat sign a peace treaty and agree terms for Israel's withdrawal from the occupied territories. Gaza and Jericho are granted autonomous status.

1995: Israel withdraws from all Palestinian cities except Hebron. On 4 November, Prime Minister Rabin is assassinated by a Jewish extremist.

1996: Benjamin Netanyahu, the candidate of the right wing Likud party wins the elections.

1999: Ehud Barak, leading a centre-left party, wins the elections.

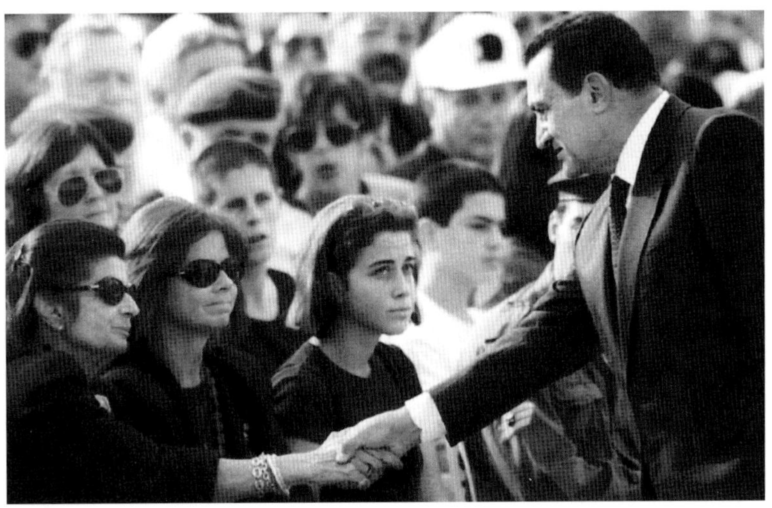

President Mubarak of Egypt expresses his sympathy to Yitzhak Rabin's widow.

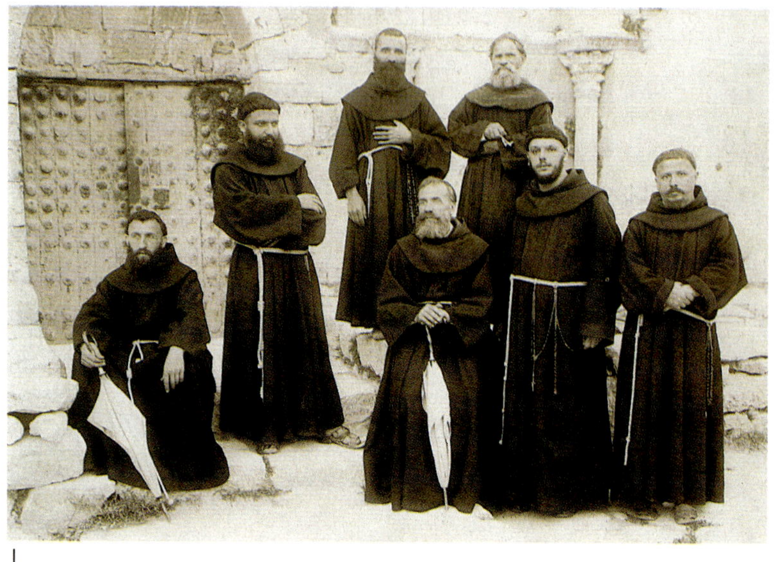
1

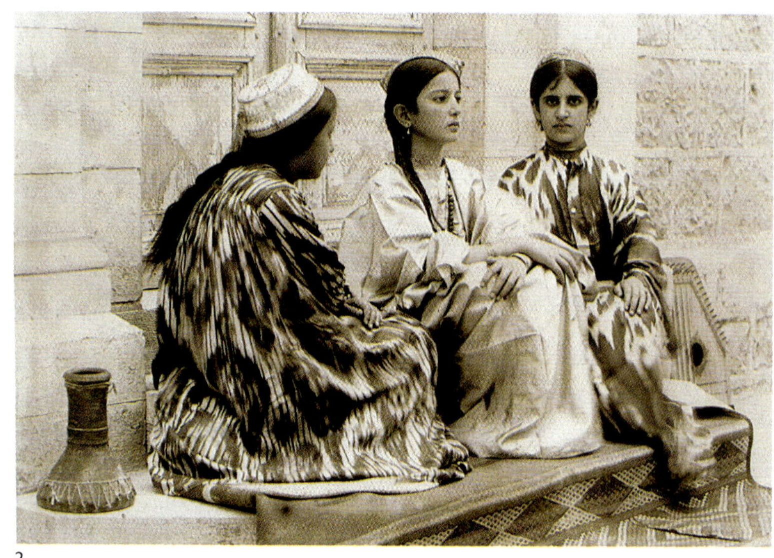
2

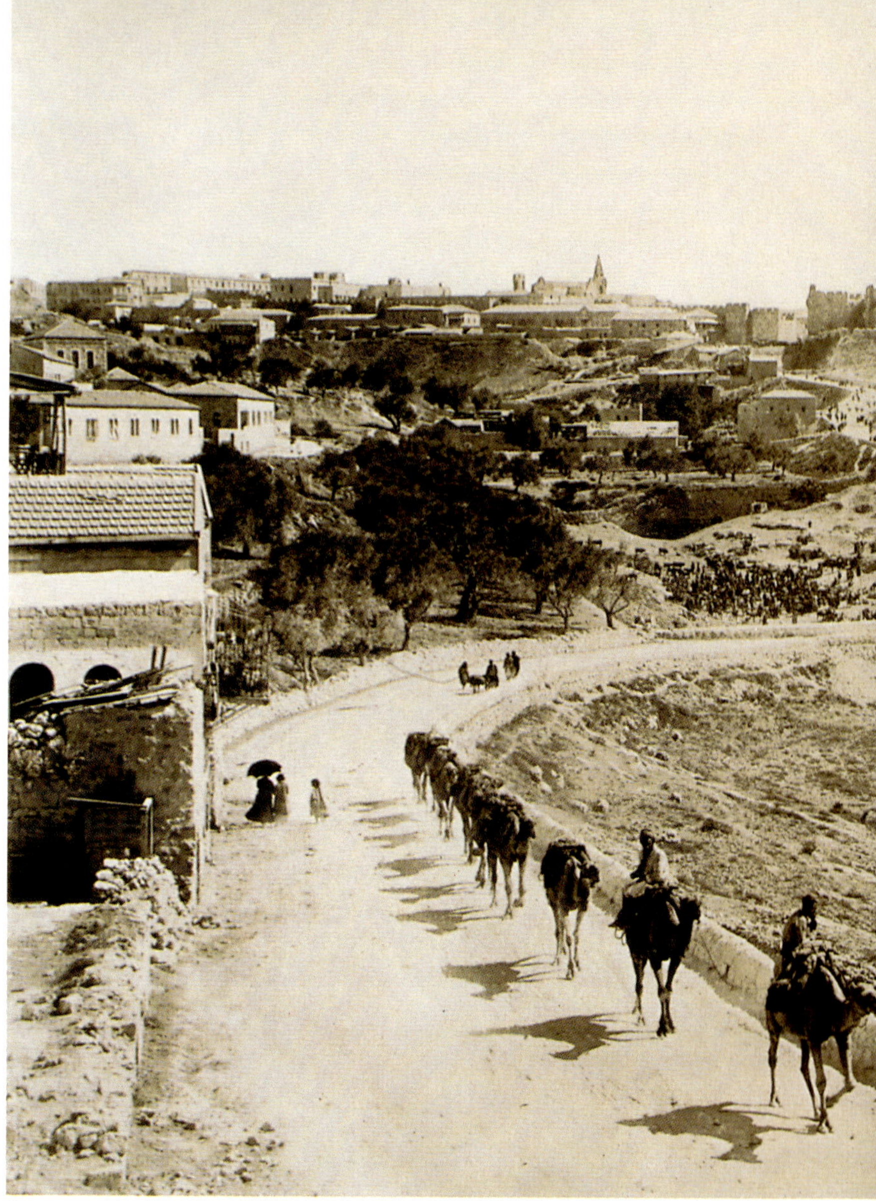
3

the ghetto and become a 'normal' country, a nation like many others. But since the founding of the State, Israelis have lived in highly abnormal circumstances, isolated from their neighbours and forced to defend their very existence through three major wars. And these are not the only contradictions. Israeli society is fixated on history at the same time as looking to the future with a near-obsessive belief in progress – the Middle Ages intertwined with the twenty-first century.

Jerusalem's Mea She'arim district is the home of ultra-Orthodox Jews who still wear traditional garb, speak Yiddish and reject the State of Israel as a 'Zionist Blasphemy'. As far as they are concerned a Jewish State can only be established by the Messiah. At the same time, Israel plays a leading role in the high-tech industry of today, an example of which is its position at the forefront of the development of modern communications technology.

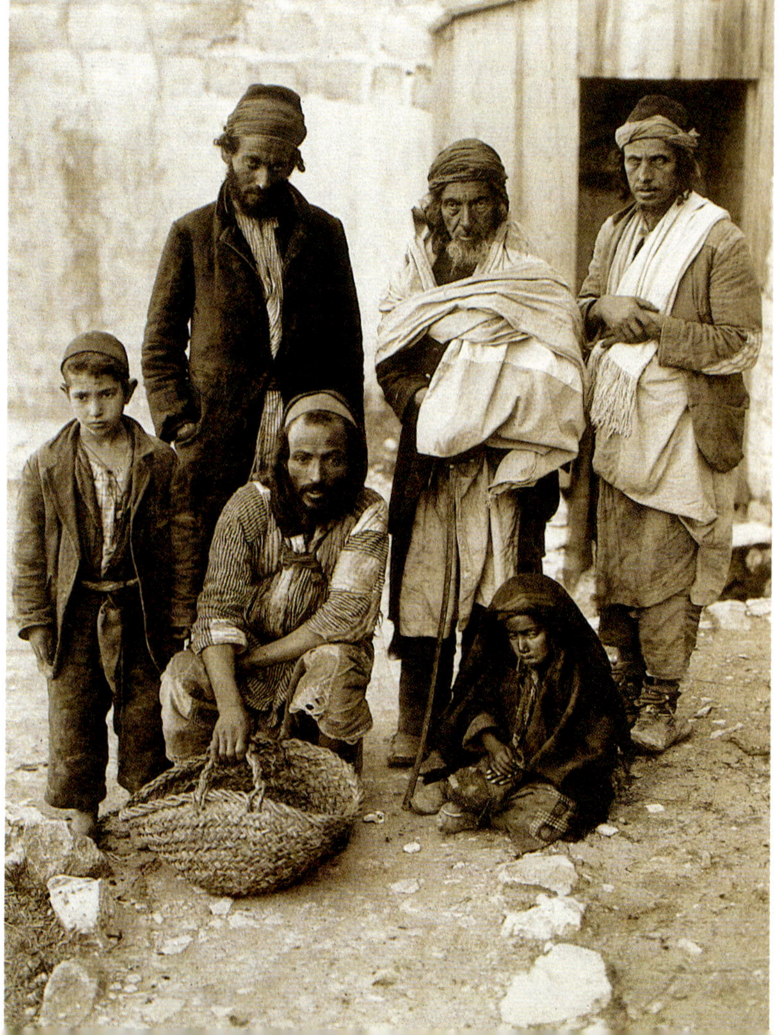
4

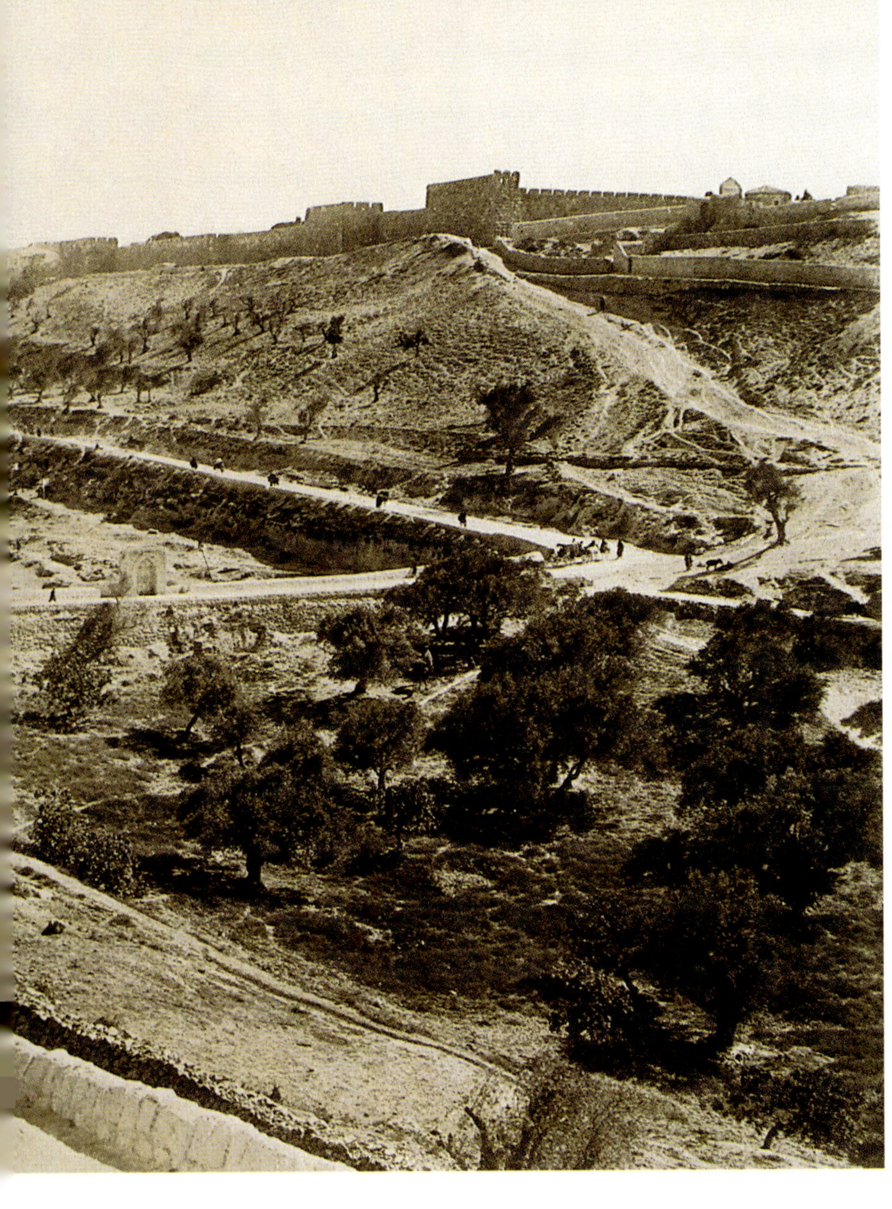

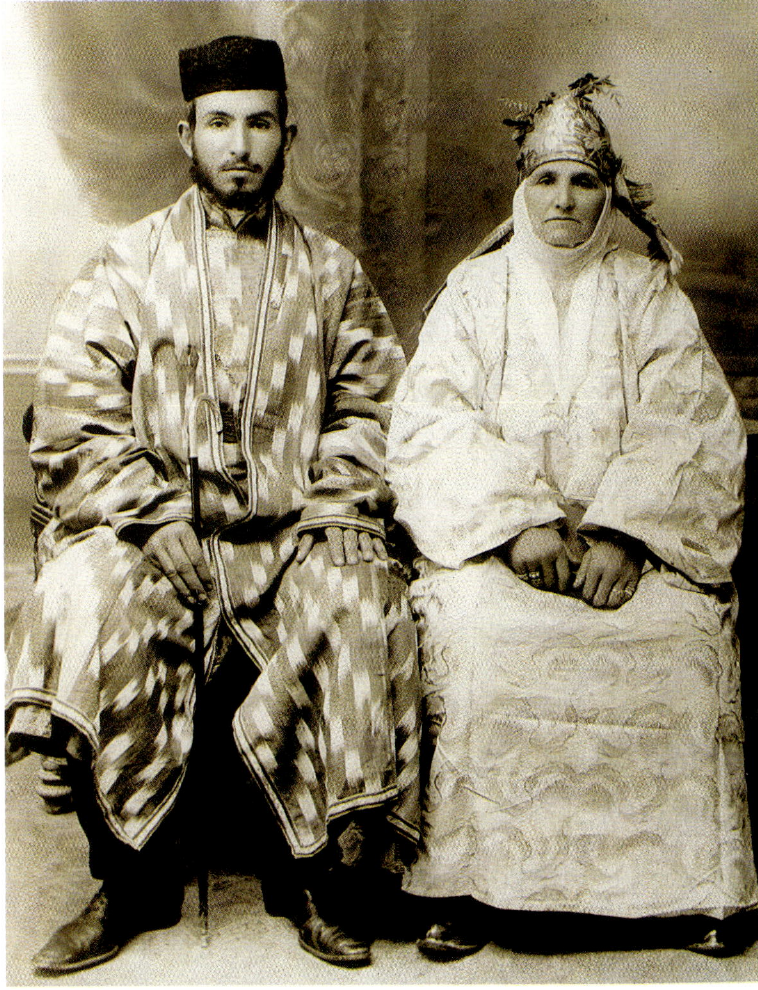

7

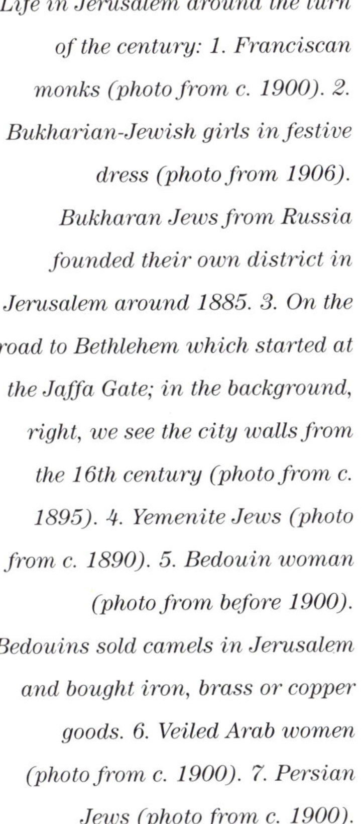

Life in Jerusalem around the turn of the century: 1. Franciscan monks (photo from c. 1900). 2. Bukharian-Jewish girls in festive dress (photo from 1906). Bukharan Jews from Russia founded their own district in Jerusalem around 1885. 3. On the road to Bethlehem which started at the Jaffa Gate; in the background, right, we see the city walls from the 16th century (photo from c. 1895). 4. Yemenite Jews (photo from c. 1890). 5. Bedouin woman (photo from before 1900). Bedouins sold camels in Jerusalem and bought iron, brass or copper goods. 6. Veiled Arab women (photo from c. 1900). 7. Persian Jews (photo from c. 1900).

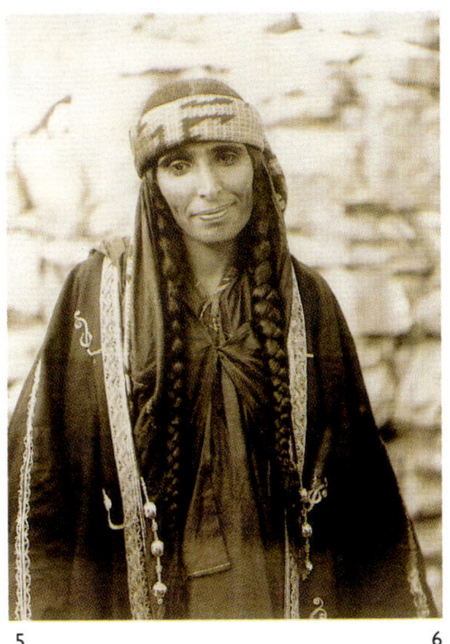

5 6

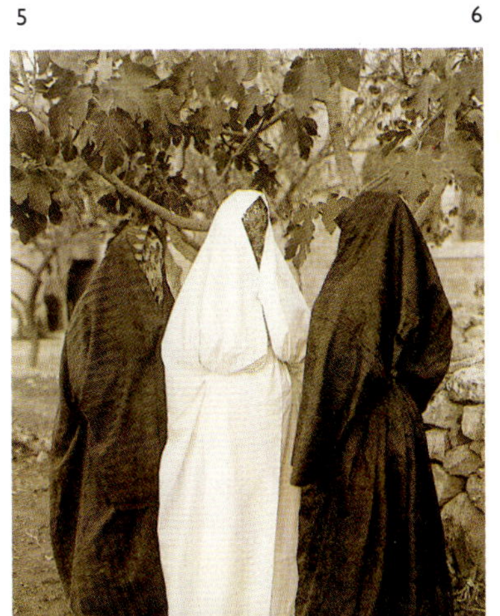

Israel is truly a challenge. And the visitor who is bound to leave this country more confused than when he arrived can still truthfully say that he has learned a great deal during his visit.

Travelling in a Land of Contrasts

Israel is not just at the crossroads of three religions, it also marks the crossroads of three continents: Europe, Asia, Africa. Excluding the Occupied Territories the State covers just over 7720 square miles with a landscape as full of diversity as an entire continent.

Skiing can be enjoyed on Mount Hermon in the north, while in the south at Eilat on the Red Sea the season is always right for swimming. The nature reserve of Tel Dan at the northernmost outpost of the country, where one of the Jordan's three tributaries rises, is an area of swamps and bubbling ice-cold streams while the southern half of the country consists almost solely of desert fed by water from the Sea of Galilee by means of a complicated system of pipelines stretching more than

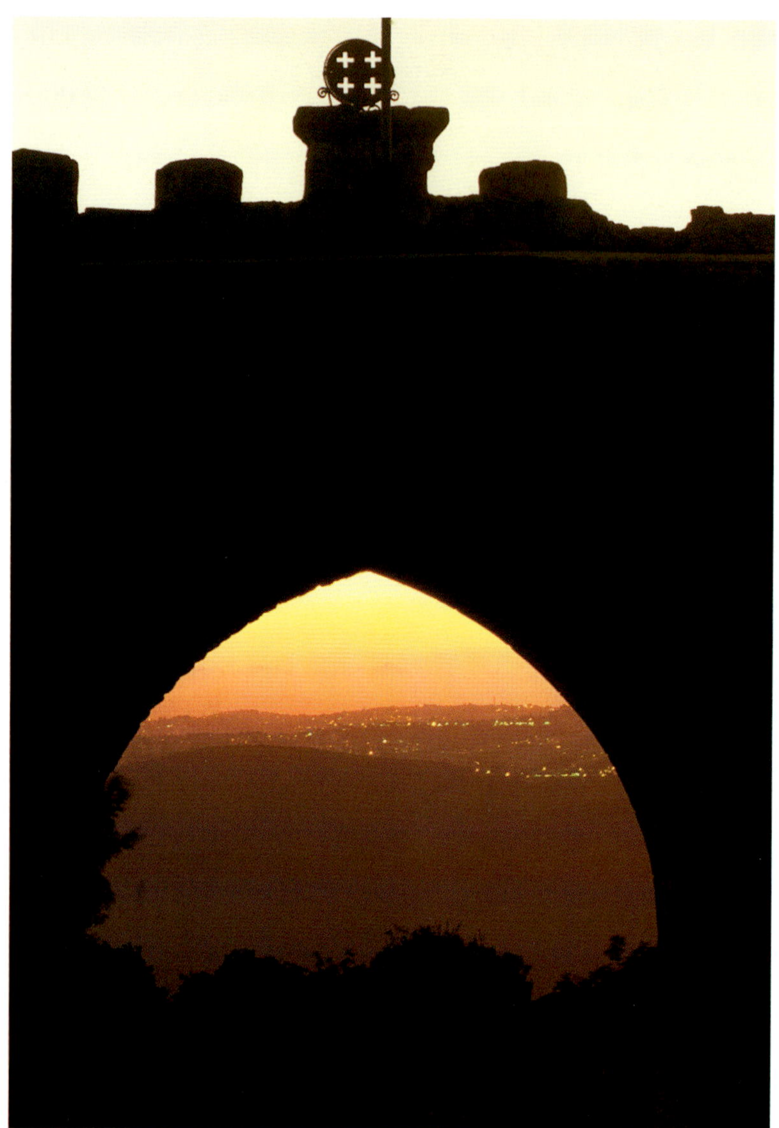

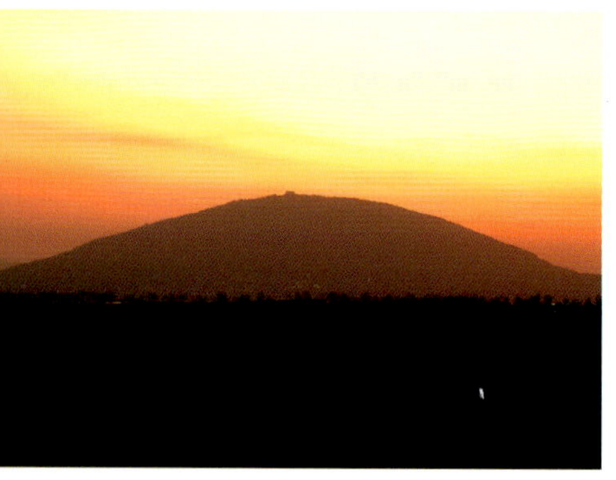

Mount Tabor, a sacred mountain for Christians, situated in Lower Galilee rises to a height of 588 metres (both pictures). On its distinctive hemispherical summit we find a Greek Orthodox and a Franciscan monastery from the roof of which a splendid panorama can be enjoyed.

186 miles and converting some of the land into lush green plantations. The hills of Galilee, Samaria and Judea stretch throughout the country from north to south separating the conurbations along the Mediterranean beaches from the Jordan Valley, where the Sea of Galilee and the Dead Sea lie as low as 400 metres below sea level.

It is not just that such diverse landscapes lie in such close proximity that makes dealing with Israel so difficult – sometimes there are only a few miles between the traffic chaos of the main towns and the contemplative spots surrounded by nature. Where once milk and honey flowed, we now have the flow of traffic which can be quite aggressive: there's beeping and overtaking and braking. In fact, one gets the impression that the Darwinian law of the survival of the fittest (and fastest) has become the predominant traffic regulation. And then, of course, it's not as though the Israelis are reluctant about showing their emotions – spontaneous gestures and verbal outbursts

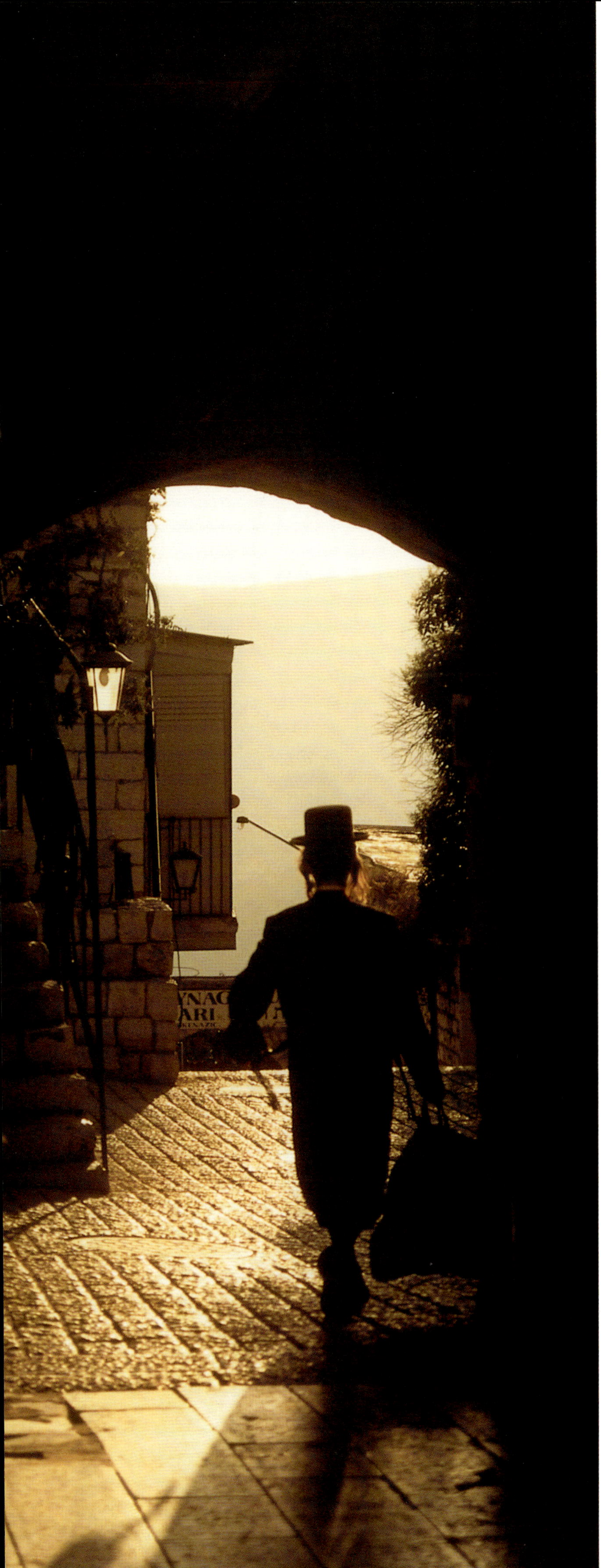

The hilltop town of Safed in Upper Galilee in the early evening is filled with an air of mysticism (left). Fishermen on the Sea of Galilee (right).

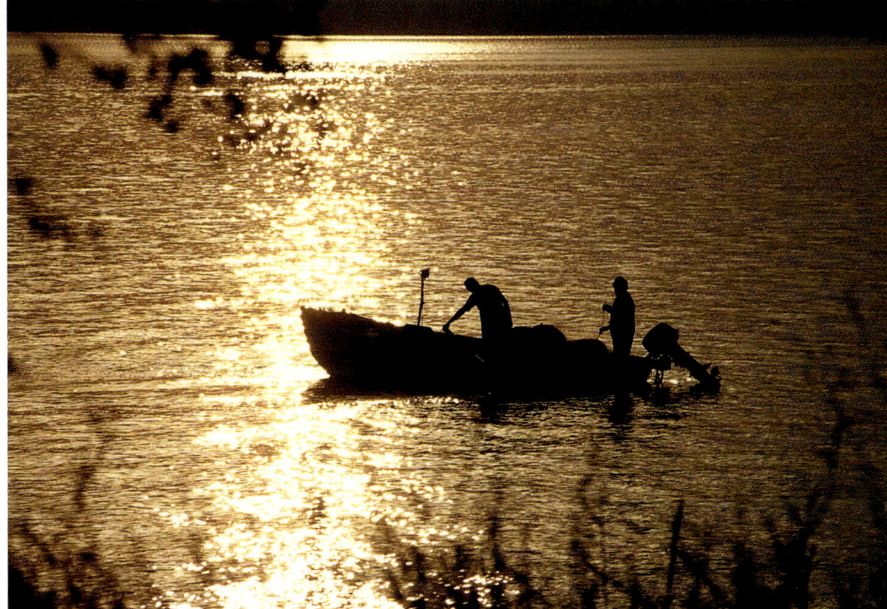

rich in colourful vocabulary are the order of the day. Politeness can easily fall by the wayside. Sitting in a restaurant in Tel Aviv, for example, when a customer is on his mobile phone, he makes no effort to lower his voice. The entire town can hear what he has to say – that is, if all the other customers aren't on their own mobiles!

Even before you arrive you should be prepared to exercise a great deal of patience. You will have barely touched down on Israeli soil when you will be faced with strict security checks at the local airport carried out by young Israeli men and women, who go through a ritual of questioning anyone wishing to enter their country. They will want to know whether you have packed your suitcase yourself, even if you're travelling here for the first time, and finally they will want to know why you've come to Israel at all. Whatever your reply, your security expert isn't going

A prickly pear (sabra), the symbol for the children of Jewish immigrants born in Israel, who call themselves Sabras.

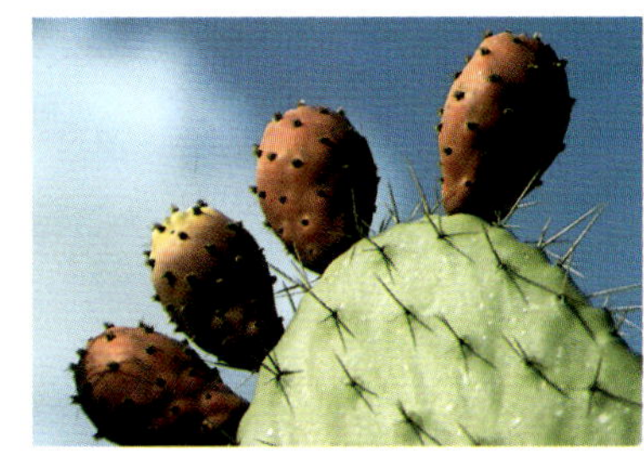

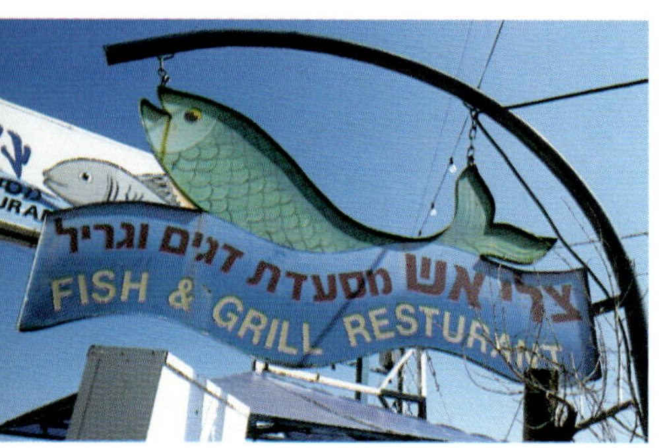

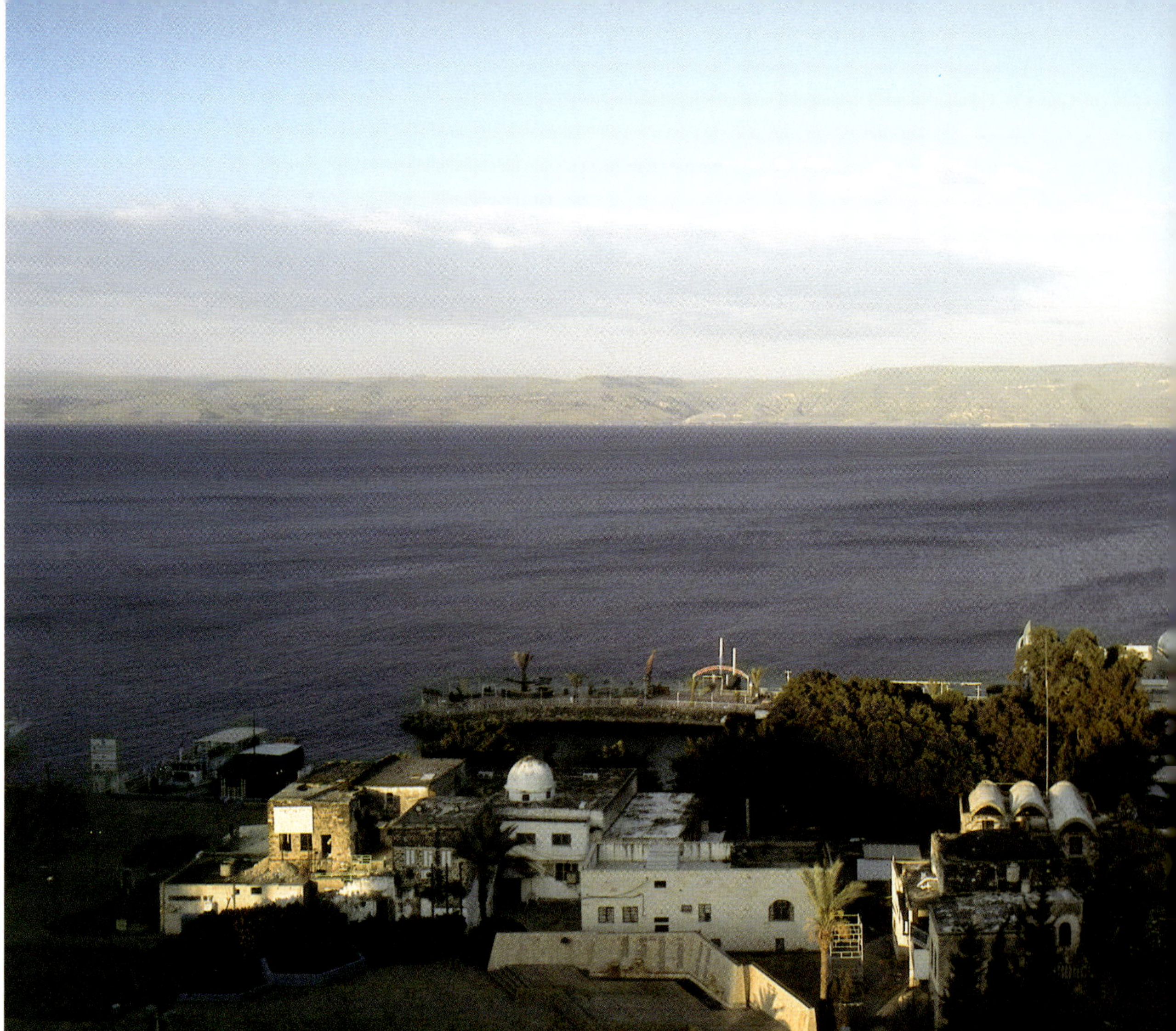

A religious centre for Jews since the 3rd century AD, and today an important tourist centre on the Sea of Galilee: Tiberias is synonymous with rest and recreation – and fresh St. Peter's fish from the lake (left, centre and below).

The Israeli Kibbutz

The Kibbutz movement was the result of an ideological aim of creating an egalitarian society on the one hand and, on the other, economic necessity. When the first settlers after 1882 fell prey to plagues of locusts, malaria and attacks by Bedouin it was decided to join the available forces into a collective. In 1909 the first kibbutz was established in Deganya (see also page 80f.). This was followed by many more. Everything in the kibbutz is owned communally. Instead of wages, members receive accommodation, food, clothing, medical care, social security and schooling. Nowadays many kibbutzniks live in their own houses equipped with television and other mod cons, and families live together with their children, who formerly would have been living in children's quarters.

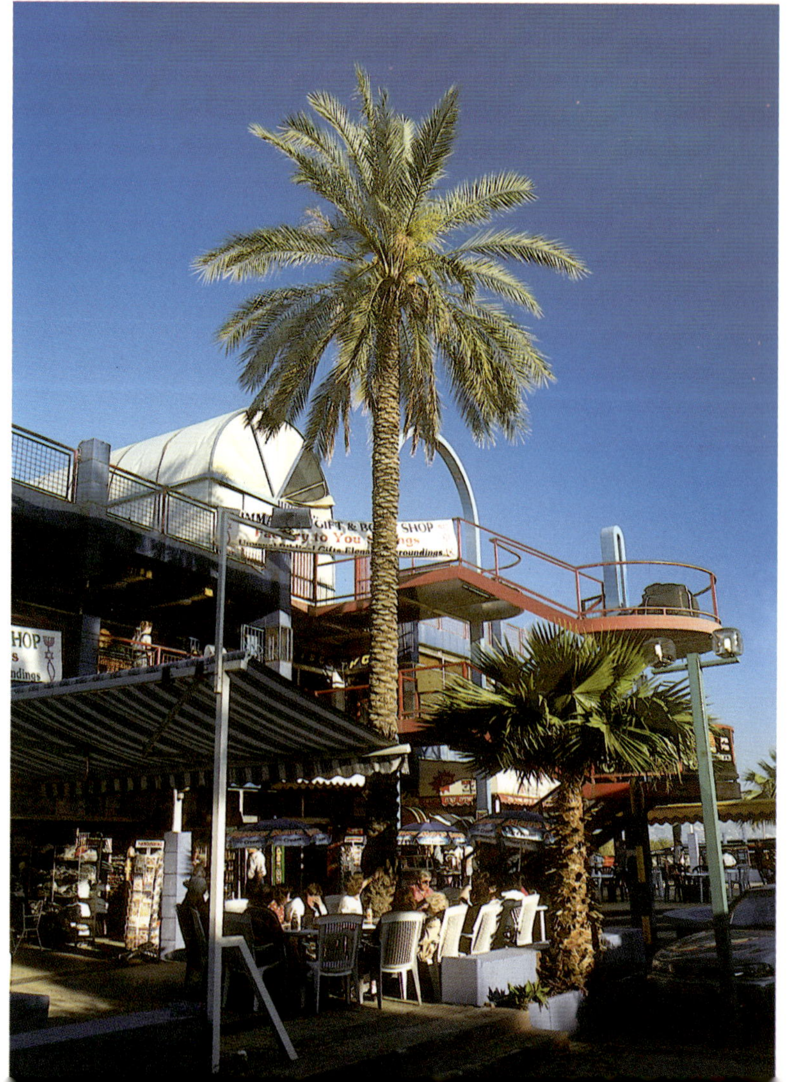

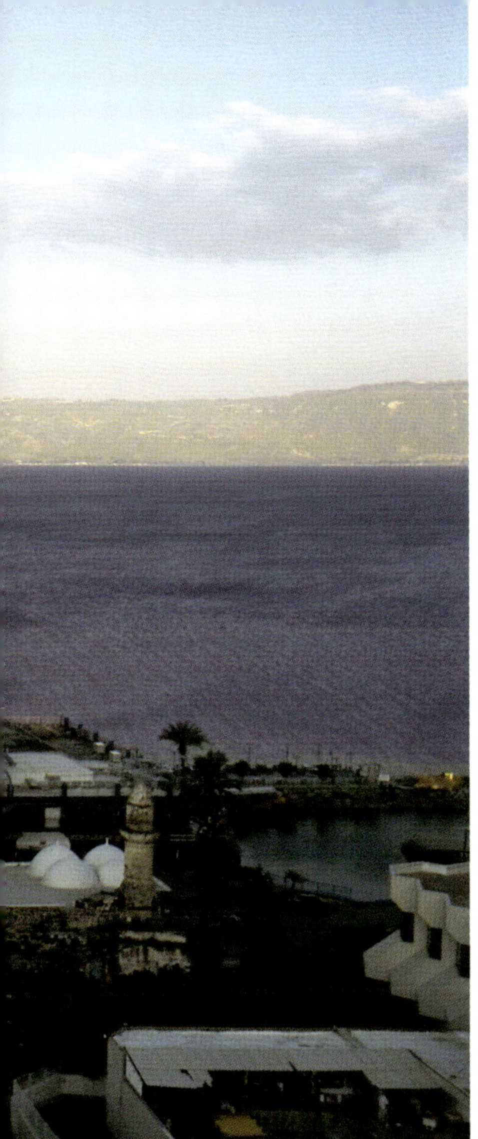

to believe you anyway, but will reply with a sceptical 'aha', wish you a good flight in an offhand sort of way and let you get on with your first experience of Israel.

There are hundreds of reasons for visiting this country and Israel will be ready to come up with thousands more. You might decide to spend a holiday on the beach, on the Mediterranean or in Eilat, diving, snorkelling and lazing in the sunshine – but you'd be missing a great deal. For example, you shouldn't pass by the opportunity of stepping into the Dead Sea: the feeling of bobbing about like a cork and the difficulty you'll experience when you try to put your feet down on the ground is quite unique. The Sea of Galilee, on the other hand, with the winding mountain road which indicates when you've arrived at sea level is just as remarkable.

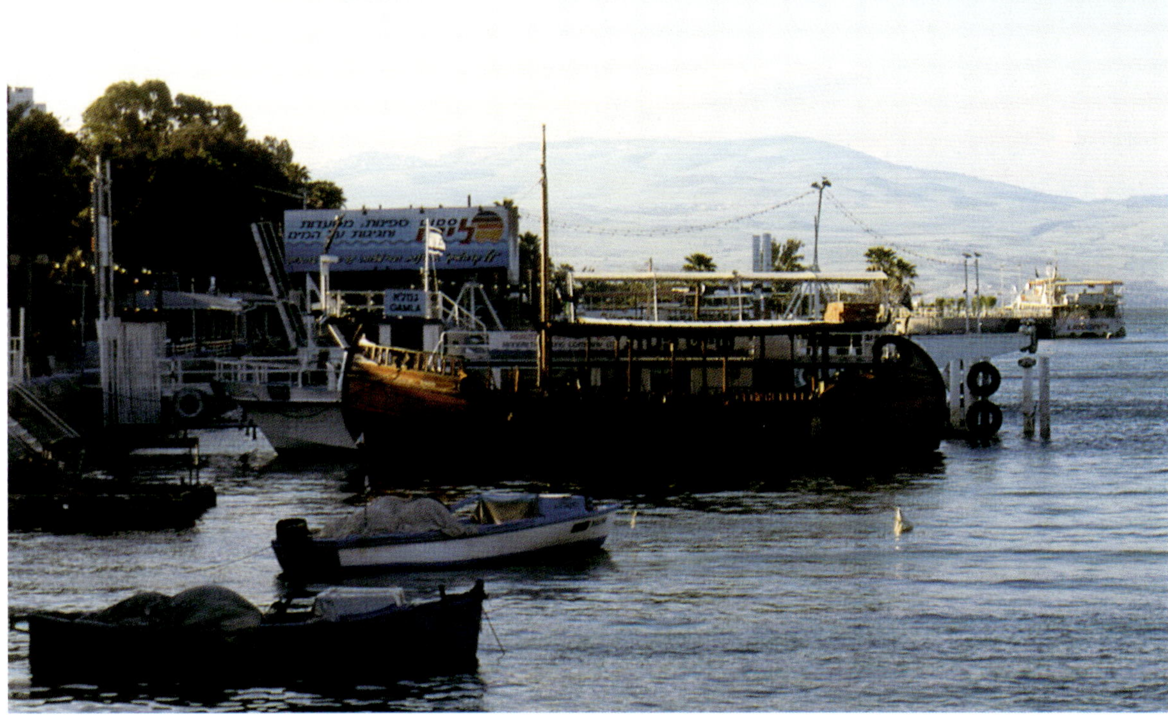

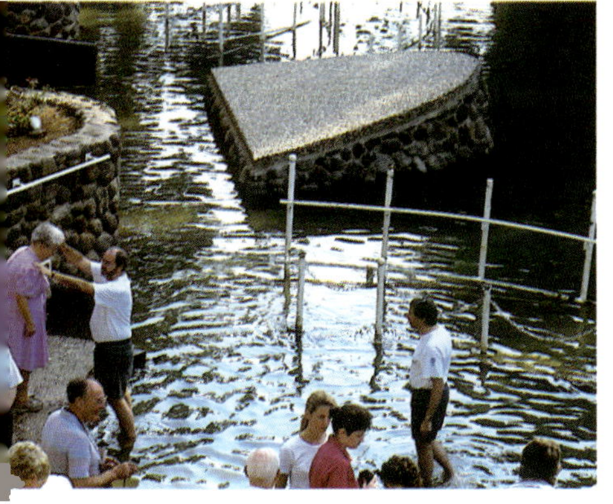

The special attraction on the seafront promenade in Tiberias is the Jesus boat replica, the original of which was found near Ginosar (right). At the Yardenit Baptismal Site where the Jordan flows out of the Sea of Galilee, pilgrims are baptised with holy water (above).

Experiencing Israel can touch your very soul and this may have something to do with its biblical sites. But it's not all pure bliss. Some of these places, the Via Dolorosa in Jerusalem, the Church of the Nativity in Bethlehem or St Peter's fisherman's hut on the Sea of Galilee are usually overcrowded. Other experiences can have a more lasting effect, such as when the evening sun sets on the salt pillar known as 'Lot's Wife' in the Mt Sodom Range and the silence of the desert becomes palpable: then the biblical tales seem to be wonderfully near.

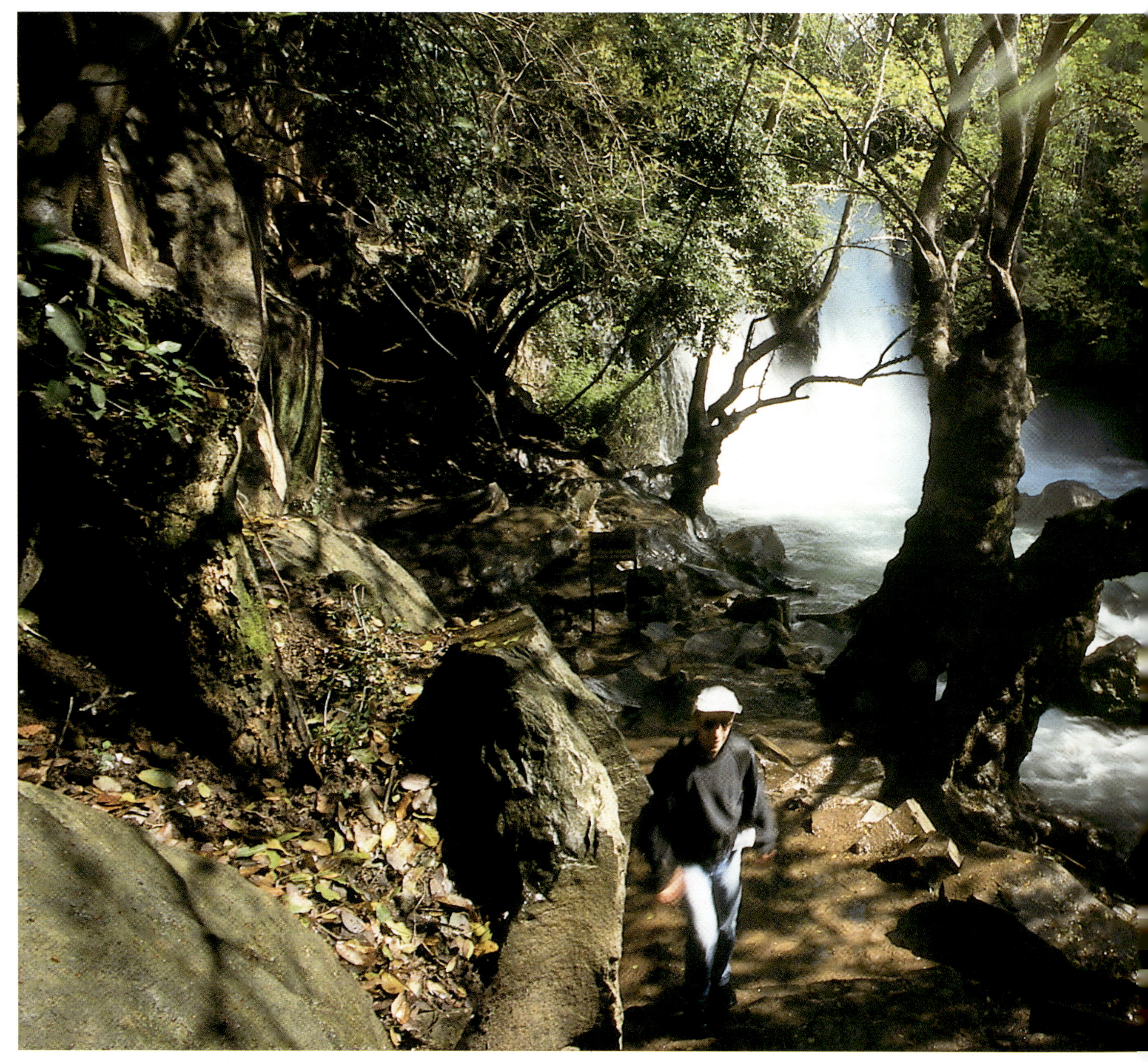

The Tribes of Israel – A People full of Mystery

It began, as is so often the case in the annals of the Jewish people, with a revelation; and there followed – as also often in its history – a journey. Countless researchers and archaeologists have asked themselves what it was that made the patriarch Abraham leave his home in Ur of the Chaldees and break away from his old religion, the worship of the Mesopotamian Moon God, Sin. According to Jewish scholars it was the profound realisation that there is only one true God of Creation. Scientists offer a rather more prosaic explanation for the fundamental change in Abraham's life.

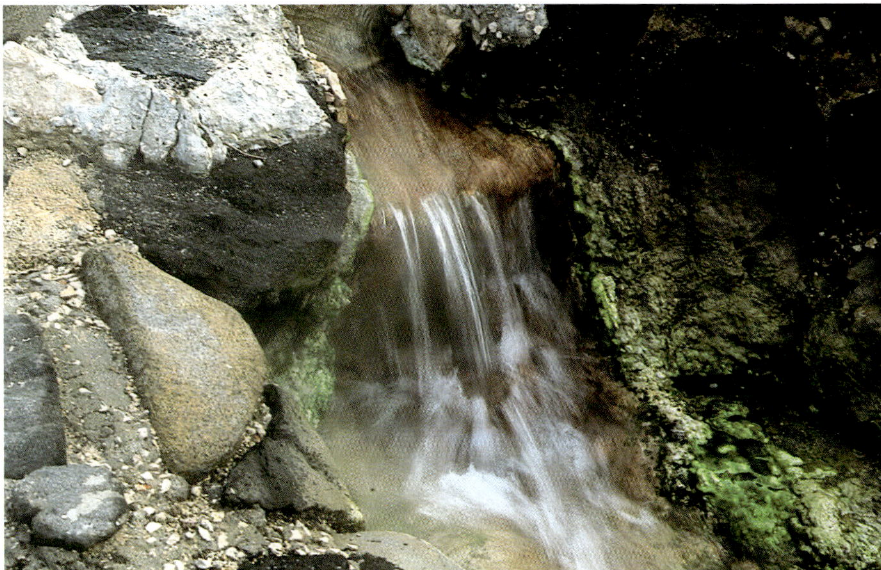

Mesopotamian sources tell of clashes between the western Semitic tribes which invaded Mesopotamia, the 'land between the rivers' of the Tigris and Euphrates, contributing a great deal towards the fall of the cultural metropolis of Ur. They presume that some time around the first half of the twentieth century BC, some of the local people fled from these clashes seeking quieter regions further north, places like Haran in what is today the Syrian-Turkish border area. However, Abraham did not remain in Haran but moved on to Canaan. According to biblical prophecy this was the land that God had promised to Abraham: 'Lift up now thine eyes, and look from the place where thou art, northward, and southward, and eastward, and westward. For all the land which thou seest, to thee will I give it, and to thy seed for ever.' (*Genesis* 13: 14–16). Abraham, however, did not live in only one place. He was the leader of a nomadic tribe which roamed between Shekhem (Nablus) and Hebron,

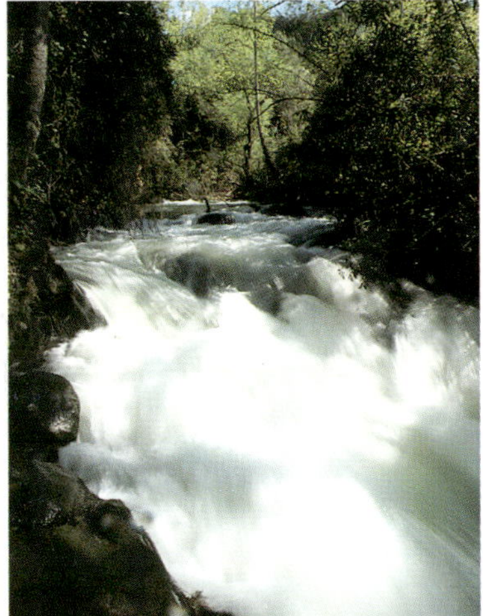

A secluded path at Banyas, where a stream feeding the River Jordan in the Golan area leads up to the Jordan waterfalls.

Beersheba and even Egypt.

His son Isaac, allegedly born to Abraham by his wife Sarah in his 90th year and who became the second patriarch of the Israelites, had a more settled way of life. He settled in Beersheba. Isaac's son Jacob, the third patriarch, on the other hand, returned to the nomadic way of life, living for a long time with his uncle Laban in Haran until he followed his son Joseph to Egypt, where he died. Jacob's uncle Ishmael, Abraham's first son by Sarah's Egyptian handmaid Hagar, was driven into the desert together with his mother as a result of the jealousy of Sarah. Arabs believe that they are the descendants of Ishmael and therefore of Abraham (Ibrahim).

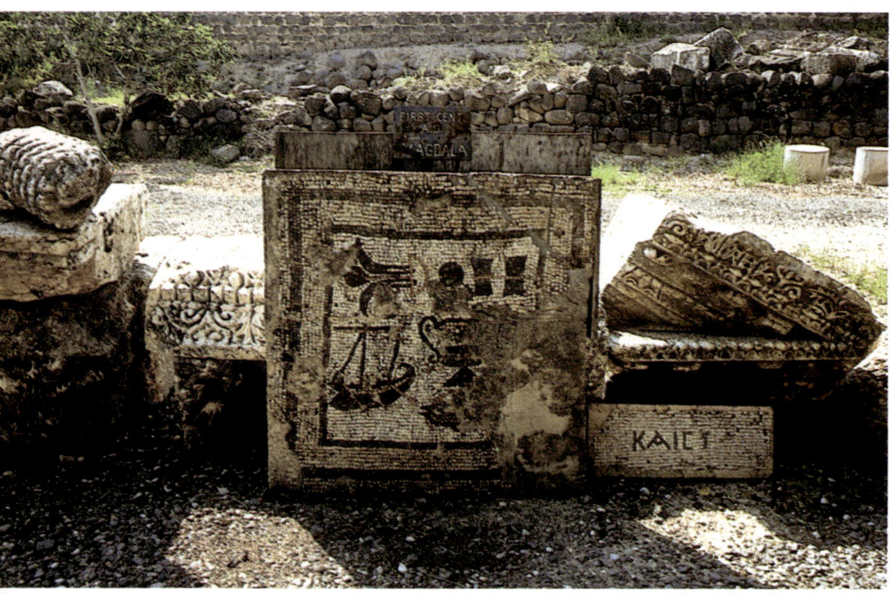

Despite all the promises, the Israelites' connection with the land which had been promised to them by God was by no means strong. It was not common land which was to weld together Abraham, his followers and descendants, a loose association of nomads, into a nation. It was the belief in a single God, the enormous steadfastness of defending this belief against all enemies, and the experience of slavery in Egypt.

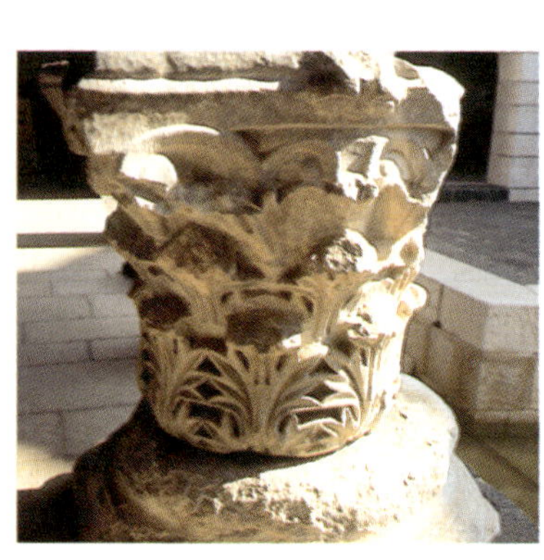

Archaeological treasures around the Sea of Galilee: many of the mosaics and architectural fragments in Capernaum date back to the fourth century AD (top); capital of a column in Tabgha where churches were built in the fourth and fifth centuries AD (below); the Roman colonnade in Bet She'an leading towards the semi-circular theatre (right).

Originally, Jacob and his 12 sons, after whom the Tribes of Israel are named, were drawn to Egypt for economic reasons – the failure of the grain crop. In Egypt, according to the second Book of Moses, *Exodus*, the family of Jacob 'increased abundantly, and multiplied ... and the land was filled with them'. In fact, the time came that they were seen as a threat by the rulers of Egypt, who forced these strangers into slavery. Under Ramses II who ruled between 1279 and 1212 BC the Hebrews had had enough of servitude. With the help of Moses they prepared a revolt against their slavery and an exodus out of Egypt. According to the Book of Exodus, 600,000 men left Egypt. Observant Jews believe that this section of the Bible is based on historic fact, and celebrate it every year in the Feast of Passover. Scientists, however counter with the theory that there is no Egyptian source describing such a mass exodus. There is only one column with inscriptions of the Pharaoh Menephta dating back to around 1207 BC and which says that in Canaan

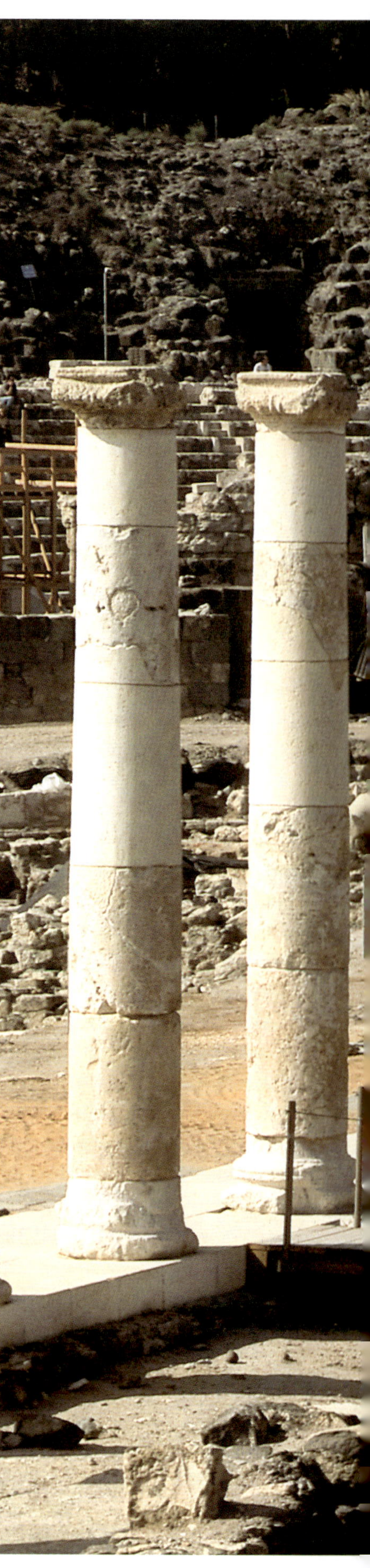

Continues on Page 40

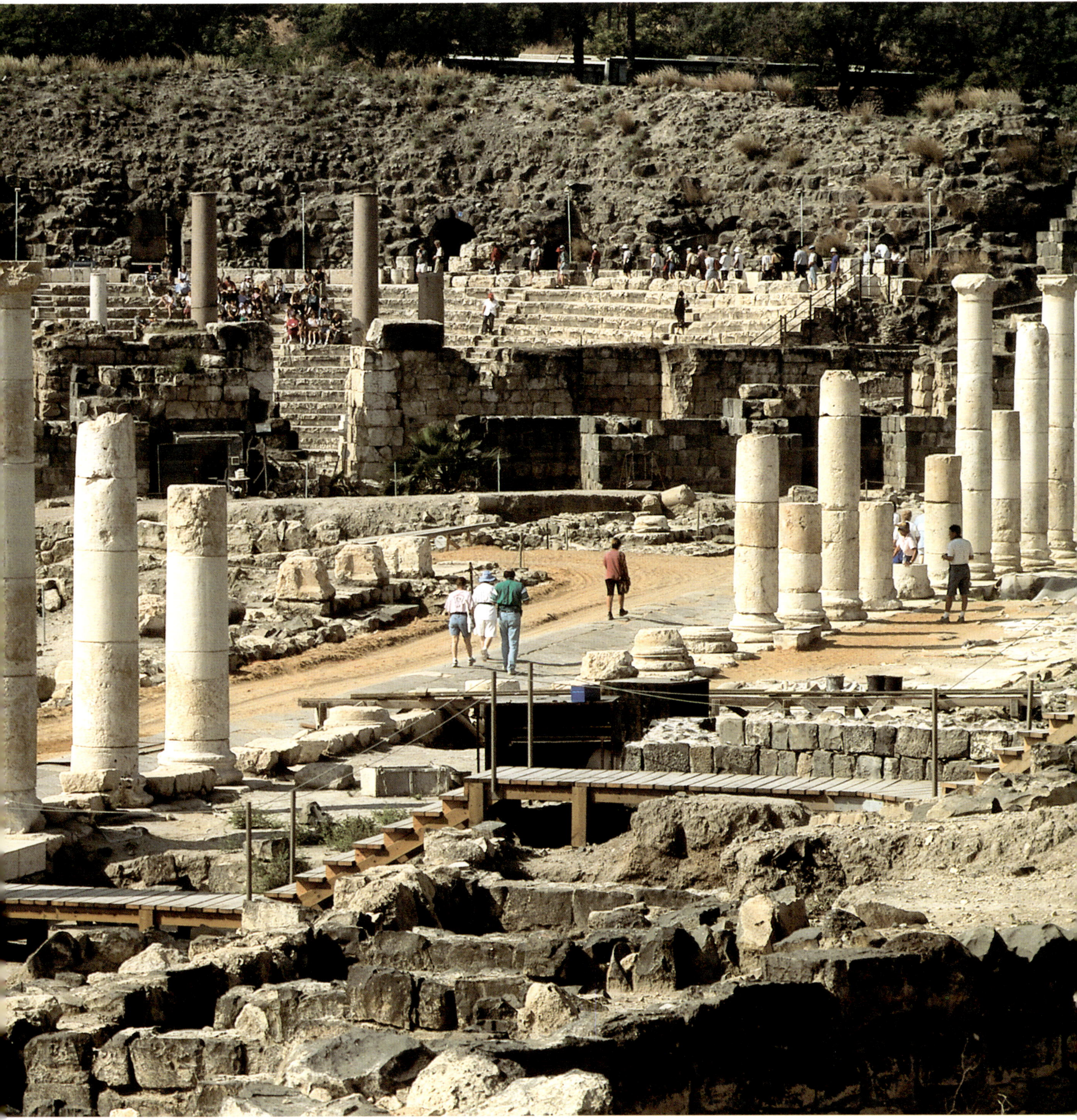

Ashkenazi, Sephardi, Bahai

Israel – a multicultural society

If a survey were to be conducted of the number of languages spoken by the residents of any single Israeli block of flats, it would frequently include more than ten languages. Most of Israel's inhabitants have arrived in the country within the last 40 years and they have frequently learnt Hebrew not only from the 'ulpanim', the language schools for immigrants, but from their children who have attended Israeli kindergartens and schools. Even before the state of Israel was founded, Jews emigrated to Israel from Poland and Russia, Germany, Austria and what was then still Czechoslovakia. After 1948, waves of immigrants came from Yemen and Iraq, from Morocco, India and Ethiopia, and more recently, again from the former Soviet Union and even Anglo-Saxon countries such as the USA, New Zealand and South Africa. After the USA, Israel is probably the first truly multicultural country in the

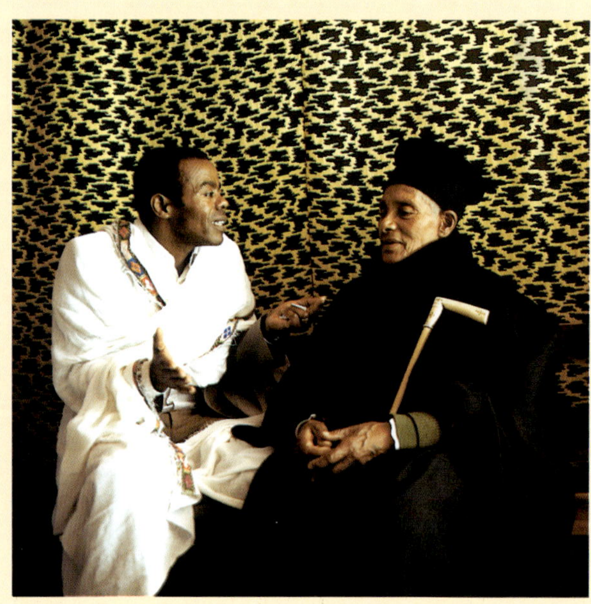

1

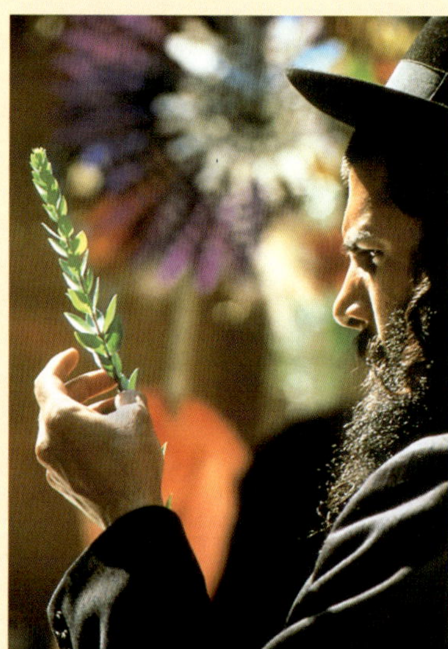

2

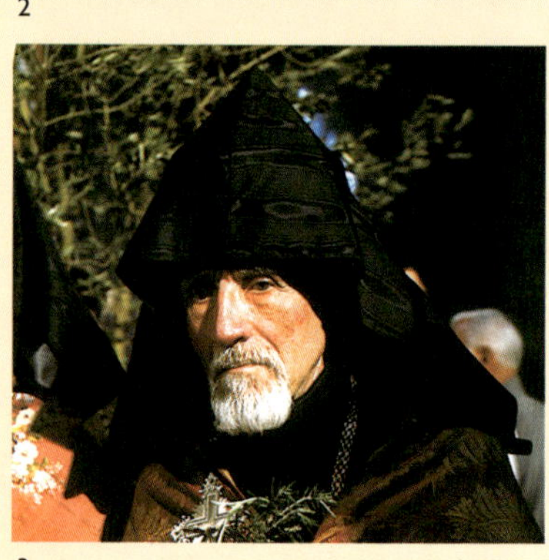

3

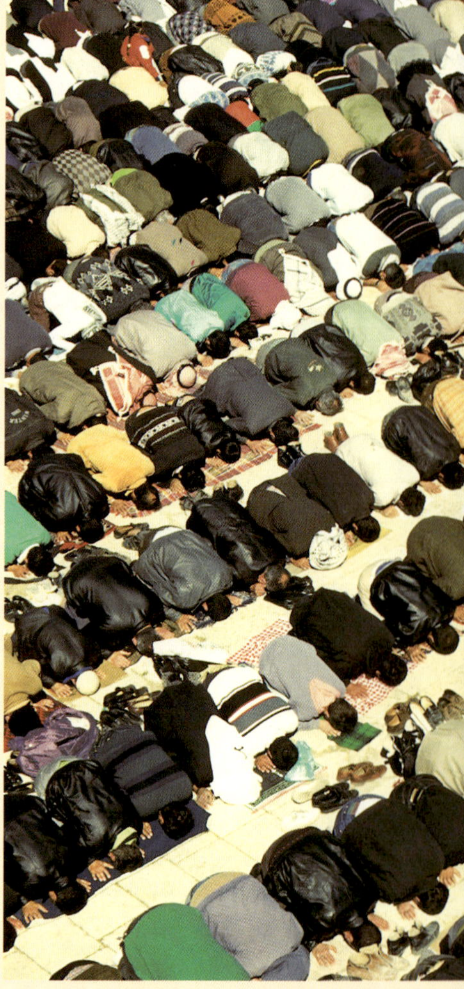

4

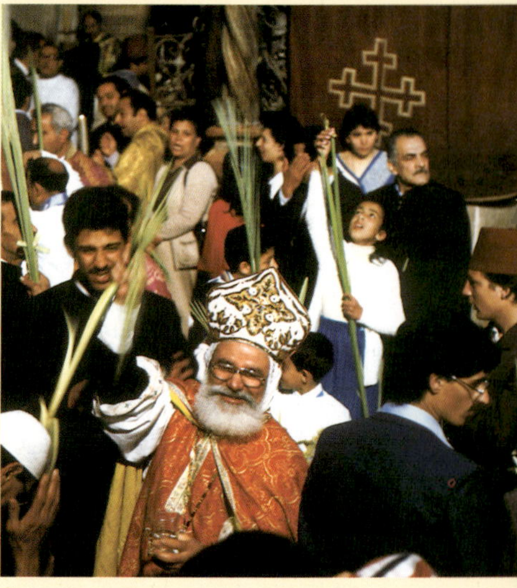

5

Representatives of various religious communities: 1 Pilgrims from Ethiopia. 2 Orthodox Jew. 3 Armenian monk. 4 Muslims praying on Temple Mount in Jerusalem. 5 Coptic Bishop in a procession.

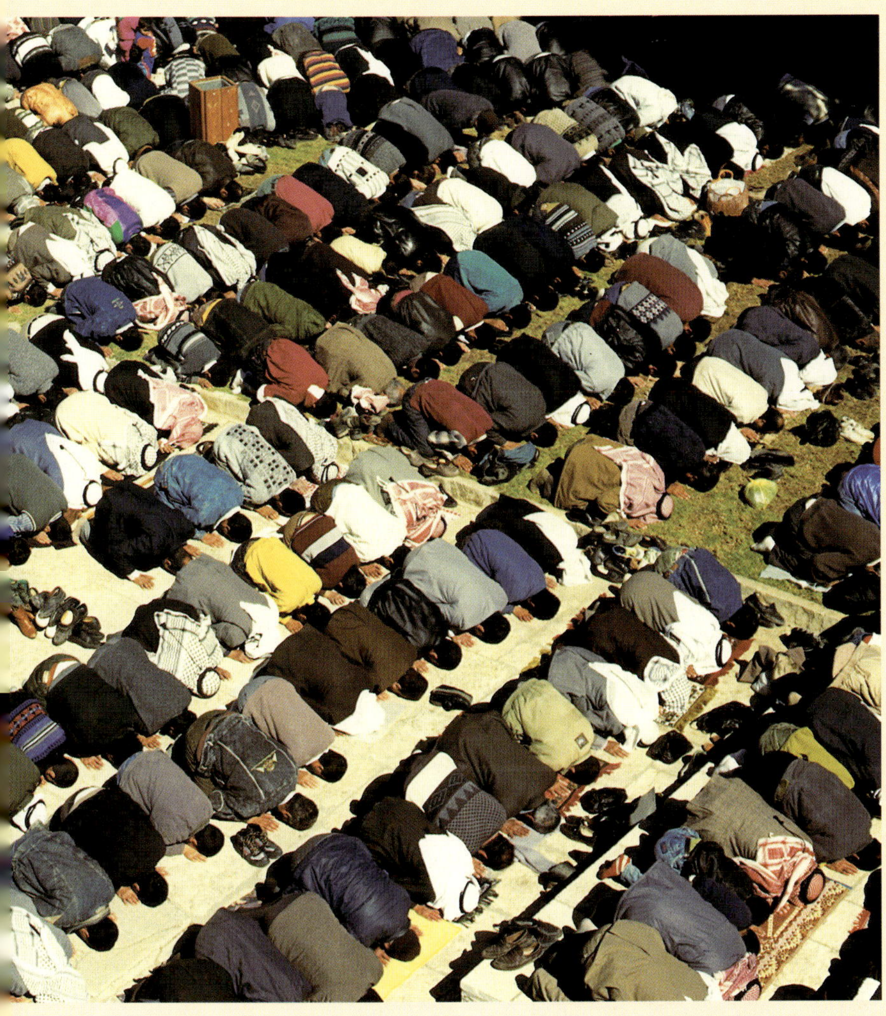

are referred to the authority of their places of worship.

However, as well as Jews, Israel is home to Muslims, Samaritans, Protestants, Anglicans, Catholics, Copts, Armenians, Russian Orthodox Christians, Druze, Bahais and the 'Black Israelites', Afro-Americans who regard themselves as one of the lost tribes of Israel. Each of these groups is guaranteed religious freedom and the right to conduct their own affairs.

Also, since the recent influx of migrant workers from Southeast Asia, we can assume that every religious community and almost every ethnic group is represented on this tiny strip of the planet.

world – with one difference: most Israelis are Jews, which should be a unifying force, despite differences in tradition, culture and language. Not a bit of it! Since the immigration of 'Sephardic' Jews from Arab countries, there have been quarrels with the European Anglo-Saxon 'Ashkenazi' Jews who, the Sephardis feel, discriminate against them.

Some of the citizens of this country see themselves as Israeli first and foremost, for whom Judaism is no more than a fading historic memory of the time of the Diaspora, or the occasional practice of attending synagogue, at least during the most important Jewish festival, Yom Kippur. Others define themselves primarily as 'Jews' for whom religion is more important than nationality, and who do not wish to see the old traditions watered down by secularisation. Whatever their views, by the time their thoughts turn to marriage, Israelis remember their religion. Since there is no strict separation between state and synagogue in Israel, it is not possible to conduct civil marriages or divorces. Jewish Israelis can only be married or divorced by a rabbi and in accordance with Orthodox Jewish ritual. Christian and Muslim couples

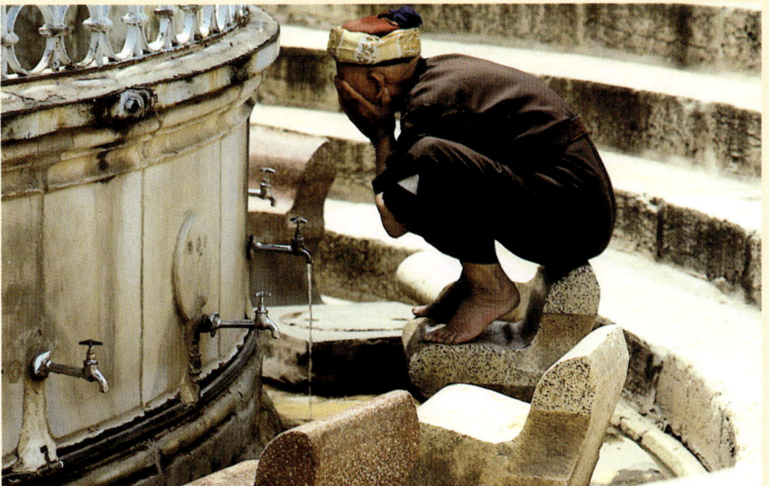

6

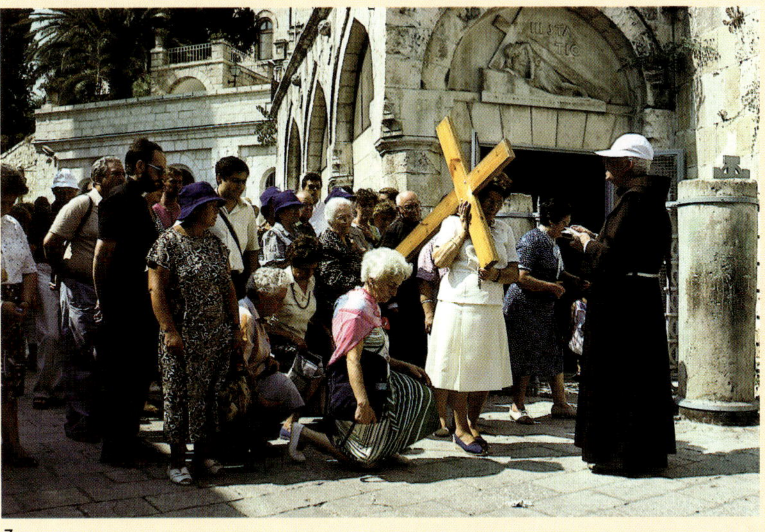

7

6 A religious duty for Muslims: ritual washing before entering the mosque.
7 Christian pilgrims on a procession along the Via Dolorosa in Jerusalem.

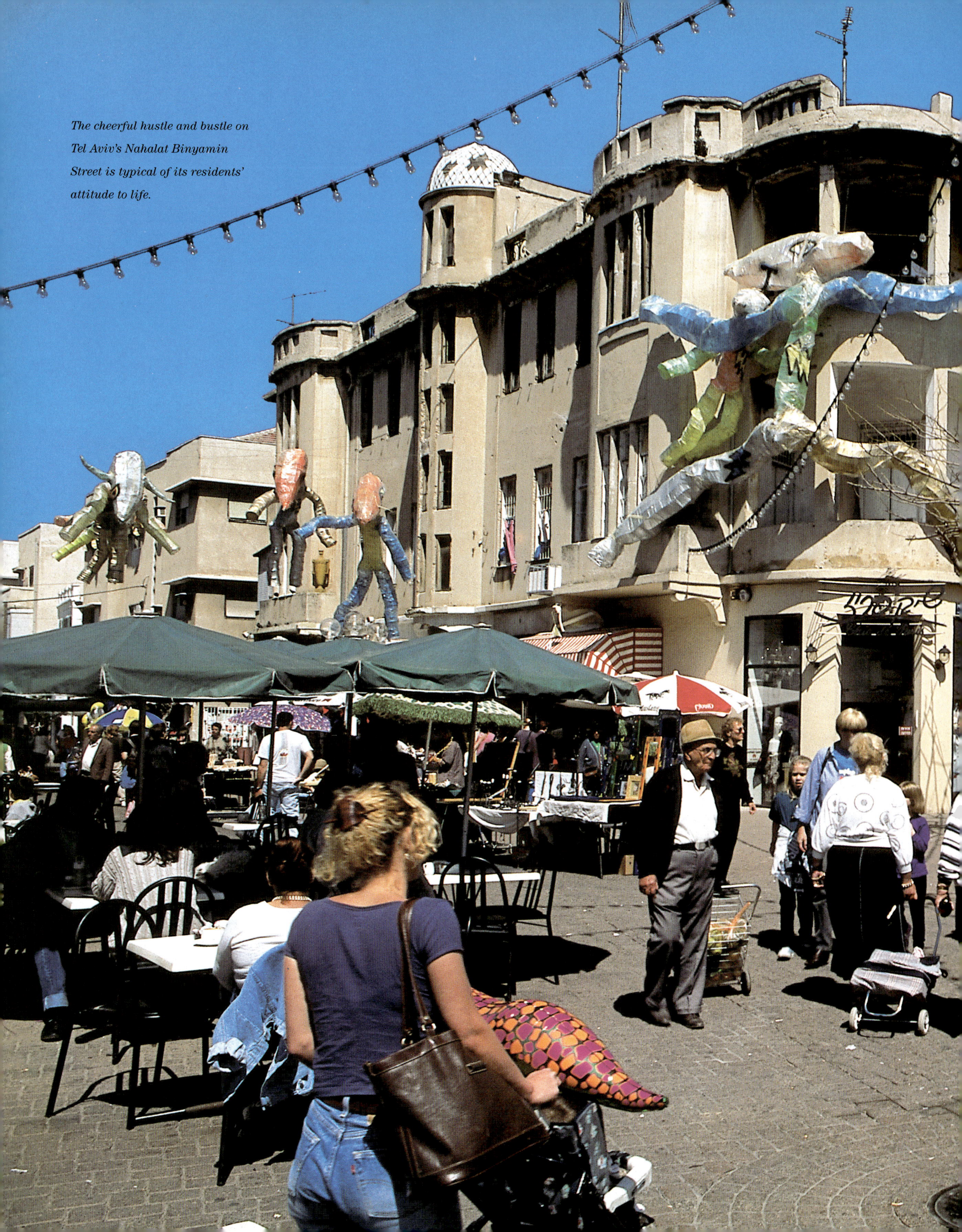

The cheerful hustle and bustle on Tel Aviv's Nahalat Binyamin Street is typical of its residents' attitude to life.

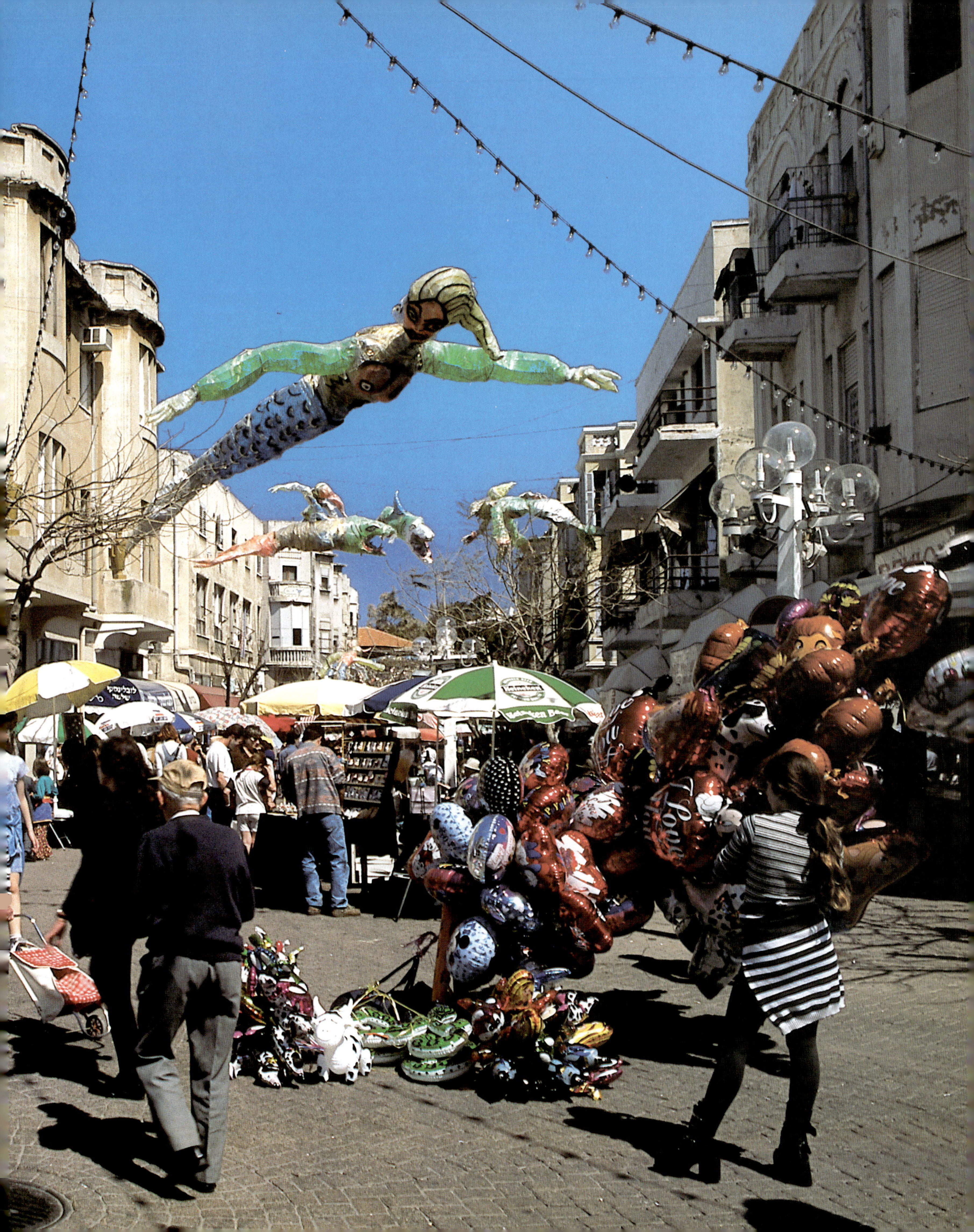

Tel Aviv is a thoroughly modern city where people live for today. The religious ambiance of biblical sites has no significance here, and the Israeli-Palestinian conflict is as far away as can be. In this city's lively centre it is easy to forget that we are in Israel.

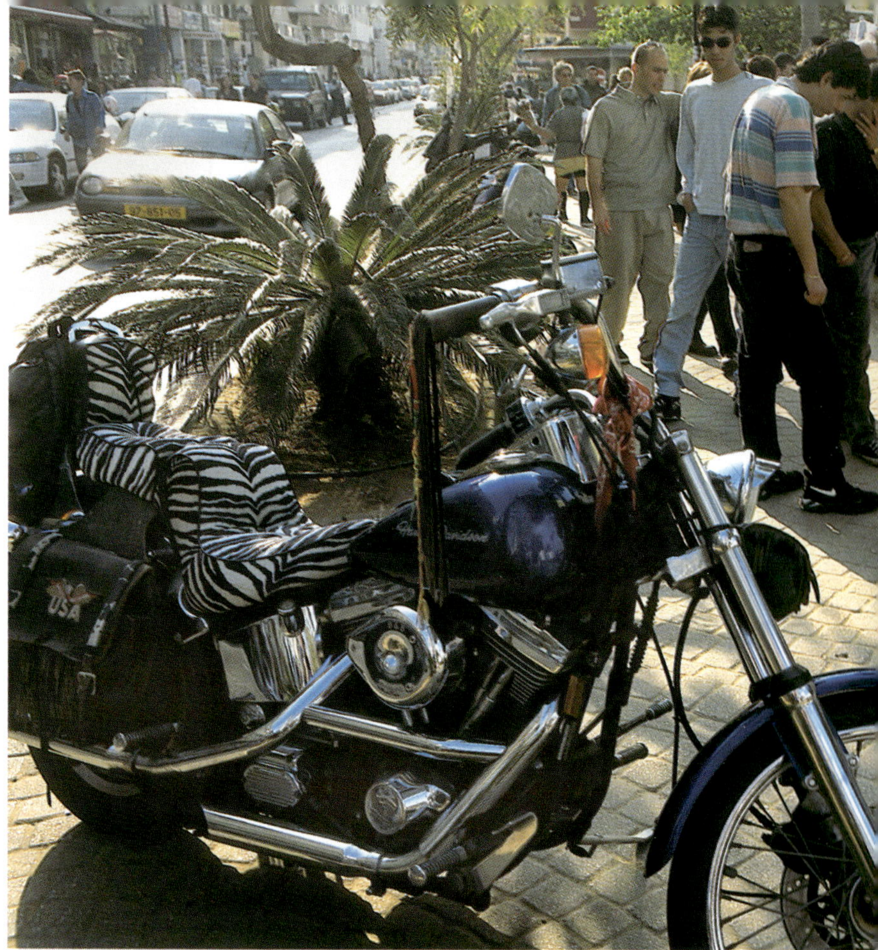

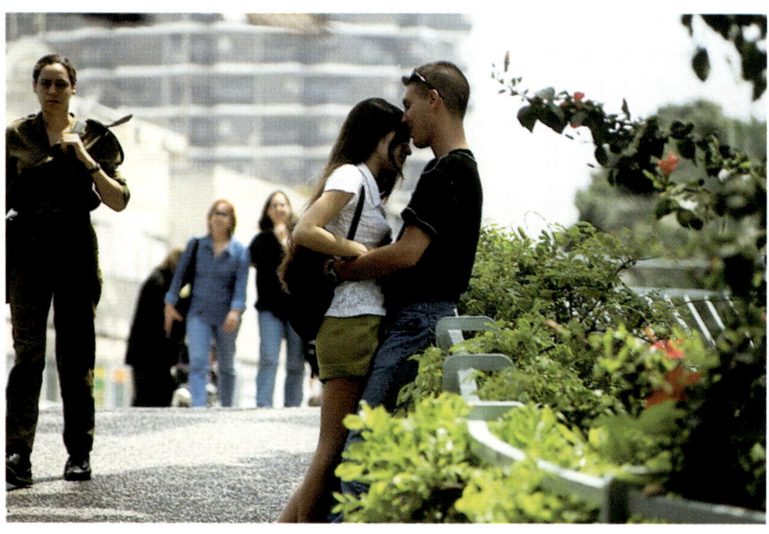

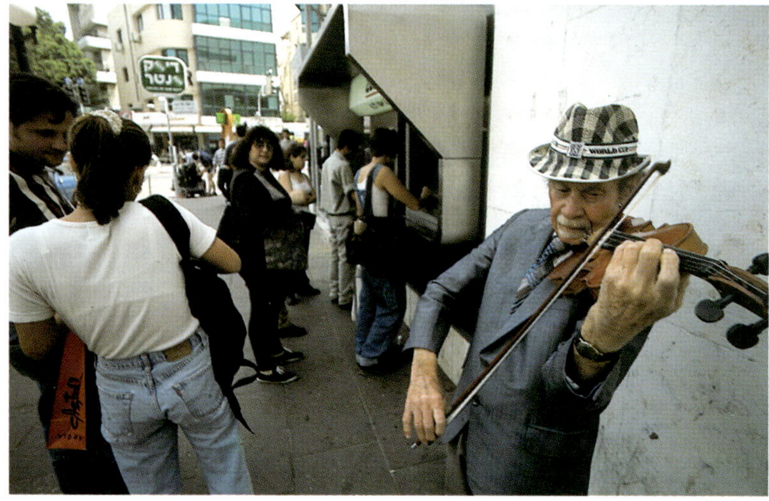

there may have been something by the name of 'Israel'. But it is difficult to determine what this Israel was, whether it was a tribe, a nation or a place. 'We don't even know to this day' says the Israeli writer Yoram Kaniuk, 'what we Jews actually are. A people, a nation, a religion or possibly even a race.'

Moses' military commander Joshua was to conquer Canaan. Israel's claim to this land is based on God's promise to Abraham and Joshua's conquest of it. However, as though history has a peculiar sense of irony, it is today's West Bank – including the cities of Jericho, Hebron and Nablus – which was conquered and settled by the Israelis in those days. The coastal strip, the real heartland ofcontemporary Israel, was enemy territory – the land of the Philistines, a tribe whose riders and chariots were considered to be almost invincible. During this period, the Israelites were ruled by tribal leaders known as judges. The Old Testament book of *Judges* describes the Israelite society of the period in words that could just as easily apply to contemporary Israel: 'In those days there was no king in Israel: every man did that which was right in his own eyes.' It was in the battle against the Philistines that the tribes united and became one kingdom.

United in the Promised Land

Every Israeli child can tell several tales of King David's heroic accomplishments. As a youth he slew the giant, Goliath, in single combat. This is ideal material for all the parallels of the small country of Israel in combat with the 'Arab Goliath'. David is credited with writing the Psalms. He also defeated the Philistines and conquered the Canaanite city of Jebus, which he renamed Jerusalem and made it the capital of the Kingdom of Israel which was established around 1000 BC. Above all, he was a charismatic political realist. He succeeded in doing what few other Jewish politicians have done, namely, uniting the Jewish people for a period of time under a policy of common interests and cleverly defending his country against larger neighbouring powers, using both military and diplomatic means.

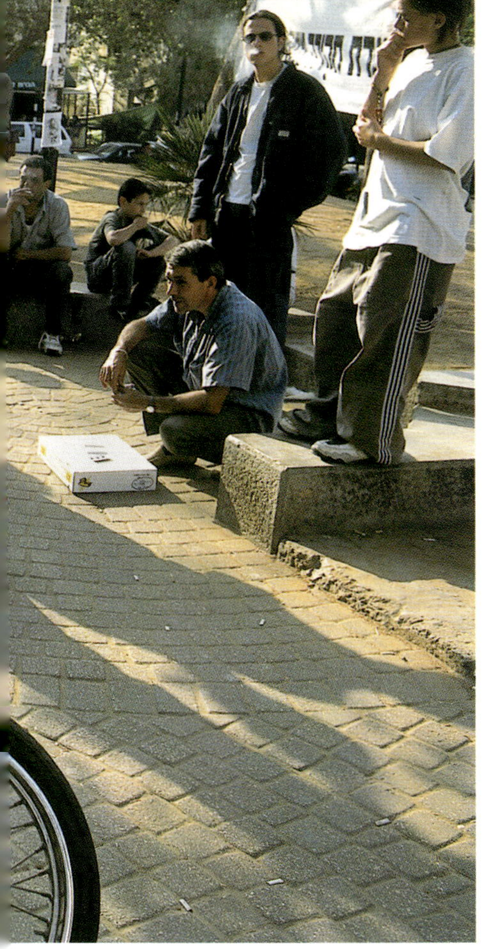

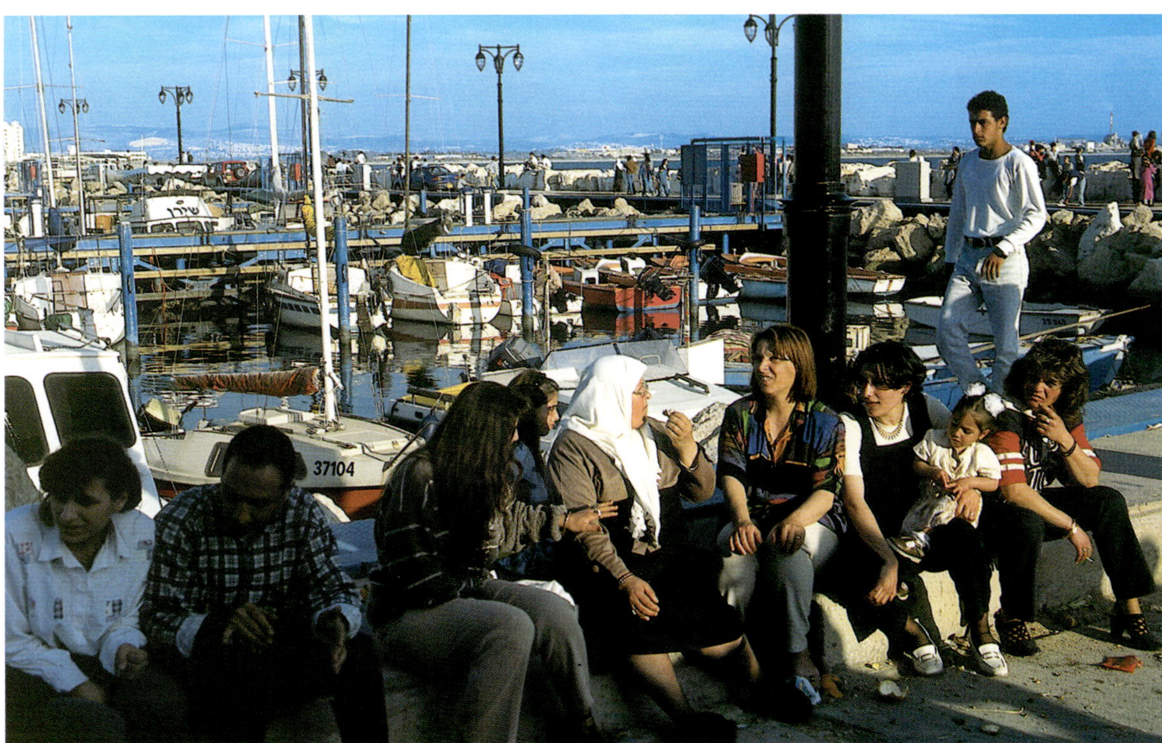

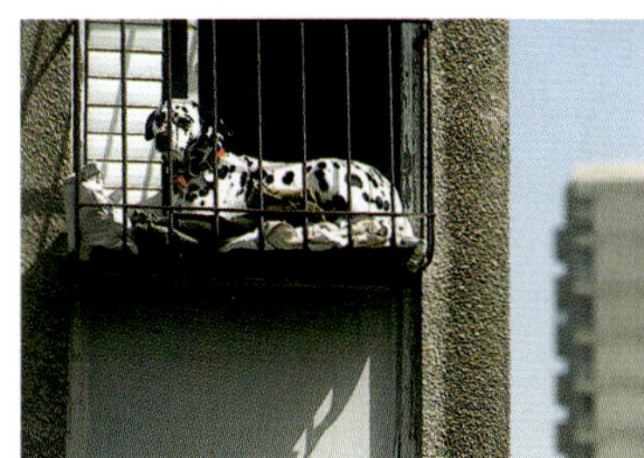

During the period of the crusades, Acre was a major harbour town, whereas today commercial shipping has moved to Haifa. Nowadays it's just fishing and sailing boats and yachts along the pier.

Mostly Kosher: Israel's Cuisine

The Jewish cook can learn what is kosher by reading the Old Testament which states: 'Thou shalt not seethe a kid in his mother's milk.' Meat and milk should therefore never be combined. Pork is forbidden, as is the meat of camels and horses and lobster and crabs. A kosher Israeli breakfast may only include meat-free delicacies such as cottage cheese with olives, salads, cake and egg dishes. Lunches tend to be snacks – for example falafel, delicious little chickpea balls which are served in pitta bread and garnished with salads and sauces according to taste. Humus and tahina, spiced chickpea or sesame pastes are also very popular. In the evenings, however, Israelis are drawn to the many ethnic restaurants which various immigrants have established, where the food ranges from A for Arabic to V for Vietnamese. That is quite typical of the Israeli cuisine: its diversity, the fact that it consists of foods from all around the world.

In 970 BC, after a reign of 40 years, David left his son Solomon a well-organised kingdom and the knowledge of how to administer it successfully. Under Solomon a number of fortified cities such as Megiddo and Chazor were built, whose ruins can be partly seen today. He also succeeded in strengthening Israel's political and economic alliances. And finally, he built the Temple in Jerusalem. Both King David and King Solomon brought an end to the nomadic existence of the Israelites. By conquering Jerusalem and building the Temple in the new capital city they created a spiritual and a new tradition which was to have an effect on thousands of years of Jewish history.

If deep conflicts between religious and nationalistic versus secular parties are visible in Israeli society today, it is by no means a new phenomenon in Jewish history. The kingdom created by David and his son barely survived Solomon's death. It then broke up into the two kingdoms of Judea and Israel, which continued to wage bitter wars with each other.

The Kingdom of Israel, whose capital was Samaria, was destroyed and occupied by the Assyrians in 722/721 BC – an

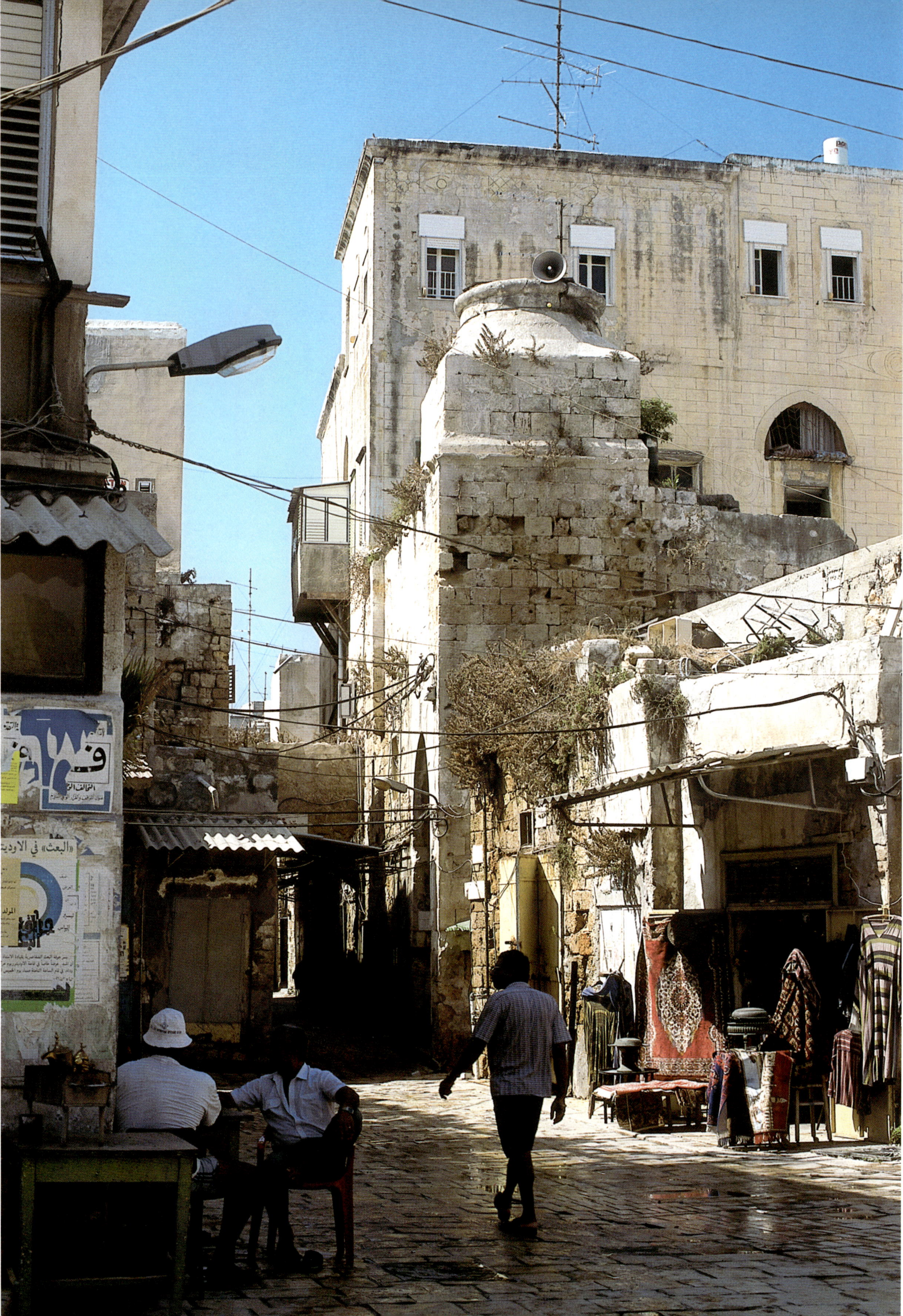
«البعث» في

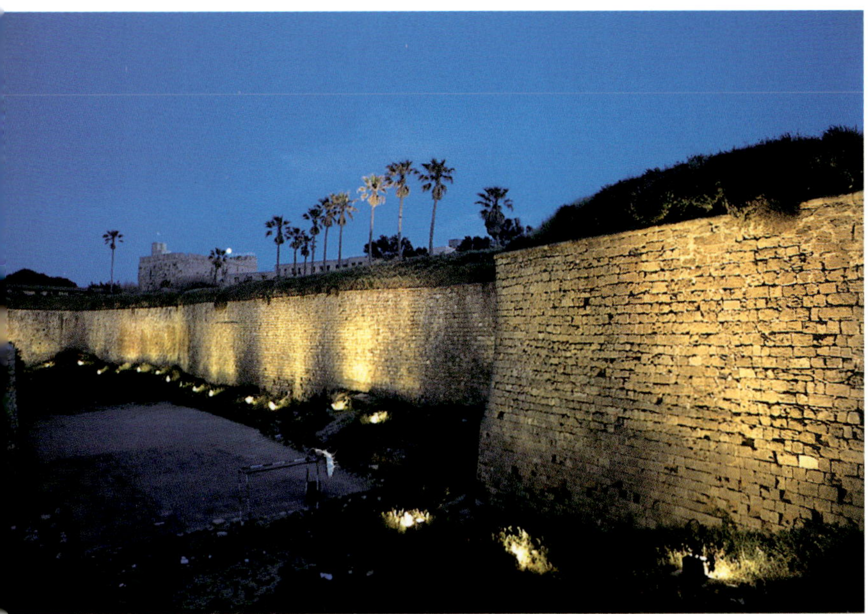

event which was mentioned for the first time in non-biblical sources. A large part of the people of Israel was then lost. Even the Kingdom of Judea, weakened by wars, did not last much longer. Together with its capital Jerusalem, it was conquered by the Babylonians, and the Temple was destroyed by Nebuchadnezzar in 587 BC. The first exile had begun.

Only 50 years later thousands of Jews returned to Jerusalem. Twenty years after that, in 516 BC, the second Temple of Jerusalem was consecrated. A large section of the Jewish upper class remained in Babylon, and another group went to Egypt where a large Diaspora community developed in Alexandria. These places were to play an important part in ever-changing Jewish history. Both communities ceased to exist for a while when the State of Israel was declared in 1948, and the Iraqi and Egyptian Jews had to leave these countries during the Arab-Israeli conflict.

Diaspora, Sects and Overestimation – the Temporary End

Throughout its history, the Jewish people has always had to decide between pure self-assertion and armed resistance. They did not always make the right choice, which sometimes had fatal consequences. As long as the many rulers who continued to conquer and then lose the small strip of land between the Mediterranean and the Dead Sea acknowledged the right of Jews to practice their religion freely, the Jewish people came to terms with their situation. If, however, they felt they were in danger of losing their national and religious identity through

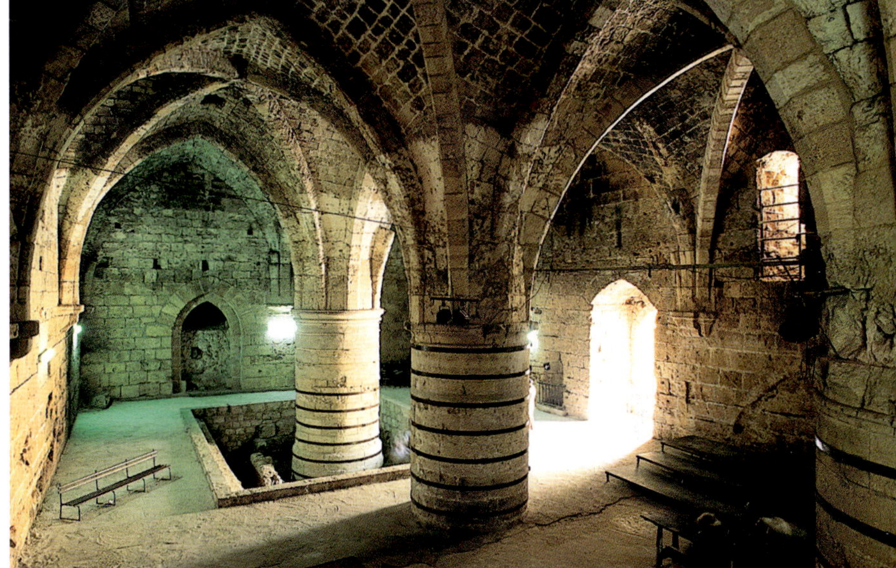

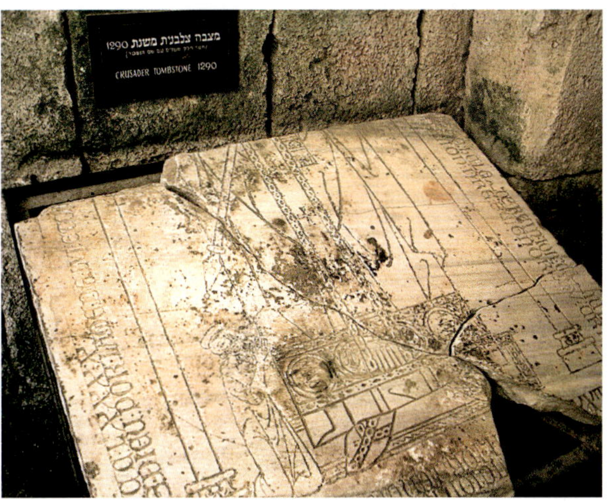

For anyone wishing to follow in the footsteps of the crusaders in Acre (left page), the first step is to go underground. The crusader town lies under the citadel (left) which was built by Ahmad al Jazzar in the 18th century. Memorial slabs (below) and the refectorium or the dining hall (above) were excavated in the 1950s.

assimilation into a tempting new culture or through submission or subjugation, they did not choose diplomacy and compromise, but rather violent confrontation, regardless of any realistic chance of success. And they would always lose in the end.

Alexander the Great, who conquered the region in 332 BC, granted the Jews considerable religious and political freedom. However his successors attempted to Hellenize the Jews, forbidding the observance of the Sabbath, circumcision and the dietary laws. The priest Mattathias and his five sons rebelled against these sanctions. Under the leadership of the eldest of his sons, Judas Maccabeus, the rebels led a skilful guerrilla war against the Greeks and regained Jerusalem and the Temple in 165 BC. The victory of a small, but well-organised rebel army

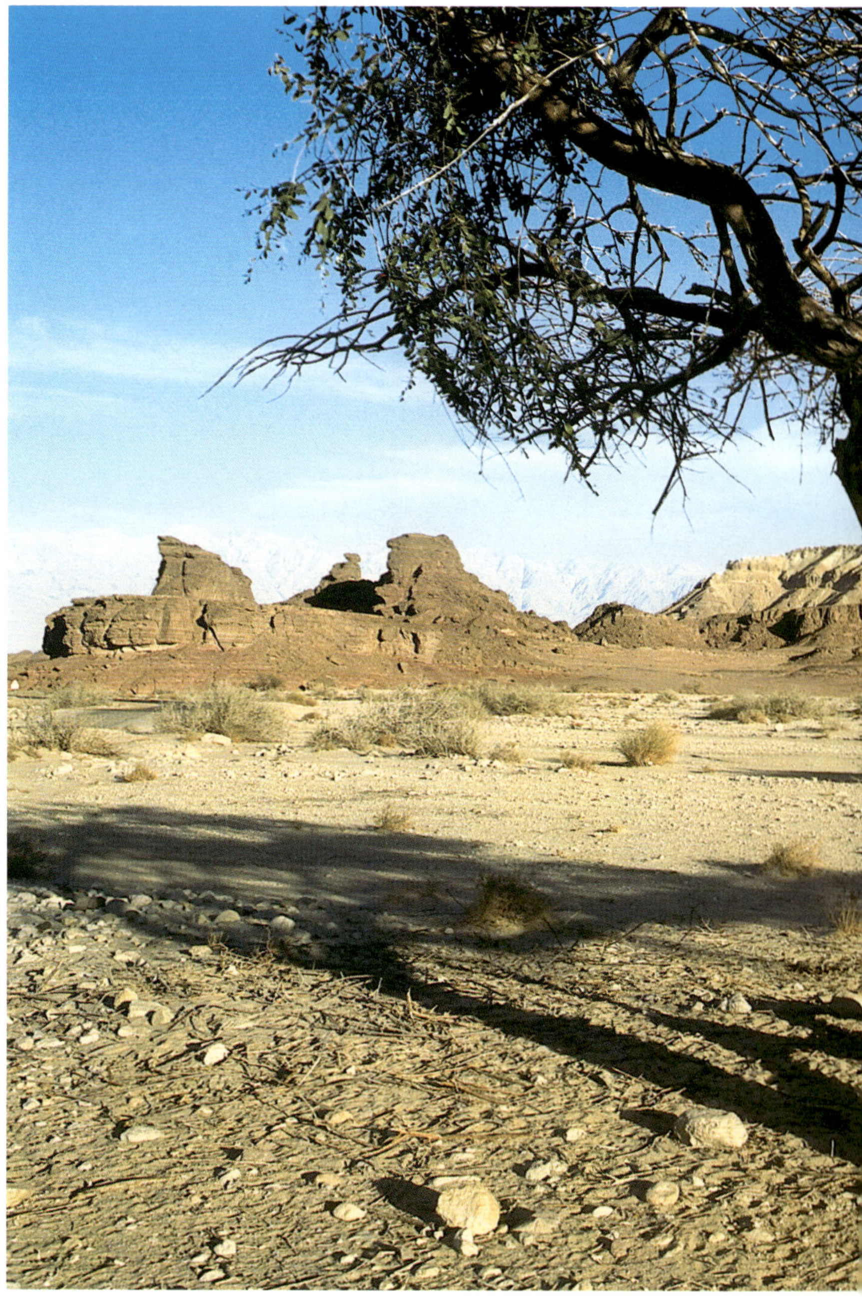

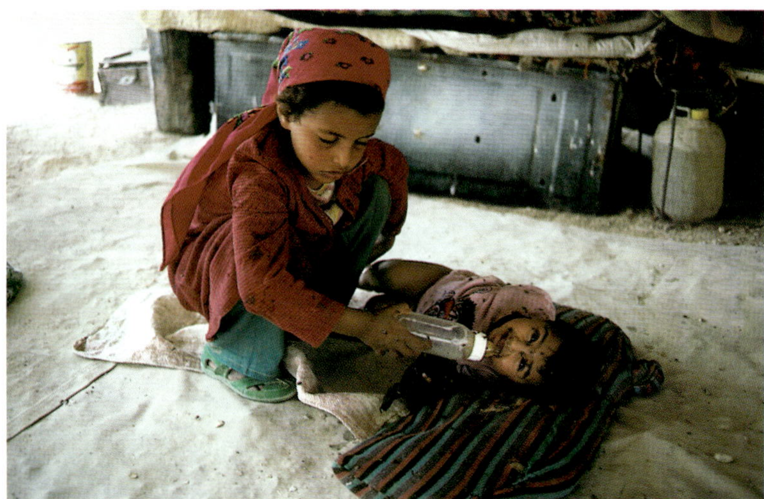

Until the founding of the State of Israel nearly 100 Bedouin tribes lived a nomadic life in the hills of the Negev Desert. Today many live in reservations around Beersheba where a Bedouin market is held on Thursdays (pictures below). Only one tribe continues to wander through the barren region with its 'ships of the desert'.

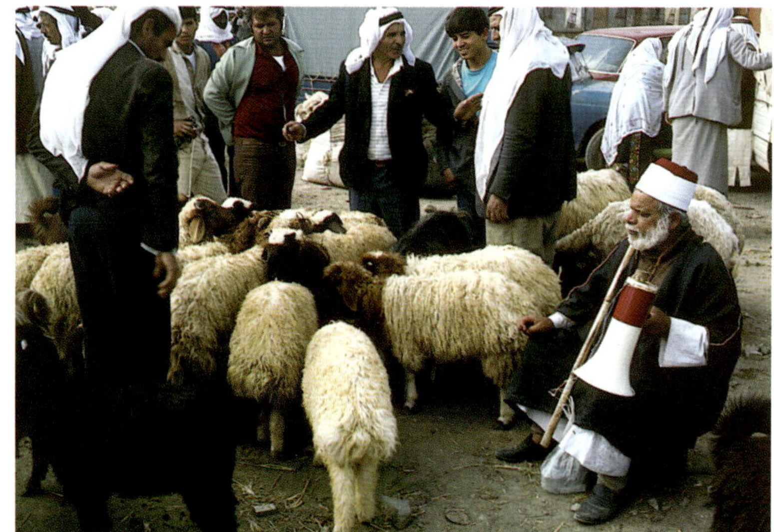

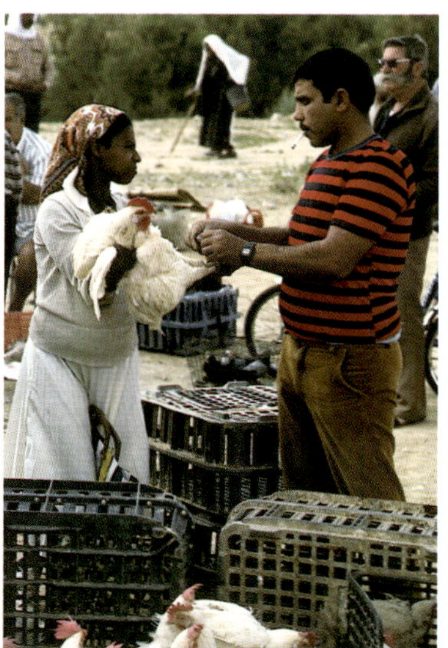

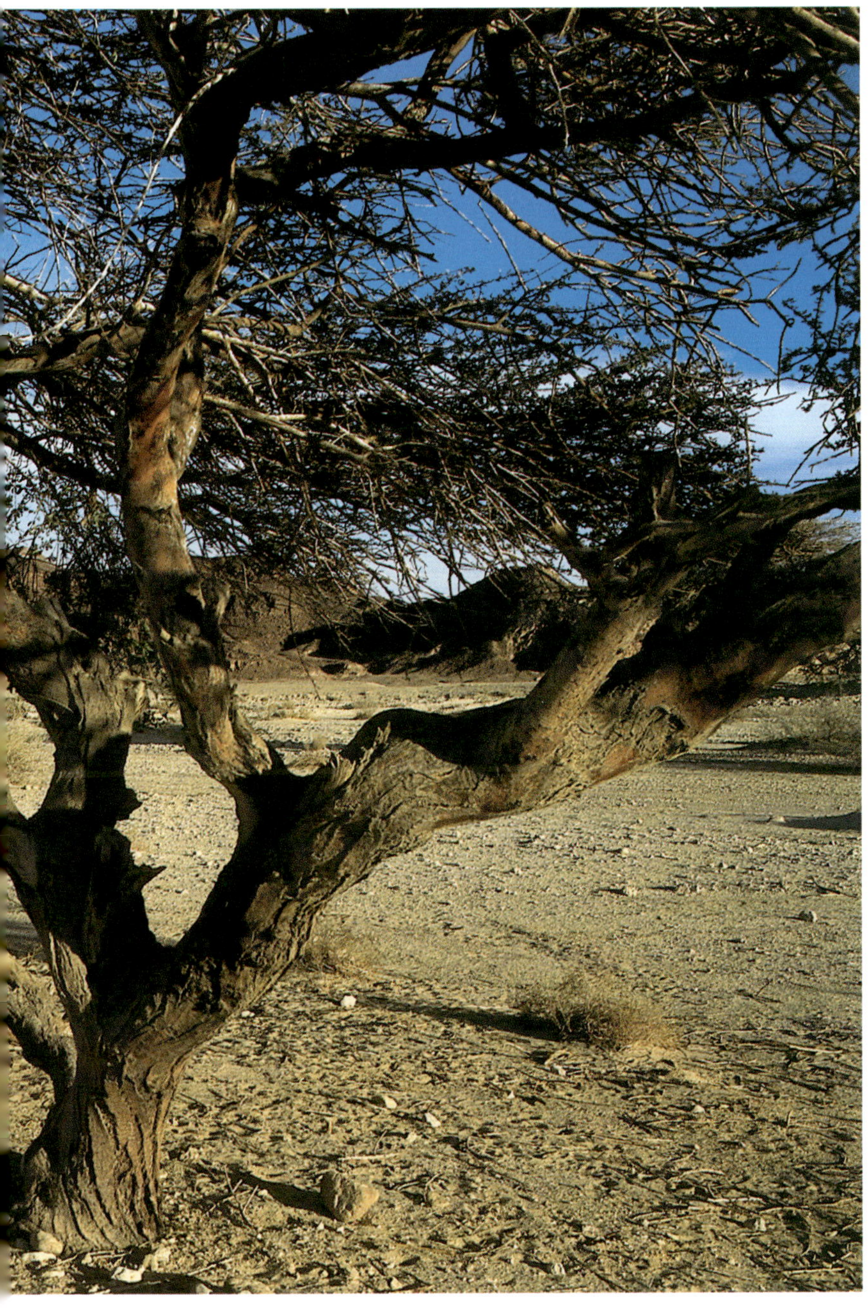

The Negev covers more than 60 per cent of the surface of Israel. Its only populated area is in the north where it is artificially irrigated. A trip through the desert to Timna (centre) and Eilat is very impressive.

against a military world power would have been enough of a miracle. But the Book of *Maccabees* also describes a religious miracle. For the rededication of the Temple a supply of special candle oil was required for eight days. In the plundered stocks, however, enough oil was found for only one day. The Maccabeans lit it and it burned for the prescribed eight days. This miracle of the candle is commemorated every year during the festival of Hanukkah.

The Maccabeans had hoped to convert Jewish society into an aristocratically structured unit as it was during the time of the Judges. The battle against Greece, whose kingdom was slowly crumbling, was a much simpler task than trying to unify this people. In 63 BC the mighty military machine of the Roman Empire under the leadership of its commander, Pompey the Great, finally captured the small country of Judea. It was faced with a Jewish society more fragmented than ever before. Countless self-appointed prophets predicted the only true salvation out of this crisis in which the Jewish people found themselves. Some, such as the Essenes who are referred to in the scrolls found in Qumran (see pages 68, 136, 140f.) withdrew to a life of solitude and asceticism. Jesus was one of many teachers who tried to reform Judaism during that period. It was not just in religious matters but also in questions of politics that agreement could not be reached. There was, however, consensus on one thing: that they would not allow themselves to be subjugated by Rome without any resistance.

That might not have been absolutely necessary. The Romans, in their pragmatism, hardly wished to interfere in internal Jew-

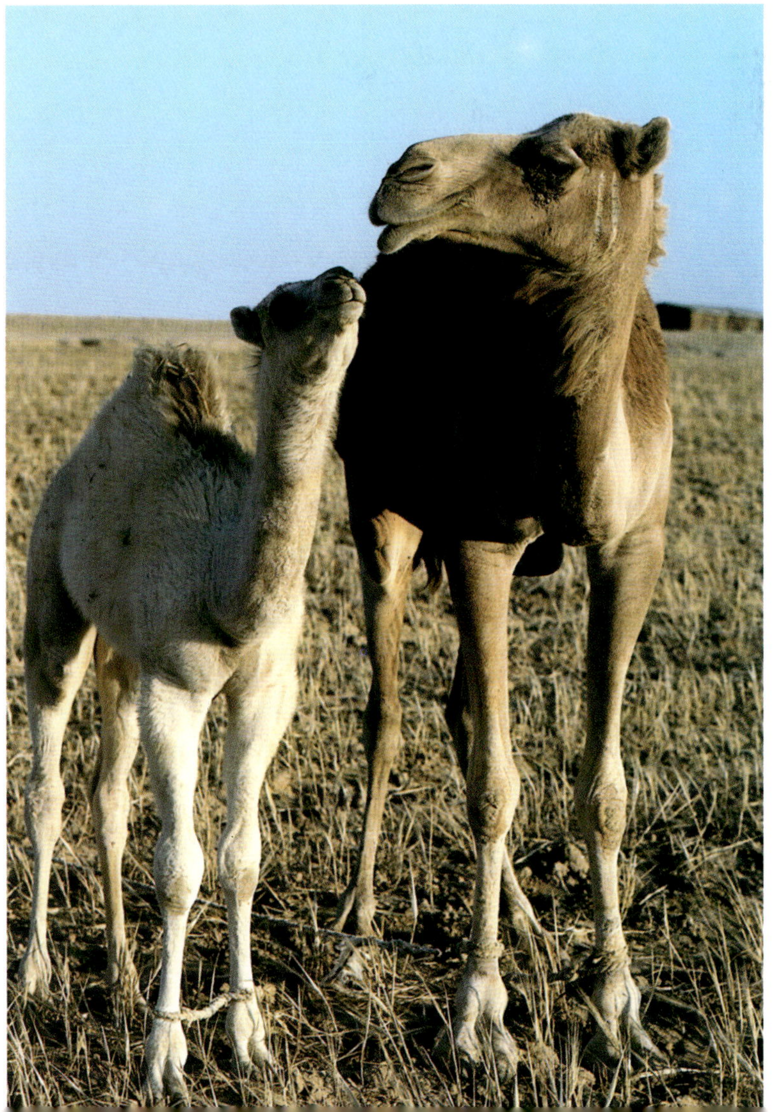

Between February and April and from August to October white storks fly over the country.

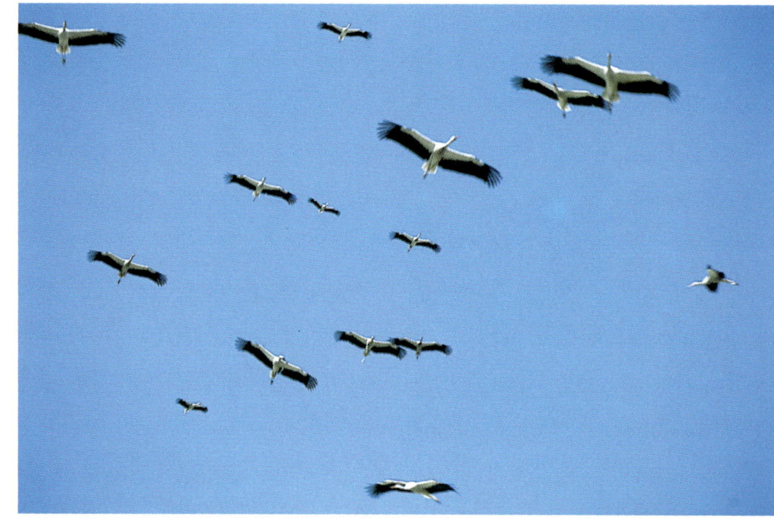

From white to ochre to red, these are the colours that play in the changing light of the desert: Mt Sodom, south of the Dead Sea (left), rocks in the Timna Valley (centre), in the Desert of Judea near Masada (below right).

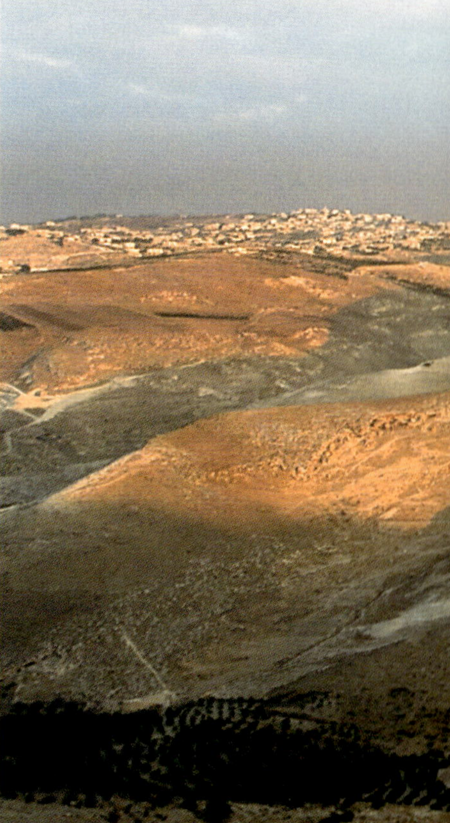

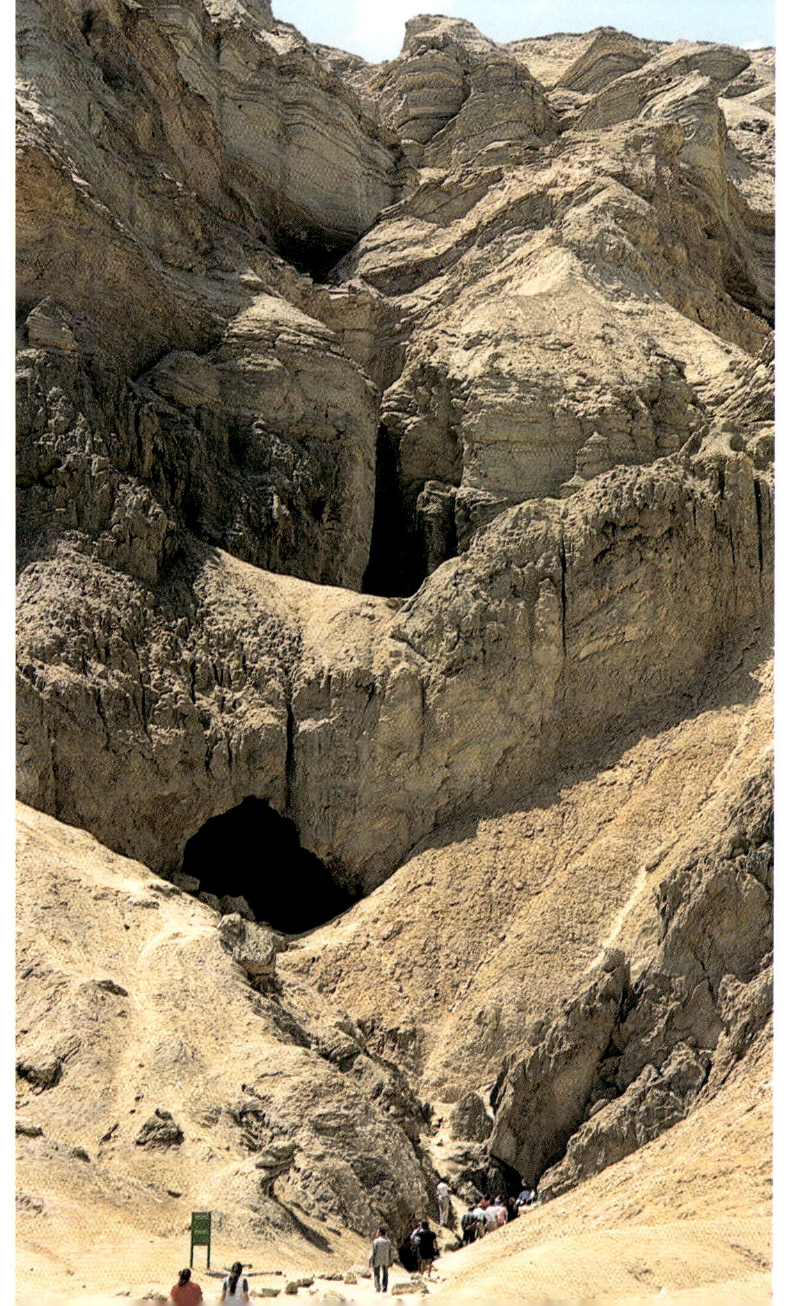

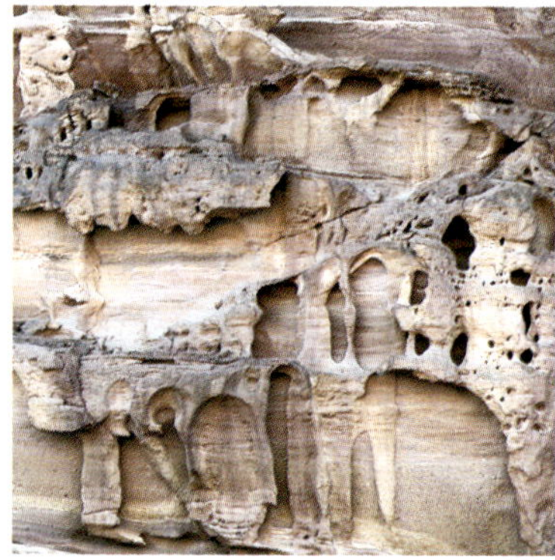

ish strife and guaranteed their province of Judea a great deal of autonomy. Permanent friction between the Jews and the mostly corrupt Roman rulers, within the split Jewish society itself and between the Greek and Roman population and the Hebrews brought matters to a head. In the latter period, no one, not even the Jewish historian Flavius Josephus who followed the beginning of the 'Jewish War' against Rome, first as a fighter and later as an observer, could work out what the original causes really were.

Rome sent three legions with a total of 60,000 well-trained professional soldiers. Judea stood up with a handful of rebels who preferred to die in their Messianic zeal rather than submit to Roman heathens. Seven years, from 66 to 73 AD, was how long this first war against the Romans lasted. The aim of the Jewish rebels was to throw off the yoke of Rome and above all to protect Judaism's most holy site, the Temple of Jerusalem, from being desecrated. The opposite happened. The uprising

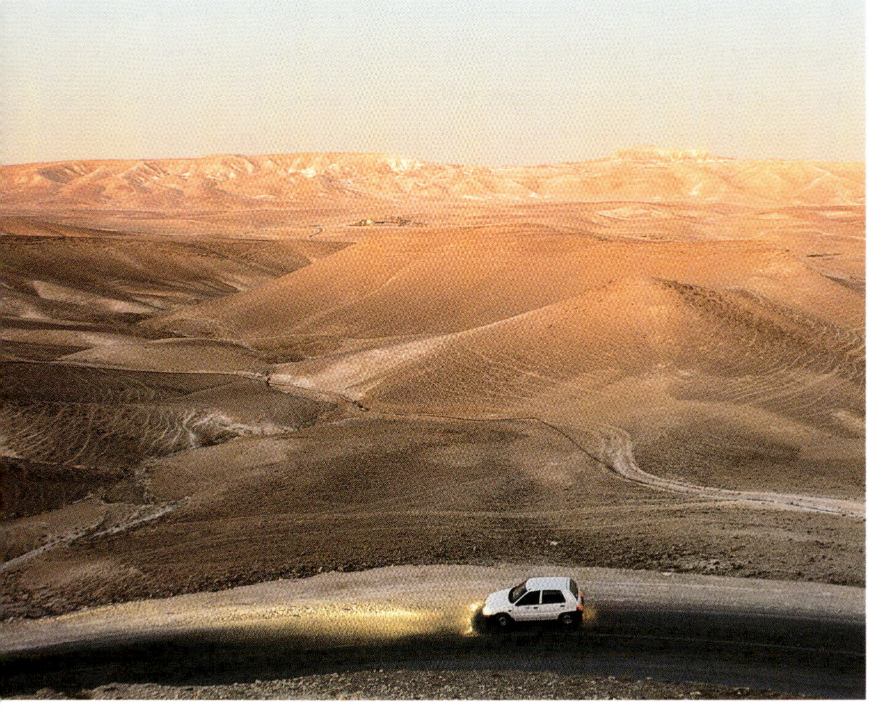

ended with the destruction of the Temple in 70 AD and the collective suicide of 960 rebels on the fortress of Masada (see page 138f.) in the year 73 AD. Thus the rebellion of the Jews was put down, but even in the years that followed the region remained an area of unrest.

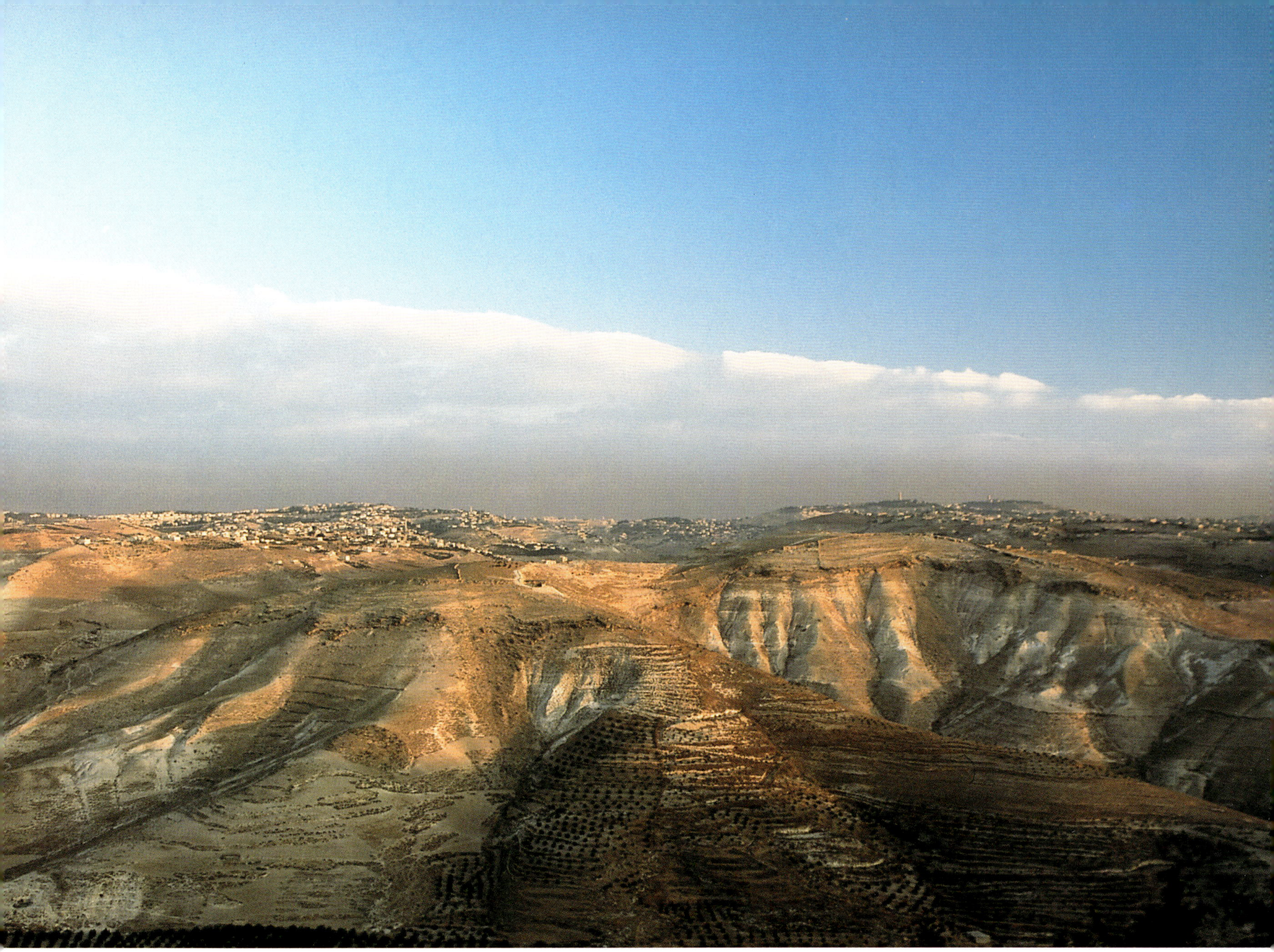

Being conquered and losing their land was something that the Jews were still able to cope with. Judea had witnessed too many rulers coming and going to believe that the Jewish people would not survive. However, without their spiritual centre, without the Temple of Jerusalem, the very foundations of Judaism seemed to be shattered. With the ending of the last of the Jewish uprising against the Romans under the leadership of Bar Kochba in 135 AD, Israel ceased to exist as a nation. As a people, however, it created for itself a new spiritual centre which it would protect from assimilation in the two thousand years of exile that followed, until in 1948 it would enter the world stage as a nation once again.

New Beginnings

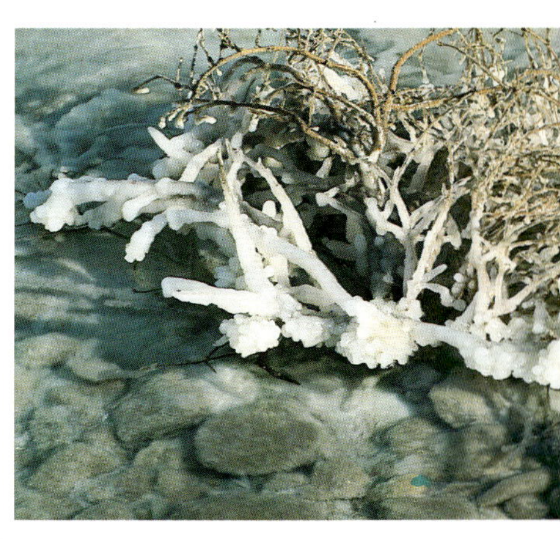

During the first of the uprisings against the Romans one man was responsible for a greater change than all the other rebels put together. After the destruction of the Temple, from about 74 AD, the scholar Johanan Ben Zakkai founded a school at Jabneh (Yavne), some 31 miles west of Jerusalem, which was to replace the former centre. Johanan and the rabbinical scribes became the new elite who took on the leadership of the people. Studying the sacred scrolls became a matter of course for large

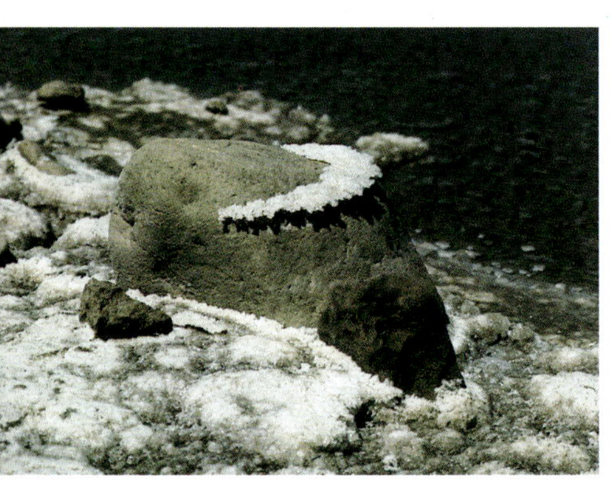

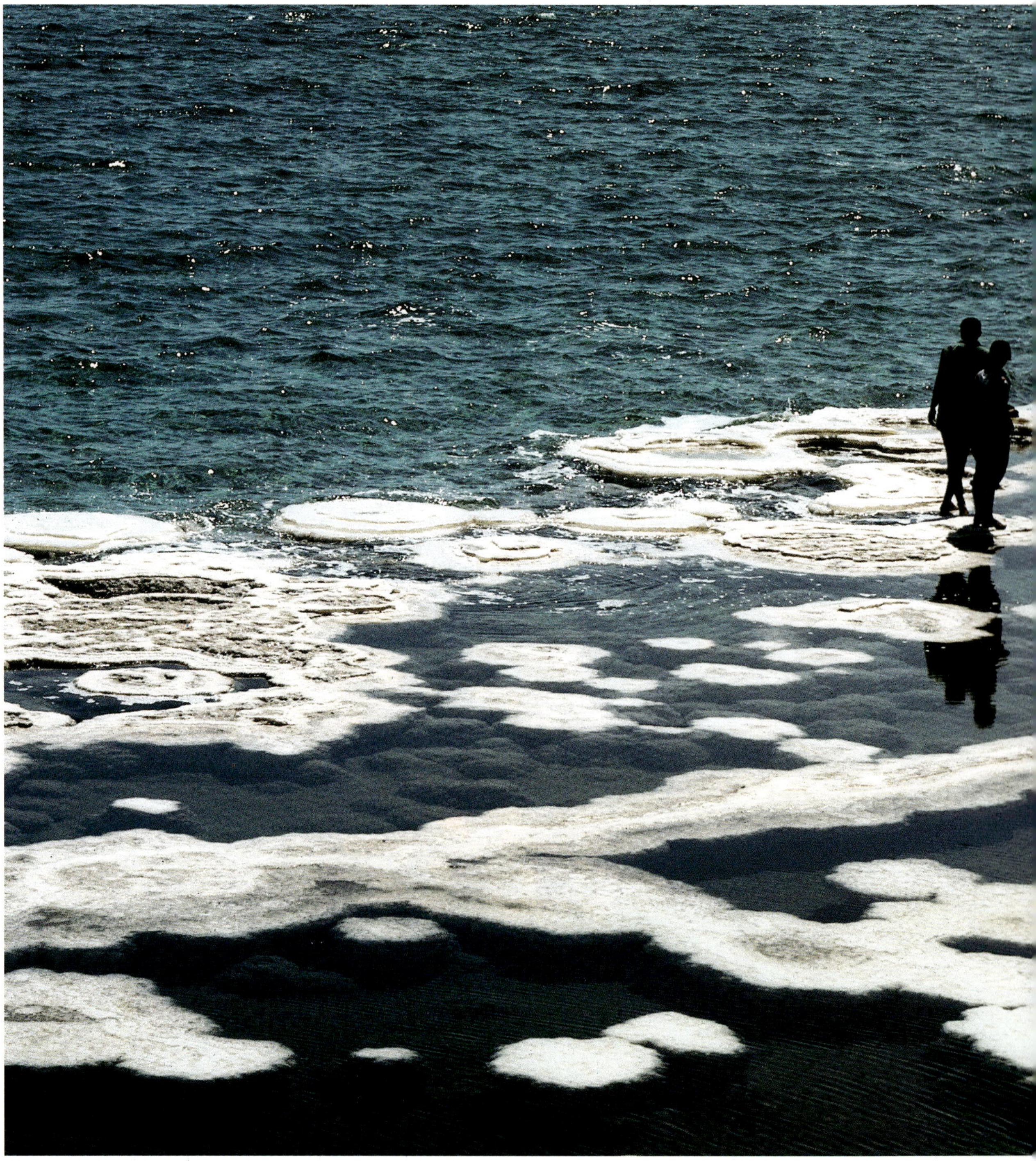

Neither animals nor plants can exist in the Dead Sea. But along its shores the high evaporation of the water results in the formation of flower-like shapes made of salt crystals. At its southern end the waters are only 13 to 22 feet deep. Lumps of salt reach up as high as the water's surface.

sections of the Jewish population. Jabneh marked the beginning of a new era: the synagogue replaced the Temple as the spiritual centre of the community. The spirit and study of the Torah, the five books of Moses and their interpretation became the cornerstone of Judaism.

Even during the Diaspora Jews continued to live in the Holy Land as insignificant communities. The region was governed by Rome and Byzantium until the seventh century, after which came Arab princes, then Christian crusaders in the eleventh century, Turkish sultans from the sixteenth century and then, after the First World War, the British. But the spiritual impulses came from the Diaspora. Whatever else happened throughout the history of the Jews dispersed around the world, in spite of all resistance and persecution, they steadfastly upheld their doctrine of a single God. Hope was concentrated on the arrival of the Messiah who would appear one day to redeem the Jews, lead them back to the Promised Land and rebuild the Temple. The memory of the Holy Land is expressed as a devout prayer every year on the eve of the Passover Festival with the words, 'Next year in Jerusalem!'

Israel's colourful history makes it even more attractive as a travel destination: Canaanites, Philistines, Assyrians, Romans, Byzantines, Crusaders, Arabs, Mamelukes, Turks, have all left behind eloquent traces of their presence. Israel is one of the few countries in the world in which we find impressive witness to thousands of years of diverse cultures cheek by jowl with the most modern infrastructures, the shopping mall next to an Oriental bazaar – Europe and the Orient united.

'Salaam' say the Arabs when they greet someone. 'Shalom' say the Jews. Both words mean Peace. May this wish come true in the near future.

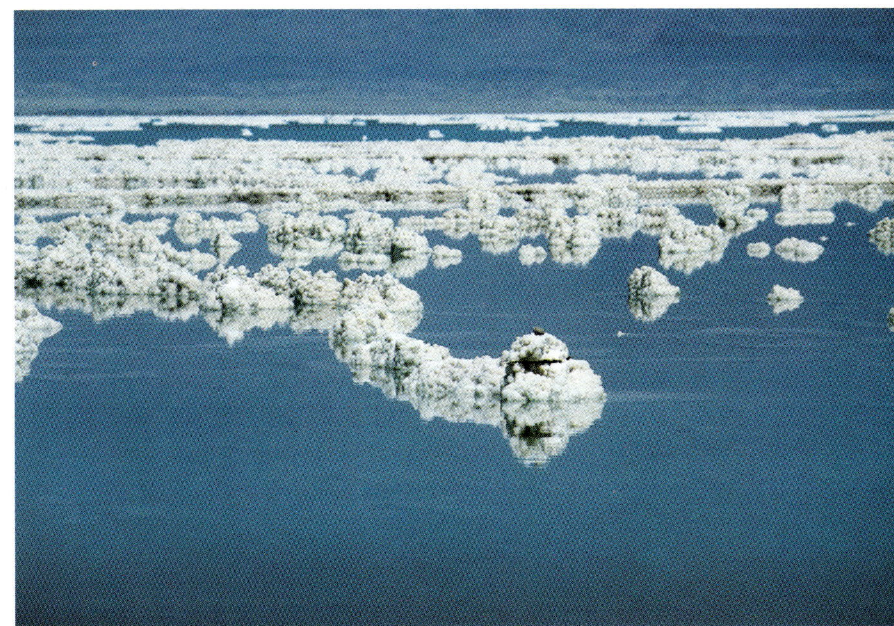

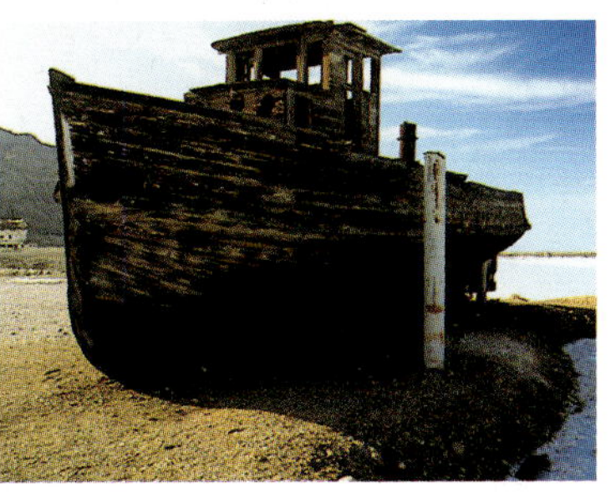

The wooden ship lying in solitary splendour on the southern shores of the Dead Sea reminds us of Noah's Ark.

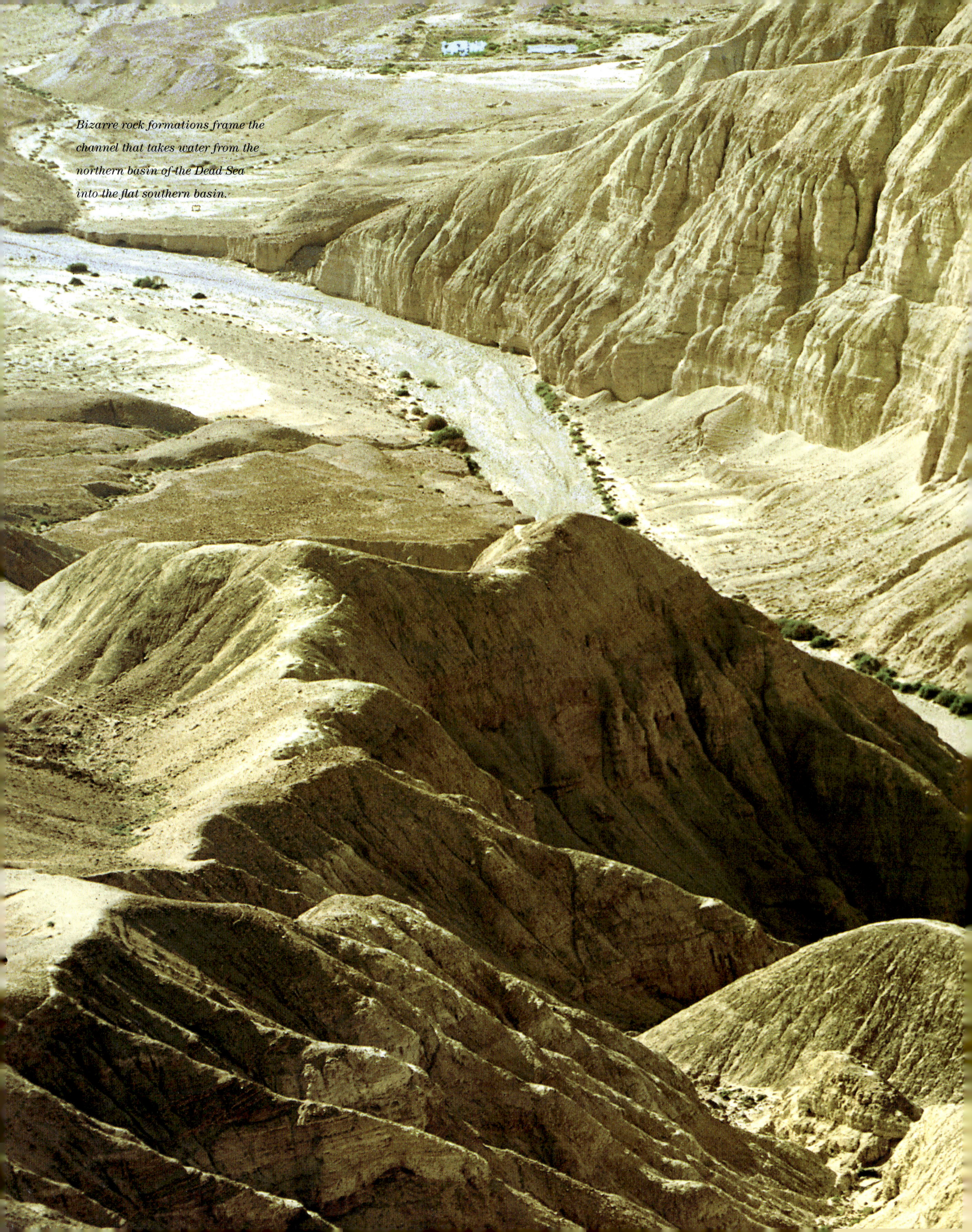

Bizarre rock formations frame the channel that takes water from the northern basin of the Dead Sea into the flat southern basin.

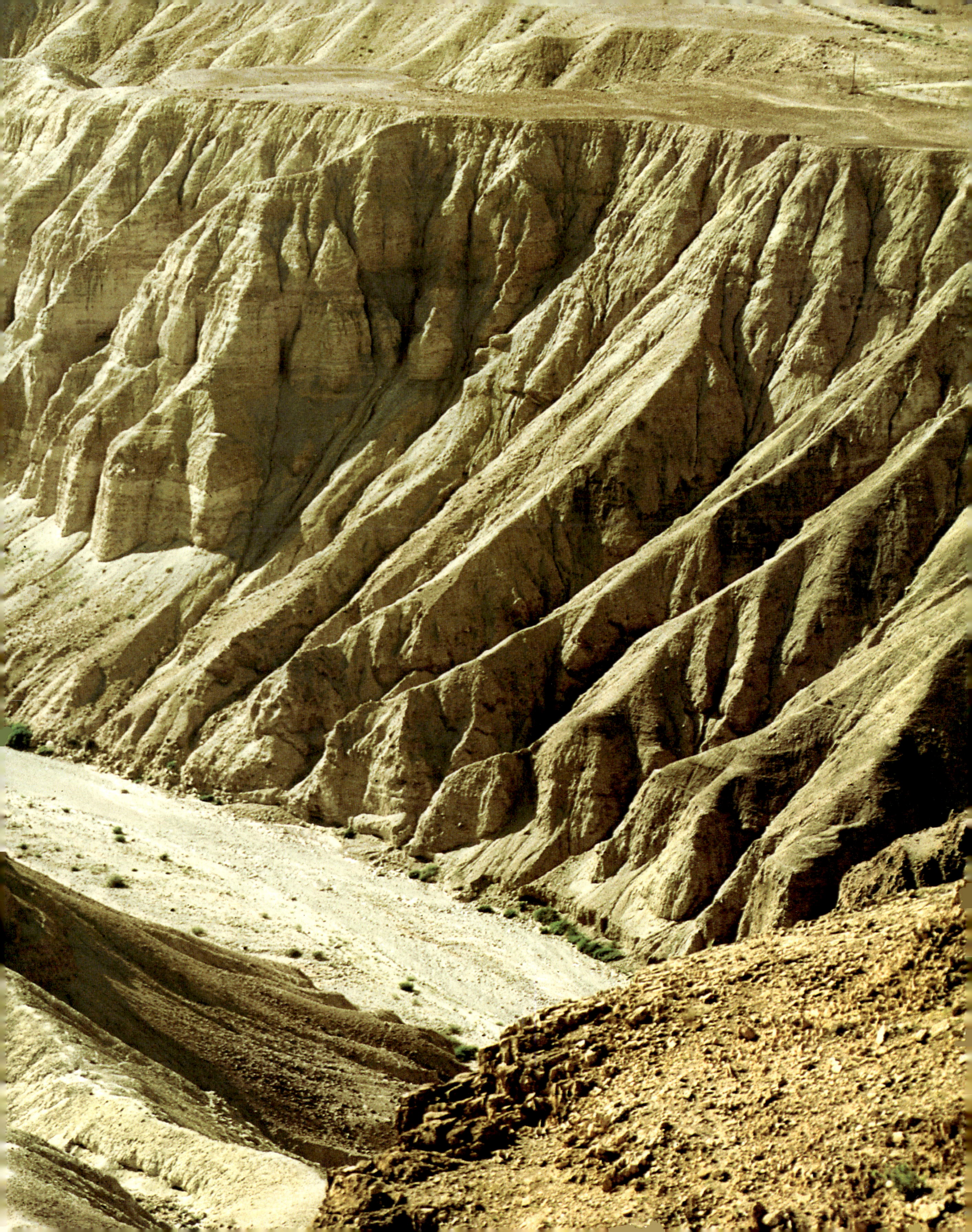

City of Three World Religions

Ancient and Modern Jerusalem

The world has seen cities that have been more magnificent and more powerful, but none has been the focus of so much yearning and so many hopes as Jerusalem. It is sacred to all three monotheistic religions – Judaism, Christianity and Islam – representing nearly a third of the world's population. However, throughout its history, it always had to pay a high price for its holiness, for the wishes and aspirations of its inhabitants, visitors and conquerors. 'And it shall come to pass in the last days, that the mountain of the Lord's house shall be established in the top of the mountains, and shall be exalted above the hills; and all nations shall flow unto it. ... and they shall beat their swords into plowshares, and their spears into pruninghooks'. This was prophesied in the Bible by the prophet Isaiah some 700 years before the birth of Christ, inspiring us to this day with the hope of a peaceful co-existence of all people and all religions. But even the Jewish history of this city started with a war – a conquest: King David defeated the Jebusites around 1000 BC, capturing the small city of Jebus, renaming it Jerusalem and declaring it to be the capital of his kingdom. David's successor Solomon built the Temple and made Jerusalem the political as well as spiritual centre for the Jewish people, and so it remained for centuries to come.

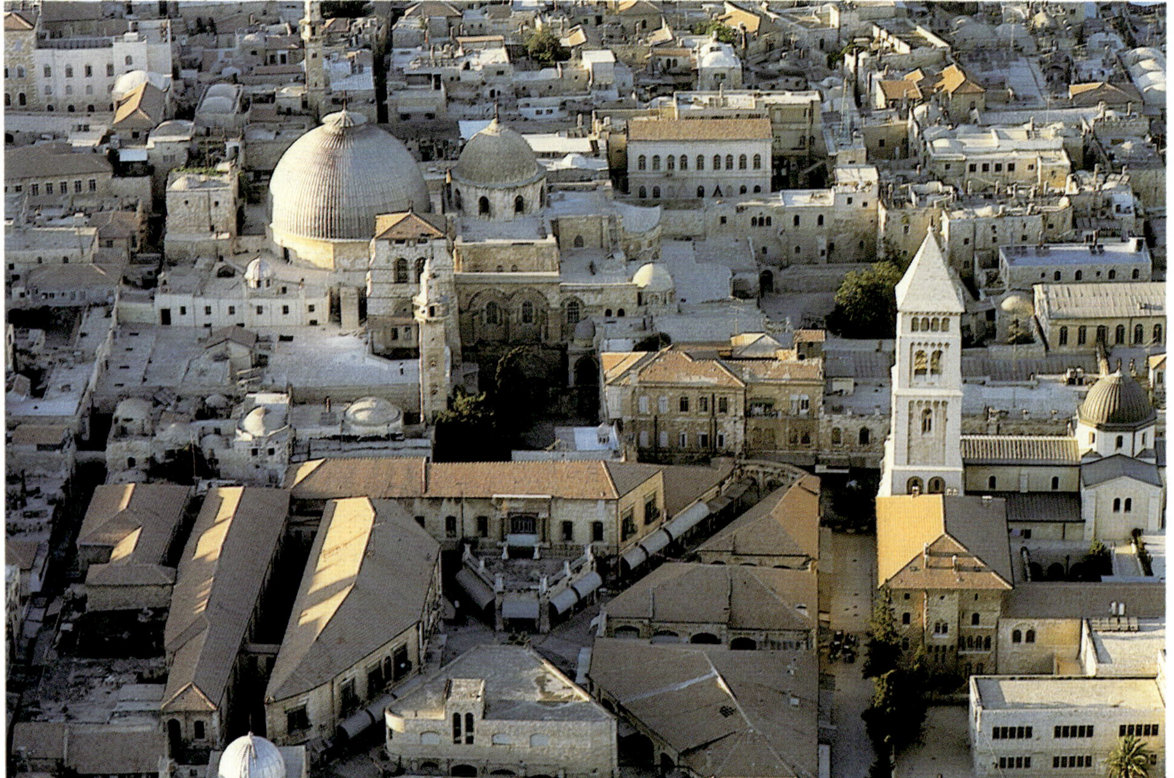

Jerusalem, the Holy City. No where else do we find the most hallowed locations for Jews, Christians and Muslims lying so close together as in the capital of Israel. The Church of the Holy Sepulchre with its prominent rotunda is said to be the site of the last Station of the Cross and of Christ's resurrection (the slim tower of the Church of the Redeemer, right).

Titus, the Roman general, razed the city to the ground in 70 BC, destroying the Temple and releasing a bloodbath among its inhabitants. Sixty-five years later and following another revolt against the Romans, the Emperor Hadrian prohibited all Jews from entering the city. Even Rome's first Christian emperor, Constantine, did nothing to change this verdict. It was not until 637, when Jerusalem was taken by the Muslims under the Caliph

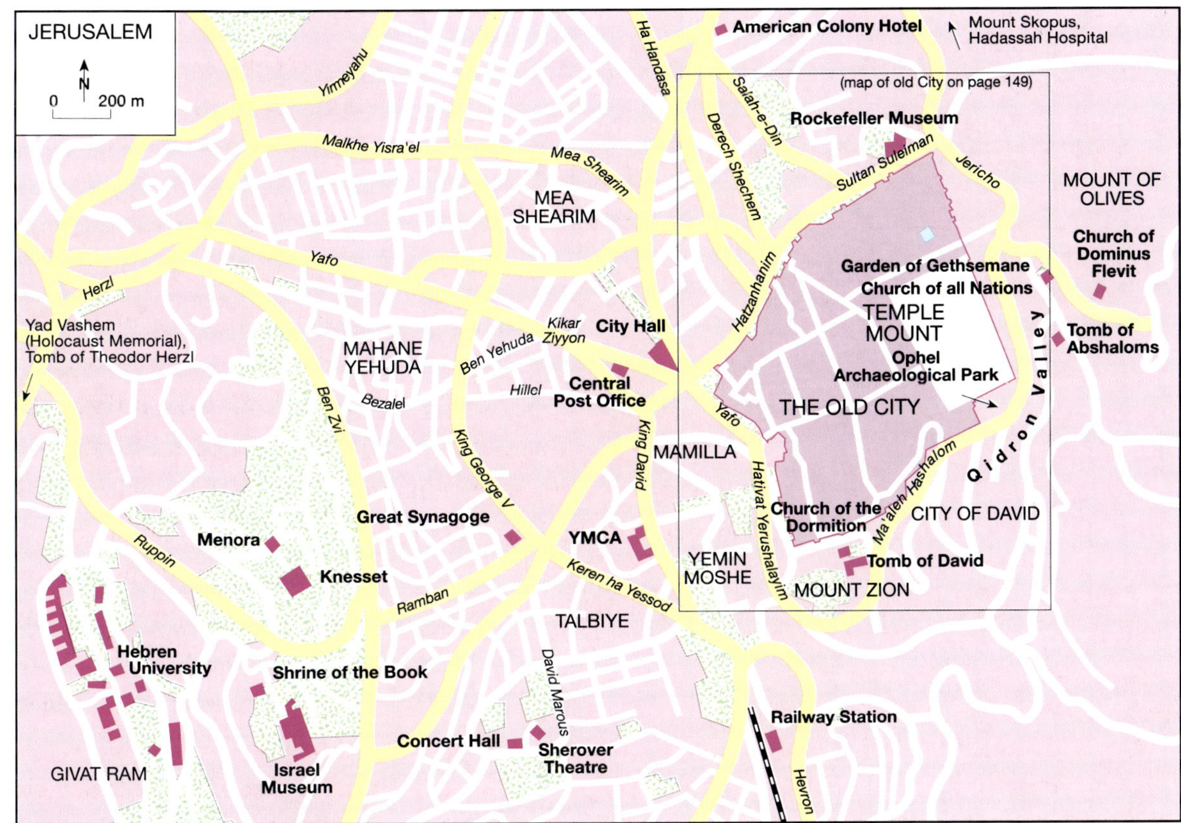

Umar I, that Jews were allowed to settle in the southern part of the city. For centuries they remained a minority in what had once been their capital, packed together in a small district of the Old City.

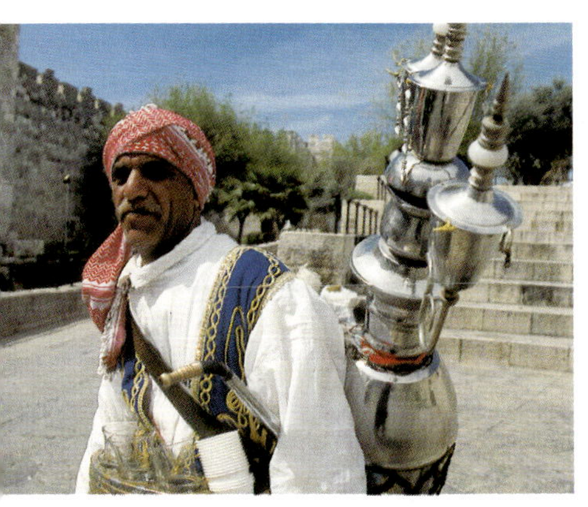

In the alleyways of the Old Town, surrounded by Arab street traders, one feels as though one is on an oriental journey of discovery with tea and water sellers.

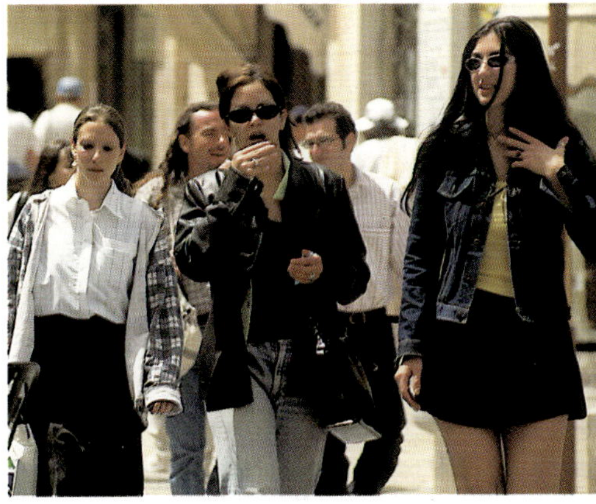

Ben Yehuda Street is the centre of modern Jerusalem. Pedestrianised in 1982, it invites people to shop and stroll among its many shops, cafés and street musicians.

The Muslim Arabs ruled over Palestine with tolerance, unlike the Christian crusaders who, between the ninth and twelfth centuries slaughtered anyone who was not of their religion, all 'in the name of the Lord'. This relatively short era ended when the Mamelukes conquered Palestine in the mid-thirteenth century, driving out the last of the Crusaders as well as the few remaining Jews of Jerusalem. It was only when the Ottomans defeated the Mamelukes in the fifteenth century and gained control of Palestine, which they maintained until the twentieth century, that the Jews dared to return to the Holy Land. Thousands had fled from Spain where they had been mercilessly persecuted by the Inquisition. They continued to be a minority under the Ottomans in Jerusalem, but at least were assured a safe refuge.

It is only since the Zionist immigration movement towards the end of the last century that Jews represented a majority again in their former capital city. After the declaration of the Jewish State in 1948, bitter fighting broke out between Jews and Arabs in the wake of the War of Independence. During these battles the former Jewish quarter of the Old City was almost

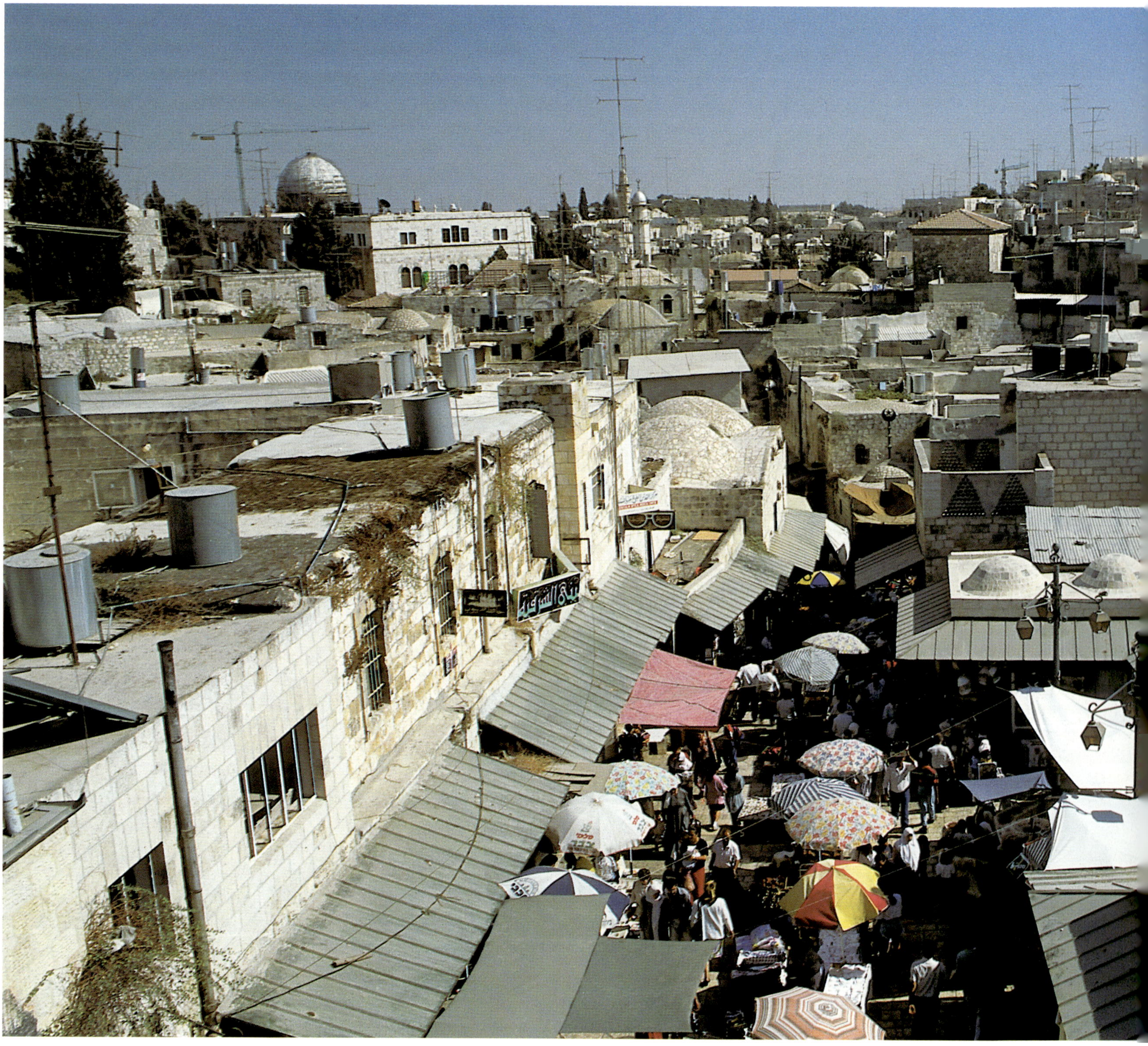

The Damascus Gate along the Ramparts is the perfect place to observe the goings-on in the Old City or for climbing down to join in the hustle and bustle of the Muslim Quarter.

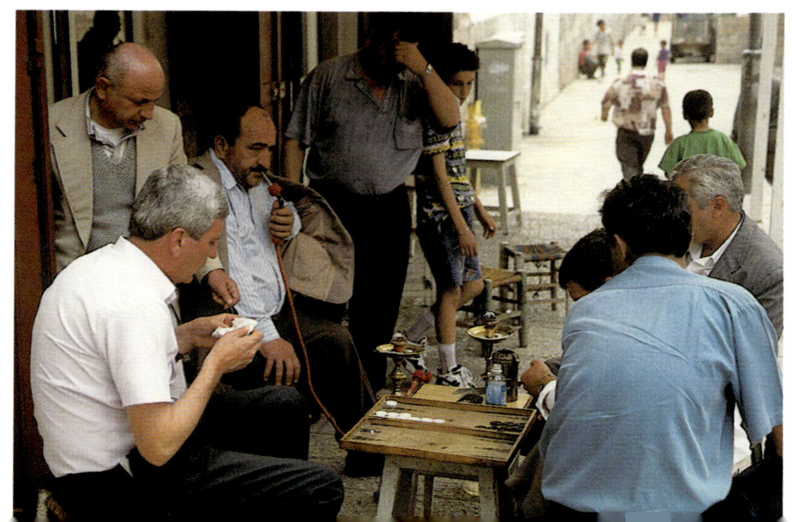

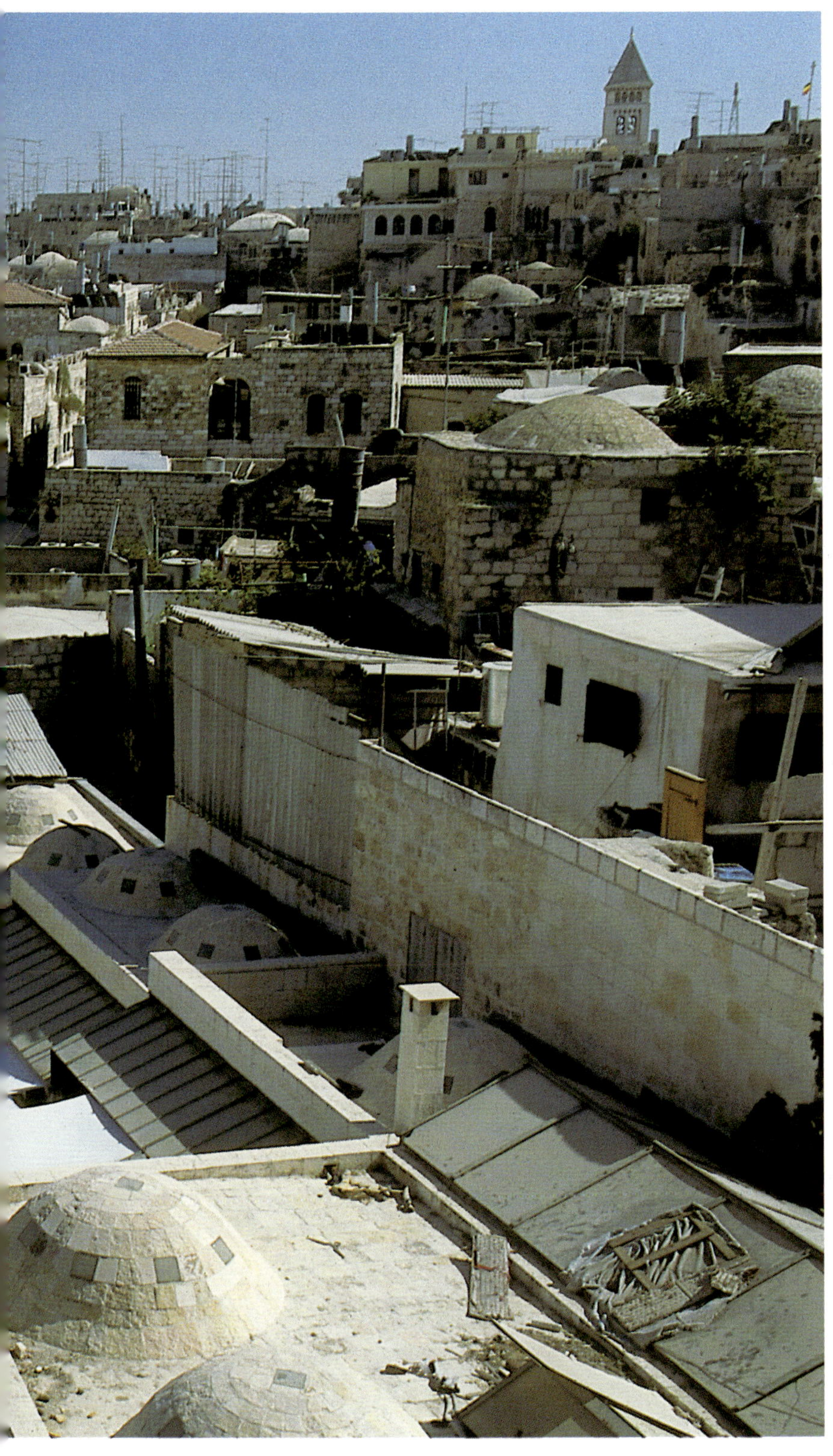

totally destroyed. What remained was razed to the ground by the new victors, the Jordanians. The city was divided, and the Dome of the Rock, the Al-Aqsa Mosque and the area known today as East Jerusalem went to Jordan's King Abdullah. West Jerusalem, the relatively new city outside the walls, went to Israel. Once again, observant Jews were only able to look at the Old City and the Western Wall from distant vantage points such as Mount Zion, until the Six Day War in June 1967 when the Old City was recaptured. The pictures of Israeli soldiers crying at the Wailing Wall were seen around the world. 'Never again', Israelis swore, would the city be divided. Thirteen years later, in June 1980, the Israeli government, in accordance with the 'Law of Jerusalem' declared the city to be 'the eternal capital of the Jewish State'.

Bone of Contention for Christians, Jews and Muslims: The Old City

The centre of the Old City surrounded by a 40 foot high wall is the focus of all political as well as tourist interest. It is quite easy to wander through all the ages of Jerusalem's history, to sites which are sacred to Jews, Christians and Muslims. Eight gates lead into the city, seven of them are open to visitors. Best known is the *Jaffa Gate*, which had to be adapted to the requirements of the German Kaiser Wilhelm II in 1889: as the imperial ruler was not minded to bow his head to anyone or anything, even in Jerusalem, a gap was cut into the portal to the right of the gate so that he could travel through with his spiked

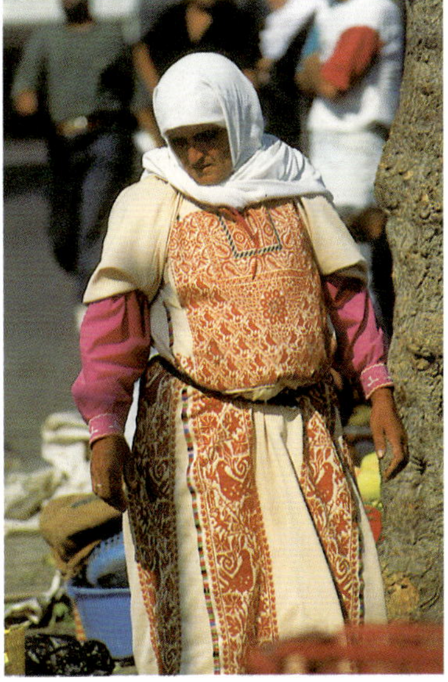

While Arab women occupy themselves with ordinary everyday tasks, the men sit around with their hookahs and backgammon.

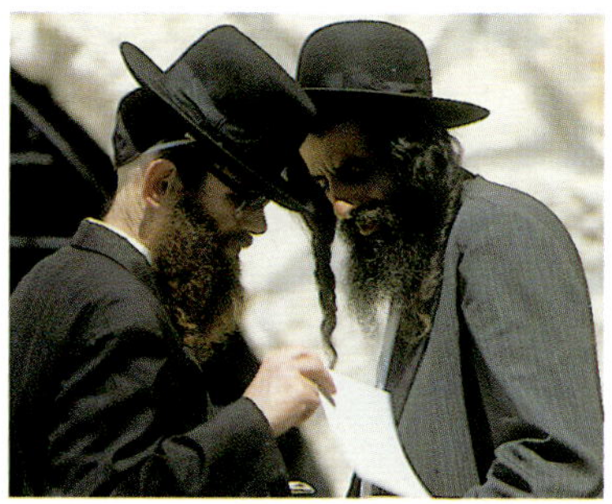

Black coats, black hats, long beards and long curling sidelocks – orthodox Jews in their typical garb can be seen especially around the Wailing Wall and the Mea She'arim district.

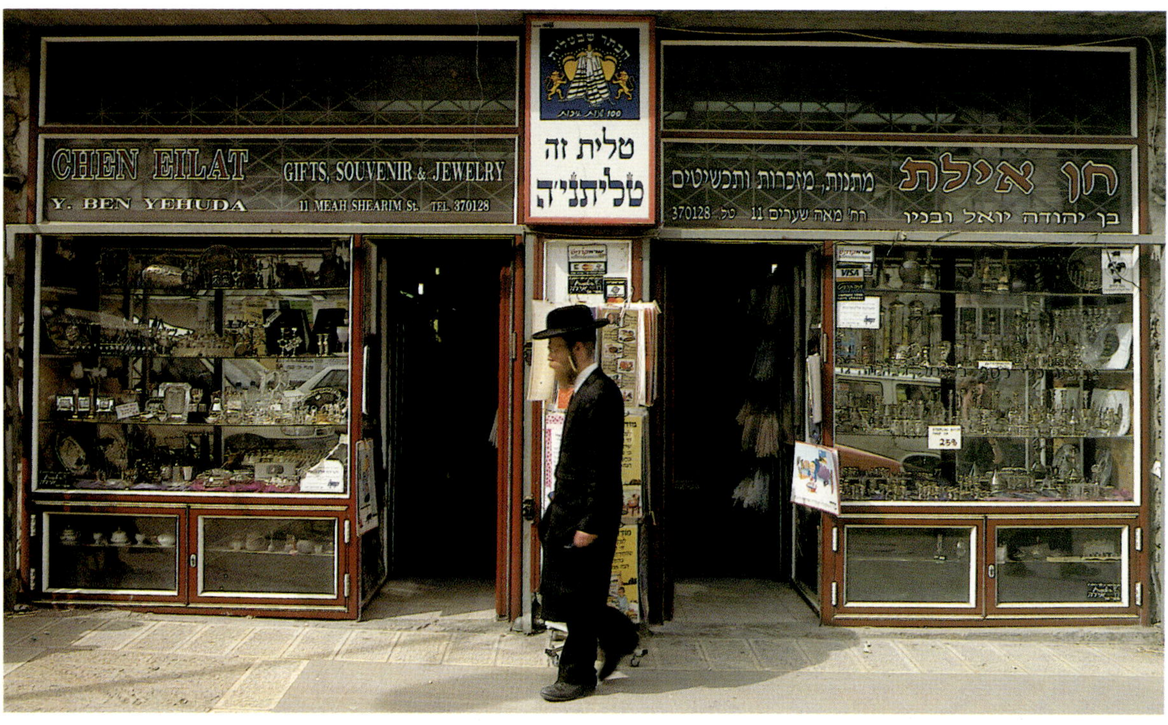

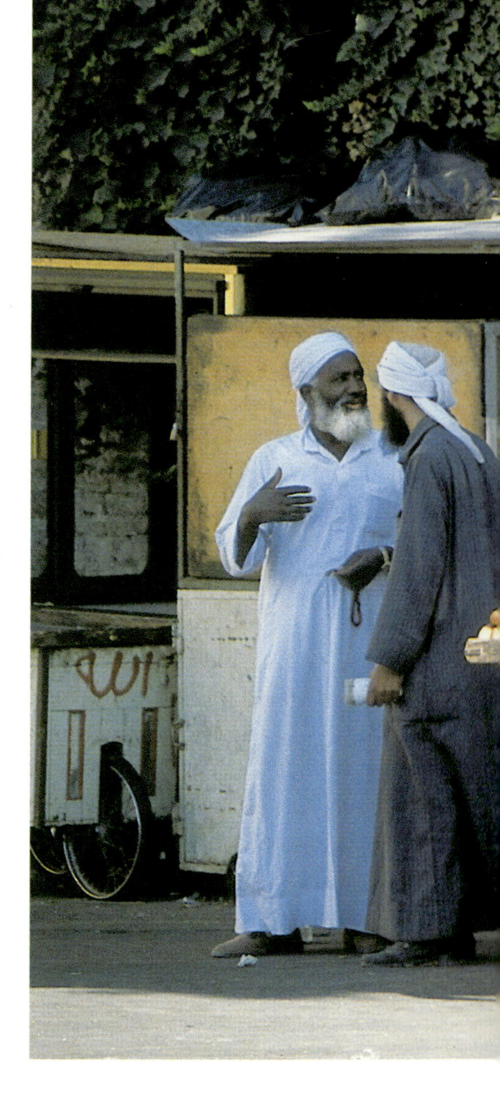

helmet, horse and carriage and Empress. It must be said, however, that the Kaiser did bestow upon the town not only a widened portal, but also the *Augusta Victoria Hospital* with its distinctive square tower, whose silhouette slots in between the Franciscan Church of *Dominus Flevit* with its tear-shaped cupola on the Mount of Olives and the tower of the old *Hebrew University* on Mount Scopus.

In those days it was mostly pilgrims who visited the city, often suffering enormous hardship during their trip to the Near East and not being spoiled with comfort in what was then quite a run-down area. Nowadays, many groups are guided easily through the town. But one should also roam the narrow alleyways on one's own, from the *Jaffa Gate*, for example, towards the *Bazaar* in *David's Street* just to see the astonishing collection of religious and ethnic accessories. Or take a break in one of the unobtrusive cafés and enjoy the diversity of humanity that passes by: religious Jews scurrying through the Old City on their way to the Wailing Wall or to a yeshiva (religious seminary for teaching the Talmud and the Torah); elderly Arabs with the traditional keffiya wrapped around their head; or even the Israeli soldiers with machine-guns casually slung over their shoulders who demonstrate the ever-present threat to security. Here, in Jerusalem's Old City, every alley, every corner, offers a different smell, a new sight, another slice of history.

Herod's Gate and *Damascus Gate*, like the Jaffa Gate, also lead straight into the centre of the oriental maze of the Muslim quarter. A few feet beneath the Damascus Gate you can see several layers of the Old City. It is also there that we can see remains of the Roman *city walls*.

The *New Gate* was built only in 1889, to make the entry into the Christian Quarter somewhat easier. You will, however, get a better feel for this district if you approach it through

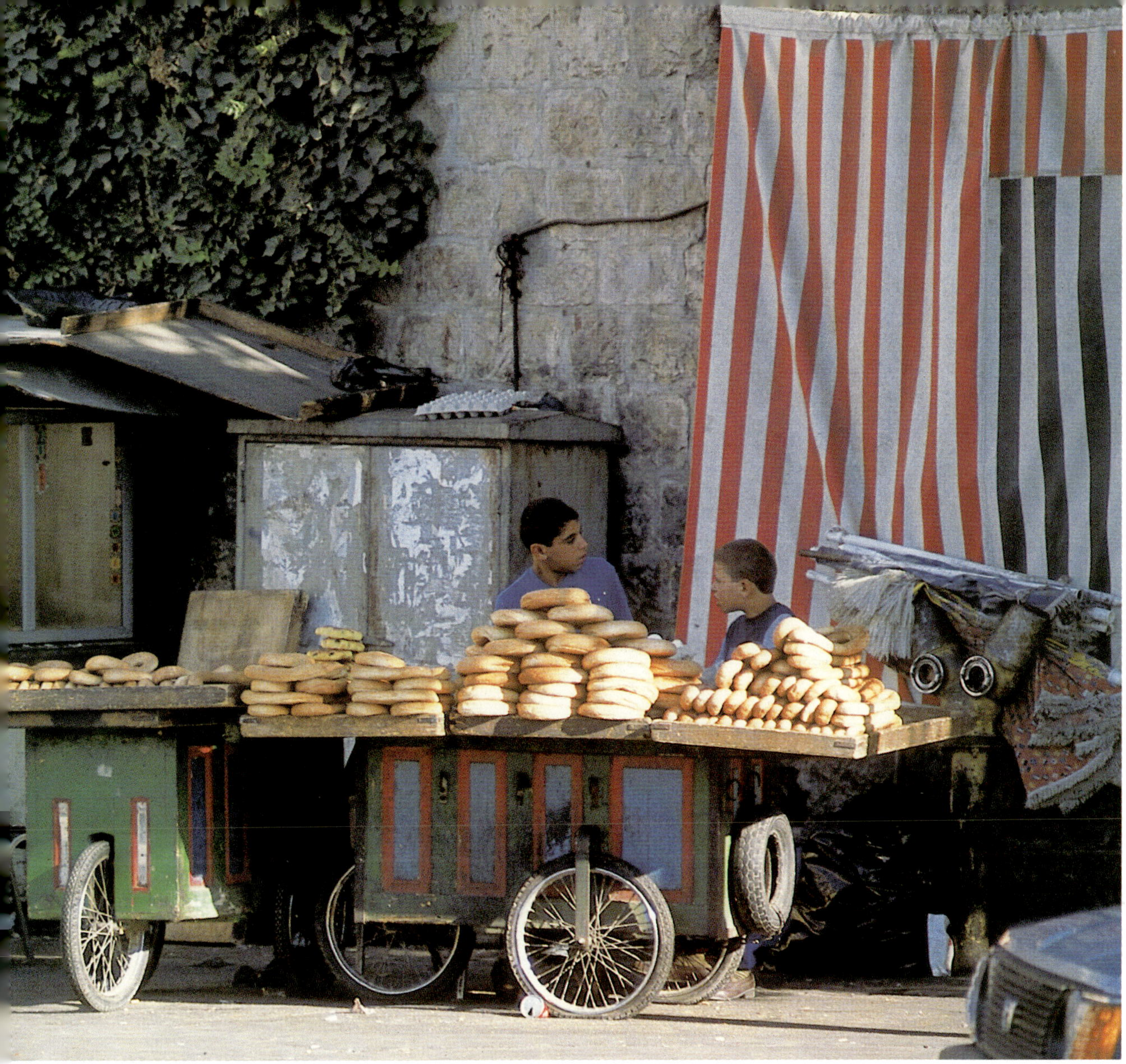

An alternative to the restaurant and perfect for those little snacks between meals are the travelling snack stands offering sesame buns. Strictly observant Jews must make sure that they only eat kosher foods, the ingredients and preparation of which are strictly in accordance with the Old Testament.

the *Lions' Gate*, also known as *St Stephen's Gate*. That is where the street which later turns into the *Via Dolorosa* begins and which marks the Stations of the Cross – even if more recent archaeological research has stated that they have been found some distance from this route.

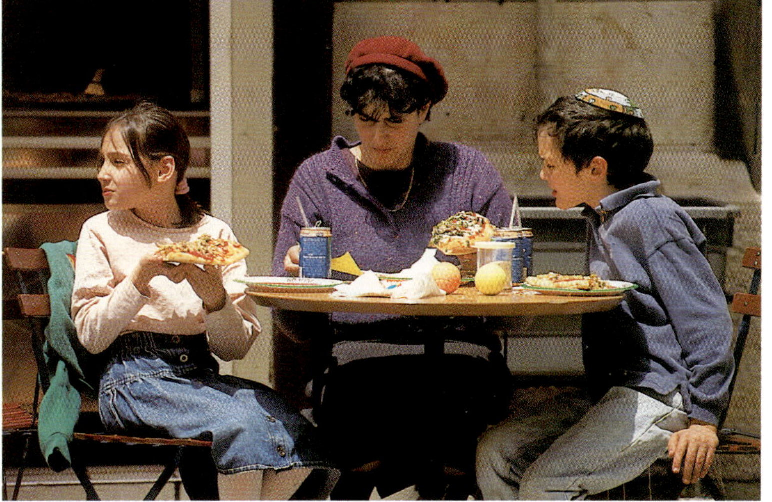

Not far from this gate, pilgrims worship at the *Church of St. Anne*, a well-preserved Crusader building, the alleged birthplace of the Mary the mother of Jesus, and named after Mary's own mother. Within the church grounds, surrounded by a hidden garden, we come across the *Pool of Bethesda* where Jesus performed a healing miracle – a good place to relax before rejoining the lively Via Dolorosa which is lined with numerous shops selling every sort of religious *kitsch*. Most of the nine Stations of the Cross can be described quite briefly. After the second station, the mighty *Ecce Homo Arch* spans the street. It is named after Pontius Pilate's cry 'Behold the man!' identifying Jesus to the crowd, although it is, in fact, a Roman triumphal arch from the second century AD.

The Via Dolorosa ends inside the *Church of the Holy Sepulchre*, the holiest site for Christians. Traditionally said to be

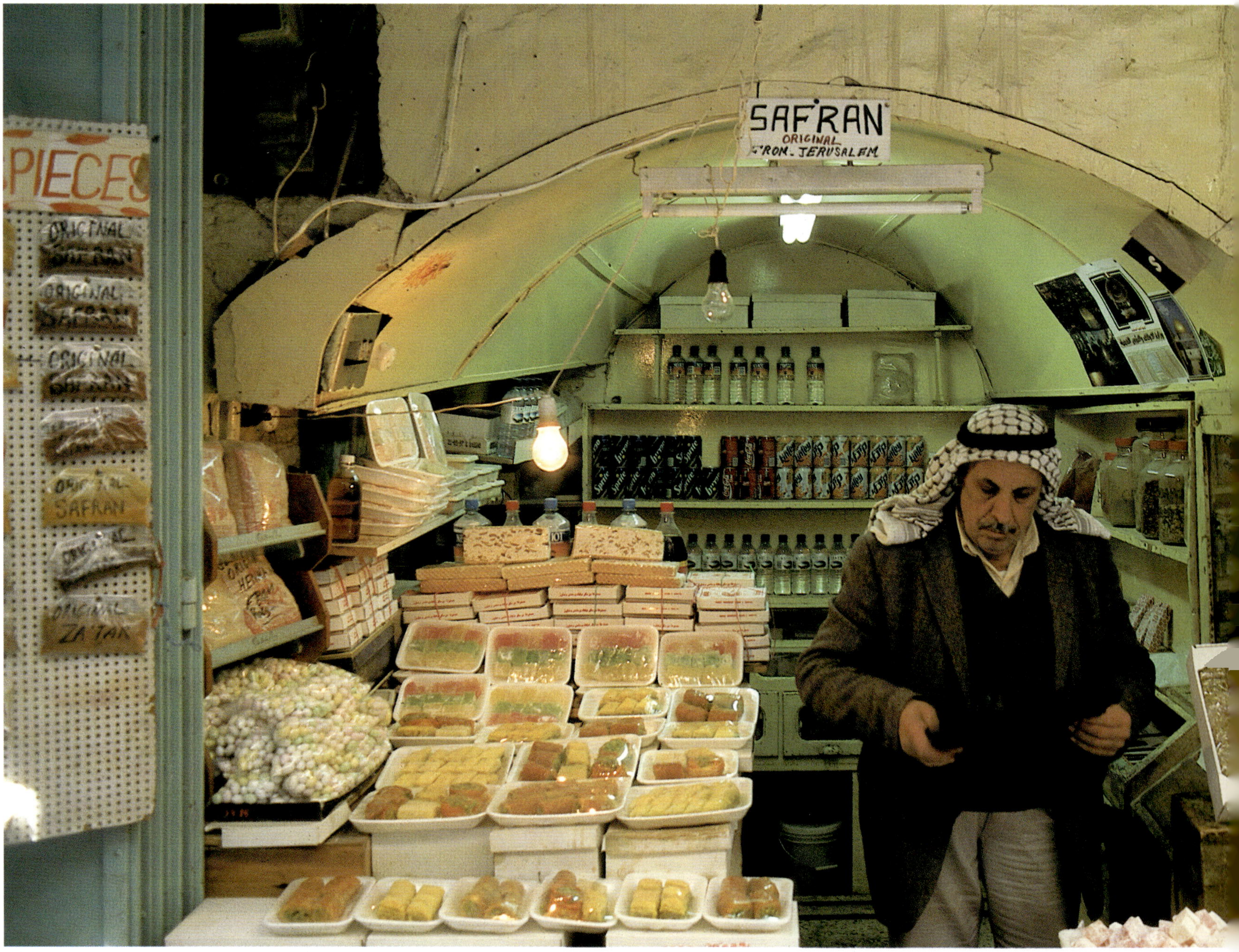

The bazaars in the streets of Jerusalem are a feast for the eyes and nose. It is easy to believe that one is wandering through a fairy tale from A Thousand and One Nights *with its combination of busyness and leisure.*

the site of the crucifixion, burial and resurrection of Jesus Christ, this has been disputed by archaeologists and historians for many centuries. The first Christian Roman emperor, Constantine, built this church in 335 AD in honour of his mother, Helena. Since then it has been one of the holiest sites in Christendom and the focus of an intense religious fervour which remains unmoved in the face of the strongest scientific evidence. Here, at the much visited destination of thousands of pilgrims praying devoutly at the religious services, visitors are so affected by the air, heavy with incense, the dark rooms filled with countless icons and votive pictures from the four corners of the Christian world that they are readily persuaded to buy 'miracle' candles at highly inflated prices from the professional servants of God.

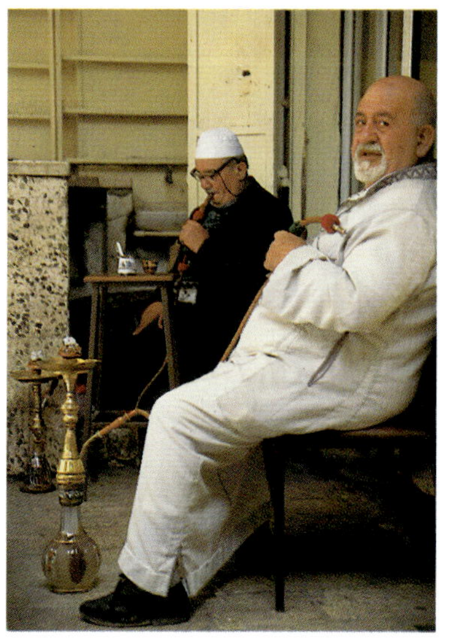

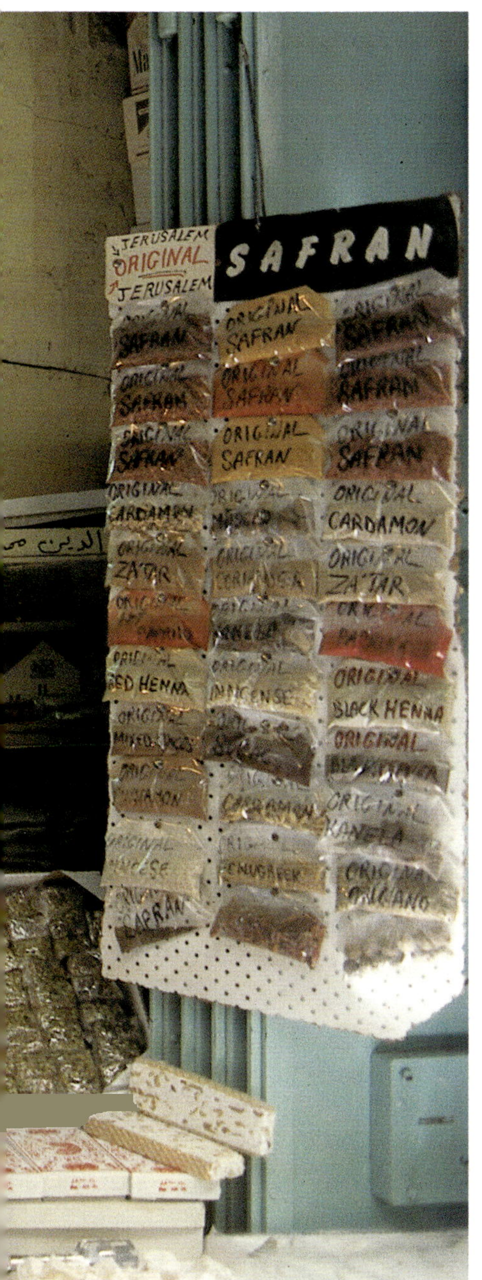

The fact that in years gone by, violent and deadly wars of faith have been waged for centuries still finds an echo in the Church of the Holy Sepulchre despite decades of ecumenical efforts, as various members of the same religion continue to make life difficult for themselves with petty jealousies. Six Christian communities share the church – Ethiopians, Copts, Armenians, Syrians, Greek Orthodox and Roman Catholic – and their main purpose in life seems to be to pray or sing louder than the others, and to make their section even more beautiful and more lavish through renovations. Thus the church can hardly ever be seen without scaffolding; cement dust is everywhere and moments of prayer in an atmosphere of peace and seclusion are near impossible. To ensure that there are no underhand attempts to change the status quo, as far back as the twelfth century the famous Sultan Saladin, a wise and forward-looking man, took

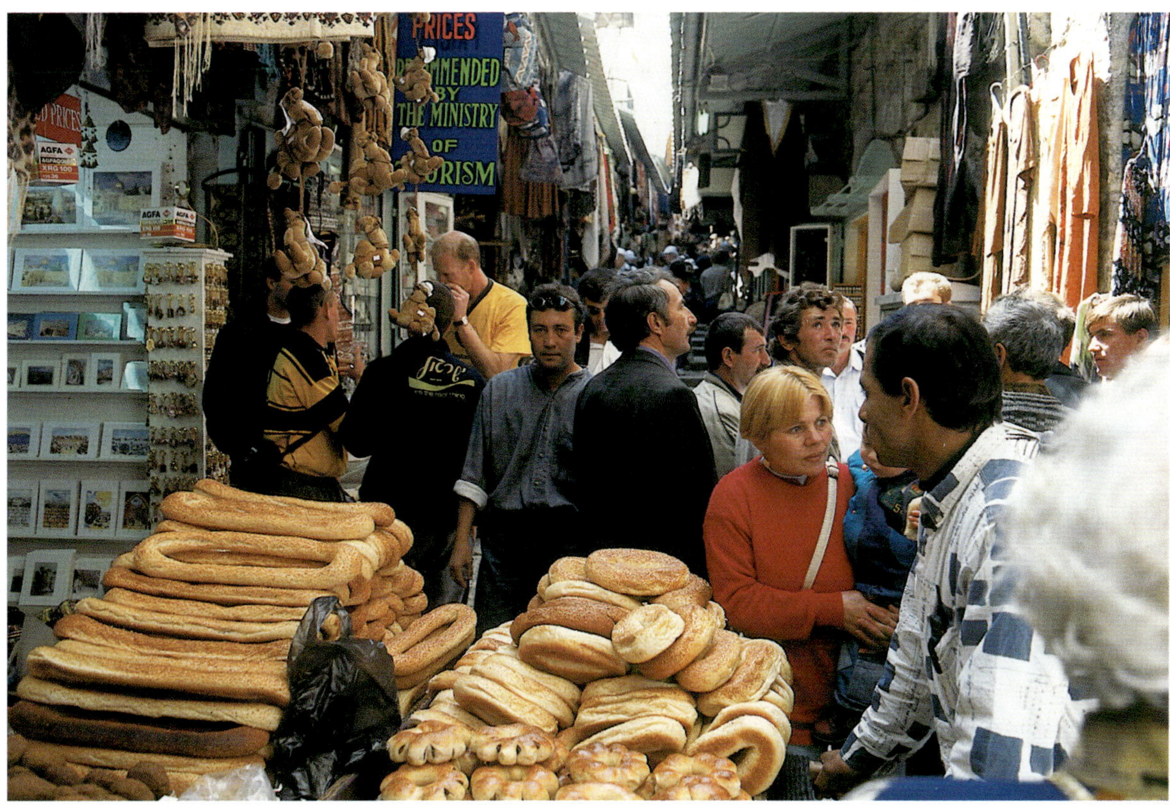

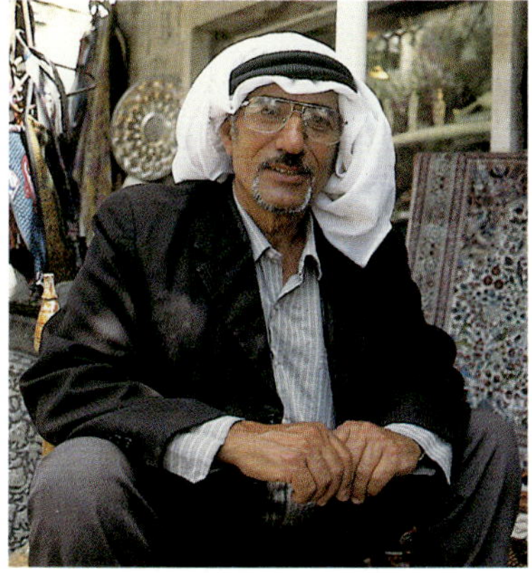

the decision to have the church locked up by a Muslim family every night. And that is what happens to this day.

Churches of all factions surround the Church of the Holy Sepulchre, including the Lutheran *Church of the Redeemer*, notable for the impressive view one has from its tower over the Old City of Jerusalem.

A crash course in haggling would not go amiss if you intend to purchase some favourite item from the rich array of rugs, leather goods, brasswork, jewellery or clothing on offer.

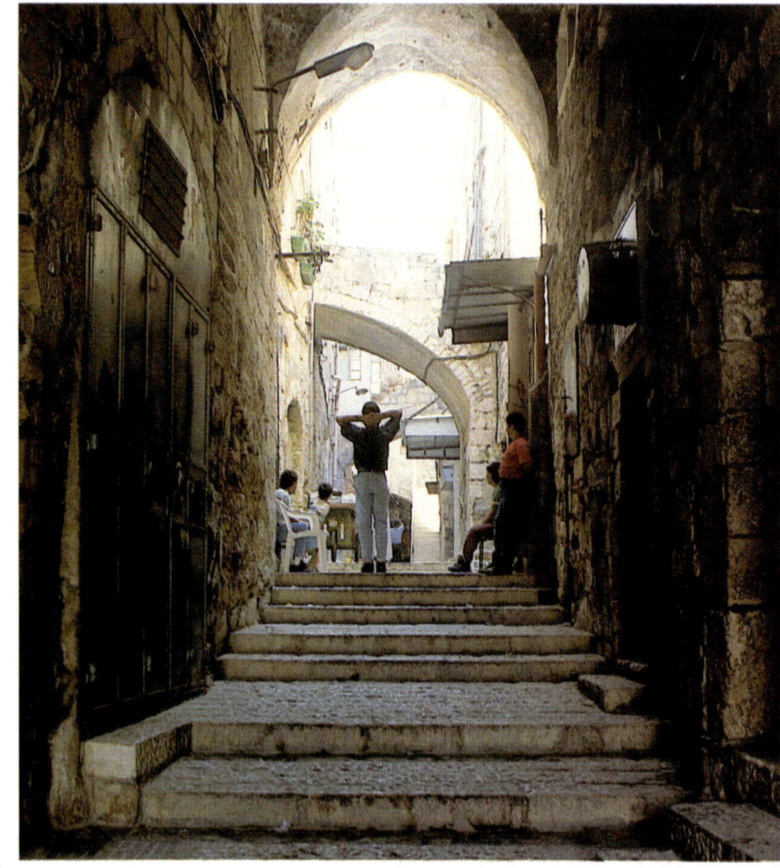

The Old City of Jerusalem consists of the Armenian, Christian, Jewish and Muslim quarters – a basis for the ethnic and religious diversity which gives this city its unique atmosphere.

Brand New and yet Quite Ancient: Jewish and Armenian Quarters

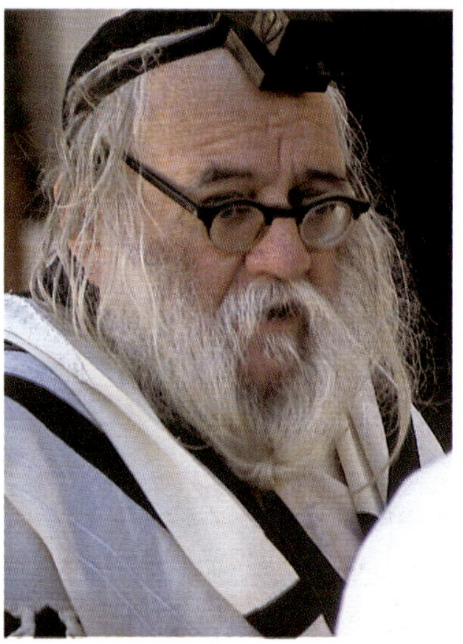

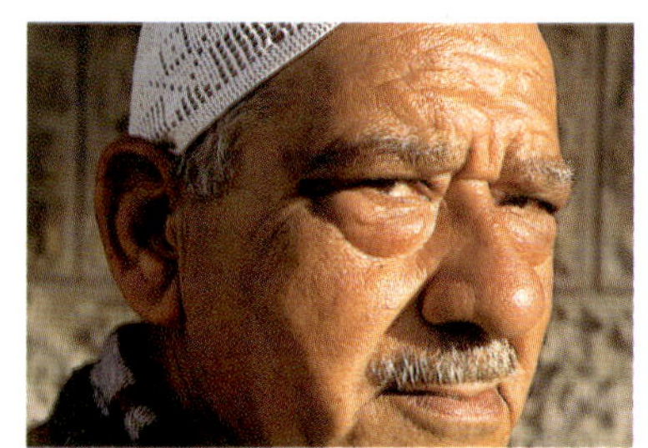

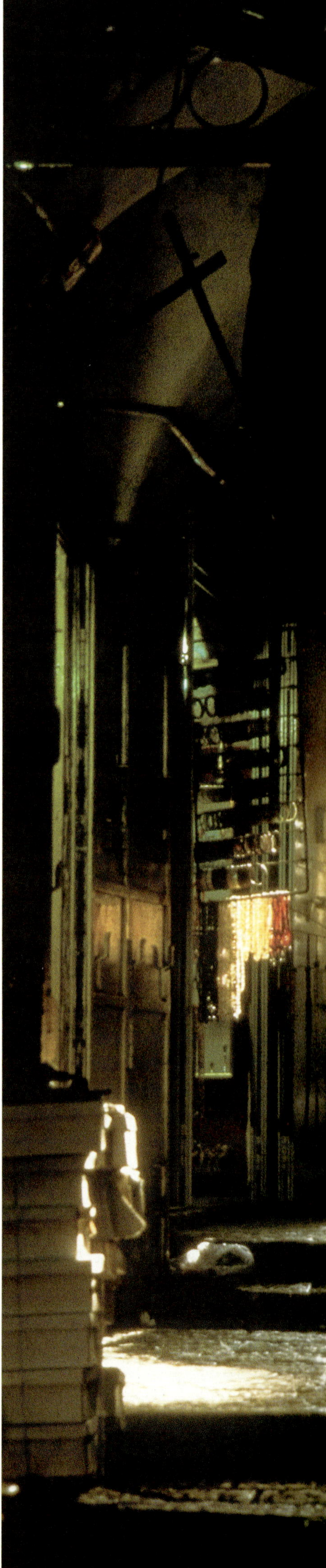

Destruction and reconstruction - there is nowhere better to see the unfolding of Jerusalem's history than in the *Jewish Quarter*, which you enter through the *Dung Gate.* The road leads directly to the *Wailing Wall* (see p. 62), a vast, cleared area behind Israeli security barriers, maintained with good reason. Time and again fanatics have tried to smuggle themselves on to the Temple Mount through this route to disturb its religious peace. However, such extremists are the exception rather than the rule in the quiet and sedate Jewish Quarter, which in style and substance wishes nothing more than to prove that it has always been here.

And yet, hardly a stone was left standing when the Israeli army conquered the Quarter in 1967. The last of the ruins in which Palestinian refugees found their refuge were soon levelled to the ground without further ado so that Israel's best architects could begin with the reconstruction of the Jewish Quarter – on condition that each new house be faced with the natural gleaming straw-coloured stone, 'Jerusalem stone', and that wherever a new building was erected, excavations would first be carried out under the watchful eye of archaeologists. This also happened

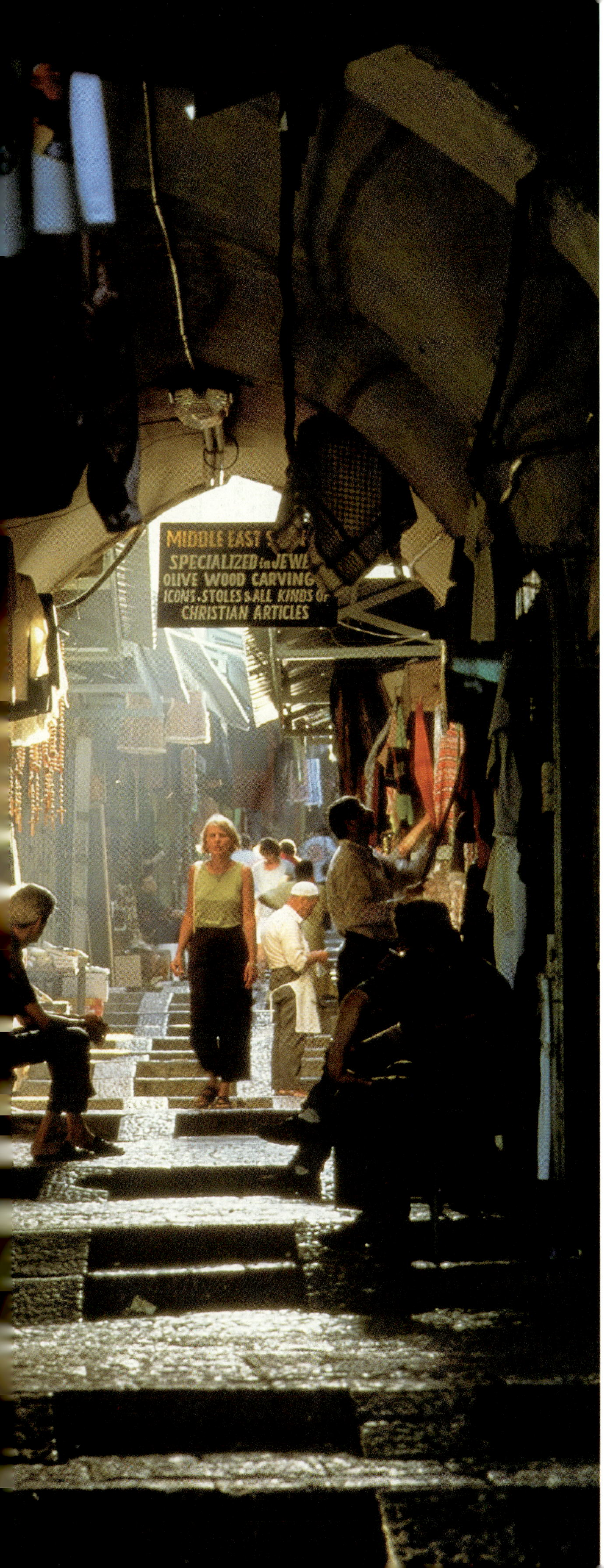

The Muslim Quarter covers the largest area within the walls of the Old City. It is a labyrinth of residential streets and bazaars, each with its own unmistakable character.

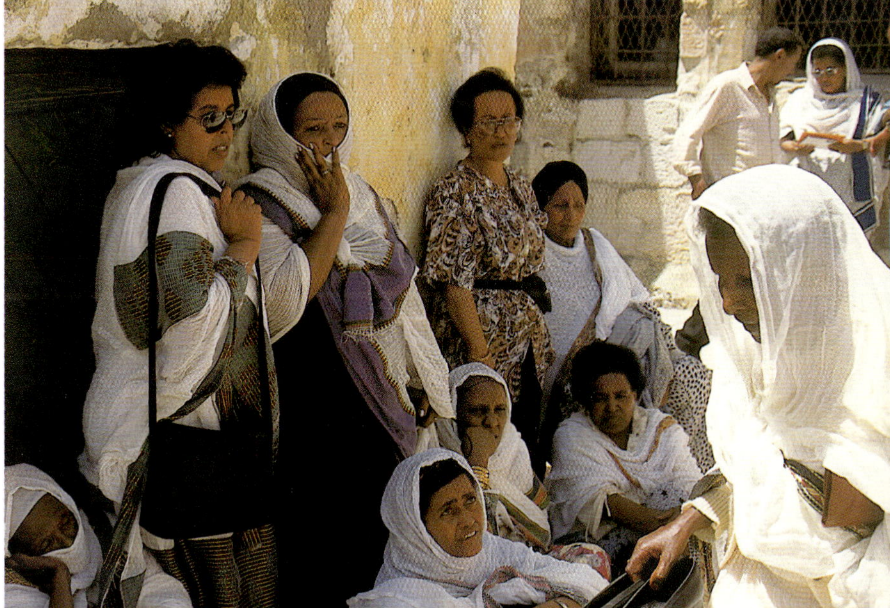

for political reasons, since each and every excavation would reveal historical evidence of Jewish existence on this spot, which would substantiate and thus strengthen Israel's claim to Jerusalem.

In Tiferet Y'Israel Street we see the remains of the *Burnt House*, whose owner was a Jew who lived there during Titus's destruction of the city in 70 AD. In HaYehudim Street, below the ruins of the *Hurva Synagogue*, the thirteenth-century arch of the *Ramban Synagogue* was found and incorporated into the new building. To the west, steps lead up to the *Cardo* where the remains of the Cardo Maximus or main thoroughfare of Roman-Byzantine Jerusalem, can be viewed. The Cardo has been restored and is once again a main street of the Jewish Quarter. These days its upmarket boutiques have turned it into one of Jerusalem's most expensive addresses. Although architecturally it has been carefully adapted to the older parts of the Old City, it looks like a piece of mosaic put in as an afterthought, missing the necessary patina. The Cardo is a beautiful, but also an alien, stone in the masonry of Jerusalem.

Continued on Page 64

Judaism's Holiest Site

The Wailing Wall

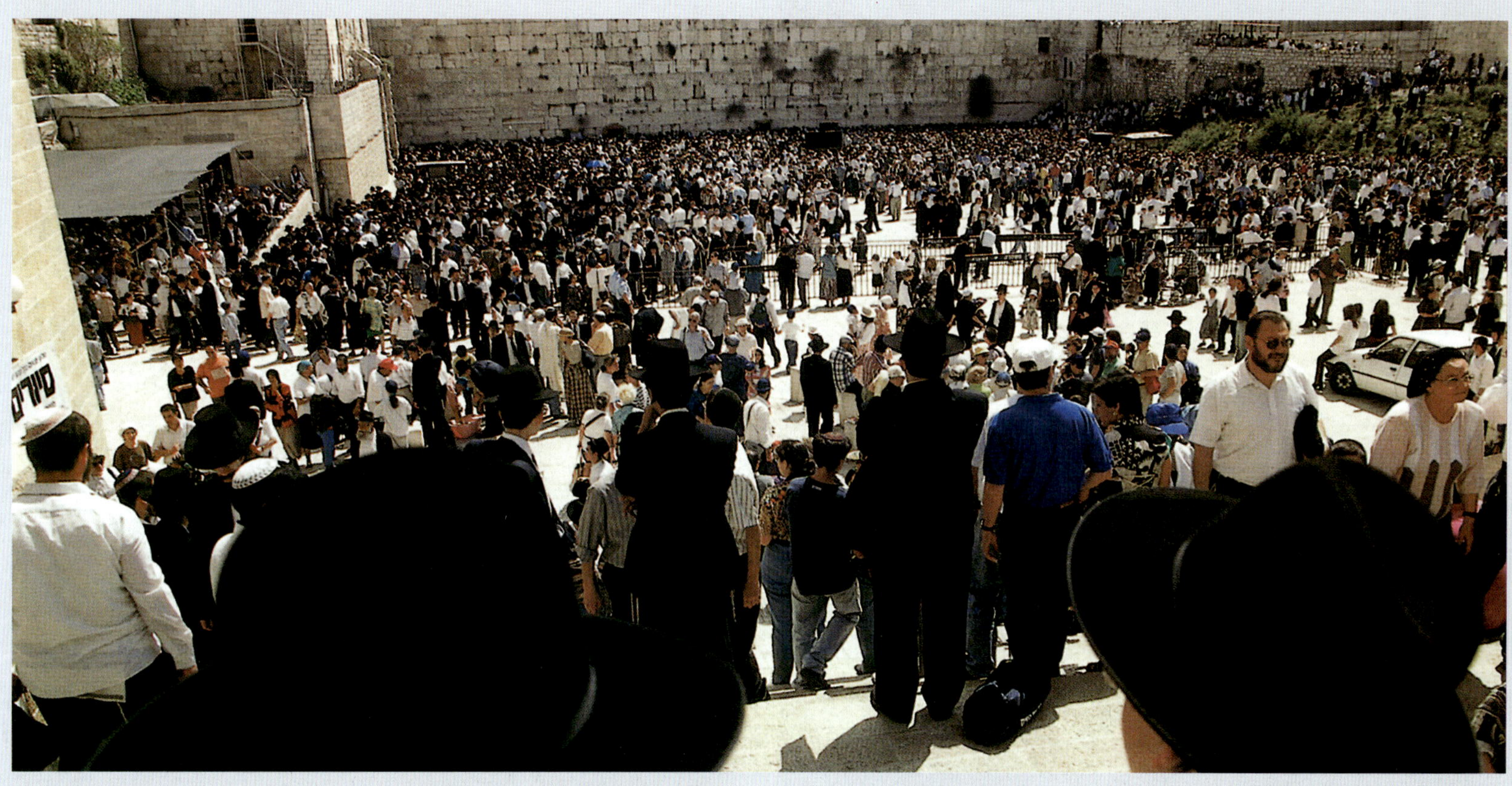

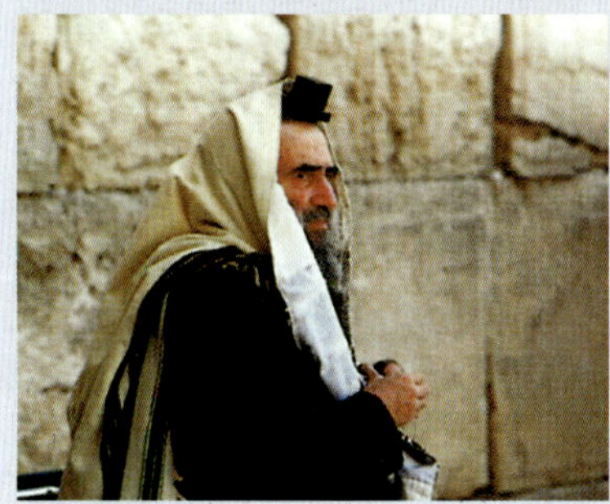

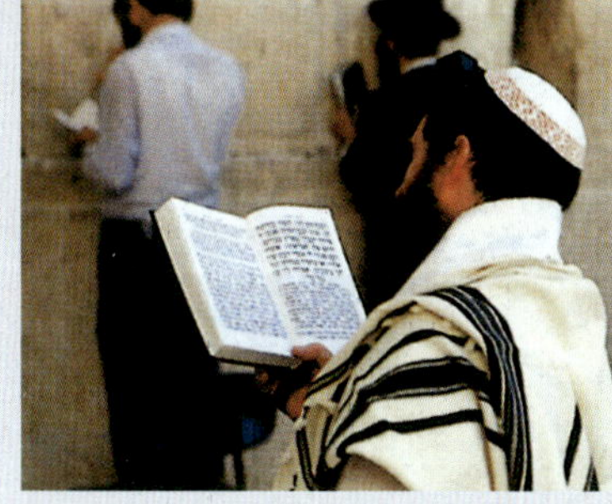

The area around the Wailing Wall is always crowded on Fridays when Orthodox Jews come to pray and chant to welcome the Sabbath. On other days too, people gather to pray or study the Torah.

Following the capture of Jerusalem's Old City by the Israeli army in June 1967, Israelis streamed to their most important historic monument, the Western Wall, the only fragment of the Second Temple remaining after its destruction by the Romans in 70 AD. Because Jews during the first century were only permitted to visit Jerusalem once a year in order to mourn the loss of their Temple, it has popularly become known as the 'Wailing Wall'.

After 1948 their right to enter this part of Jerusalem, which had come under Jordanian rule, was revoked. They could no longer pray at the Wall or insert into its cracks the little pieces of paper on which were written pleas for intercession which, according to popular legend, an angel could deliver directly to God.

It was only after East Jerusalem was captured that 560 feet of the wall, which had originally been 1640 feet long, became freely accessible. Since then, people again started congregating at the Wailing Wall. Men have to cover their heads and women must keep their shoulders and legs under wraps. There is one aspect however, in which modernity has made inroads. A fax machine was recently installed so that pleas from Jews the world over could be inserted into the Wall's cracks without incurring delays.

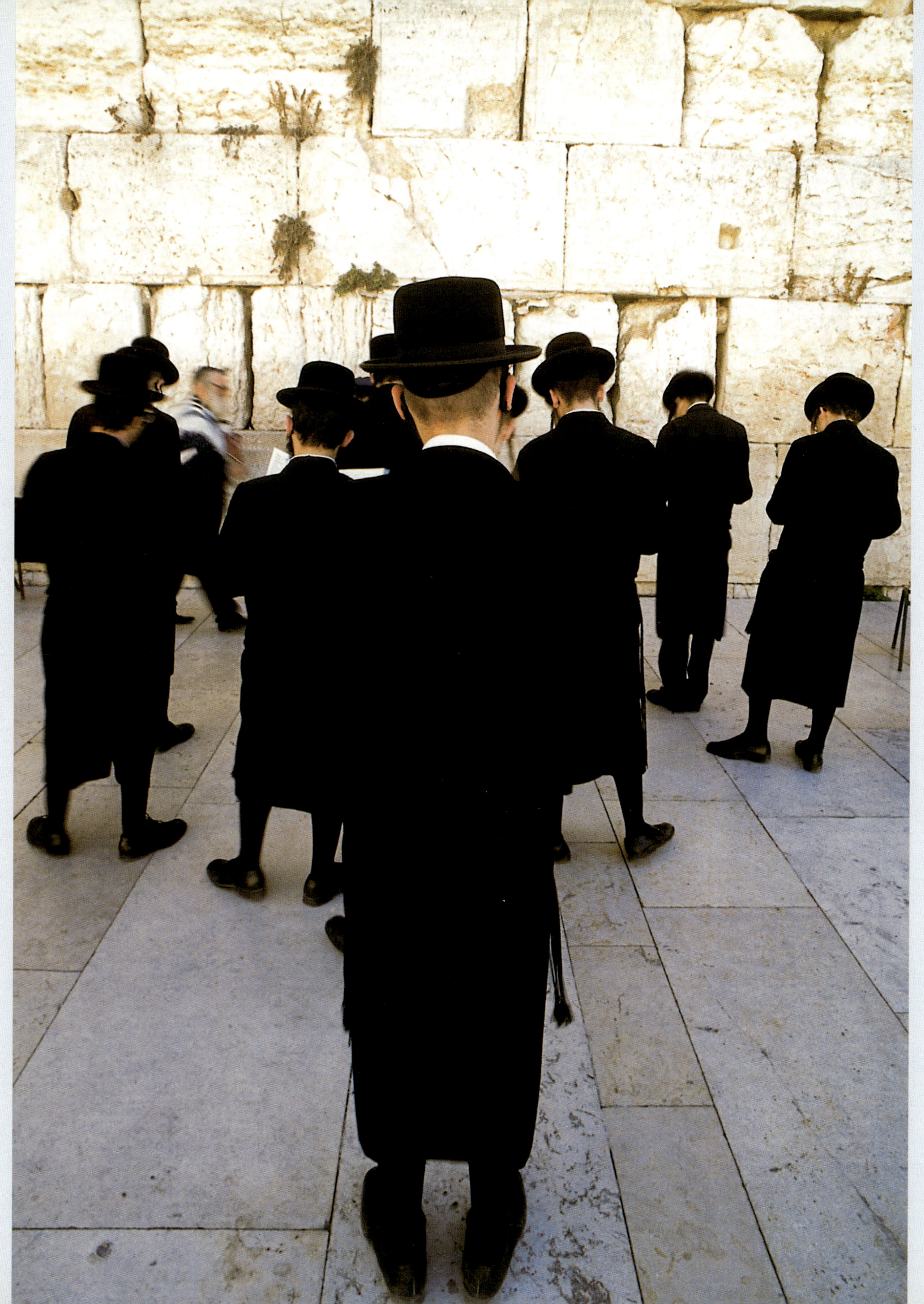

If you are seeking an oasis of peace, you should enter the Old City through the Zion Gate which leads into the *Armenian Quarter*, the smallest and probably one of the most mysterious areas of Jerusalem. Visitors are rarely allowed a glimpse of what goes on behind the walls, or in the interlocked rear courtyards and Armenian monasteries and convents. Nobody knows much about the Armenians, and those who were gruesomely persecuted by the Turks at the beginning of the century and found refuge here do not give much away about themselves. In contrast with the other admirers of the Holy City who proclaim their love from the rooftops, this smallest of all the groups in the Old City quietly keeps itself to itself. Even the *Armenian Museum* gives only scant information about the history, religion and traditions of its people. The *House of the Patriarch* contains one of the city's oldest libraries; countless valuable

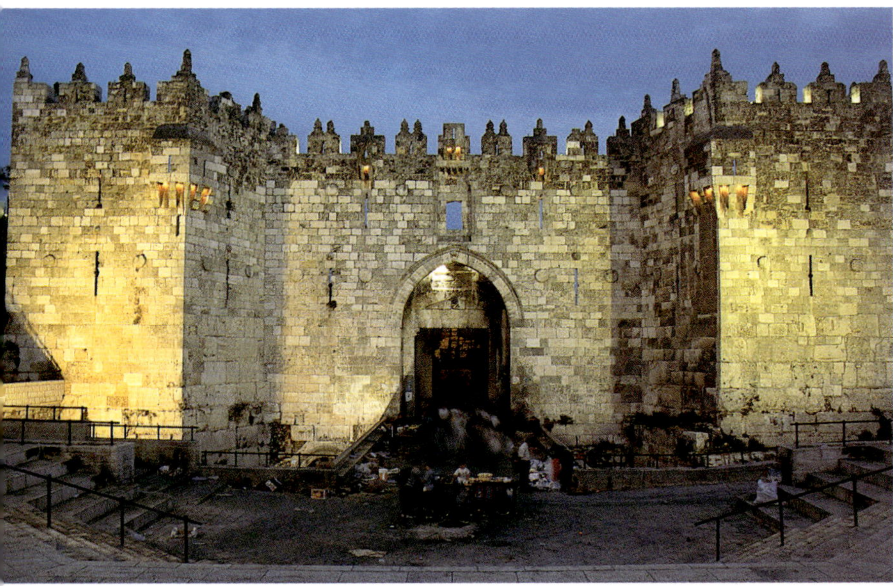

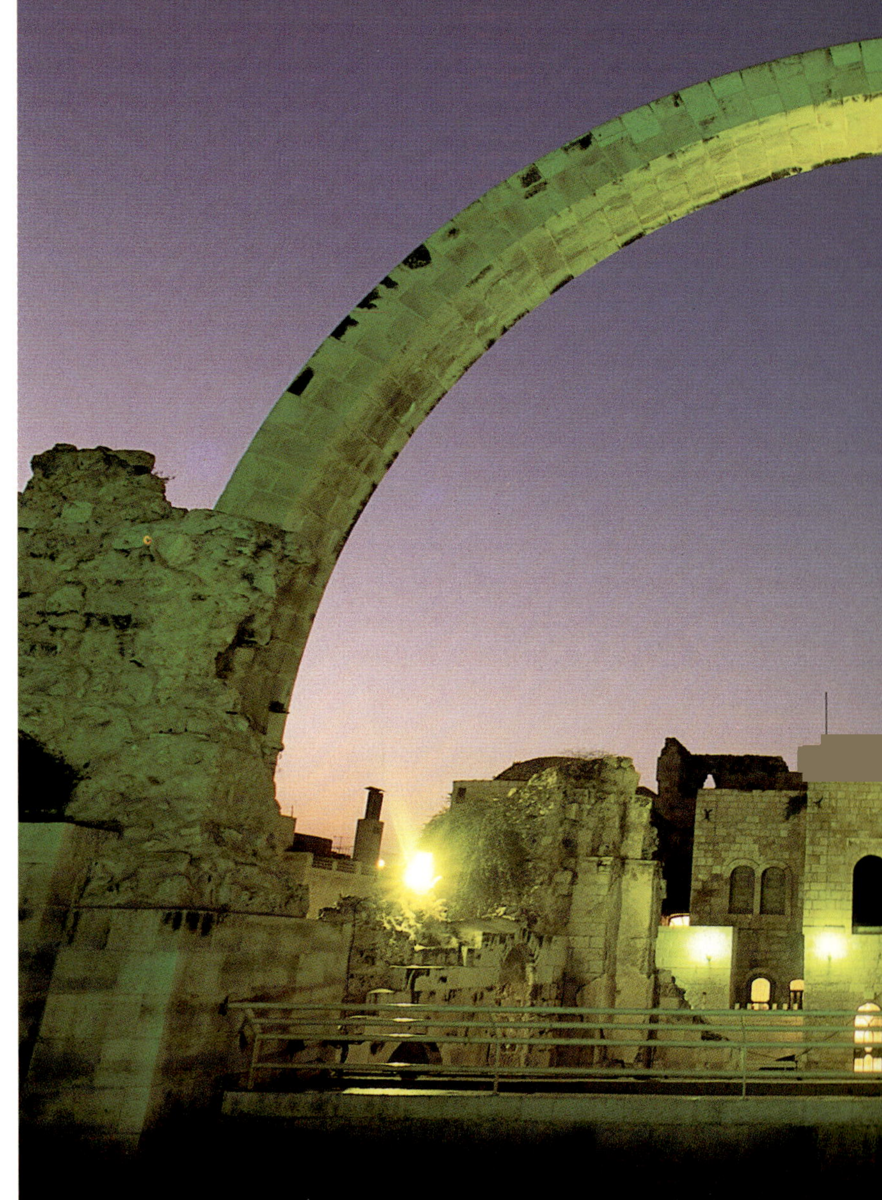

manuscripts are stored there, jealously guarded by an ancient librarian. The walk through the quarter usually ends with the magnificent *St. James's Cathedral*, which was erected by Crusaders on the spot where St James, the brother of Jesus, died a martyr's death in 44 AD.

The last of the gates, the *Golden Gate* facing the Mount of Olives, is blocked off and, according to legend, will only be opened again when the Messiah appears. In 1530, Suleiman the Magnificent established a Muslim cemetery in front of the gate, allegedly for the following reason: it is more than likely that the Messiah will be a Cohen, a descendant of the Jewish high priests. As a Cohen, he is forbidden to enter a cemetery. Access to the city would therefore be denied him and the might of the Sultan would be unchallenged by any divine claims. If

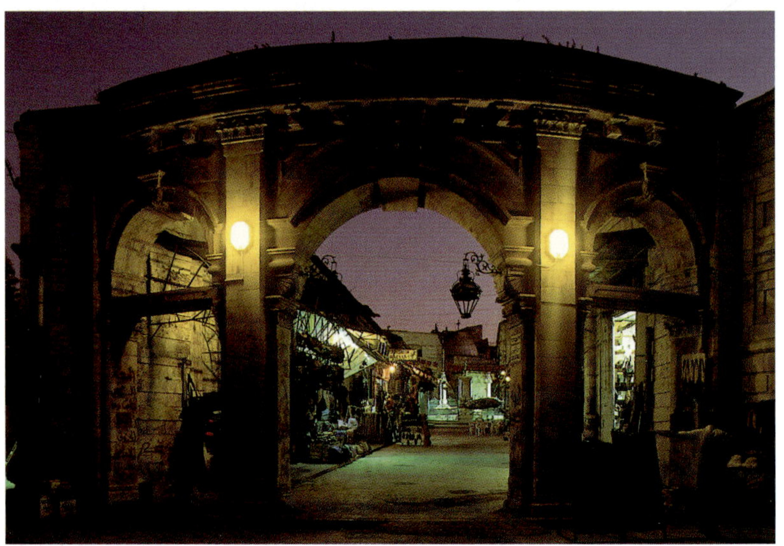

Jerusalem in the evening: the Damascus Gate (1537–1540, left); the reconstructed arch of the Hurva Synagogue which was destroyed in 1948 (above); the entrance to the leather market in the Christian Quarter (below).

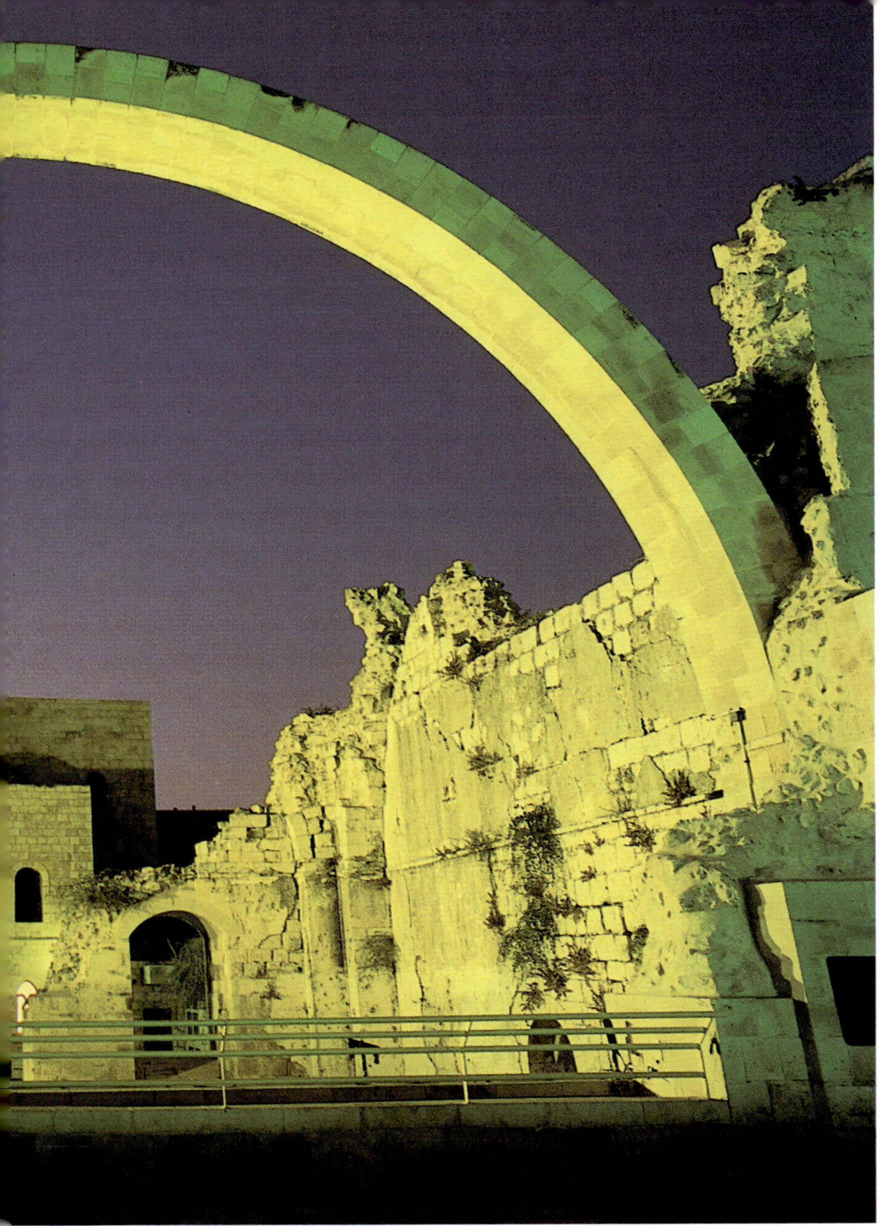

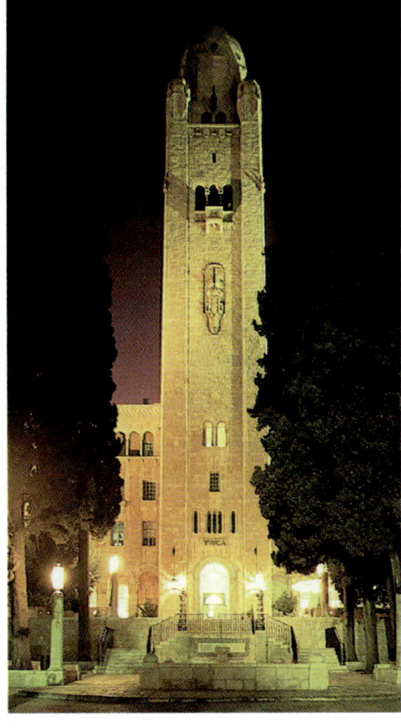

From the 150 ft high observation tower of the YMCA building which was built in the 1930s there is a panoramic view over Jerusalem (above).
The splendidly coloured glass windows created by Marc Chagall in 1962 for the synagogue of Hadassah Hospital symbolise the 12 tribes of Israel (below)

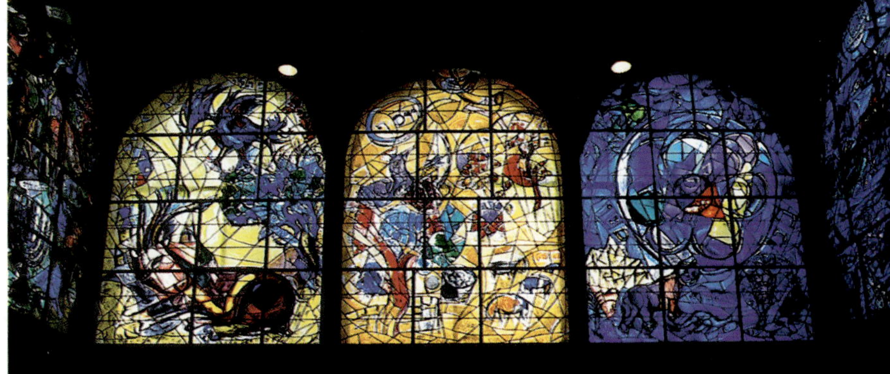

Yad Vashem

One of the most important sites in Jerusalem leaves the visitor with feelings of horror, shame, anger, sadness and bitter helplessness. The national Holocaust Memorial Yad Vashem to the west of the city reminds us of the 6 million Jews – of whom nearly 2 million were children – who were murdered by the Nazis. The Avenue of Righteous Gentiles starts at the car park, a memorial garden of trees with the names of the non-Jews who played a role in the resistance during the Nazi regime and saved the lives of Jews. The avenue leads to the main room of the memorial, the Hall of Remembrance. An eternal flame burns in semi-darkness, throwing a ghostly light on the names of the death camps: Buchenwald, Dachau, Auschwitz ...

true, this story is a perfect example of how one can worship the Almighty, while at the same time attempting to create an advantage for oneself.

A walk through the historic collection in the *Citadel* museum between the Armenian and Christian Quarters tells the history of this city. Added to this are magnificent views over the Old City from its two giant towers.

Outside the Old Walls

It is not just within the walls of the Old City that Jerusalem is exciting and mysterious. The biblical *Garden of Gethsemane*, situated east of the Old City gates, with its ancient olive trees is where Jesus is said to have prayed just before he was captured after he had been betrayed by Judas. The tour up the Mount of Olives can begin at the *Church of All Nations* with its colonnaded portico of Corinthian columns, built in 1924 on the site of a former Byzantine basilica. The walk continues up the *Mount of Olives*, past the *Tomb of the Virgin*, the *Church of St Mary Magdalene* and the *Church of Dominus Flevit* up to the *Observation Terrace*. Below that, at the south-eastern foot of the Temple Mount, we see the *Ophel Archaeological Park*. The oldest of the visible excavated remains dates back to the tenth century BC. It is here that the first Jerusalem, the city of the Jebusites, is said to have stood more than 3000 years ago. To the south lies *Mount Zion*, which remained a part of

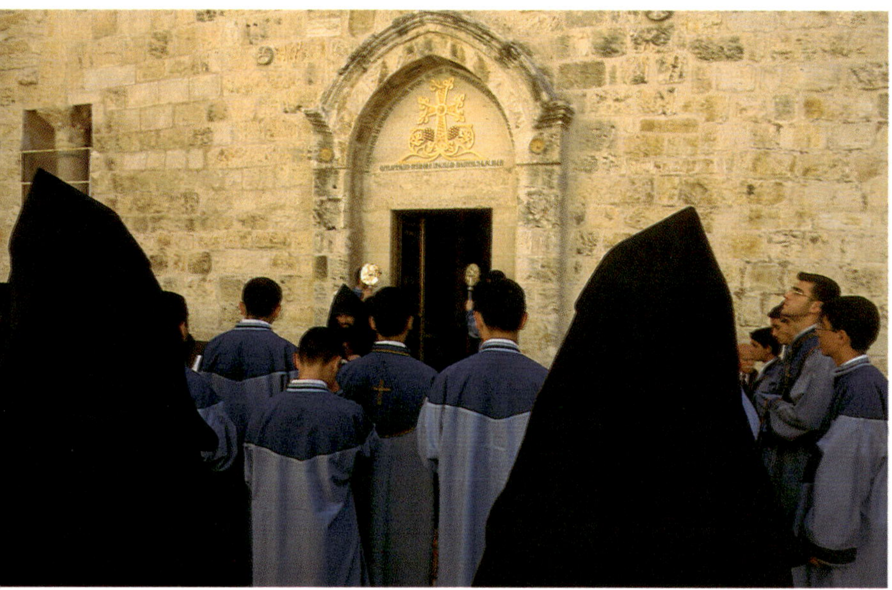

Israel when the Old City was occupied by the Jordanians. As a result, the hill became a pilgrimage site where people came to look yearningly across to that part of city beyond their reach. Archaeologists doubt whether there is any historical basis for the view that King David was buried here at the *Tomb of David* – but don't let this stop you worshipping at the mysterious site awash with ancient legends.

One of the first districts outside the fortified city was *Mea She'arim*, originally founded between 1874 and 1881 for Orthodox Jews who came from Poland and Lithuania. Here the Law still reigns supreme, not that of the secular State of Israel, but that of the Talmud with its divine commandments. The ultra-Orthodox inhabitants of Mea She'arim reject the State of Israel as a 'Zionist blasphemy' which has tried to pre-empt the work of the Messiah. Here they speak Yiddish, not Hebrew, which they regard as the sacred language of the Bible.

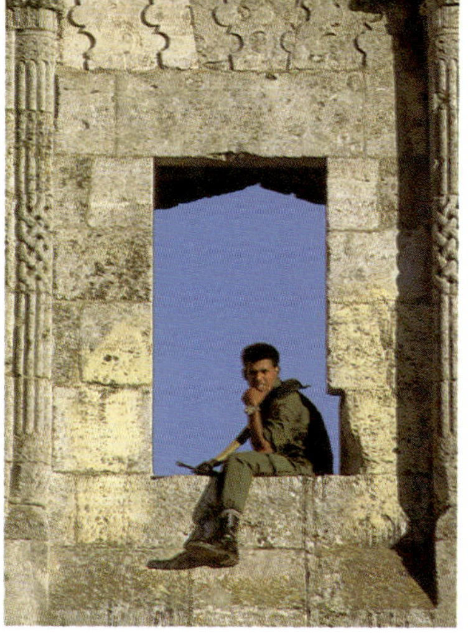

Yerushalayim – 'Place of Peace' – is the definition of the name Jerusalem. This peace is zealously guarded (top). Six different religious communities compete for the true faith at the Church of the Holy Sepulchre (below).

From the age of three, young boys go to the Cheder where they learn God's commandments in the songs of their teacher. Girls with their heavy plaits and modest dresses are prepared for their role as housewife and mother – which often means that they will one day be responsible for the care of a large family. For the most brilliant students among their husbands-to-be will never leave their religious school or yeshiva, but will spend their whole lives studying the Talmud and the Torah. They are the advocates of God, their task is to question, to study and to interpret His will. How, for instance, are we to understand God's simple rule: 'On the seventh day ye shall rest'? For example, it is forbidden to light a fire on the Sabbath, as this is clearly a form of work.

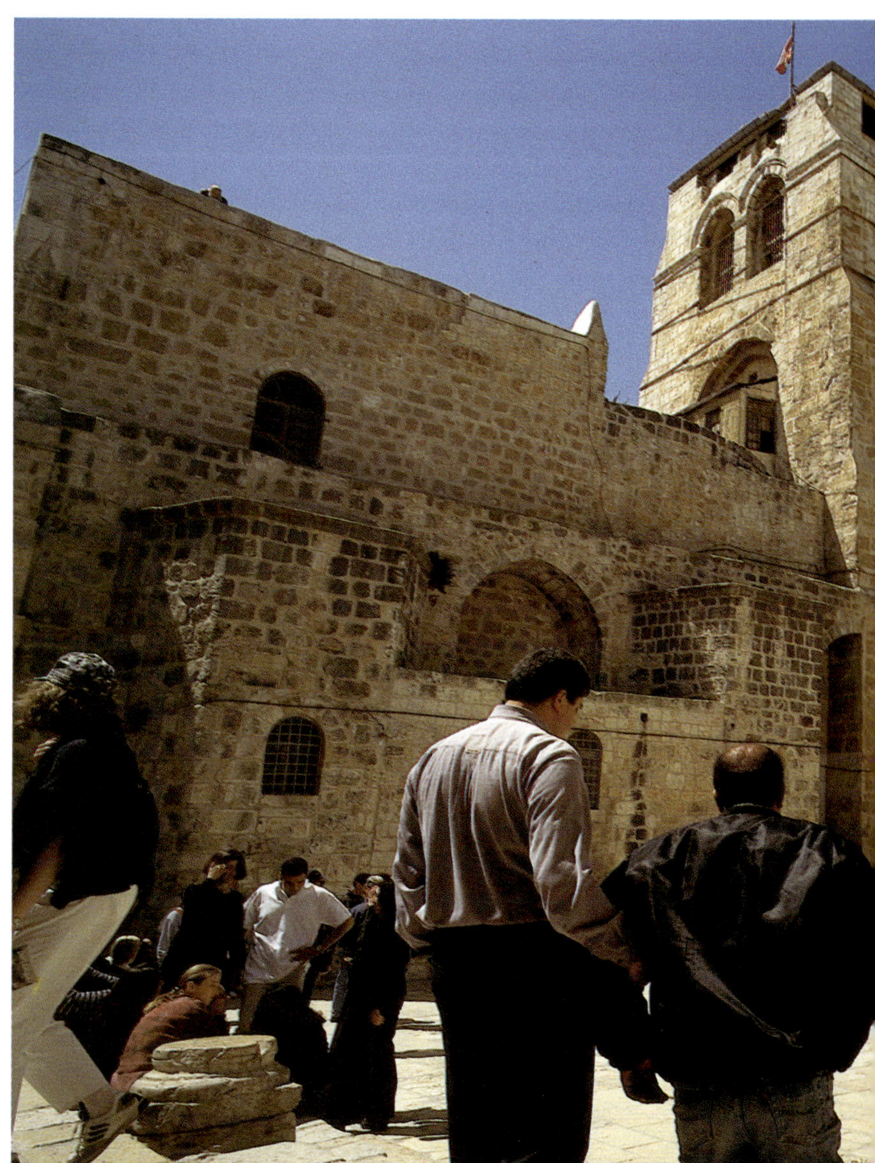

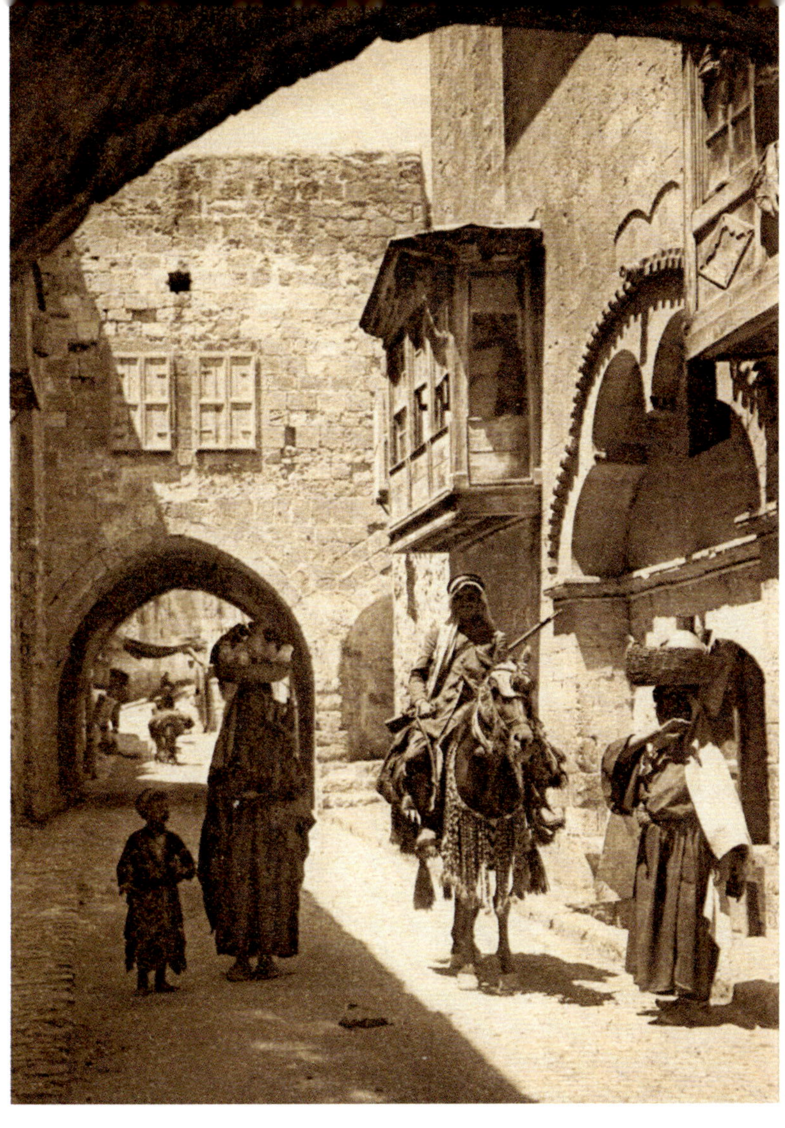

People in the Jerusalem of the 1920s: during this period Great Britain governed Palestine under a League of Nations mandate.

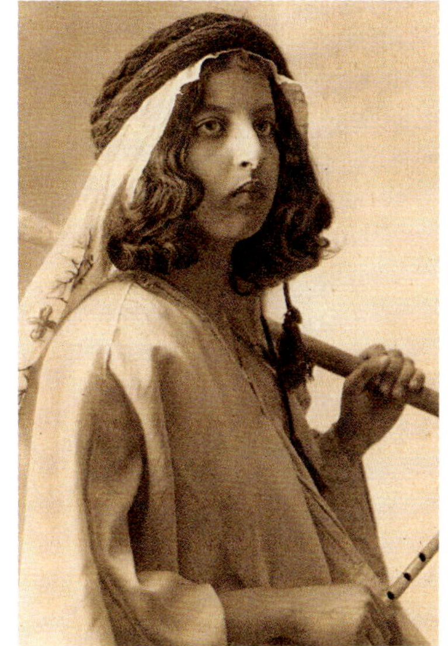

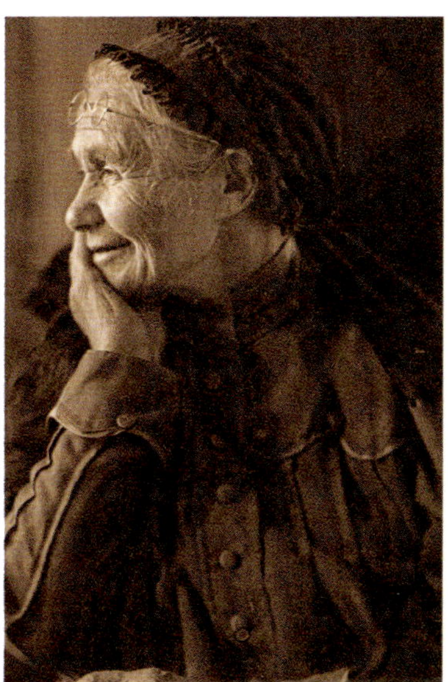

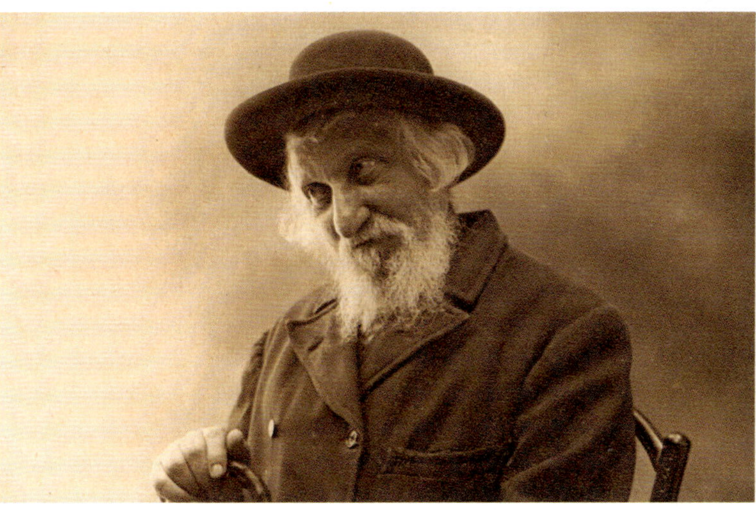

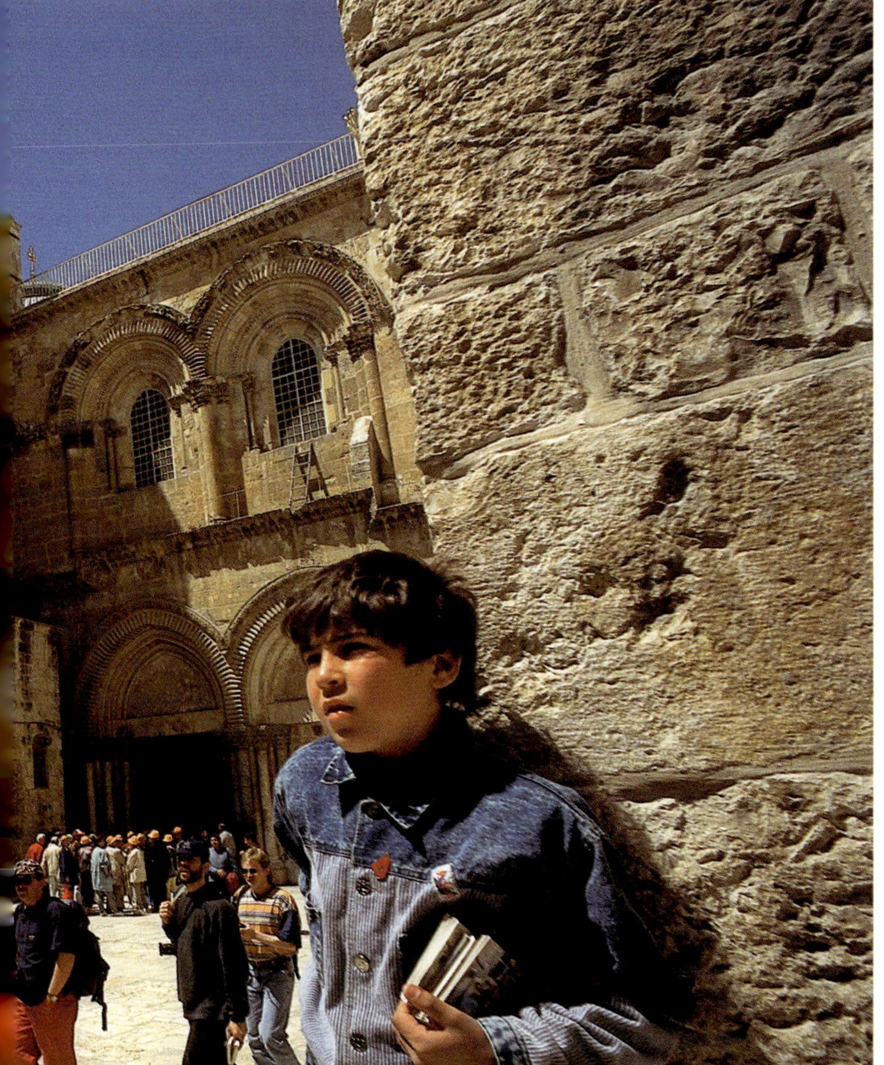

However, so as not to transgress God's laws unknowingly, the ban has been adapted to the present day – and indeed applied even more strictly. Lighting or making a fire can include starting a car, using a light switch or turning on the oven. On the other hand, technology is freely used to make life a little easier. In Mea She'arim's dusty old electrical goods shops one item is particularly popular: the time switch. With its help, lights can be switched on in the long, dark winter nights of Jerusalem without transgressing God's law. Such forays into the modern world apart, people stick to the very traditional ways in Jerusalem's religious districts. Traditional east European clothing is worn both summer and winter: the men dress in black caftans and wide-brimmed hats, women wear wigs, thick stockings and long sleeves.

Many of Jerusalem's museums contain collections reflecting the history of the city and its religious communities. In the Israel Museum you will see copies of the Dead Sea Scrolls from Qumran (right) as well as archaeological finds such as this silver vase from the 5th century BC *(left).*

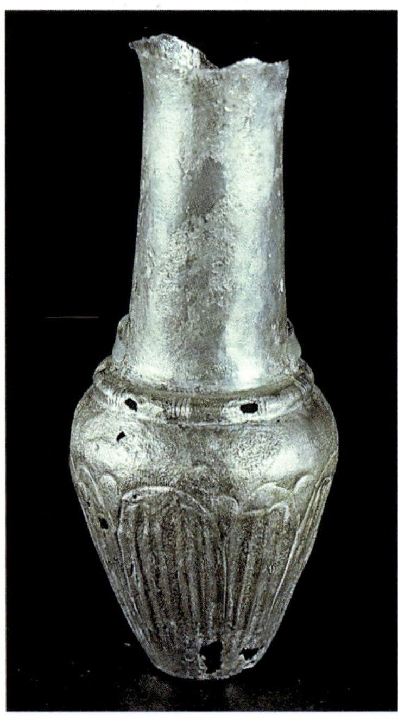

The Shrine of the Book

*The gleaming white, distinctive roof dazzles in the sunlight. It was designed to resemble the lid of one of the clay jars in which the Qumran scrolls were discovered on the Dead Sea (**see page 136 ff.**). The underground entrance to this section of Jerusalem's Israel Museum is in sharp contrast to the mystical, dark exhibition room and the high, black basalt block standing next to the dome – allusions to the text of the Essenes about the 'battle of the children of light against the forces of darkness'. The famous scrolls of the sect known as the Essenes were discovered in the early spring of 1947 by a shepherd in the hill caves of Qumran. In complete ignorance of the value of his find, he sold it, including the Book of Isaiah – the only known original Book of the Bible – to an Arab dealer in Bethlehem. Via a circuitous route the scrolls ended up in the hands of Professor Sukenik of the Hebrew University in Jerusalem. He was able to purchase three of them, and a further four were purchased by his son in 1954 on behalf of the State of Israel.*

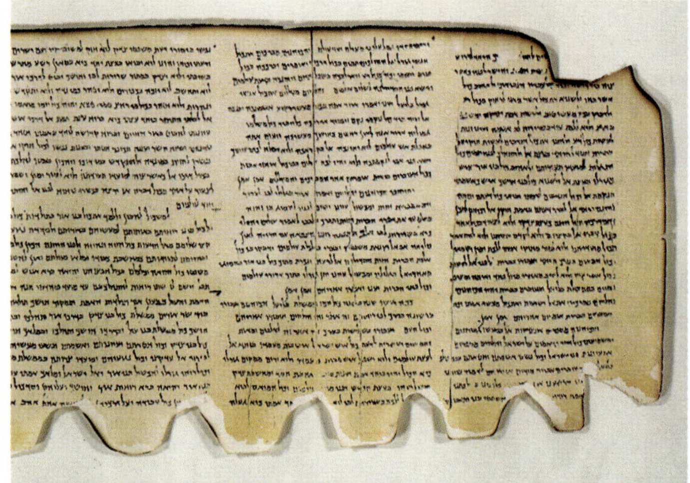

Near the Church of St Anne lie the Pools of Bethesda, originally believed to have medicinal qualities. Jesus is said to have healed a sick man here. Excavations show the remains of two churches.

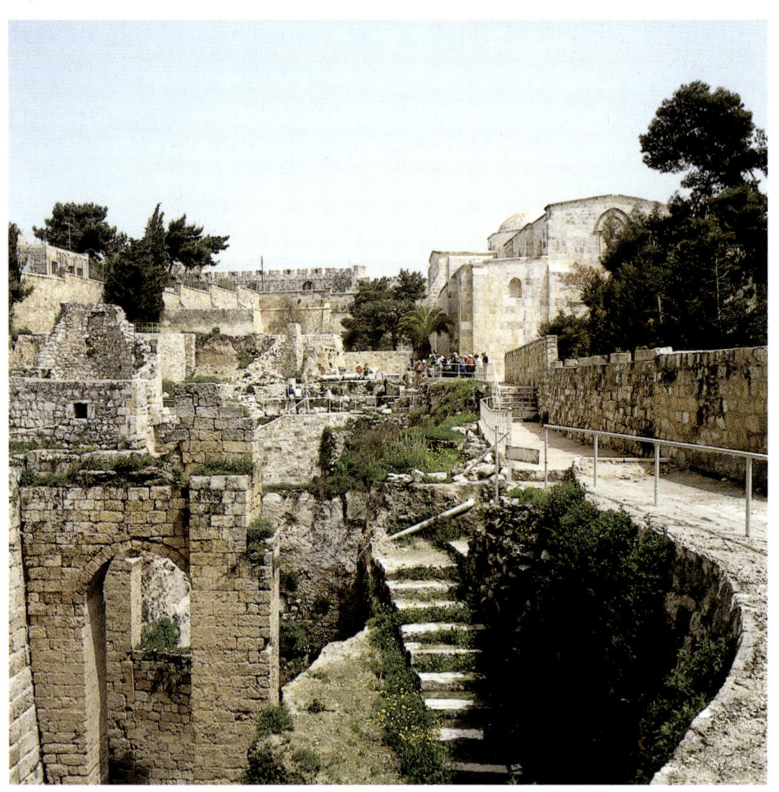

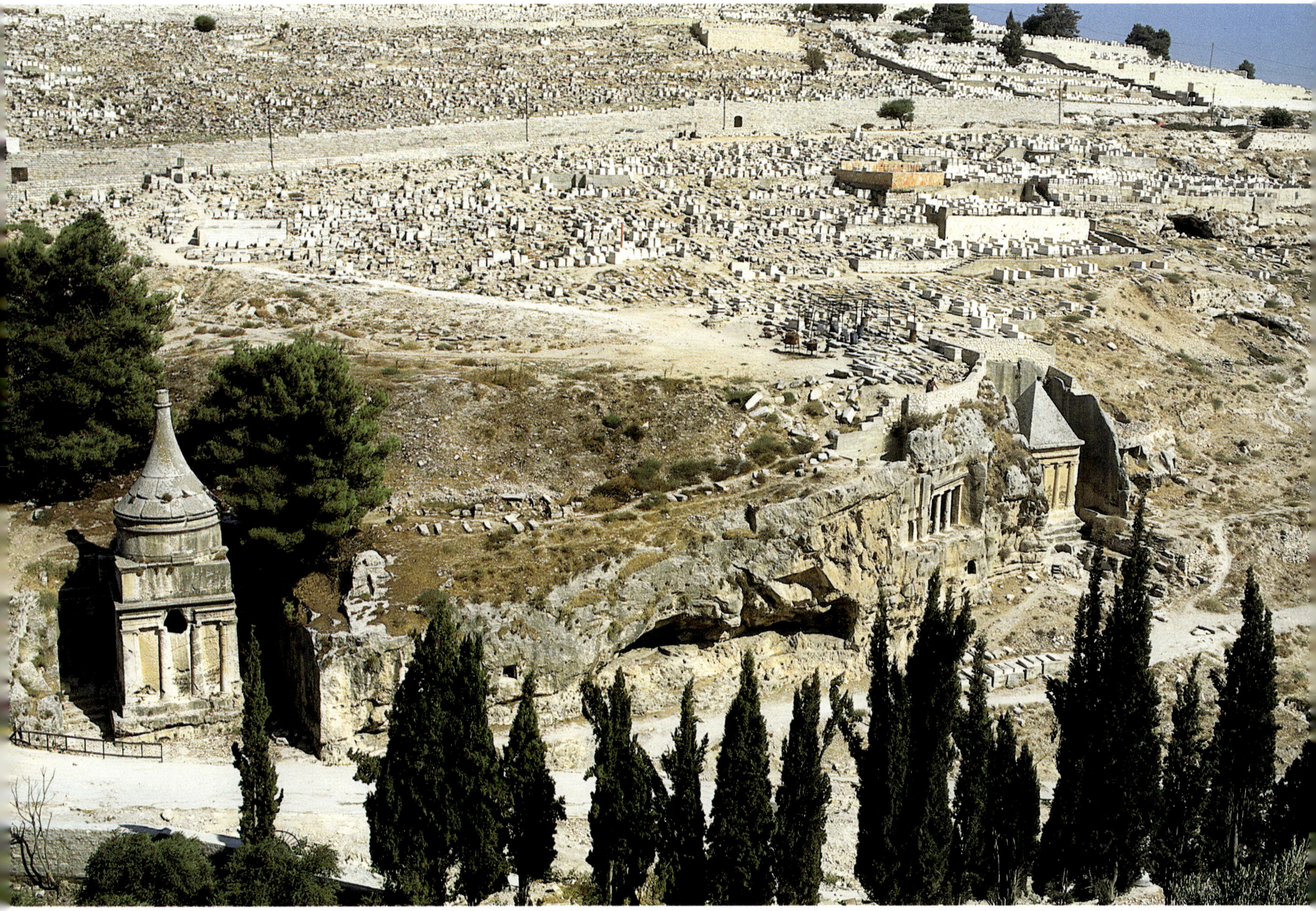

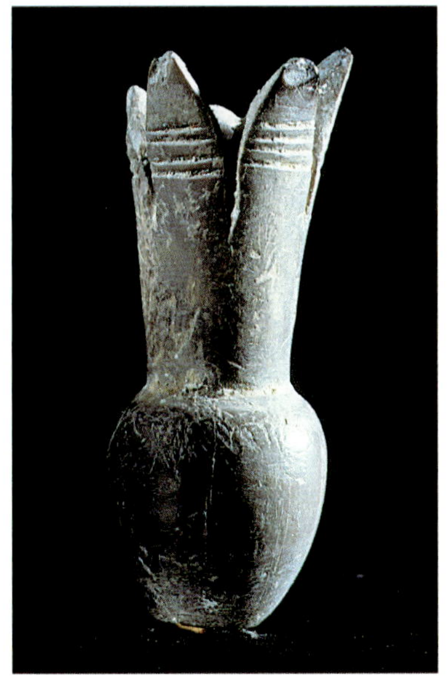

Around Mount Herzl, some way to the west of the old city walls, is where the sights of the modern city are concentrated. The simple black granite *Tomb of Theodor Herzl* is situated at the top of the hill. *Government Buildings* occupy an area to the east of the hill with its parliament building *(Knesset)* and the *Menorah* – a 16 foot high, seven-branched candelabrum, the symbol of the State of Israel. Further to the south, the pavilions of the *Israel Museum* are situated and display a number of different exhibitions: the *Bezalel National Museum* which houses an excellent collection of French Impressionists, the *Samuel Bronfman Archaeological Museum* containing a treasury of archaeological finds, the *Billy Rose Sculpture Garden* with outstanding sculptures by Henry Moore and Auguste Rodin, and the unusual domed building of the *Shrine of the Book.*

Between the Old City and the Mount of Olives in the Kidron Valley (above), the so-called tomb of Absalom (1st century BC, left in picture) and other tombs have been excavated. A vase from the period 1550 to 1200 BC in the Rockefeller Museum (below).

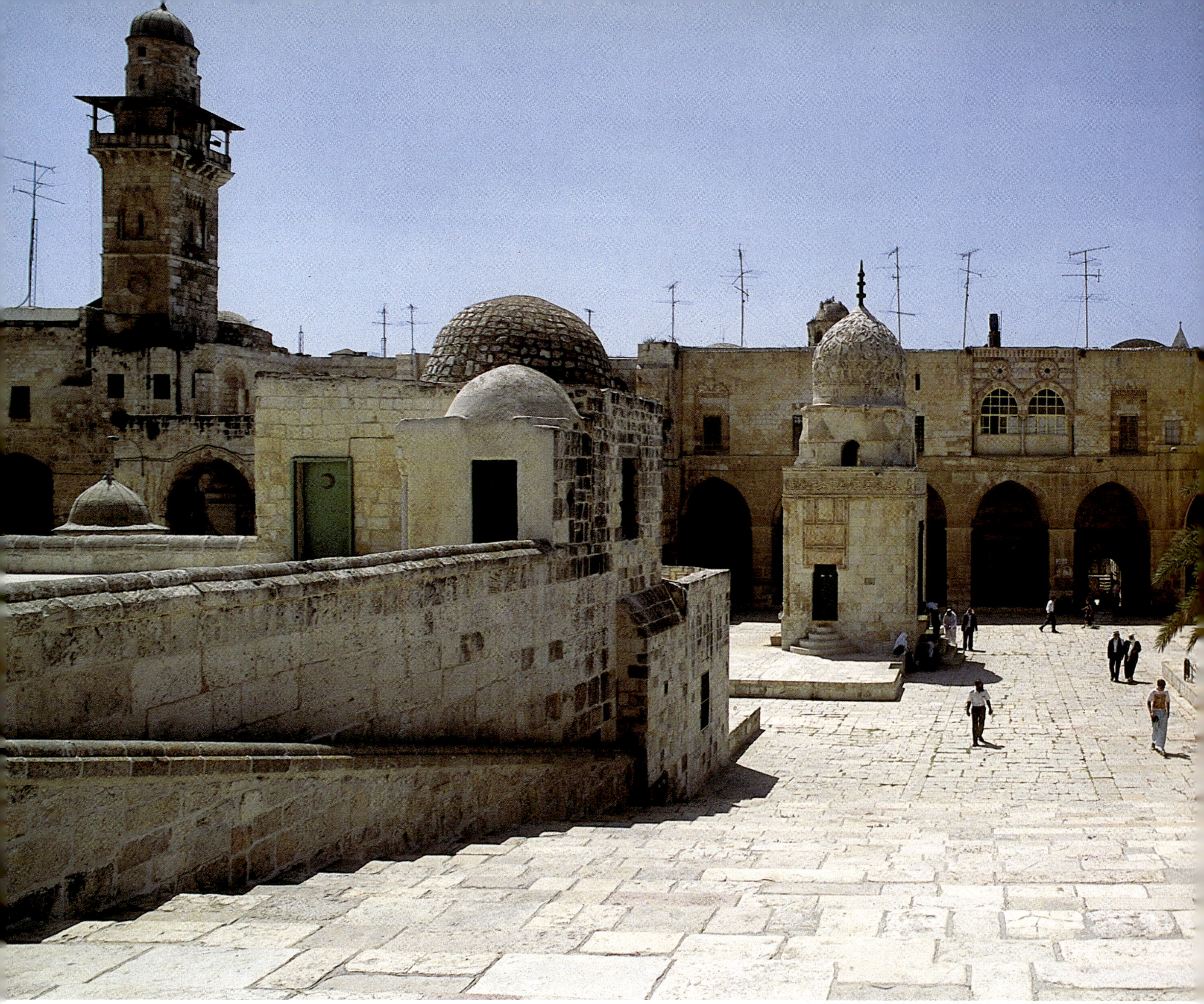

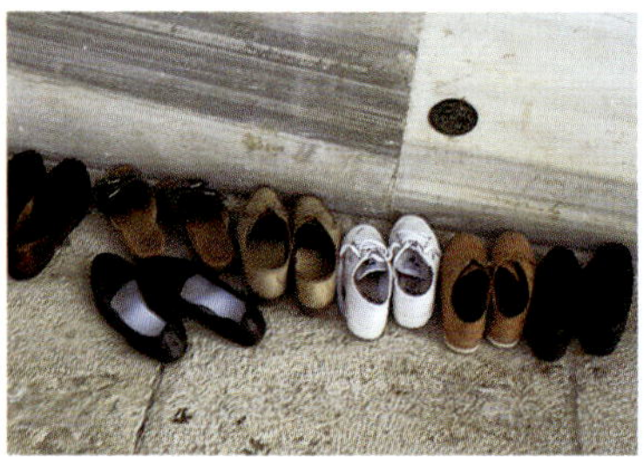

Divided City

Jerusalem is to be the 'eternal, undivided capital' of the Jewish State. In view of the city's history it is not just the attribute 'eternal' that is asking rather a lot. The word 'undivided' is more hope than reality. Jerusalem conceals a number of cities within itself: religious Jews living separately from secular Jews, Christians apart from Muslims and Muslims from Jews. Two nations claim entitlement to Jerusalem as their capital: Israelis and Palestinians, whose name for it is Al Quds (the Holy One). Since the conquest of Al Quds by the Israelis in the Six Day War in 1967 not much of their former town has been left to the Palestinians: the Muslim Quarter of the Old City and a few streets

After Mecca and Medina, the Dome of the Rock and the Mosque of Al-Aqsa on the Temple Mount are the most significant sites in Islam and have stood here for 1300 years. To enter you must take off your shoes. Jewish religious law forbids Jews to enter the Temple Mount.

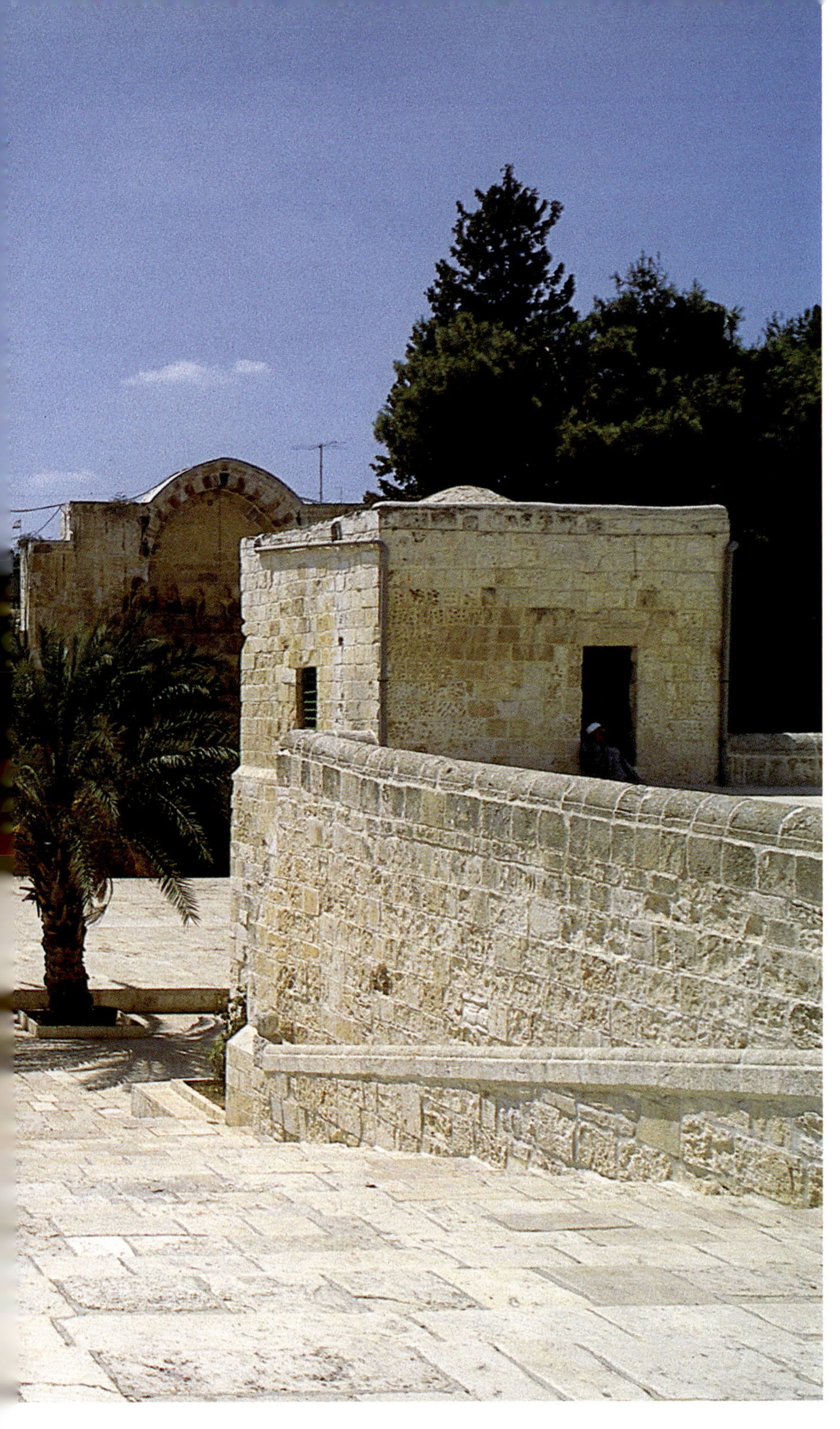

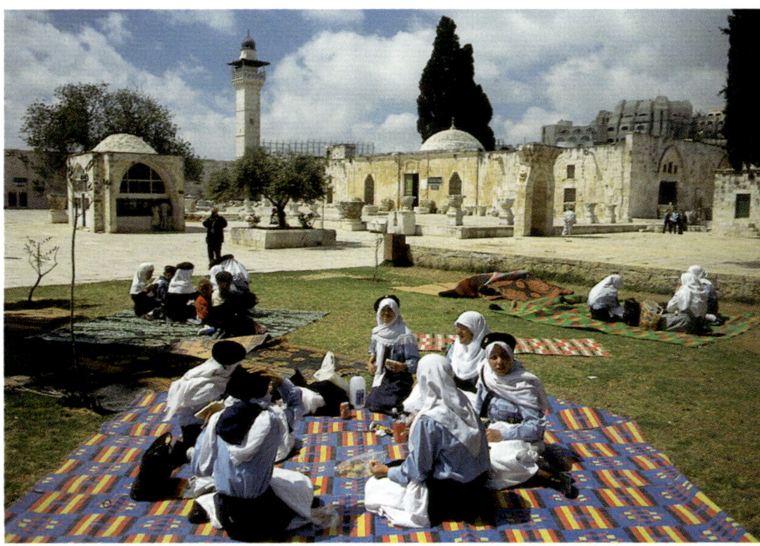

between the Damascus Gate in the south and the Sheikh Jarrah area in the north, between the Arab Bus Station in the west and the last check point beyond the Kidron Valley, the village of Silwan, and the Mount of Olives in the east. The Israeli government built new Jewish residential areas all around. The signs with the inscription 'Attention, Frontier ahead' which stood here before the Six Day War have been absent for 30 years. However, when tensions start building the police erect barricades and checkpoints around Muslim East Jerusalem.

The short period of euphoria after the Six Day War when Israelis sought out old Arab shops to buy non-kosher meat and Palestinians came to West Jerusalem to look at the houses they had left behind in 1948, has long gone. In recent times, the city has returned to a more violent language. For example, when the State of Israel declared Jerusalem as its capital in 1980, violence broke out. The conflict between Israelis and Palestinians reached new heights in December 1987 with the outbreak of the Intifada, the uprising spearheaded by Palestinian youths throwing stones. Since then, clashes and violent acts of terrorism have not been unusual occurrences in Jerusalem.

Jerusalem has two city centres, one at *Ben Yehuda Street* in West Jerusalem, the other at *Salah al-Din Street* in East Jerusalem. Double standards apply here, because the municipal authorities seem to treat Arab East Jerusalem as second-class citizens. The people of East Jerusalem rarely visit West Jerusalem to savour its cafés and bars, cinemas and museums.

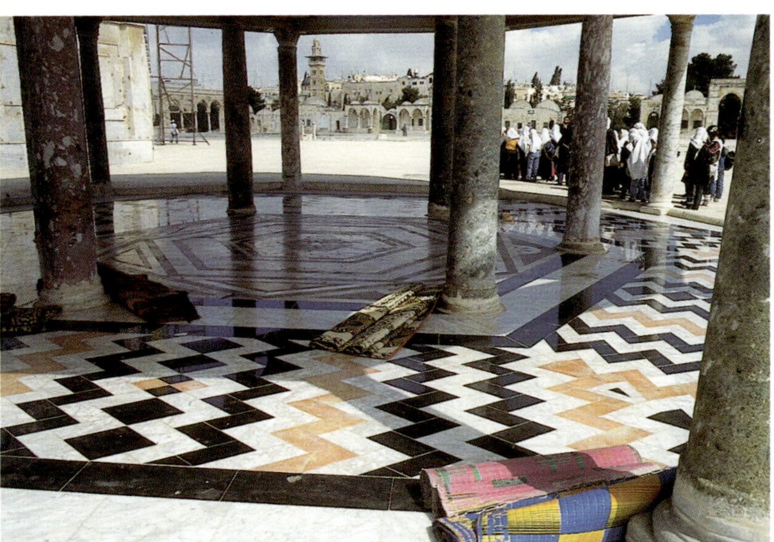

Conversely, since the Intifada, Israelis are diffident about entering East Jerusalem. Visitors to the Holy City, however, should not hesitate about making a sortie into the Arab part of the city – it has an atmosphere and rhythm all its own.

A Perfectly Normal Miracle

Jerusalem is a city full of miracles – in history as in the present. Nowhere in the world is the light clearer than in the 'Holy City'. Nowhere is there a more magical view than the one towards the surrounding bare hills of the Judean Desert. And nowhere is the star-studded night sky more enchanting. For many people, Jerusalem is the epitome of the place nearest to heaven – even if they do make life hell for one another in the meantime. The greatest miracle in this city of exceptional features is its

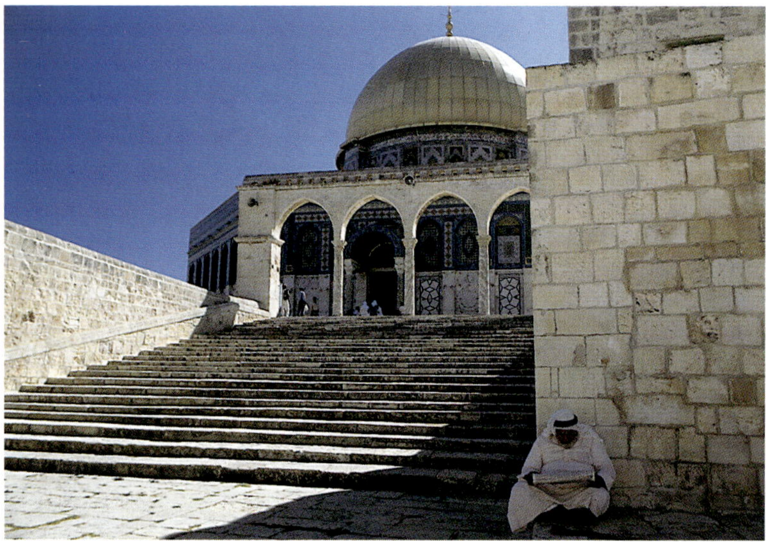

inhabitants who love Jerusalem quietly. The ones who see things in a clear light, the modest ones who are excited about simple, unspectacular events, such as the opening of a new restaurant or a new shopping mall and indeed anything that helps to make Jerusalem a perfectly normal city which simply wants to survive and develop. All the people filled with divine inspiration, the eccentrics and zealots, may be the spice of Jerusalem. But no meal can consist solely of spices.

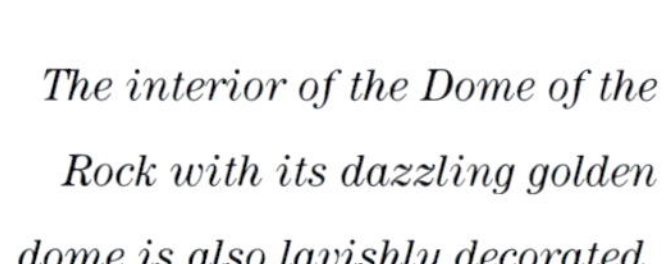

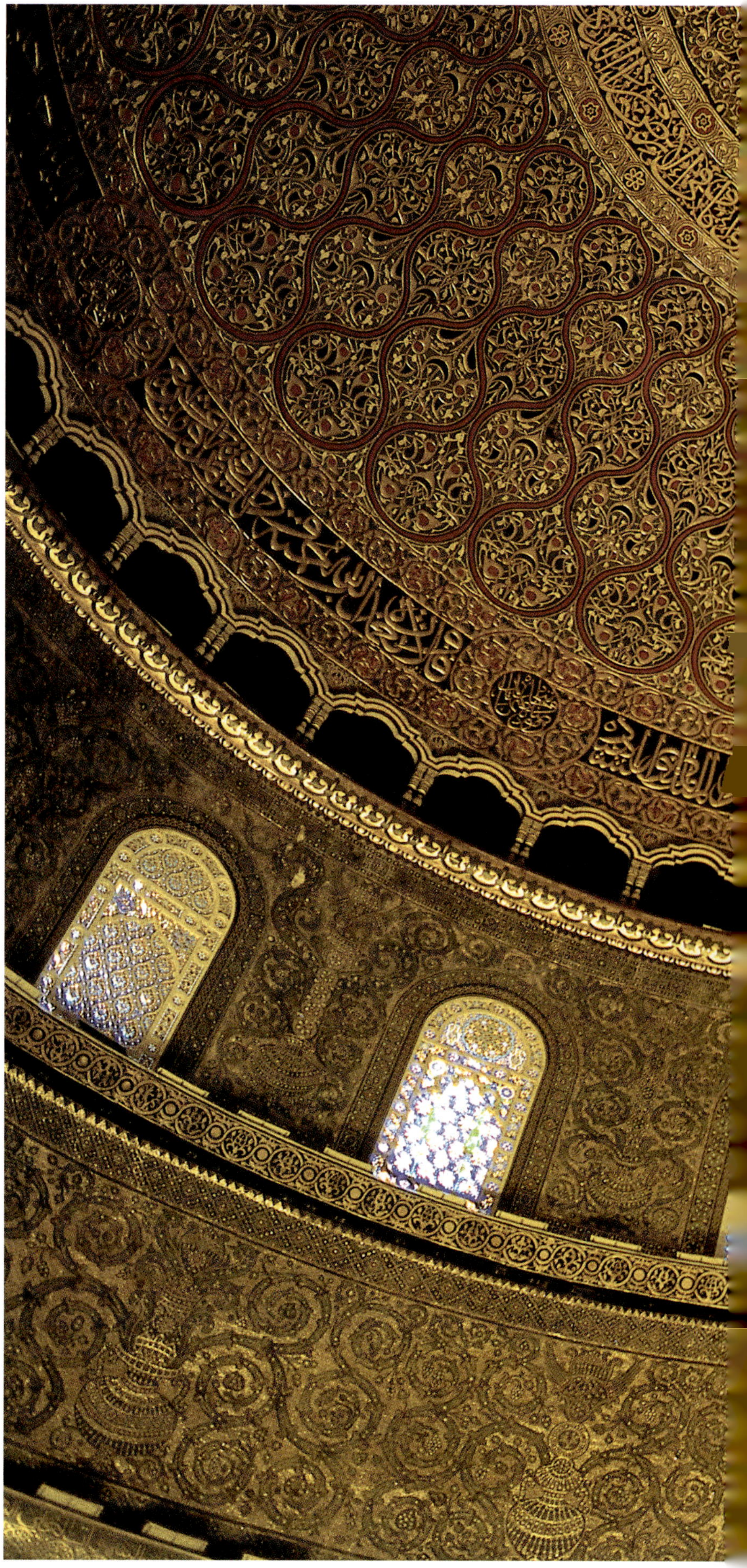

The interior of the Dome of the Rock with its dazzling golden dome is also lavishly decorated.

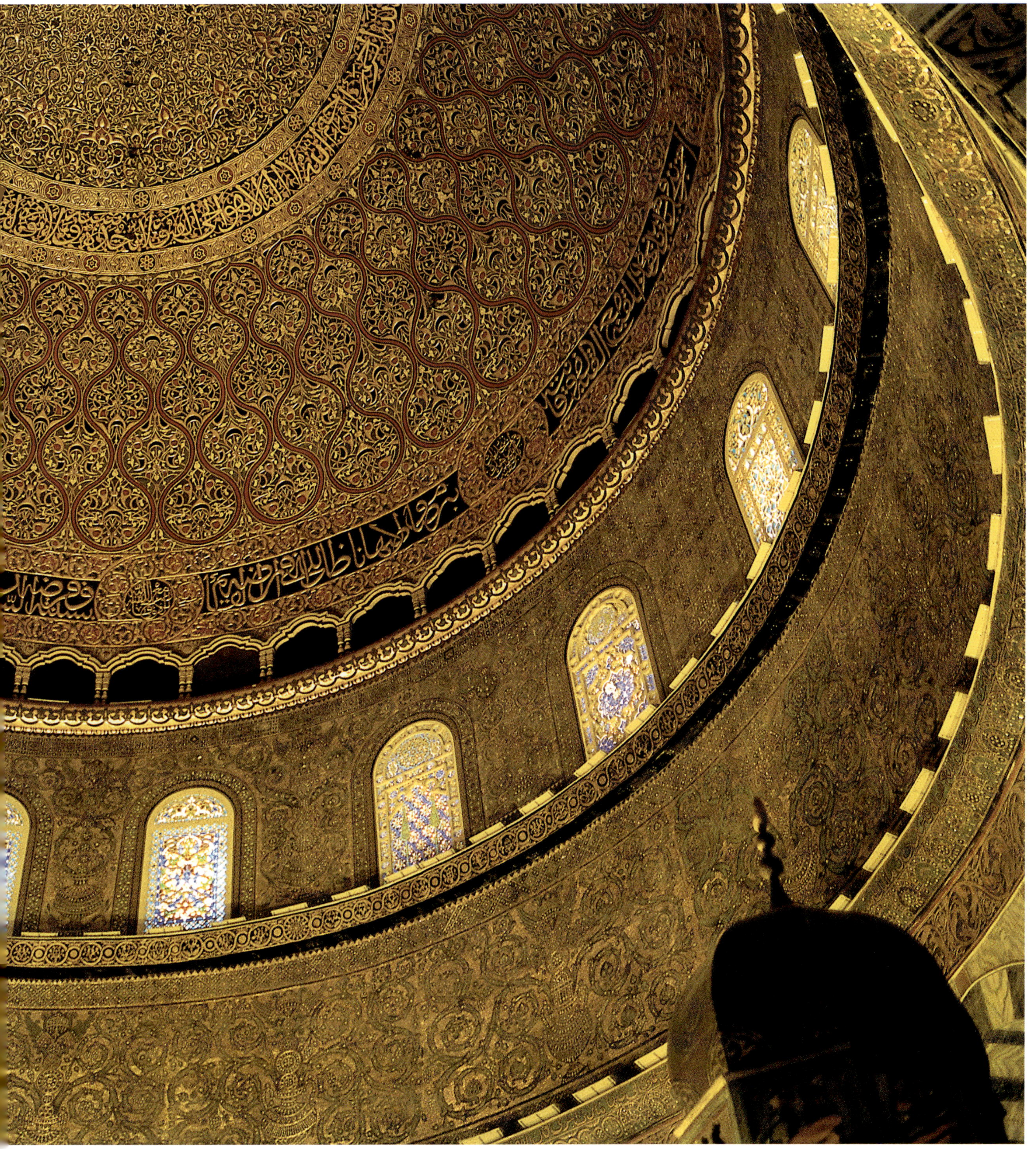

Holy Rock, Golden Glory

On Temple Mount

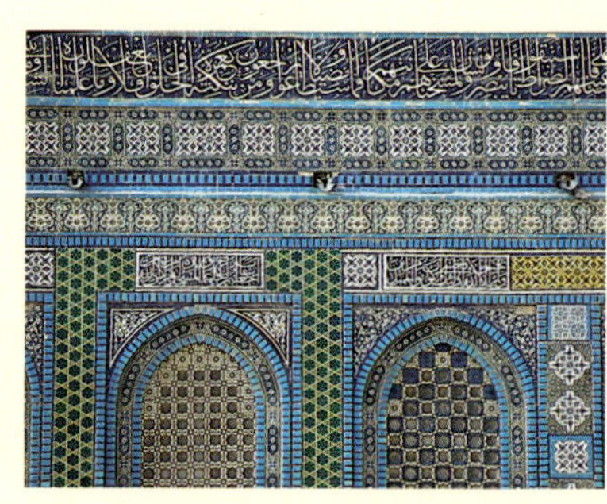

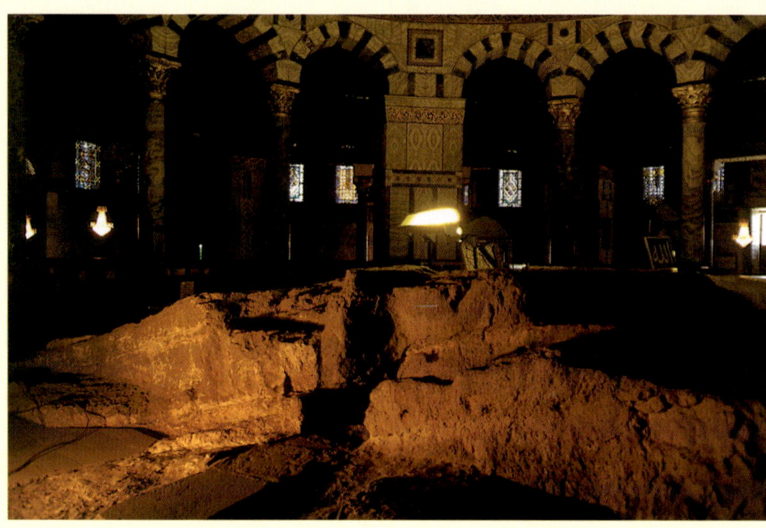

The Dome of the Rock is named for the golden yellow 'sacred rock' within (left). Highly ornate faience tiles with verses from the Koran adorn the Dome (right) with its gilded aluminium roof (page opposite).

It is said that this is the spot where the first light fell after God created the world. Here, on Mount Moriah or the Temple Mount as the Jews call it, is where Abraham offered his son Isaac as a sacrifice on a rock. For Muslims, an impression left on the same block of stone proves that this is the precise place from which the Prophet Mohammed ascended to heaven on his horse al-Burak several centuries later.

This is where Solomon built the First Temple during the 10th century BC, which was to be destroyed by the Babylonians in the 6th century BC. Nehemiah built the more modest, Second Temple, later extended to gigantic proportions by Herod in 20 BC. After the Romans destroyed the Second Temple in 70 AD, only ruins remained of this most important Jewish sacred site. In 687 AD, Caliph Abd al-Malik began the construction of the *Dome of the Rock*, which today counts as one of the world's most beautiful buildings and is a landmark of the city of Jerusalem. Christian craftsmen and architects from Syria and Byzantium assisted the Caliph in achieving a true squaring of the circle. The octagonal form unifies the square, symbol for the earth, with the circle, which symbolises heaven. Inside and out, the walls are lined with Persian faience tiles. Colourful mosaics, gilded ornamental plasterwork and columns taken from Roman and Byzantine buildings join to form a splendour found nowhere else in Jerusalem.

Whereas the Dome of the Rock provides pilgrims with a

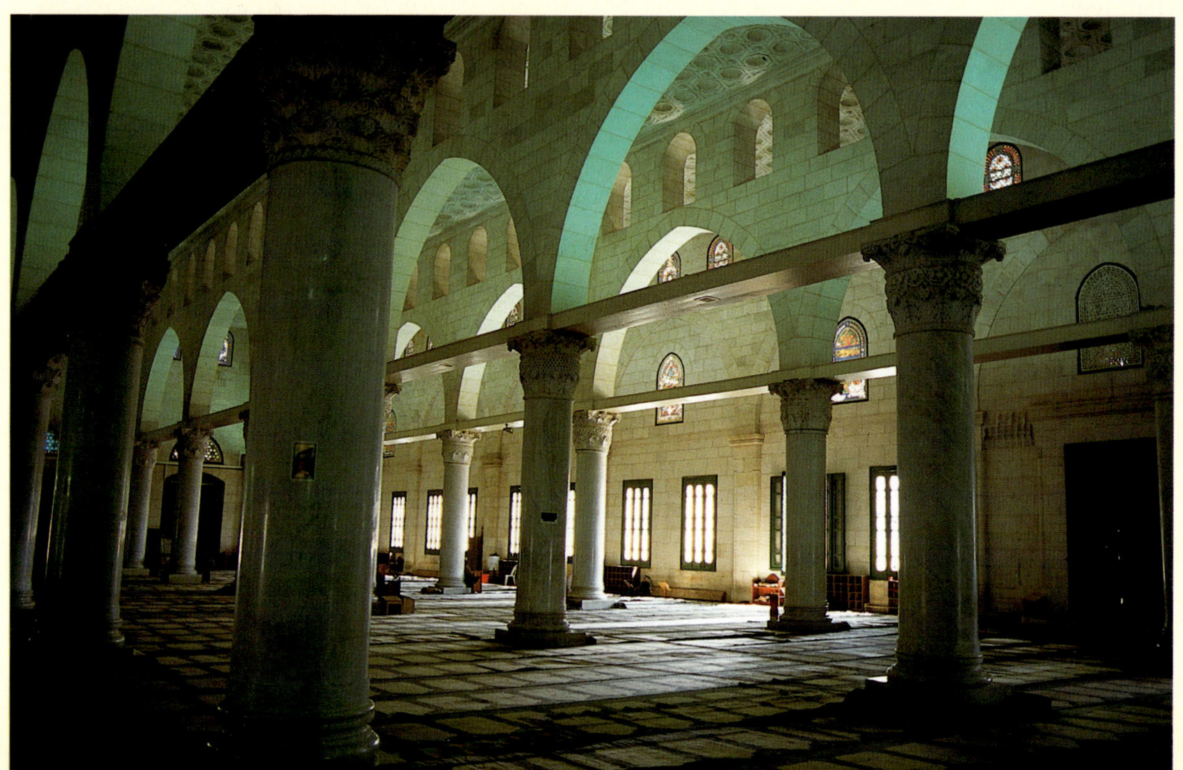

Carpets are laid out on the floor of the Al Aqsa Mosque which offers space for 5,000 worshippers. This is the largest mosque in Jerusalem.

quiet and contemplative space, the *al-Aqsa Mosque* is a place for communal prayer. Although this building was erected shortly after the Dome of the Rock, between 705 and 715, it has been rebuilt so often as a result of the destruction caused by repeated earthquakes, that today only a few parts of the building are older than 60 years.

After the Dome of the Rock, a building of almost equal splendour is the *Sabil of Sultan Qaitbey Fountain*, built in 1482. One has to imagine this example of Mameluke architecture and artistry with external stone troughs situated beneath the windows into which flowed water from the fountain inside the building.

At the south-eastern end of the Temple Mount, opposite the *Museum of Islamic Art*, visitors should take time to enjoy the panorama stretching across from the walls: the Mount of Olives and Kidron Valley, the ancient Holy Land, will lie at their feet.

The Mount appears so very peaceful when the sun is mirrored in the golden dome and worshippers stream to say their prayers in the al-Aqsa mosque. Yet the 3,000 year old history of the Temple Mount, has been anything but peaceful, proving that beauty alone does not satisfy.

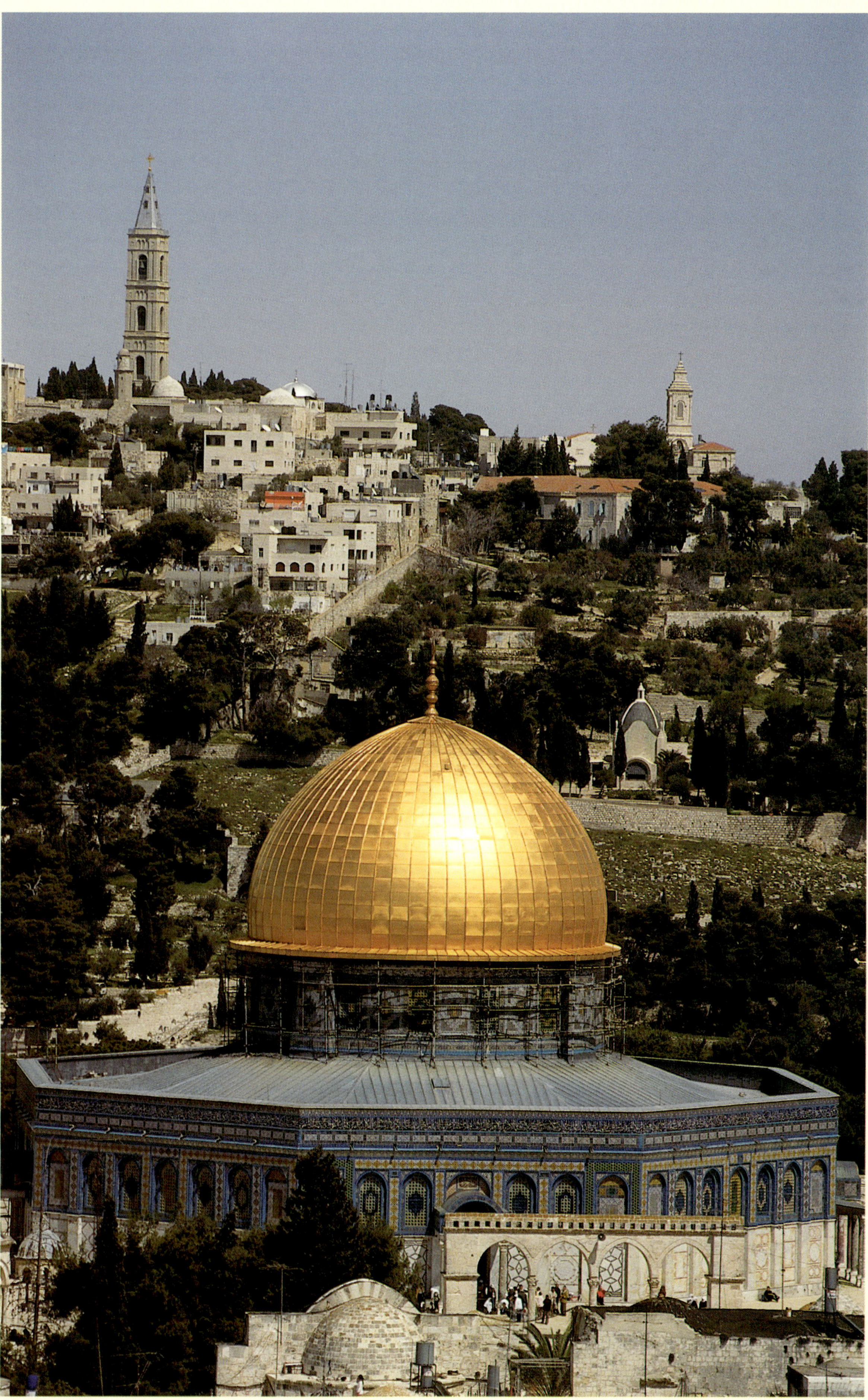

Biblical Sites in the Green Land

The North and Galilee

The Galilee in northern Israel stretches from the Mediterranean coast to the Golan Heights and Jordan Valley and from the border with Lebanon to the so-called Green Line, where the mountainous and rocky area of the West Bank begins. The Galilee offers something that the rest of Israel cannot offer: wild highlands in upper Galilee north of the road that runs from Acre to Safed, gentle hills and fertile valleys in the lower part, as well as snow-covered Mount Hermon where Israelis and tourists can ski in winter, (while others are swimming in the sea in Eilat), springs

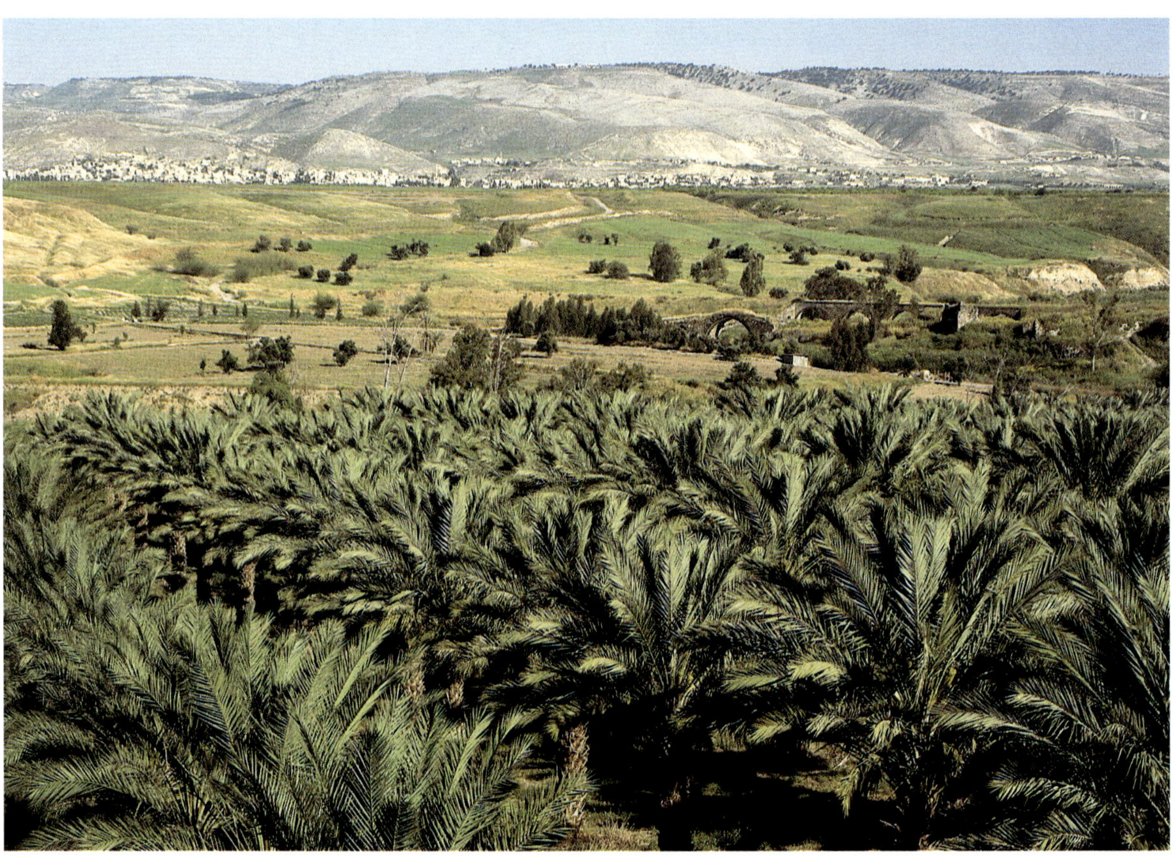

The River Jordan contains more water than any other river in Israel. Date palms grow in the fertile soil of the Jordan Valley and fruit, vegetables, grain and cotton are planted here.

and river sources, forests and probably the most famous lake in the world, the Sea of Galilee, as it has been called by Christians since New Testament times, or Yam Kinneret, 'Harp Lake' as it is known in Hebrew on account of its shape.

The lake is part of the 250-mile long Jordan Valley which is itself part of the Great Syrian-African Rift Valley between the Arab and African continents stretching from Africa all the way to southern Turkey, with its lowest point in the Dead Sea. This geological peculiarity transforms a drive to the Sea of

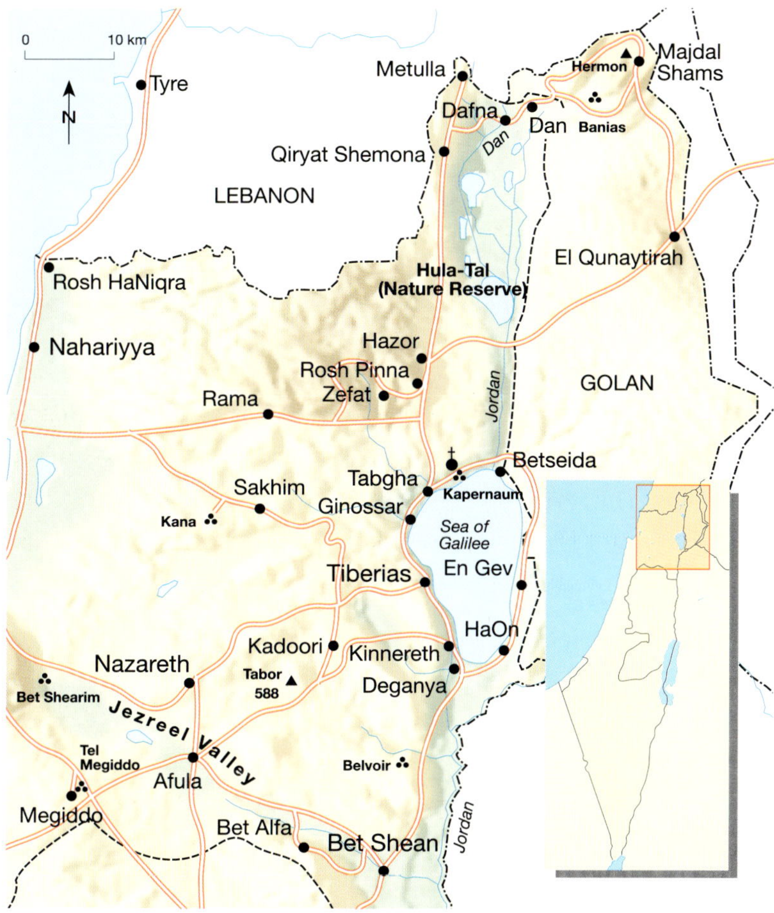

Kibbutz Deganya at the southern tip of the Sea of Galilee made an international name for itself for the success of its intensive agricultural efforts.

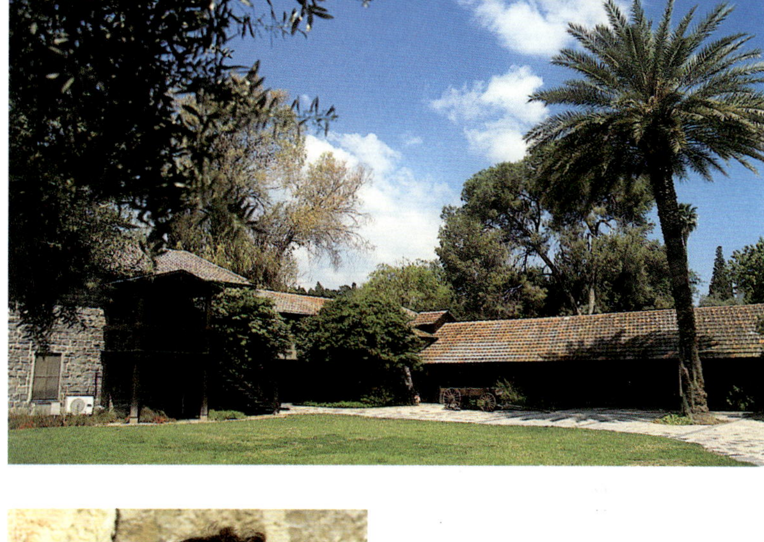

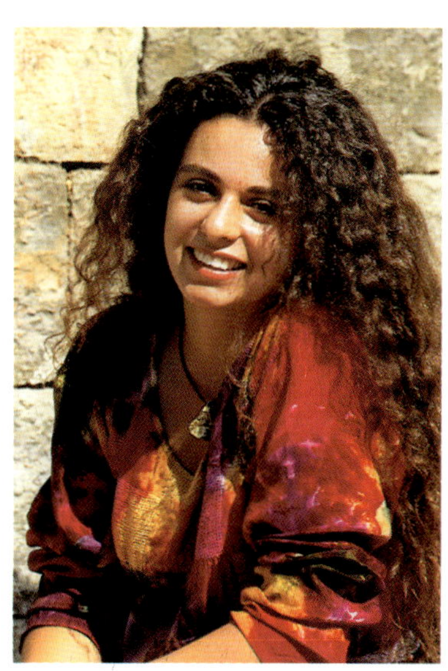

Galilee into a bizarre experience: suddenly, out of the blue, a street sign appears stating that you are at sea level, after which you are faced with a dramatic descent down a winding road.

If one assumes that a landscape can shape man and his relationship with God and the world, then it is easy to imagine that monotheism could only have been 'invented' and maintained in the grandiose sparseness of the Judean desert. The strip of land in the North on the other hand has been called 'heathen Galilee', and this is not just because 'heathens' such as Greeks, Romans or Mamelukes settled here to make use of the Via Maris, the old trade route between Egypt and Mesopotamia. Or because the Druze, Muslim and Christian Arabs who live here today make up the largest non-Jewish minority in Israel. In this region, with its Mediterranean flora and varied landscape kept green by the highest rainfall in Israel, there is even talk about the existence of elves and river spirits – good enough reason to attract spiritualists and mystics from all over the place. Galilee may be said to be the cradle of Christianity, but beneath its monotheistic facade a number of pagan customs are concealed, such as the worship of fertility symbols. Furthermore, the North has always been and still is the centre of the Cabbalistic and mystical movements of Judaism, which are centred on Safed.

Safed – City of Cabbalists and Artists

Safed or Zefat, pronounced 'Tzfat' by the locals, moulds itself along the foothills of Mount Meiron in terraces up the steep, narrow roads. When the hill town disappears under a veil of fog on rainy winter days or under a jungle of subtropical vegetation during the warm summer, there are times that one feels Safed is not of this world.

History and fairy tales live side by side here. Many, many years ago, perhaps in the sixteenth century, a poet, returning home to Safed was set upon by a group of murderous bandits outside the city gates. They granted him one last wish: to play a tune on his flute. The melancholy melody moved the camels so much that they began to dance, and the bandits fled in horror.

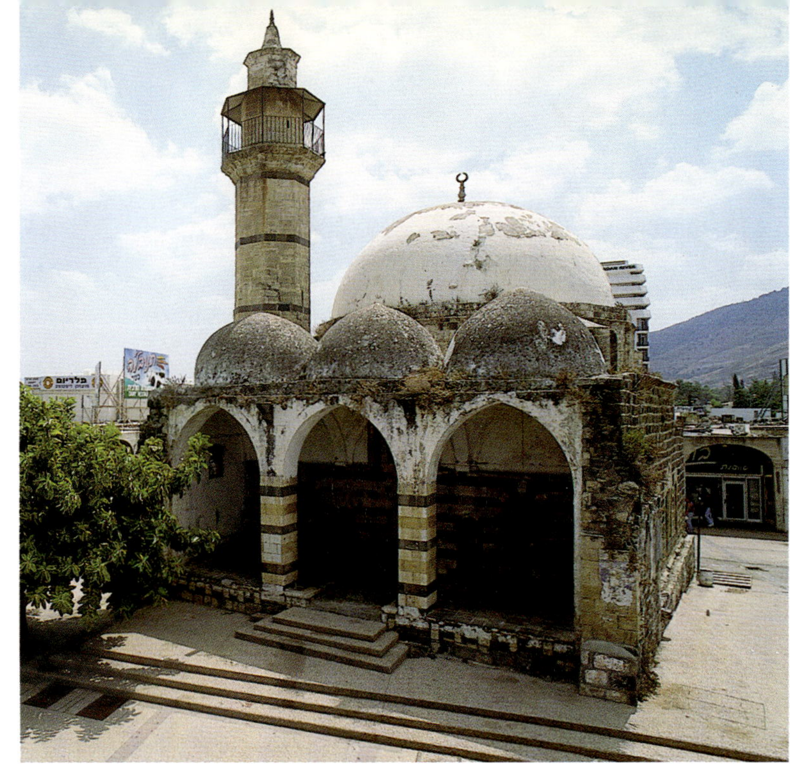

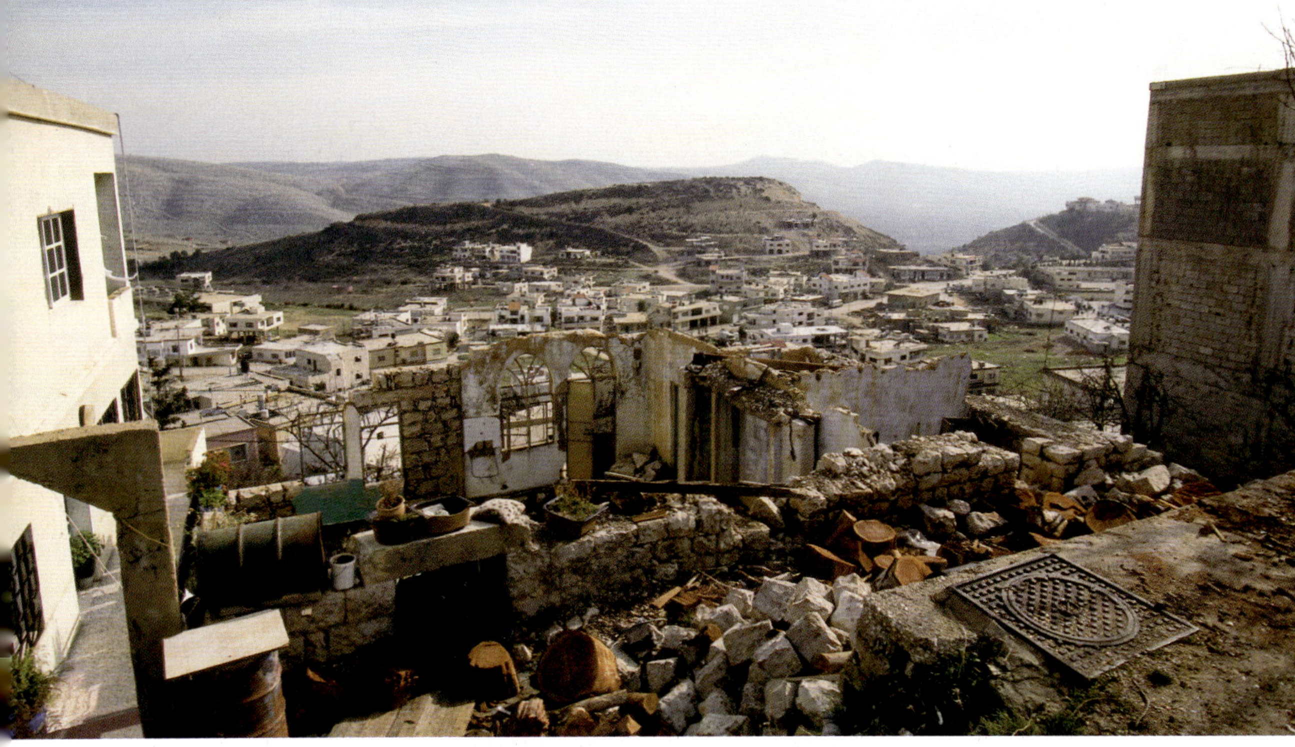

The hot thermal baths south of Tiberias were much appreciated by the Romans (see page right, below). The city was destroyed in 1247. In 1738 the ruler of Acre had Tiberias rebuilt and erected a mosque here (top). Majdal Shams, situated at 3900 feet on the eastern slope of Mount Hermon is the largest of the Druze villages in the Golan (below).

There is still a slight air of melancholy in Safed today which you will feel as you wander through its warren of twisting alleyways – especially if you walk in the direction of the *Hametzuda*, the citadel high above the city. The remains of an old Crusader fortress standing here are visited primarily for the outstanding view over the Sea of Galilee and the Golan Heights.

Safed, however, is a place where people come to worship at *tombs* and *graves*, from the cemetery at the entrance to the city where the prophet Hosea is said to be buried to Mount Meiron with the grave of Rabbi Shimon Ben Yohai. He survived the Bar Kochba uprising against the Romans in the second century and was the spiritual leader of the 'new' Judaism which was forced to continue without its spiritual centre after the Temple of Jerusalem was destroyed. The *Book of Zohar*, which is attributed to him, is the central work of the Cabbalists and covers the Five Books of Moses or Torah using tales, monologues or dialogues by means of allegorical and almost unintelligible explanations. It is, however, more likely that exiled Jews from Spain brought the work with them in the fifteenth century. During that period, Safed was the spiritual and religious centre of Judaism and was the largest Jewish community in the Holy Land for about 100 years.

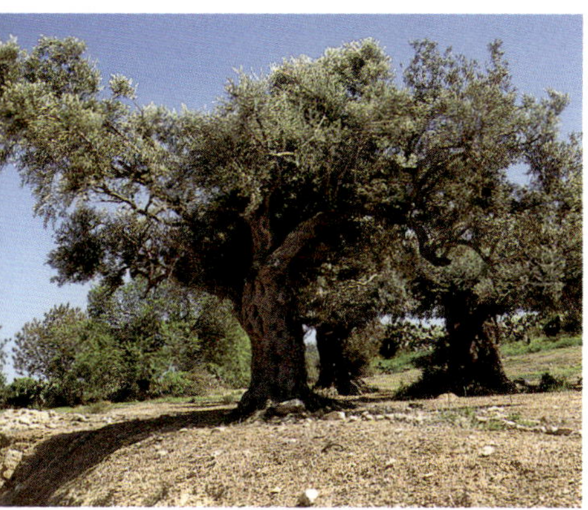

In 1882 Romanian immigrants established the first Jewish settlement east of Safed in Galilee. It was called Rosh Pinna, the 'cornerstone' (right).

In 1563, the brothers Ashkenazi established the first Hebrew printing works in the Orient. It was from here that religious and mystical scripts were distributed to Jews around the world. Numerous Talmudic schools and synagogues were built around here. Many of them are located in the Old City centre which is also known as the 'Synagogue Quarter' (Kiryat Batei Ha Knesset) for this reason, and many can still be seen here, despite an earthquake which almost totally destroyed the city in 1837. Two of them, the two *Ari Synagogues* built in honour of Rabbi Ari, the 'Lion', who lived in Safed in the sixteenth century, are truly worth a visit. As small and insignificant as these buildings may look from the outside, their magnificent interiors are reminiscent of Gothic architecture and were clearly influenced by European immigrants of the day. Even when only a handful of Jews lived in Safed between the period when the earthquake struck and the War of Independence in 1948, when the Israelis captured the city, the old traditions have always been maintained. Students continue to study the mystical theories of the Torah far into the night in their little prayer rooms and Talmudic schools.

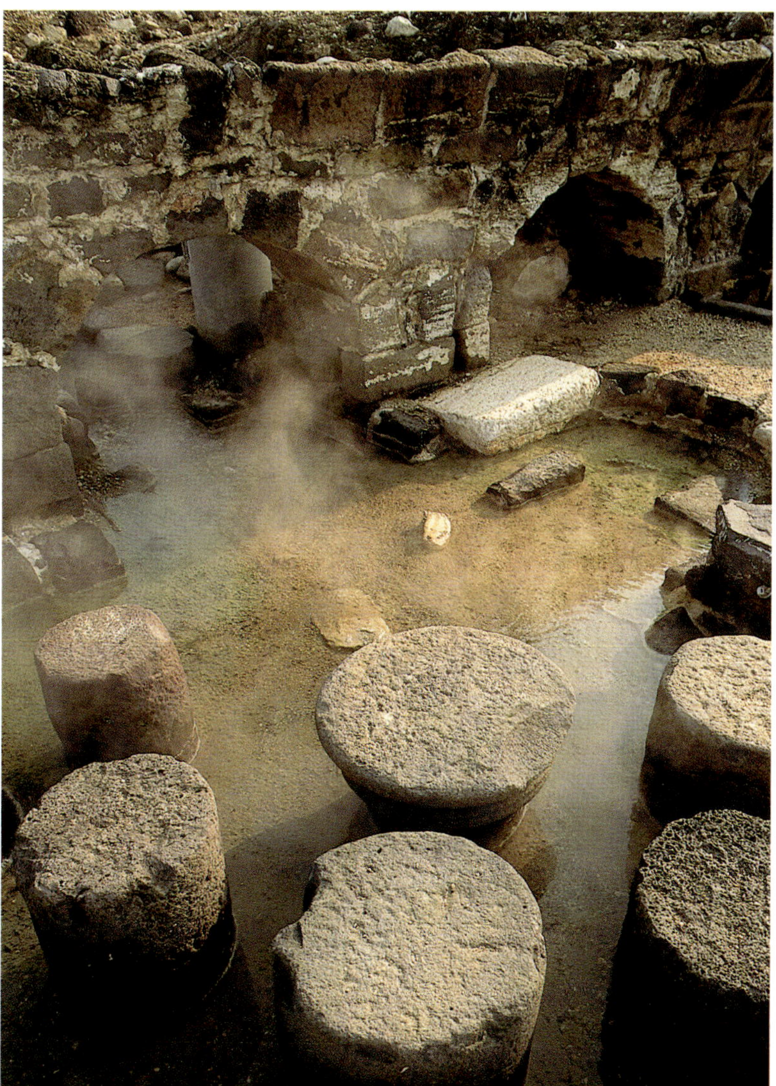

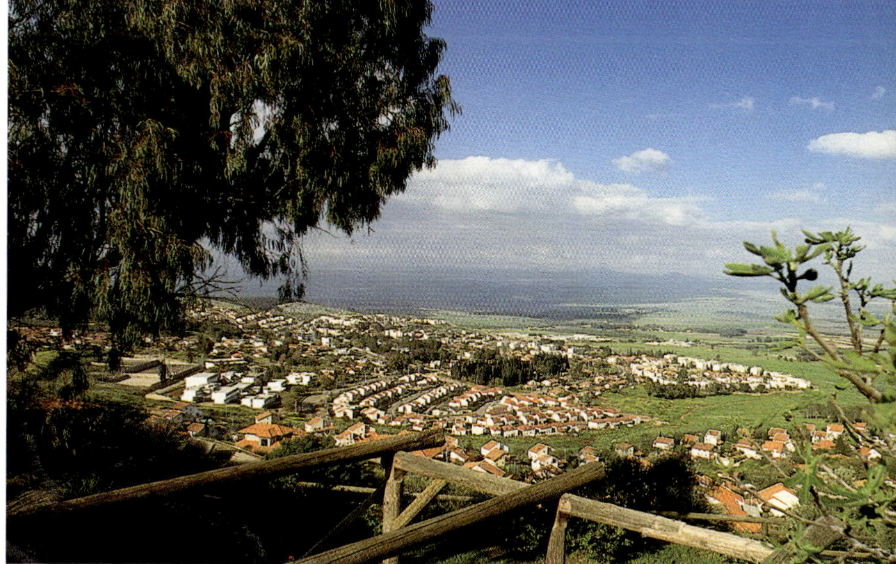

It may well have been this very atmosphere that drew the most famous painter from the eastern European Shtetl, Marc Chagall, back to Safed again and again. Chagall used to visit the capital of Galilee once a year, every year, from the 1920s up until his death in 1985. His influence is felt to this day. Not only in the many souvenir shops where you can buy Chagall posters, postcards, prints and much more. A whole colony of artists followed him here. They are to be found within the old Arab Quarter whose inhabitants fled or were driven away after the War of Independence. These days you will find studios and little galleries in the old Arab houses and modern sculptures where olive trees used to grow.

Continues on Page 82

Beaches of Antiquity

Around the Sea of Galilee

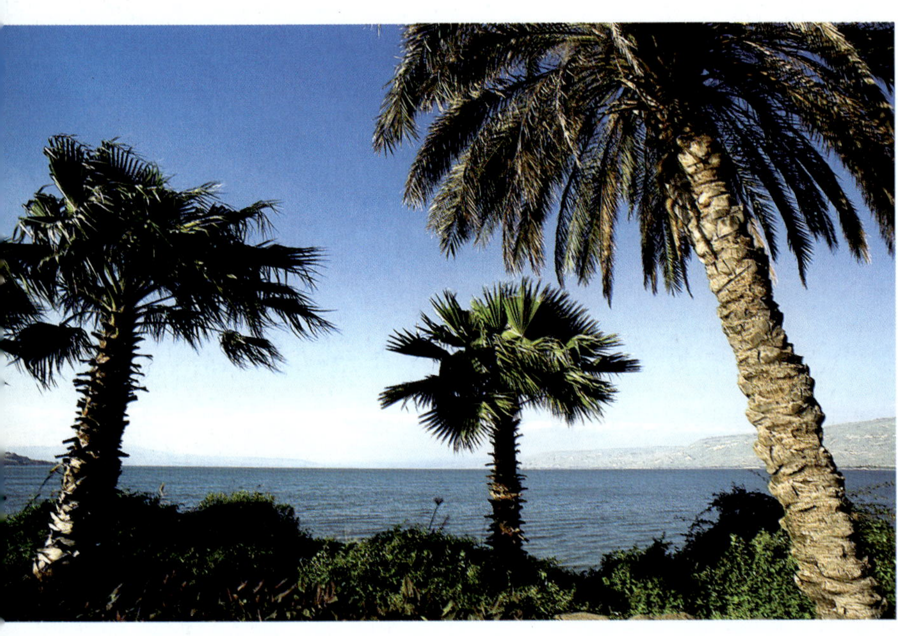

Although it is only 7 miles wide and 13 miles long, the mere existence of a deep blue, freshwater lake, smooth as glass, in this dry land is of enormous importance, and not just aesthetically. The shape of this, the largest fresh water reservoir in the arid land of Israel, has given rise to its Hebrew name 'Kinneret', or harp. Israel's first kibbutz was founded at its southern point, where the River Jordan leaves the lake to snake its way to the Dead Sea along innumerable twists and turns. As in many later kibbutzim, the intention in *Deganya*, the 'cornflower', was to test socialism in practice. Everyone pulled together to make the marshland arable, combating malaria and typhoid as well as beating back Syrian attacks. Nowadays, socialism is no longer taken quite so seriously. The mud huts belonging to the first settlers have made way for comfortable

It is said that when God heard the sound of the waves on the Sea of Galilee, it seemed to Him that He could hear a harp playing.

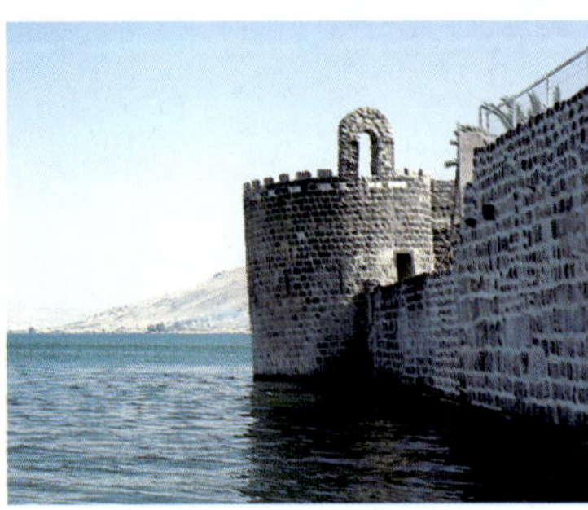

A fabulous panoramic view of Tiberias and the Sea of Galilee stretches before the hills of Galilee; above, a section of the old city walls.

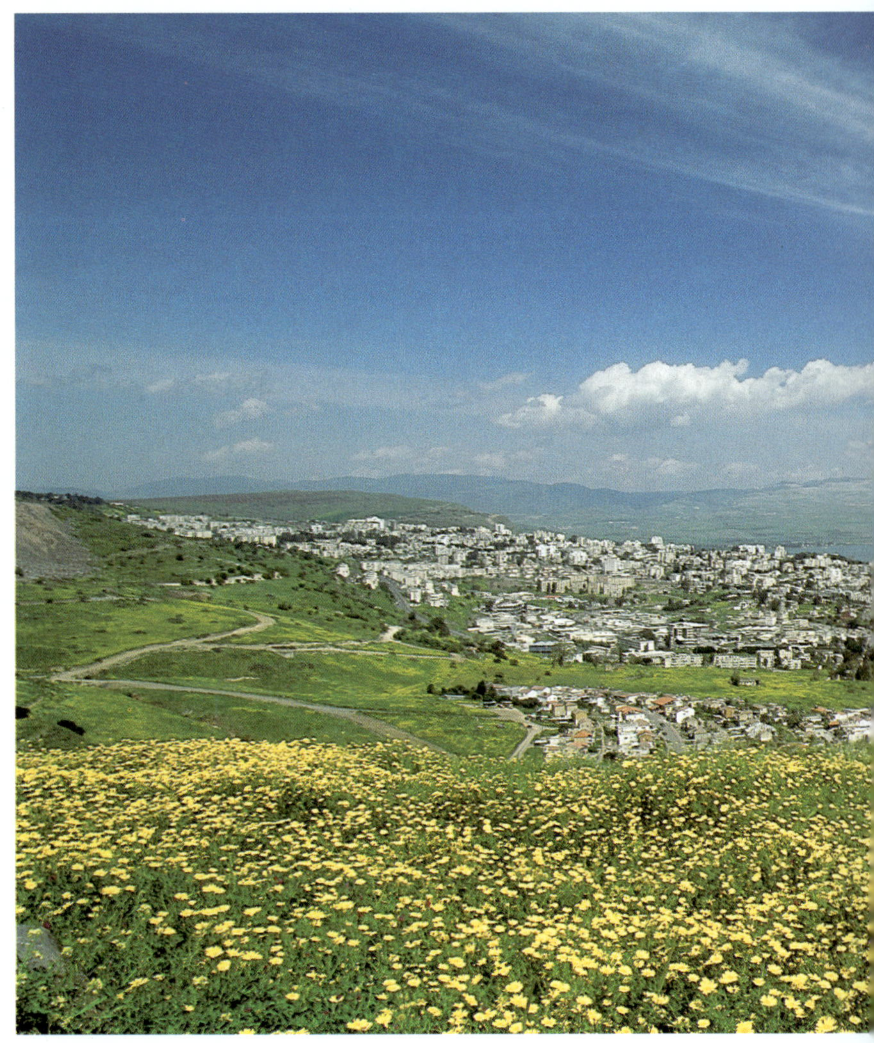

houses, and Deganya has expanded to become two kibbutzim, *Deganya Aleph*, which continues to be a farming community, and *Deganya Bet*, which earns its living from diamond cutting.

Inventiveness is the motto for all the kibbutzim around the lake. For example, *HaOn*, which lies to the east of Deganya, is dedicated to breeding ostriches. However, it remains questionable whether this is a profitable business or merely a tourist attraction. Ostrich meat is not kosher, and therefore not licensed for export.

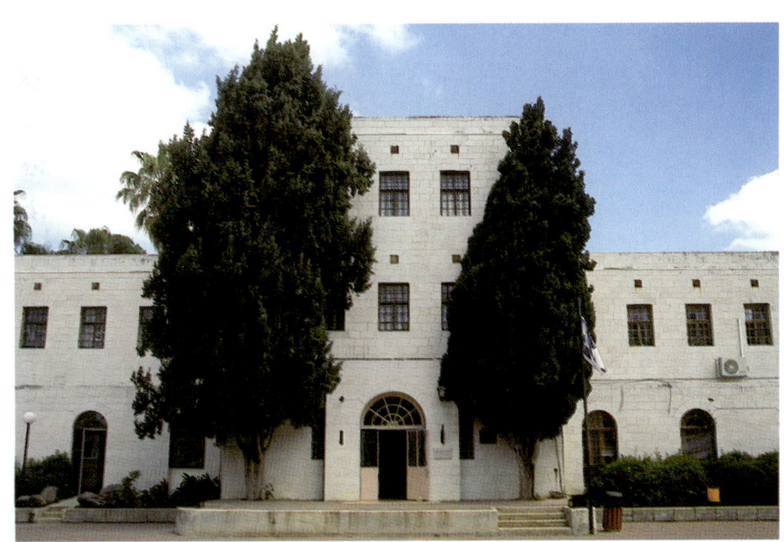

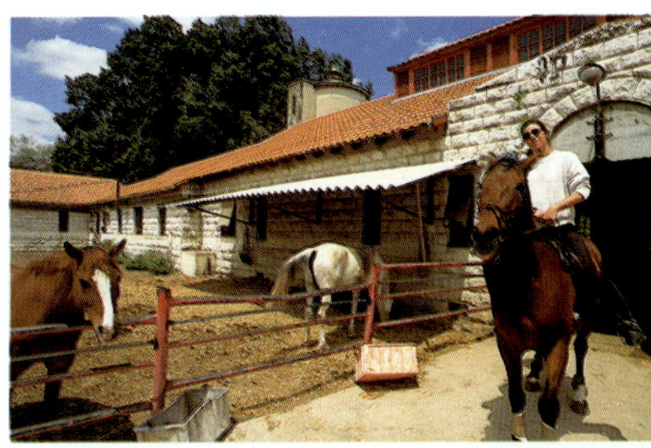

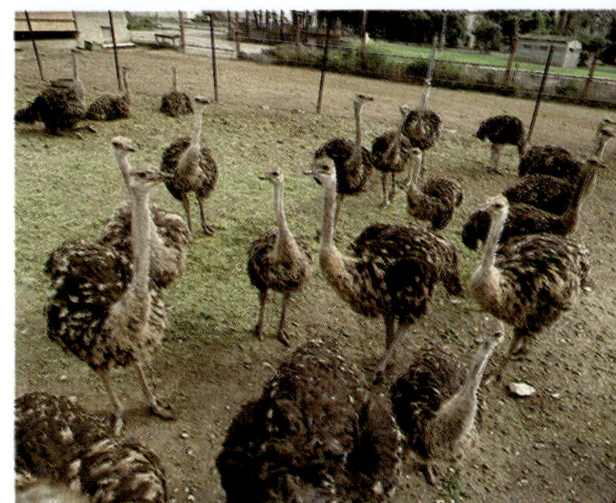

Kibbutz Kadoori, which nestles between the lake and Mount Tabor, is famous for its stud farm (above left and right). Emus in kibbutz En Gev on the eastern shore of the lake (right).

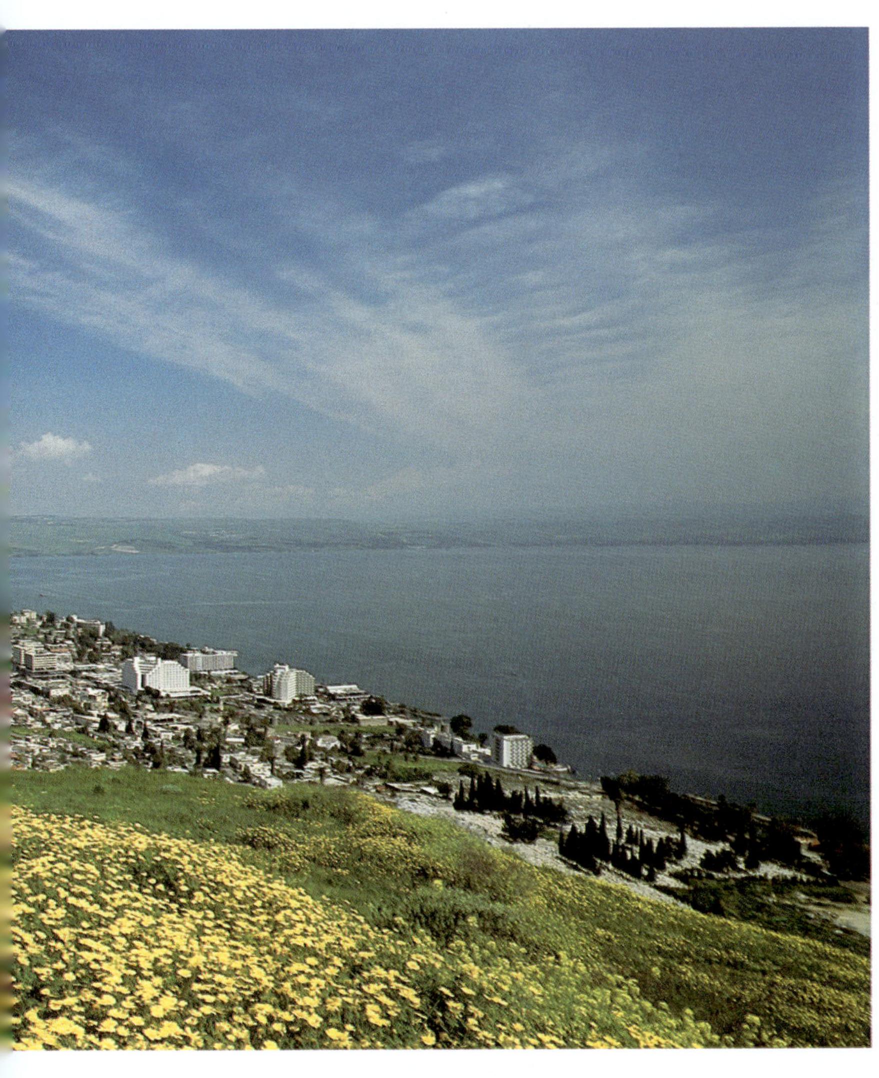

The *En Gev* Kibbutz on the eastern shore of the lake was founded in 1937 and every year celebrates its famous music festival. And Kibbutz *Kinnereth* caters to the visiting pilgrims' religious fervour. Situated opposite Deganya, it also lies close to where the Jordan leaves the lake and where Peter, and presumably John the Baptist, underwent the ritual of becoming Christians. Naturally, Christians from all over the world are keen to be baptised again in such a symbolic place, especially with genuine water from the Jordan. The kibbutzniks have erected a baptismal site for this purpose. And for the relatives back home, a few shekels will buy a plastic bottle full of the very same genuine Jordan water.

Tiberias is the region's economic centre, a spa with numerous thermal springs well-known in antiquity, and a beach and watersport resort. The city was razed to the ground after a battle in the thirteenth century and destroyed again by an earthquake in 1837. Con-sequently, there are scant remains of historic buildings.

There is, therefore, very little sightseeing to be done in Tiberias. It is a place for rest and relaxation, for enjoying the renowned culinary delights of the John Dory fish served in local restaurants, added to which is the view of the port, the sea and the numerous passers-by. All this makes it well worth paying the higher prices charged here as compared to less developed areas in Israel.

Signs and Miracles in Galilee

You need to believe in miracles just a little bit if you wish to study the difficult texts of the Zohar and learn to understand the secret meaning behind each and every word of the Bible, however insignificant, just as the mystics and Cabbalists of Safed do. But miracles do not seem to be so unusual in Galilee. The area around the Sea of Galilee, according to the New Testament, is where Jesus performed the very miracles that had even the sceptics among his followers believing that he really was the Messiah. On the north coast of the Lake is *Capernaum*, where Jesus chose to live after he had left Nazareth. It is here that he began his missionary work, and here he met Peter, the fisherman whom he wanted to convert into a 'fisher of men'. This town was probably founded in the thirteenth century BC and was already inhabited primarily by Christians in the second century. Later it was destroyed by an earthquake and never rebuilt. When Franciscans bought the site in 1894 excavations started to reveal an old synagogue from the 4th century AD and, under the remains of a basilica, a house was found which is believed to be the house of St. Peter. A church cantilevered

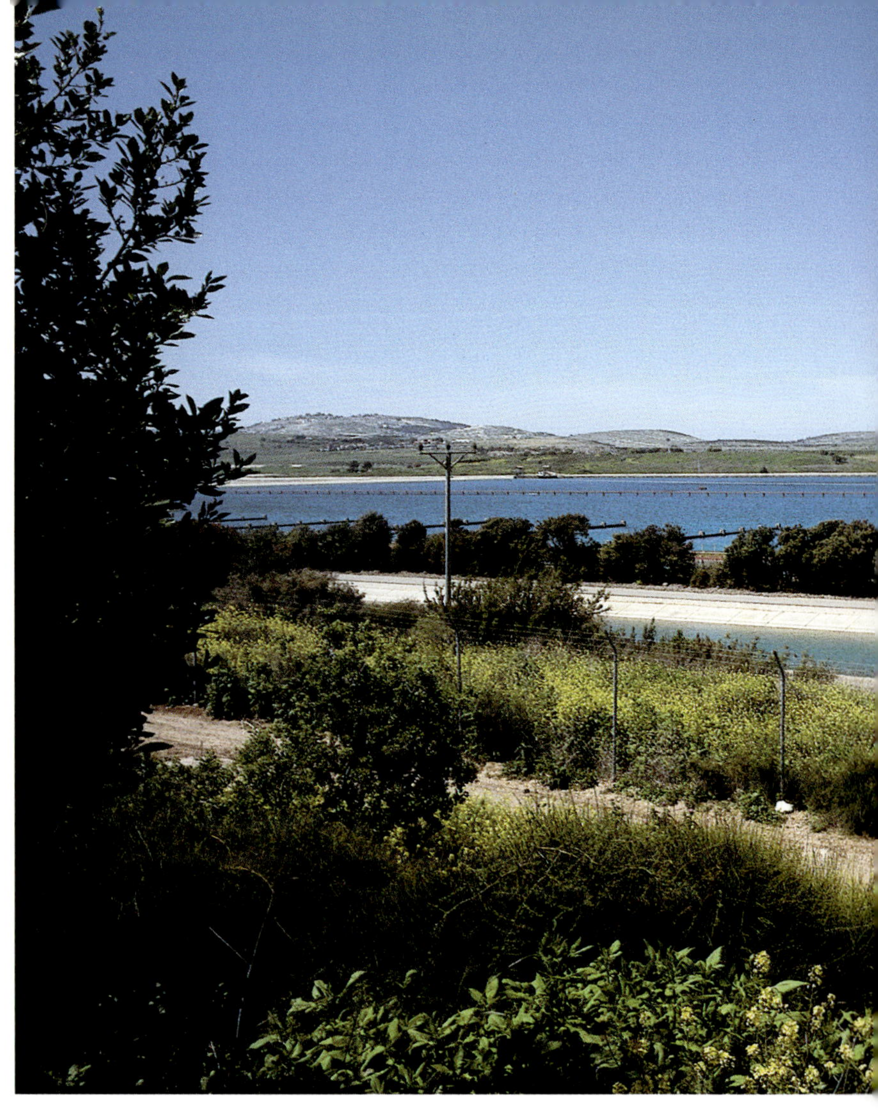

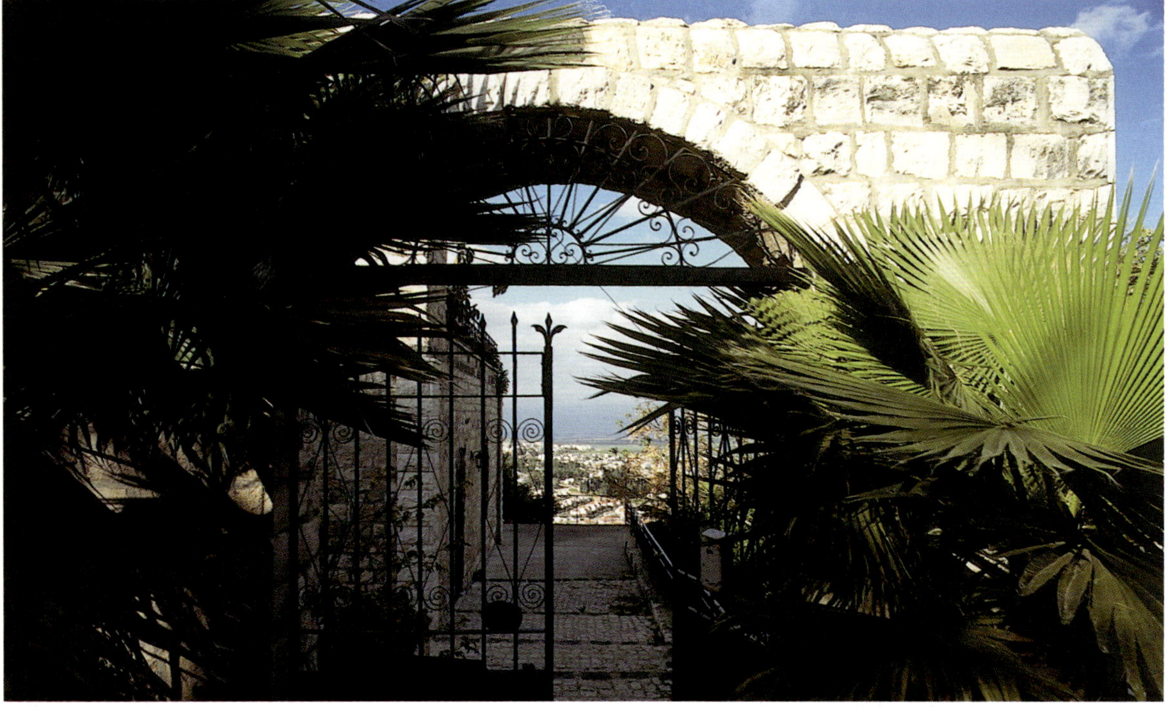

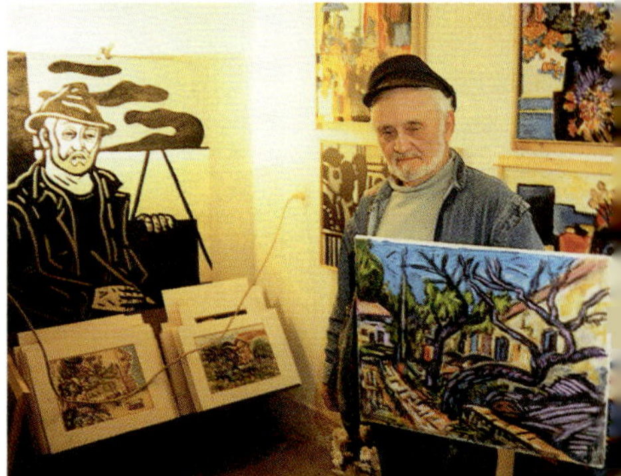

Reservoirs were built in Galilee to provide continuous irrigation for the fields (above). Artists can be visited in their studios in Rosh Pinna (below left, and right).

over the site on stilts built in 1991 offers a view of the remains of buildings from previous centuries.

Like Capernaum, where Jesus performed healing miracles for Peter's mother-in-law, a lame man, the servant of a Roman centurion and a leper, *Tabgha* which lies a little to the south-

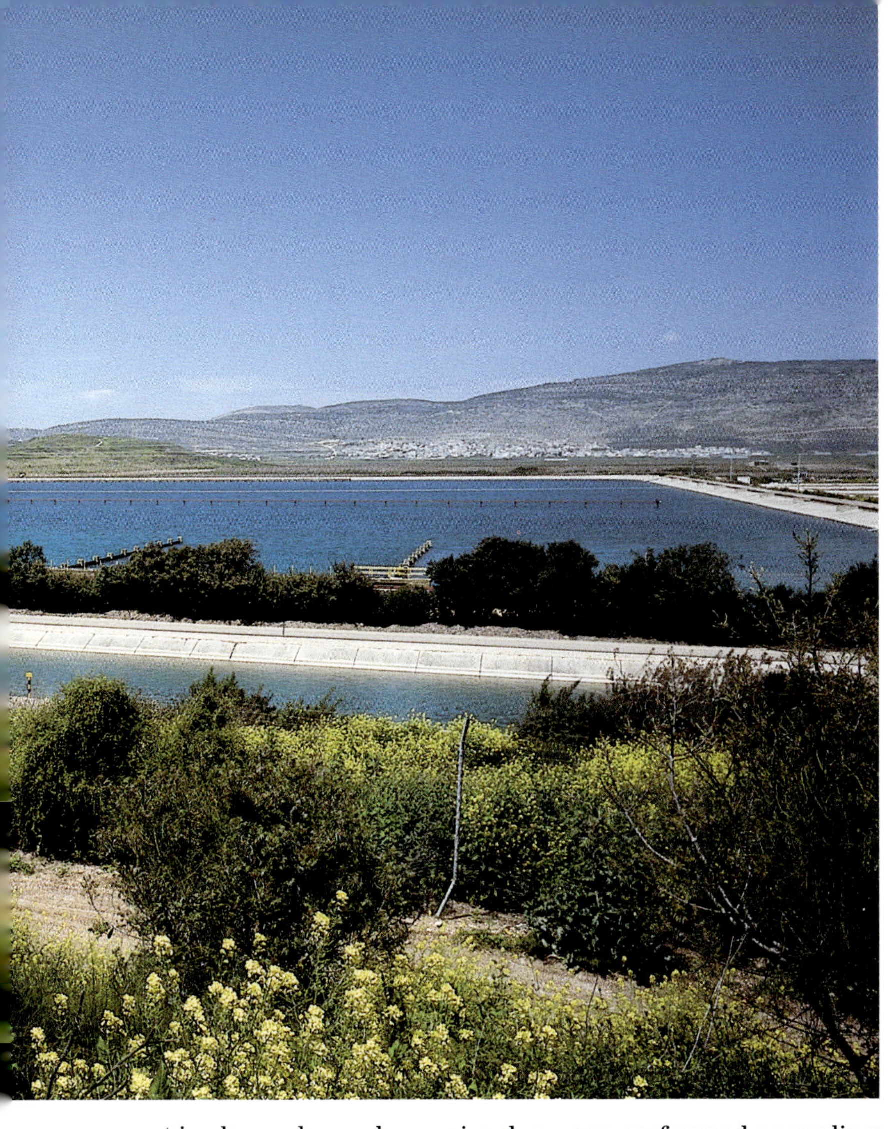

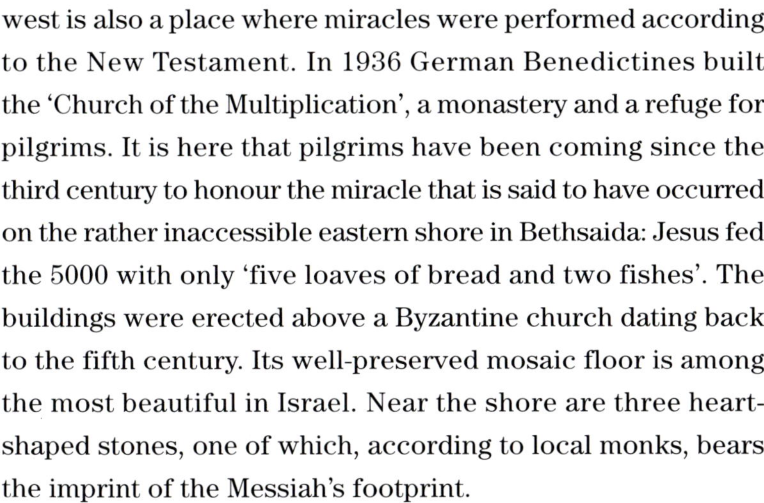

west is also a place where miracles were performed according to the New Testament. In 1936 German Benedictines built the 'Church of the Multiplication', a monastery and a refuge for pilgrims. It is here that pilgrims have been coming since the third century to honour the miracle that is said to have occurred on the rather inaccessible eastern shore in Bethsaida: Jesus fed the 5000 with only 'five loaves of bread and two fishes'. The buildings were erected above a Byzantine church dating back to the fifth century. Its well-preserved mosaic floor is among the most beautiful in Israel. Near the shore are three heart-shaped stones, one of which, according to local monks, bears the imprint of the Messiah's footprint.

A little to the north of Tabgha, on the Mount of Beatitudes, Jesus is said to have preached the Sermon on the Mount. Fans of Monty Python will remember that the film *Life of Brian* starts with a parody of the Sermon on the Mount and will be amused to learn that it was actually filmed on the original location.

Continuing on our way past the *Kibbutz Ginosar* which runs a luxury guest house and *Tiberias* (see Page 81), a cheerful summer resort and centre on the lake, we soon arrive at the southern end of the Sea of Galilee. The ruins of the Crusader castle of *Belvoir* are definitely worth a detour for the stunning views over the lake and valleys all the way to the mountains of Jordan.

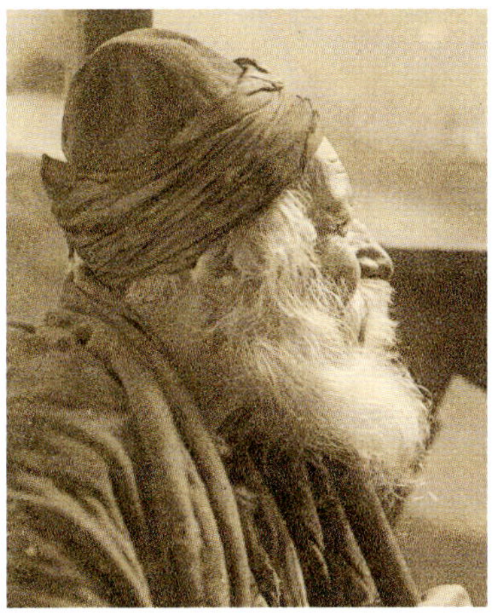

A picture reminiscent of biblical times: shepherds tend their flocks on the shores of the Sea of Galilee (1921 photo postcard). You can escape the noisy beach life by seeking out the eastern shoreline.

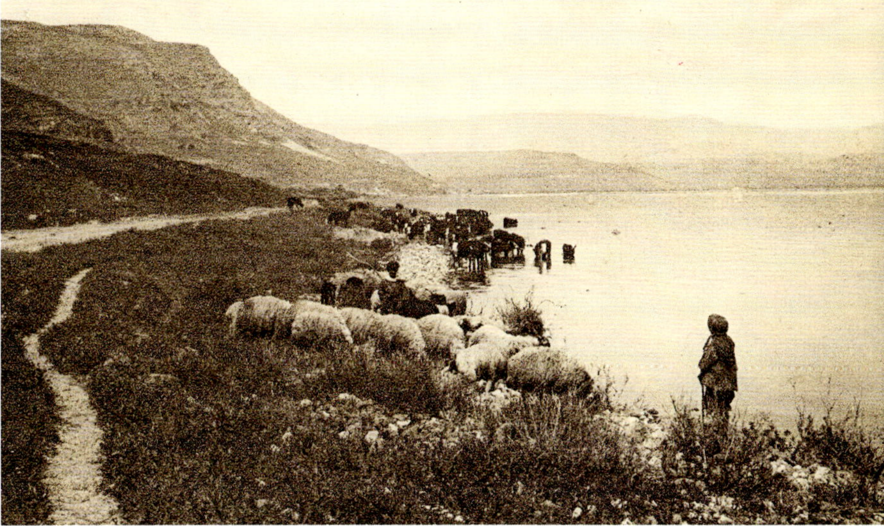

Another 12 miles further south brings us to Israel's largest archaeological site at *Tel Bet She'an* (see Page 85) where the earliest ruins date back to the fifth century BC.

Land of Shepherds and Farmers around Nazareth

The traveller to this part of the world tends to associate Galilee with Nazareth, but this quiet, verdant region with its gently rolling hills has much more to offer. The best views of this area so rich in agricultural produce can be obtained from Mount Tabor. History was made in the Jezreel Valley. Throughout the centuries, battles were fought here by dozens of rulers at the strategic trade route between Egypt and Mesopotamia. The best-fortified fortress was situated in *Megiddo* which was even mentioned in Egyptian hieroglyphics as a battle site. Today it is better known for the peaceful work of the archaeologists which has drawn visitors by the thousand: in the ruins of the biblical Armageddon, impressive remains from the period between 4,000 and 400 BC were found including a rather clever underground irrigation system which is no less than 2,800 years old. *Bet She'arim* is another place of subterranean wonders. The sight of the hundreds of sarcophagi has you catching your breath in awe and lowering your voice in respect. When the Romans had closed Jerusalem to the Jews after the Bar Kochba revolt they came to She'arim, where they established a spiritual centre. Jews continue to come here on pilgrimage from all over the world.

North of Nazareth lies *Cana*, another biblical town with two small churches which remind us of the occasion when Jesus turned water into wine at a wedding feast. *Nazareth*, one of the

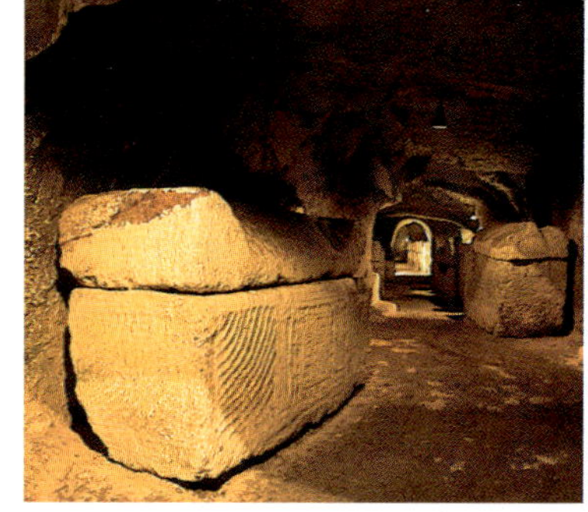

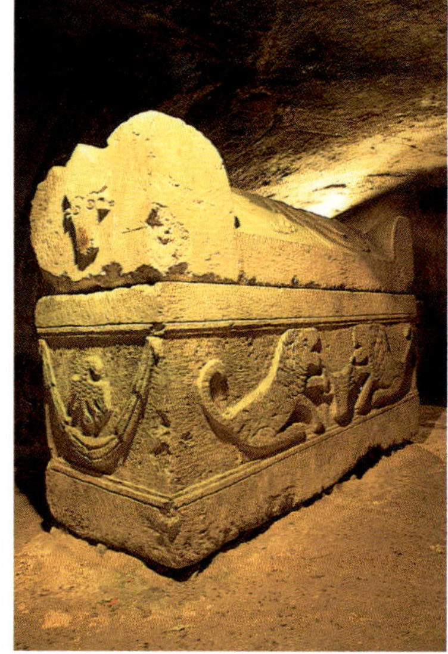

North of Safed there is a synagogue from the second or third century in the deserted village of Bar'am (left). Since 1936, catacombs with hundreds of sarcophagi were excavated (above). A museum was established in one of the catacombs (page right, right).

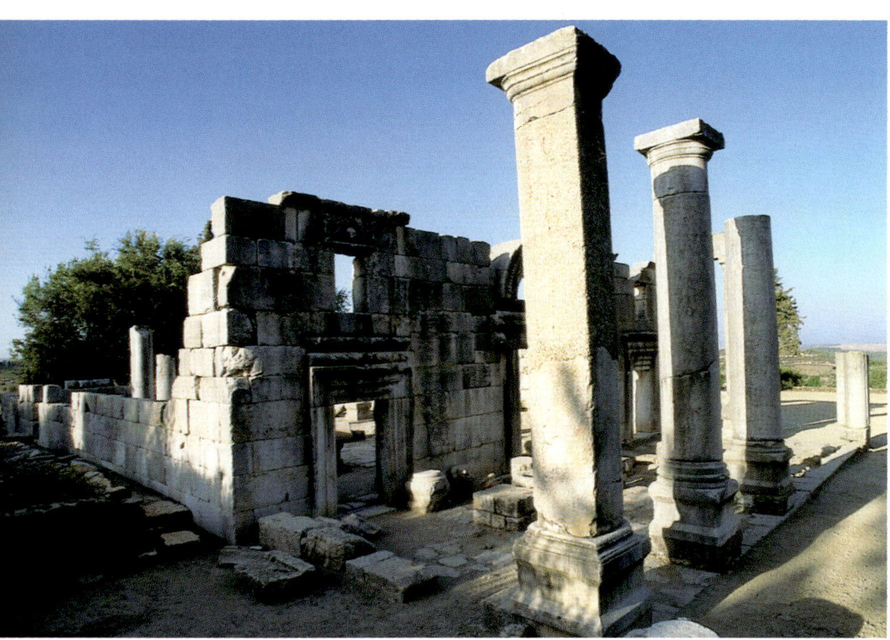

most important sites in the Holy Land for Christian pilgrims is a purely Palestinian town. The historic old city is inhabited by about 50,000 Arabs today with around 30,000 Jews living in the new part of town known as Nazareth Illit. Tourists usually make a beeline for the Basilica of the Annunciation, the largest church in the Middle East. It stands on the site where the Archangel Gabriel announced to Mary that she would give birth to a divine Son.

In biblical times, during the lifetime of Jesus, Nazareth was a totally insignificant town. It was only after the Emperor Constantine declared Christianity to be the official religion of the empire that Nazareth began to come into its own. The church built by Constantine in 326 lasted as short a time as many churches after it. The present church is only about 30 years old and was designed by Giovanni Muzio, an architect from Milan. Today, the various treasures found during the course of the building

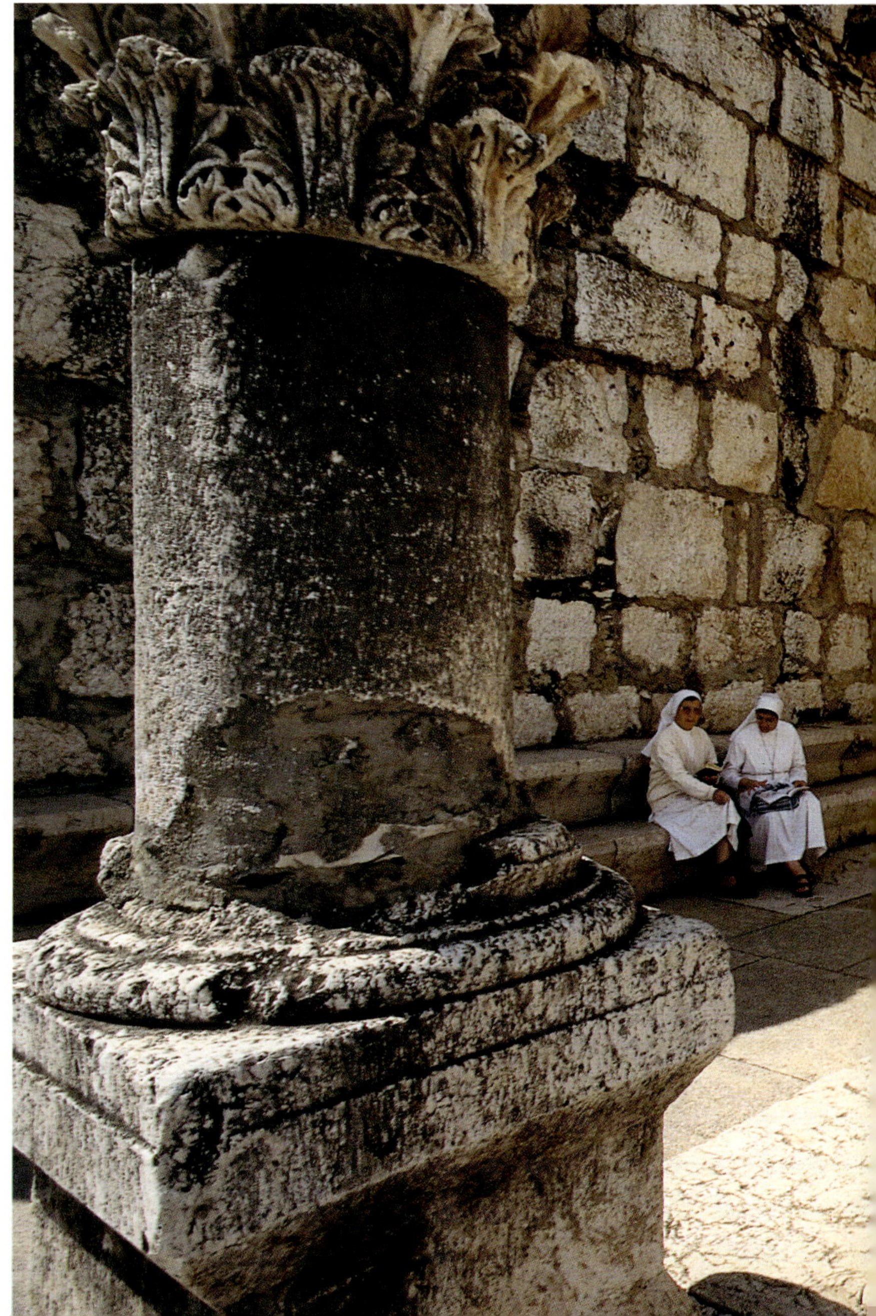

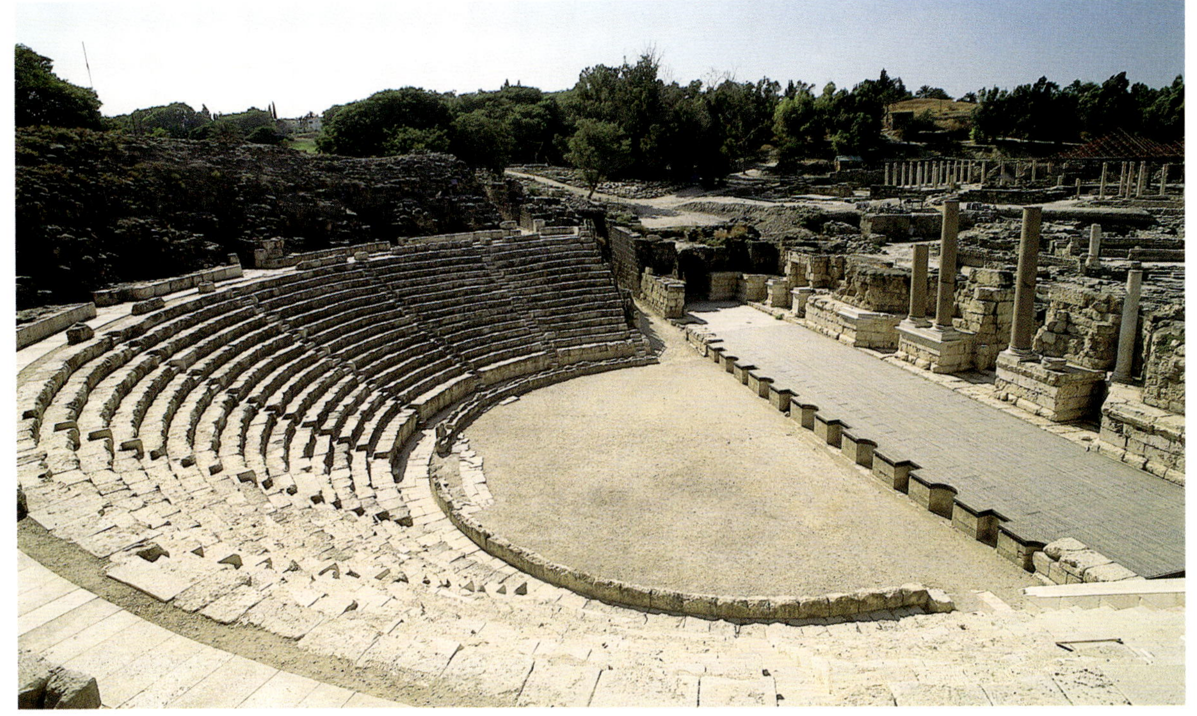

A treasure-trove for archaeologists: Bet Sh'ean's impressive Roman Theatre (left). The synagogue of Capernaum was built of white limestone (below).

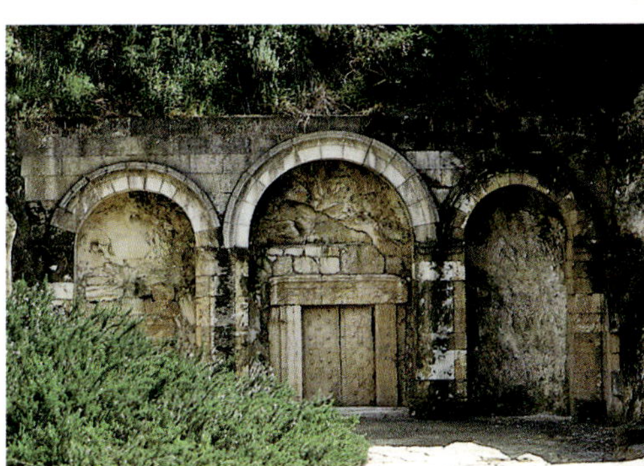

Bet She'an

'If Paradise is located in Israel, then Bet She'an is located at its main entrance', is how the Talmud refers to the quality of life in this city. Archaeologists have found remains from more than 6,000 years of history and more than 20 cities at Tel Bet She'an (Arabic: Tell el Husn). The Greeks named this place Scythopolis, City of the Scythians. During Roman times Bet She'an was the only city west of the Jordan and it was, of course, heavily populated; the Romans left behind Israel's best preserved Roman amphitheatre. As many as 8000 people could watch the spectacles here!

works can be viewed in the Franciscan Museum which lies within the enclosure of the Basilica. St. Joseph's Church, consecrated in 1914, is situated next to the Basilica of the Annunciation and can also be visited as can the eighteenth century Greek Orthodox Church of St Gabriel built over a spring from which the Virgin Mary is believed to have drawn water. You may also enjoy a walk through the labyrinth of narrow streets of the Arab souq, buying herbs and spices and watching the colourful comings and goings while sipping a cool drink.

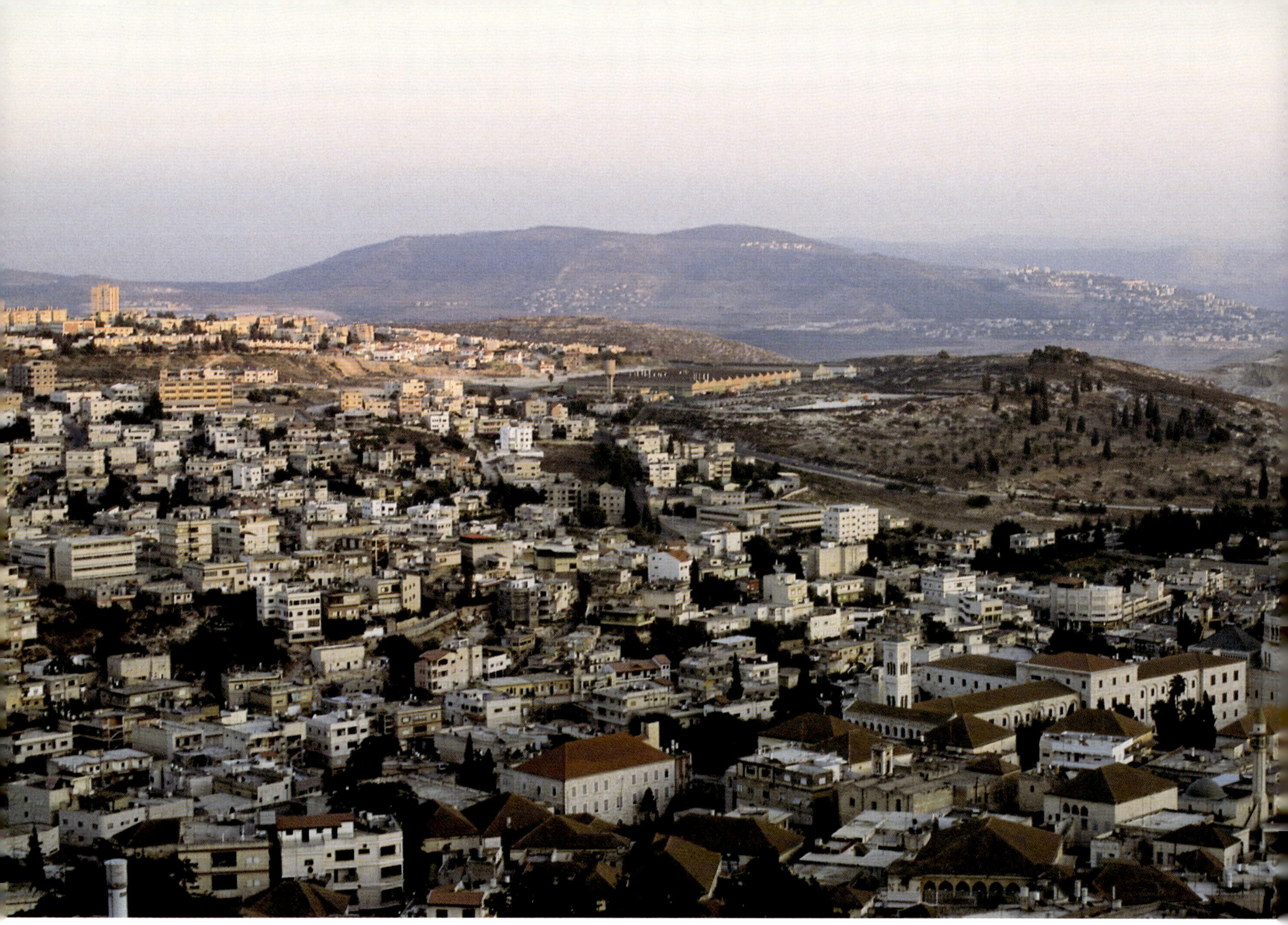

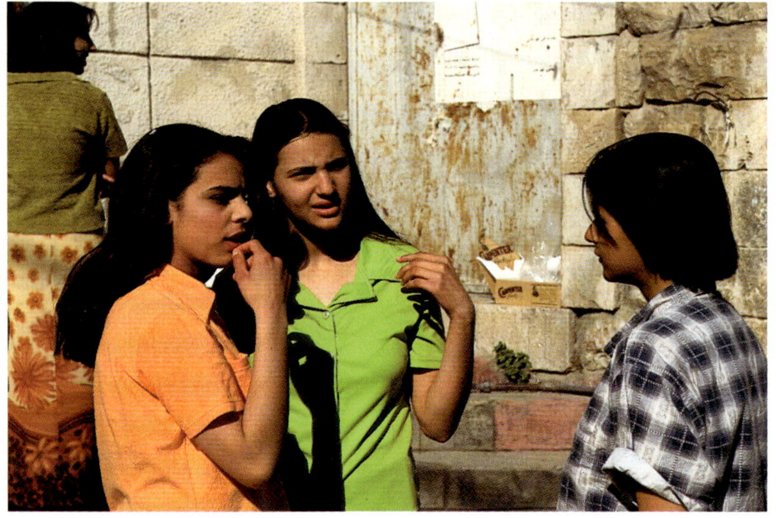

For and against Nature: In the Hula Valley

According to an Arab legend, the Hasbani, Dan and Hermon rivers were quarrelling with each other as to which of them was the most beautiful. God therefore made them an offer: if they would unite at a source and become one he would make them the most famous river in the world. And so the River Jordan was born. As with the Sea of Galilee, it is not size that makes it so significant. The Jordan is more of a narrow stream when it is not swollen by the waters of a plentiful winter rainfall. But apart from the three source rivers which spring from the Golan Heights – which up until 1967 were in Syria – and its most important tributary, the Yarmuk, it is the largest river in the otherwise arid land of Israel. No wonder, then, that it has always taken on an almost mystical significance for the people living around it, be they Jews, Christians or Muslims.

The River Jordan was not always a blessing to those liv-

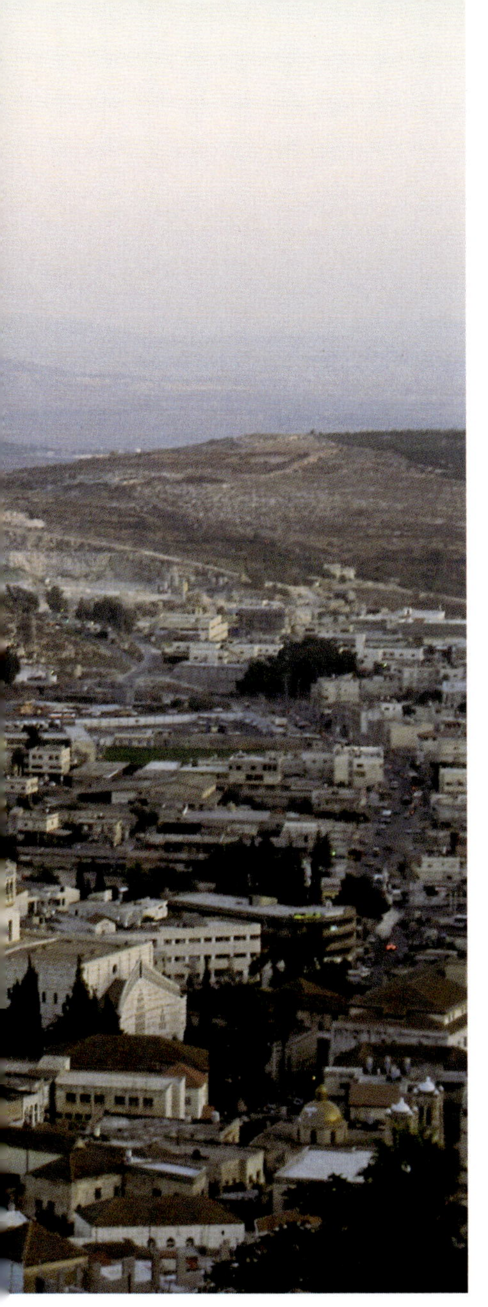

Nazareth (left), at the southern edge of the Hills of Galilee, is the city in which Jesus grew up. The Church of St Gabriel (right) and especially the Basilica of the Annunciation (below) attract streams of Christian pilgrims every day. Many couples come to get married at the Basilica of the Annunciation.

ing on its shores. Between Hazor, some 15 miles north of the Sea of Galilee, and Dan at the Lebanese border lies the *Hula Valley*. It used to be synonymous with swamps, malaria and wild animals such as bears and water buffalo. The Lebanese owners believed that the land could not be tilled and towards the end of the nineteenth century sold it to Zionist pioneers. The settlers' efforts to reclaim and cultivate the land continued into the middle of this century – not an easy task. Syrian troops, stationed at the 1,000 metre high plateau of the Golan Heights, frequently shot at Israeli farmers in the Hula Valley. This continued until 6 June 1967 when an attack on the two kibbutzim of Dan and Dafna triggered the Six Day War. Just three days

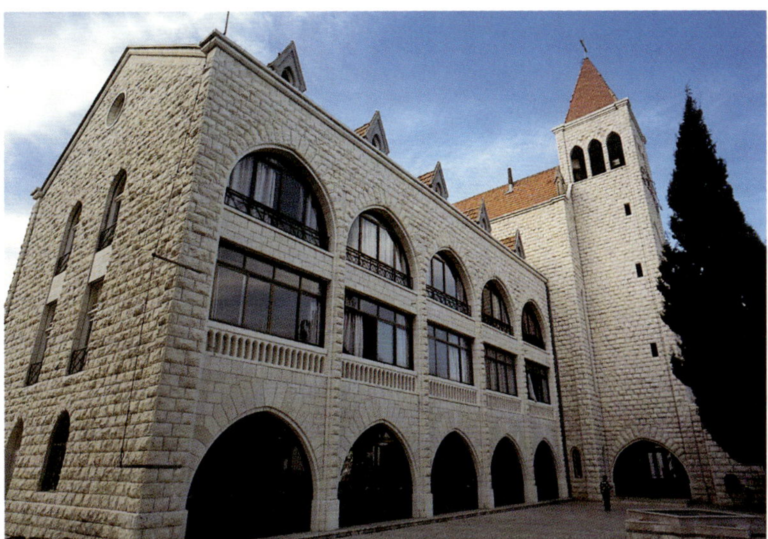

This mosque in Nazareth serves the people of the Muslim minority.

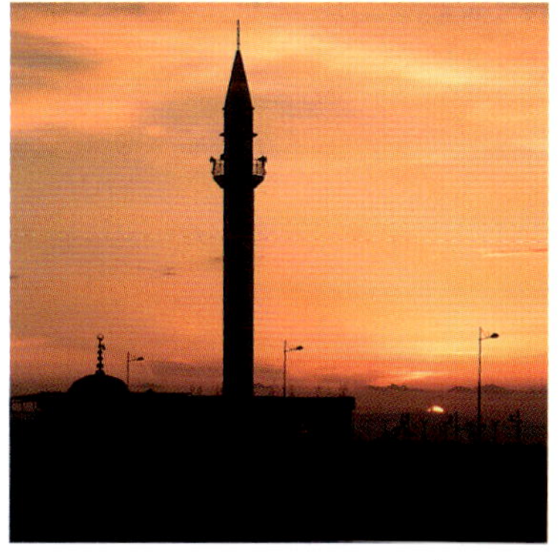

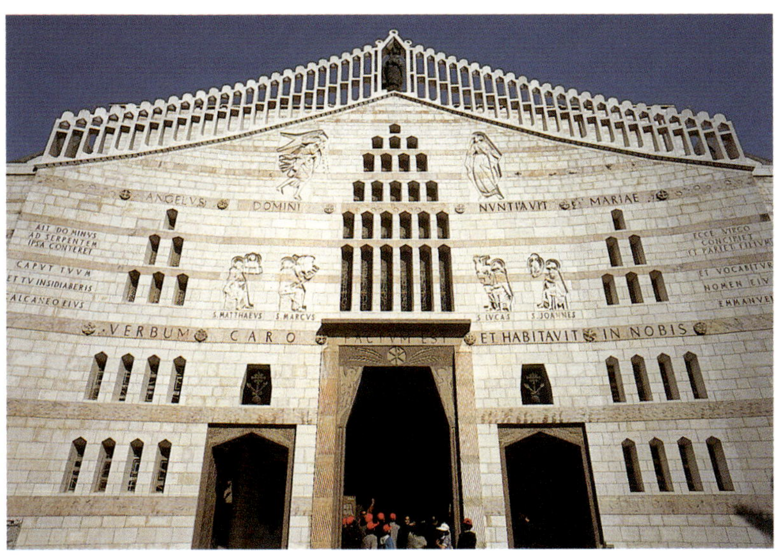

later, the Israelis conquered the Golan Heights, thus gaining overall control of Northern Galilee, and by acquiring the tributaries of the River Jordan they were assured of at least one third of their water supply. Few signs are left of these battles today. Agriculturally, the Hula Valley with its reserves, its fish ponds and the canalized Jordan River has become one of Israel's most productive regions. Its cultivation is considered to be the one of the greatest success stories of Zionist settlements. At the same time it is the birthplace of the Israeli environmental movement. In the mid-1950s, when it became apparent that cultivation of the land was threatening the fragile ecosystem where papyrus thickets and water lilies grew and pelicans, otters, waders and sea eagles made their home, environmentalists succeeded in having the north-western part of the valley declared a nature reserve – at just under 1000 acres it is the oldest nature reserve in Israel. Another reserve which is worth a visit is named after one of the sources of the Jordan River, at Banias (or Banyas) on the Golan Heights in the Nahal Hermon Nature Reserve.

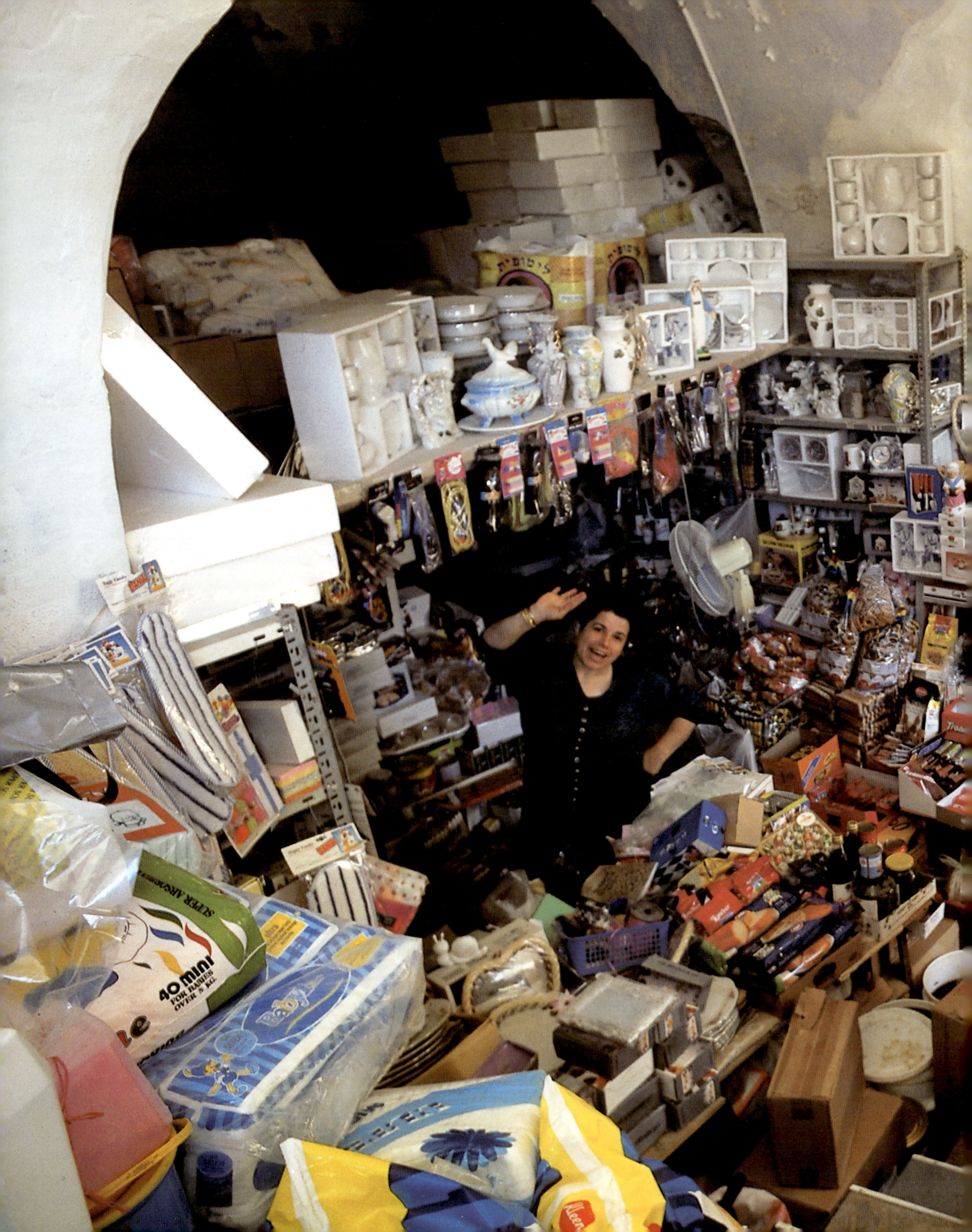
40 mini
FOR BABIES
OVER 5 KG.

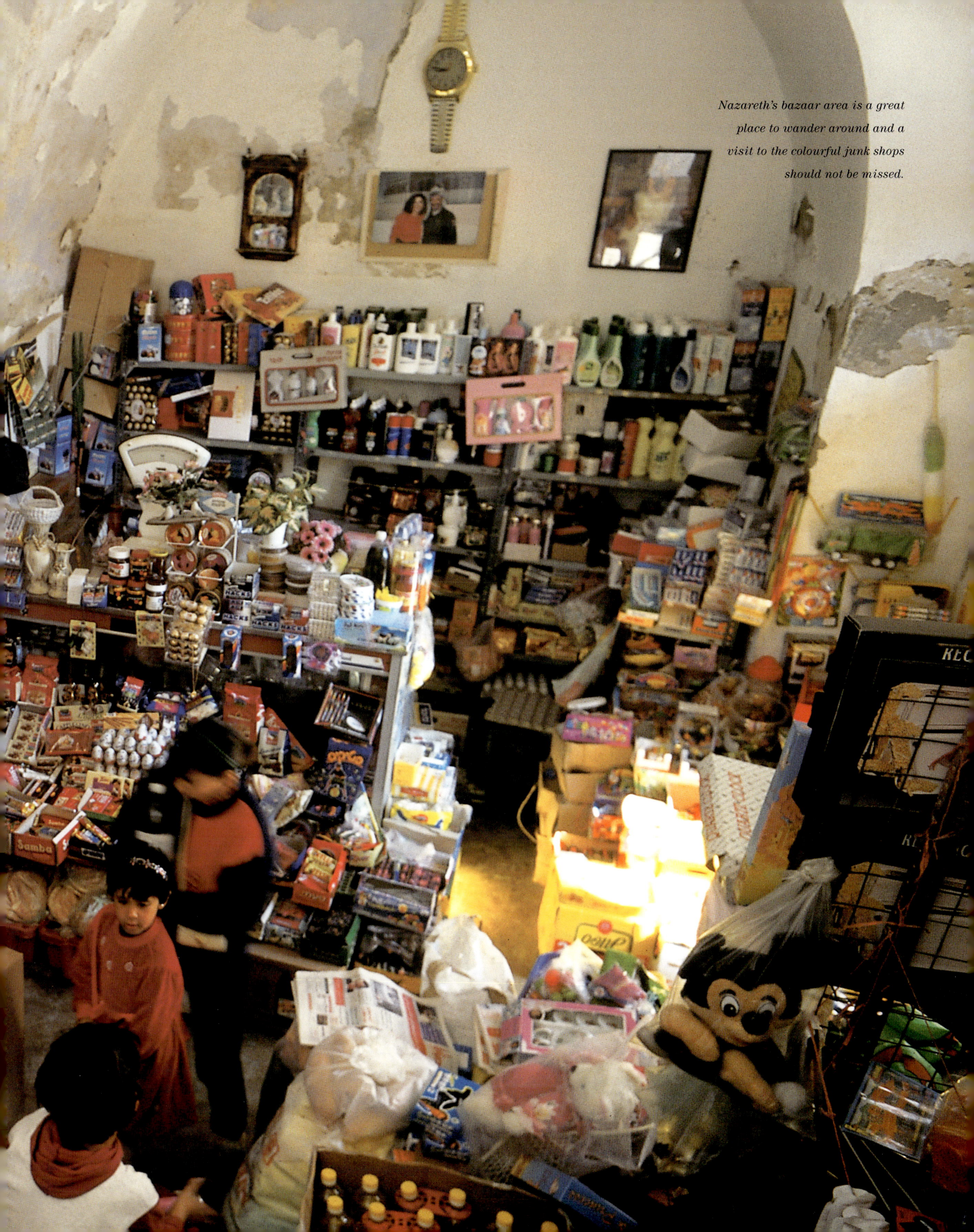

Nazareth's bazaar area is a great place to wander around and a visit to the colourful junk shops should not be missed.

Fasting, Eating, Celebrating

Traditional Jewish Festivals

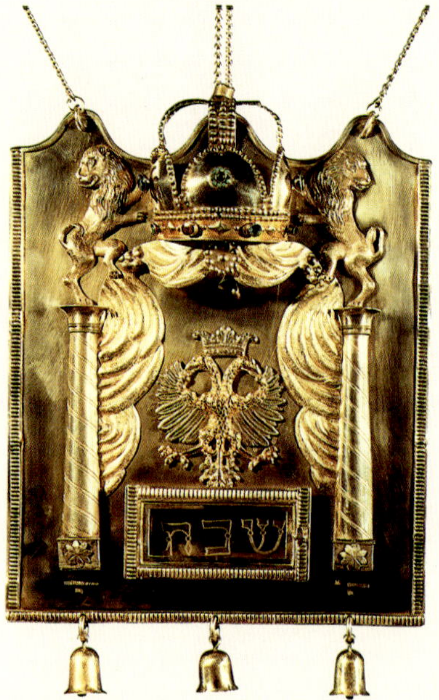

1 *A silver Torah plate (early 18th century, Vienna, Max Berger Judaica Collection). The Torah, or Five Books of Moses, tells the story of the Hebrew people from their beginnings to the death of Moses.*

Not a museum warden to be seen? No breakfast, even at the hotel, and the staff are conspicuous by their absence? In that case, it may well be *Yom Kippur* (Sept/Oct), because on this, the holiest Jewish holiday, everything and everyone rests and the pious fast for up to 25 hours. Yom Kippur concludes the period known as the Ten Days of Awe which determine life and begin on the Jewish New Year's Day of *Rosh Hashanah*.

Succot, the Feast of Tabernacles (later in Sept/Oct), commemorates the Exodus from Egypt, when the Israelites built huts in the wilderness where they slept. During the week of Succot, religious Jews construct huts made of branches in which they eat and sleep, and it is not unusual to see restaurant tables also decorated with bowers. *Simchat Torah* is the day on which joy is expressed for the Torah, the Rejoicing of the Law, and is on the last day of Succot, when the annual cycle of readings of the law comes to a close. The religious celebrate, dance, eat and drink, and there is an exuberant mood in the streets and squares. The candlelit children's processions held on this occasion are full of atmosphere.

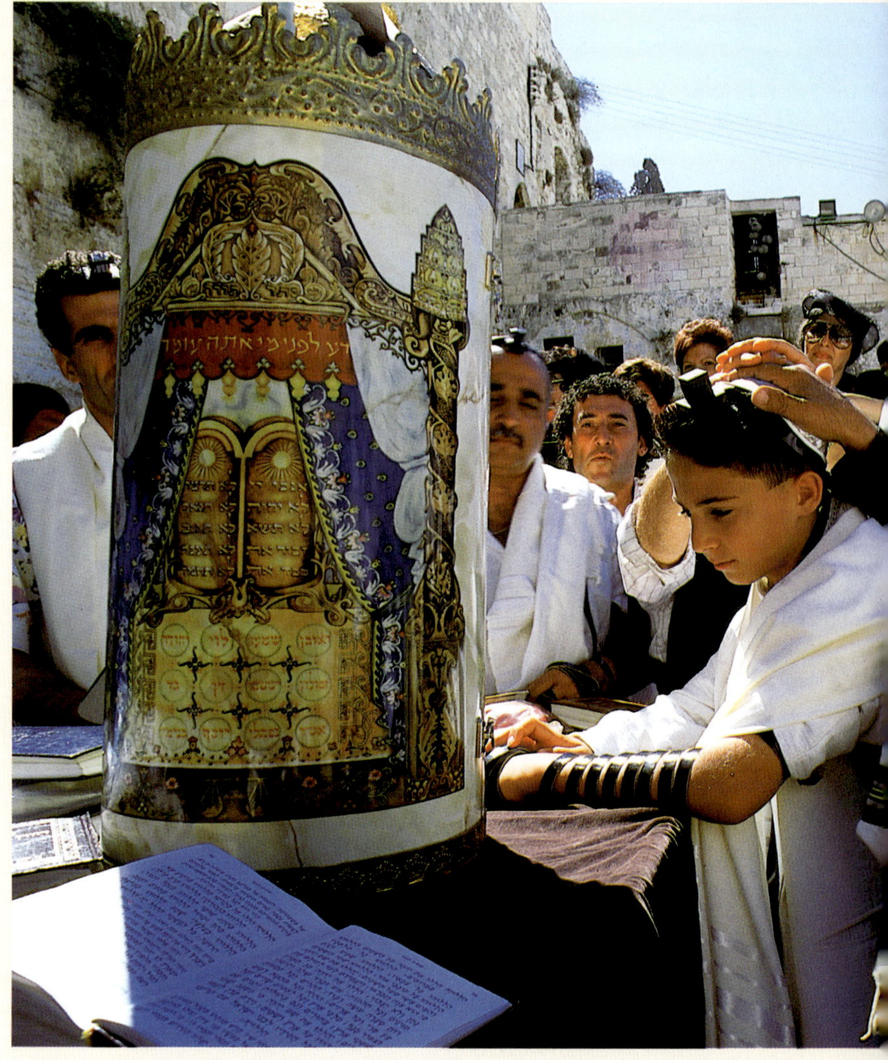

2

The Festival of Lights is *Hanukkah*. For one week in December, a new candle is lit on the eight-branched candle-

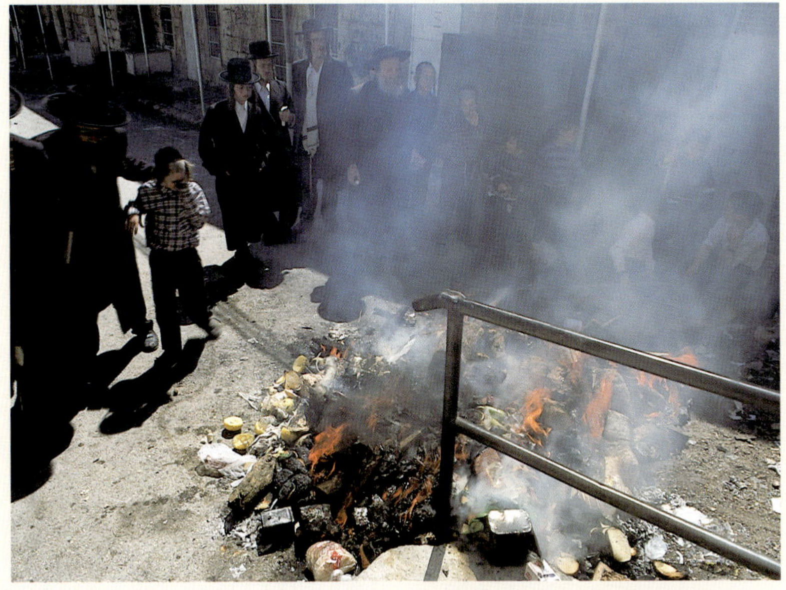

3

3 *Burning leavened bread before the feast of Passover.* 4 *Purim, a festival for children.* 5 *Many foreign Jews visit Israel to celebrate the Feast of Tabernacles.* 6 *Bar Mitzvah celebration.*

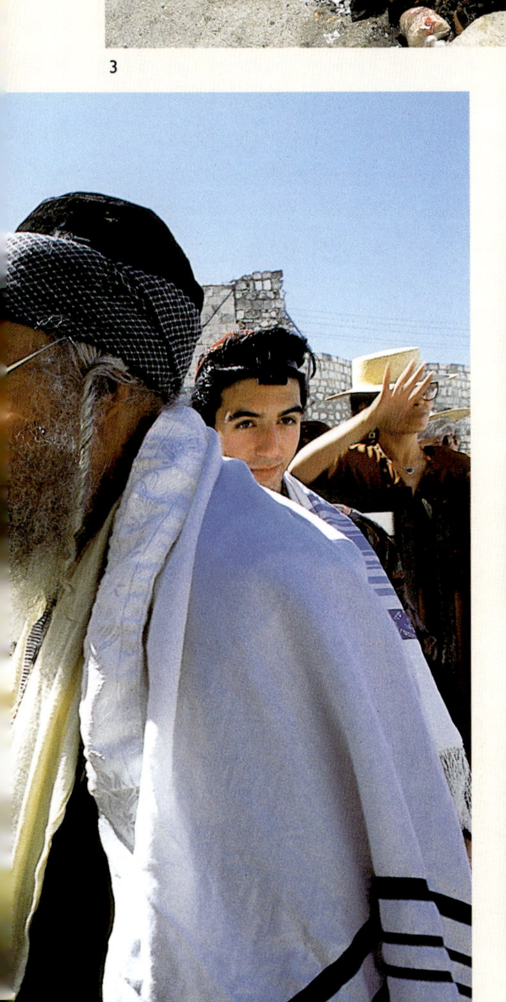

2 *At a Bar-Mitzvah, the official initiation of thirteen-year-old Jewish boys into the Jewish community.*

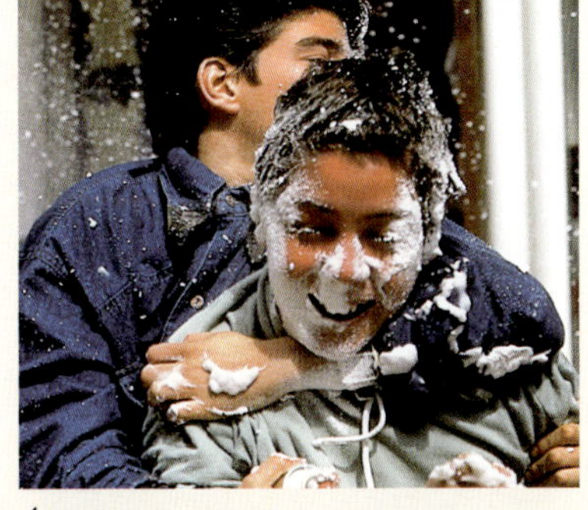

4

6

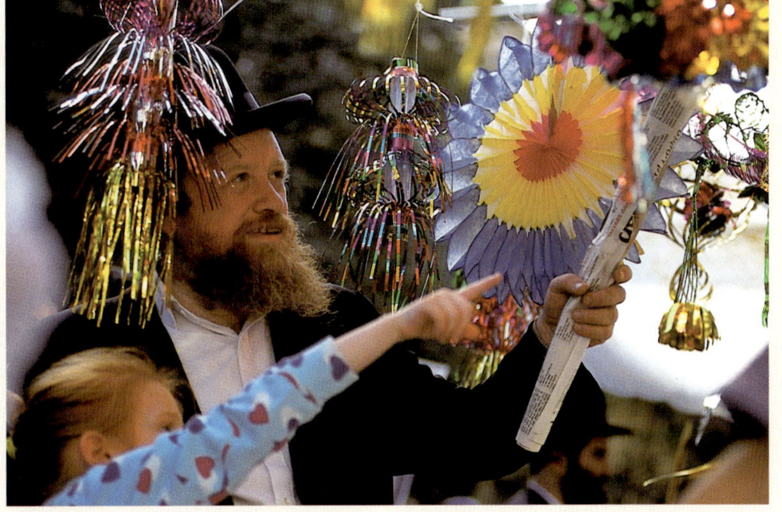

5

stick, the Hanukkah lamp. This festival is celebrated to commemorate the Maccabeans' victory over the Greeks more than 2,100 years ago. Children and adults wear historic costume, visit friends and give each other gifts of home-made doughnuts and potato pancakes. Eight-branched candlesticks are put up in offices, banks and post offices, department stores illuminate their displays – the entire country is bathed in light.

Food, or the conscious renunciation of food plays an important role in all Jewish festivals: during the spring festival of *Tu B'Shevat* (Jan/ Feb), fifteen different kinds of fruit are tasted, thanks are given to God for nature and her plentiful gifts to humanity. On this day, children plant saplings. The whole family assembles for *Passover*, probably the best known of all Jewish festivals. In accordance with tradition, the patriarch reads chapters from the Bible which deal with the Exodus from Egypt, and in between the family enjoys a feast of traditionally prepared dishes.

During the Jewish carnival celebrations of *Purim* (Feb/ March), children dress up as Queen Esther or the villain Haman. This is to commemorate the rescue of Persian Jews by the courageous Jewess Esther during the 6th century BC.

Over One Hundred Miles of Beaches

Tel Aviv and the Mediterranean Coast

The men in their black suits probably looked a bit out of place as they gathered around in the sand dunes on the beach for a group photograph. Behind them, the ancient harbour town of Jaffa which had become too constricting for them and 60 other Jewish families. Before them, the Mediterranean Sea and the vision of something extraordinarily new. On this day, in the year 1908, the foundations were laid for the first city in modern Palestine. At first, its founders gave it the modest name of 'Achusat Beit', meaning 'estate'. Fifteen years later Meir Dizengoff, Tel Aviv's mayor, renamed the few streets by the rather flowery name of Tel Aviv or 'Hill of Spring'.

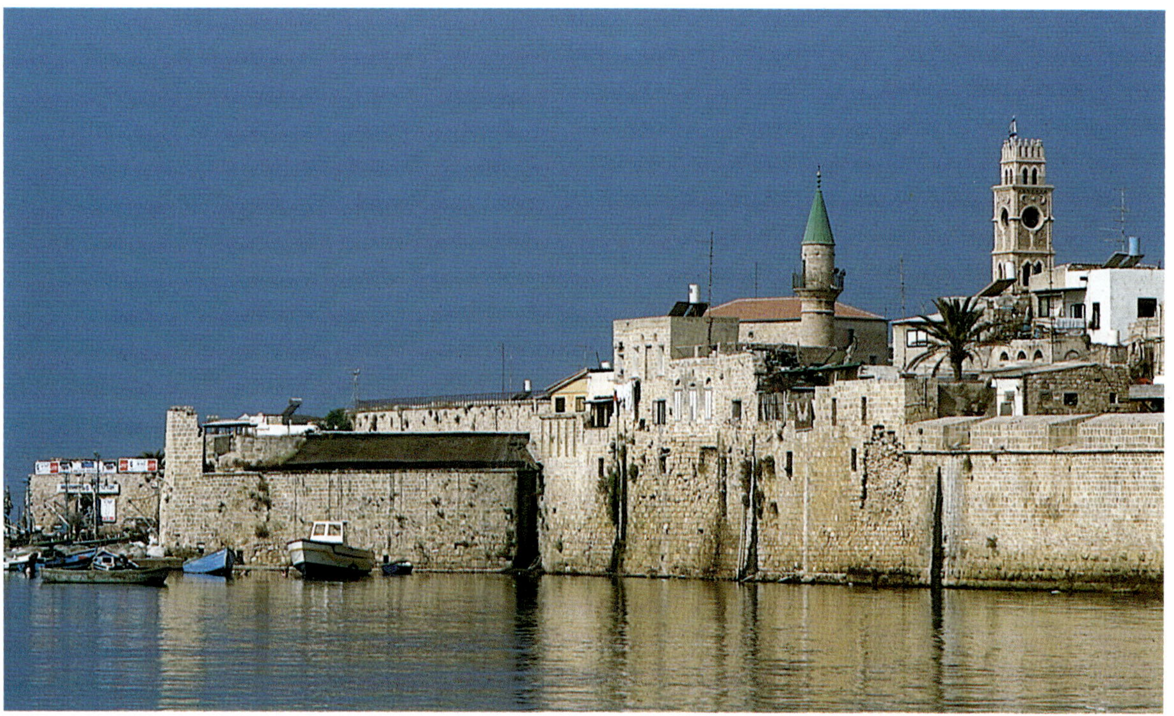

Acre – historic town on the Mediterranean: Crusaders and Turks have all left their mark in Acre by building churches, mosques and a spectacular city wall.

The immigrants of the first *aliya*, or wave of immigrants, (1880–1903) built large, collectively farmed estates on this coastal strip. This was former 'enemy territory', the land of the Philistines which had been conquered by King David, but then lost. From an ideological perspective it offered ideal possibilities, because the immigrants to this territory did not want to conquer the land by the rule of the Bible, but 'by the sweat of their brow'. In fact, this region had always been inhabited and was not a blank page with no history and no people as the Zionists had hoped.

Idyllic Harbour Town of Jaffa

Jaffa is full of history. When Noah's Ark had finally landed on Mount Ararat after its long journey, Noah's youngest son discovered a hill with a splendid view on to a wide bay. He named this favoured place Jaffa, after the Hebrew 'yafo' meaning 'beautiful'. Even if the ancient seafaring town, one of the oldest cities in the world, is almost swallowed up by the pulsating neighbouring city of Tel Aviv, it still stubbornly maintains its orien-

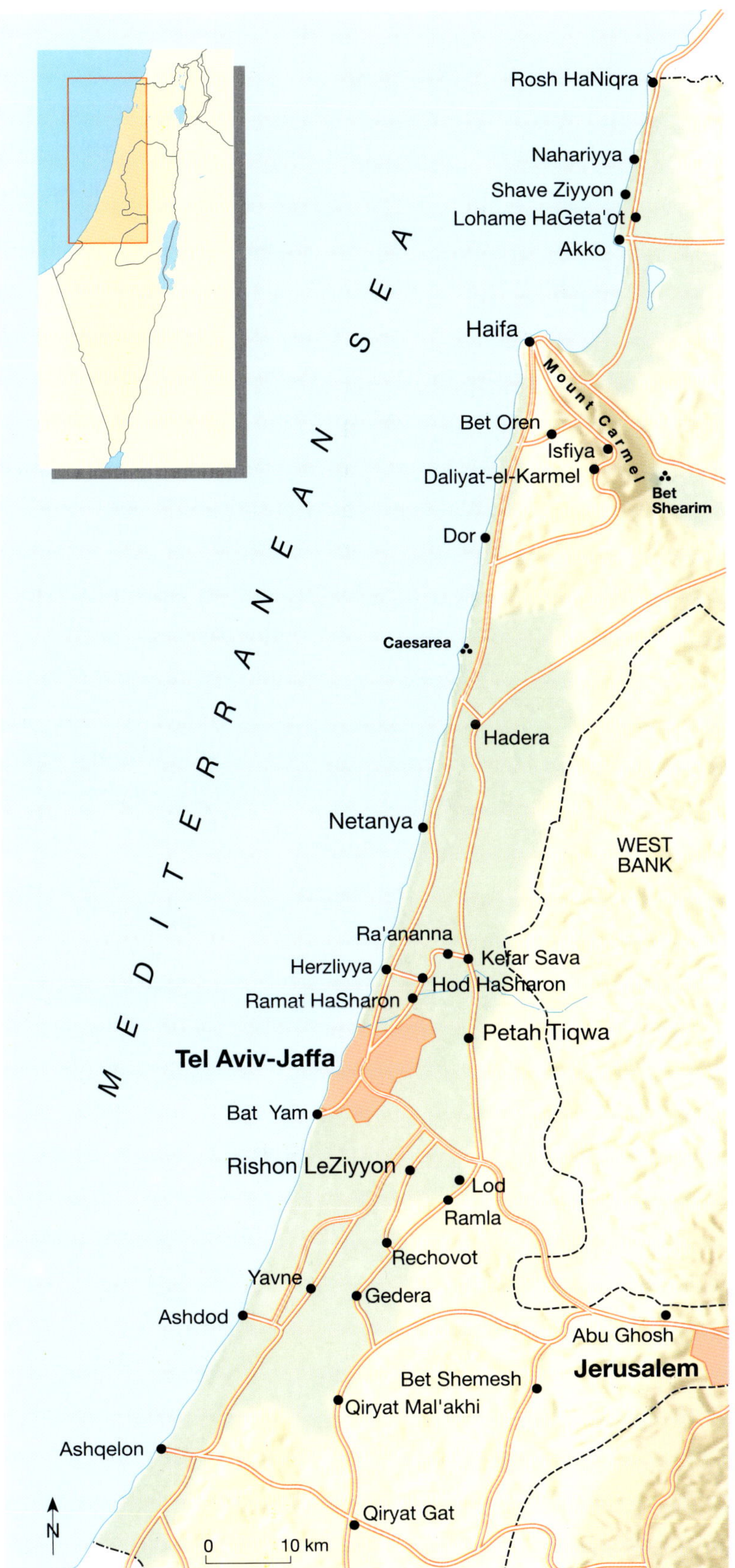

tal identity in the winding, narrow alleyways. The entrance to the Old City is marked by the *Clock Tower*, a proud landmark of its rich history. Each of the windows depicts a historic event. The *Museum of Antiquities* also manages to arouse enthusiasm for this city's convoluted history. The *Church and Monastery of St Peter* next to it was built on the remains of a Crusader fortress. From here is a spectacular view onto *Andromeda's Rock* where, according to legend, Perseus rescued Andromeda. Those of you still dreaming of ancient times will be brought into the twentieth century with a jolt when you see the ultra-modern *Tourist Centre* on Pasteur Street. On *Kikar Kedumin*, Jaffa's main square in the renovated part of the town you might be studying simple labels describing the excavation site when you are suddenly startled by a bombastic multivisual show. Exciting contrasts which make this ancient and yet young country so charming.

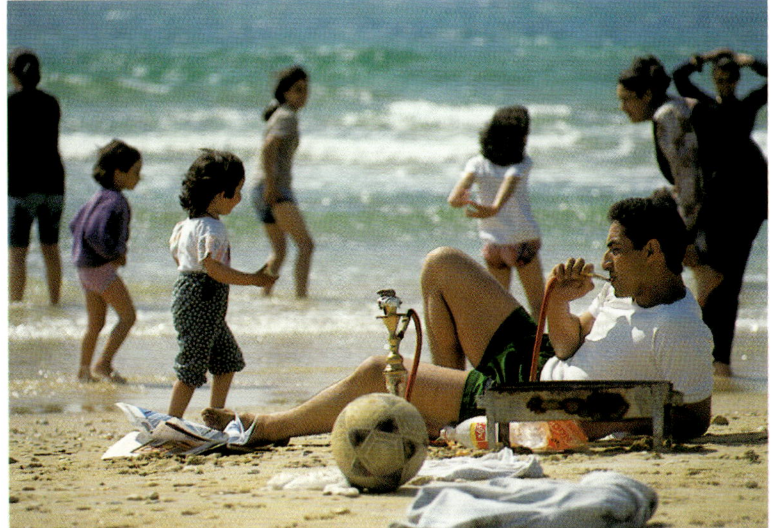

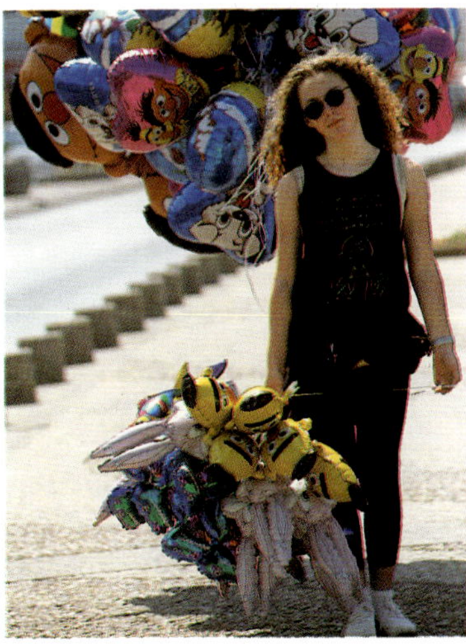

Haifa, situated between the Mediterranean Sea and Mount Carmel is described as the 'Water gate into the Promised Land' and also as the 'City of work'. However, the people here still know how to relax and enjoy themselves.

Modern department stores and oriental markets, young people on mobile phones and orthodox Jews – there's nothing you won't see in Tel Aviv.

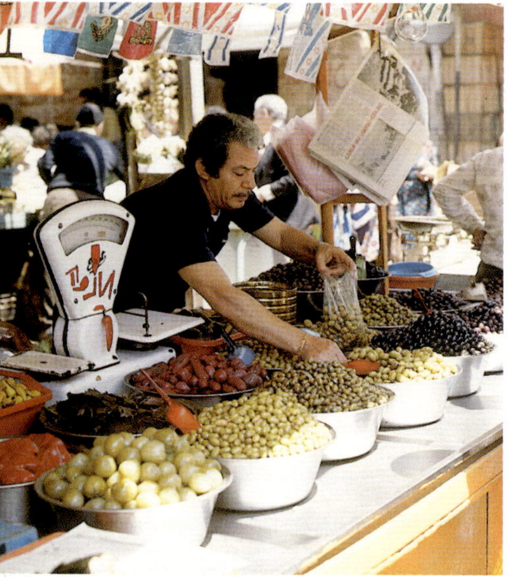

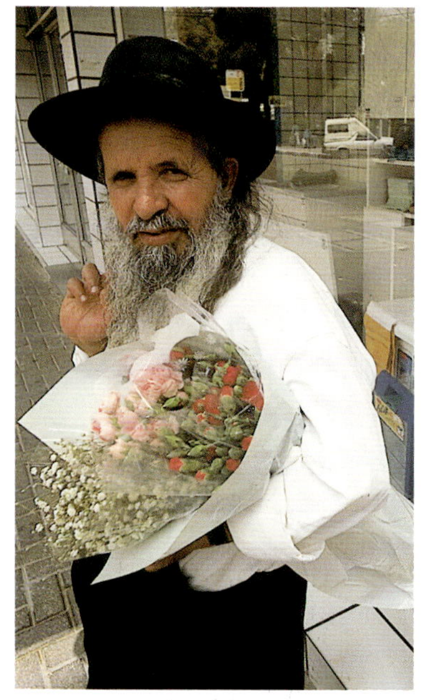

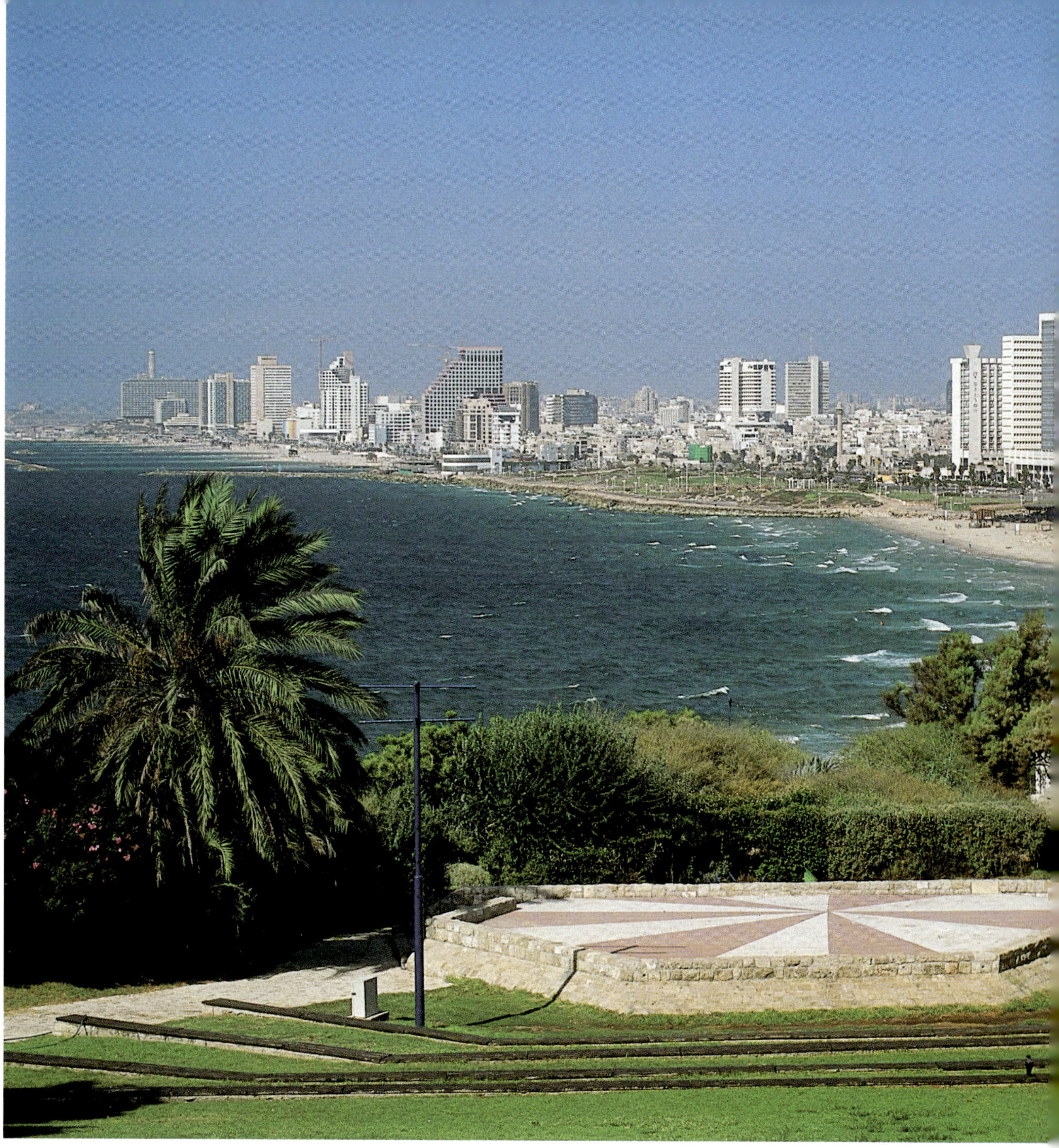

The City that Never Sleeps: Tel Aviv

Tel Aviv is a metropolis which reinvents itself every day and whose people couldn't care less about its historic past. Not many of the original houses built by the city's founders in a hotch-potch of oriental and colonial styles are still standing. Here, in a city literally built on sand, which does not rest on thousands of years of history, only the young, the new, the current count for something. No fashion is crazy enough, no trends so outlandish as not to be snapped up by Tel Aviv. And the people of Tel Aviv build as they live: avoiding irritating decrees where possible, only change and growth is relevant. Where there were just a few streets in 1908, by 1926 some 40,000 inhabitants were living in 3,000 houses, and there was a power station making Tel Aviv the first city in the land with electricity. There are still some architectural relics of this period, mostly in a fairly

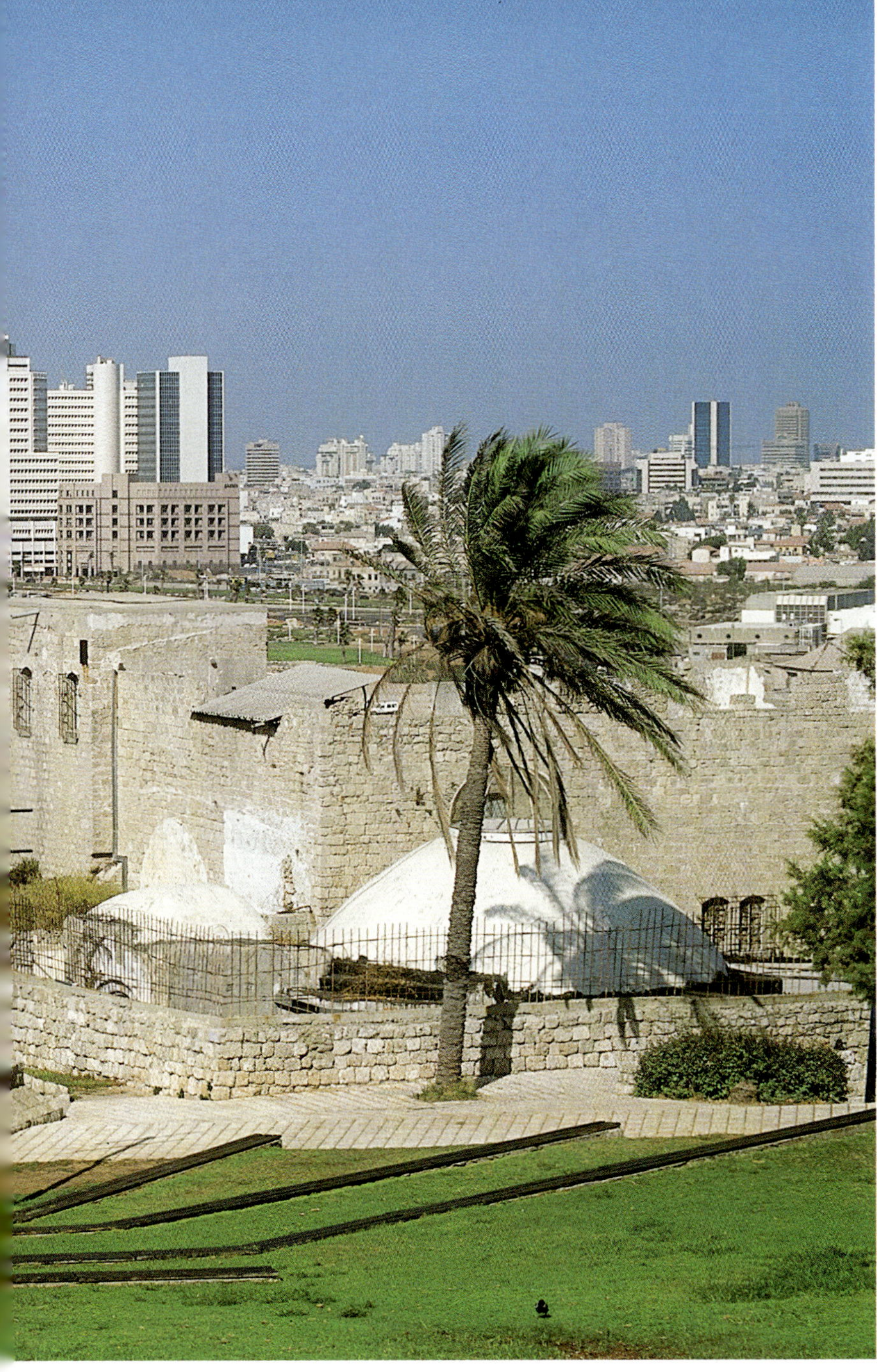

run-down condition in the southern part of the city, which today boasts a population of some 350,000 people. Have a look at the *Nahalat Binyamin* pedestrian mall, at *Rothschild Boulevard* and *Allenby Street*.

The refugees from Nazi Germany brought a new style with them. Tel Aviv has the world's largest and most beautiful array of Bauhaus architecture. But other than the examples of *Bauhaus buildings* there is not much left of the culture of the yekkes or German Jews. However, at the *Café Vienna*,

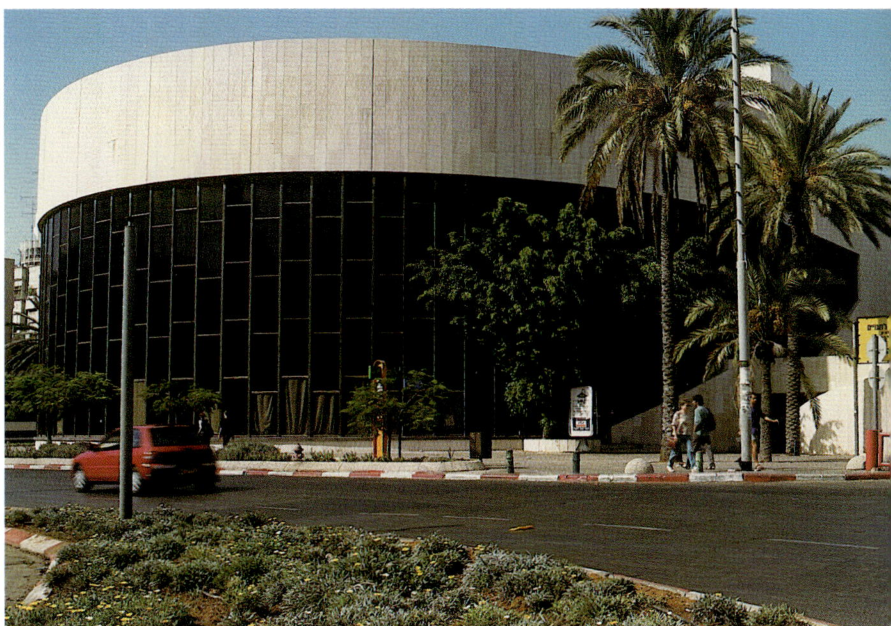

the last of the yekke restaurants, of which there were once so many, one or two of the old guard still meet to be greeted in German by the Hungarian head waiter and to order a Wiener Schnitzel which tastes better than any you will be served in the whole of Austria.

But don't think Tel Aviv is a sentimental place. Tel Aviv mourns nothing and no one, at least not for long. Here, people are far too preoccupied with finding out which café, which restaurant, which bar is the current 'in' place to be seen at. When the muezzin calls devout Muslims to evening prayer in Jerusalem and the ringing of church bells ushers in the peace and quiet of the evening, that is when Tel Aviv really wakes up and gets going. Traffic jams way beyond midnight are not unusual in the City that never Sleeps, where everyone and everything is always on the go. Various parts of town which had been declining for years and turned into slum areas are suddenly being rediscovered by artists followed very soon by yuppies seeking out the trendiest new areas. A good example is the neighbourhood of Neve Zedek, originally built in 1887. No one would have willingly set foot

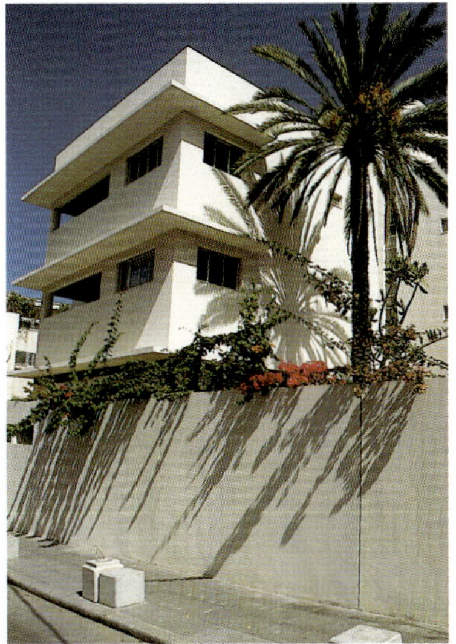

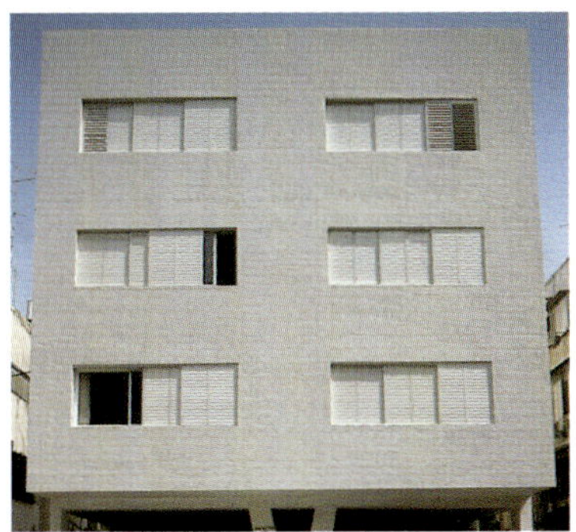

Skyscrapers are one aspect which defines Tel Aviv's skyline (above). The other is the Bauhaus architecture which was developed in the thirties (below left and right). Tel Aviv's 'Temple to the Dramatic Arts', the Habimah Theatre (right)

in this corner of Tel Aviv until recently. It was an area tightly controlled by drug dealers and pimps until the Bat Sheva Dance Company came along one day and used a old colonial house to establish their cultural centre. Once restoration began on the *Suzanne Dellal Centre* young artists started moving into this area. These days it is being renovated at great expense.

Even in the chaos of Tel Aviv with over one million inhabitants, there are a number of outstanding places from which a comfortable walk takes you to the centre of town. These include

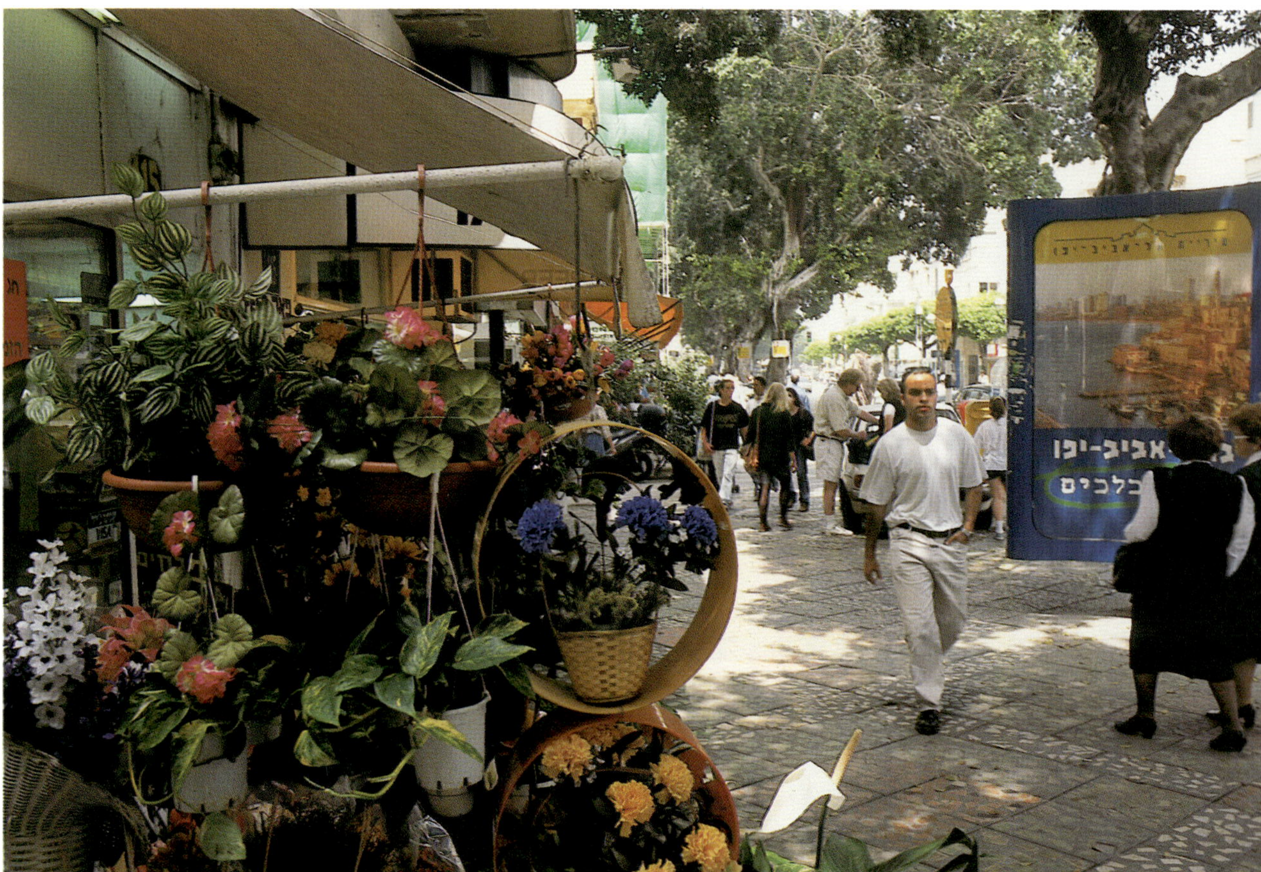

Dizengoff Street named after Tel Aviv's first Mayor Meir Dizengoff is where people come to stroll and people-watch. There are restaurants and cafés one after another. Kassit,(page right top) one of the oldest coffee shops in town, is the meeting place for writers, actors, politicians – and perfectly ordinary people.

Dizengoff Square and the street of the same name, perfect for a stroll to the *Cultural Centre* with the Helena Rubinstein Pavilion and its collection of modern Israeli art. Then there is the *Tel Aviv Museum of Art*, also worth a visit. Starting at the *Habimah Theatre* built in the Bauhaus style one can walk along Rothschild Boulevard to Tel Aviv's tallest building. The *Migdal Shalom* towers over the city and the Observatory on the 34th floor offers a tremendous panoramic view. Immediately behind the Tower is the start of the *Yemenite Quarter*: exotic, narrow, full of enticing smells of herbs and spices – Arabia in miniature.

The most extraordinary thing about this mixture of the Levant and the USA named Tel Aviv is how normal it all is. Nowhere else in Israel is such an effort made to concentrate on life

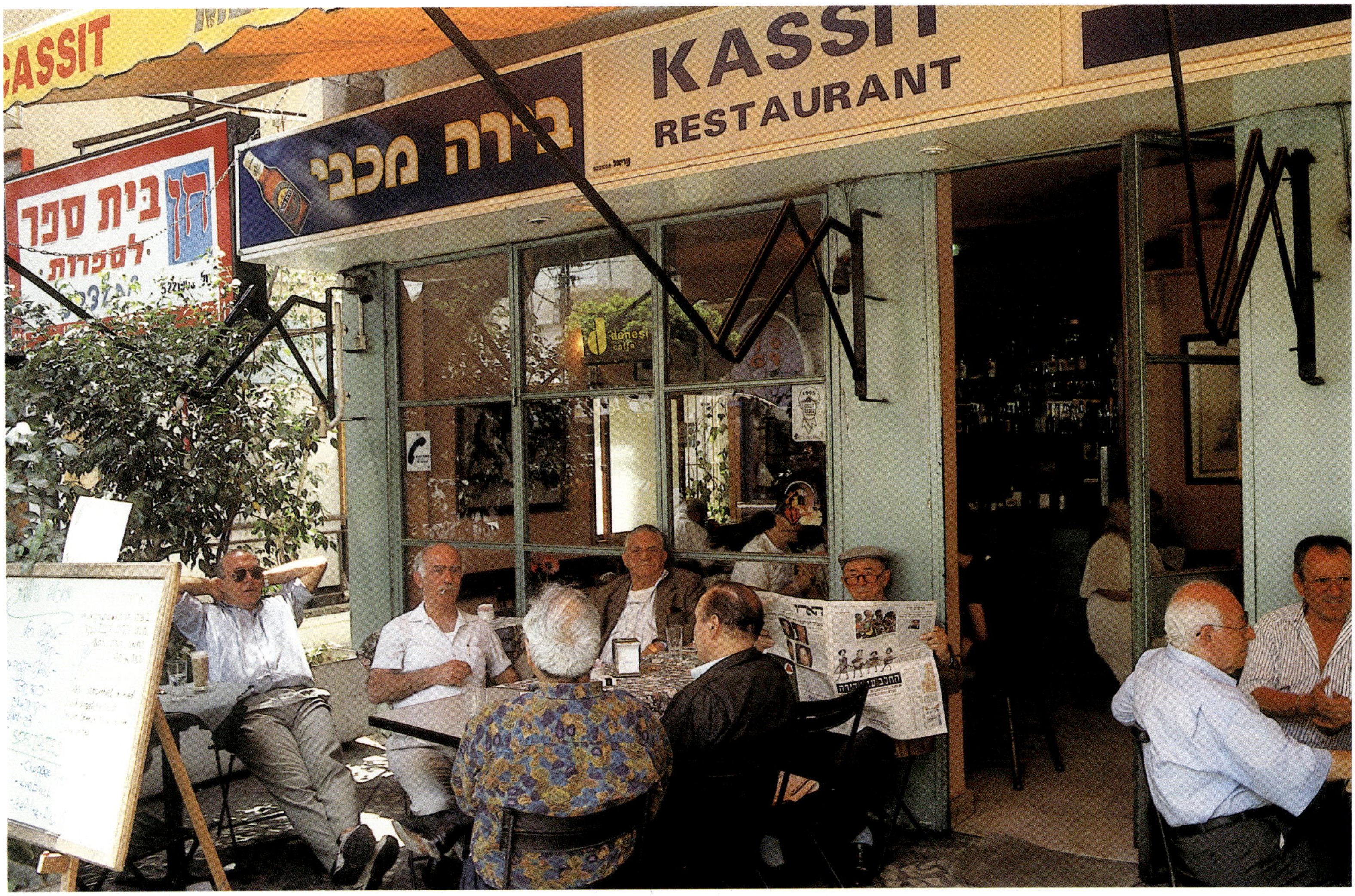

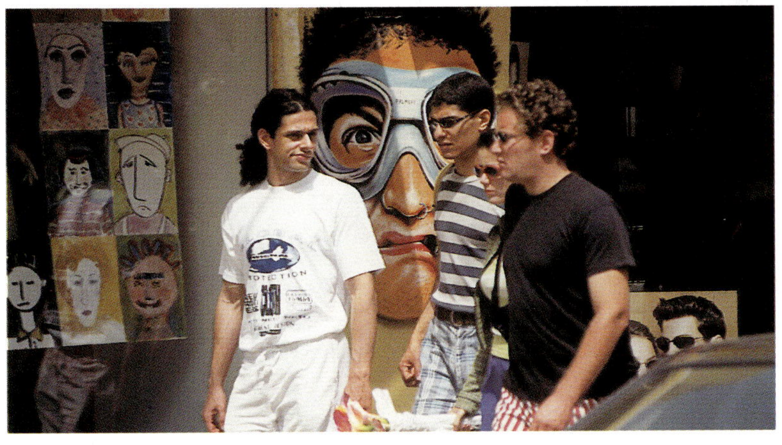

Tel Aviv is a young city. It is here that the latest fashions are designed. It is here that culture and entertainment reign supreme.

outside the Israeli-Palestinian conflict. The best example of this is on *Sheinkin Street* in the evening. Trendy joints are situated next door to shops from the earliest days, young people with no thought of politics enjoy an evening out with friends or go shopping in the new boutiques, and old peace activists meet up at the *Café Tamar* which is decorated with all the old political caricatures and slogans ever thought up by Israel's left-wing. Even the most orthodox fanatics are gripped by the spirit of tolerance in these surroundings. If Herzl had lived to see the founding of the Jewish state he might have settled right here.

The Mediterranean Coast – Pioneer Country and Illegal Immigrants

When the pioneers first arrived, the coastal region consisted primarily of sand dunes and malaria-infested swamps. Many people died here before orange groves, banana plants and cotton were established. Yet just a few years later, citrus fruit from Palestine became the leading export. When the con-

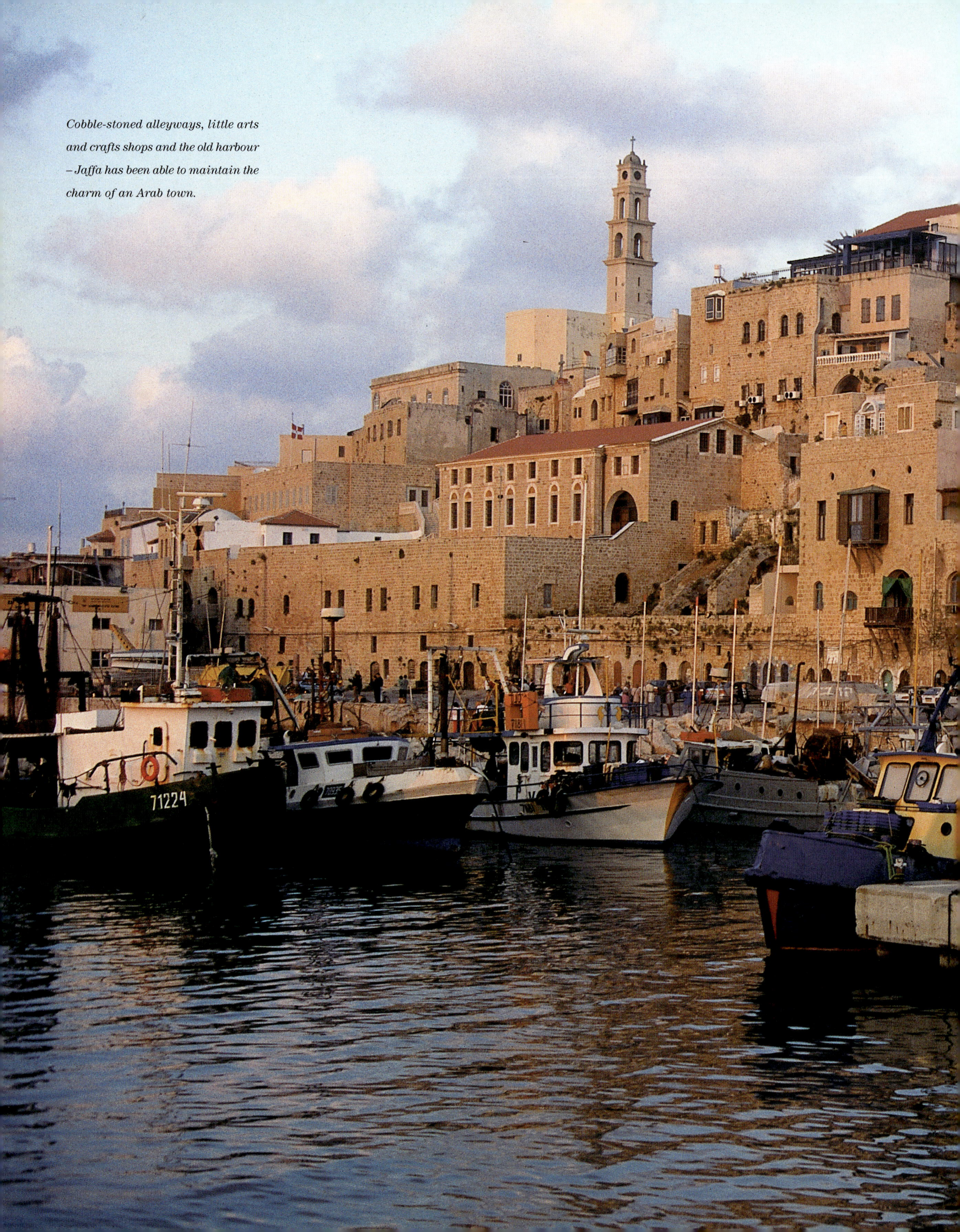

Cobble-stoned alleyways, little arts and crafts shops and the old harbour – Jaffa has been able to maintain the charm of an Arab town.

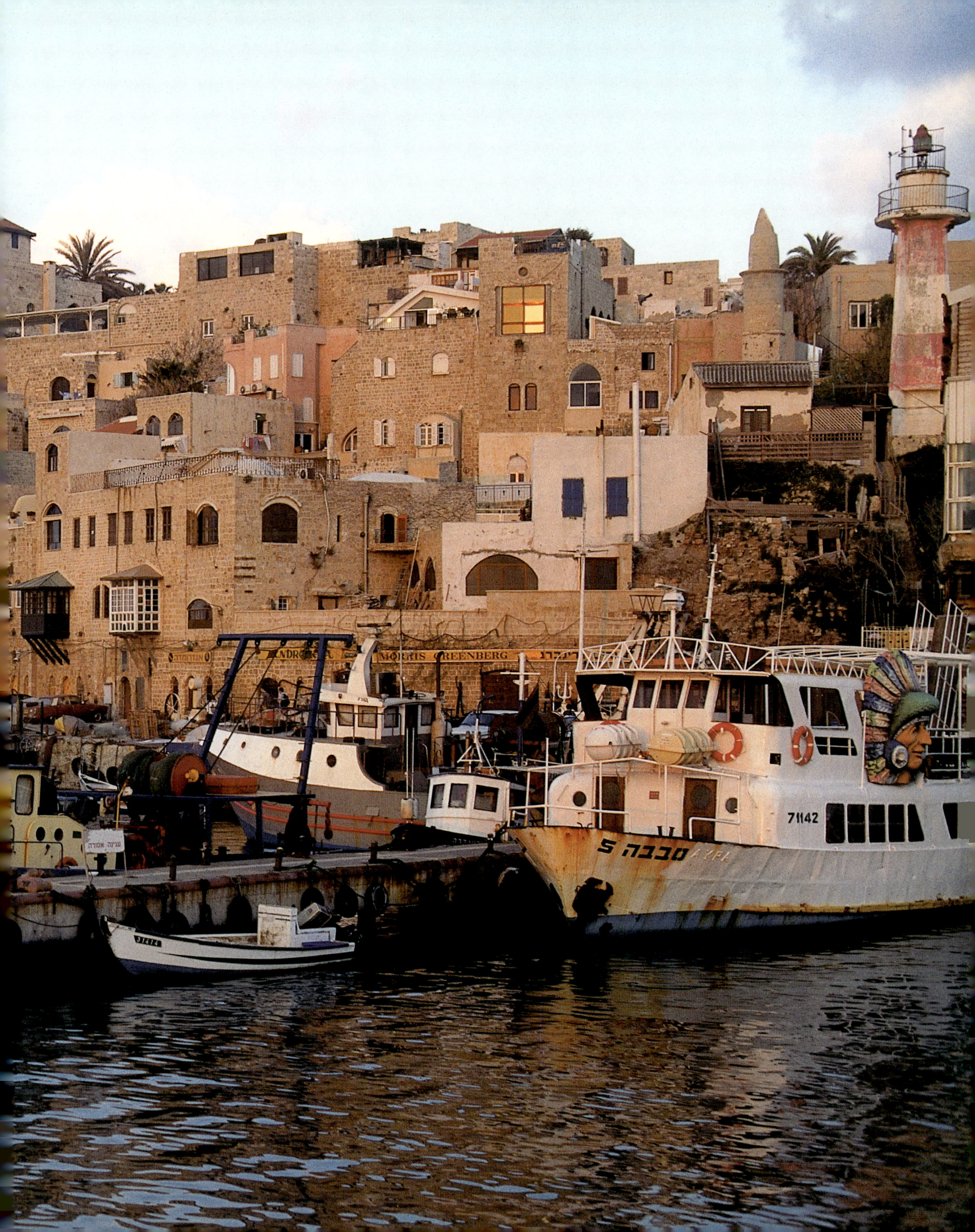
MORRIS GREENBERG
סבבה 5
71142

Caesarea offers a perfect holiday combining swimming with culture (right). The aqueduct provided the Roman city with spring water (centre). Ruins are waiting to be discovered even in the sea, some immediately visible, some under water (below).

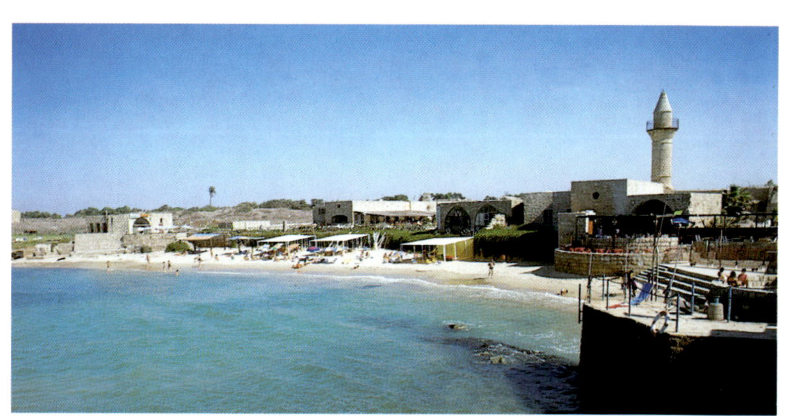

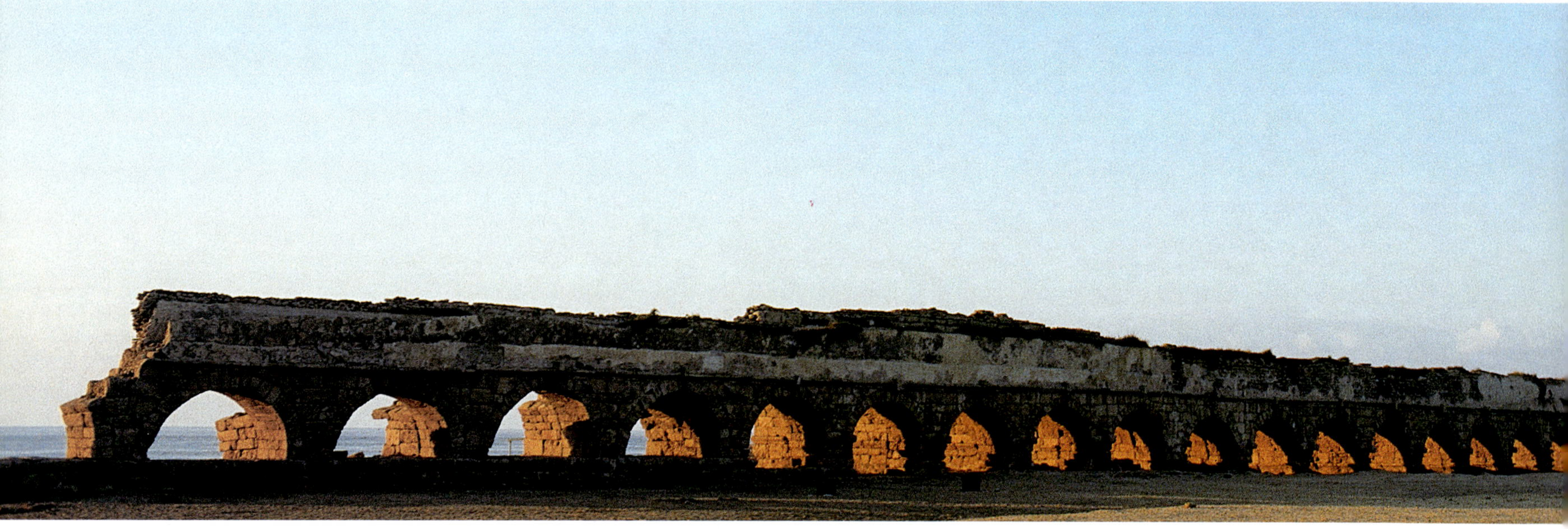

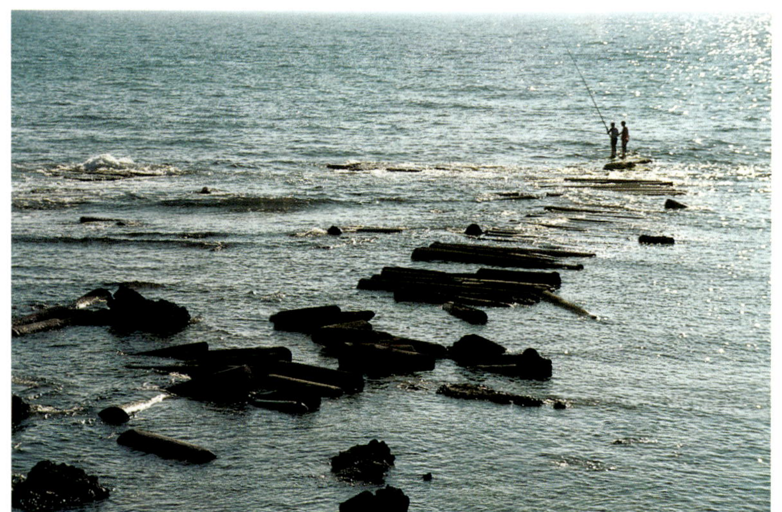

flicts between Arabs and Jews intensified, the British Mandate decreed that the influx of Zionist immigrants should be limited and prohibited the establishment of further settlements. But the Jews didn't pay much attention to this decree. New settlements continued to be created in secret and immigrants were brought into the country illegally, mostly on derelict freighters always attempting to evade the patrolling British ships. This was how a group of German Jews established *Nahariya* in 1934, quickly discovering that life on one of the Mediterranean's most beautiful coastal areas was good. The little town offered the refugees a new home and fast developed into a popular seaside resort.

Creativity and an Enterprising Spirit: in the former country of pioneers

Viewed superficially, there is not much left of the pioneer country on the coast. What were once small individual towns have

Ruins on the Beach

The Excavations of Caesarea

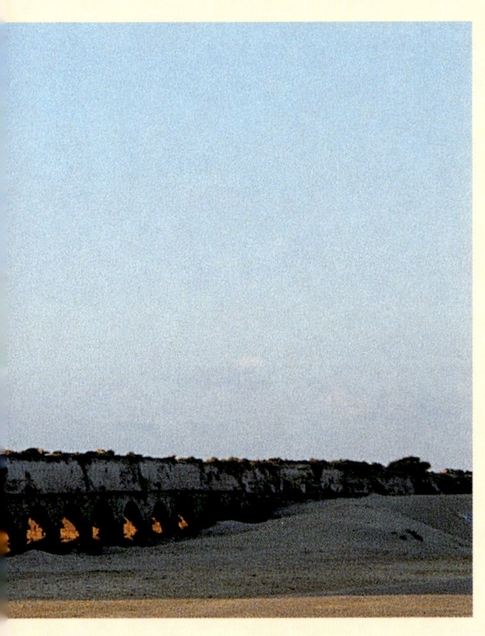

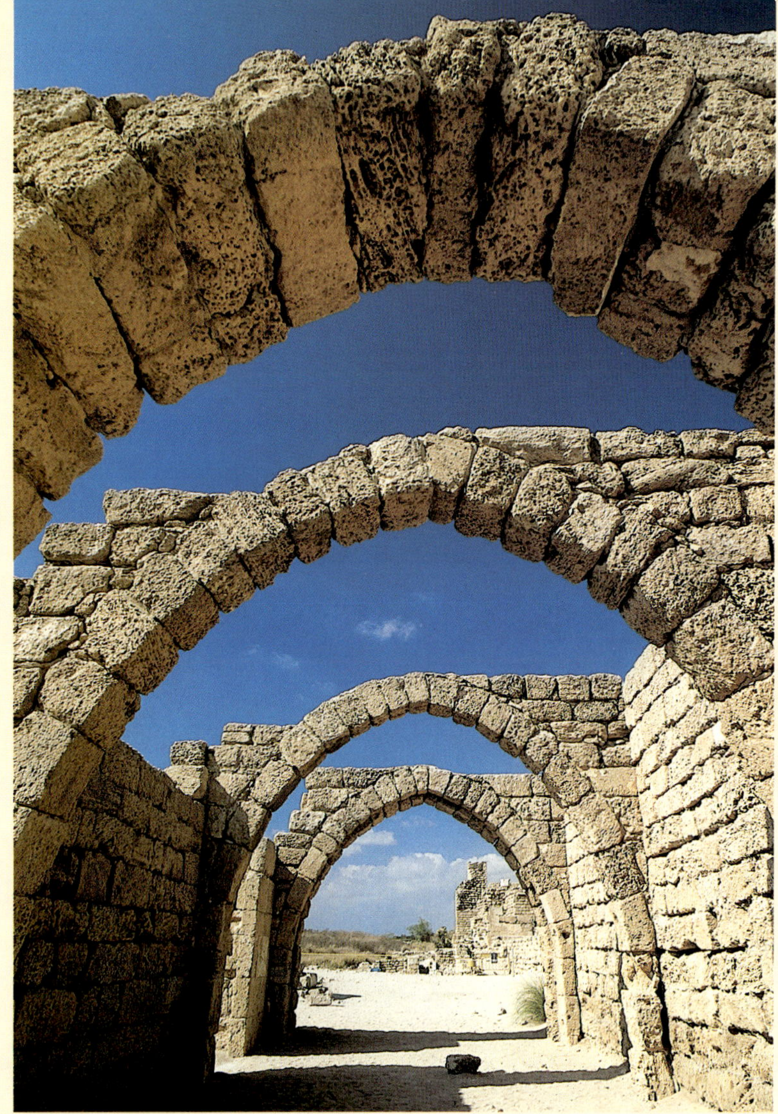

Flavius Josephus was one of the early historians to attest to King Herod's 'extraordinarily difficult and arduous task'. Herod the Great began building a city in 22 BC by 'sinking vast boulders to a depth of 20 cubits [about 38 ft] into the sea' and called this town Caesarea in honour of his patron, the Emperor Augustus. In the sixth century BC, Caesarea became the headquarters of the governors of Judea and for 500 years it remained the headquarters of the Roman administration of Palestine. During the Pax Romana the city became the centre of Greek and then later of Christian culture. It was captured by crusaders in 1101. In 1187 Saladin the Kurd captured Caesarea, but it was regained by Richard the Lionheart in 1218. For 200 years it changed rulers so frequently that even the most knowledgeable tourist guides give up at this point in their historical narrative and simply point out that Caesarea was captured and plundered time and again; in the 18 eighteenth century, Ahmad al Jazzar, the ruler of Acre purloined its antique columns for his buildings and, finally, the ancient city was freed from the sands of the sea and the sands of time in the mid-1950s.

There is not much left of the Roman remains. A slight rise in the ground is the last vestige of the *hippodrome*, there are a few small pieces left of the *aquaduct* and it is only extensive restoration work that allows something of the former *amphitheatre* to be seen. These days it is used for festivals and theatre productions. Even the remains of the famous antique *library* lie, like the other Roman relics,

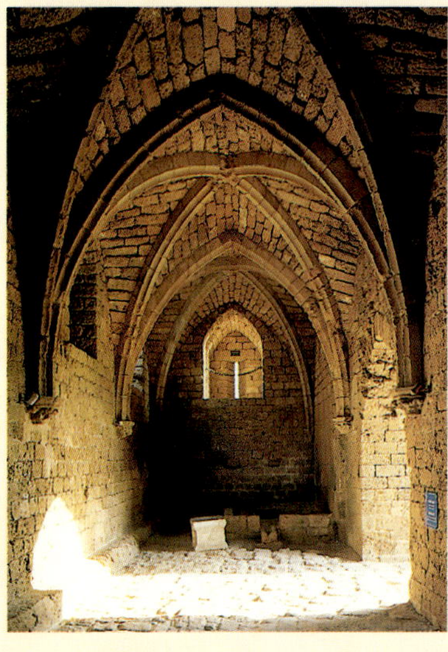

The colonnade (above) and the archway with the ribbed vault (below) are all part of the 13th century crusader city.

outside the *crusader city* with its imposing walls. The crusaders also left behind a *cathedral* and the *harbour ramparts* in Caesarea.

Some years ago, archae-ologists opened up an unusual attraction to diving visitors: where Caesarea sank to the bottom of the sea, around 13,000 square feet of land have been marked out as an *archaeological underwater park*, in which items of special interest are indicated. A nearby diving centre rents out the necessary equipment together with waterproof brochures and gives a short introduction – and then you're off to an exciting underwater exploration of the harbour of Herod the Great.

long since merged together and the coastal strip represents the most densely populated area of Israel. Only a few long-established orange groves are left, and almost the only place you can still see a sand dune is in a national park. The former pioneer village of *Herzliya* has become an exclusive residential suburb of Tel Aviv. However, the people between Ashkelon and Acre

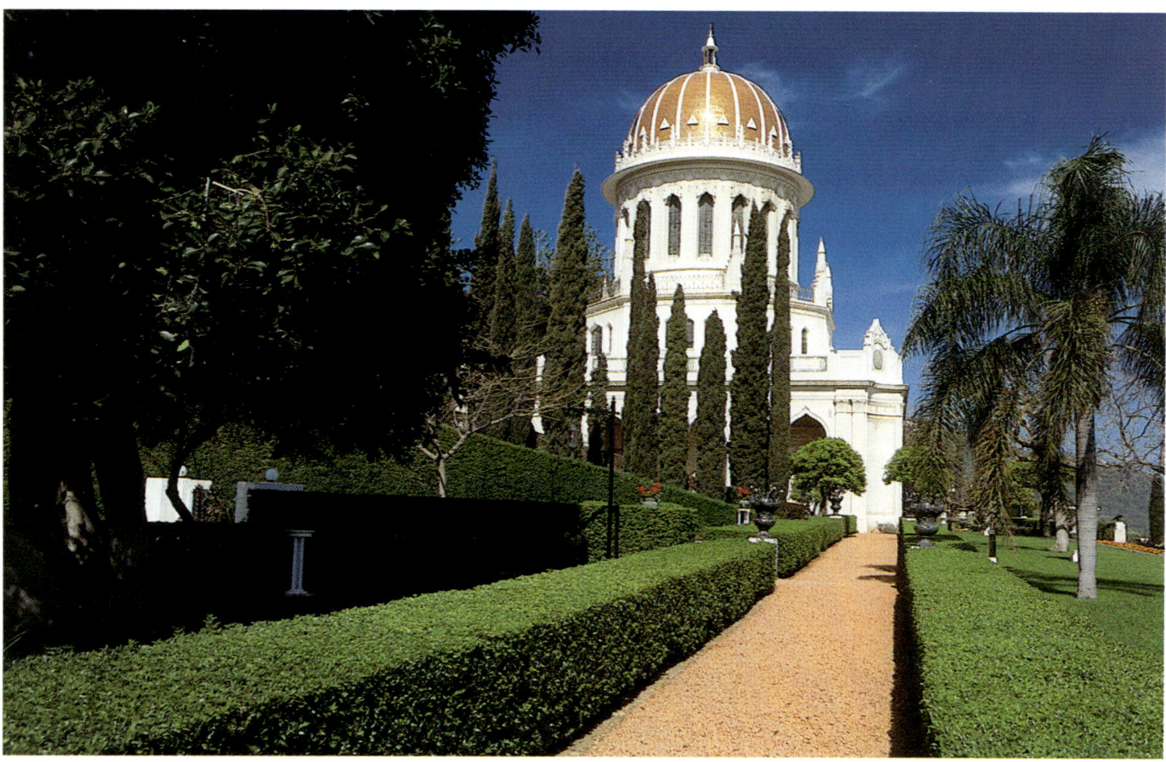

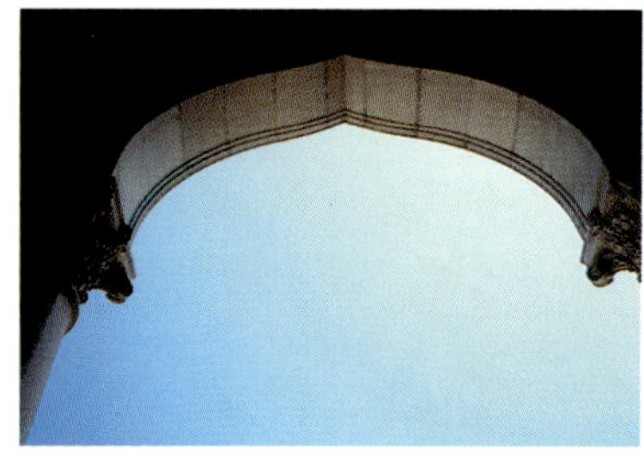

The gold-plated dome of the Bahai Temple dominates the landscape of Haifa. All year round followers of the Bahai religion, which first developed in the 19th century, wend their way to this place of pilgrimage

managed to maintain a few of their pioneering characteristics: creativity and an enterprising spirit. This part of Israel has become a sort of Silicon Valley of the Holy Land, where Israel's high-tech industry has established its base. The Weizmann Institute in *Rehovot*, for instance, has made a name for itself as one of the world's most renowned research institutes, and at the Wingate Institute, Israel's sportsmen and women are trained to Olympic standard. These are all things that Herzl and the early pioneers could only dream about. Here, in this coastal strip, is where Israel's economy flourishes. It is here that the most important part of Herzl's utopian dream for a Jewish state of the future becomes reality: it is here that Israel is just a perfectly normal country with perfectly normal inhabitants.

Starting in the South

Ashkelon, situated on the ancient Via Maris, the famous caravan route between Egypt and Syria, has always been a trading centre. Together with Ekron, Gath, Gaza and Ashdod it

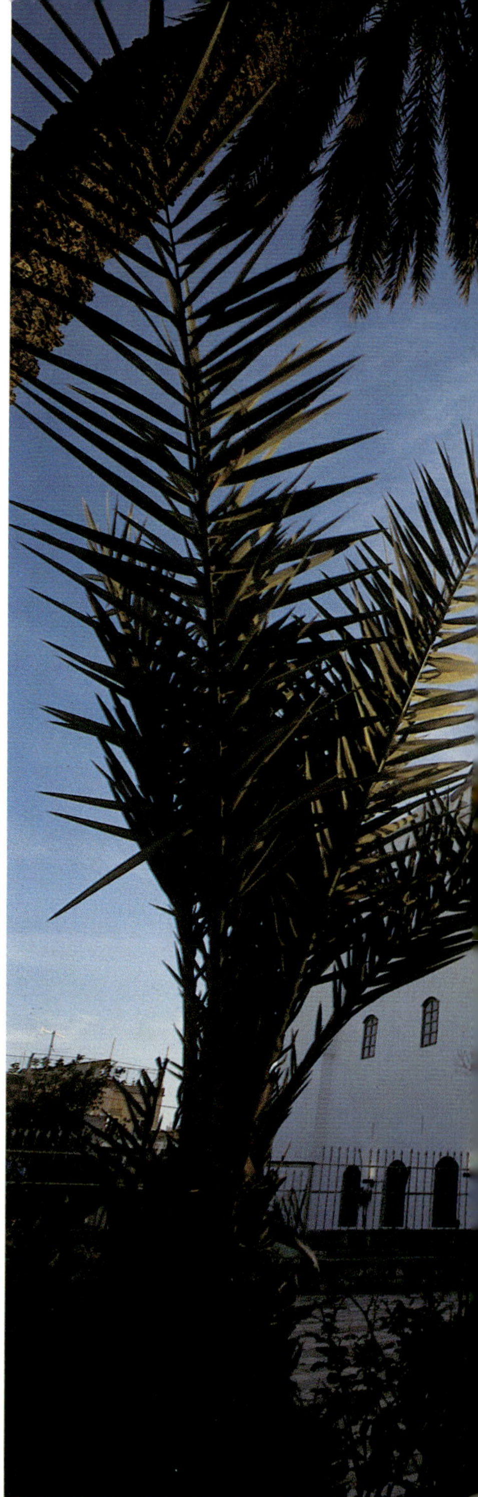

The Great Mosque of Al Jazzar Pasha is the largest and most magnificent mosque in Acre. Ahmad 'el Jazzar' ('the butcher') had it erected in 1781. A shrine containing a hair from the beard of the prophet Mohammed is preserved here where people come to worship.

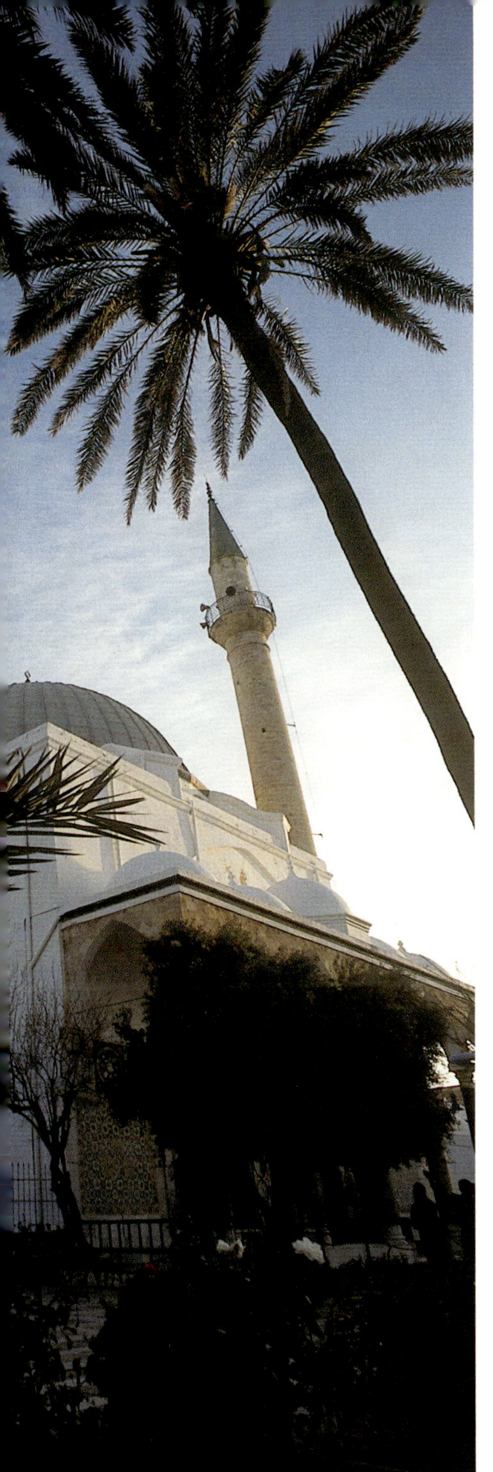

formed the Philistine confederation of five royal cities which is mentioned in the Book of Joshua. Sightseers are invited to stroll between rows of pillars from the time of Herod the Great and ancient Roman remains in a National Park surrounded by imposing walls built during the Crusades.

The little town which now has a population of some 65,000 inhabitants also offers attractive sandy beaches. Just a few miles to the north we come to *Ashdod* which was founded in 1957 and is now Israel's most important deep sea harbour.

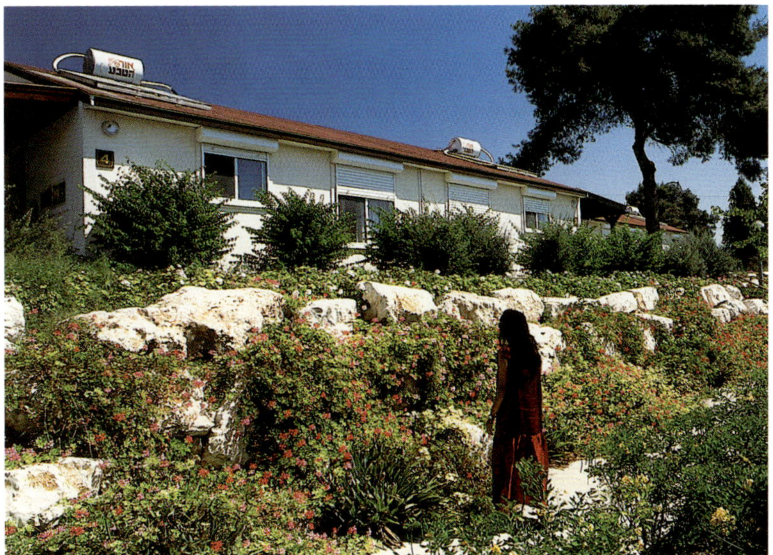

Bet Oren, which lies south of Haifa on Mount Carmel, is a kibbutz founded in 1939 which offers accommodation to guests (left). Many Druze still live in the villages of Isfiya and Daliyat-el-Carmel in the Mount Carmel area (below).

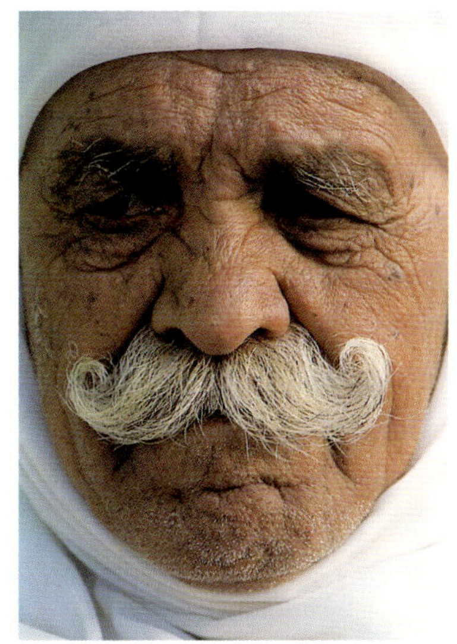

The Druze

The Druze are a religious minority who diverged from Islam in the eleventh century. They worship the Caliph al-Hakim as God's last incarnation in human form. They believe in one God and membership of their religion is inherited from the father. The Druze, who are committed to leading a life of moral rectitude, live in the mountainous regions of Lebanon, in Syria and – around 70,000 of them – in the Mount Carmel region to the south of Haifa. The Druze have become quite integrated in Israel, especially their young men most of whom do military service. However, in the villages of Mount Carmel, traditional crafts have continued to be practised and the Druze market in Daliyat-el-Carmel is both a tourist attraction and the expression of an age-old tradition.

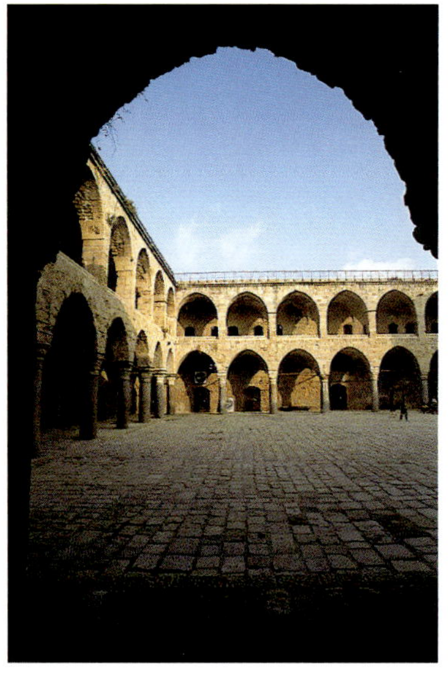

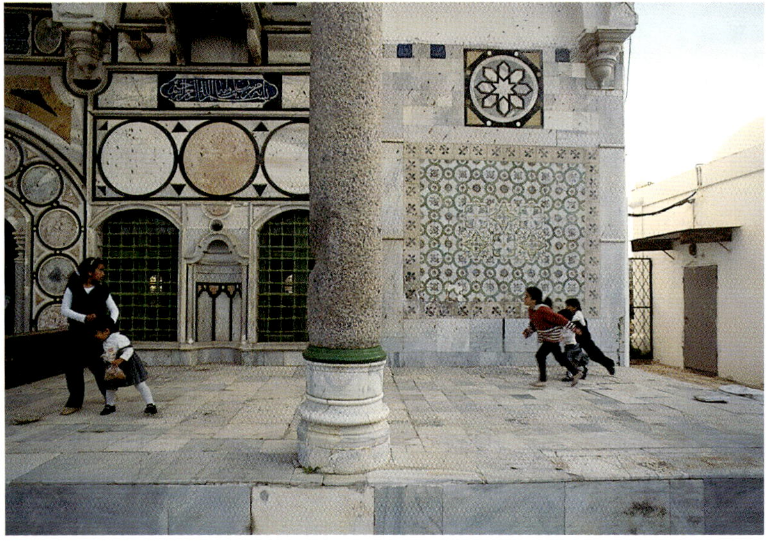

Caravanserai like Khan el Umdan with its decorated arcades (end of the late eighteenth century) in Acre were rather like a motel (above). Pack animals were housed on the ground floor while travelling tradesmen were housed on the upper floors.

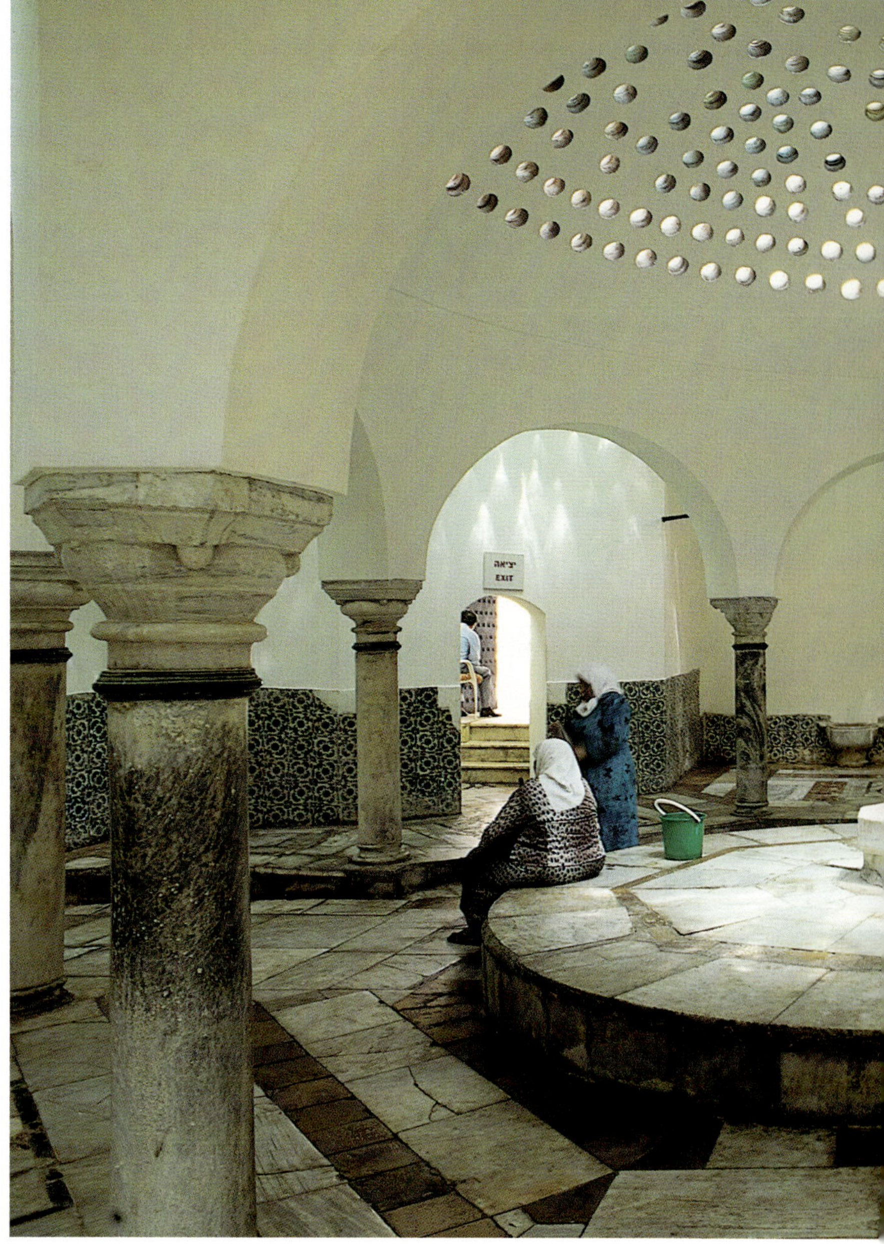

The elegant town and popular weekend resort of Herzliya has very nearly merged with Tel Aviv, while Netanya is more the sort of place where families like to relax. It is also well-known as a centre for the diamond trade developed by emigrants from Amsterdam and Antwerp. It goes without saying that a guided tour through the diamond polishing works always ends up in the tempting sales room – however, prices should be compared with those at your jewellers' back home. Beyond the excavation sites we arrive at Caesarea (see p. 101) a place of flowers and pretty little houses. Moving northwards we see before us Mount Carmel, a range of hills which is almost totally covered by Israel's largest national park and – unusually for this otherwise nearly treeless country – swathed in verdant forests. One of the largest groups of the Druze minority (see p. 103) lives on the original slopes of Mount Carmel.

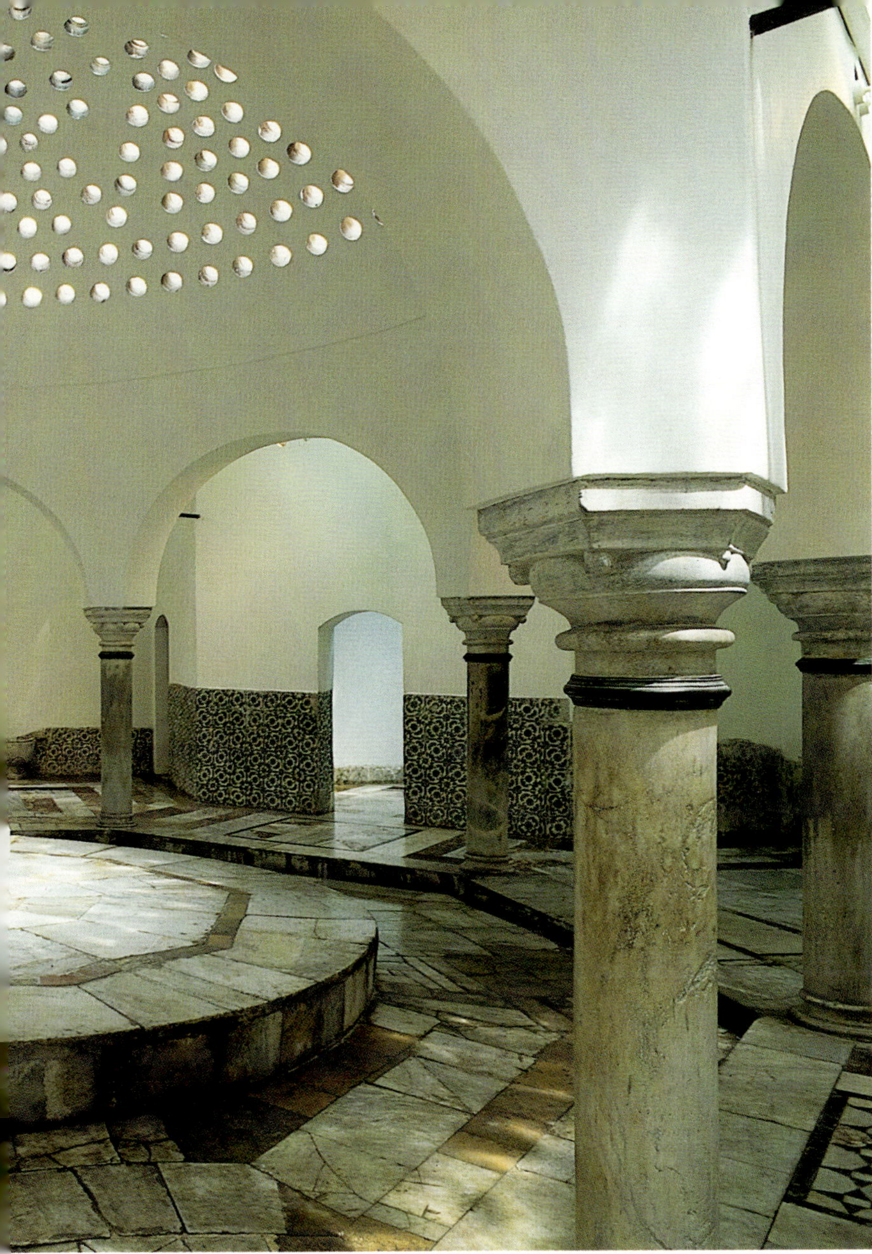

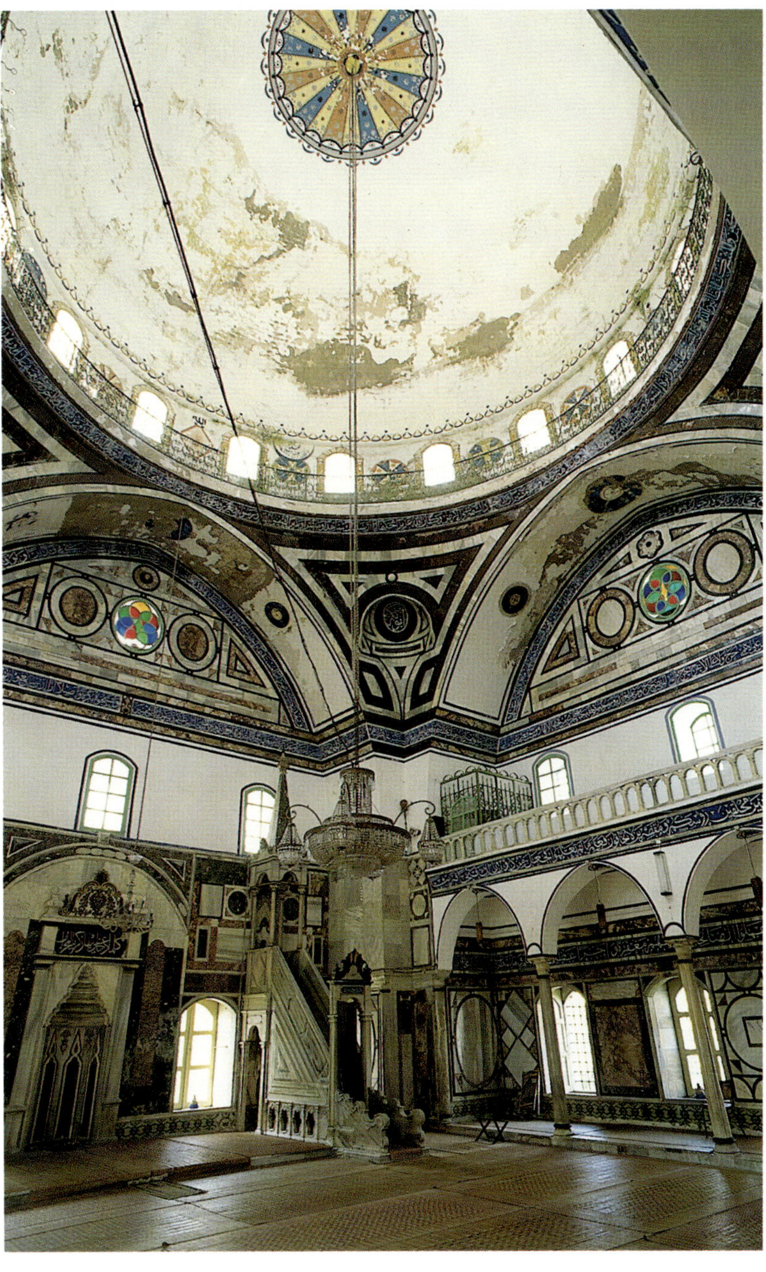

The interior and exterior of the El Jazzar Mosque in Acre is adorned with coloured marble and quotes from the Koran on a blue background (left below and right). Ahmad al Jazzar also built the Hammam el Basha in Acre, a bath-house based on the style of Roman baths. Today the town museum is located here (centre).

Haifa – City of Steps on the Slopes of Mount Carmel

It may just be a few miles away from Haifa, but the idyllic atmosphere of Mount Carmel seems to be light years away. The closer the winding road gets to the valley, the more one is enveloped by the restless and noisy, yet charming city of Haifa, the City of Steps – visiting Haifa, one has to be prepared to spend most of one's time going up and down stairways! We are offered superb views from the *Carmelite Monastery* or from the Bahai Temple over the harbour and bay. Haifa had already served the Romans as a port. It was destroyed in the 12th century during battles between the Arabs and the Crusaders, after which it suffered a fairly dismal existence until Zionist pioneers started reconstructing it from the mid-19th century onwards. Haifa quickly developed into a city of immigrants and thousands of refugees settled there.

'There are few ways in which a man can be more innocently employed than in getting money' or spending it, as Samuel

Johnson wrote in the eighteenth century. In Haifa both are done with dedication. And this may well be the reason why Arabs and Jews have managed to live here for generations side by side without major problems. According to the old saying, 'Jerusalem prays, Tel Aviv lives and Haifa works' and Haifa is known for being an industrious and bustling city. It is here, in the politcally radical harbour town, that the powerful Histradut trade union was founded in the twenties. Public buses operate even on the Sabbath. The dominant religious monument of Haifa, the *Bahai Temple*, completed in 1953, is a symbol of peaceful co-existence. The Bahai religion was founded in the mid-nineteenth century by the Persian Bab, and has some three million adherents around the world. Their main creed is that of tolerance. Bab was executed as an apostate of Islam in Tabriz in 1850, his remains were transferred to Haifa in 1909 and buried in the gardens of the Bahai Temple. The Temple with its dome consisting of 12,000 gold-plated tiles donated by Bahai communities around the world has become a symbol of the city – visually more appealing than its second symbol, the 30-storey high *Eshkol Tower* of the University of Haifa.

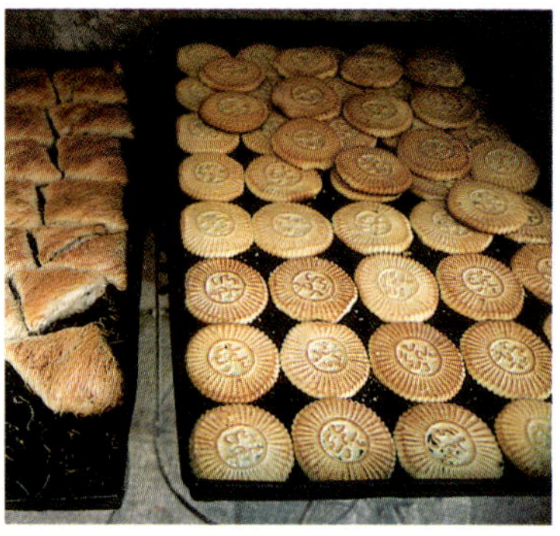

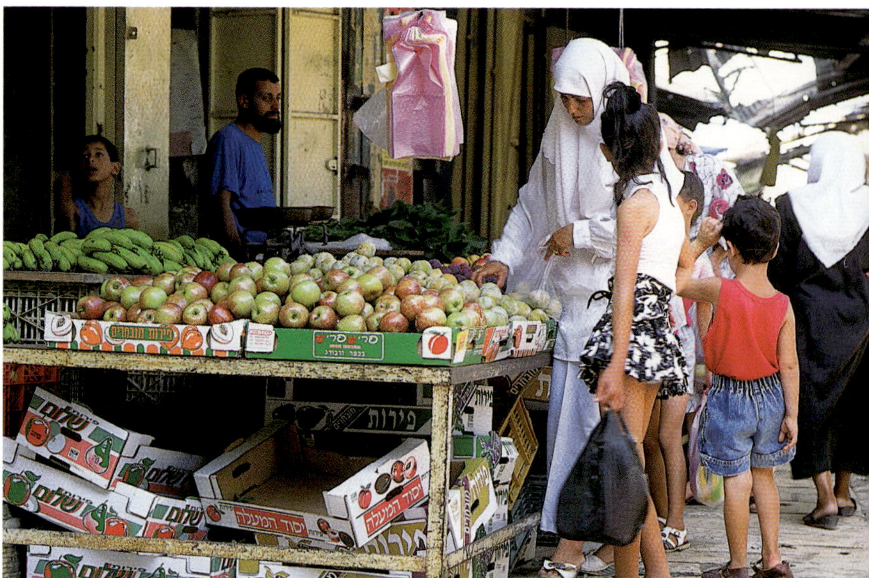

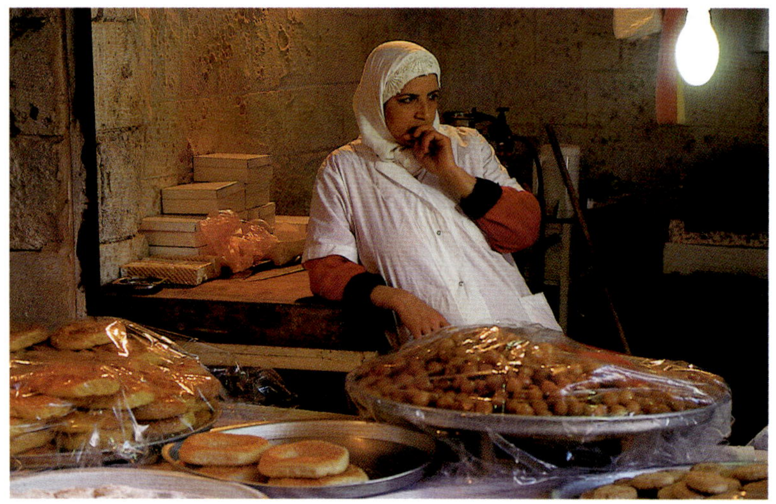

Appetising snacks and pastries, fresh fruit, vegetables, fish and meat – in the market place of Acre the local people go shopping for their daily requirements

Picturesque Acre – Citadel of the Crusaders

Acre too experienced the usual history of destruction and reconstruction familiar in this part of the world. As early as 2000 BC it served as a port to the Assyrians, then to the Phoenicians, the Egyptians and finally to Alexander the Great. This little town reached its zenith towards the end of the twelfth century AD under the Christian knights, who made it the capital of their Crusader Kingdom, developing Acre into the most important harbour and trading centre on the Mediterranean. However, after the horrific massacres committed by the Crusaders on the Muslims and the equally gruesome revenge taken by the Mamelukes who conquered Acre in 1291, the city fell into decay, remaining devastated for a long period of time.

It was the middle of the eighteenth century before a Bedouin sheikh by the name of Dahr el 'Omar made Acre into his capital city, fortifying it with a *town wall*, which is still fully preserved today, and building a new *fortress* together with a *clock-*

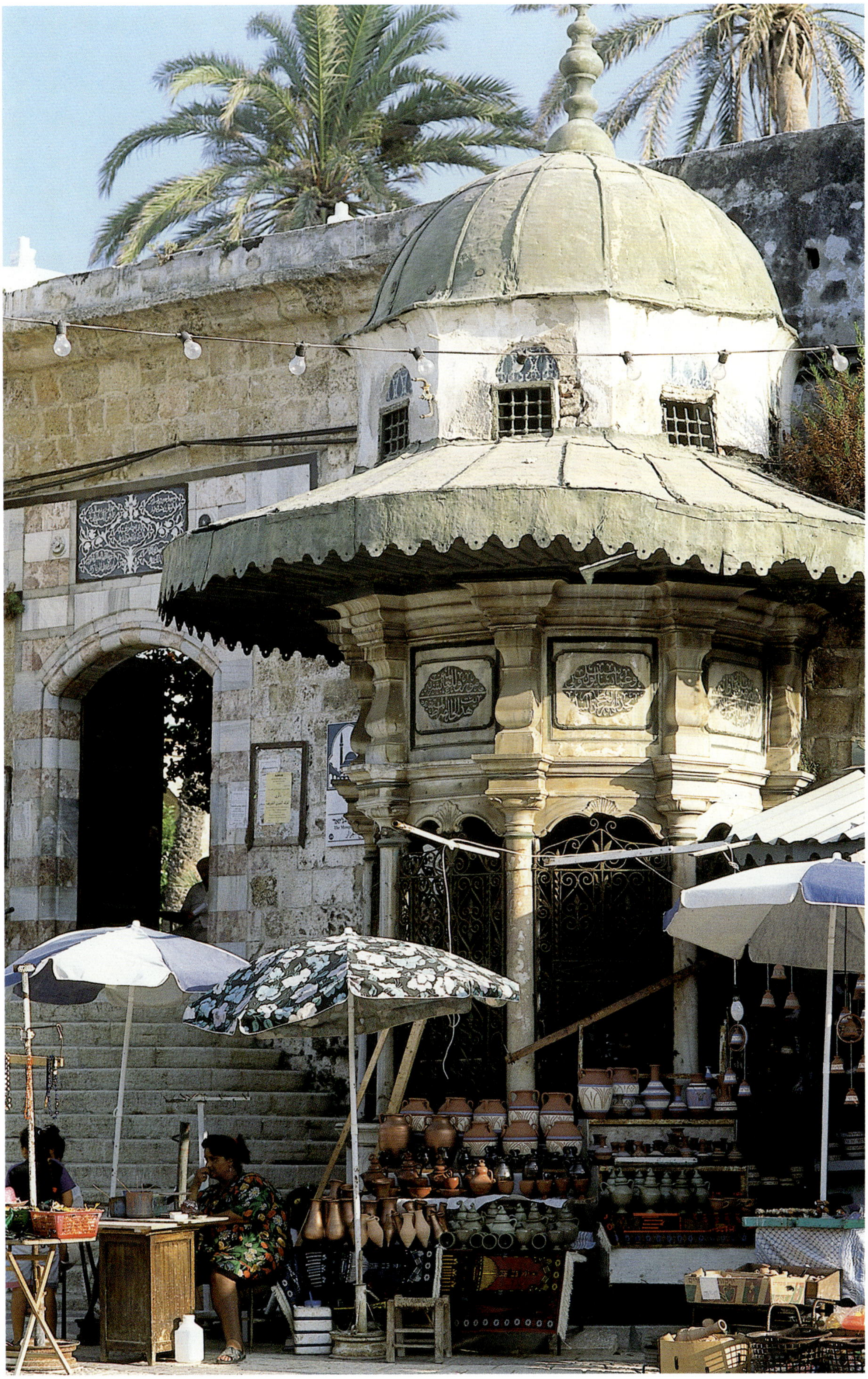

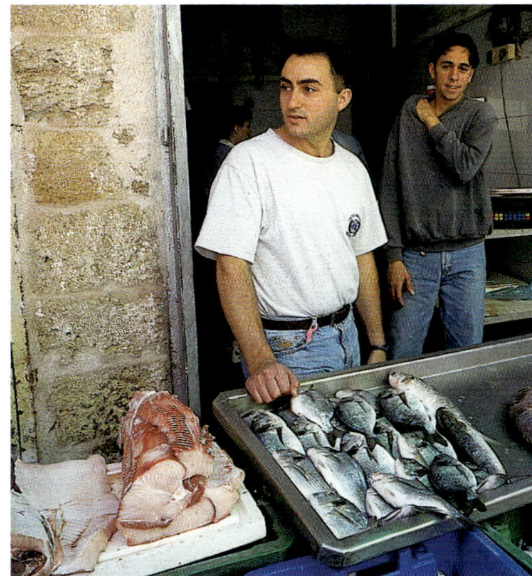

It is not just in the market place that the craftsmen offer their wares, they also set up their stands outside the main entrance of the Al Jazzar Mosque with its delicate well for ritual cleansing. After all, the mosque is one of the major tourist attractions.

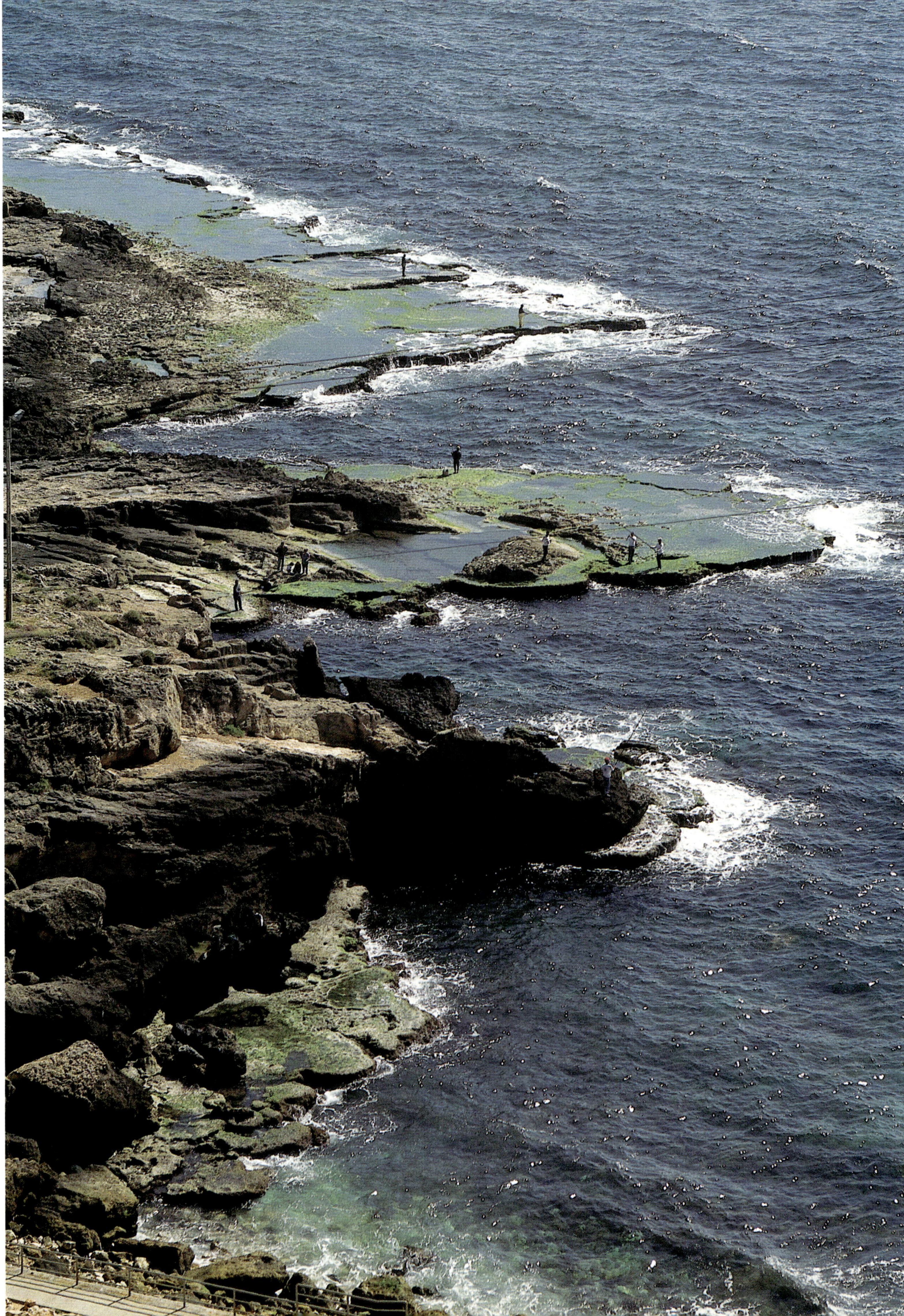

tower. The sheikh did not live to enjoy his buildings for long: he was poisoned by Ahmad al Jazzar, a Turkish Pasha of Bosnian origin who bore the dubious nickname 'the butcher' – not undeservedly. Al Jazzar did not kill only Sheikh Omar, but also his wife and numerous other enemies. However, he did give the town many of its most magnificent buildings which are preserved to this day: an *aqueduct*, the bath house which serves

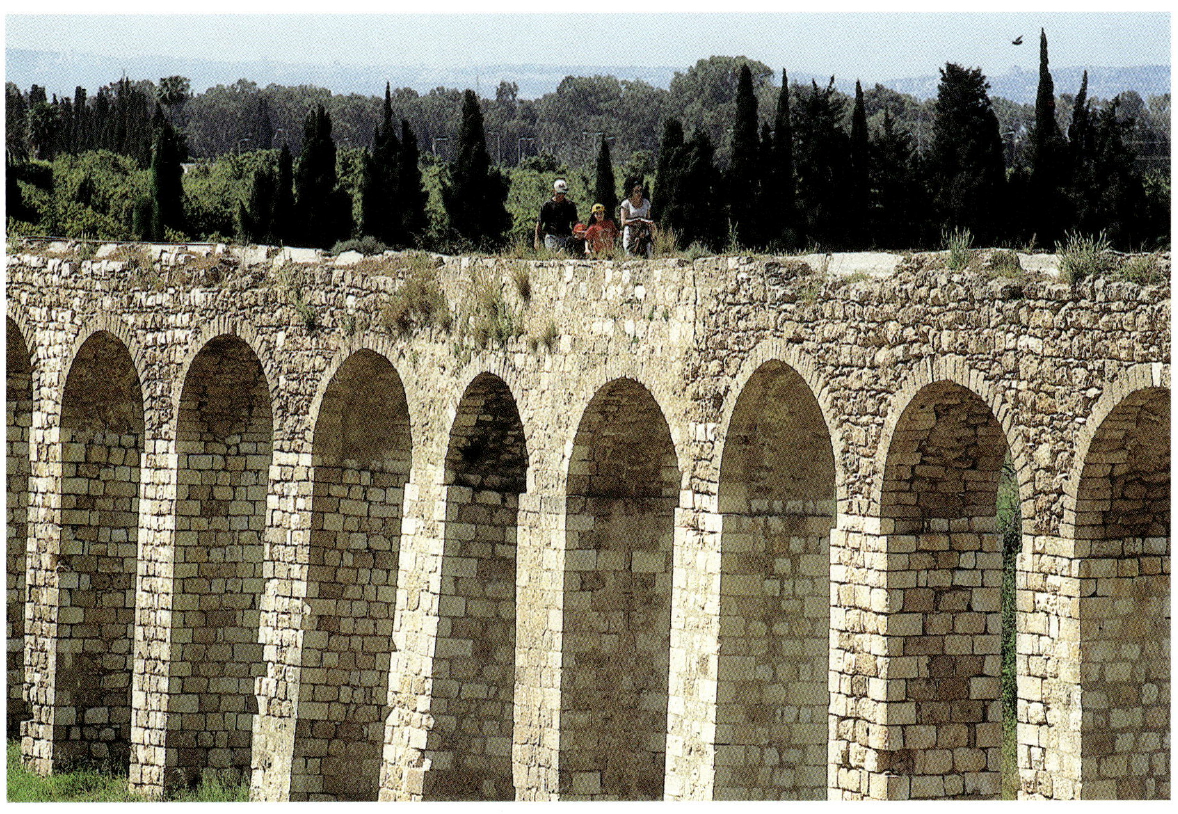

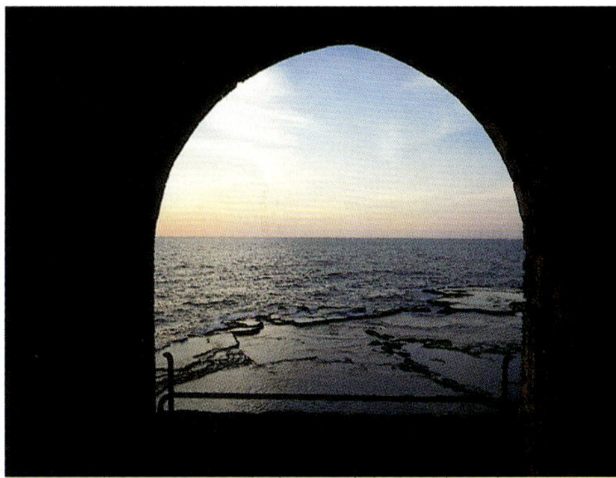

Cliffs, rocks and grottoes – at the foot of the Rosh Hanikra chalk cliff near the border with Lebanon, the sea has created a fascinating labyrinth of caves (left page). On the land of the Kibbutz Lohamei Hageta'ot north of Acre, there is an aqueduct from the Ottoman period (centre).
From the sea walls of Acre, the eye is always drawn out to the Mediterranean (right).

as Acre's *City Museum* today, and the splendid *Mosque of Al Jazzar* with its secluded inner courtyard framed by arcades and palm trees. The *Khan el Umdan Caravanserai* once offered stabling for camels and accommodation for their drivers; however, it looks more like a palace than a simple shelter.

It is easy for superlatives to trip off the tongue when describing Acre: the most magnificent mosque, the most harmoniously beautiful old town centre in the land.However, many of Acre's treasures are out of sight, several levels underground. Today, a visitor can wander 33 feet below street level through imposing arched cellars of excavated *Crusader buildings*.

Acre also has a wonderfully soothing effect after the nerve-wracking traffic jams of Tel Aviv or the cacophony of car horns in Haifa and gently leads you to the quiet coastal resorts of the north. In *Rosh Hanikra*, erosion has carved caves and grottoes out of the cliffs which can be reached by means of a small cable car – this is the gentler side of Israel.

Sand, Sea and Falafel

Swimming in the Mediterranean

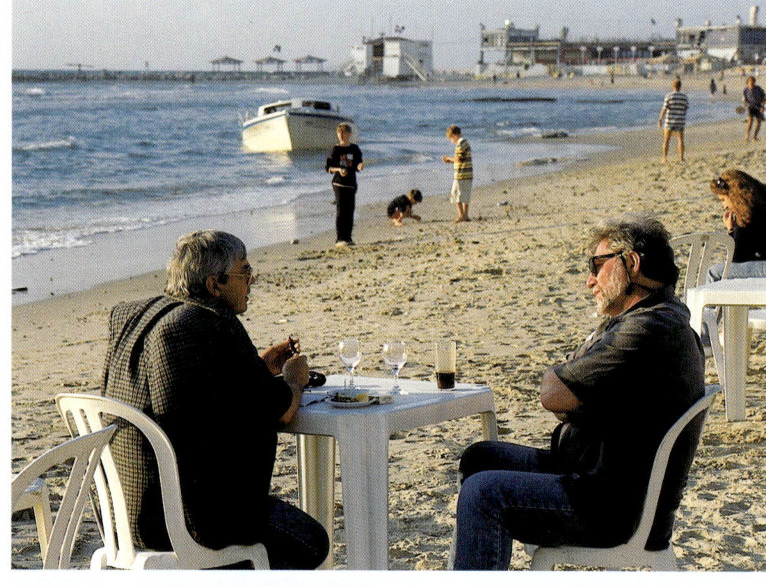
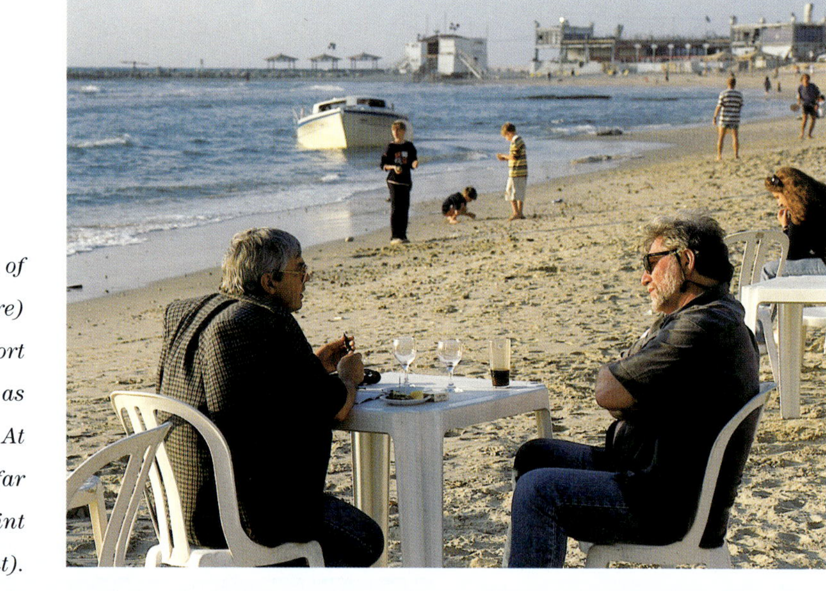

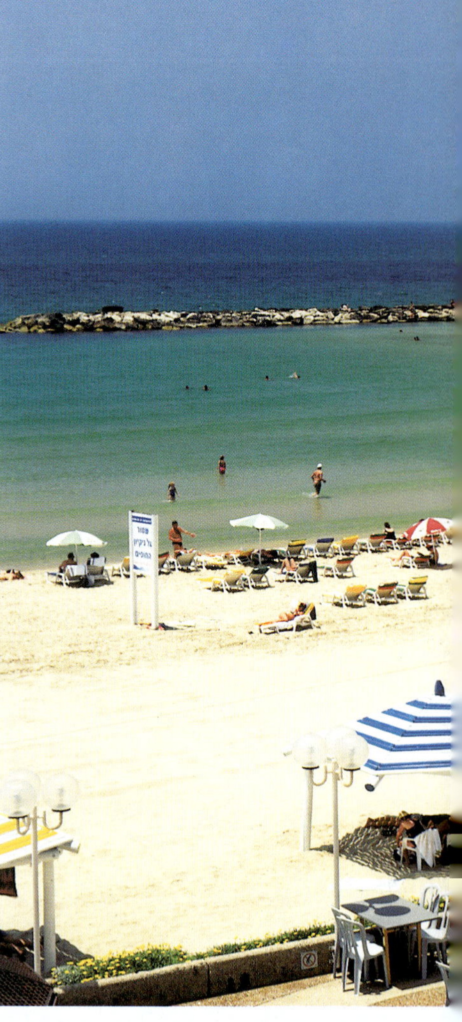

On the beaches of the metropolis of Tel Aviv (above left and centre) and the popular holiday resort Netanya (below left) it is only as peaceful as this out of season. At the same time it is never very far from the nearest falafel joint (below right).

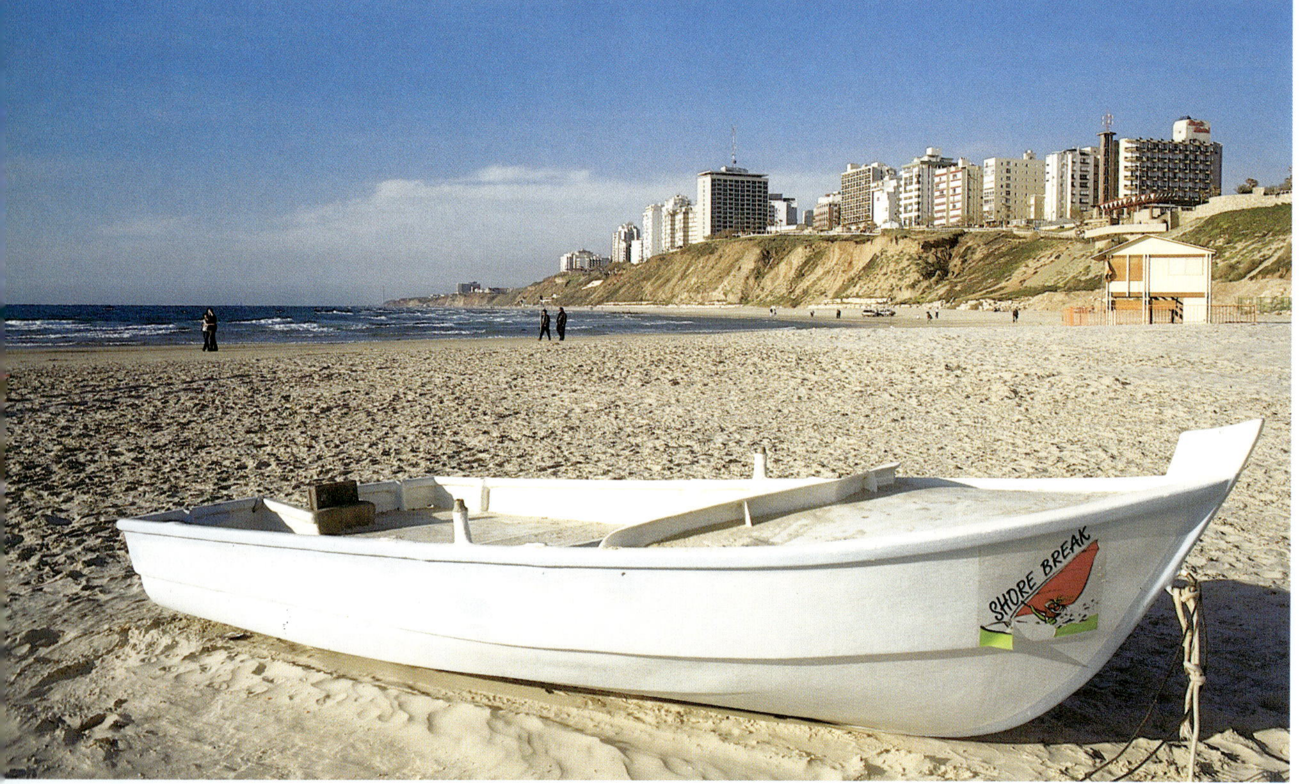

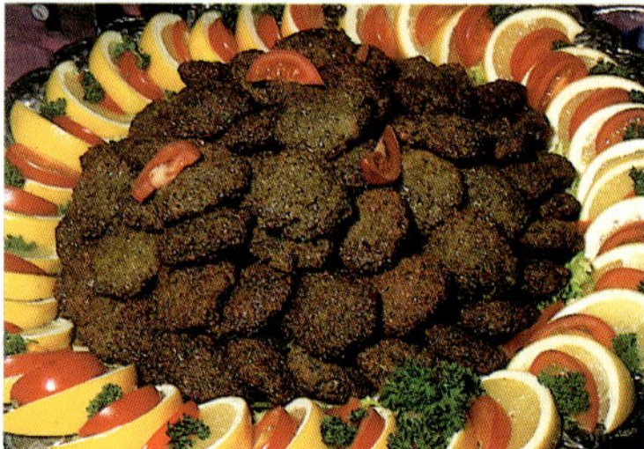

Beaches of the finest hour-glass quality sand, as far as the eye can see – that is what the 125 mile Mediterranean coast of Israel offers.

A beach holiday in Israel does not, however, necessarily mean lonely afternoons in secluded coves, for the Mediterranean coast is the most densely populated area of the country and this means that

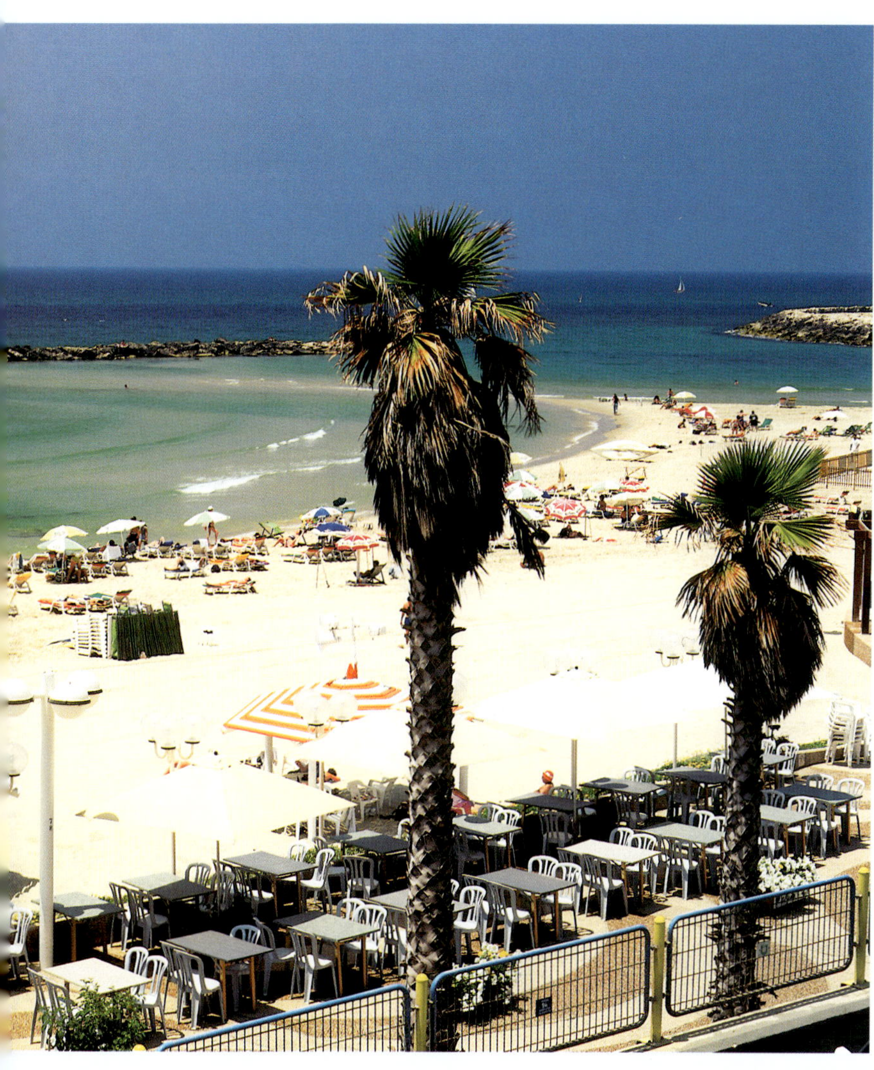

When you've managed to soak up enough sunshine, you'd be well advised to pay a visit to the chalk cliffs of Rosh Hanikra (top). And if swimming, sailing, water skiing and diving are all too energetic for you, you can always take your fishing rod out to sea near Acre (below).

cities and hotels are inching their way closer and closer to the beach. The beach isn't just a magnet for tourists from all over the world, it also attracts the Israelis, who may want to do nothing more than sit at a beach cafe, letting their gaze wander round and uttering a heartfelt prayer of gratitude: 'Toda Raba, many thanks for this gift!'.

Starting in the South, in *Ashkelon*, the beaches are part of the city. And in *Tel Aviv* and *Herzliya* before the big rush to lie in the sun, there is the big rush to find a parking space – anywhere, as long as we don't need to walk too far.

Netanya, the most important of Israel's Mediterranean resorts is blessed with all the advantages of a perfect infrastructure and the disadvantages of the hustle and bustle that its own popularity brings upon it. It is only when we get to the north of *Haifa*, whose name is often said to come from 'hof yefe' (beautiful beach), that the beaches are quieter than those further south. What is it, you might ask, that makes the Mediterranean beaches of Israel so different from those in Spain and Italy? Well, Israel fans particularly appreciate the colourful and international flavour that visitors to Israel bring with them - and the variety of the cuisine. Those falafel joints are still successfully managing to stop the spread of the fast food chains. And besides, Netanya's beaches are so long that despite everything, there's still enough room between you and your neighbour.

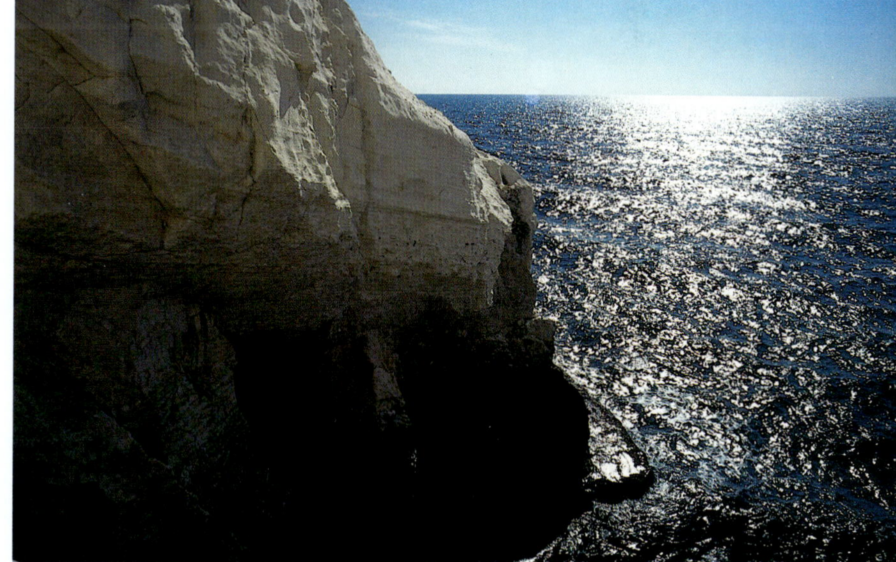

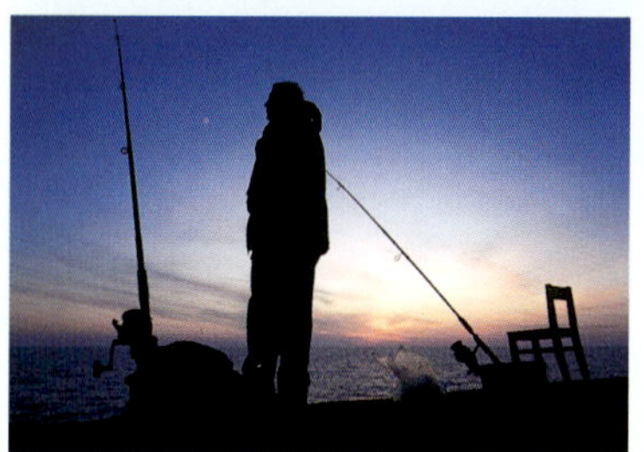

And if you enjoy culture as much as swimming, you don't have to choose between one and the other in Israel. In Caesarea or in Dor, the excavation sites are situated right by the most beautiful bathing beaches.

And if one activity still feels too energetic and the other too much like cultural hard work, then just a few kilometres to the south of Nahariya, the *Moshav Shave Ziyyon* will offer you peace and quiet – and possibly even the option of discovering a place where you can eat genuine Swabian *spätzle*. In 1938 farmers from the Black Forest emigrated here and they still cook according to Grandma's recipes. To this day *Nahariya* bears the influence of its German immigrants. The seaside resort founded in 1934 with its long boulevard lined with eucalyptus trees has the feel of a small town. Tourists who come here especially for the swimming appreciate the warm welcome they receive and along the sandy beaches walkers still exchange a friendly 'Shalom!'.

The Desert is Alive

Southern Israel from the Negev to Eilat

However many tourists fly into the seaside resort of Eilat in their charter flights, arriving by car or by bus is much more impressive. The commonest route takes you from Jerusalem southwards via Beersheba, past the impressive ruins of Mamshit, the Nabataean settlement, past the Dead Sea and along the salt swamps of Sodom into the stony desert of the Negev.

Crossing the Negev along the Israeli-Jordanian border towards Eilat one is under the impression of having landed in the middle of a very peculiar sort of mirage. Right in the middle of this mountainous desert, in-between the most bizarre cliff formations and mighty craters, just 25 miles north of Eilat we suddenly come across a herd of black and white cows grazing by the roadside. Together with the enormous cow-sheds, they belong to the *Kibbutz Yotvata*, one of the oldest kibbutzim in the Negev Desert and operating a guest house and camp site as well as an agricultural enterprise. The milk products produced here and said to be the best in the country are sold in the kibbutz's own shop.

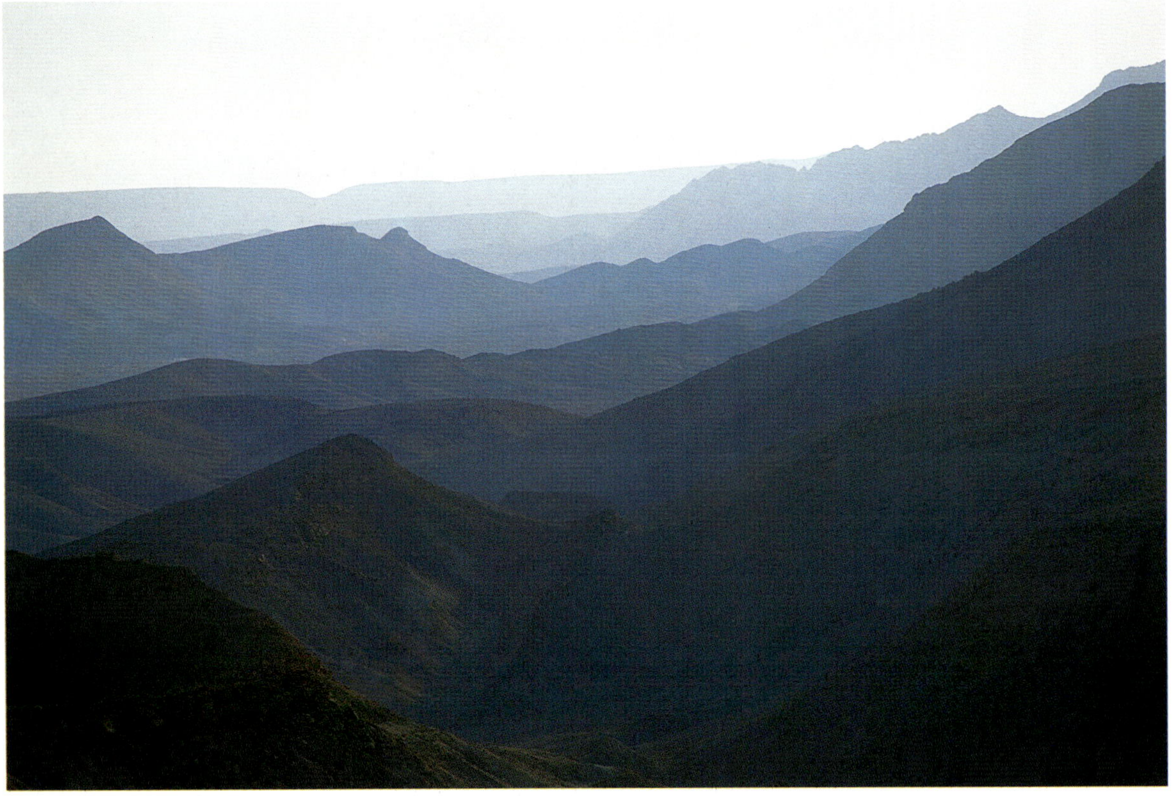

Driving along the western Negev road from Eilat to Beersheba, mountain peaks and wide table mountains come into view near Mitzpe Ramon.

The *Hai Bar Nature Reserve* also belongs to the kibbutz and is an example of the intensive ecological and greening measures that Israel has been adopting. The country's more recent history bears witness to the superhuman efforts made reclaiming land from the deserts of stone and sand as well as that destroyed by nature itself. 'Hai Bar' is Hebrew for 'animal kingdom' and represents an initiative whose goal is to repopulate the desert with all the desert animals mentioned in the Bible. You can already see wild donkeys, antelopes and ostriches from the roadside;. beasts of prey such as leopards and hyenas live in a second nature reserve. In the *Visitor's Centre* you can learn much about life in the desert.

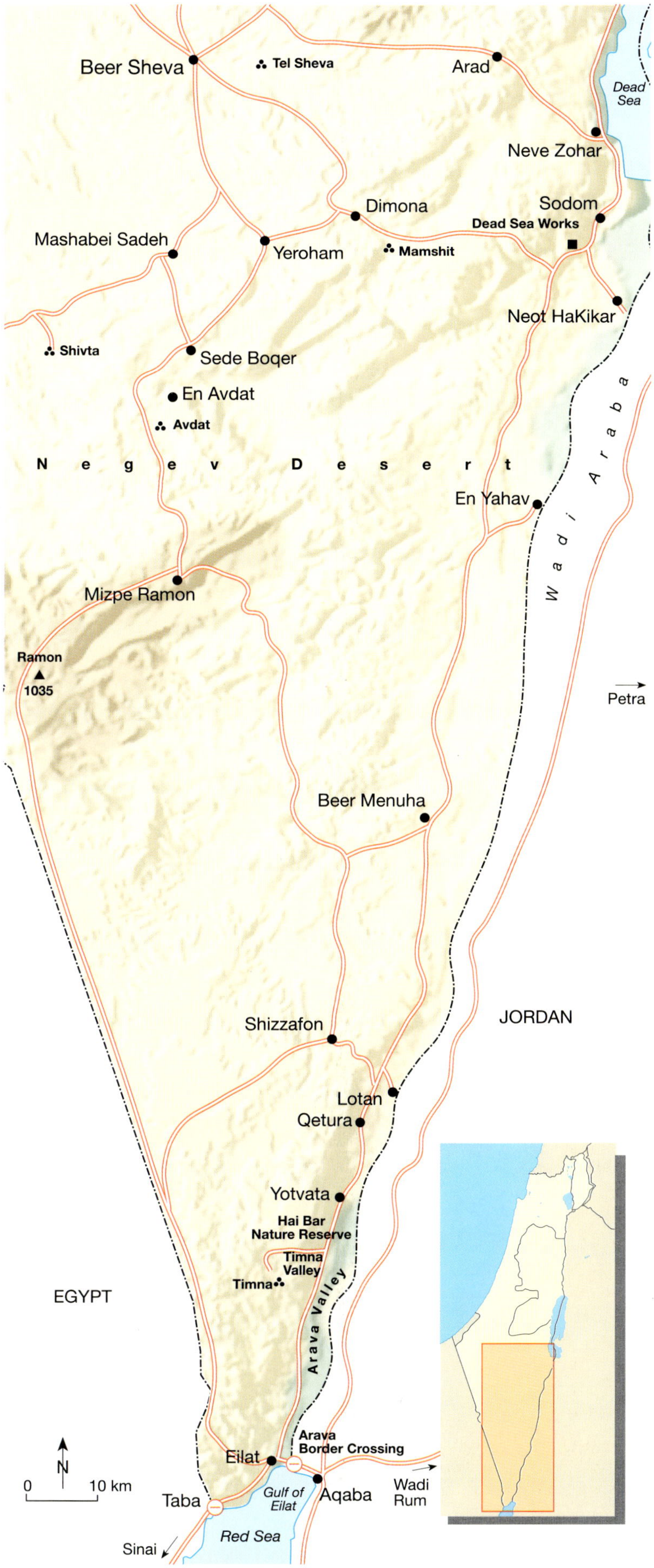

Beer Sheva
Tel Sheva
Arad
Dead Sea
Neve Zohar
Dimona
Sodom
Dead Sea Works
Mashabei Sadeh
Yeroham
Mamshit
Neot HaKikar
Shivta
Sede Boqer
En Avdat
Avdat
Negev Desert
En Yahav
Wadi Araba
Mizpe Ramon
Ramon
1035
Petra
Beer Menuha
Shizzafon
JORDAN
Lotan
Qetura
Yotvata
Hai Bar
Nature Reserve
Timna
Valley
Timna
EGYPT
Arava Valley
Arava
Border Crossing
Eilat
N
0 10 km
Taba
Gulf of Eilat
Aqaba
Wadi Rum
Red Sea
Sinai

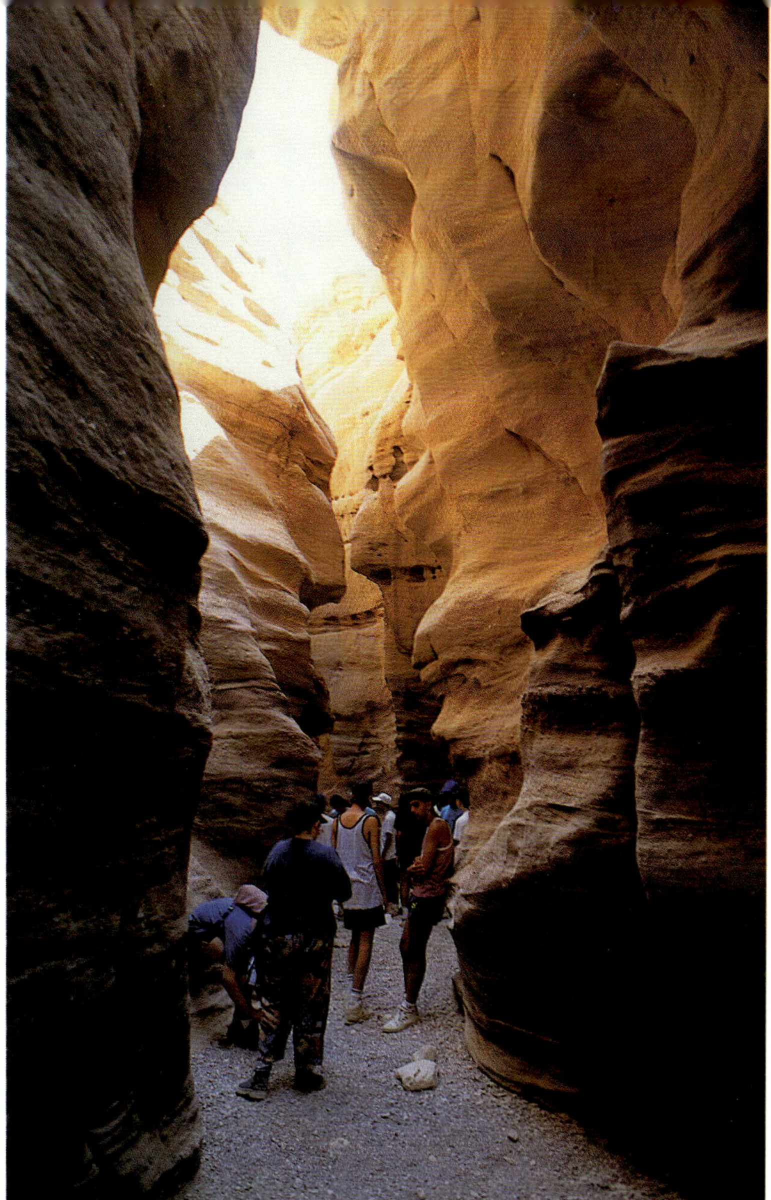

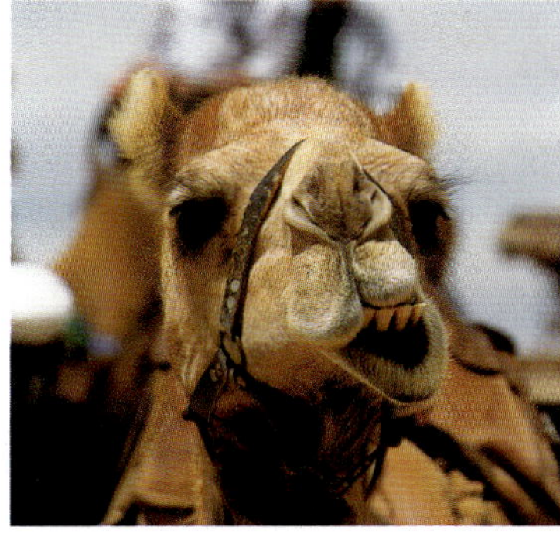

Excursions from Eilat take you to the gorges of the surrounding massifs (above), by camel into the desert (below) or by bus to St Catherine's Monastery.

The founders of Yotvata took David Ben Gurion, Israel's first Prime Minister seriously when he told his people to reclaim the desert, which, after all, covers 60 per cent of the country but is inhabited by only about 500,000 people, many of whom are Bedouin. For 'if the State of Israel does not conquer the desert' according to the founder of Israel, 'the desert will conquer the state'.

A few miles further south we arrive at the *Timna Valley*, a stunning desert landscape and significant archaeological site where copper was mined as early as 4000 years BC in vast mines. (see p. 118).

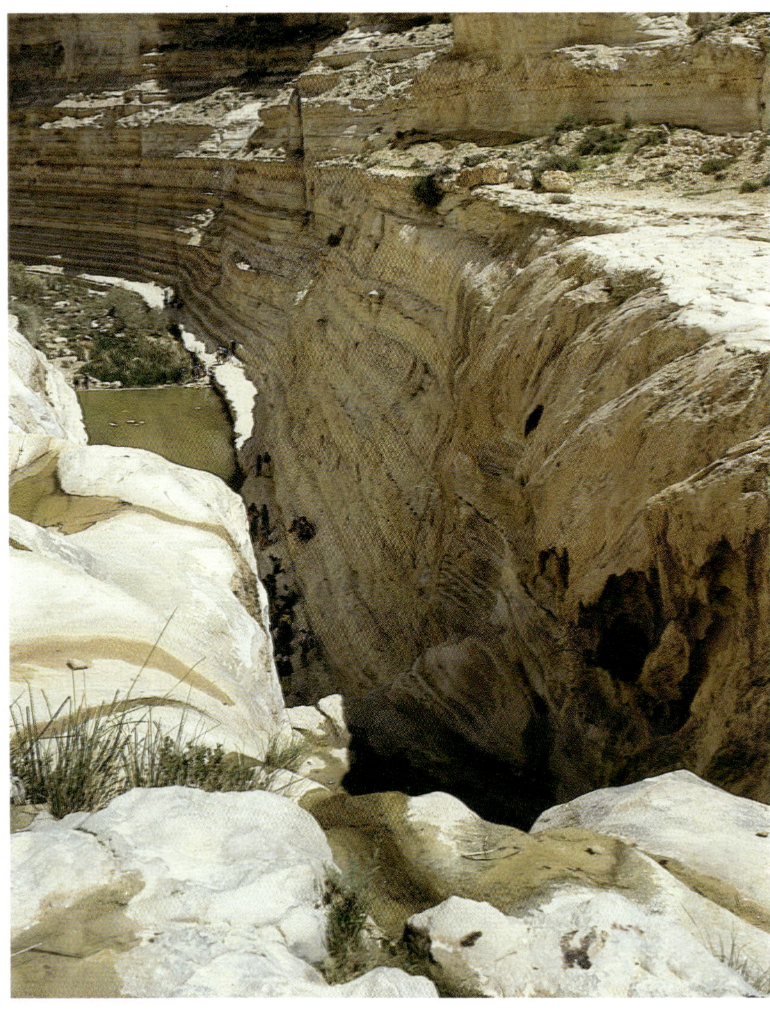

In the middle of the Negev Desert lies the fertile Ein Avdat Oasis. A walk along the steep walls of the narrow gorge follows the path of the stream which leads to a pool fed by a waterfall.

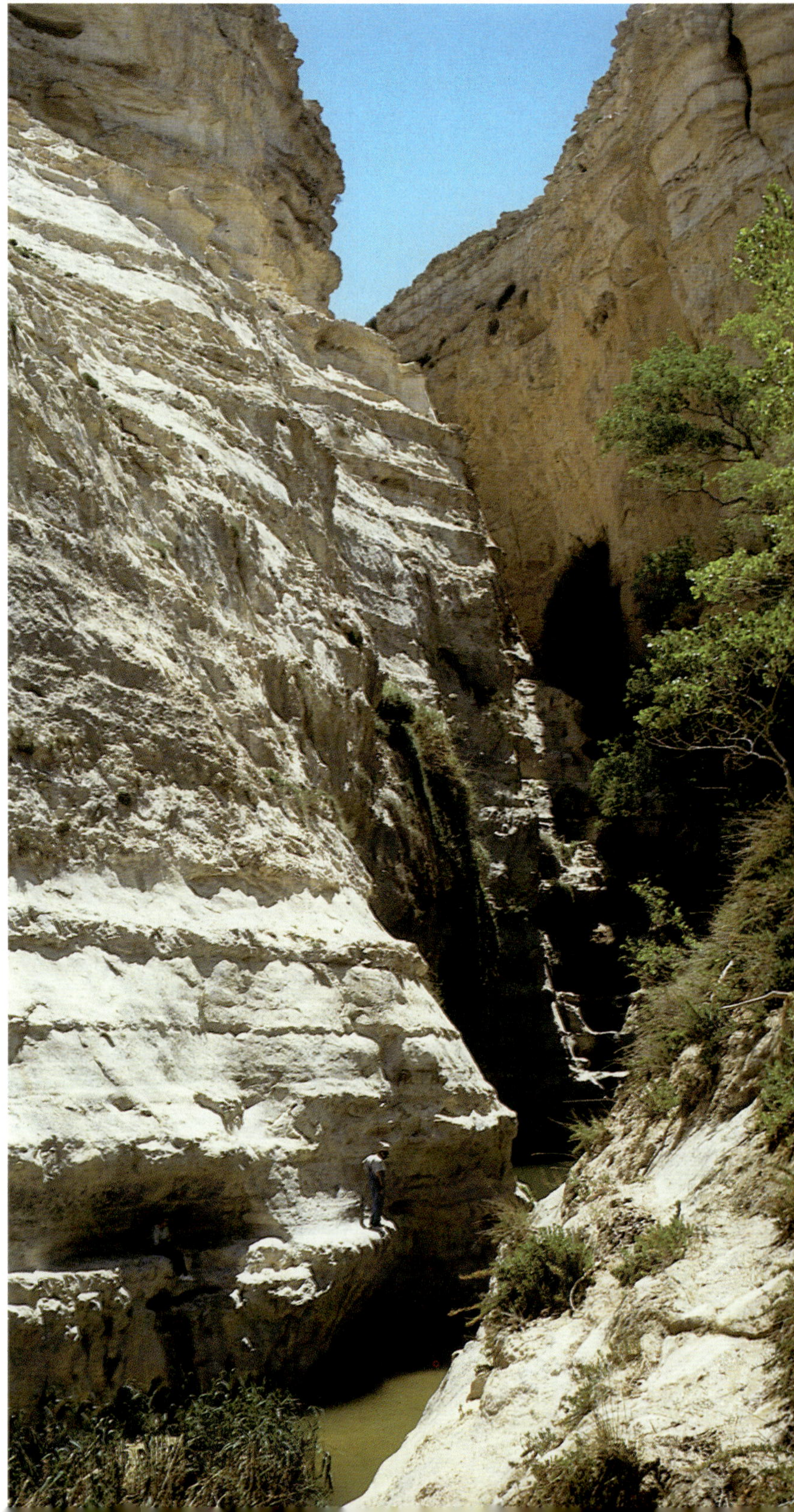

Despite Israel's enthusiastic and successful efforts to cultivate the desert, this breathtaking landscape will not disappear so quickly. Just one fifth of the 46,000 square miles of the Negev is to be reclaimed. Most of the desert is used by the Israeli army as training ground. There is, however, still enough room for tourism-related enterprises. Several agricultural settlements like *Ein Yahav* and *Neot Hakikar* in the Arava Valley, which lie off the main road from Sodom to Eilat, offer visitors camel or jeep tours of the desert in conjunction with the Israeli Nature Reserves Authority. These excursions can be tiring, as a ride on a camel for several days is something one needs to become accustomed to, but it is certainly worth it. The tour guides, mostly biologists, geologists or botanists really know their subject and are keen to pass on their enthusiasm for the surrounding landscape and the special characteristics of the desert. Accommodation on these tours is under the stars, in sleeping bags around the camp fire and they usually include a visit to a Bedouin encampment.

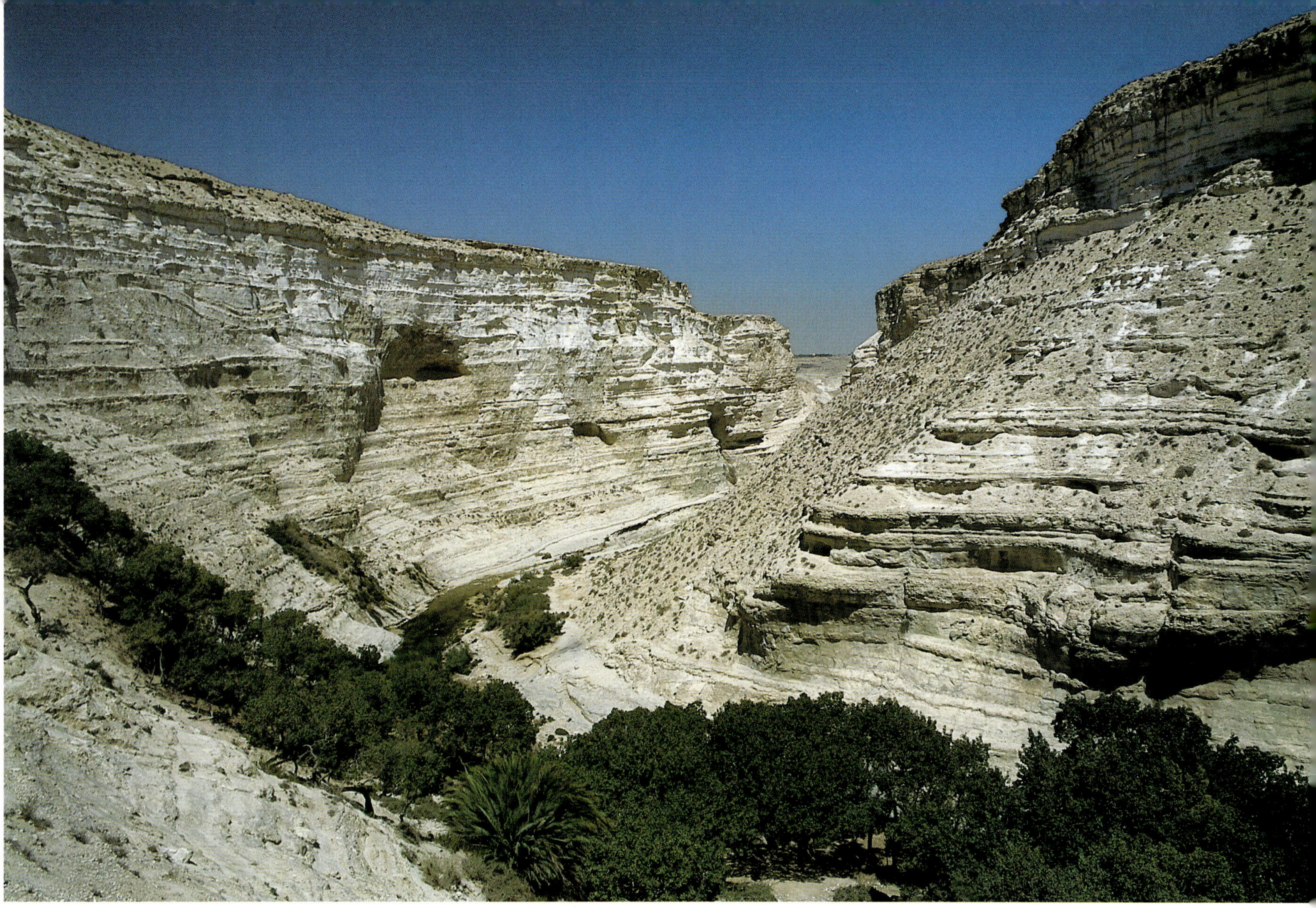

The Southern Route – Crater Landscape and Bedouins

The southern route from Beersheba via Mitzpe Ramon to Eilat is far more interesting than the road from Sodom on the Dead Sea to Eilat. It winds through mighty craters and over barren high plateaux, past bizarrely shaped rock formations and wide gorges.

It is well worth stopping at the *Kibbutz Sede Boqer*, a blooming agricultural settlement where Ben Gurion settled after he retired from politics – it is also his final resting place. In the neighbouring research institute botanists, geologists and farmers are seeking out ways to 'make the desert bloom' and ensure that Ben Gurion's vision does come true. Some of their achievements are beyond the wildest dreams of the great statesman: in *Kibbutz Mash'abbe Sade*, fish ponds breed up to 50,000 St. Peter's fish at a time under gigantic green plastic tents. Right next to this we find the small, sweetly-flavoured tomatoes being grown which are sold at European and American markets for as much as £3 a pound. And in the northern part of the Negev, a bright green carpet of winter grain grows between Kiryat Gat

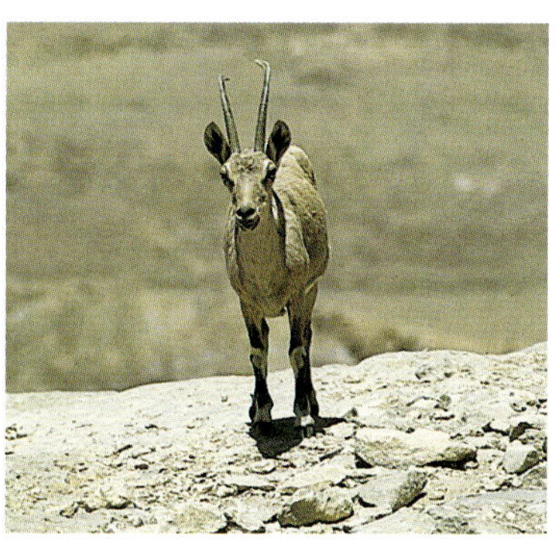

In the glorious valley of Ein Avdat tamarisk and pistachio trees grow (top), herds of gazelles (below) wander around and there are many different species of birds.

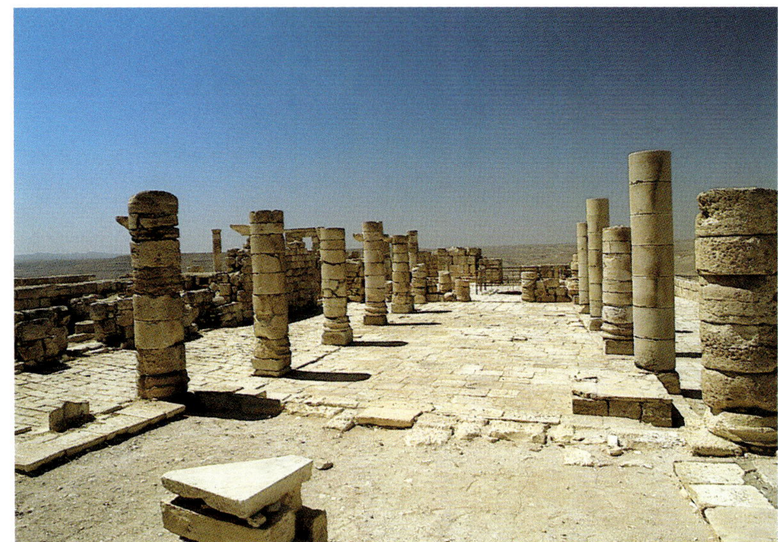

After the Nabataeans and the Romans, the Byzantines brought prosperity to Avdat. They built the North Church (above). There is a splendid view of the excavation site in the desert (below) from the observation balcony.

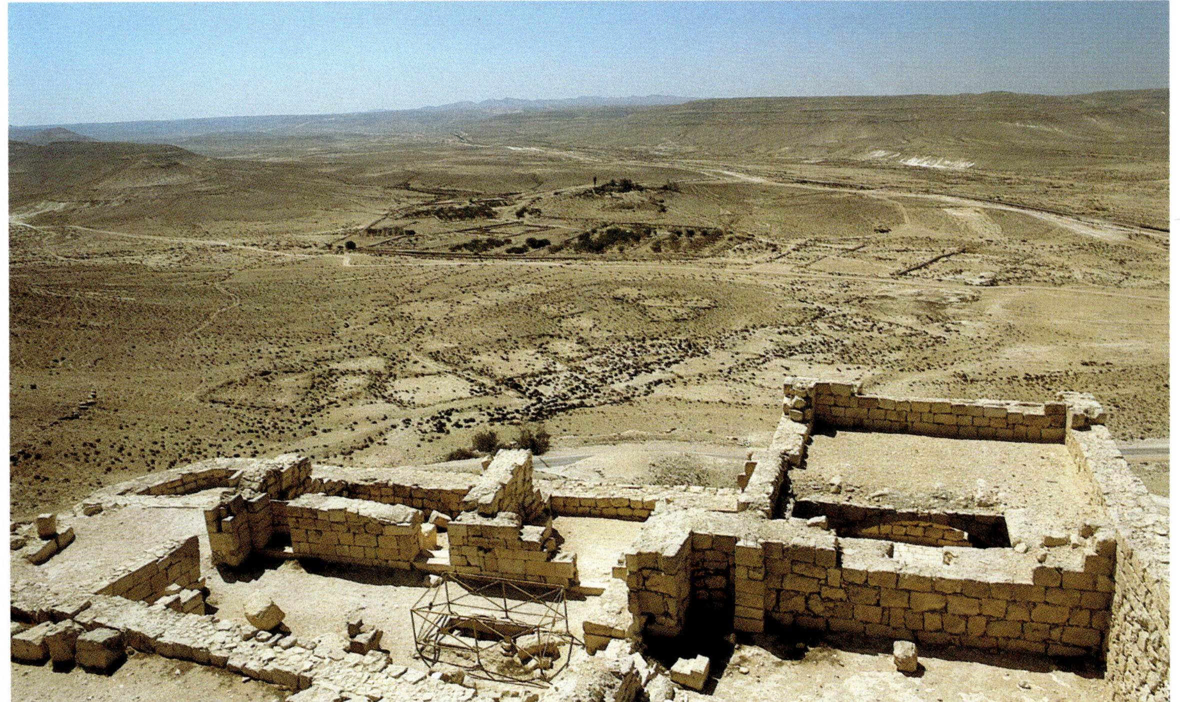

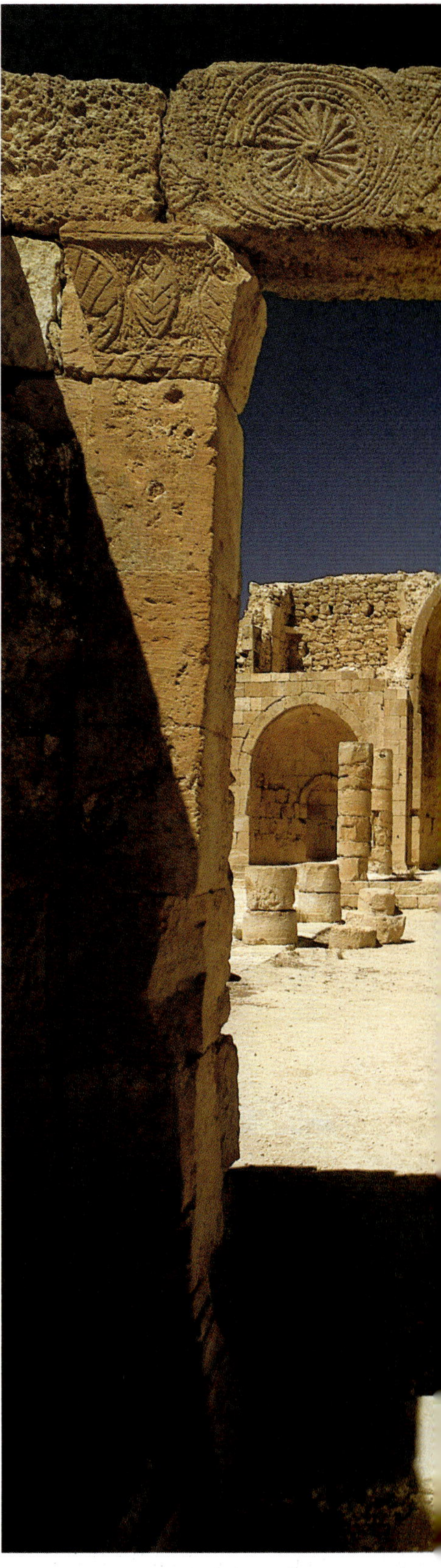

The South Church in Shivta, originally built with three naves, was built in the 4th century. The remote town of Shivta was once a major agricultural centre.

and Beersheba, the capital of the Negev. This raises the question of how the farmers of the Negev manage to raise cattle in the middle of the desert, farm fish in ponds and find water for tomato plantations and fields of grain. Nearly half the water that is required, some 115 million cubic metres per year is recycled water which is fed into the Negev from the north. However, about 20 years ago, geologists discovered a further source of water. At least 3300 feet under the desert is an enormous, ancient reservoir of salty, hot, brackish water. At first it was thought that this water was not usable. However, the residents of the Kibbutz Mash'abbe Sade proved that it was. Today they fill their fish ponds with this water, and then from time to time they drain it and divert it to the tomato fields, with aston-

Continued on Page 119

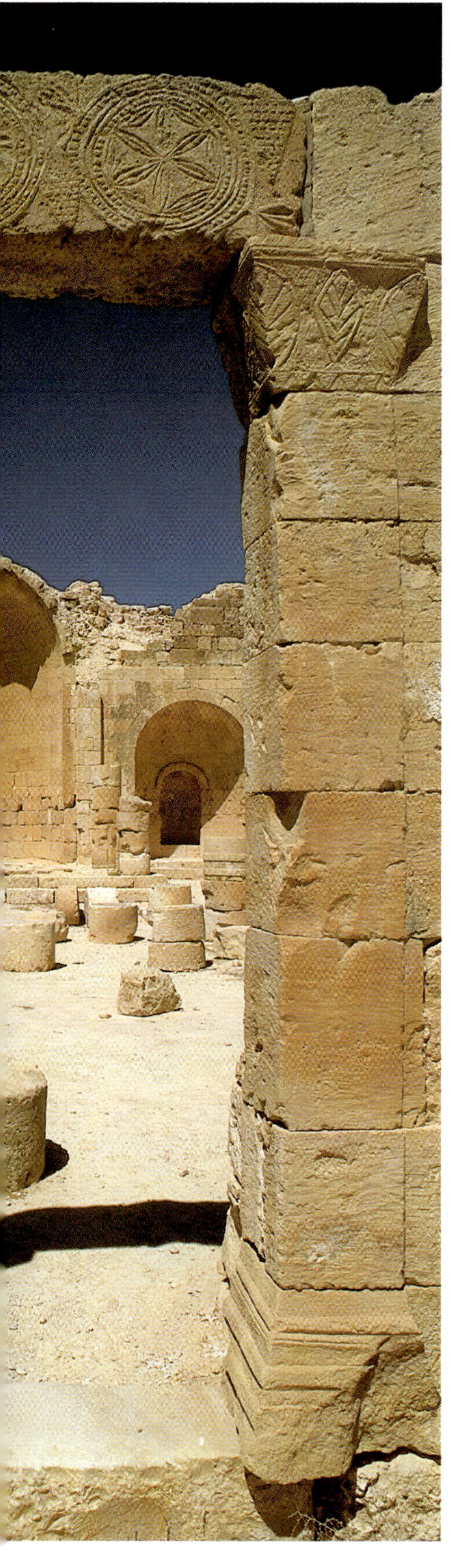

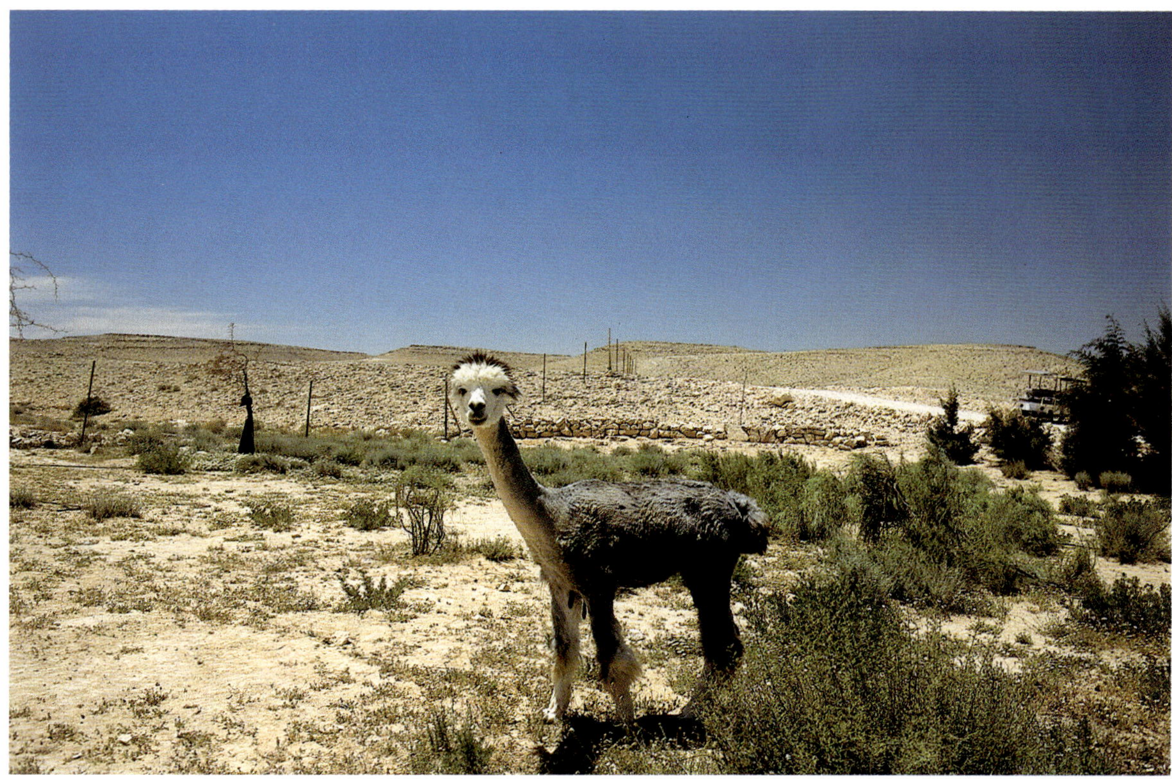

The Nabataeans

The Nabataeans, a tribe of Arab origin, probably arrived in the area of the present day Negev around the first century BC. After their subjugation by the Romans in 106 AD, they left the cities of Mamshit, Shivta, Avdat and famous Petra in Jordan. These cities were repopulated in the Byzantine period and these days it is possible to see and admire Byzantine churches and castles as well as pre-Christian structures. There are reconstructions in Avdat which show how highly developed agriculture and fieldwork was in those days – there are even some antique winepresses on view in Mamshit. An impressive picture of the lifestyle of this people who were important to the history of Israel for no more than the twinkling of an eye is conveyed by all three archaeological sites, through the remains of domestic buildings, burial caves and public buildings.

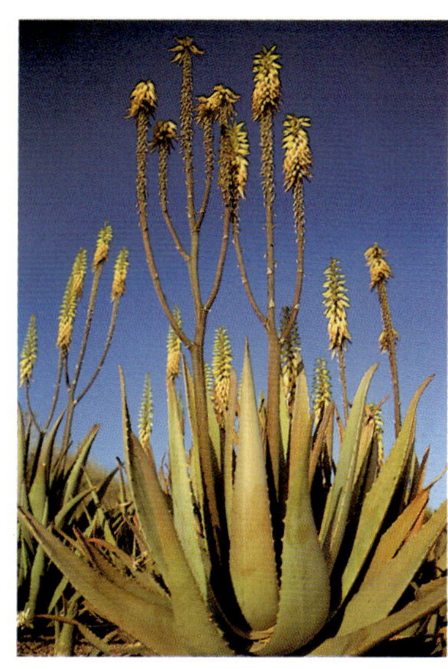

Many of the plants and animals mentioned in the Bible are no longer to be found in Israel. The alpaca originally comes from America (above, on a farm in Mitzpe Ramon) as did the Agave plant (below).

On the Trail of King Solomon

In the Timna Valley

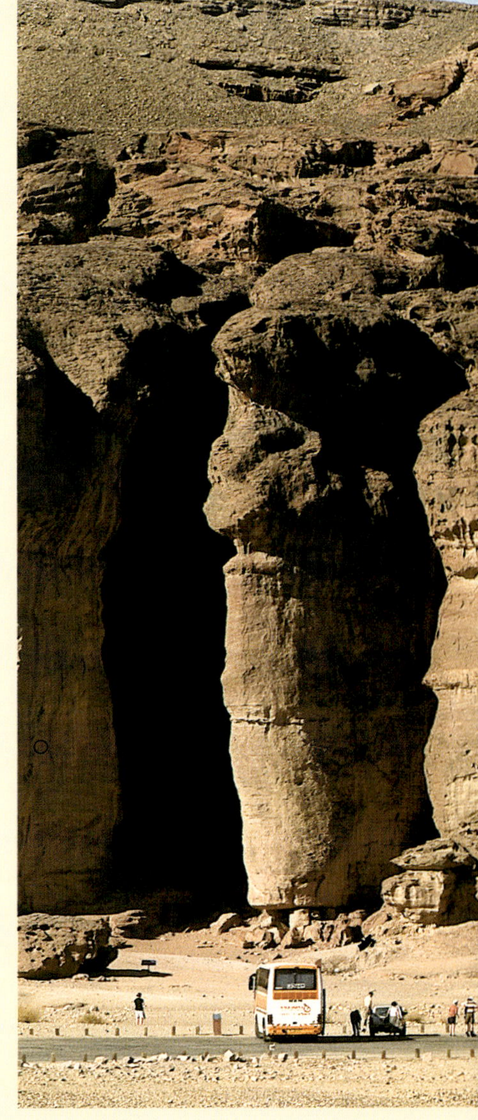

Approximately 25 kilometres north of Eilat, Israel once again proves to be quite perplexing. As is so frequently the case, the distances between modern industrial plants and historic sites are short, in this case it is the distance between the new *Copper Mines of Timna* and the ancient mines attributed to King Solomon. A circular route, which runs underground for part of the way, leads past an impressive display which illustrates how the precious ore was won in earlier times. Archaeologists have been able to demonstrate that copper mining was practised here from the 4th millennium before Christ until the Roman era. First the copper was smelted in round stone furnaces, then carried along stone channels to collecting vessels after which it was left to cool. Artfully constructed ventilation ducts caught the north wind and accelerated the cooling process. The area surrounding the archaeological site is now a 50 square kilometre expanse of national park.

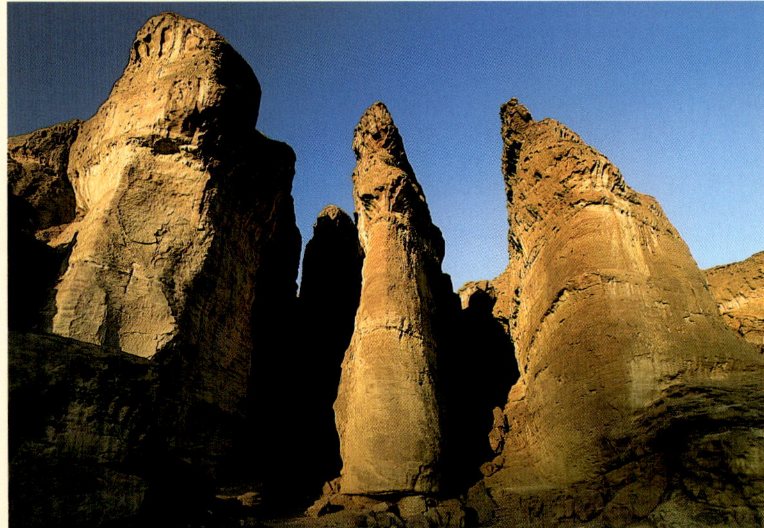

In the Timna Valley, you can see and admire the bizarre formations of reddish sandstone; the Pillars of Solomon which rise to about 50 metres.

Nubian sandstone erodes very quickly, which is how the *Pillars of Solomon* came to be. These are gigantic weathered rock towers of red stone. A stroll through the bizarre rock formations cannot but stimulate the imagination. However, one of the most impressive of these natural monuments permits only one interpretation; it is a monumental *Mushroom Rock*. The phenomenon of such formations is known the world over: wind and weather wear away the soft outer layer of stone which surrounds the granite core until only the harder material remains.

As in many other parts of the Negev and the Sinai, *rock paintings* from various historical periods are found here: in one cave, researchers found ceramics of Byzantine and Roman origin, stone implements dating back to Neolithic and Aeneolithic ages, as well as rock walls covered in pictures. The oldest are very simple line drawings of animals, mainly Nubian goats, next to which there are also images of people armed with spears. In another cave in the northern Timna Valley, scientists are researching two walls that are also carved with images: most depict draught animals pulling carts with hunters and their game: animals with enormous horns, probably Nubian goats. Scientists date these drawings back to the 2nd millennium BC. It is thought that they were made by hunters, gatherers and herdsmen who either lived in these caves or found shelter for themselves and their animals. If these early artists had not covered the cave walls around them with thousands of drawings there would be no trace left of their existence.

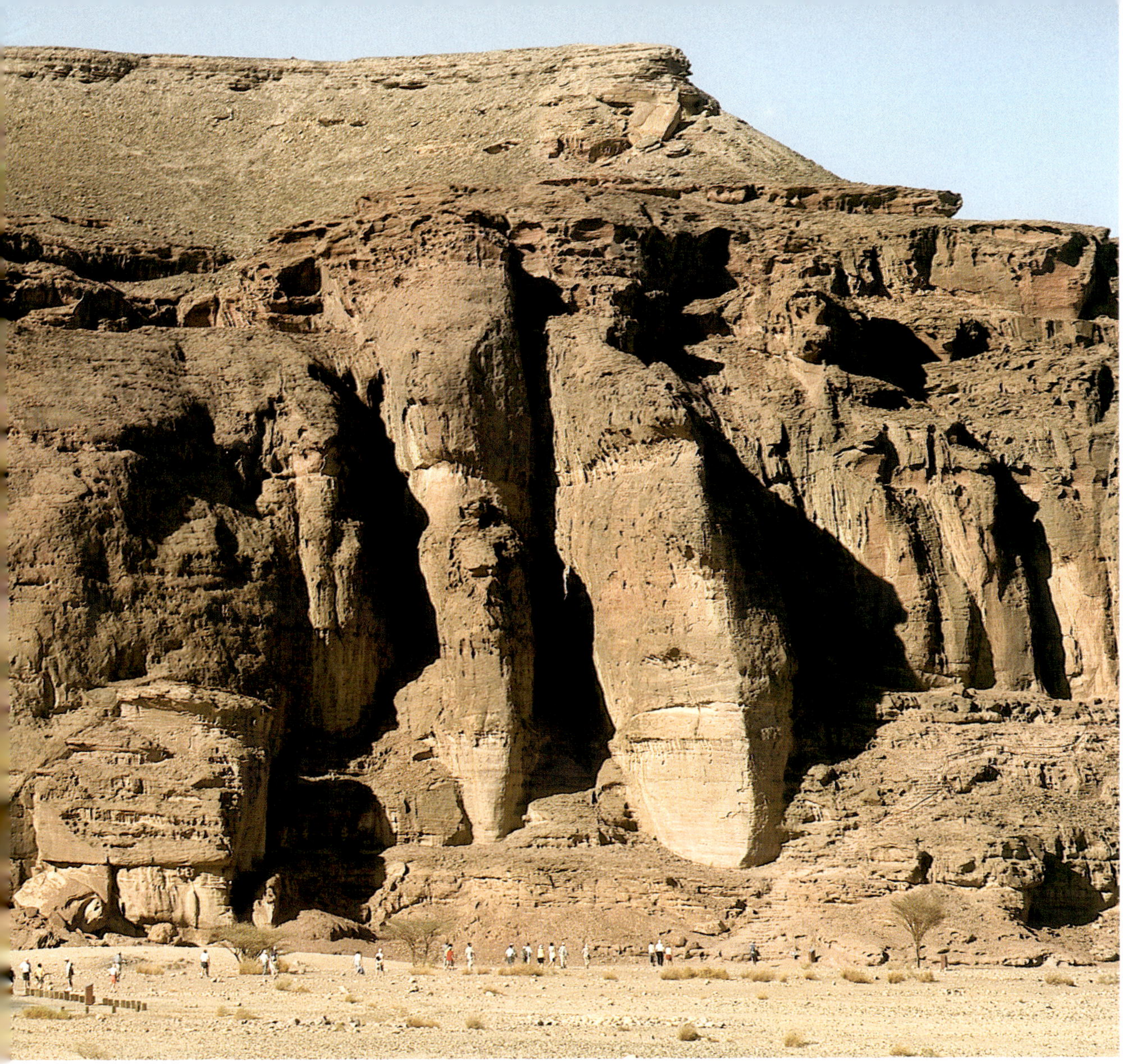

Many of the plants and animals mentioned in the Bible are no longer to be found in Israel. The alpaca originally comes from America (above, on a farm in Mitzpe Ramon) as did the Agave plant (below).

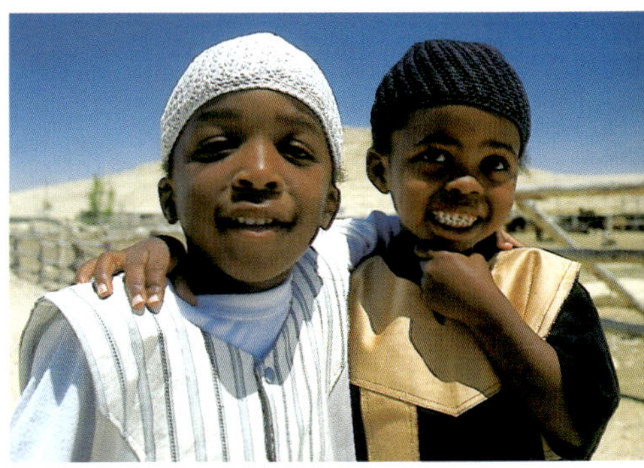

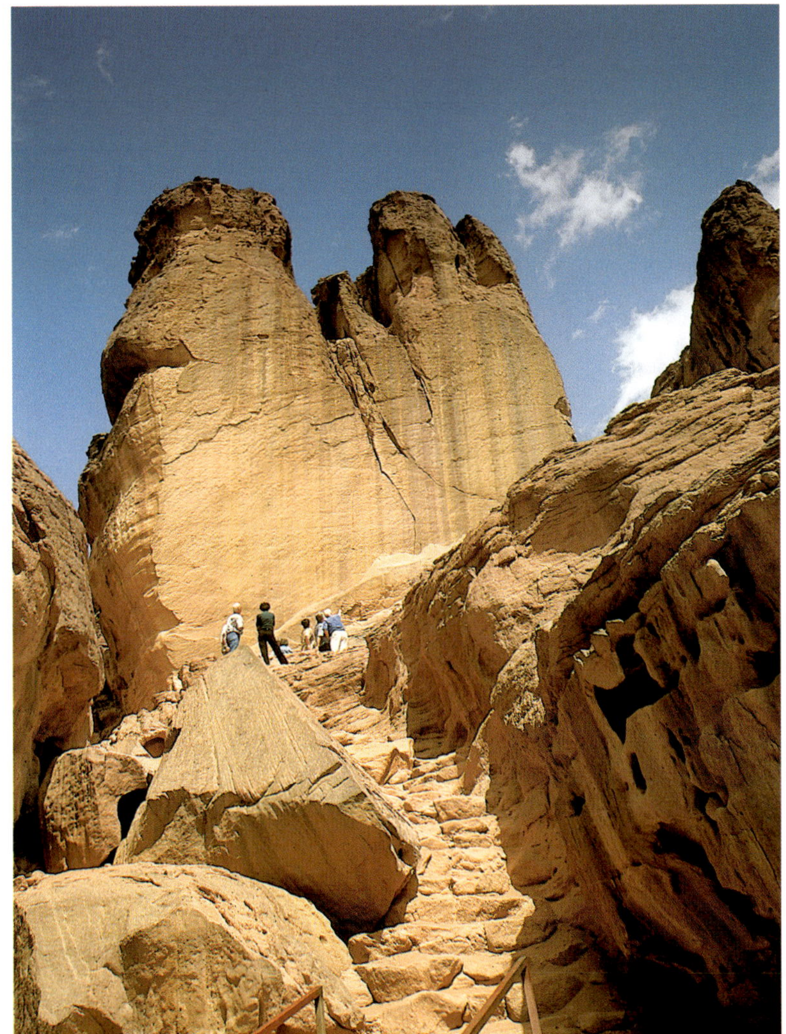

ishing results. The tomatoes, according to kibbutznik Itzik Levy, develop a form of 'stress' when treated with salty water and react by developing a higher sugar content – creating the sweet tomatoes from the Negev Desert which are popular the world over.

Five miles south of Kibbutz Sede Boqer it is possible to swim in the cool waters of the *Ein Avdat Oasis* even in summer. The whole of the Ein Avdat region with its four natural springs was declared a nature reserve where gazelles and ibex graze and drink and happily ignore the tourists.

Ein Avdat means 'the source of the Avdat' and takes its name from a city of great antiquity, the most important Nabataean-Roman-Byzantine settlement in the Negev, settled between the third century BC and the eighth century AD. The excavations of *Avdat* point to the fact that in ancient times this city was very prosperous – which is not really surprising, as the Nabataeans (see p. 117), being clever merchants, bought spices and perfumes in Yemen and sold these luxury goods at great profit to the Romans. The Israeli botanist Michael Evenari has reconstructed a Nabataean desert farm below the excavations of

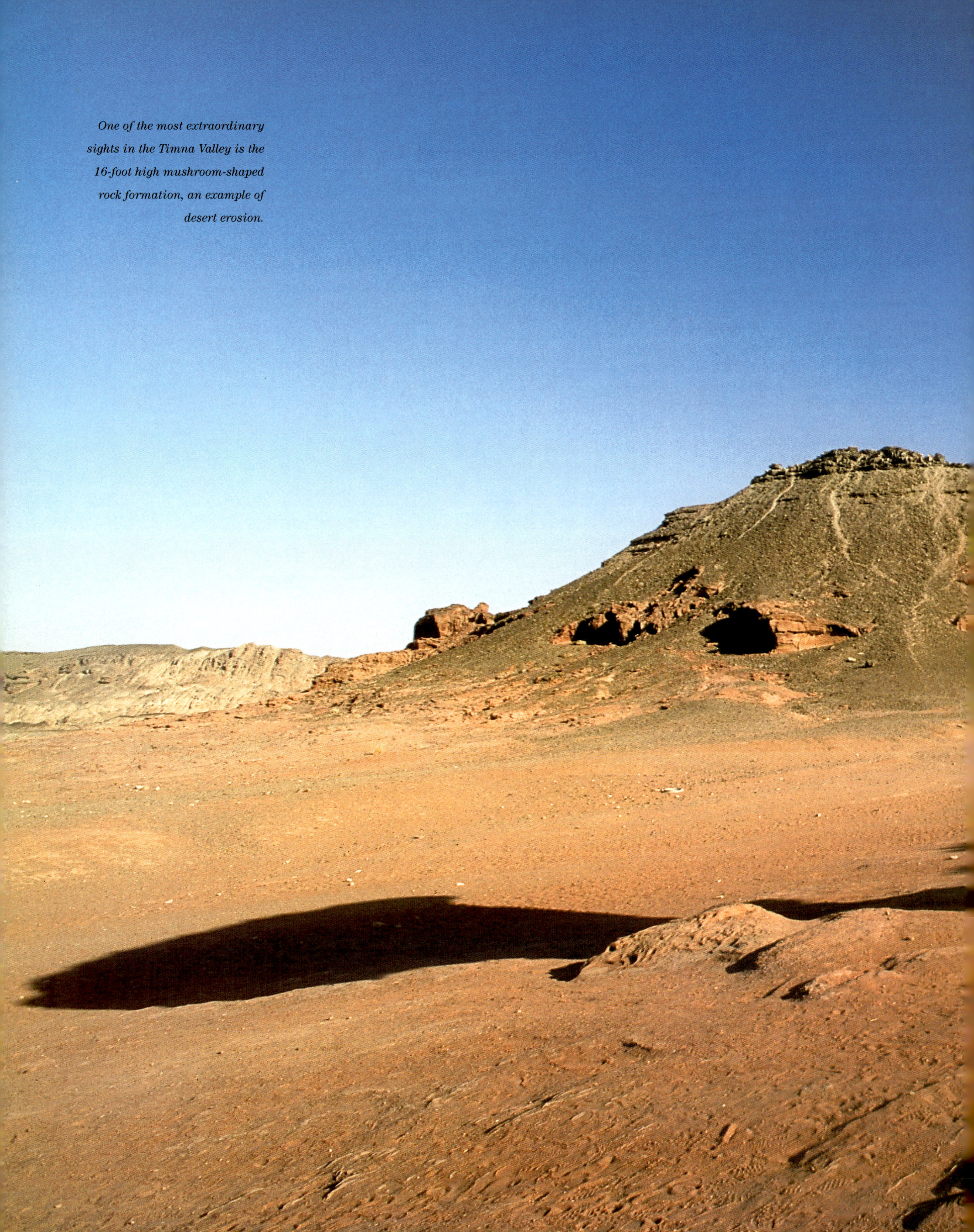

One of the most extraordinary sights in the Timna Valley is the 16-foot high mushroom-shaped rock formation, an example of desert erosion.

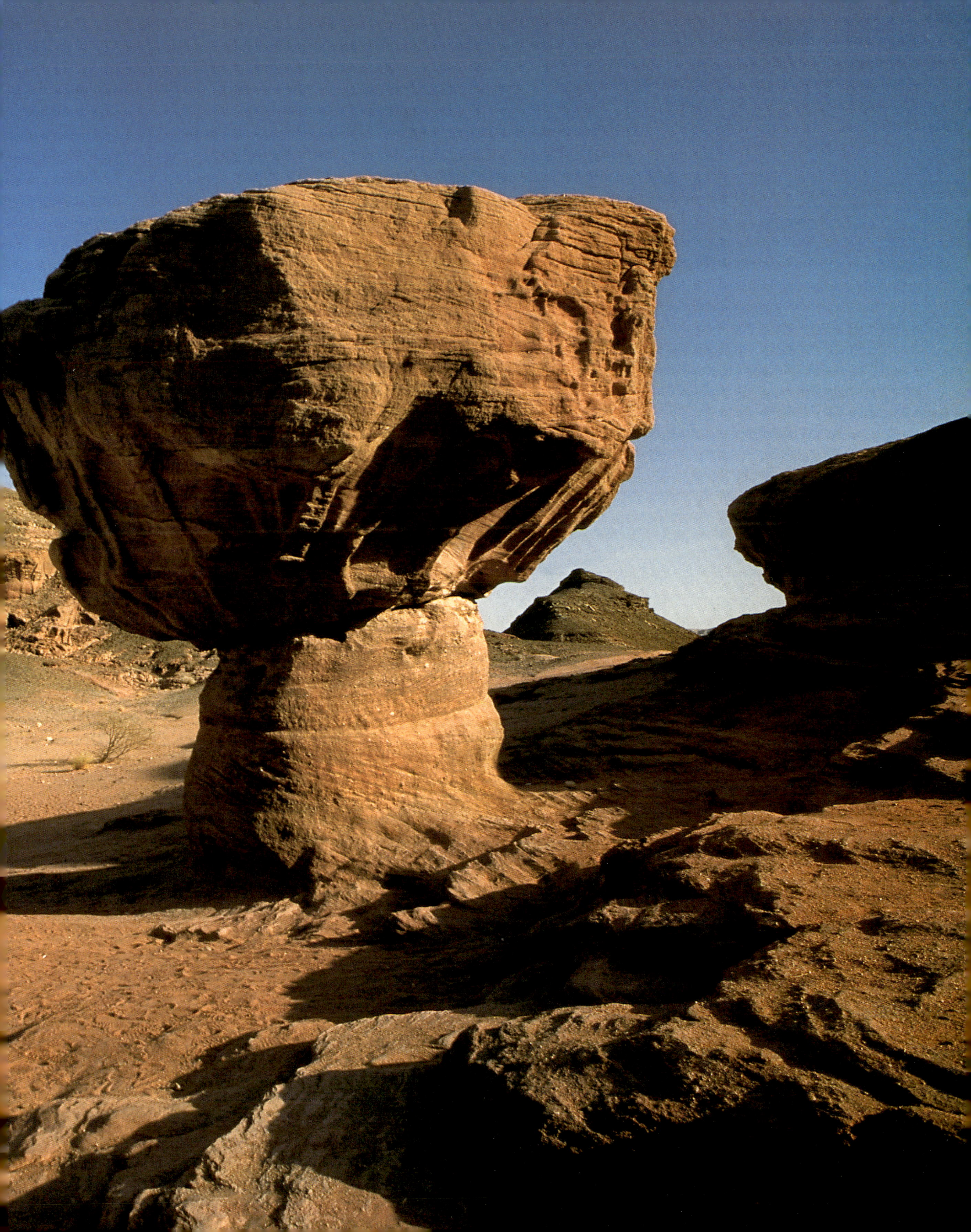

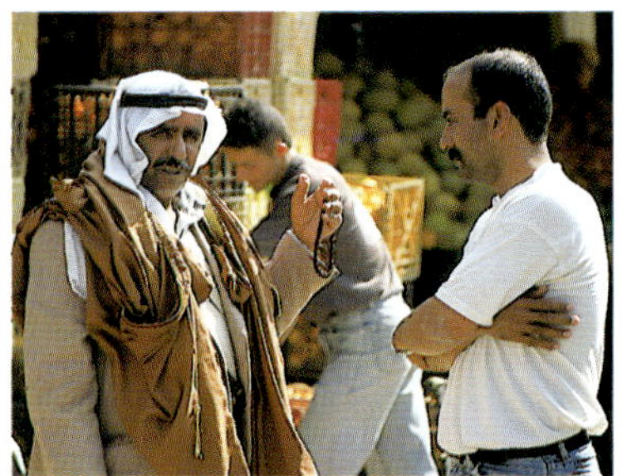

The faces here look like something from an oriental fairy tale and the variety of goods on offer turns the visit to the Bedouin market in Beersheba into an adventure.

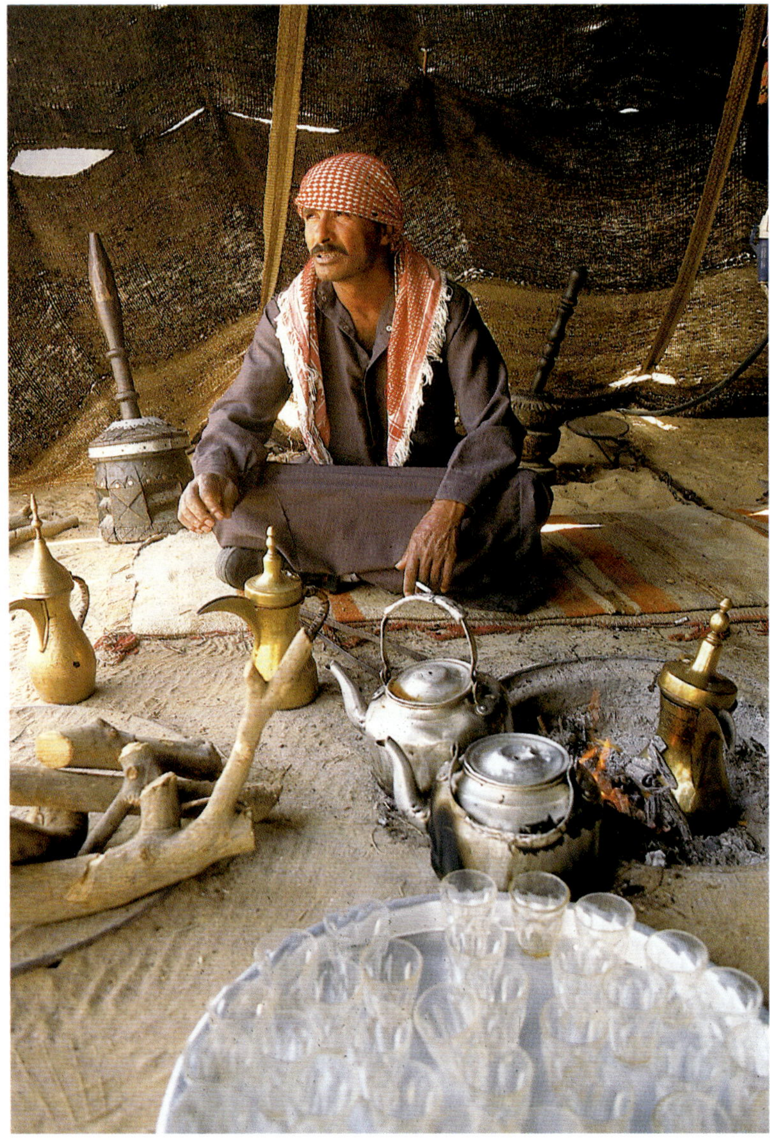

If you're going to buy something at the Bedouin market, be prepared to haggle and make sure you don't pay the first amount that's mentioned. A nice strong cup of tea helps revive the spirits.

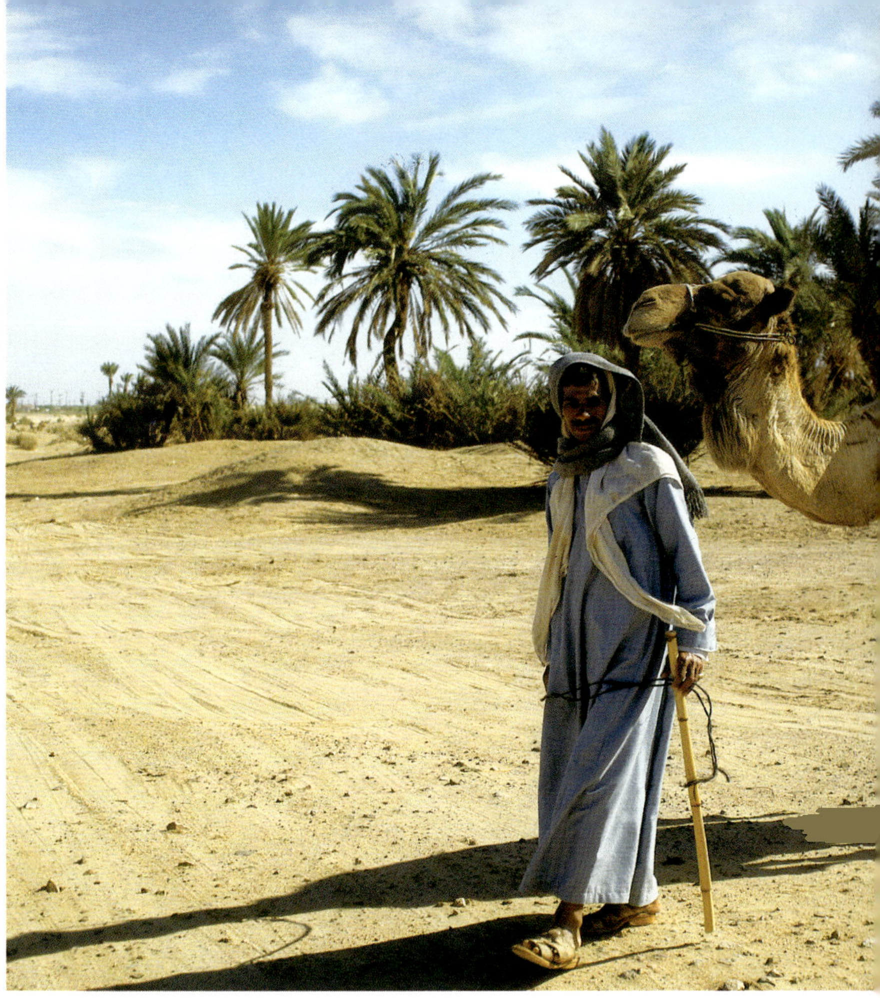

this greatest and grandest of Nabataean archaeological sites. It is obvious that the Nabataeans were very resourceful in dealing with the lack of water in the Negev. They trapped whatever water there was from the rain and channelled it through a system of dams and canals into the terraced fields. By copying the old canal systems, Evenari and his team are able to grow fruit and vegetables all year round without the use of an underwater reservoir and without using recycled water.

The most impressive spot on the southern route is *Mitzpe Ramon*. More than 1300 feet deep, 5 miles wide and 25 miles in length – these are the dimensions of the *Makhtesh Ramon*, the 'mortar' of Ramon, a gigantic erosion crater formed some 70 million years ago through earth movements over hollow areas. At the edge of the crater there is a visitors' centre with a terrace from where one can enjoy superb views of the stone-strewn desert. A multivisual show available in several languages presents the history of the earth's development in such simple terms that even the most uninformed person can understand and appreciate it. There is also an exhibition of the regional geology, flora and fauna. If you wish to explore the area yourself, be sure to take enough water and remember that a head-covering is essential to protect you from the sun. There are numerous marked trails taking you past the various layers of rock all the way into the heart of the crater.

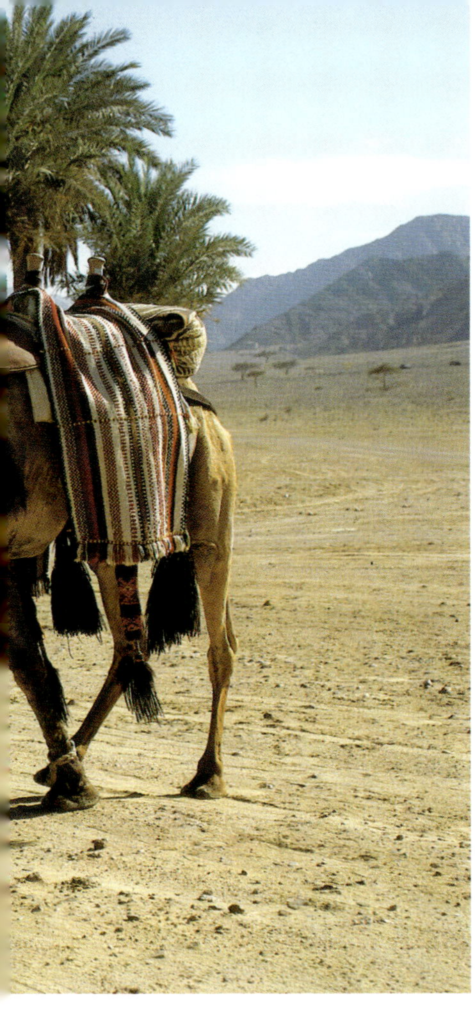

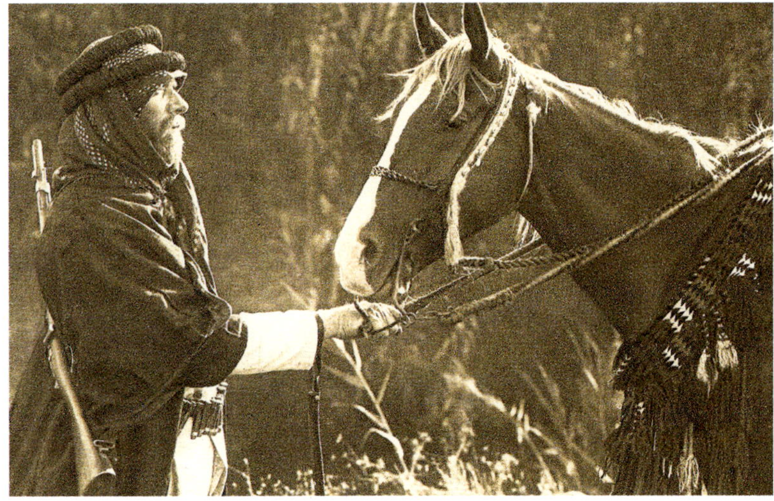

Although most Bedouin have given up their nomadic lifestyle they still keep up the old laws and customs of their forefathers (photo postcards from 1921).

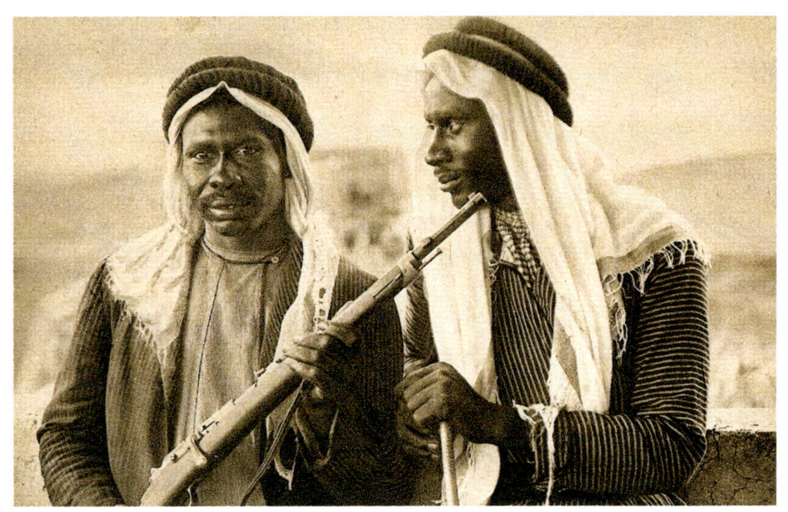

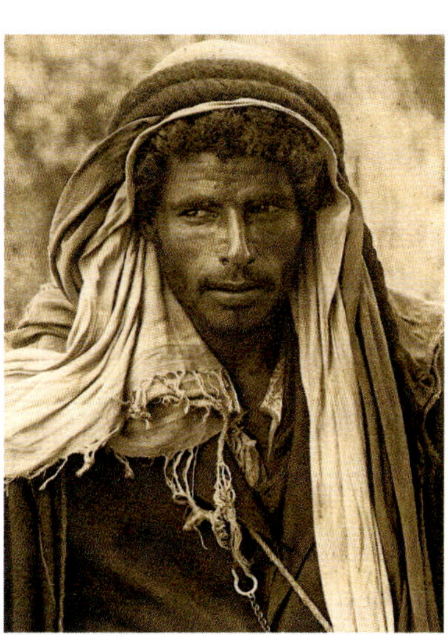

It has, however, not been possible to 'domesticate' the whole of the Negev. At least not as far as its inhabitants are concerned. Of Israel's 100,000 Bedouin, around 60,000 live in the Negev Desert. Many of them fled to Jordan during the 1948 War of Independence from what was to become Israeli territory. Those who remained were granted Israeli citizenship, but parts of their Bedouin lands were confiscated by the Israeli government, which at the same time attempted to make the Bedouin give up their nomadic ways.

A quarter of the approximately 100 Negev settlements are inhabited by Bedouin, but about two and a half miles east of Beersheba in *Tel Sheva* there are signs of the negative side of the attempts to make the Bedouins settle in one place. The houses, kindergartens and a school which the Israeli government built there were not accepted by the Bedouin families. They preferred to set up their traditional tents or simple corrugated iron huts. The weekly Bedouin market in Beersheba is the perfect place to observe how the twentieth century has infiltrated their traditional lifestyle. Bedouin arrive from near and far on their camels, donkeys and occasionally in rickety old VW buses to bring their goods to market. What you will see here are chickens, goats, food, rugs, engraved brass bowls, embroidered cushions, camel saddles or the traditional handmade silver jewellery. But take care, because among all the above there will be the occasional trinket 'made in Taiwan' on offer.

Beersheba – the 'Well of the Oath'

Not far from the Bedouin Settlement Project are the ruins of the biblical Beersheba which look a little out of place in a city which, at first sight, seems rather faceless, even transient. In fact, Beersheba, this energetic outpost of civilization is very old and is mentioned in the Bible as the Well of the Oath. This refers to a dispute between Abraham and Abimelech, the Philistine, about a well, the dispute over which was settled by that very oath.

A contract between the heads of the two tribes secured for Abraham the right to use the well he had dug, an agreement

The attractions of Eilat lie around and under the water. This modern holiday resort on the Red Sea boasts long beaches, every conceivable water sport and a fascinating underwater world of fish and corals.

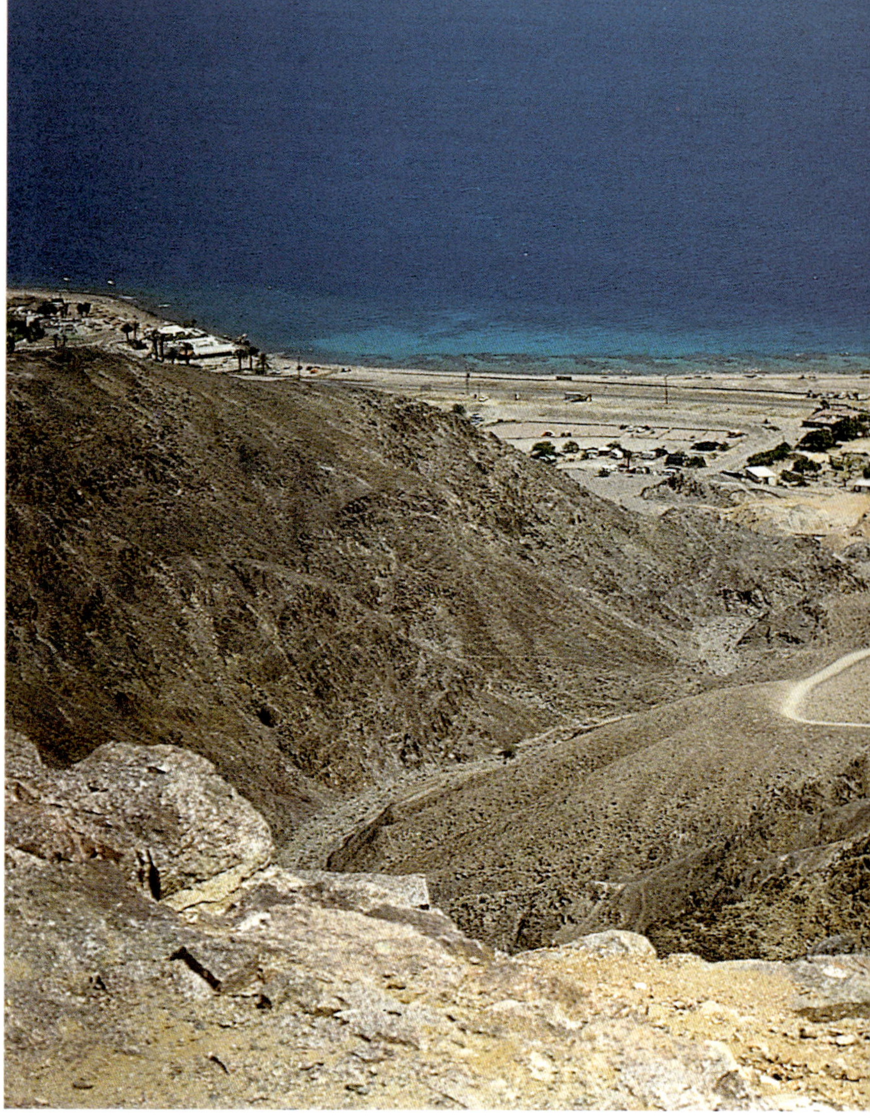

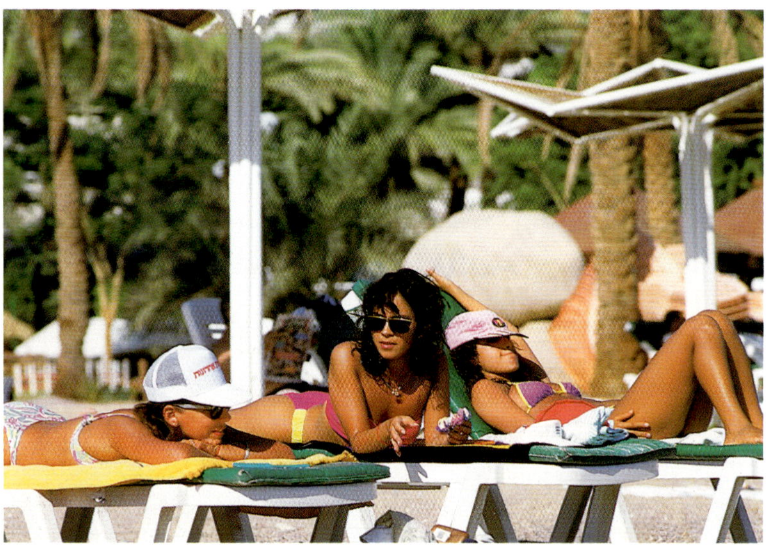

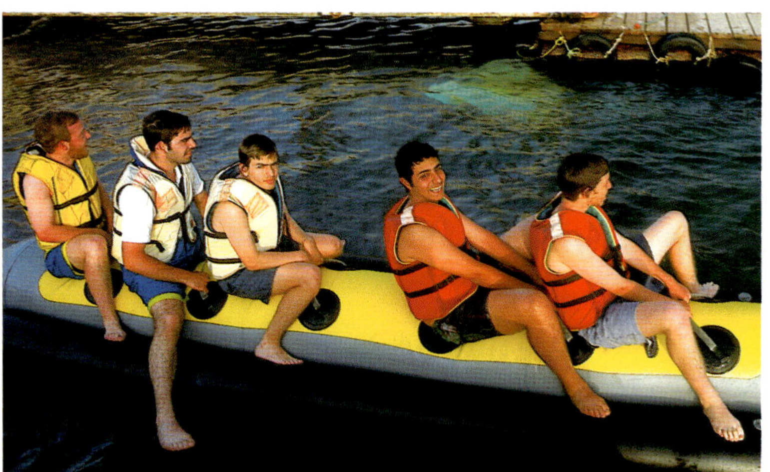

which was confirmed by Abraham's son, Isaac, and documented in the Bible. Resourceful businessmen have picked out a well in Beersheba's Old City and identified it as *Abraham's Well*, but this particular construction, dates back only to the Ottoman period.

Until the mid-nineteenth century, Beersheba was no more than a collection of springs and streams being used by local Bedouin tribes. The Ottoman rulers finally built a small police station and a mosque here. It is easy enough to see the whole of the Old City of Beersheba. The main street through the Old City is the Keren Kayemet Le-Israel Street; it has a few narrow roads off it with slightly crooked houses looking for all the world as though the wind had given them a slight shove to one side. The former mosque is located within the Old City, as is the *Museum HaNegev* which has some interesting exhibits dating back to the fourth century BC. These exhibits were excavated on the Tel, the old settlement hill outside the city.

It was only after the Israelis conquered Beersheba during the War of Independence that a speedy programme of resettlement was started. Apartment buildings of very little charm were built here in the 1950s to house immigrants from Arab countries. In the 1970s, immigrants from the Soviet Union joined

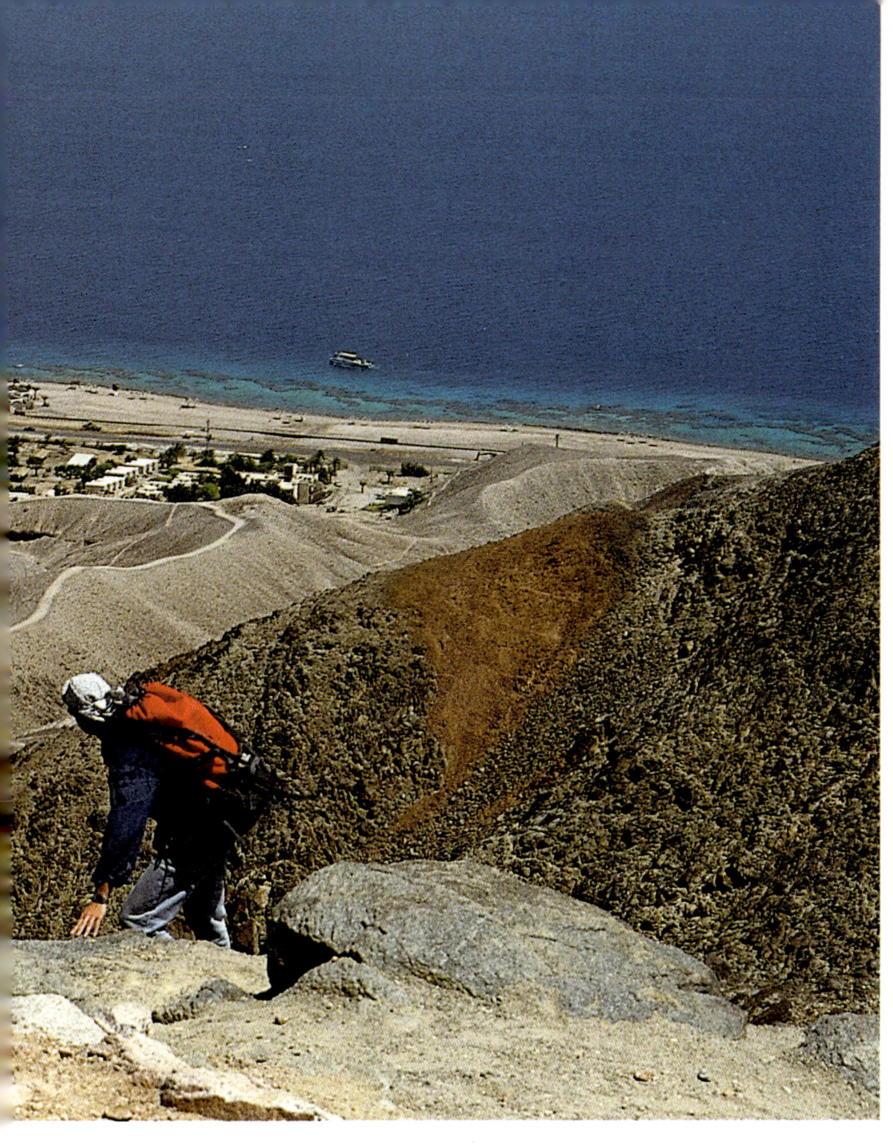

them, and now make up about a quarter of the 150,000 inhabitants. Today it is the *Ben Gurion University* which reigns supreme here. With its students and professors it is the intellectual centre of the Negev region. Established in 1968, the university brought the city a certain level of prosperity. This is particularly noticeable around the suburbs of *Omer*, *Meitar* and *Lehavin*. Members of the university and physicists who work at the atomic reactor in Dimona live here in gleaming white houses with lush green gardens – very much like an American suburb. Little wonder that this is an area which is regularly found at the top of the list of desirable places for those looking for a better quality of life in Israel.

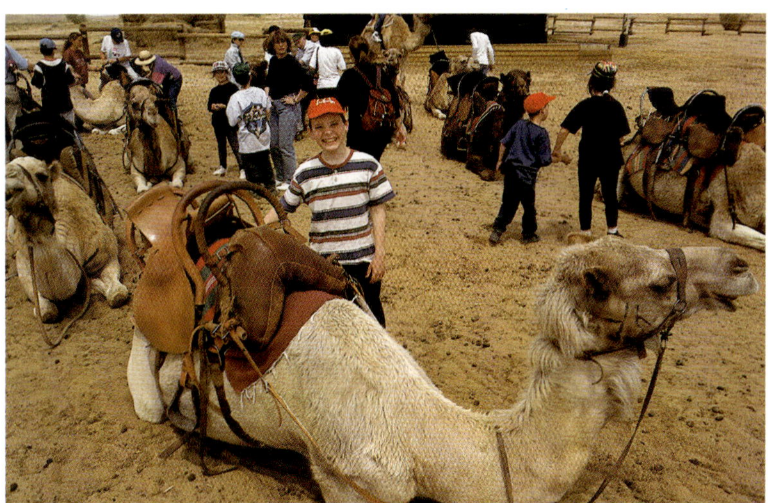

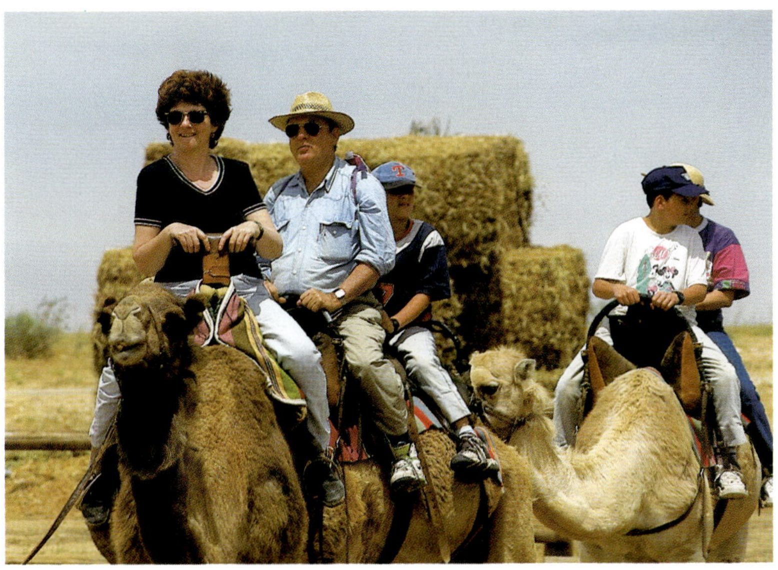

A whiff of adventure: join a camel tour from Eilat to gain a sense of what it must have been like to be a trader on the old caravan routes through the Negev Desert.

Fun, fun, fun: Eilat

The more recent history of Eilat, like that of Beersheba, started with a small police post – not a Turkish one, but a British one. Umm Rashrash, as it was then called, was a totally forgotten place at the northern tip of the Gulf of Aqaba with no plans that it became part of a future Jewish state. The UN Partition Plan of 1947 awarded the Zionists a large part of the Negev Desert, but no access to the Persian Gulf – the only shipping route from Palestine to Africa and Asia. The Israelis conquered this area in the War of Independence and, as in Beersheba, first settled Jews from Arab countries there – in apartment buildings which were just as unattractive as the ones in Beersheba. These buildings were not even on the beach but in the hilly hinterland. It was only after Israel had repelled the attempts by the Egyptians to reconquer this land during the Six Day War and when they had taken the whole of the Sinai

Peninsula, that a group of resourceful managers decided to turn this little town at the southernmost point of the country into a holiday paradise. With only five days of rain a year, temperatures of up to 21°C in winter and miles of coral banks it is only surprising that no one had come up with the idea sooner.

Meanwhile this town grows before your very eyes. Hotels elbowing each other for space, a daily influx of new tourists arriving on the Israeli charter airline Arkia, that is, if they don't prefer arriving overland from Jerusalem, driving through the desert for three or four hours. Once in Eilat these are the priorities: relax, laze around and have fun. Tourists in Eilat do not want to know about the tensions, the challenges or whatever else is going on in the rest of Israel. The hardest decision will

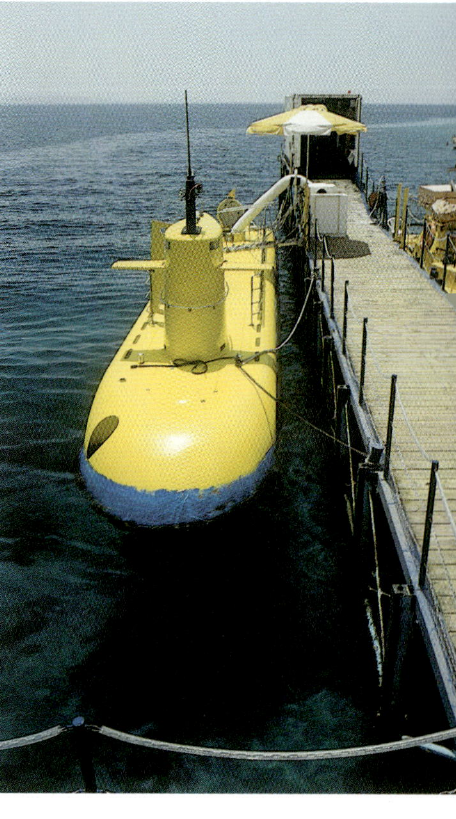

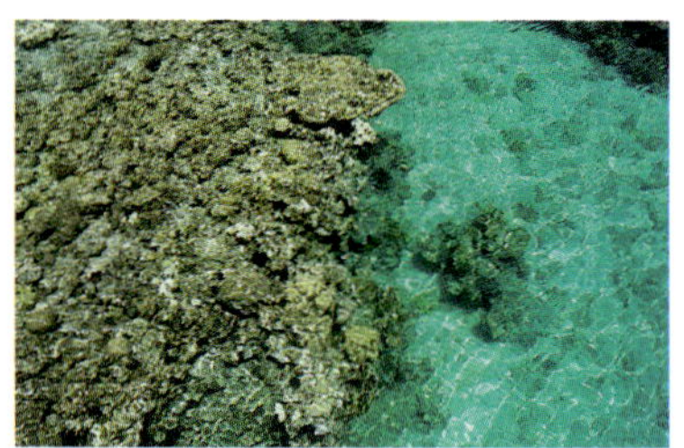

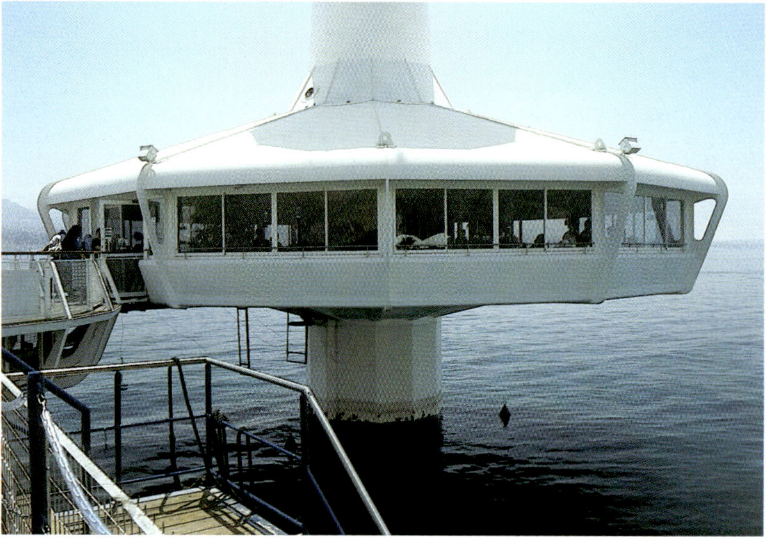

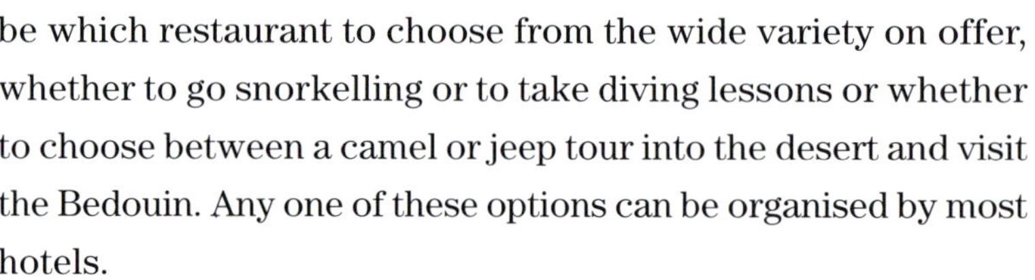

A chance to see the shimmering underwater world with brilliantly coloured shoals of fish and coral reefs from the Coral World Underwater Observatory (left and below centre). A trip on the 'Yellow Submarine' takes you down 60 metres (centre top).

be which restaurant to choose from the wide variety on offer, whether to go snorkelling or to take diving lessons or whether to choose between a camel or jeep tour into the desert and visit the Bedouin. Any one of these options can be organised by most hotels.

On the other hand, one might choose to see the fish without getting one's feet wet – south of Eilat towards the Egyptian resort of Taba there is the *Underwater Observatory* from where one can view the crocodile fish and red fire weevers, yellow parrot fish and the graceful lion fish. Not far from there is the *Dolphin Reef* which is well worth a visit. Psychologists work with autistic children here, allowing them to swim with the dolphins. This exercise helps the children learn to make body contact. It is extremely successful. Dolphins have proved to be outstanding and very sensitive psychologists.

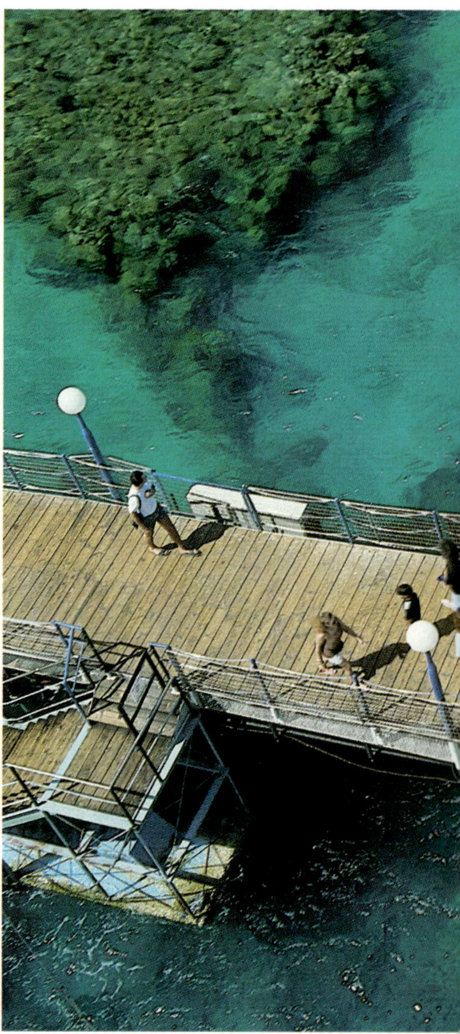

Where three countries meet: Egypt – Israel – Jordan

Even while life seemed quite carefree in the holiday resort of Eilat, in years gone by Israelis still felt a longing for something that seemed out of reach: They could see the lights of Jordan's Aqaba only from a distance, and could only imagine what it would be like to visit the mythical city of *Petra*, the former capital of the Nabataeans. However, since Jordan and Israel signed the long overdue Peace Treaty in 1994 everything has become very simple – even for independent travellers. You just find a taxi to take you to the *Arava Border Crossing*, pay a nominal exit tax, hand over a few dinars on the Jordanian side for a visa and take a taxi from there to *Aqaba*. Most drivers will offer visitors the option of a trip to *Wadi Rum*, a picturesque desert valley surrounded by rock faces of up to 1300 feet high where Bedouin have made their homes. It is here, the taxi drivers will tell you with pride, that the classic film *Lawrence of Arabia* was filmed. It is even possible to take a day trip to Petra by taxi, so long as one is prepared to start very early and cross the border shortly after it opens at 8.00 a.m. It is perfectly feasible to be back before the border closes at ten in the evening having made the two hour trip to Petra and taken in the spectacular town of the Nabataeans.

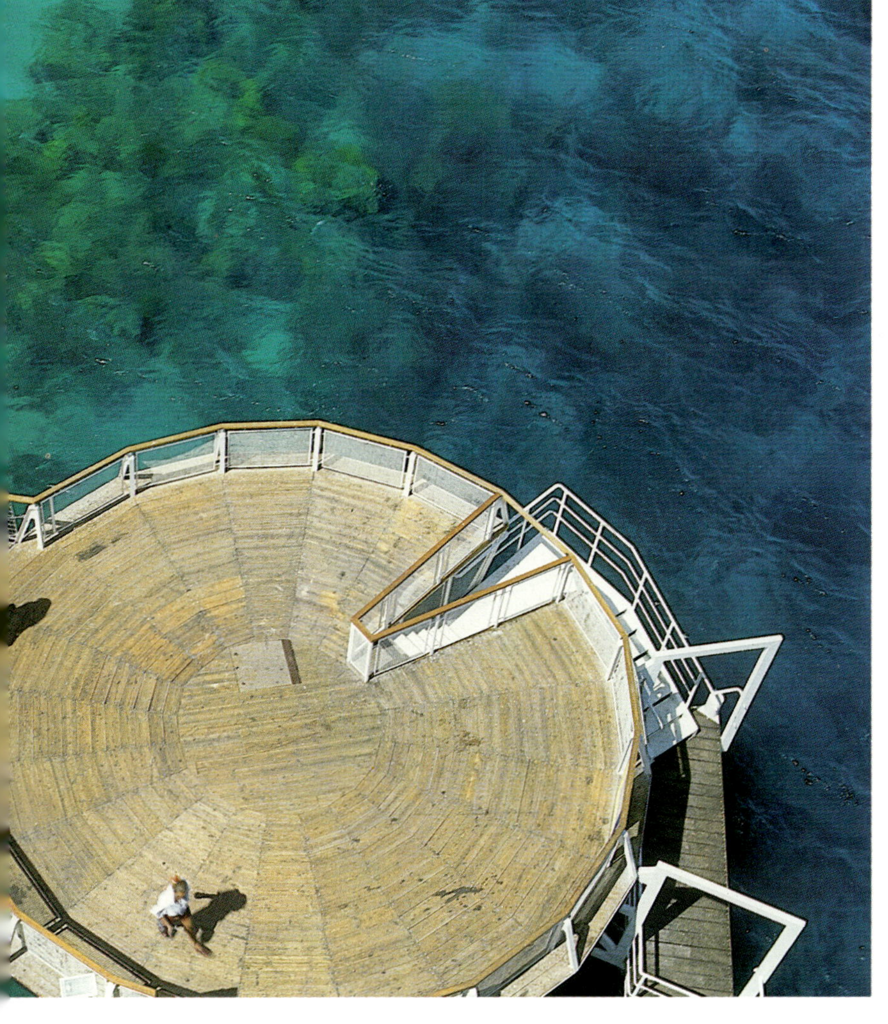

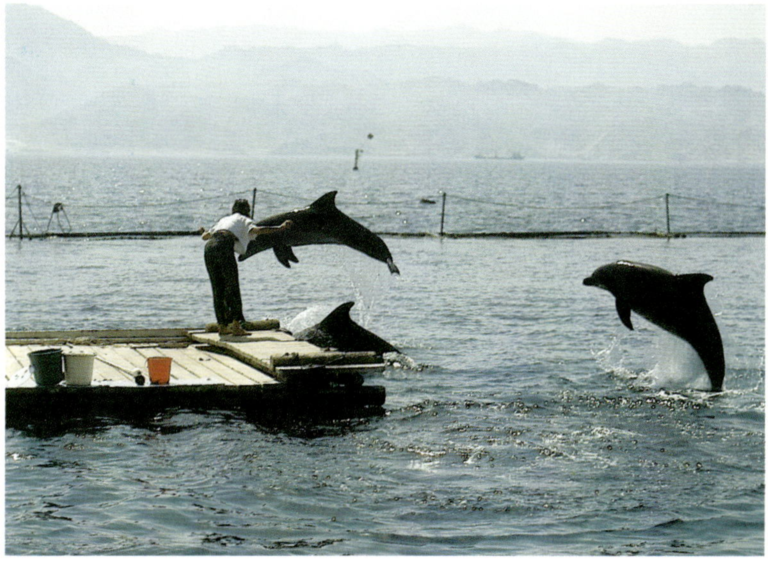

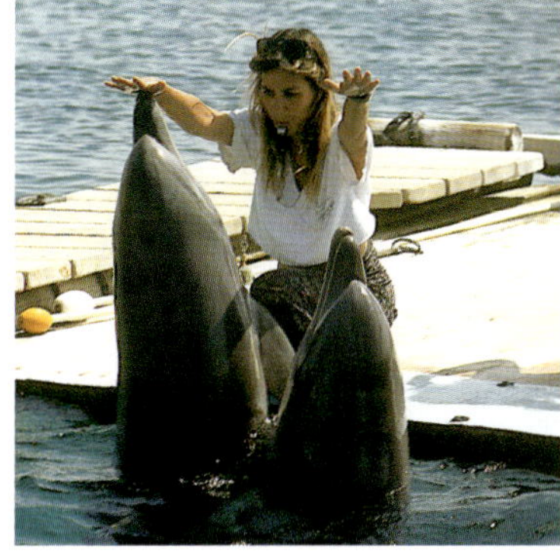

These extraordinarily intelligent and nimble dolphins are the main attraction at Eilat's Dolphin Reef. It is possible to watch the training sessions of the animals from a stage.

For those who would like to add an Egyptian stamp to their passports, nothing could be easier. The Egyptian border is just south of Eilat. The only difference between visiting Egypt and Jordan is that visas to Egypt have to be applied for 24 hours in advance. If you book a tour, for example to *St Catherine's Monastery*, built in the sixth century on the site where God appeared to Moses in the burning bush, the travel agency will make the necessary arrangements. It is also possible to pick up your visa personally at the Egyptian Consulate and by doing so you will be able to discover some lovely, isolated beaches with clear water and coral reefs along the *Sinai Peninsula* on your own. Regardless of whether you are in Jordan, Israel or Egypt, when you go to the Red Sea it is not difficult to put behind you all the political quarrels that affect this area and simply enjoy a lovely vacation.

An Underwater World of Colour

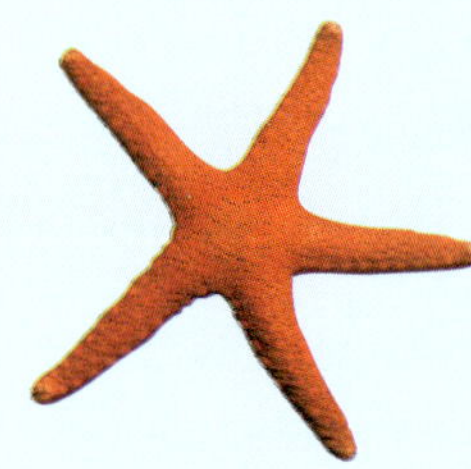
1

The Red Sea, a Diver's Paradise

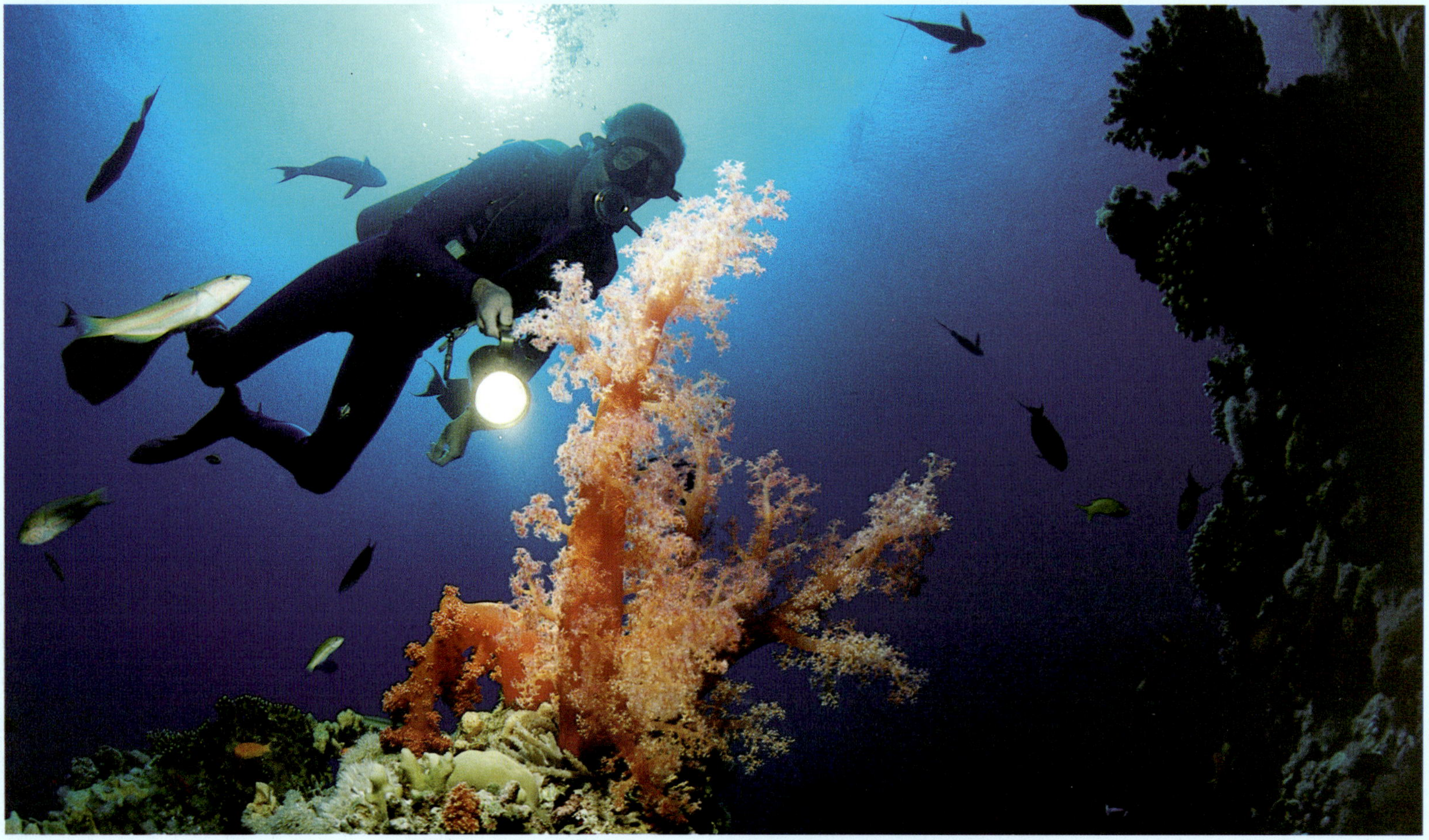

2

Diving equipment can be hired from any of the many diving schools in Eilat. The water is so clear and shallow, a snorkel and diving mask are often all the gear needed to admire the underwater fauna: 1 Starfish. 2 Diving among the corals. 3 Red coral.

If you have just come from the wasteland of the Negev and go diving below the surface of the Red Sea, you will be overwhelmed by the colour and breathtaking beauty before you.

The world's northernmost coral reefs are located in the Gulf of Aqaba, or Gulf of Eilat as it is known on the Israeli shore. Minute master builders have been creating natural

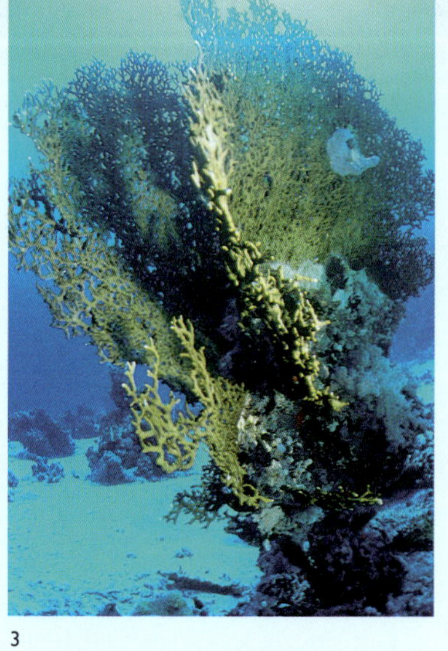
3

stone monuments of singular shapes and colours ever since the Red Sea was formed in the Tertiary Period approximately forty million years ago.

Around 6,500 different types of microscopically small coral polyps take part in the construction of this marine wonder world. Only at night, when these creatures, known scientifically as anthozoae, stretch out their tentacles to take in food, does it become apparent that they are animals. Other than a few types of algae, there is no plantlife in the Red Sea.

If one looks closely enough, it is possible to distinguish between corals with six actinoids and those with eight, depending on the number of starlike chalk deposits and tentacles present. Among those with six actinoids are the crustaceans and sea anemones that exist in symbiosis with the brightly coloured anemone fish. The eight rayed sea fans of the Gulf of Eilat are particularly impressive as they jut out majestically from the steep slopes into the sea. There are another million or so different species of invertebrates: jelly fish, snails, shellfish, crabs and all the little creepy-crawlies in the coral reef. This immeasurable diversity and the colourful multitude of the swarms of coral fish combine to make a splendid kaleidoscope of the tropical submarine world.

So long as we do not touch anything in the underwater world and are there purely as observers, we do not need to fear the sea dwellers who will often swim right past our diving masks, seemingly devoid of fear. Naturally some of the fish, such as the rock fish or the red fire weever, are dangerous, and their venom is by no means harmless to humans. However, they will only ever make use of it if directly challenged.

The extraordinary fringing reefs before the Israeli coast are popular with both snorkellers and divers. They offer steeply dropping coral walls where divers can experience exhilarating descents, as well as lagoons closer to shore which form ideal snorkelling areas with many interesting things to see in the protected shallows. One of the world famous highlights for enthusiastic divers is *Dolphin Reef* south of Eilat, where dolphins may be encountered below the sea and, to the north of the Underwater Observatory, the *Moses Rock*, overgrown with brightly covered soft coral. To the south this is joined by the *'Japanese Gardens'* whose magical coral landscapes slope to a depth of more than 40 metres.

Christian Mietz

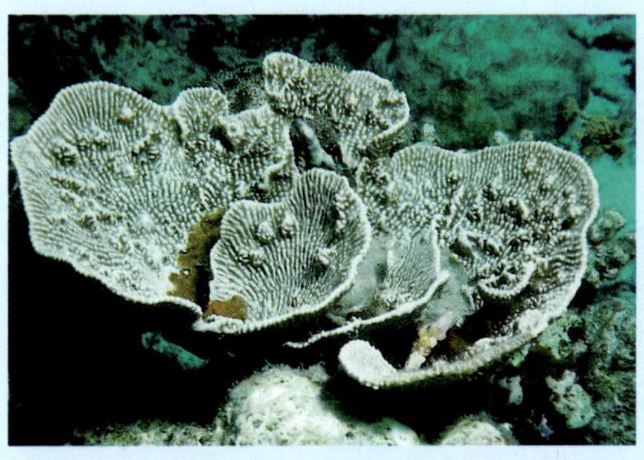
4

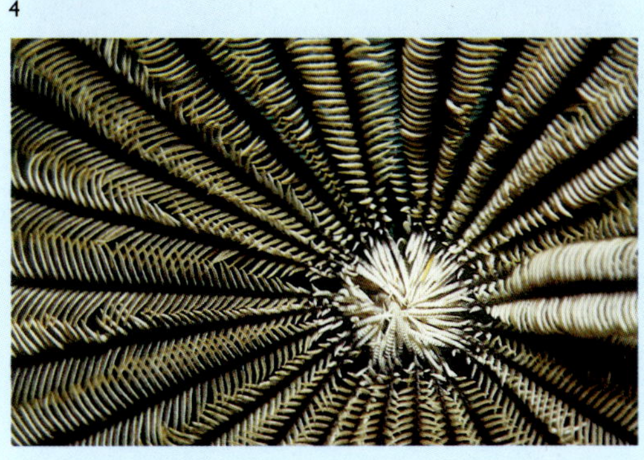
5

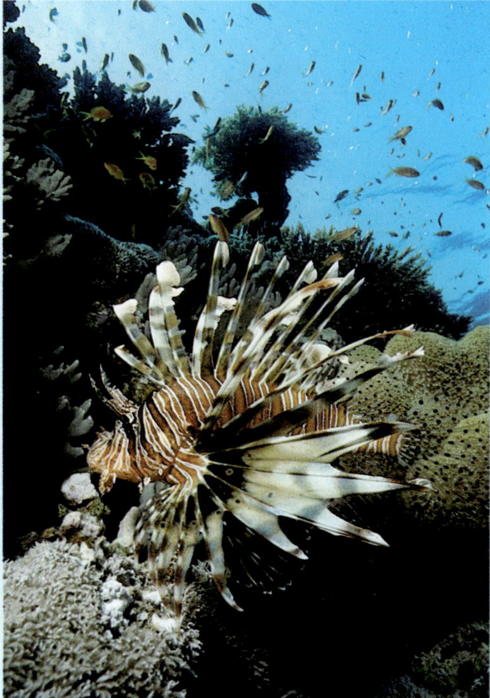
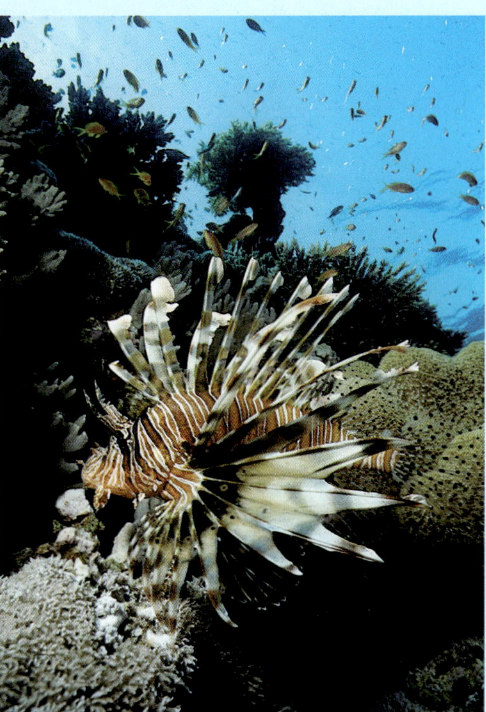
6

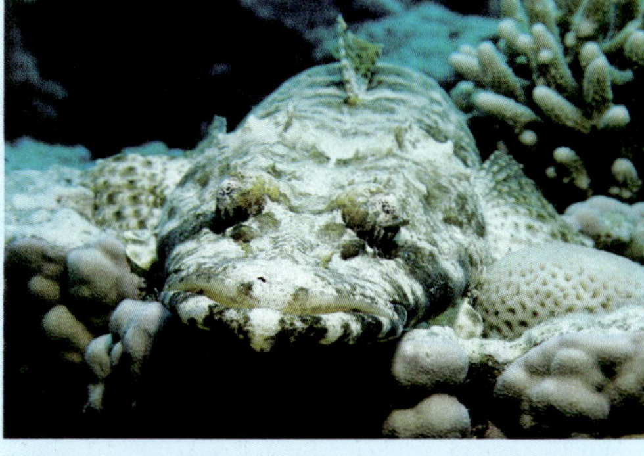
7

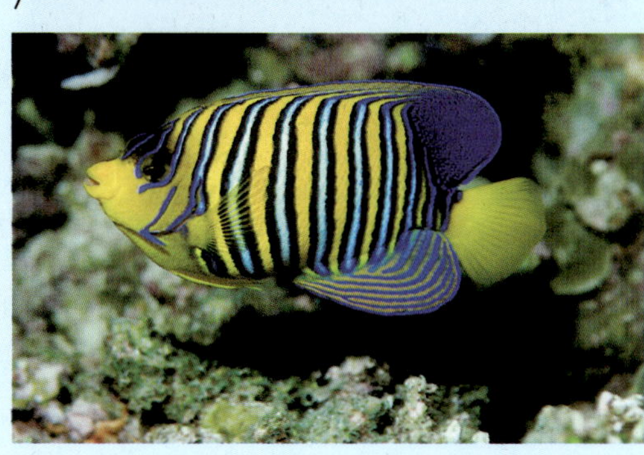
8

There is always an immense variety of fish in the vicinity of coral reefs: 4 foil coral. 5 the mouth of a plume star. 6 a dangerous red fire weever. 7 Crocodile fish. 8 Peacock emperor fish.

Red Fire Mountains on the Salt Sea

Dead Sea and the Judean Desert

The initial impression is one of burning sun, rugged mountains and a lake in which nothing can thrive. Early Christian pilgrims were so horrified at the lifelessness of the lake known as the Salt Sea in Hebrew that they gave it the name the Dead Sea. Both the Dead Sea and the Judean Desert which starts in Judea, the northern part of the West Bank, and stretches along the mountain range east of Jerusalem as far as Sodom, are captivatingly beautiful. It does, however, take a little time and effort to appreciate their full beauty. The view changes according to the time of year and time of day. The mountains of Moab and Edom, red flintstone hills on the eastern, Jordanian shore of the Dead Sea, are barely visible in the early morning light. But in the afternoon the rugged cliffs and valleys start appearing in the fading mist until they glow in the disappearing light of the setting sun in spectacular shades of purples and pinks. In summer, when the temperature rises to well above 40° C in this valley at 1300 feet below sea level, the hills look like unassailable fortresses – austere, forbidding and barren. Then the sunlight reflects the blindingly white salt-flats along the shores of the Dead Sea so brightly that the eye can barely make out clear contours.

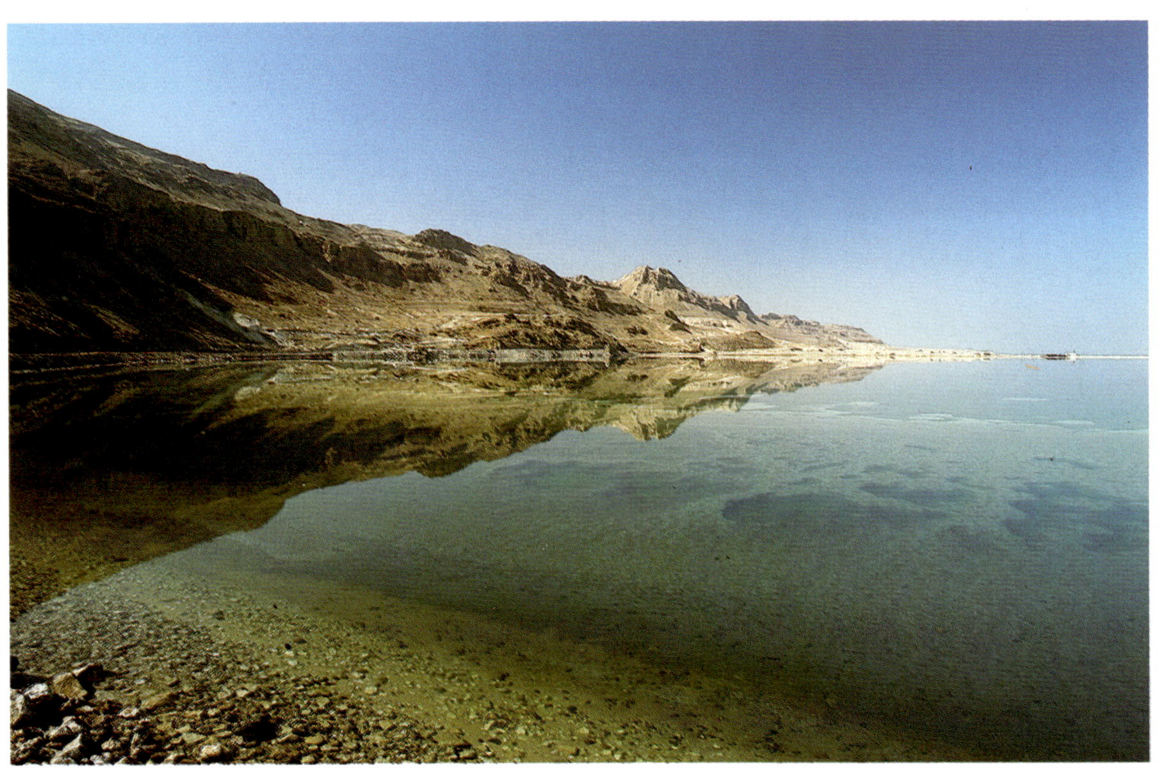

The fascinating Dead Sea is situated at the lowest point on earth. Each and every litre of water from this landlocked sea contains ten times as much salt and minerals as that in other seas. The Nabataeans were among the first to recognize its healing properties.

In late autumn when the denizens of Jerusalem have donned their rain jackets and winter coats, temperatures at the Dead Sea are still pleasantly warm – until the first major winter rains fall over the Judean Hills. Low-hanging clouds gather over the mountain ridges and the dramatic atmosphere of winter light gives the Dead Sea the look of a heavy lead-grey asphalt surface. During this time of year even the Judean Desert sees

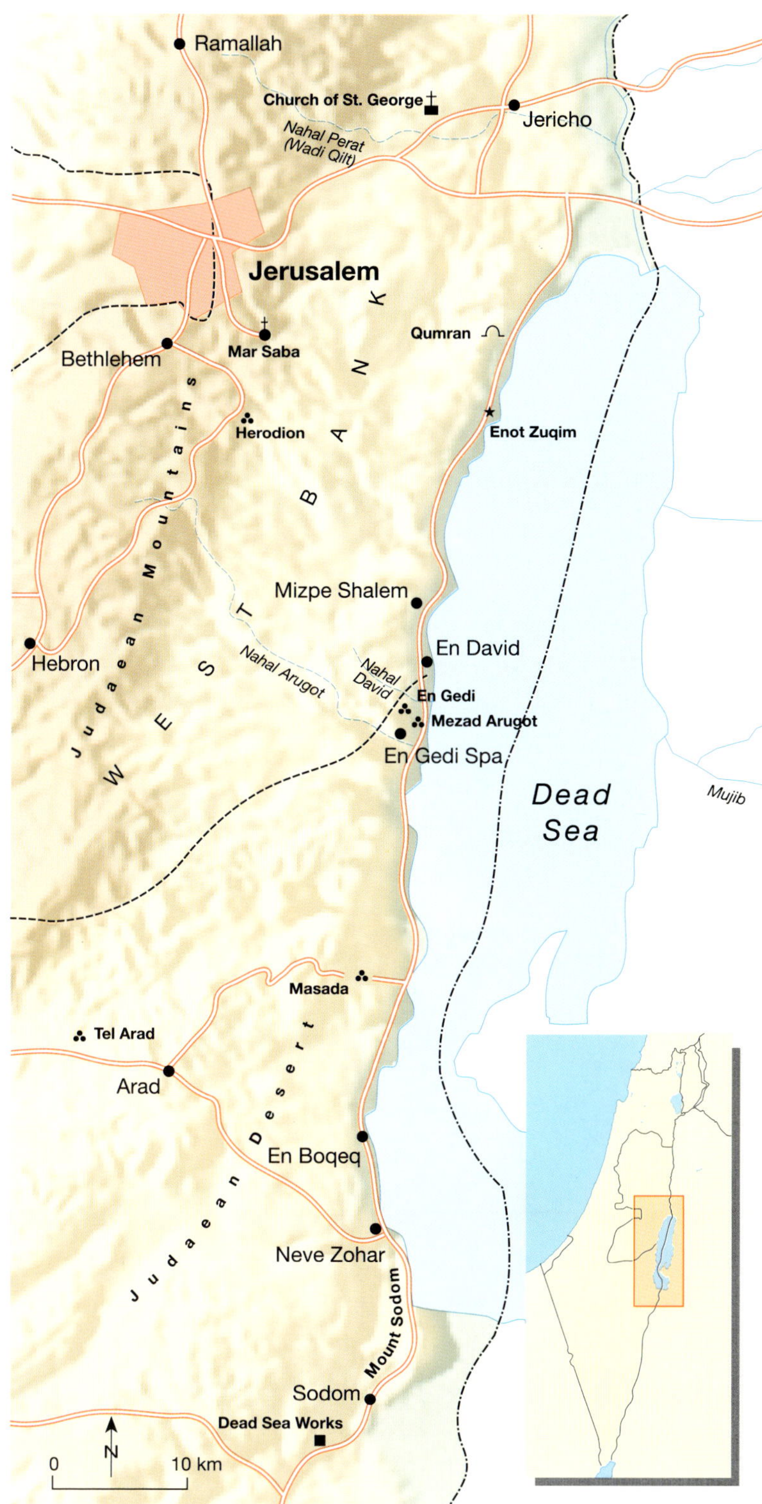

the rain – not as ordinary rain showers, but rather as torrential rain storms. The water seeps into the porous limestone of the desert until stopped in its tracks by the impermeable rock. It is then fed into the wadis or valleys eroded into the rock before ending up in the Dead Sea as flash floods. The Judean Desert is at its prettiest in the spring when it is covered by a lush green carpet on to which white anemones, blue cornflowers and red poppies add their own dash of bright colours.

The most impressive route to the Dead Sea goes from the West through the rocky desert into the modern city of *Arad*. Built in 1961, it was the first planned city of Israel. *Tel Arad* the old settlement site has a history going back 5,000 years. One of King Solomon's fortresses from the tenth century BC was discovered here as was a temple in which were found traces of animal fats in its Holy of Holies. This gave rise to the theory that it may have been used as a sacrificial site – a view that is substantiated by reports in the Old Testament. A Canaanite city from the third century BC was excavated nearby and revealed some surprising discoveries: clay jars from the first Egyptian Dynasty were found, leading us to the conclusion that the residents must have already been involved in active trading with their southern neighbours.

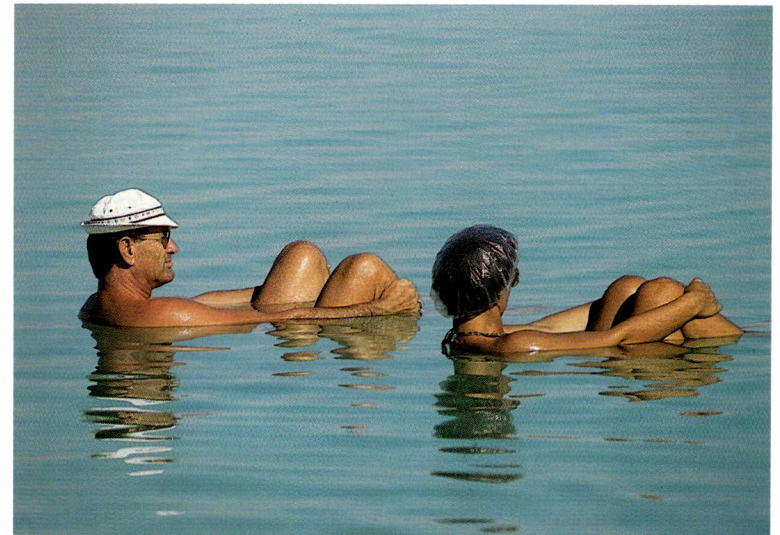

Relaxing in the water, or having mud rubbed into your skin from head to toe – the Dead Sea is a perfect place for a spa holiday. There is a variety of cosmetics available made from the mud that contains all the salts and minerals – something to take home!

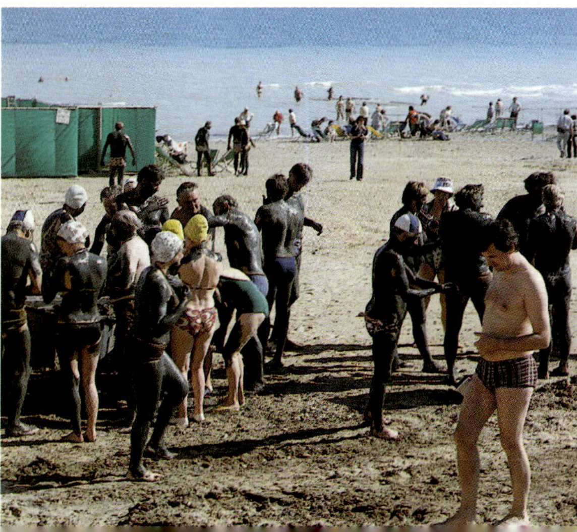

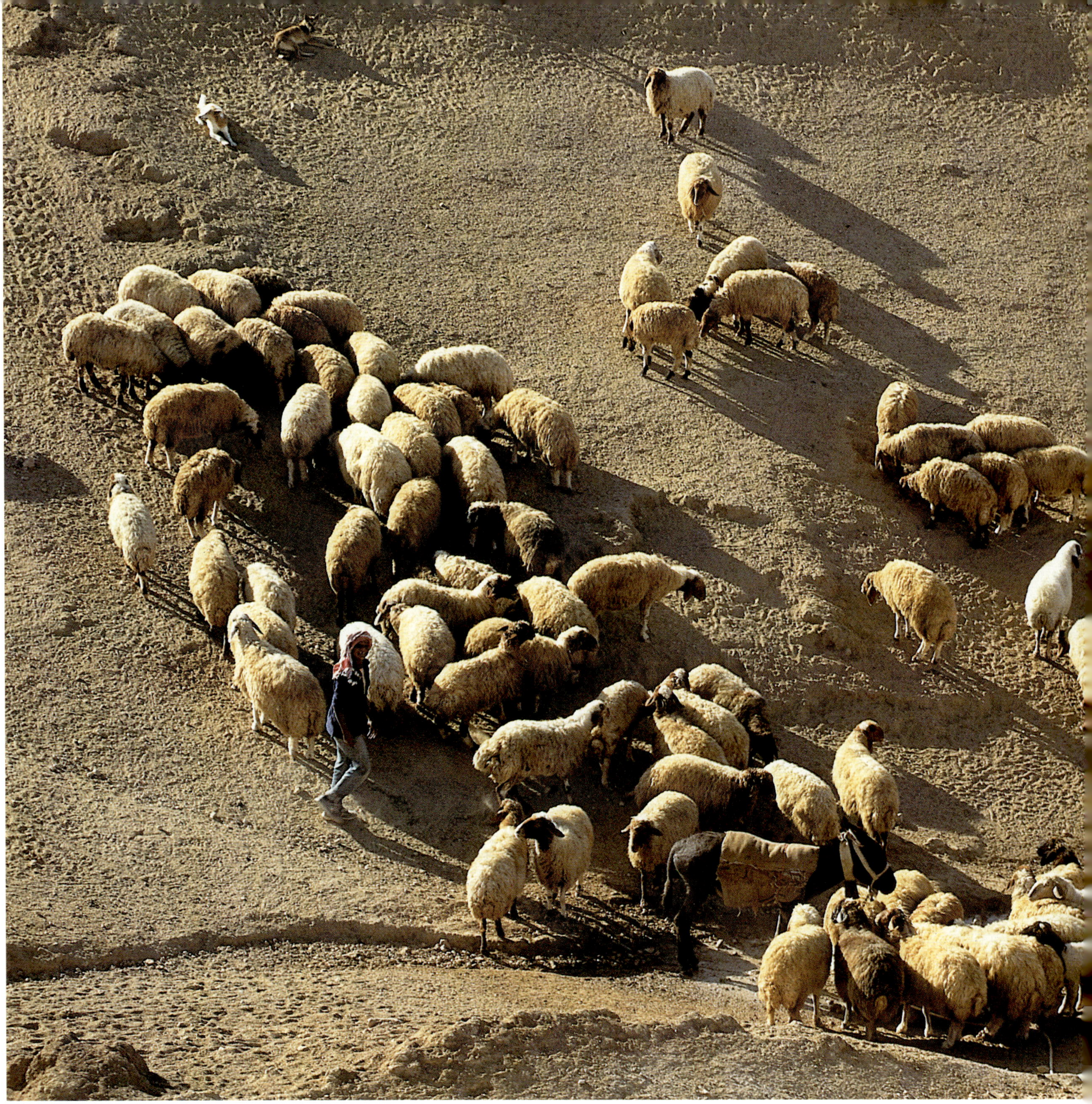

With the exception of oases such as Ein Gedi on the Dead Sea and Jericho, the arid Judean Desert can only be used for grazing sheep and goats. Camels don't much mind the dry conditions either.

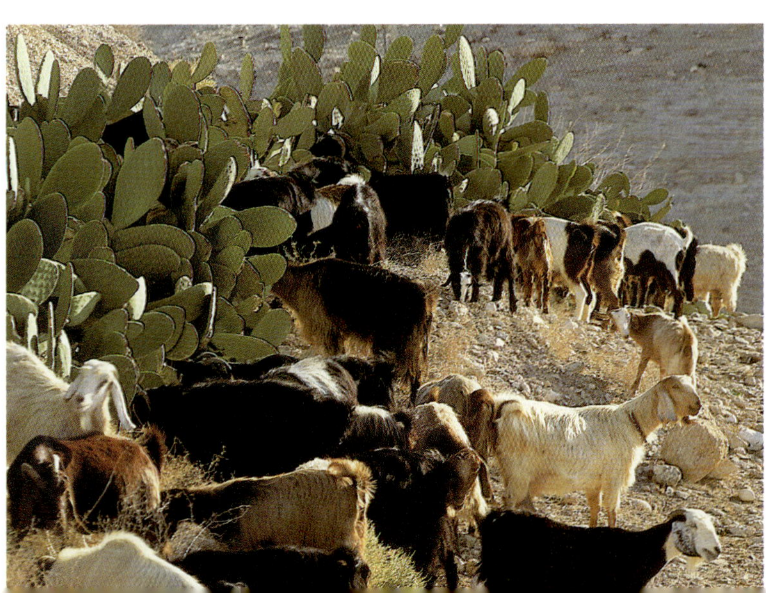

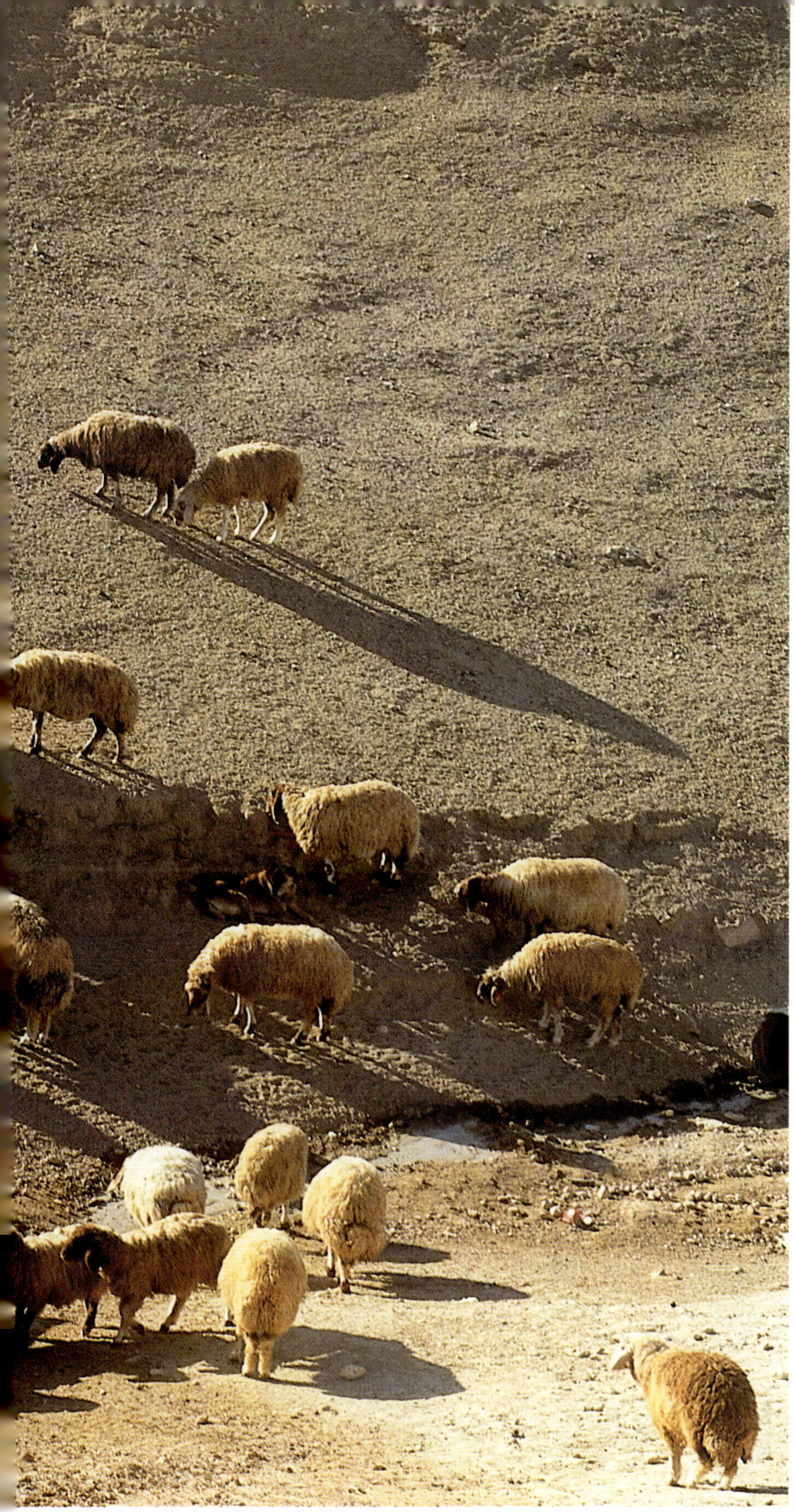

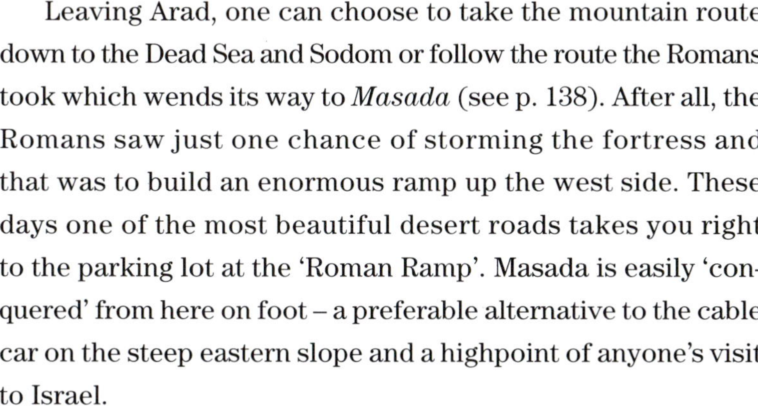

Leaving Arad, one can choose to take the mountain route down to the Dead Sea and Sodom or follow the route the Romans took which wends its way to *Masada* (see p. 138). After all, the Romans saw just one chance of storming the fortress and that was to build an enormous ramp up the west side. These days one of the most beautiful desert roads takes you right to the parking lot at the 'Roman Ramp'. Masada is easily 'conquered' from here on foot – a preferable alternative to the cable car on the steep eastern slope and a highpoint of anyone's visit to Israel.

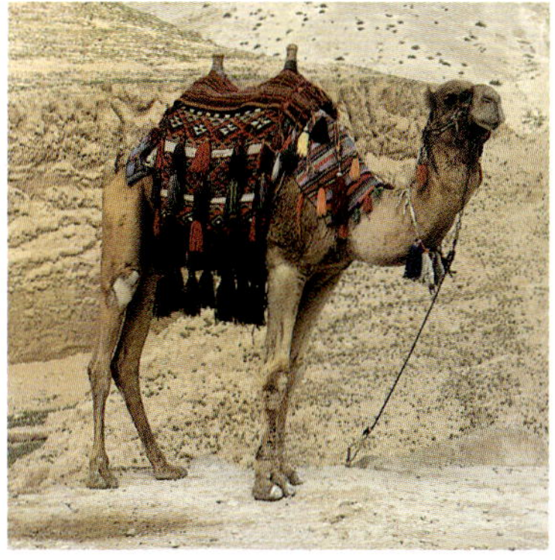

Although the Judean Desert enjoys more rainfall than the Negev, not many plants grow here. However, as soon as it does rain, there is a burst of colour.

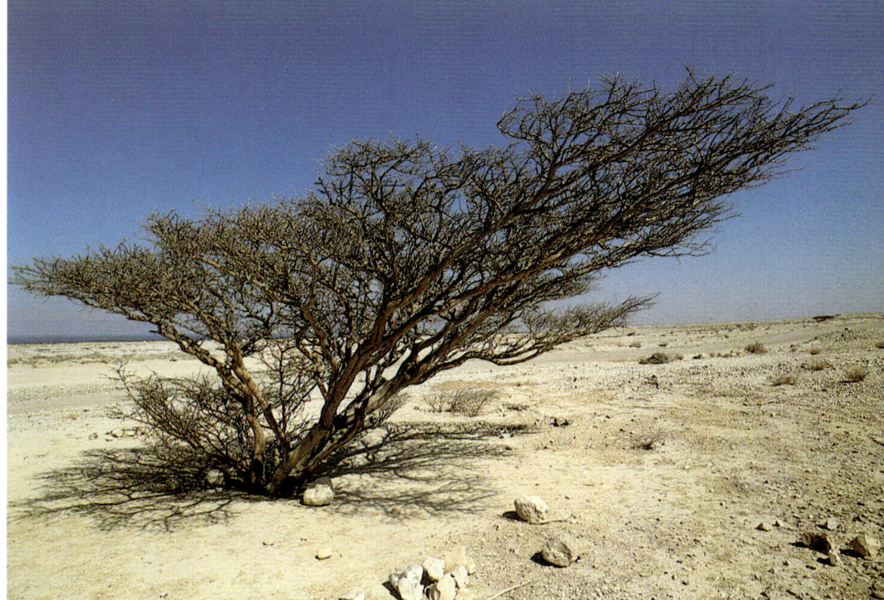

Spas since Antiquity: on the Banks of the Dead Sea

The Judean Desert does not give things up easily. You can only take from it what nature is willing to release and these include some of Israel's most important mineral resources. The rather bright, futuristic looking industrial complex at the southern end of the Dead Sea is the *Dead Sea Works*, a processing plant for magnesium and calcium bromide, common salt and potash which are then exported throughout the world as fertiliser.

The curative properties of the Salt Sea are world famous: the springs which flow into this lake are said to cure arthritis and rheumatism, while the totally pollen-free bromide-rich air is effective for asthma sufferers. The oily black mud taken from the bed of the lake is effective against psoriasis and is exported abroad for use in skin conditions. It is said that even Cleopatra, well known for the interest she took in her appearance, sent her slaves to the Dead Sea to bring back the mud. Like Cleopatra, other rulers of antiquity, such as King Solomon and Herod knew about the benefits of using the Dead Sea and its springs as a spa more than 2000 years ago. Another phenomenon clearly amazed the people of ancient times as much as it amazes tourists who come here today: the Jewish historian, Flavius Josephus reports that the Emperor Vespasian had slaves with their arms tied behind their back thrown into

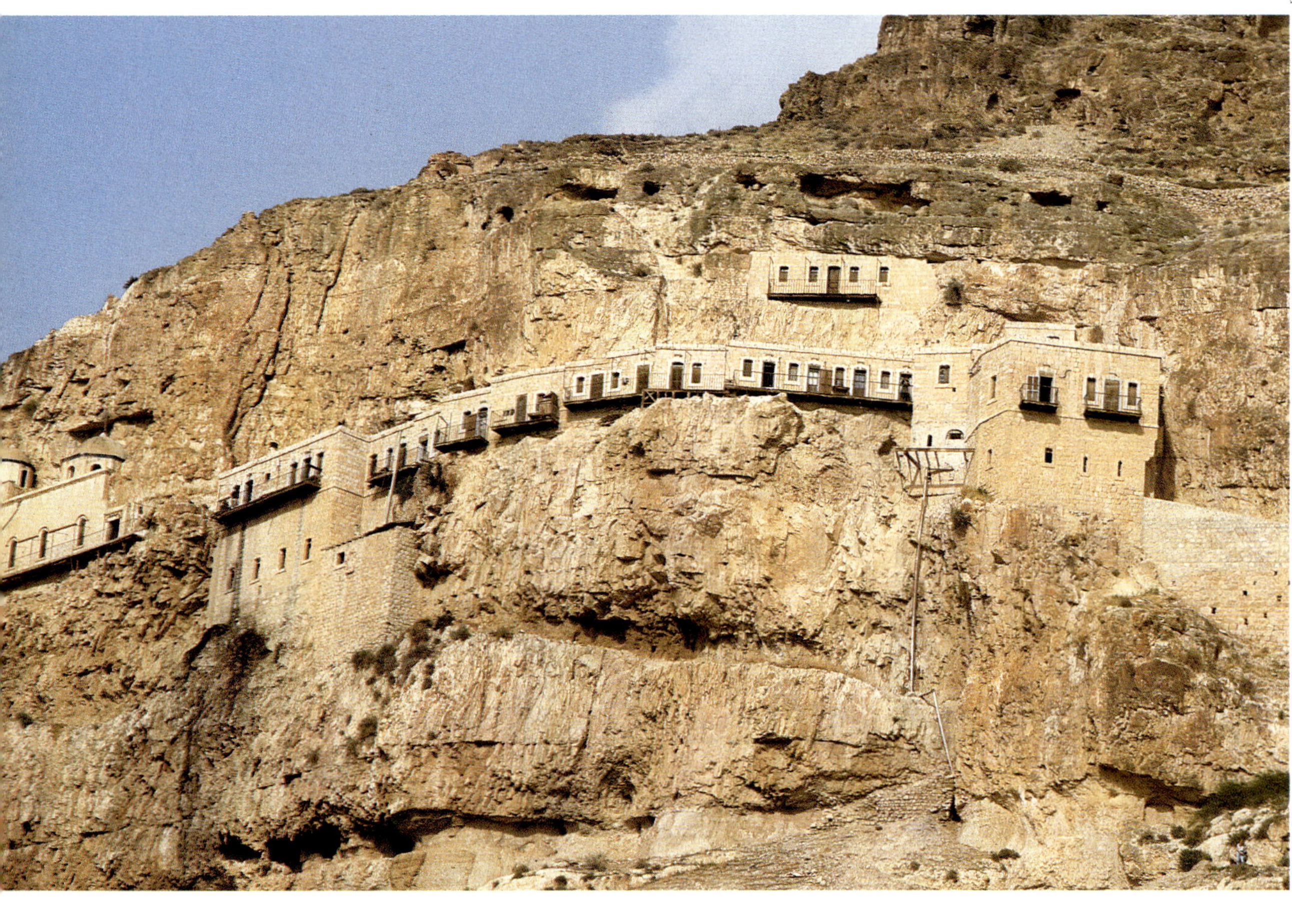

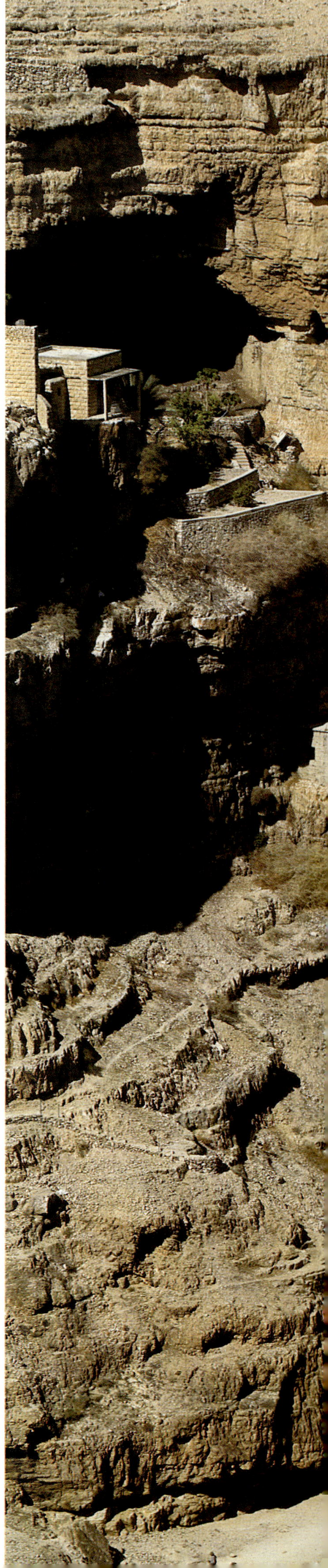

The Judean Desert has always been a magnet for those who wanted to live their lives in seclusion. Greek Orthodox monks built their monasteries around Jericho, clinging precariously not unlike eagles' nests on the Mount of Temptation (left) and in the Wadi Qelt (centre).

the Dead Sea only to prove how impossible it was to sink in water with a salt content of more than 30 per cent. This is not something that anyone should try to do today. This oily water burns painfully on broken skin, and under no circumstances should you let it get into your eyes. For this reason, not every part of the Dead Sea is suitable for swimming, but only those areas provided with fresh water showers, like the beach at *Kibbutz Ein Feshka* at the northern end, the oasis Ein Gedi, and further south the Ein Gedi Health Spa with its sulphur bathing pools.

The southern end of the Dead Sea has a series of bathing spots starting with *Sodom* near the mountain range of the same name. Its extraordinary landscape of canyons, caves and crystallised shapes was formed over the centuries as a result of erosion. One of the more bizarre formations, according to legend, is said to be that of Lot's wife who was 'turned into a pillar of salt'.

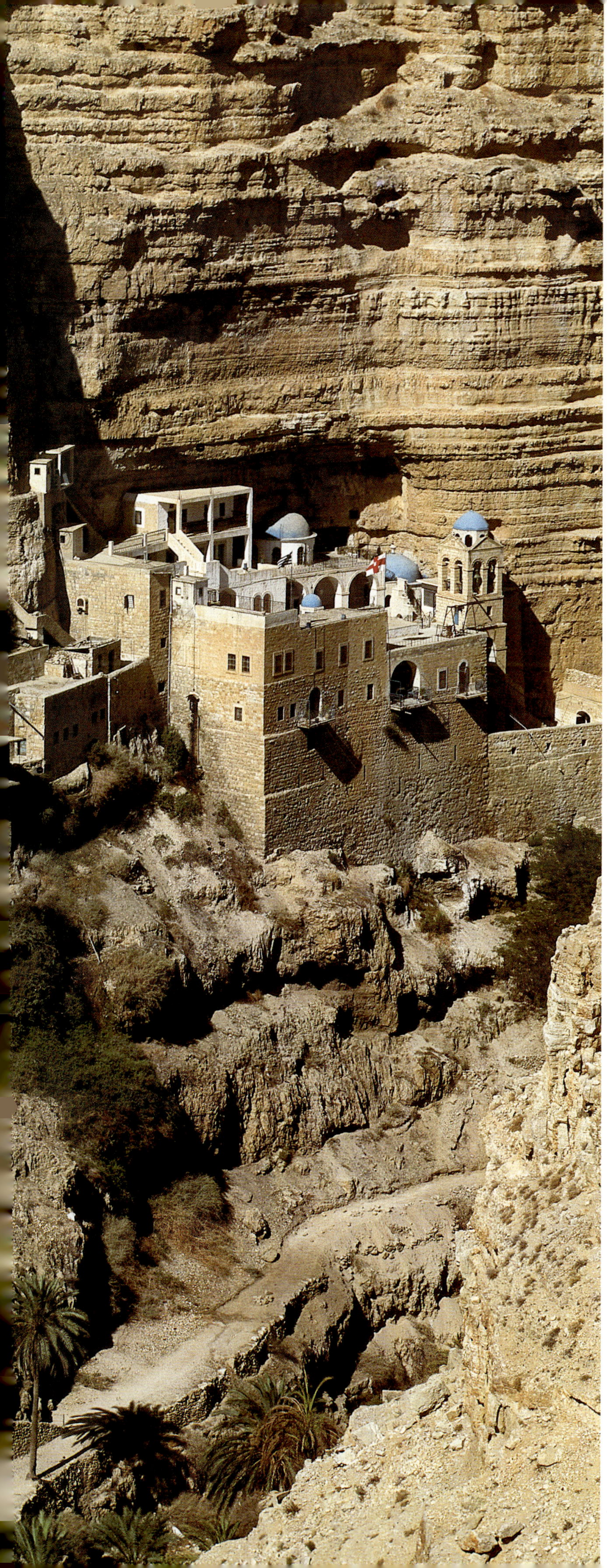

Beyond Sodom we come to *Ein Boqeq* and *Neve Zohar* with their famous sulphur baths and mud packs. Everyone should treat themselves to the luxury of a break here whether they have a medical need for it or not. *Ein Gedi*, beach, nature reserve and kibbutz which operates a guest house and youth hostel as well as running an agricultural farm, offers the perfect conditions for a break. The Ein Gedi Nature Reserve in the *Nahal David* valley is open all year round and is definitely worth a visit. It is blessed with springs and lush green vegetation along the cliffs, and waterfalls splashing behind dense reed caves down the smooth cliffsides end in inviting looking ponds and pools. After a walk of about an hour one finally arrives at David's Falls, near which David is said to have hidden from King Saul.

If one is looking for a little more solitude, there is the walk of about a mile further south through the *Nahal Arugot*. Here too one comes across a few ponds which are deep enough for swimming. This is, in fact, the better place to see animals such as ibex, gazelles, antelopes, foxes and a variety of birds.

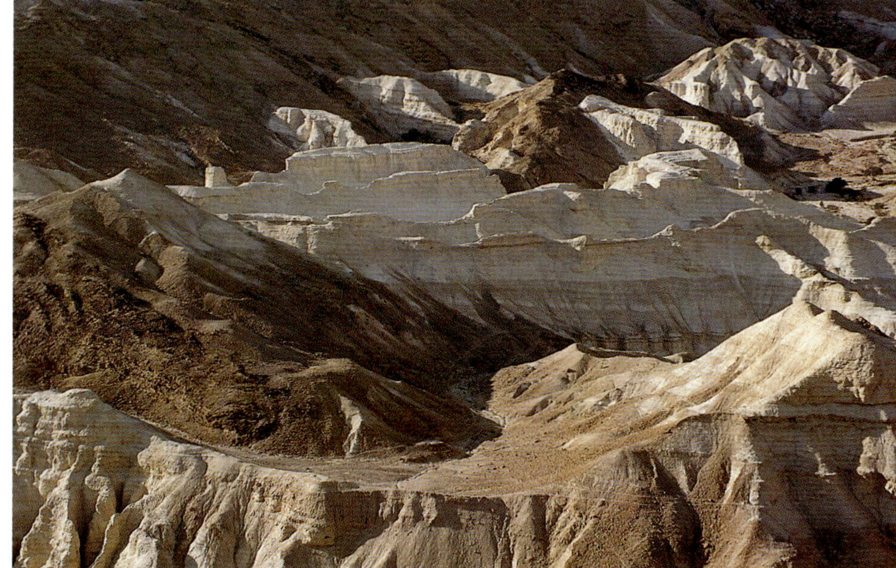

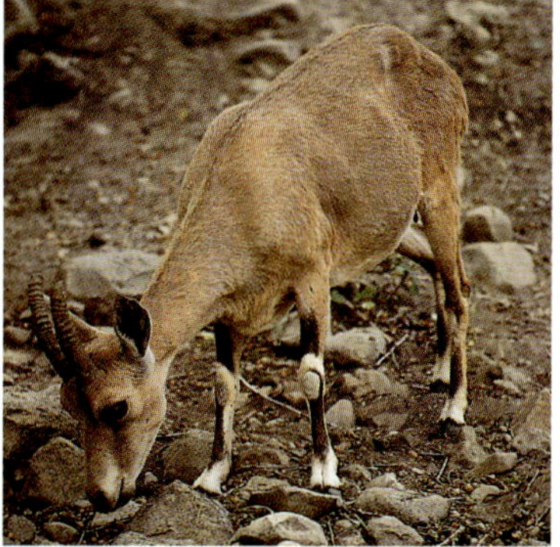

The Dead Sea is the starting point for a large number of day trips. Barren desert landscape (above, near Arad) and nature reserves like Ein Gedi (below) show the extreme diversity of this region.

The remains of the circular walls of Herodion, one of Herod the Great's fortresses and a place of refuge, gives an impression of what life was like under siege (left and page right).

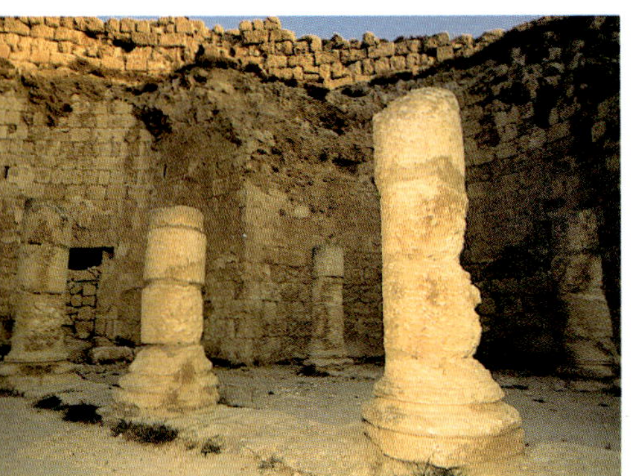

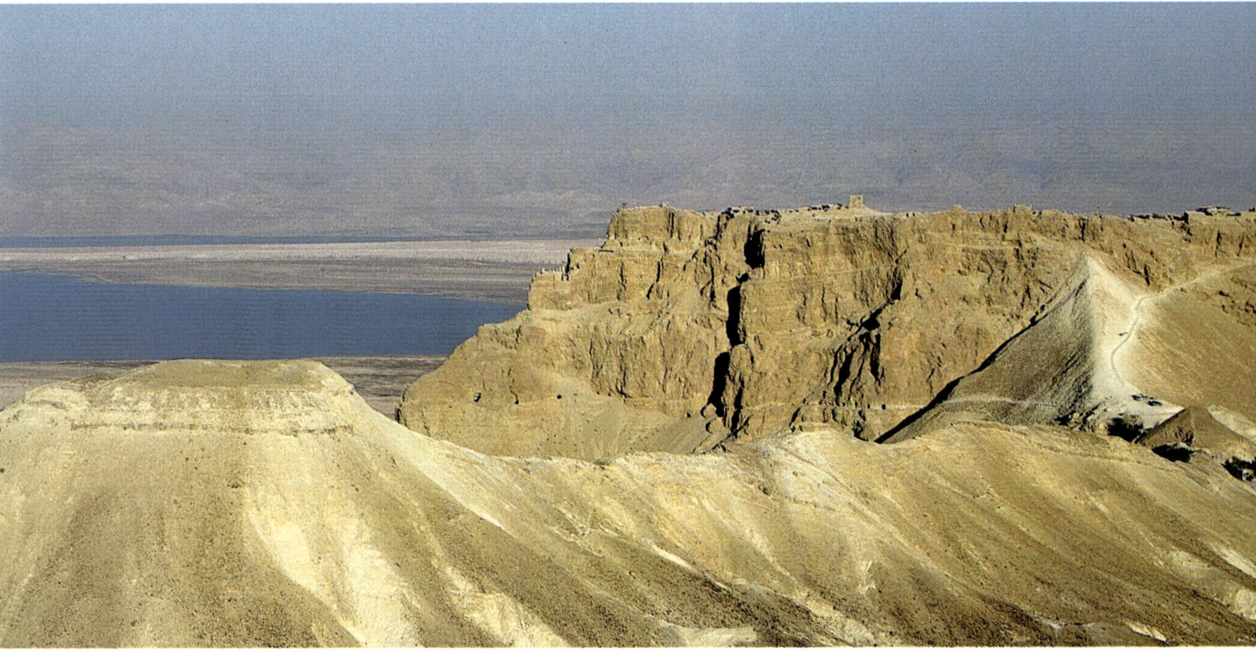

Masada, national pilgrimage site, in its grandiose setting on a cliff edge above the Dead Sea (top and below). Half a day should be set aside to visit this famous fortress.

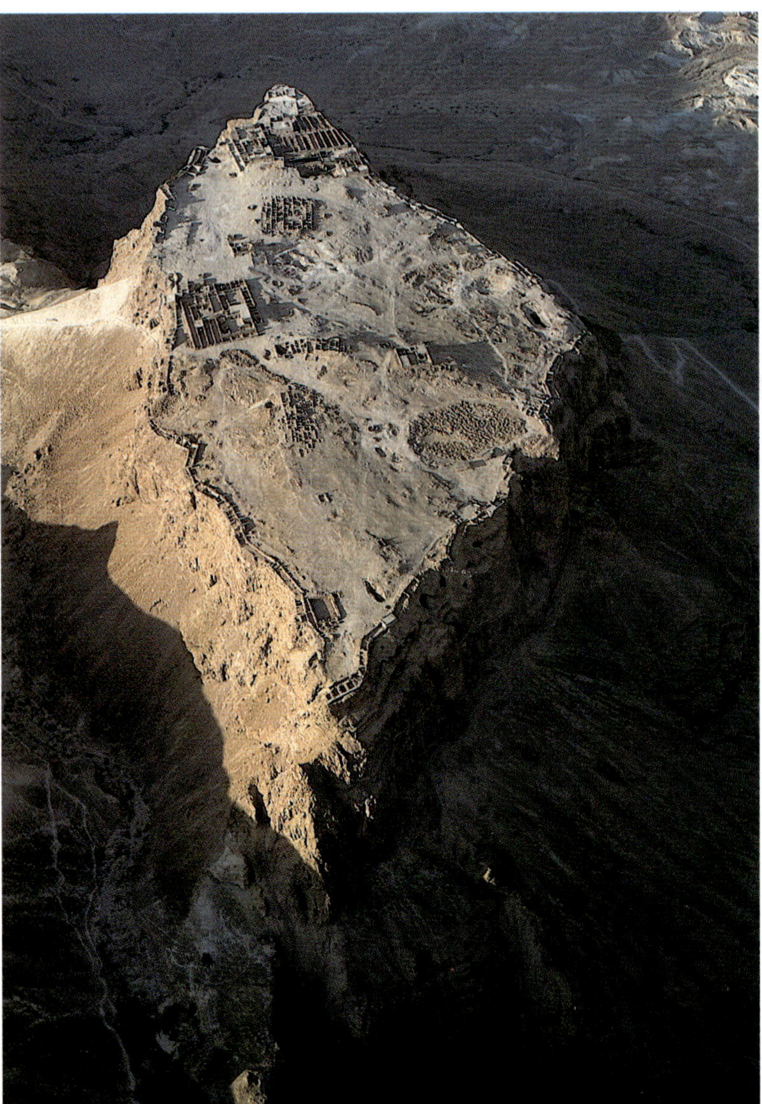

But the most relaxing option of all is a visit to the *Ein Gedi Health Spa*. This resort has only recently been built by members of the kibbutz. At the time it was built it was right at the water's edge. However, in the past 20 years the water level of the Dead Sea has fallen by about 20 feet. At the northern end it still reaches a depth of about 1300 feet, but at the southern end the level has fallen to a point where it is often only about 13 to 23 feet deep due to the extraction of the mineral resources. The peninsula which always jutted out into the lake has now become a land bridge to Jordan. Hydrologists even predict that the Dead Sea, which is about 47 miles in length and up to 10 miles wide, may shrink from 500 to 160 square miles in as little as 300 years. This development is easy to identify at the Ein Gedi Health Spa. Only a few years ago, tourists could walk the distance from the sulphur pools to the beach. Nowadays a small railway is being used to cover the ever-increasing distance, even stopping on the way at the fresh water swimming pool near the bathing pools, at the containers where the dark brown mud is kept for the visitors who wish to rub it on themselves from head to toe, and finally at the beach where tourists pull out their cameras to film each other unable to sink.

Mysterious Scrolls

Even if you are only here for the cure, a visit to *Qumran* at the northern end of the Dead Sea is a must. This city has become world famous since a young Bedouin shepherd boy discovered the first scrolls of the Essenes in 1947. The scrolls can be viewed

Continued on Page 140

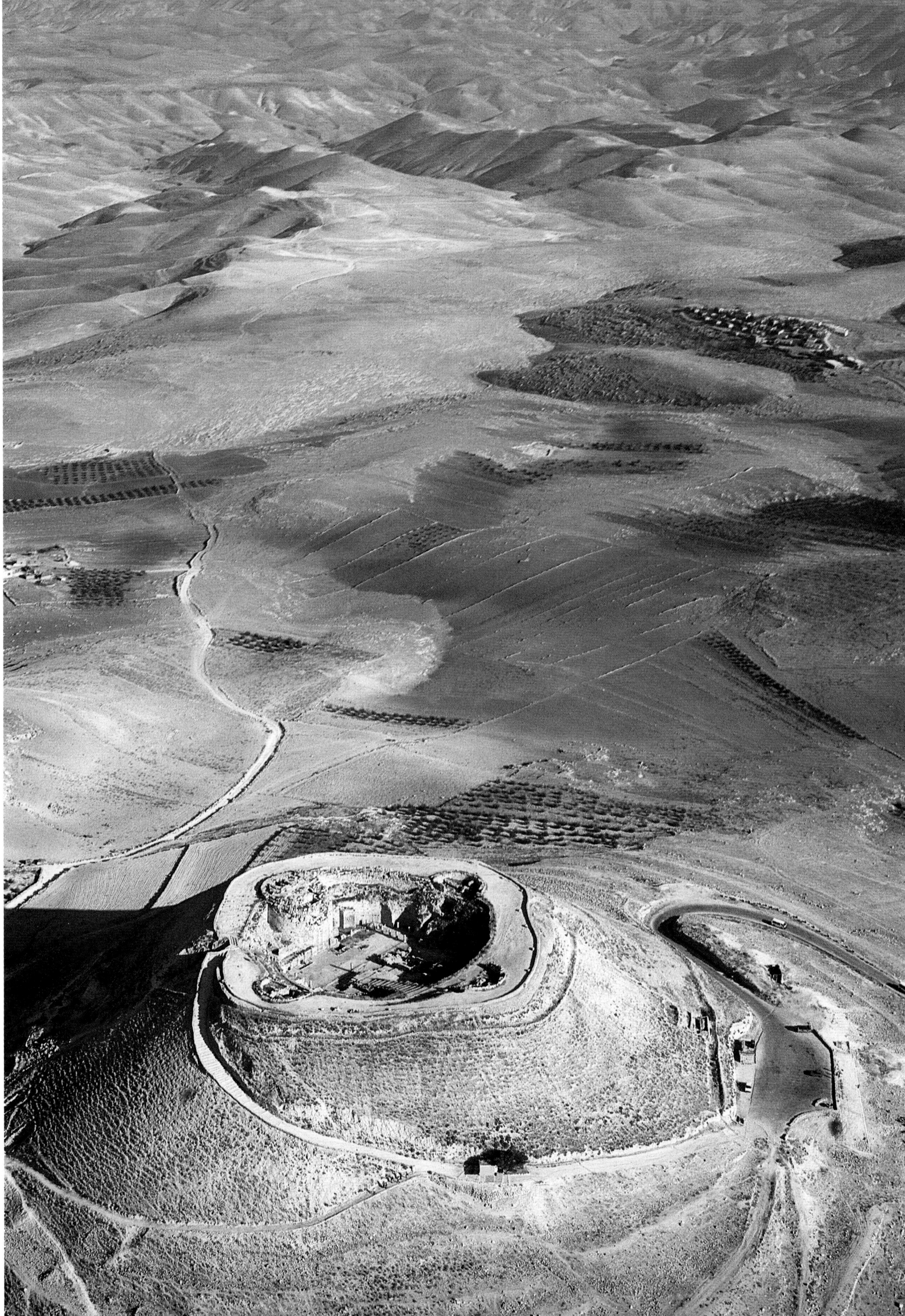

The Myth of Masada

Herod's Refuge in the Desert

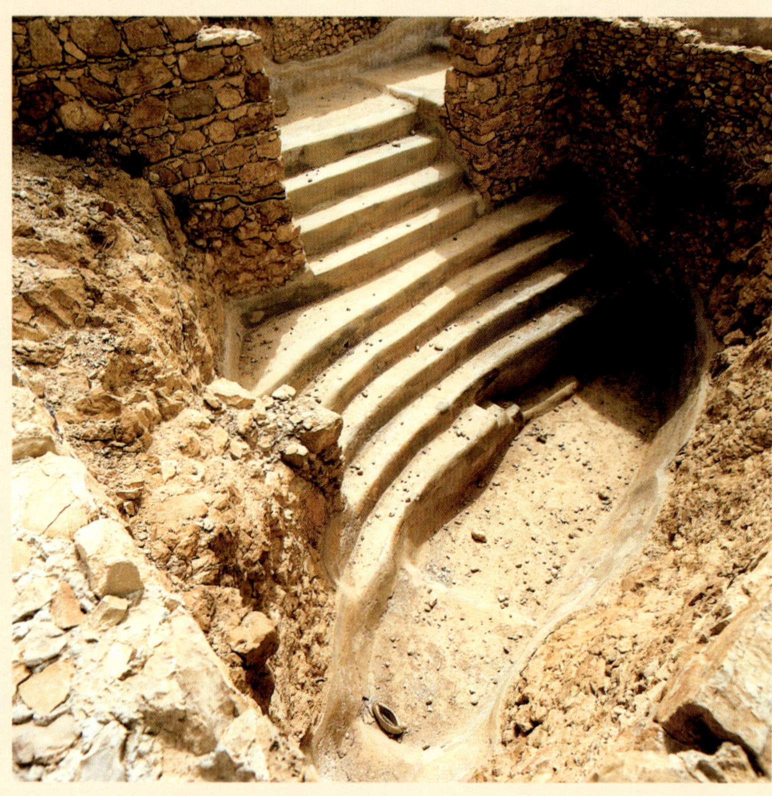

The ruins of the bath house provide an indication of the former luxury of Masada (above and right). It was equipped with under-floor heating and decorated with sumptuous mosaics. The western palace was also adorned with floor mosaics based on geometric and plant motifs (below and above right).

Herod the Great, King of Judea from 40 to 4 BC, was a skilful tactician whom the Romans favoured with territory and power. He was also a ruthless despot who ordered the murders of many of his opponents and even members of his own family. Furthermore, he is regarded as a great master builder of his time, and his choice of Masada as the site for his refuge fortress is deemed to be inspired since it affords both protection and camouflage.

Many mountains on the western shore of the Dead Sea are similar to Masada in appearance. So, despite the historian Flavius Josephus' detailed descriptions, Herod's palace remained undiscovered until 1838 when a biblical scholar came across it. Herod erected another refuge fortress, the *Herodion*, which lies to the east of Bethlehem and was also well hidden. This is probably where he lies buried. This fortress, also subsequently destroyed by the Romans, was built on the top of a mountain which for a long time was believed to be a volcano until, that is, the Herodian buildings were discovered.

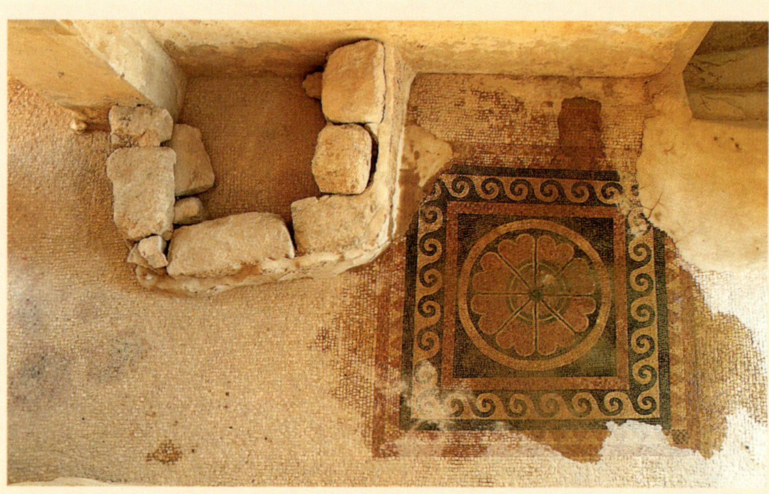

The rock of *Masada*, which towers around 440 metres over the Dead Sea, was very nearly impregnable. It presents sheer rock on its western, northern and southern faces, although nowadays visitors can reach the summit from the east in the

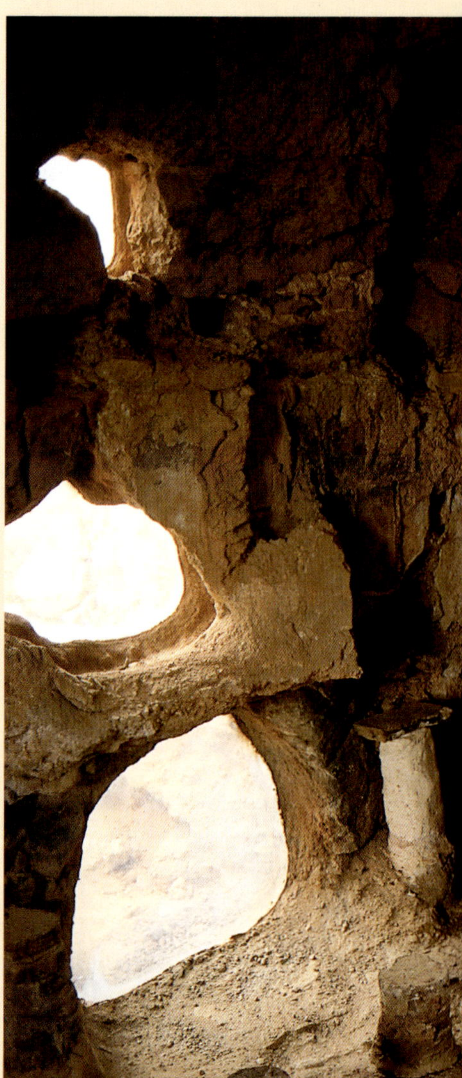

comfort of a cable car. Here, the Roman minion could feel protected from his enemies, where he could hold out for sev-

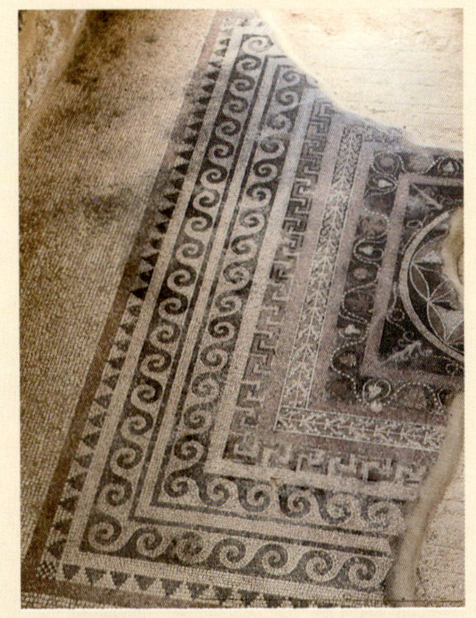

eral years. Adjacent to the three storey *palace*, which clung to the north face like an eagle's nest, Herod built numerous *store houses* as well as a sophisticated *water supply system* which permitted the installation of a *bath house* in the Roman style.

Herod never did have cause to seek refuge in his fortress. It was only an event which took place around a hundred years after its construction that gave the fortress its importance in Jewish history. Following the defeat of the rebellion against the Romans in 70 AD, a last group of anti-Roman zealots – 967 men, women and children – entrenched themselves on Masada. Thereupon the Roman emperor dispatched the experienced general Flavius Silva with 10,000 soldiers and 500 Jewish slaves. Silva set up eight camps all around Masada, whose foundations are still clearly visible from the summit.

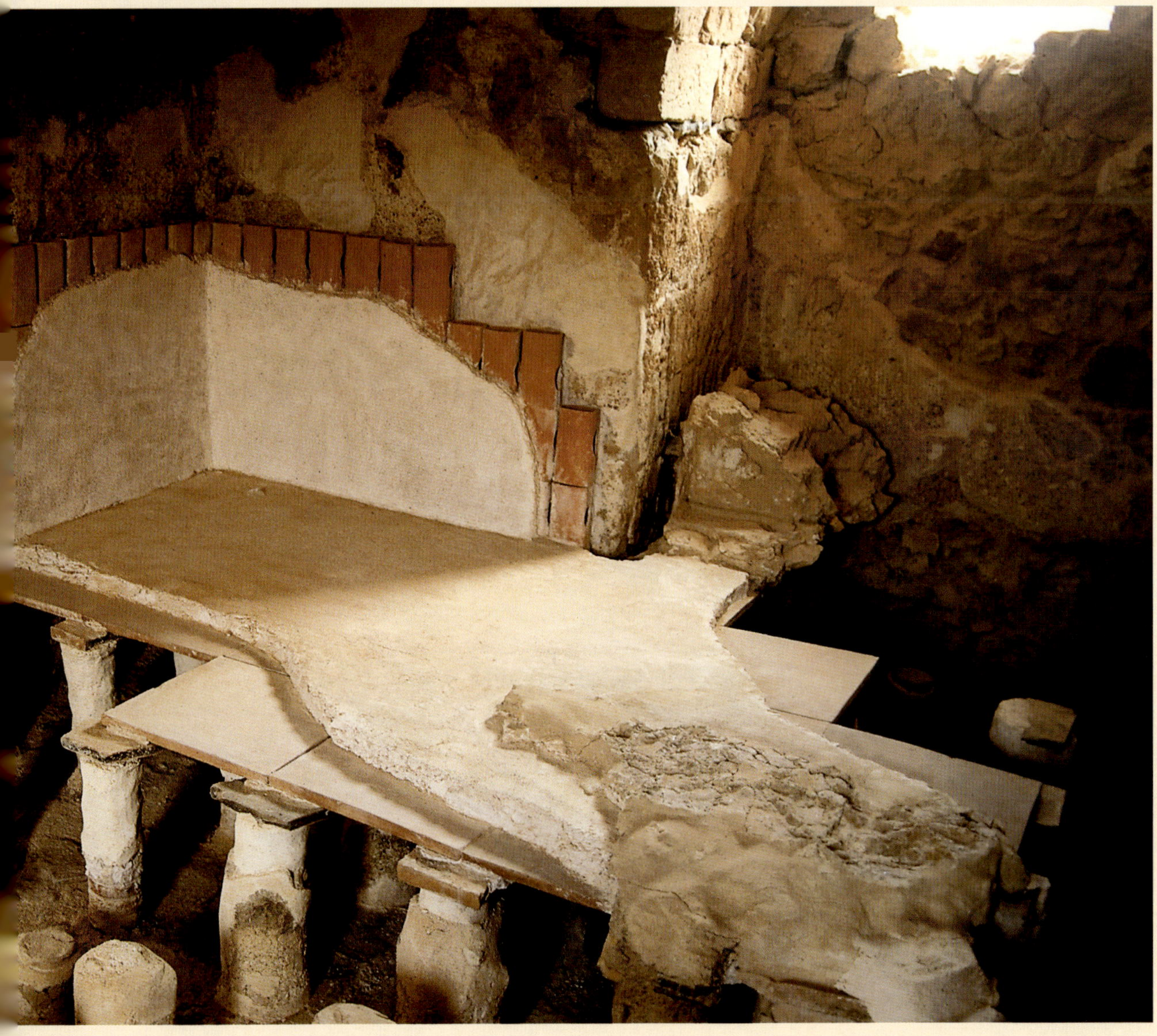

The siege lasted for three years until Silva succeeded in damaging the wall with the aid of a *ramp* and a battering ram. At this point the rebel leader Eleazar ben Jair realised that the battle was lost. With an impassioned speech he called upon the rebels to commit collective suicide. Two women and five children who survived the massacre by hiding in a cistern described the events that followed. Ten of their own men had to kill the besieged. The last to remain set the palace on fire before himself committing suicide. However, he spared the store houses in order to prove that 'we did not give up for lack of food but because we choose death over slavery'.

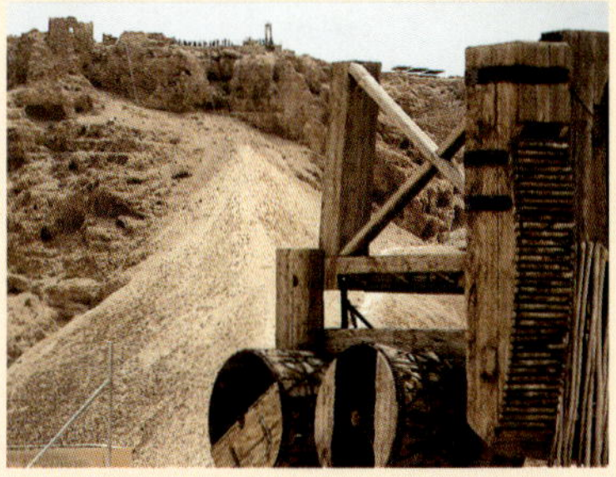

During the siege, the Romans built a ramp on the west face of the fortress, which enabled them to breach the wall with a battering ram.

Such a tale of heroism was perfectly suited for inclusion in the mythology of the Jewish state. Today, elite Israeli army troops swear their oath of allegiance at the top of the rock and vow: 'Masada shall not fall again!'

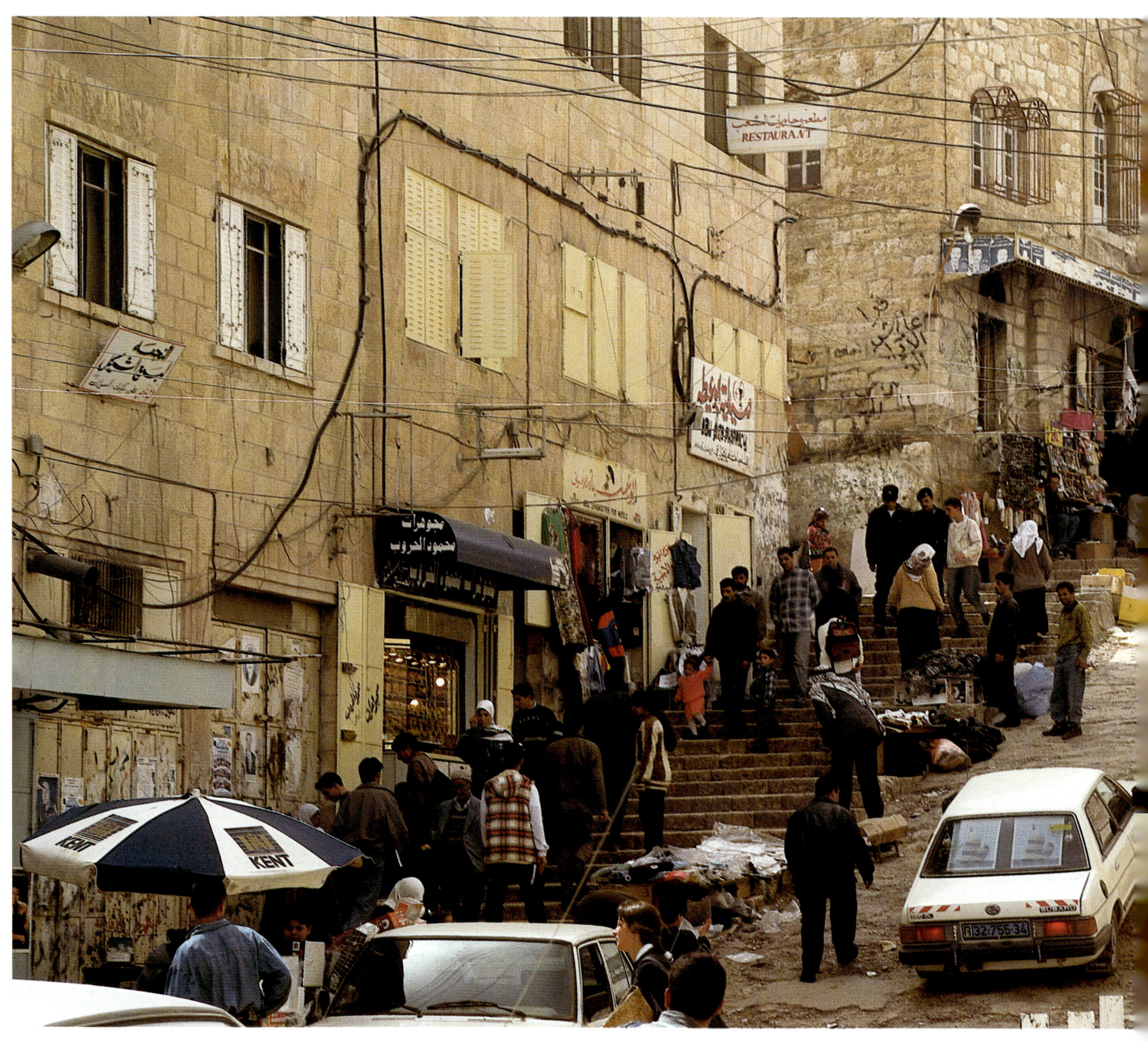

These pictures of colourful bazaars and Arab markets in Bethlehem do not conceal the fact that this city lies on the West Bank, a centre of the conflict in the Middle East.

in the Shrine of the Book (see p. 68) in Jerusalem where they arrived after a convoluted trip halfway around the world. Since then many more fragments of scrolls have been discovered around the caves of Qumran, revealing information about the life of the Essenes.

It is presumed that this religious splinter group cut themselves off and set up isolated communities in the desert because of disputes with the ruling class of scholars. The Roman his-

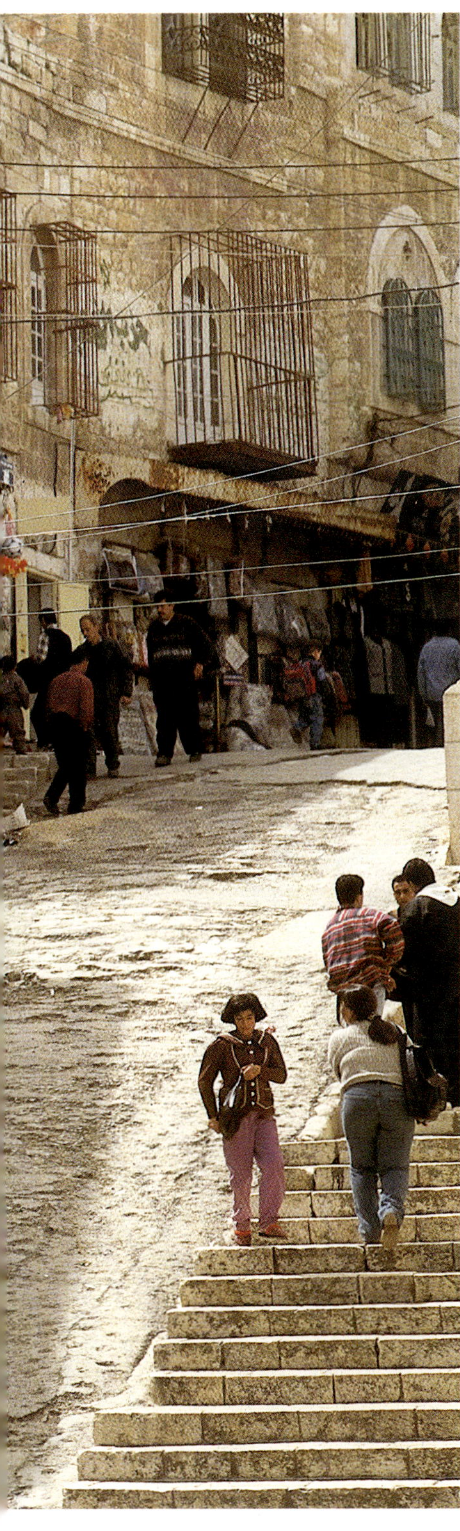

torian, Pliny the Elder (23/24–79 AD) was one of the first to describe the Essenes in his *Historia Naturalis*: 'On the western side of the Dead Sea there lives a race by themselves, more remarkable than any other in the wide world. They live without women and abstain from love. They are without money and live near the palm trees. Their numbers increase by the day through those who come to join them for there are many who have grown weary of life. That is how a nation [...] within which no child is born continues through the centuries.'

This Roman historian was mistaken in one point, that of how long the Essenes survived, which was actually only from the beginning of the second century BC till the war between the Romans and the Judeans which destroyed Qumran in 68 AD. It is possible to see almost all the excavated remains of the city – and the caves within which the most important scrolls were quickly concealed from oncoming troops.

As the birthplace of Jesus, Bethlehem draws crowds of pilgrims. The souvenir business, whether in items of plastic or wood, icons, jewellery or toys, is doing well.

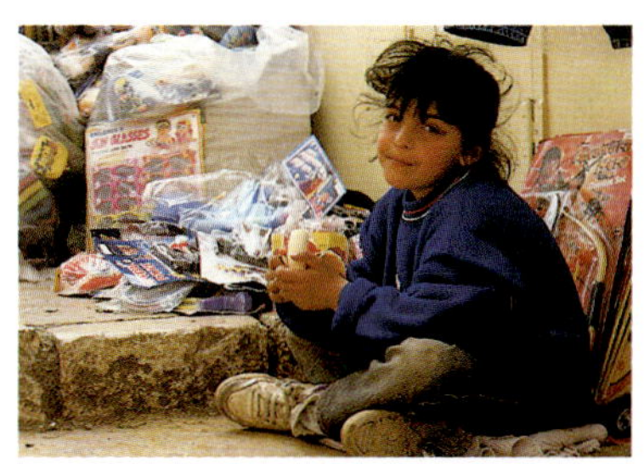

Monks, Hermits and Ascetics

It may be that the nearby metropolis of Jerusalem where political and religious interests have always clashed, drove into the desert those of a more sensitive nature. It may be that they were attracted by the sparse beauty of the desert. For thou-

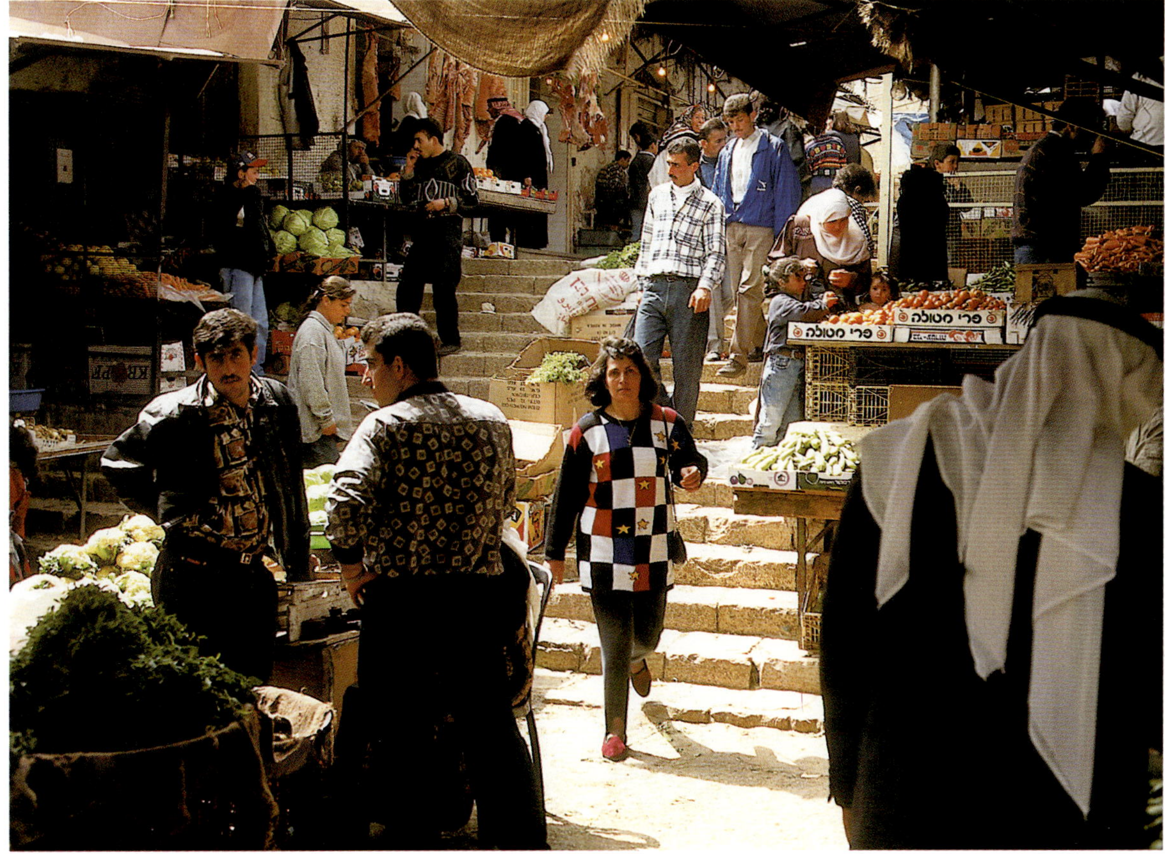

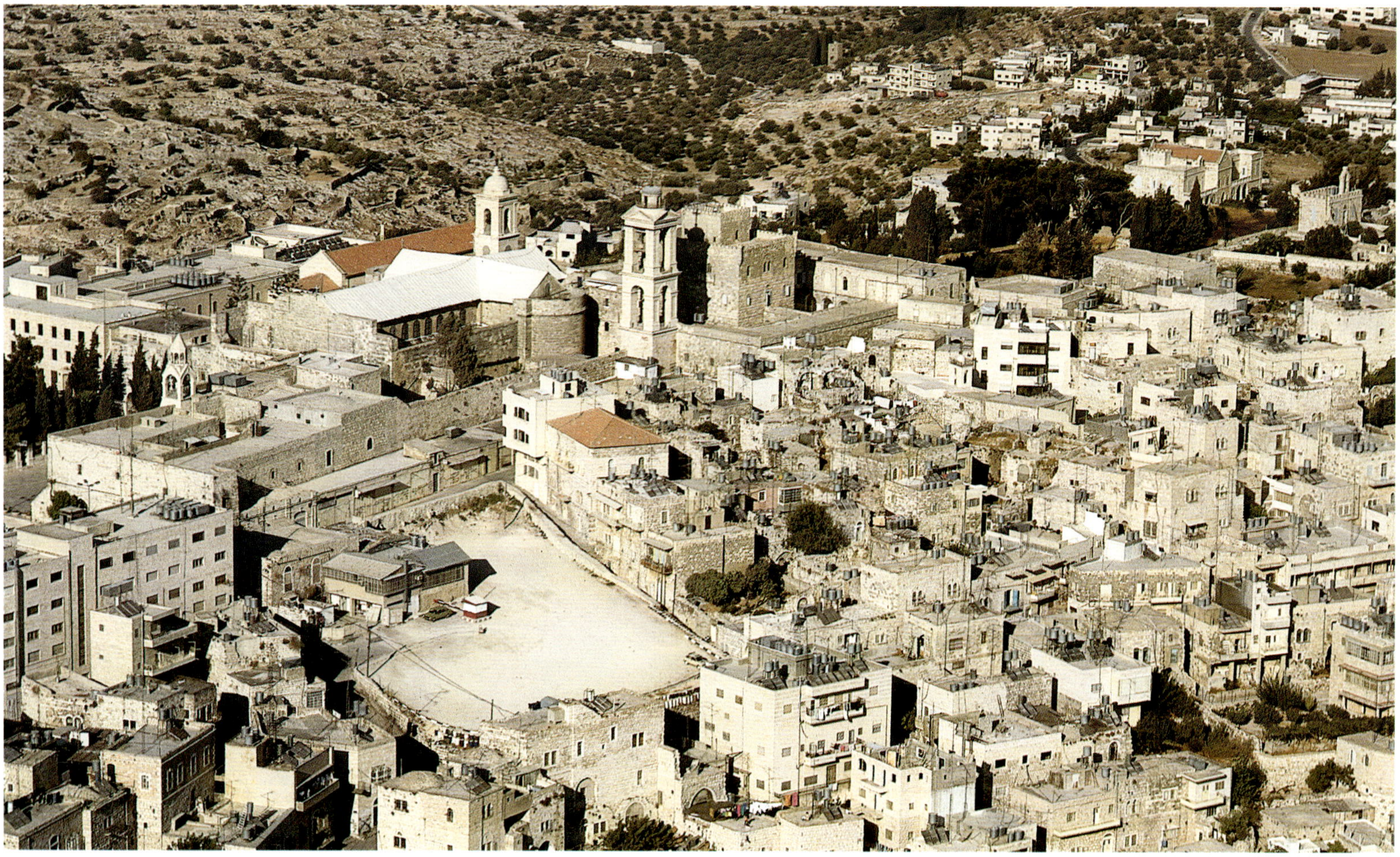

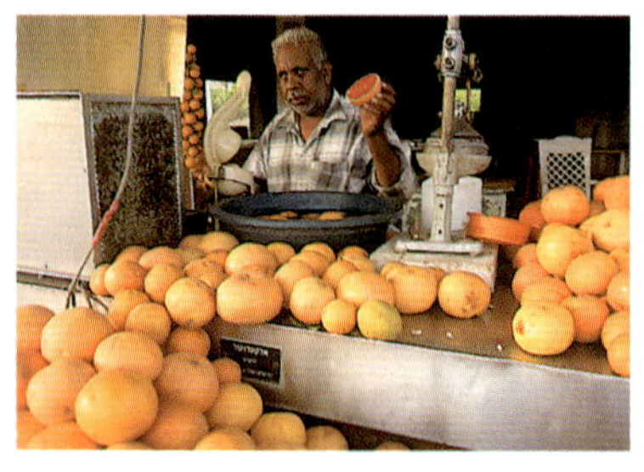

The compound of the Church of the Nativity in Bethlehem looks like a fortress with the Catholic Church of St Catherine and the Armenian and Greek Orthodox churches and monasteries adjoining it. (top). It is not far from Manger Square in front of the Basilica to the market where you are offered a refreshing glass of freshly squeezed orange juice (below).

sands of years, hermits, prophets and rebels lived in the Judean Desert. These were people who had to hide from whoever was in power at the time. Close to Jericho (see p. 144), on the *Mount of Temptation*, Greek Orthodox monks built a monastery which is perched precariously on a rocky ledge halfway up the mountain. It is here that Jesus is said to have come to fast and pray for 40 days and 40 nights and where he was tempted by the devil with the words: 'If thou be the Son of God, command that these stones be made bread'. To this day, the monks point to the very stone on which Jesus reputedly sat. Not far from here the old Roman road wends it way through the gulch of *Wadi Qelt* from Jerusalem to Jericho. In those days, highwaymen used to lie in wait for the merchants and pilgrims who travelled through the deep, dark crevice in the hills. The 15 mile long, astonishingly beautiful canyon is littered with ruins. hermitage caves, ponds and waterfalls. The course of the wadi continues deeper and deeper until it brings you to another Greek Orthodox monastery, the *Monastery of Saint George of Koziba*. The present building was built towards the end of the nineteenth century. But monks have been living in this oasis with its view over Jericho for more than 1,600 years.

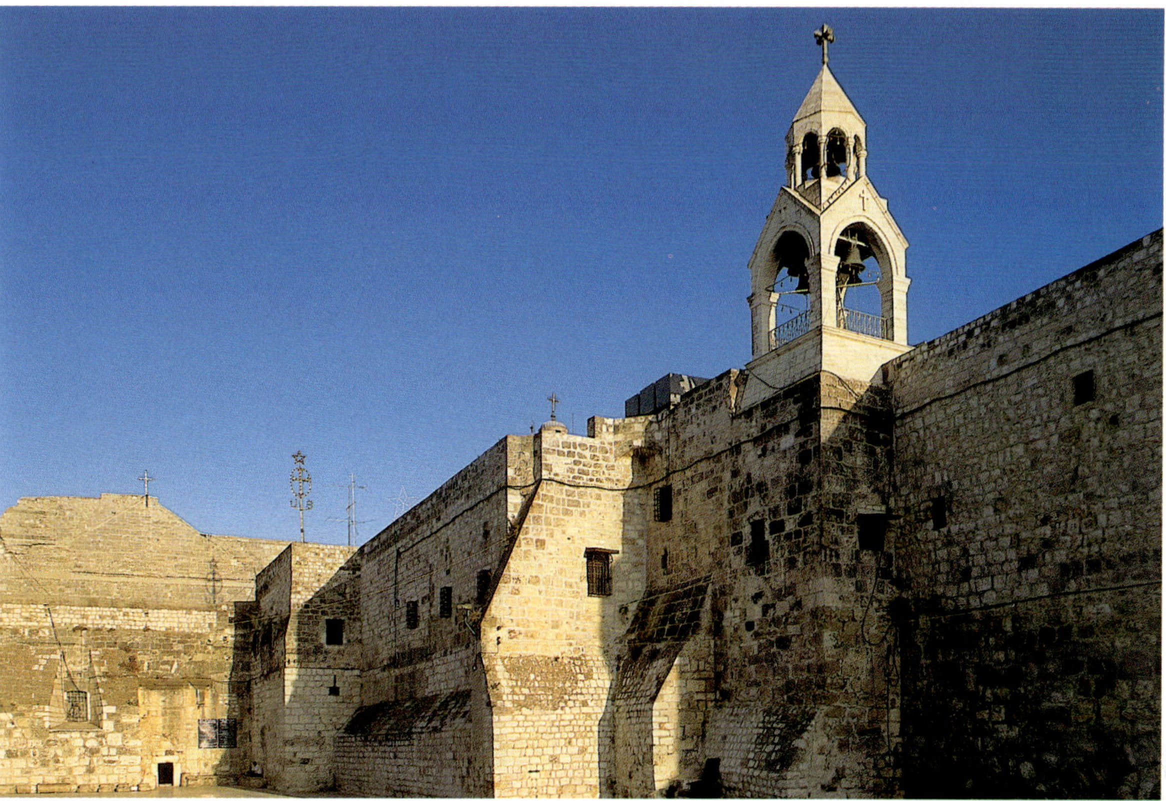

The Church of the Nativity in Bethlehem was originally built in the sixth century, but has been restored and expanded numerous times over the years. The Grotto of the Nativity attracts the most visitors.

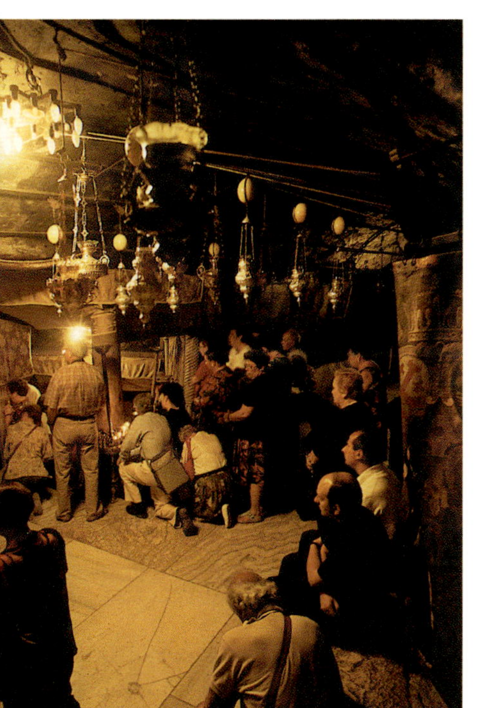

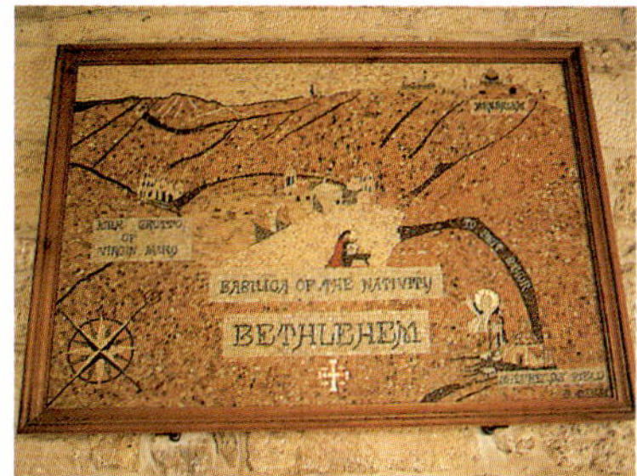

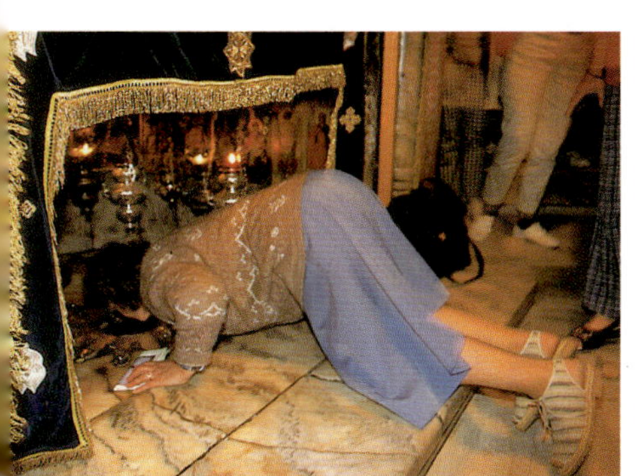

In the southern part of the Judean Desert, in the Kidron Valley east of Bethlehem, a monastery founded by Saint Sabas (439–532 AD) seems to be growing straight out of the cliff-face. This is *Mar Saba*. Very near the monastery is the Women's Tower from where women who are forbidden to enter the monastery proper can have a look at it. Ida Pfeiffer from Vienna who was one of the first women to travel in this area on her own described her enthusiasm of the view in her diary in 1842 as follows: 'I saw a place bustling with activity, there were Bedouins in the courtyards and Arabs busying themselves with their horses, others prostrated themselves to worship the very same God I too worship [...] This evening will give me many beautiful hours filled with rich memories.'

Bethlehem

The tradition of Bethlehem as the birthplace of Christ was established by the early Christians. The church over the Grotto of the Nativity was originally built here in 325 AD and has since become the most important pilgrimage site in Christendom. Groups of travellers jostle with pilgrims and vendors of devotional items and all cluster around the entrance, only 4 feet high, leading into the interior of the Basilica, which is surrounded by fortress-like monastic buildings. On the northern outskirts of Bethlehem is the Tomb of Rachel, wife of Jacob, one of Judaism's holiest shrines and venerated by Jews and Muslims alike. A field near the village of Beit Sahur south-east of the city is traditionally where 'shepherds watched their flocks by night' when they were given the news of the birth of Jesus.

An Oasis straight out of 'A Thousand and One Nights'

Jericho, the World's Oldest City

Every oasis is a jewel, yet Jericho is the most beautiful of them all. At least it is if one takes the time to discover it thoroughly Like a forgotten relic from an oriental fairytale, Jericho lies in the Jordan valley between the hills of the Judean Desert and the precipitous Moab mountains. Irrigation is provided by small, above-ground canals which carry spring water through the oasis which is overgrown with lush banana plants and orange trees, sycamores with outstretched branches and an abundance of bougainvillaea. 10,000 years ago, people had already settled in this city which is located 250 metres below sea level and is therefore the lowest lying city in the

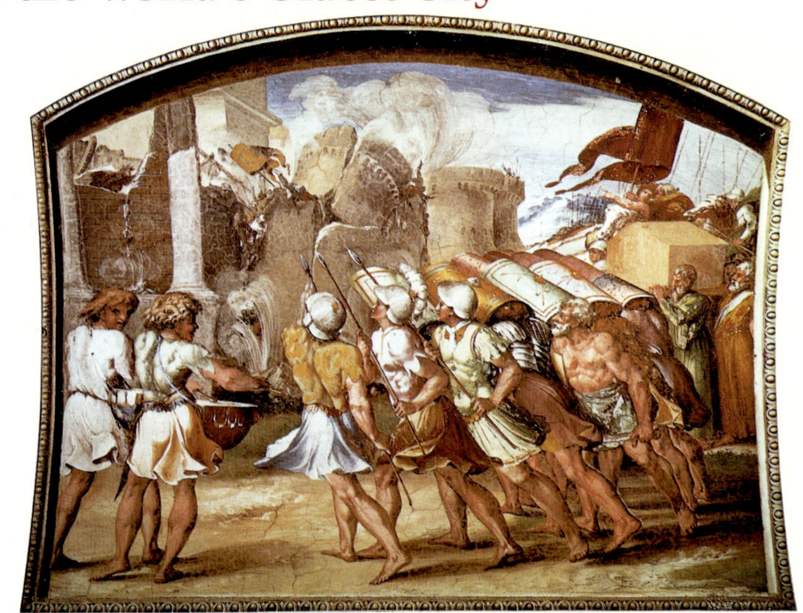

According to the Bible, the walls of Jericho were brought down by the sound of trumpets (detail of the Rafael fresco in the Vatican, Rome, around 1515–1518).

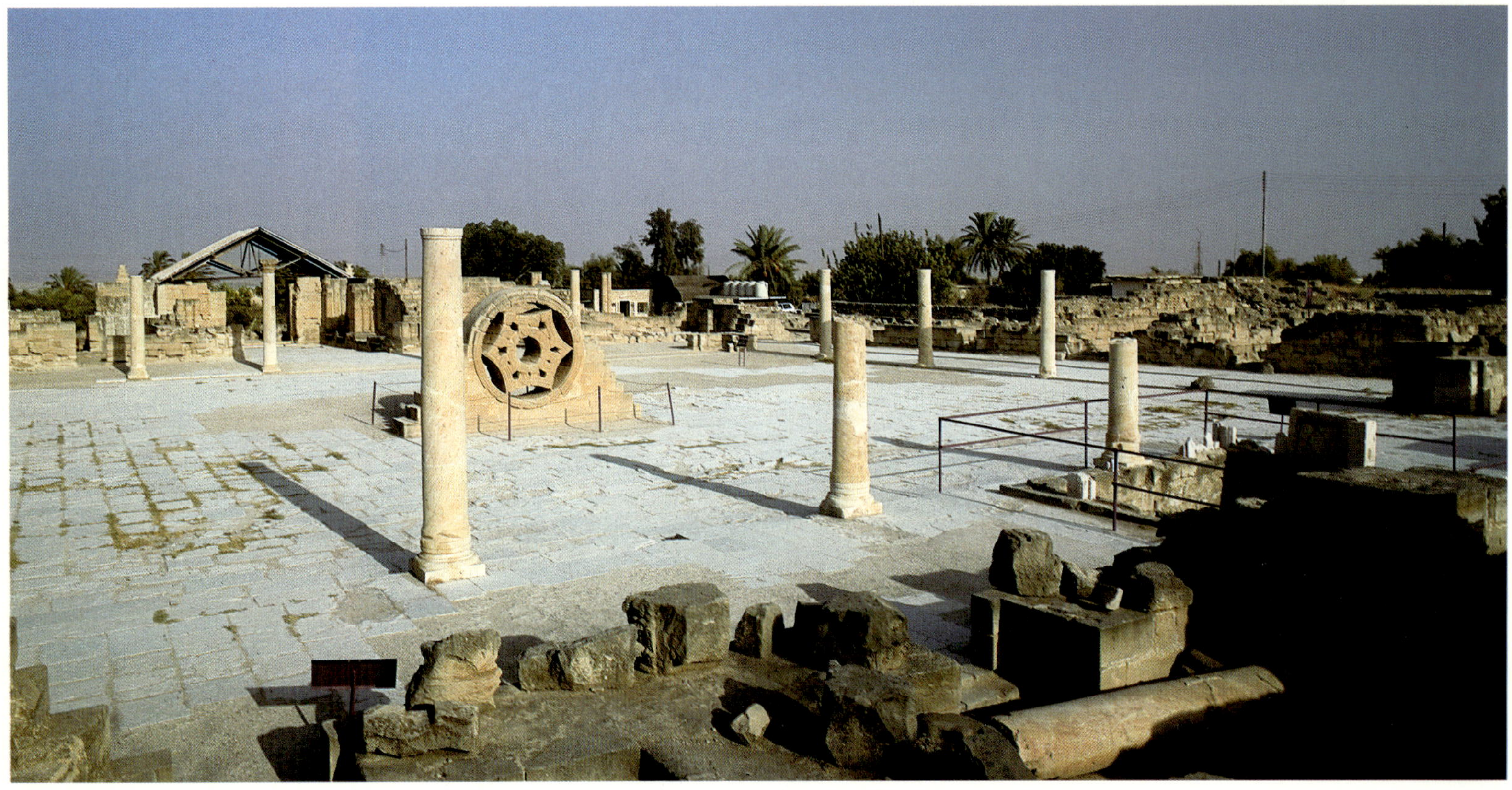

world. Excavations at *Tel es Sultan* brought to light a stone tower with a staircase from the 8th century BC. This proves that Jericho is the earliest settlement and perhaps even the oldest city in the world.

Very much later, wealthy rulers built their winter palaces in this earthly paradise. Among them was Hisham Abd'el Malik: In 742 AD, the Caliph begun work on the construction of his *Palace*, two miles north of Jericho. It was fitted with steam baths, a private mosque and audience rooms. However, an earthquake left behind only the ruins of a domed building and the private bathroom which features colourful mosaics.

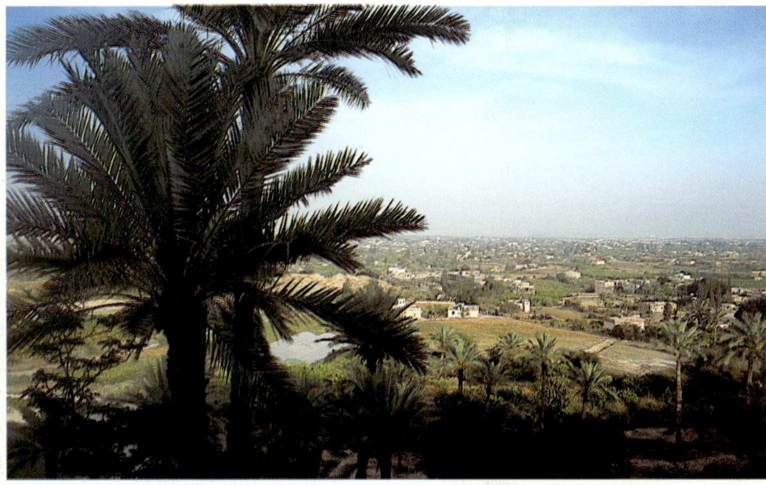

The banana plants and orange trees of Jericho.

In Jericho, leisure and pleasure were the order of the day. In the meantime in Jerusalem, which was merely 22 miles away, religious fanatics and secular rulers fought bitter battles. King Hussein of Jordan built himself a winter villa in Jericho during his reign. And even in 1987, at the beginning of the Palestinian rebellion against the Israelis, things stayed relatively calm in this area. So calm in fact, that Jericho's selection as the first city to be given over to Palestinian autonomous rule after the peace agreement of 1993 was probably not due entirely to chance. On the day that the Israeli occupying forces left, the citizens expressed their joy loudly and publicly.

Since then, Jericho has calmed down again. Young people cycle around the main square, people sit, shaded by orange trees, in restaurant gardens and wait. They wait for guests, Palestinians, foreigners and maybe even the Israelis who stayed away following the Intifada. Or maybe they're just sitting for the sake of it. For in ancient Jericho everyone knows that time will pass with no help from anyone.

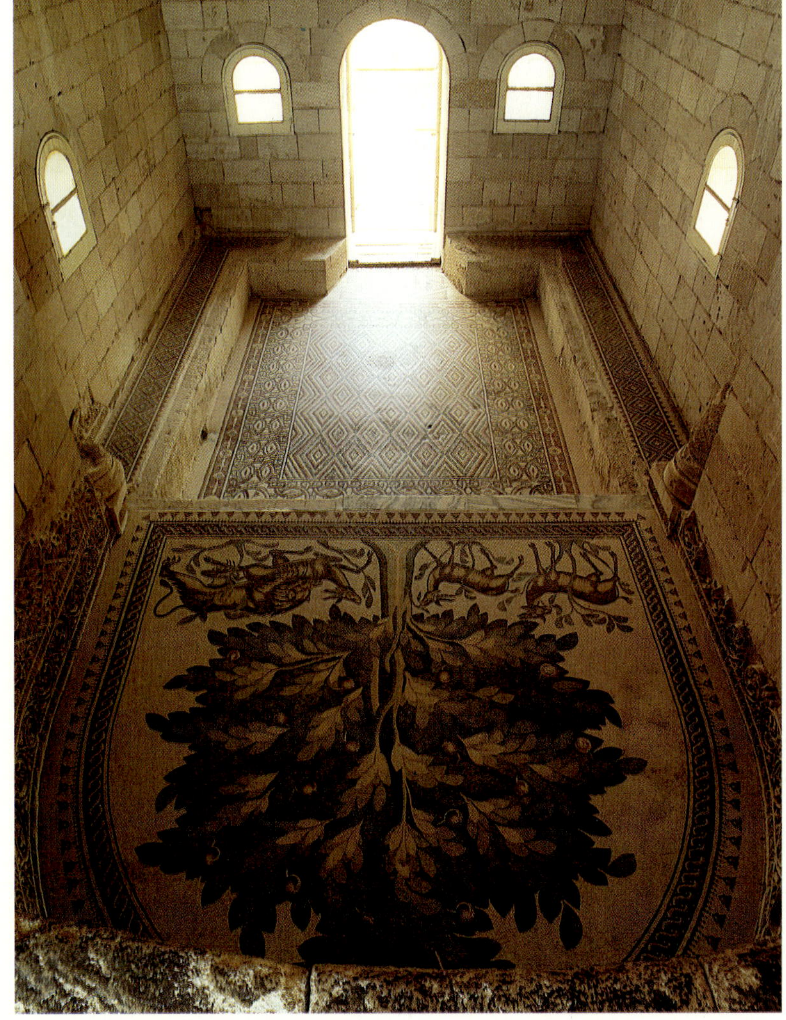

Hisham's Palace: the courtyard and tracery windows (left), the mosaic depicting the tree of life in the bath house (centre), section of a richly adorned colonnade (right).

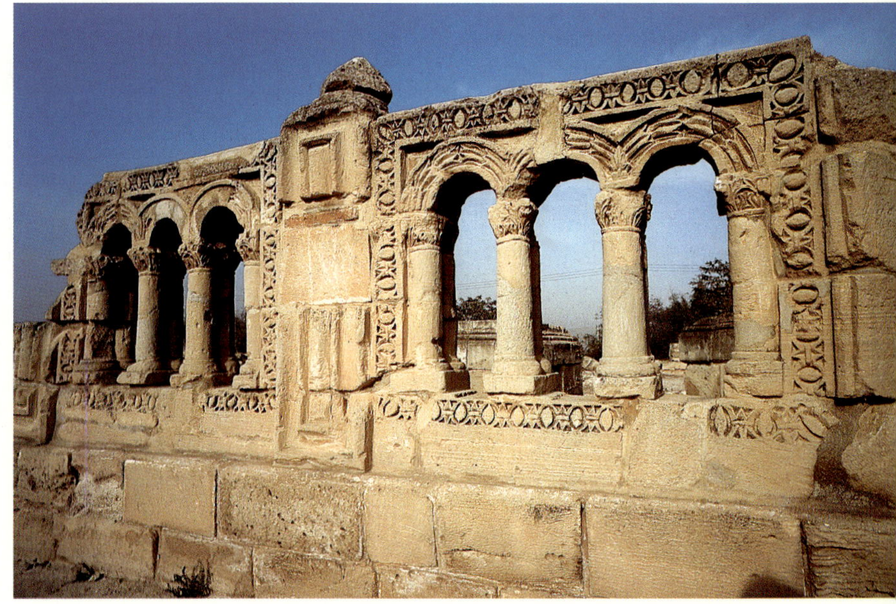

Planning and Travelling

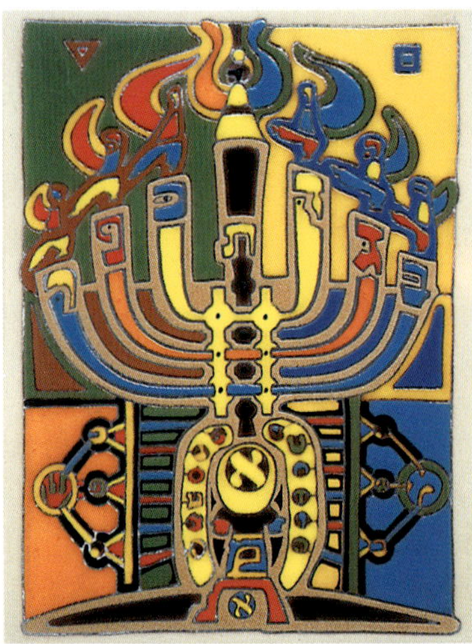

Seven-branched candelabrum painted on a door in Safed.

Geography

Israel lies at a point where three continents meet. In the west it borders onto the Mediterranean, to the east lies the great African Rift Valley and to the south it borders onto the Red Sea. Including the occupied territories, Israel covers an area of 13,639 square miles. At its widest point it stretches 84 miles across from east to west, and 345 miles from north to south. At 392 metres below sea level, the Dead Sea is the lowest point on earth. The country can be roughly divided into four geographic regions. The coastal plain with the large cities Tel Aviv and Haifa stretches out to the west. This is where the majority of Israel's 5.5 million inhabitants live. In the east are the Jordan and Arava valleys, where the subtropical Jordan valley connects the Sea of Galilee with the Dead Sea. A mountain range stretches out to the north, which reaches from the Galilean highlands, over the areas of the West Bank known as 'Judea and Samaria' with Jerusalem in between, to the Negev mountains. And in the south lies the desert of the Negev with the cities of Beersheba and Eilat.

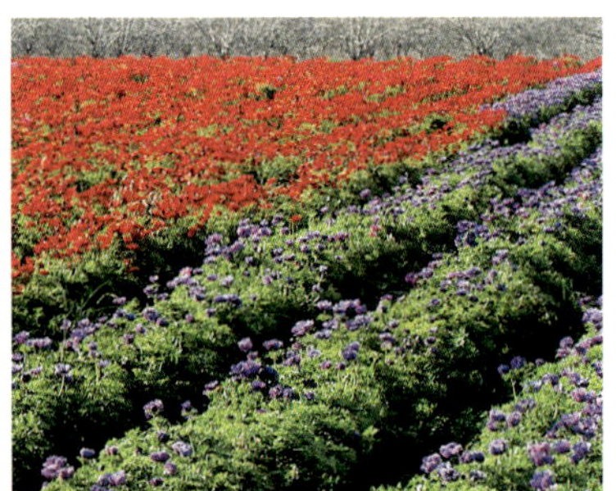

Artificial irrigation produces an abundance of flowers.

Flora and Fauna

Intensive land cultivation and the Israeli's love of hunting have wiped out many animals or dangerously decimated their numbers. Nowadays there are several reserves where attempts are being made to reintroduce Israel's indigenous animals such as the ostrich and wild donkey. The flora too has suffered at the hands of man. A large amount of timber was needed to construct the railway through the desert, both for building sleepers and for burning. As a result, Israel's forest declined to three percent of its area. Since the founding of the state, there has been intensive reforestation and now the forest once again covers ten percent of the country. In 1964, the Hula Valley in the Jordan Valley was the first area to be declared a nature reserve and since then 1864 square miles of the country have been thus designated. The Nature Conservation Authority (SPNI) has visitor centres at Arad, Mizpe Ramon, Yotvata and the Hula Valley where natural history tours are on offer.

Population

Israel's population, including the occupied territories where around 1.5 million Palestinians live, has grown – partly due to immigration from the former Soviet Union – to over 5 million. In 1994 the population had reached 5.41 million. Israel may be the 'Jewish State', but it remains a multi-national and multi-religious country with major religious minorities such as Moslems, Samaritans, Christians, Druze and Bahai. Not counting the occupied territories, there is a large Arab minority of 800,000 people, who live in Galilee, Jaffa, Lod, Ramle and East Jerusalem.

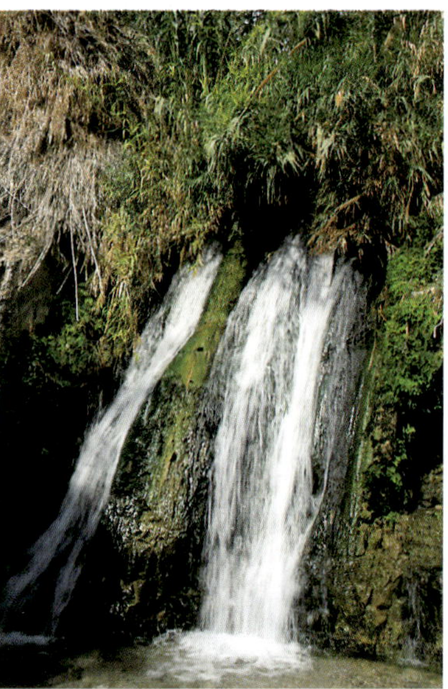

En Gedi National Park near the Dead Sea.

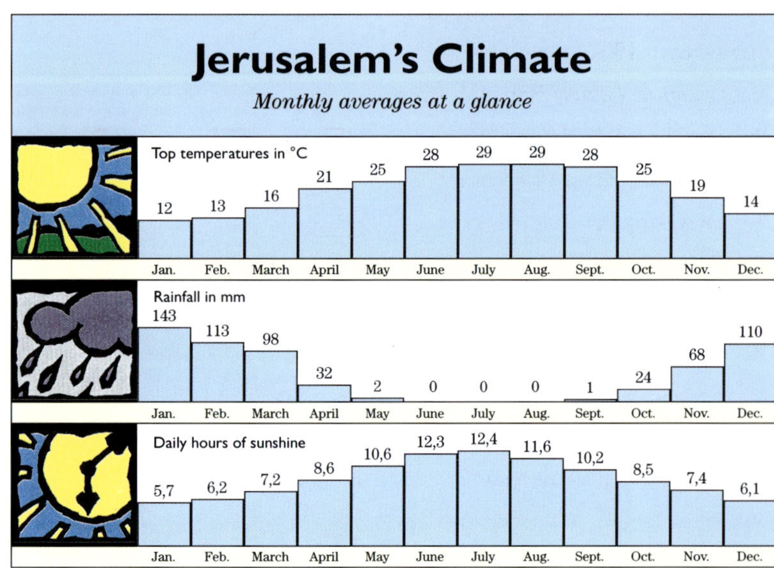

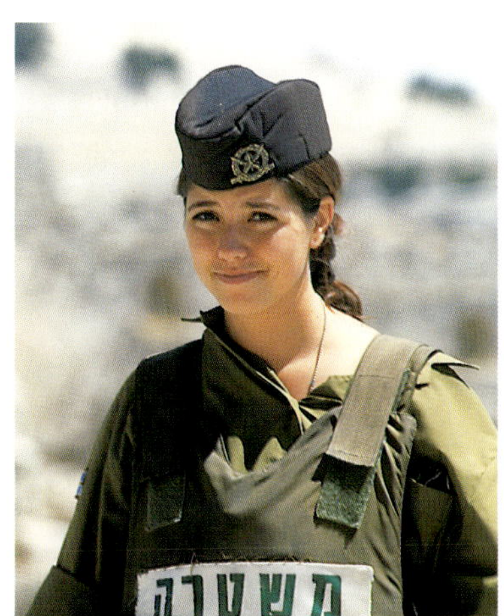

Nothing unusual: female soldiers.

Politics and Economy

Israel is the only democracy in the Middle East. The government is elected every four years by proportional representation; there are 120 seats in the Knesset. Following the founding of the state, the left leaning Labour Party remained in power for a long time. In 1977, the right-wing Likud block won the elections for the first time and thus began the controversial settlement policy under Prime Minister Menachem Begin. The Labour Party did not return to power until 1992 under the leadership of Yitzhak Rabin. With the new Prime Minister came the signing of the Peace Agreement with PLO-chief Arafat in 1994. On 5 November 1995 the world was shaken by the assassination of Rabin. His successor Benjamin Netanyahu was not able to convince international doubters that the peace process would continue. Israel's politics always have an effect on tourism, which, with around two million visitors every year, represent one of the country's main economic factors, along with agriculture, the armaments and diamond industries and the service sector.

Language

The official national languages are Hebrew (Ivrit) and Arabic. Many Israelis also speak English and, because of immigration, Yiddish, Russian, Polish, Hungarian, French, German and Spanish are also common languages.

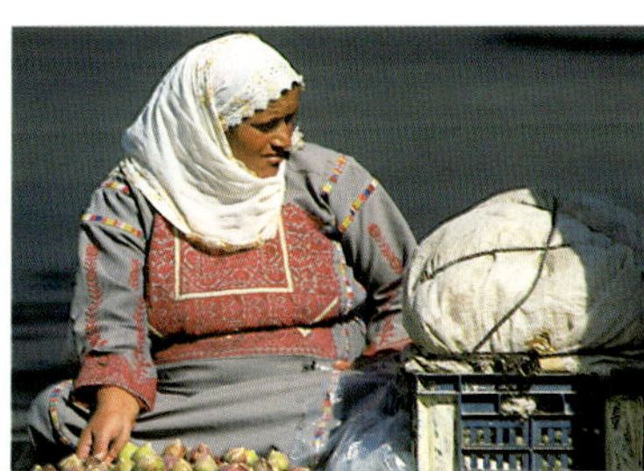

This Moslem woman is selling fresh figs.

The main linguistic problem is that written place names have not been standardised. Therefore Acre may also be written as 'Acer' or 'Akko', Safed as 'Sfad' or 'Zefat'.

Best Times for Travel

Israel is blessed with a Mediterranean climate; warm, dry summers from May to October and cool, rainy winters from November to April. The wettest period is between December and February. There is no rainfall to speak of during the summer months. Therefore, trips to Israel can be undertaken at any time of the year, and Eilat in particular provides a year-round holiday destination. If visiting the northern regions during the winter, travellers should remember to bring warm clothes and waterproof gear.

Time Zones

Israel is an hour ahead of Central European Time. Watches have to be put forward on arrival. Summer time applies from the middle of April to the middle of October and is one hour ahead of Central European summer time.

Public Holidays

The lunar year is observed in Israel. The Jewish New Year, Rosh Hashanah, occurs in September/October; this is the first day of a ten-day period of atonement which ends with Yom Kippur. The dates on which Jewish holy days (see also pages 90 and 91) occur are different every year. In parallel to the Hebrew

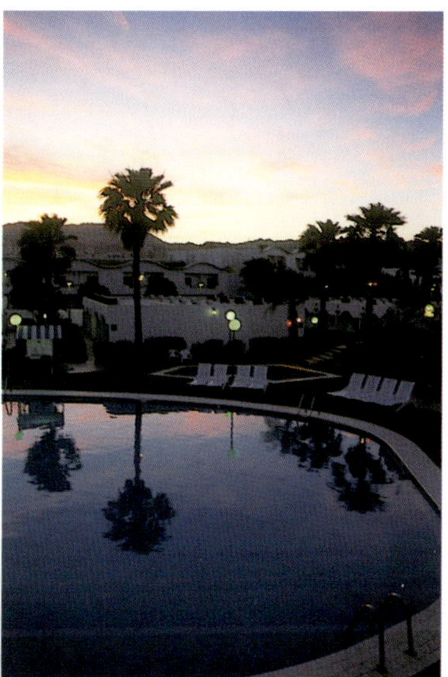

There are many luxury hotels in Eilat.

calendar, the standard Gregorian system is also in use everywhere. Holidays and the Sabbath (Saturday) are days of rest, shops do not open, there is no public transport, and offices are usually

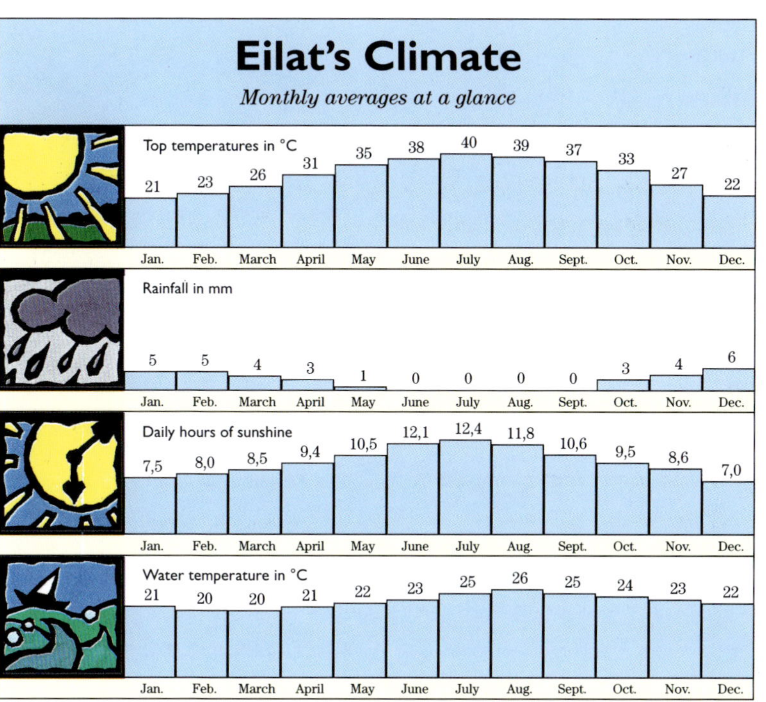

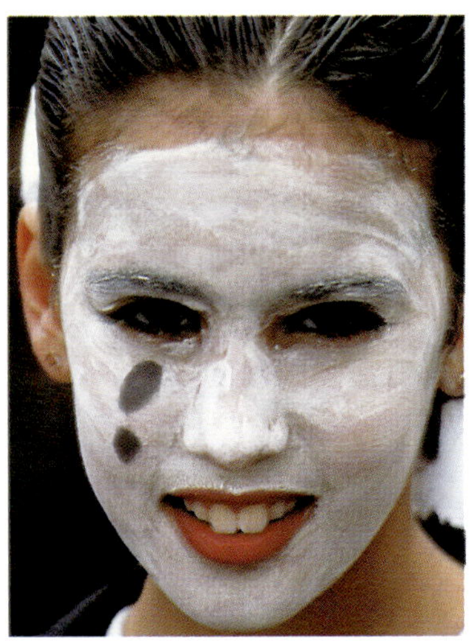

Children wear fancy dress for Purim.

open from Sunday to Thursday, and on Fridays or before holidays they close at lunch time.

Sept/Oct: Rosh Hashanah, Yom Kippur, Succot, Simchat Torah
Nov/Dec: Hanukkah
Jan/Feb: Tu B'Shevat
Feb/March: Purim
March/April: Passover
April/May: Independence Day, Lag B'Omer
May/June: Jerusalem Liberation Day, Shavuot
July/August: Tisha B'Av

Weights and Measures

The metric system is used in Israel.

Getting There

Flying time to Israel's 'Ben Gurion' airport is about four hours. Various shipping and ferry lines offer sailings from Athens to Haifa. Cypriot ships have stop-overs in Rhodes and Limassol. Israel can be accessed overland via Jordan or Egypt, but these routes can only be taken by bus or train and not by car.

Medical Services

Most places in Israel have good medical services, most doctors speak English or another foreign language. Dial 101 to summon the 'Magen David Adom' (Israeli Red Cross) ambulance service in Haifa, Jerusalem or Tel Aviv. The daily papers such as the English language 'Jerusalem Post' have lists of ambulance stations operating at night, during holidays and weekends in various cities.

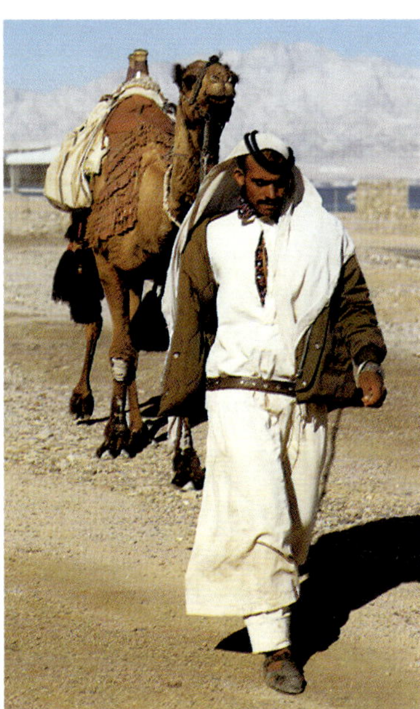

Most Bedouins have settled in one place.

Information

Israel Ministry of Tourism, 24 King George Street, Jerusalem,
Tel. 02/675 48 11

Beach Resorts

Israel has many beaches. Almost the entire Mediterranean coast is lined with sandy beaches, and those between Bat Yam and Netanya, as well as in Nahariya are well developed (see also page 110). Although the water temperature rarely drops below 17° C, air temperatures can be rather fresh in winter. The same applies to the Sea of Galilee. The Red Sea is most suitable for a winter beach holiday. Although the beaches are pebbled, the lowest water temperature of 21° C is still very pleasant. The Dead Sea with its rocky beaches is also pleasantly warm throughout the year.

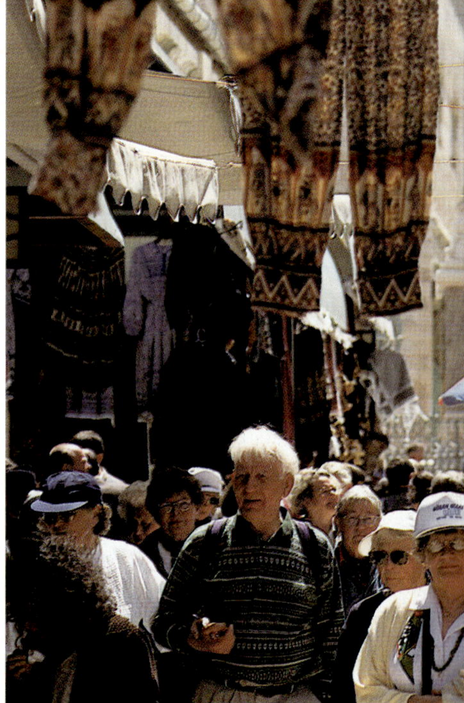

Christian pilgrims walk along the Via Dolorosa in Jerusalem in remembrance of Christ's passion.

In the Heart of the Metropolis

A beautiful walk around Jerusalem

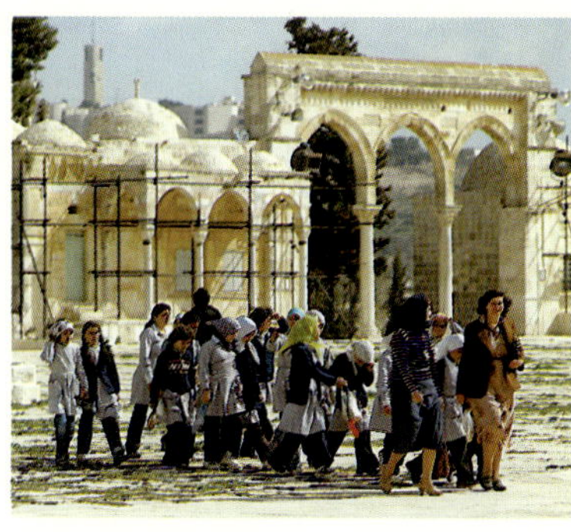

School outing to the Dome of the Rock in Jerusalem.

aThe best place to start a walk through Jerusalem's Old City is at the Jaffa Gate. It may be crowded, but the tourist information office nearby is stocked with plenty of information material. The Museum

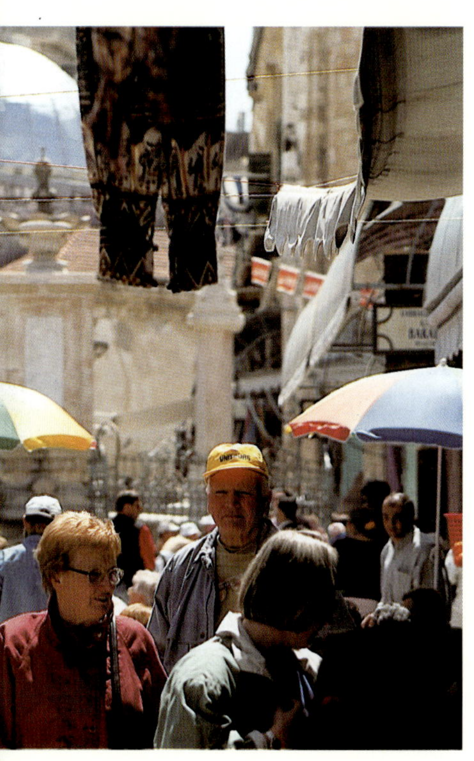

of the City of Jerusalem inside the Citadel is right next door and contains displays which illustrate the tumultuous history of the city. A stroll through the Armenian Quarter gently guides you towards this intriguing city. This area is calm and relaxed. The Zion Gate to the south provides access to Mount Zion, the Tomb of David and the Church of the Dormition. Turning back one soon comes across the 'Cardo' in the Jewish Quarter. Today the former north-south axis of the Roman garrison town is a shopping street with expensive boutiques. The southern end of the Cardo is open to the sky and the ruins of ancient buildings are visible underneath new apartment buildings. Tiferet Street leads past both the Hurvah and Ramban Synagogues and, at its eastern end, to the Burnt House, which was destroyed by the Romans in 70 AD. Stone steps guide us down to the Wailing Wall and past Porat Yosef Yeshiva, Israel's most famous Talmudic school. While on the stairs, it is worth having a camera to hand to take a picture of the Dome of the Rock on Temple Mount. Visitors should take some time to visit the Mount; half a day should do it. St Stephen's Gate leads up to Mount of Olives and a magnificent view of the city walls and the Old City. Finally, the Via Dolorosa leads through the busy crowds of the Moslem Quarter to the Church of the Holy Sepulchre. Leaving the Citadel through the New Gate and walking a short distance along the city wall the walk brings you back to the Jaffa Gate. For a chance to relax and unwind in peaceful surroundings after the long walk, a drive to Mount Scopus is recommended, here you can watch the sun setting behind the silhouette of the city. As an alternative for those who prefer to engage in cultural activities, Jerusalem's Sherover Theatre in Talbiye or the YMCA in King David Street are popular performance venues. And if all this culture makes you hungry, go down to Ben Yehuda Street where Jerusalem's lively night life is found in the bars and restaurants.

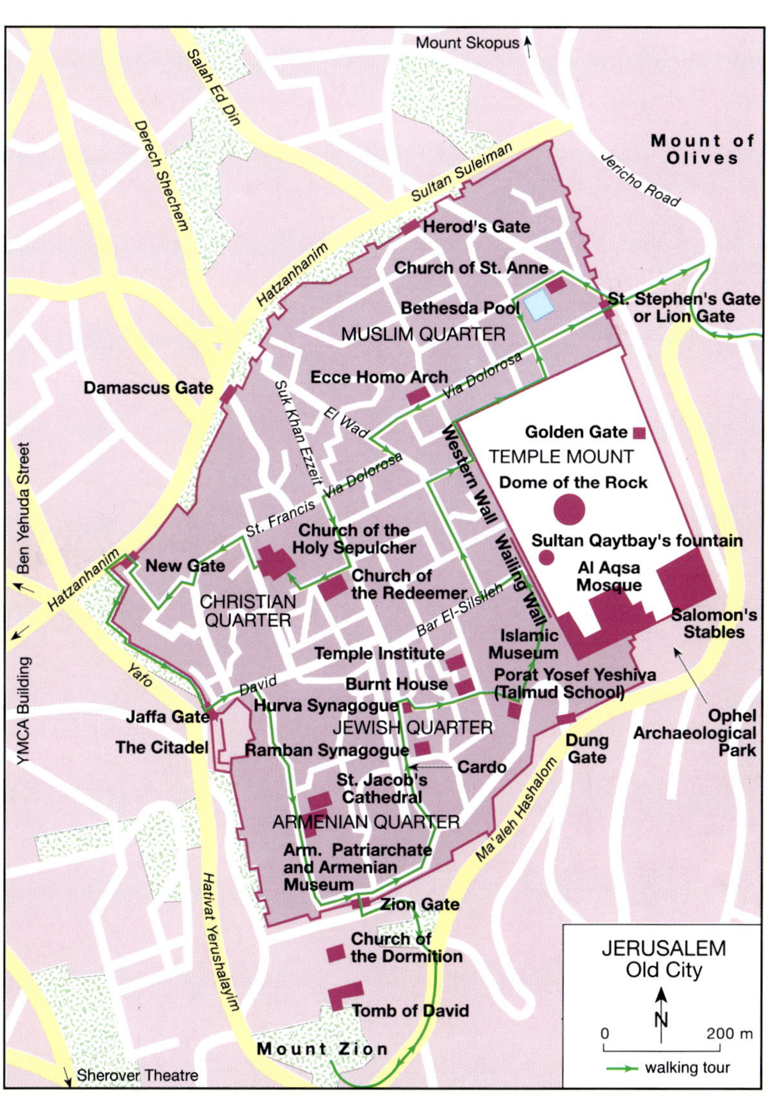

Banks

Opening times for the major banks are Sunday, Tuesday and Thursday from 8.30 a.m. to 12.00 p.m. and from 4.00 p.m. to 5.30 p.m., Monday and Wednesday from 8.30 a.m. to 12.30 p.m., Friday and on the eve of a holiday from 8.30 a.m. to 12.00 p.m. Most cash dispensers will accept EC or credit cards.

Shopping

There are no fixed closing times for shops. Some supermarkets are open 24 hours a day. Small shops generally open at around 8.30 a.m., close for lunch between 1.00 p.m. and 3.00 p.m., and open again until late in the evening. Jewish shops are closed on Saturdays and during Yom Kippur, Arabic shops shut on Fridays, and Christian shops on Sundays.

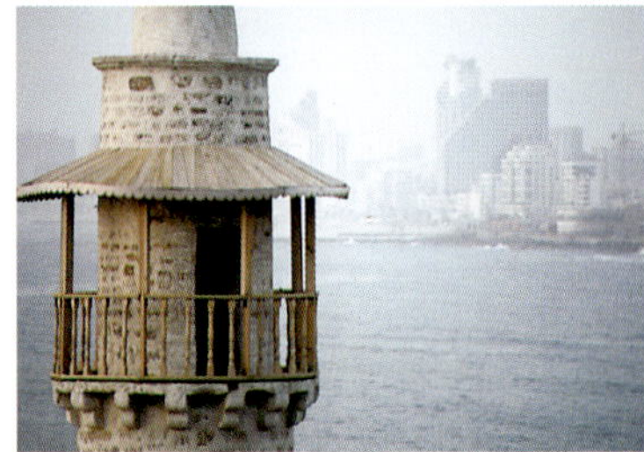

Minaret in Jaffa and the skyline of Tel Aviv.

Electricity

Israel uses 220 Volt AC current. Sockets are usually suitable for three-pin plugs, so visitors from the UK will not usually need an adaptor.

Entry and Exit Formalities

All visitors to Israel have to be in possession of a valid passport on entering the country and are required to fill an entry form, AL17, on arrival. This is usually handed out during the flight. Passport control then stamps it and it must be handed back on departure.

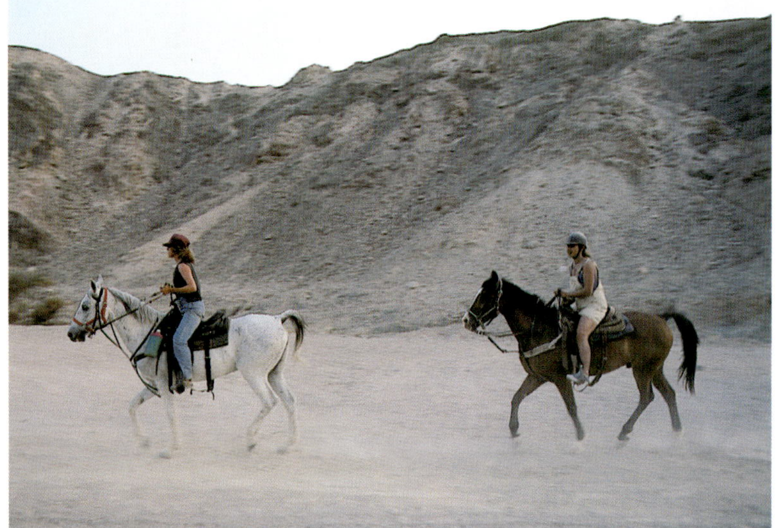

Short forays into the Negev desert or trips lasting several days – riding holidays are becoming increasingly popular in Israel. Others treat themselves to a short holiday at the En Gedi Kibbutz.

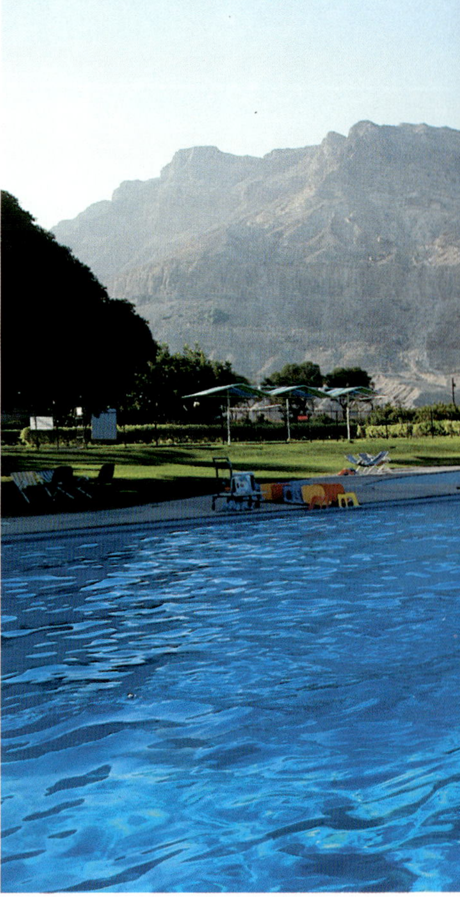

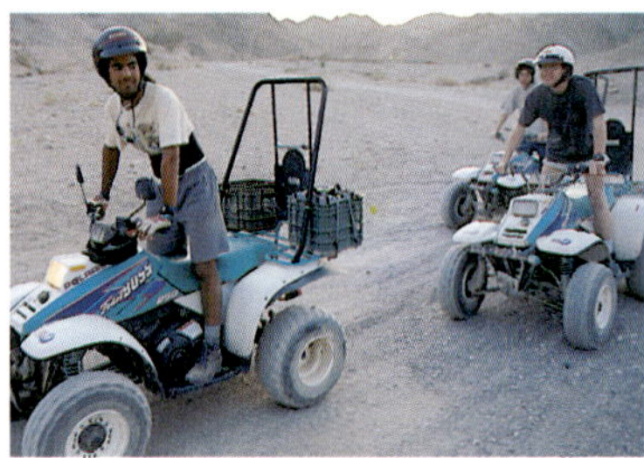

Motorised fun in the Negev desert ...

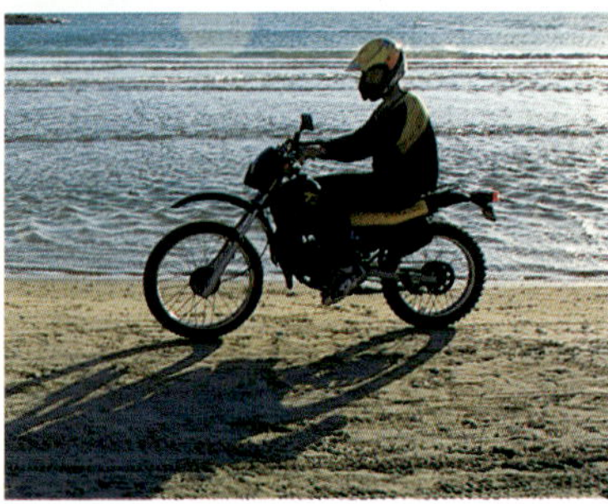

... and along the beach at Netanya.

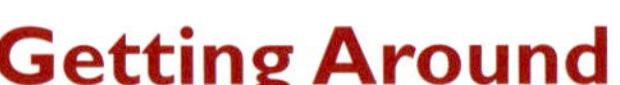

Getting Around

By car: All the major car hire firms are represented at the airport and in many cities. An international driving licence is required or a national licence if issued in a country which accepts Israeli driving licences. Drivers must be 21 years old and have had a minimum of one year's driving experience. Israelis drive on the right hand side of the road, and speed limits are 50 kilometres per hour in urban areas, 80 kilometres per hour outside of urban areas and 90 kilometres per hour on motorways. There is a strict seat belt rule.

By taxi: A particularly Israeli mode of transportation is the 'Sherut', which usually operates on Saturdays too. Up to seven passengers share a six door Mercedes and the price is equivalent to the bus fare. Sheruts often cover the same routes as buses.

By bus: Buses are the most important means of transportation in Israel. Services depart from local central bus stations, are regular and the fares are reasonable. Buses from Tel Aviv to Jerusalem for example run at ten minute intervals. It is advisable to make reservations before longer journeys. Apart from in Haifa, there is no bus service from Friday afternoon to Saturday evening and on Jewish holidays.

By Train: Rail services operate only from Haifa/Nahariya and Tel

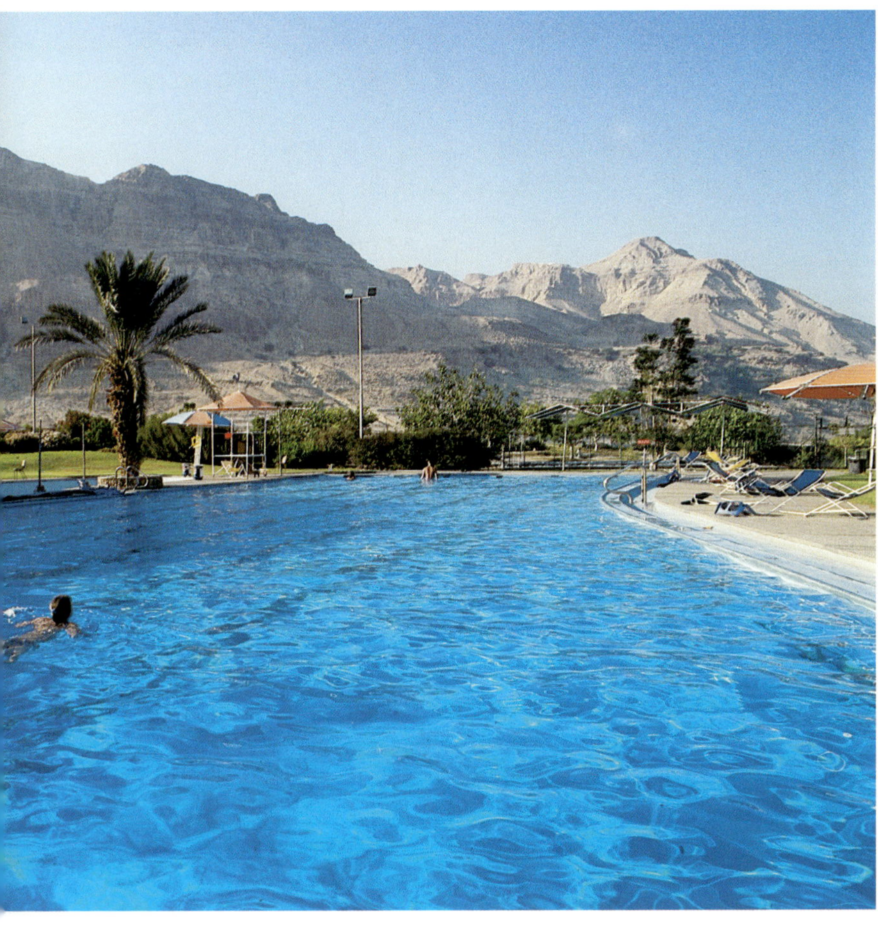

Aviv to Jerusalem. The journey from Tel Aviv to Jerusalem is particularly picturesque, as the train winds through the Sorek Valley.

By air: Israel's charter airline 'Arkia' flies to airports in Tel Aviv, Jerusalem, Rosh Pina, Haifa and Eilat.

Photography

It is forbidden to photograph military installations. However, these are always clearly signposted.

Health

There are no vaccination requirements for tourists entering Israel. Hygiene standards in Israel are the same as in Europe.

Travelling with Children

Israelis love children, and Israel is a country with a high proportion of young people. In restaurants and hotels, children are treated with consideration. However, it has to be borne in mind that the intense sunshine in Israel can be much more harmful to children than adults. Therefore, you should take care to provide plenty of protection from the sun, an adequate amount of liquids and rest periods in the hotel. The best way to visit Israel with children is by staying in hotels close to the beach or in kibbutz guest houses. In the kibbutz, children often make friends with the local kibbutz children. Older children will also enjoy alpaca or camel rides and the moonlit desert walks on offer by the Israeli Department of Tourism.

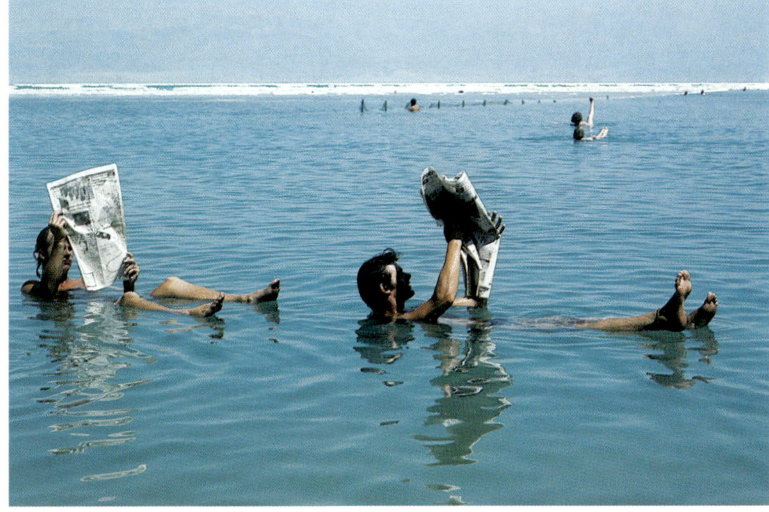

A frequently photographed image: Reading the newspaper whilst floating in the Dead Sea.

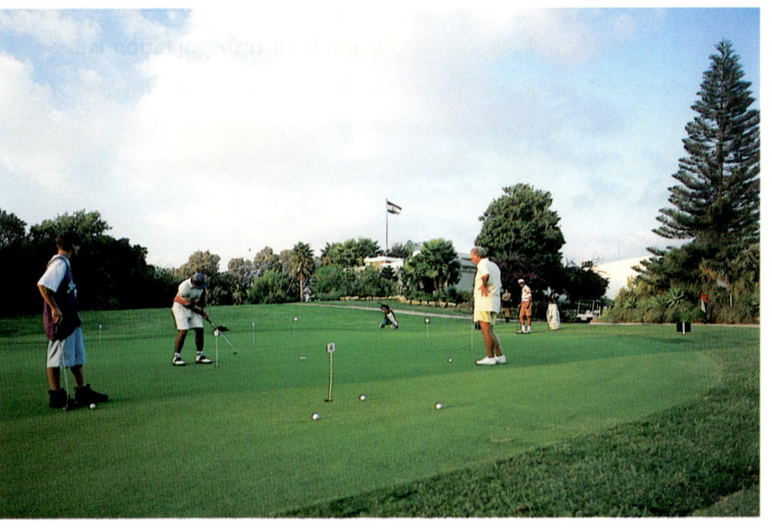

The only 18 hole golf course in the Middle East is situated close to the ruins of Caesarea.

Health Resorts

Israel has an excellent reputation for spa holidays. There are health resorts on the Sea of Galilee and by the Dead Sea. The hot mineral springs in Tiberias on the Sea of Galilee are said to be beneficial for muscle and joint ailments and psychosomatic complaints, whereas the resorts on the Dead Sea, above all Neve Zohar and En Boqeq, are among the most famous for curing psoriasis and other skin diseases as well as rheumatism.

Museums

Museums and archaeological sites are usually open from Sunday to Thursday from 9.00 or 10.00 a.m. until 4.00 or 5.00 p.m.. Restricted opening times often operate on Fridays and Saturdays and some

Discovering Israel by Car

The most interesting Routes

Route 1:
Sky over the Desert
Beersheba, oasis city and last outpost on the edge of the desert, provides the starting point for an intense encounter with Israel. In the west and north, the Negev is flat and dusty and as far up as the intersection with the Nebatean city of Shivta, it seems somewhat melancholy. After the kibbutz of Sde Boker, the land begins to rise, and south of Avdat, another Nebatean excavation site, the Ramon crater forms the first high point in the landscape. The drive through the sparsely populated mountains, where chalk, sandstone and granite formations abound and where the light paints shadows in all hues from anthracite to red, is one of the most impressive experiences Israel has to offer. To avoid repeating the same drive, this route takes a right turn at Shizzafon, that is in a south westerly direction, and traverses an expanse of emptiness all the way to Eilat. The road leading north from the bathing resort of Eilat is busier. Not to be missed on the way is the semi-circular road through the Timna Valley, past its bizarre rock formations and ancient copper mines. Continue along the main route to the date palm oasis of Kibbutz Yotvata and then via Dimona back to Beersheba.

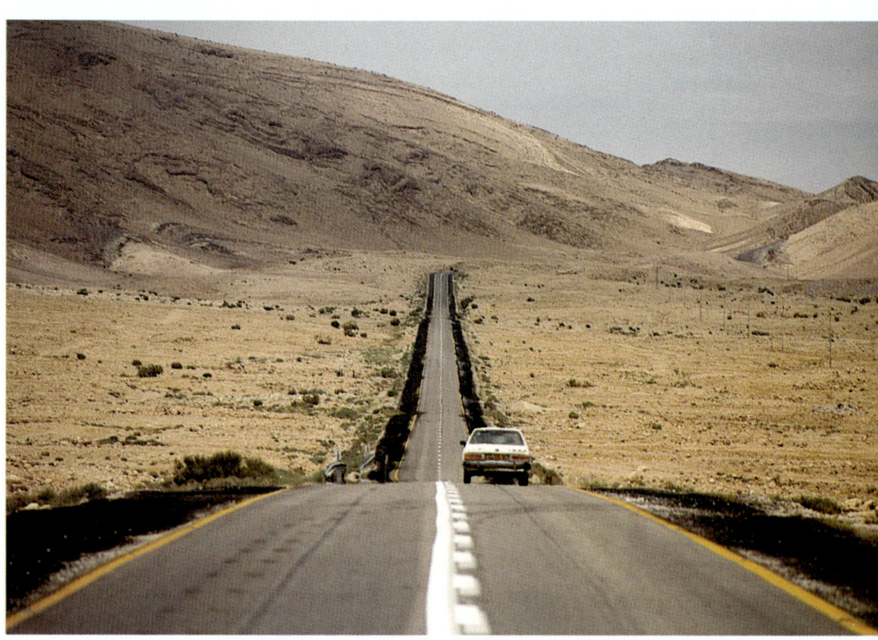

Once a malaria infested swamp, the Hula Valley is now one of Israel's largest cultivated areas.

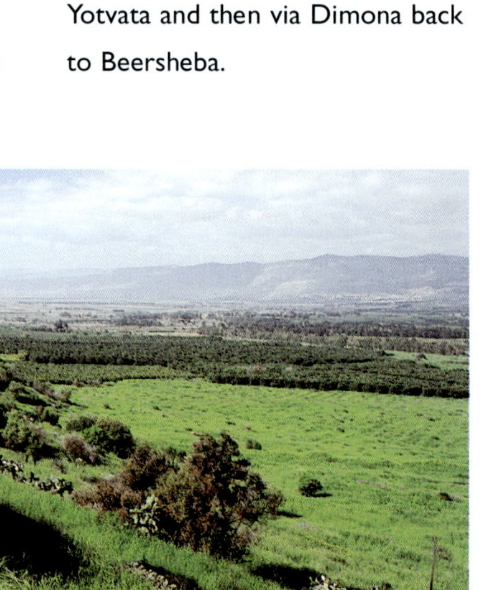

The drive from Beersheba to Eilat passes through rugged mountains and desert.

Route 2:
The fascinating Dead Sea
The first leg of the route from Ashkelon on the Mediterranean is not particularly impressive and leads first in the direction of Beersheba, but then, north of Beersheba in the direction of Arad. If you have limited time and can't fit a visit to the Negev into your itinerary, you should definitely turn off towards Masada at Arad. This route will ensure that you don't go home without having had an experience of the desert and will take you to the Roman Ramp, the best way to approach Masada on foot. You will have to take the same road to get back to the main route, but later on in the day, the light will have changed and transformed the landscape. At Neve Zohar you will have reached the Dead Sea where you should indulge in the spectacular swimming experience provided by the buoyancy of the salty water - perhaps at the resort of En Gedi. At the northern tip of the Dead Sea it is only a short trip to Jericho after which it is worth visiting the famous Wadi Kelt and the Monastery of St George. Back on the main route to Jerusalem there is a turning on the left which leads to the Qumran archaeological site. The remainder of the route to Jerusalem is a picturesque and adventurous drive through numerous rock gorges.

Route 3: Sea and Mountains, Crowds and Solitude
Netanya is a Mediterranean resort and the starting point for this journey north. The first highlight is

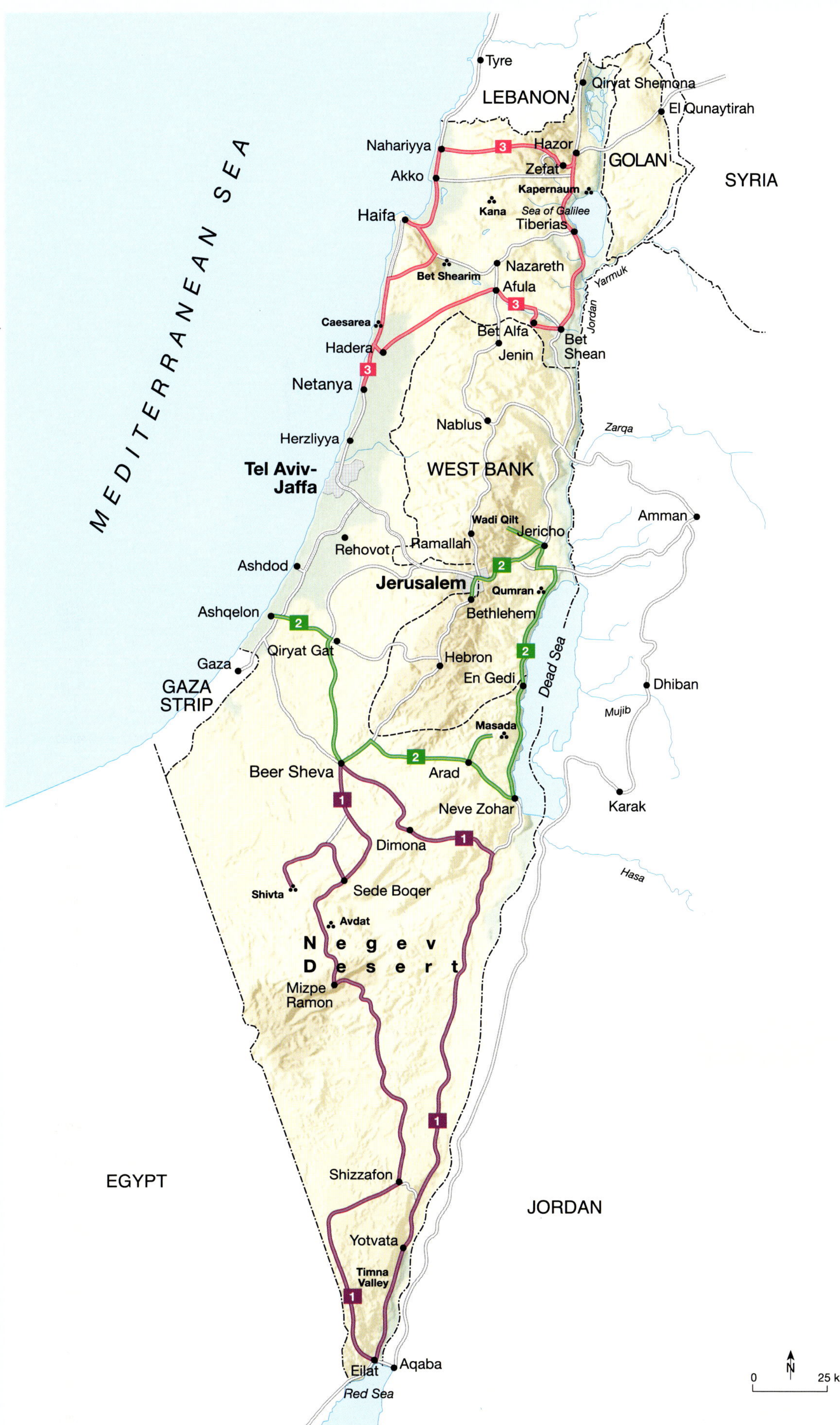

provided by the archaeological site of Caesarea. The route itself becomes more interesting as the journey progresses: The enchanted forest in the Carmel Range and peaceful Druze villages show a side of Israel which seems barely imaginable back on the Mediterranean beaches. From quiet Carmel, the route descends to the lively port of Haifa. The area between Haifa and Acre is spoilt by the indiscriminate spread of the settlements, but the ancient crusader city with its enchanted nooks and crannies soon makes up for this and the quiet sea-side resort Nahariya will make you forget the conurbations entirely. As the route turns further towards the east, it becomes increasingly lonely and mountainous, and by the time you reach Safed with its famous artists' quarter, the Mediterranean coast will seem light-years away. From Rosh Pina, the first Jewish village in Upper Galilee which was built in 1882, the roads winds down towards Capernaum on the Sea of Galilee. As the route descends to below sea level one gains the eerie sense of having just come from the highest mountain regions. Along the lake, past Biblical sites, the road follows the Jordan valley to Bet She'an. After a visit to this archaeological excavation site, the subsidiary road via Nir David and Bet Alfa is the more attractive option for a journey to Afula in the fertile Jezreel Valley. From here it is a short drive back to Hadera and the coast.

museums don't open at all on the Sabbath.

Postal Services

Post boxes in Israel are yellow (for mail within the city) or red (for out-of-town and international mail). Postage stamps can be purchased at post offices, as well

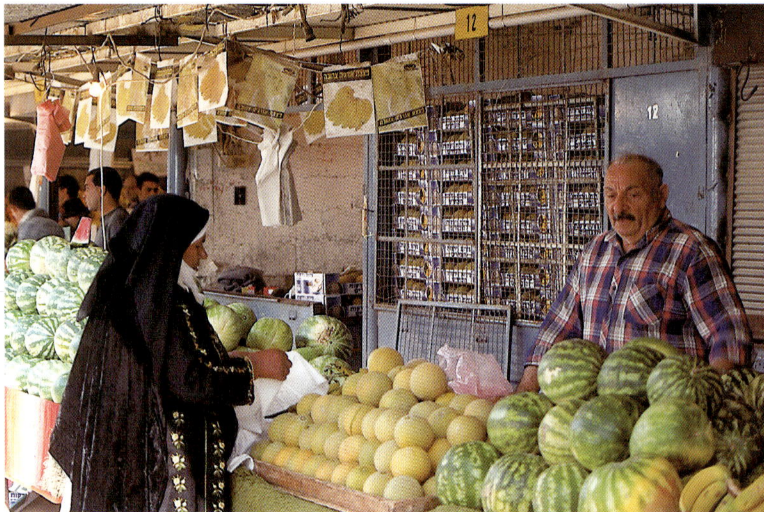

Bedouins in traditional costume are a frequent sight in Beersheba where many have settled.

as in most hotels and in stationery and souvenir shops.

Souvenirs

Israel offers everything from shopping malls to bazaars. Oriental markets are found in the old cities of Jerusalem, Acre, Nazareth and in the Druze villages in Galilee, particularly Daliyat near Haifa. The Bedouin market in Beersheba, where traditional handicrafts are amongst the items for sale, is held every Thursday morning: Olive wood carvings, jewellery, mother of pearl, leather goods, embroidered textiles are all worth looking at. Haggling is part of the deal in the bazaars. Judaica like Menorahs (seven-branched candle sticks) and Mezzuzot (Torah boxes) are available everywhere. In the diamond city

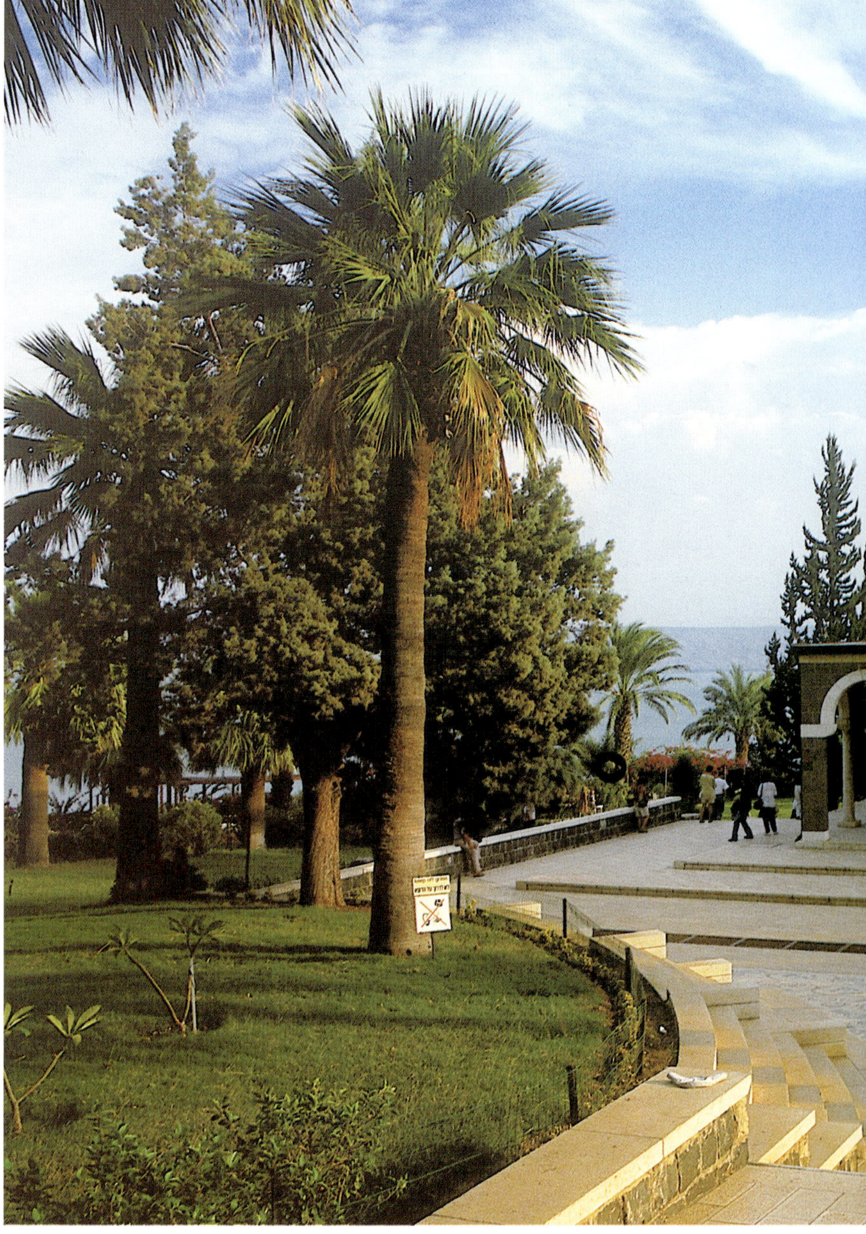

On the Seligpreisung mountain on the north side of the Sea of Nazareth, the church of Seligpreisung was built in 1937.

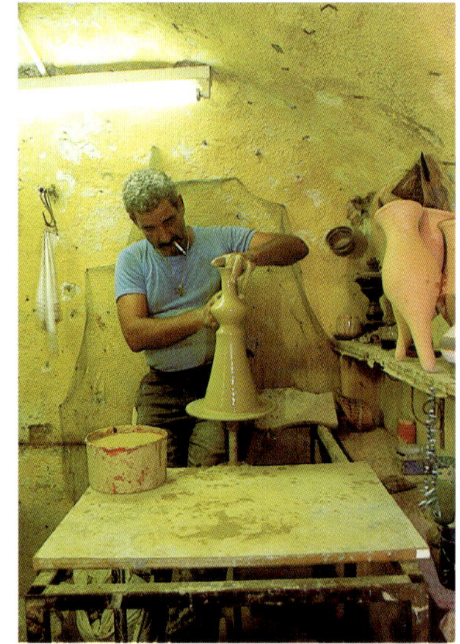

A potter in his workshop in Acre.

Netanya, diamond cutting shops sell the precious stones. Cosmetics based on Dead Sea minerals make nice gifts to take home, as do wines from the Israeli vintners 'Carmel' or the Sabra liqueur.

Sport

Israel provides ideal conditions for a number of different sports. Eilat has internationally renowned diving and snorkelling areas which are also suitable for beginners. Swimming, surfing, sailing and water-skiing are all available on the Red Sea and the Mediterranean. The eastern side of the Sea of Galilee is also popular among surfers. Skiing is available on the slopes of Hermon and ramblers enjoy Galilee and the Golan. Horse riding is also available almost anywhere in the country. Caesarea is home to Israel's only, but wonderful, 18-hole golf course which is located on a drifting sand dune on the Mediterranean coast.

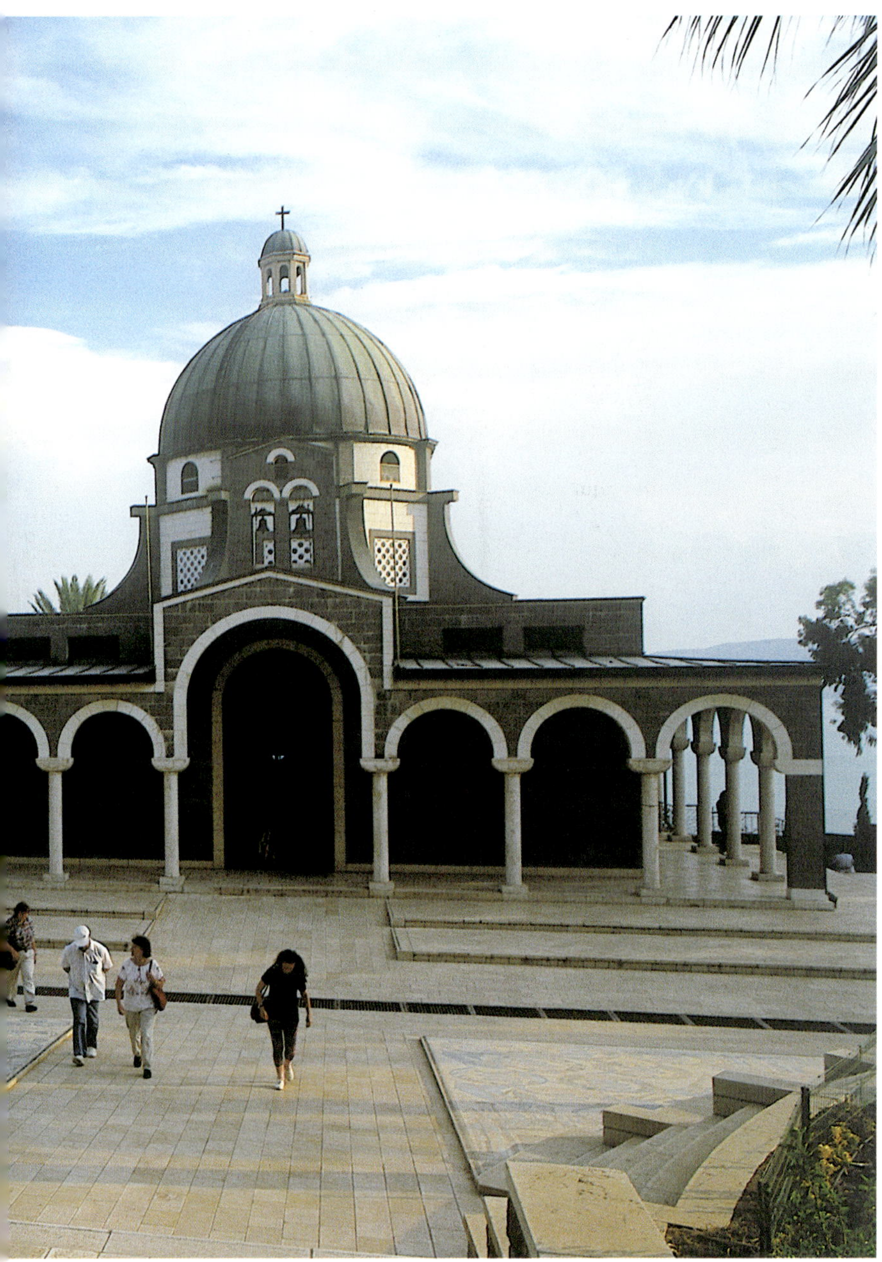

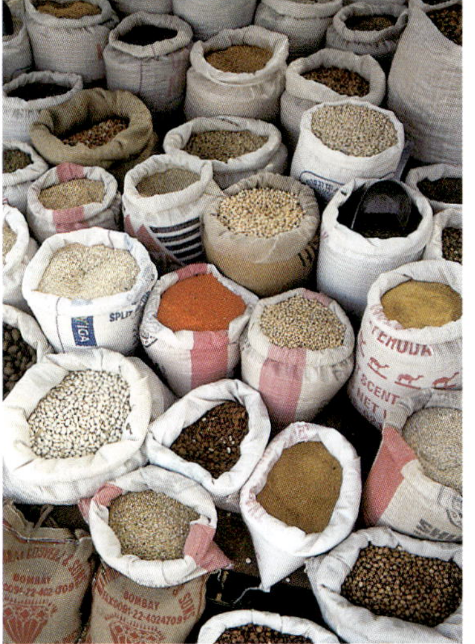

Exotic goods on offer in the local markets.

Telephones

Telephone cards are needed to operate Israel's public telephones. These are available at post offices and newsagents and can be used to make overseas calls from any public telephone. National calls are cheaper after 10 p.m. The dialling code for the United Kingdom is 00 44.

Tipping

Restaurants expect to receive tips of about 15 percent of the bill. A small tip for taxi drivers is optional, depending on level of politeness, but Sherut drivers will definitely expect a tip.

Accommodation

Hotels of an international standard are mainly available in the beach resorts and cities. These tend to be huge, modern buildings. The kibbutz guest houses offer a more personal atmosphere. Christian hospices also take in guests. Many tourist information offices will also act as agents for bed and breakfast accommodation. An international YHA card is needed to stay in any of the 30 or so youth hostels. Camping sites are of a very high standard. Some offer bungalows and tents for rent.

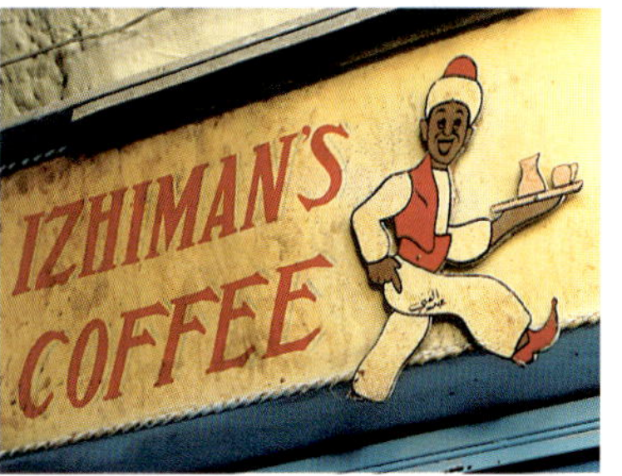

Turkish coffee is as popular in Israel as anywhere else.

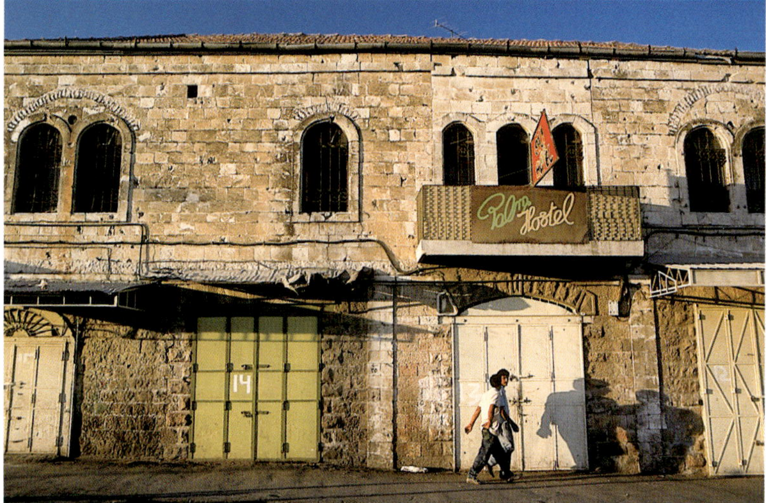

Jerusalem has hotels to suit every pocket and personal taste. Some are in historic buildings.

Currency

The national currency is the 'New Israeli Shekel' (NIS). The rates of exchange are almost the same at banks or private Bureaux de Change. Travellers cheques and international credit cards are accepted across the country.

Duty Free Shopping

Duty free allowances are: $^{1}/_{4}$ litre of perfume, 2 litres of wine or 1 litre of spirits, 250 grams tobacco or 250 cigarettes. Fresh meat and fruit, narcotics and weapons may not be imported.

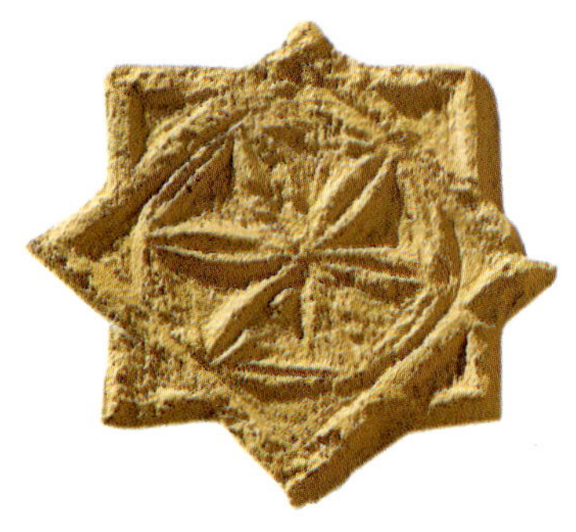

Index of People, Places, Descriptions

Page numbers in italics indicate illustrations, coloured squares and page numbers in bold indicate special interest sections, coloured bars indicate spotlights.

Index of People and Names

Ornaments for the North Church in Shivta (above). In Hebron (below).

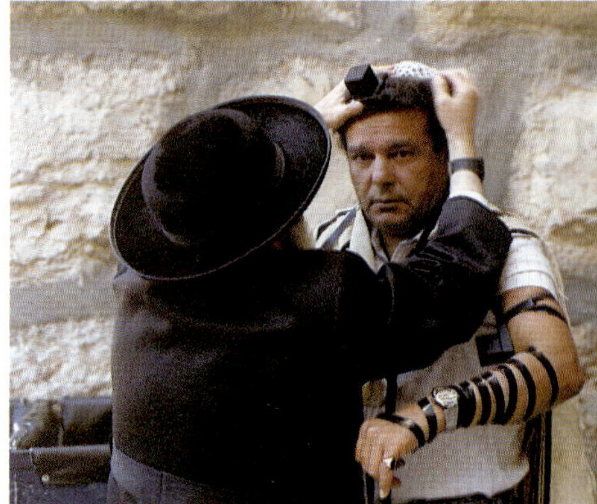

Religious duty for Jews: attaching the tefillin – leather box and straps – to head and arms.

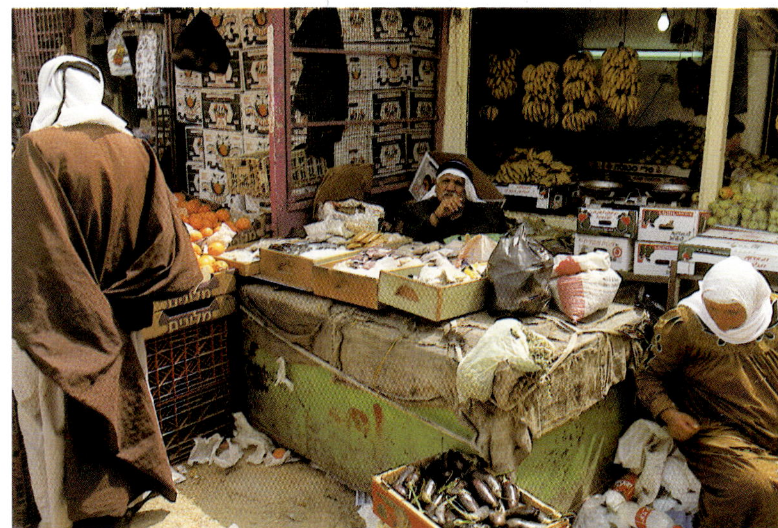

Tourists and natives hoping to strike it lucky in the colourful markets.

Places and Descriptions

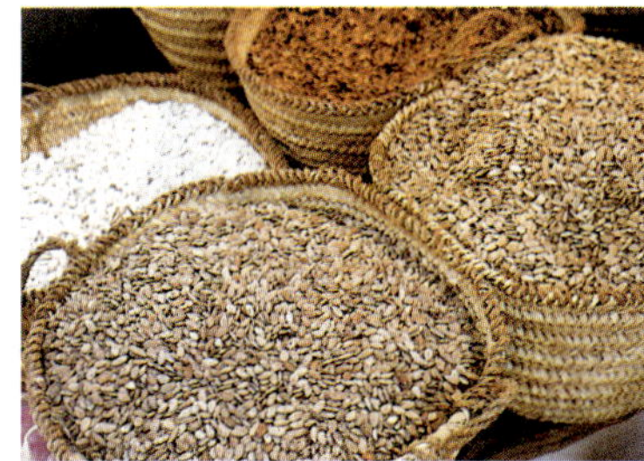

Grains, nuts and cereals.

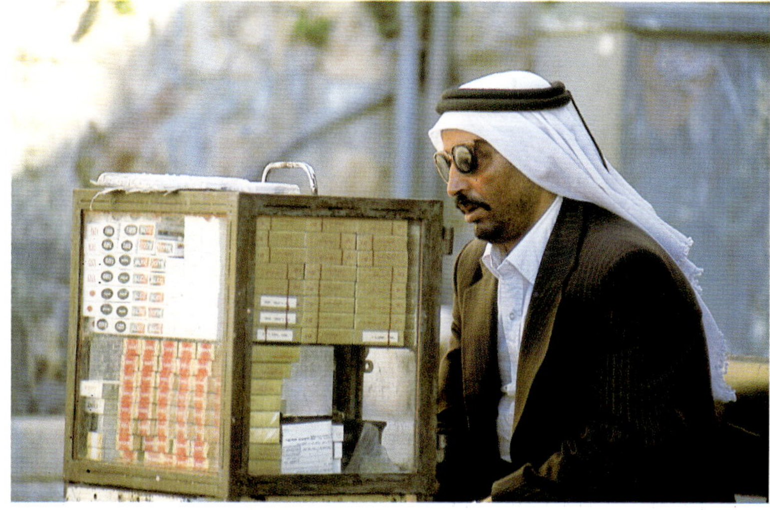

Strong Arab cigarettes are for sale.

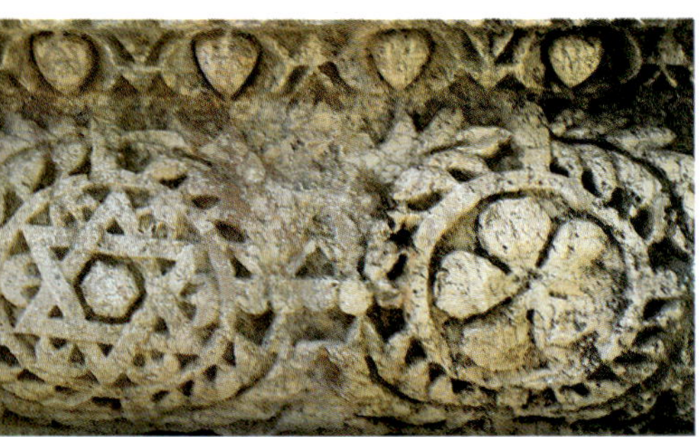

Detail of a frieze in Capernaum.

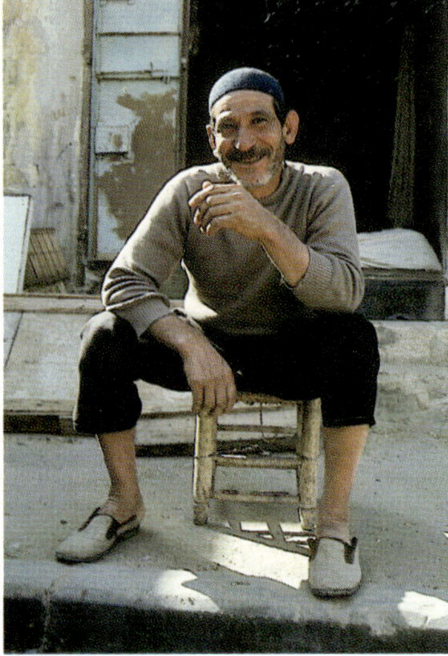

Palestinian in Gaza.

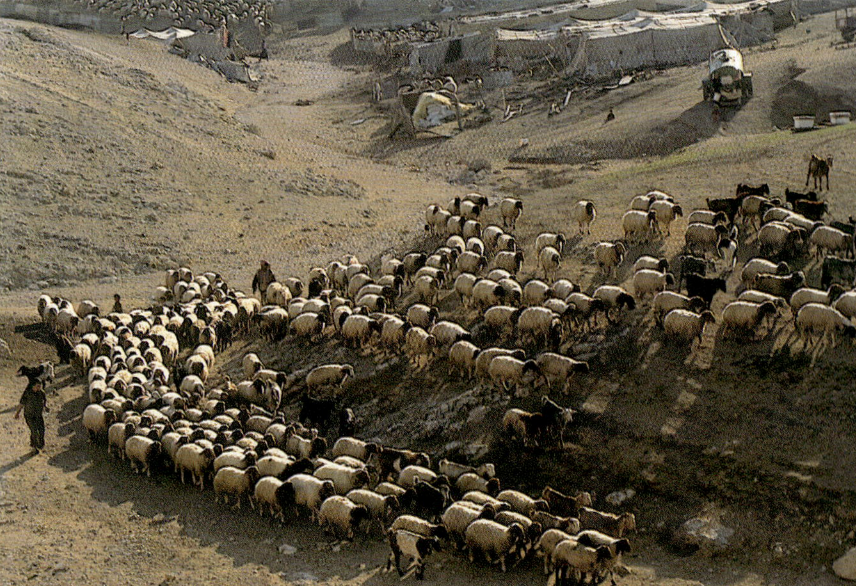

Flocks of sheep seeking nourishment in the Judean Desert.

A garden at the foot of the 'Ölbergs' in Jerusalem.

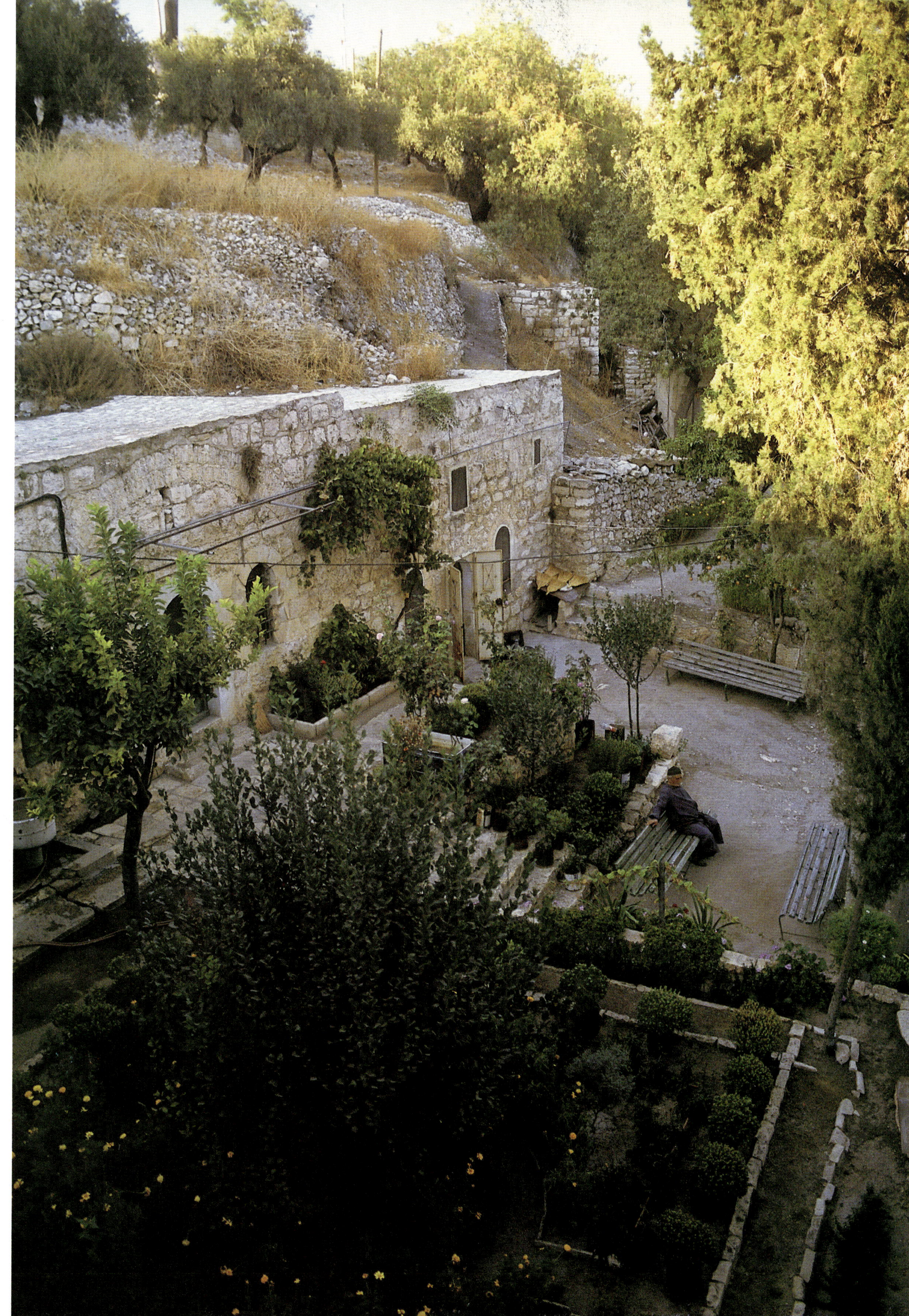

Text and picture Credits

The Authors:
Nicola Förg studied German Literature and Geography. She was the editor for a travel magazine and has been living in Munich for a number of years where she works as a freelance journalist for magazines and daily newspapers and as an author of travel books.

Rachel Goldmann studied History and Political Sciences. She lives in Berlin and Jerusalem where she works as a freelance writer.

The Photographer:
Tom Krausz studied photography in Hamburg. He has been working as a freelance photographer for magazines and book publishers since 1978. His work has been shown at numerous exhibitions in Germany and abroad.

Text Credits

The special section on Page 128 is the contribution of Christian Mietz who lives on the Starnberger See in Germany and works as a freelance writer, underwater photographer and diving instructor. He has written many books and articles on the subject of diving.
All the other texts were written by Nicola Förg and Rachel Goldmann.

The quote on page 10 was taken from a speech by Chaim Herzog at Schloss Augustusberg on 6th April 1987 based on: Eva and Zeev Goldmann, Hed Wimmer: Israel. Legend, History, Present. Munich and Lucerne, Publishers C. J. Bucher 6th Edition 1989

Picture Credits

Archiv für Kunst und Geschichte (Art and History Archives), Berlin: p. 25 t., 68 t., 69 b., 90 t., l., 144 t.
Bildarchiv Preußischer Kulturbesitz (Picture Archives of Prussian Cultural Heritage), Berlin/Israel Museum, Jerusalem: p. 24 t. (2) 68 r.
Gidal Picture Collection: p. 26/27 (7)
Massimo Borchi/Atlantide, Florence: p. 3 t., 4 c., 5 second from b., 6 t., 8/9, 10 t. and c. r., 11, 14/15 (4), 16 b. l., 19 b. r., 20 t. and b., 21 b., 42, 43 t. r., 47 t. and b., 52, 54 t., 55, 56 t. r., 60 t. l., 60/61, 64 b. r., 64/65, 65 t., 66 t., 69 t., 70/71 t., 78 t., 84 l. and t. (2), 85 t. l., 86 t., 90/91 b., 92, 93 b., 94/95, 101 (2), 104 t., 104/105 c., 105, 106 r., 107 l., 112, 113 t., 115 t., 116 (2), 116/117, 118, 120/121, 126/127 b., 130, 131 t., 133 b., 136 b. l. and t. r., 137, 138 b., 142 t., 143 t. l., 144 b., 145 b. l., 147 l. and c., 154 b., 158 l., Cover photos front r.
Hans-Ulrich Comberg, Hamburg: p. 37 b. r., 44 l., b. l. and b. r., 45 b., 48 l., 48/49, 49 t. r., 151 r., 156 l., 158 t.
Elisabeth Gilbert, Jerusalem: p. 136 t. l.
Ifa-Bilderteam, Munich: p. 36/37 t., 37 t. r., 76, 85 r., 100 c., 110/111 t., 131 b., 134, 150/151.
Interfoto, Munich: p. 24 l. t.
Udo Kefrig, Osnabrück: p. 128/129 (8).
Keystone Press Service, Hamburg: p. 24 c. r., b. l. and b. r.
Laenderpess, Mainz: p. 94 l., 100 t., 110 r., 115 b., 122/123 t., 148 b., 149 t.
Dinu Mendrea, Jerusalem: p. 4 t. and b., 16 t. l., 20 c., 36 t. c., 38/39, 77 b., 91 t. and b., 95 b. l. and t. r., 103 (2).
Radu Mendrea, Munich: p. 114 (2), 124/125 t.
Sandu Mendrea, Jerusalem: p. 5 t., 6 b., 10 second from t., 18/19, 28/29 (5), 31 b. l., 33 r., 35, 46 t. and b. l., 48 t., 50/51, 79 b., 80/81, 91 c., 100 b., 119 b., 124 t., 132 b., 132/133, 134/135, 135 t., 146 c., 148 t., 154/155 t.
Werner Neumeister, Munich: p. 36 b. l, b. c. and b. r., 80 c., 91 t. r., 138 t. l., 139 t.
Axel Schenck, Bruckmühl: p. 67 (4), 83 (2), 123 (3).
Süddeutscher Bilderdienst, Munich: p. 25 b. r.
All other photographs have been contributed by Tom Krausz, Hamburg. The photographer wishes to thank the P.I.C. (Photo Imaging Centre Laboratory), Hamburg, the ICS (Israeli Charter Service) Airline and the American Colony Hotel in Jerusalem for their kind support.
The maps on pages 11, 53, 77, 93, 113, 131, 149 and 153 were drawn by Astrid Fischer-Leitl, Munich.
The meteorological data on pages 146 and 147 were supplied by the German Weather Centre in Hamburg.

Translated into English by Monica Bloxam

We wish to thank all holders of rights and publishers for permission to reproduce illustrations. Despite every effort it has not been possible to identify all holders of rights. They are asked to contact the publishers.

Published in 1999 by
Tauris Parke Books
an imprint of I.B.Tauris & Co Ltd
Victoria House,
Bloomsbury Square,
London WC1B 4DZ
175 Fifth Avenue,
New York NY 10010
Website: http://www.ibtauris.com

In the United States and Canada distributed by St Martin's Press,
175 Fifth Avenue,
New York NY 10010

Printed and bound in Italy
ISBN 1-86064-481-3